The Mind and Faith of Justice Holmes

The Mind and Faith of Justice Holmes

HIS SPEECHES, ESSAYS, LETTERS, AND JUDICIAL OPINIONS

Selected and edited,
with a new preface and afterword by

Max Lerner

Transaction Publishers
New Brunswick (U.S.A.) and Oxford (U.K.)

New material this edition copyright © 1989 by Transaction Publishers, New Brunswick, New Jersey 08903. Originally published in 1943 by Little, Brown.

All rights reserved under International and Pan-American Copyright Conventions. No part of this book may be reproduced or transmitted in any form or by any means, electronic or mechanical, including photocopy, recording, or any information storage and retrieval system, without prior permission in writing from the publisher. All inquiries should be addressed to Transaction Publishers, Rutgers–The State University, New Brunswick, New Jersey 08903.

Library of Congress Catalog Number: 88-20137
ISBN: 0-88738-765-9
Printed in the United States of America

Library of Congress Cataloging-in-Publication Data

Holmes, Oliver Wendell, 1841-1935.
   The mind and faith of Justice Holmes : his speeches, essays, letters, and judicial opinions / selected and edited by Max Lerner ; with a new afterword by the editor.
      p.   cm.
   Reprint. Originally published: Boston : Little, Brown, 1943.
   Bibliography: p.
   Includes index.
   ISBN 0-88738-765-9
     1. Law—United States.   2. United States—Constitutional law.
I. Lerner, Max, 1902-   II. Title.
KF213.H6L46   1989
349.73′092′4—dc19
[347.300924]   88-20137
                                                           CIP

For

MR. JUSTICE FELIX FRANKFURTER

"The final test . . . is battle in some form. . . . It is one thing to utter a happy phrase from a protected cloister; another to think under fire — to think for action upon which great interests depend."

Contents

Preface	xv
Holmes: A Personal History	xvii

PART I: CAMPAIGNS OF LIFE AND LAW

Introductory	3
1. A Fighting Faith: the Civil War	5
Autobiographical Sketch (1861)	6
The Class of 1861: A Poem (1864)	8
Memorial Day (1884)	9
Harvard College in the War (1884)	17
The Soldier's Faith (1895)	18
"Parts of the Unimaginable Whole"	25
"The Class of '61": Fiftieth Anniversary Reunion (1911)	
2. Law as Calling, Life as Art	28
"Our Mistress, the Law"	29
Suffolk Bar Association Dinner (1885)	
"Your Business as Thinkers"	31
"The Profession of the Law" (1886)	
"The Love of Honor"	33
"On Receiving the Degree of Doctor of Laws," Yale University Commencement (1886)	
The Black Spearheads of Change	34
"Learning and Science" (1895)	

A Man and the Universe 35
    Speech at Brown University Commencement (1897)
"The Test Is Battle": George Otis Shattuck 37
    Answer to resolutions of the Bar (1897)
Life as Joy, Duty, End 40
    Speech at a dinner given by the Bar Association of Boston (1900)

3. Law as Civilization 44
    "Masters and Men": The Gas-Stokers' Strike (1873) 48
    Selections from *The Common Law* (1881) 51
        (1) *Liability and Revenge (from Lecture I)* 51
        (2) *Punishment, Morals and the External Standard (from Lecture II)* 56
        (3) *Torts and Social Experience (from Lectures III and IV)* 64
    The Path of the Law (1897) 71

4. Law as Judgment: Some Massachusetts Judicial Opinions 90
    The Legislature and the Weavers 92
        Commonwealth v. Perry (1891)
    "Communism" in Wood and Coal 95
        Advisory Opinion of the Justices (1892)
    Publication at Peril 96
        Hanson v. Globe Newspaper Company (1893)
    The Referendum and the Woman Voter 103
        Advisory Opinion of the Justices (1894)
    Speaking without a Permit 106
        Commonwealth v. Davis (1895)

CONTENTS   ix

Labor in the Struggle for Life   109
   Vegelahn v. *Guntner* (*1896*)
The Closed Shop and the Wage Fund   117
   Plant v. *Woods* (*1900*)
Death by Molar or Molecular Motion   122
   Storti v. *Commonwealth* (*1901*)

PART II: SUPREME COURT JUSTICE

Introductory   127
1. America as a Going Concern   134
   The First Supreme Court Case   136
      Otis v. *Parker* (*1903*)
   Allowing Play for the Joints   141
      Missouri, Kansas, and Tennessee Railroad v. *May* (*1904*)
   Herbert Spencer in New York Bakeries   143
      Lochner v. *New York* (*1905*)
   Liberty and the "Yellow Dog" Contract   150
      Adair v. *U. S.* (*1908*)
   Equal Bargaining Power for Workers   152
      Coppage v. *Kansas* (*1915*)
   "Experiments in Insulated Chambers"   156
      Truax v. *Corrigan* (*1921*)
   Paying for Pain and Mutilation   160
      Arizona Employers' Liability Cases (*1919*)
   "The Product of Ruined Lives"   165
      Hammer v. *Dagenhart* (*1918*)
   A Dogma among Scrubwomen   172
      Adkins v. *Children's Hospital* (*1923*)
   The State and the Great Public Needs   179
      Noble State Bank v. *Haskell* (*1911*)

CONTENTS

Where Police Power Ends — 185
Pennsylvania Coal Co. v. Mahon (1922)

Doctrinal Fictions and State Power — 190
Tyson Bros. v. Banton (1927)

"Pure Usurpation and Subtle Fallacy" — 193
Black and White Taxicab Co. v. Brown and Yellow Taxicab Co. (1928)

The Case of the Poisoned Pool — 201
United Zinc Co. v. Britt (1922)

Death at a Railroad Crossing — 205
Baltimore and Ohio Railroad Co. v. Goodman (1927)

Circus Lithographs and Originality — 208
Bleistein v. Donaldson Lithographing Company (1903)

"A Page on Copyright" — 213
White–Smith Music Co. v. Apollo Co. (1908)

Music with Meals — 216
Herbert v. Shanley Co. (1917)

A Great Case and Bad Law — 217
Northern Securities Company v. U. S. (1904)

Commerce as a Continuum — 231
Swift and Co. v. U. S. (1905)

Social Desires and Dr. Miles's Medicines — 239
Dr. Miles Medical Co. v. Park and Sons Co. (1911)

Free Trade in Industrial Information — 246
American Column and Lumber Co. v. U. S. (1921)

Shoddy and the Manifestly Absurd — 249
Weaver v. Palmer Bros. Co. (1926)

CONTENTS

On Legislative Motive 252
   Frost v. California (1926)
Absentee Control in Drugstores 254
   Louis K. Liggett Co. v. Baldridge (1928)
Tax Law and the Penumbra 257
   Schlesinger v. Wisconsin (1925)
"A Line There Must Be" 259
   Louisville Gas Co. v. Coleman (1928)
No Limit but the Sky 261
   Baldwin v. Missouri (1930)
Judges as a Privileged Class 264
   Evans v. Gore (1920)
The Governor and the Labor Leader 268
   Moyer v. Peabody (1909)
They Created a Nation, Not a Document 273
   Missouri v. Holland (1920)
Housing in Wartime Washington 278
   Block v. Hirsh (1921)
Spiderwebs and Presidential Power 285
   Myers v. U. S. (1926)

2. State Power and Free Trade in Ideas 289
   Clear and Present Danger 292
      Schenck v. U. S. (1919)
   A Speech by Eugene Debs 297
      Debs v. U. S. (1919)
   Two Leaflets and an Experiment 304
      Abrams v. U. S. (1919)
   The Postmaster Goes to War 313
      Milwaukee Social Democratic Publishing Co. v. Burleson (1921)

A Common Tongue and Freedom of Teaching	317
Meyer v. *Nebraska* (*1923*)	
Bartels v. *Iowa* (*1923*)	
"Every Idea Is an Incitement"	321
Gitlow v. *N. Y.* (*1925*)	
"Freedom for the Thought That We Hate"	325
U. S. v. *Schwimmer* (*1928*)	
Negro Disfranchisement in Texas	328
Nixon v. *Herndon* (*1927*)	
The Judge and the Editor	332
Toledo Newspaper Co. v. *U. S.* (*1918*)	
Peonage in Alabama	336
Bailey v. *Alabama* (*1911*)	
Trial by Mob	342
Frank v. *Mangum* (*1915*)	
Justice as a Mask	347
Moore v. *Dempsey* (*1923*)	
Malt Whisky and the External Standard	353
Peck v. *Tribune Co.* (*1909*)	
"Three Generations of Imbeciles"	356
Buck v. *Bell* (*1927*)	
The "Dirty Business" of Wire Tapping	359
Olmstead v. *U. S.* (*1928*)	

PART III: THE SAVOR OF LIFE

Introductory	365
1. Men and Ideas	367
Montesquieu (1900)	373
John Marshall (1901)	382
John Chipman Gray (1917)	386
Law and the Court (1913)	387

CONTENTS   xiii

    Ideals and Doubts (1915)   391
    Natural Law (1918)   394
    Law and Social Reform (1923)   399
    Opinions and Champagnes (1920)   401
    A Preface   401
        To the Collected Legal Papers (*1920*)

2. Letters   403
    To William James   409
    To John C. H. Wu   418
    To Lady Pollock   437
    To Sir Frederick Pollock   437

3. Last Words   450
    "Gold to the Sunset" (1932)   450
    The Arrow in Flames (1932)   451
    "Death Plucks My Ears" (1931)   451

Holmes Revisited: An Afterword Essay   453
Selected Additional Literature on Holmes 473
(Since the First edition)
Note on the Holmes Literature   479
Note on Acknowledgments   488
Note on Abbreviations   490
Table of Cases   491
Index   495

Preface

More than four decades have passed since this book's first publication in 1943. I have left the original pages untouched. I have, however, appended to them an afterword essay, "Holmes Revisited," for the intervening generations of lawyers, law students and general readers who may find my account of the Holmes legend and the Holmes reality of some interest. Since the new essay assumes some knowledge of the stages and phases of Holmes's life, the reader may wish to read it after my original introductory essay, "Holmes, A Personal History."

A vast corpus of Holmes literature has accumulated, professional and general, much if not most of it since the original publication. There is no end to the books, critiques, biographies, reminiscenses, polemics and psychohistorical and deconstructional studies that have become part of the Holmes commentary. Hence the new select bibliography as an addition to the original one.

I owe much to Professor Ronald K. L. Collins of the American University Law School, who encouraged me to offer these early Holmes labors of mine to the young generation to which he belongs. He was also most helpful in suggestions for the new bibliography. I owe thanks also to Myra L. Saunders, associate librarian at the University of California Law School, at Los Angeles, for bibliographical help. Philip Herrera, editor of *Connoisseur*, has allowed me some borrowings from my essay on Holmes as my favorite Supreme Court Justice, scheduled for publication there. It was Irving Louis Horowitz, professor at Rutgers University and President of Transaction Publishers, whose invitation for a new edition came at exactly the right time, when I had immersed myself in a Holmes reassessment for a collection of earlier constitutional essays now awaiting publication. Anita Stock, also of Transaction Publishers, was generous with her editorial help. As with all my recent writing, my assistant, Evelyn Irsay, proved indispensable in turning the idea of a new edition into a reality.

It says something about the lives of a book that I worked on the original edition with my wife, Edna Albers Lerner, during the first two years of our marriage (1941-1942), when my former Williams student, now a Pulitzer Prize winner, James MacGregor Burns, joined us in the research for it. After so long a span the book holds joyful memories for me.

Max Lerner

January 1, 1989

Holmes: A Personal History[1]

I

The social and intellectual world into which Oliver Wendell Holmes, Jr. was born was one which had cramped many of his contemporaries. Henry Adams, who was born into the same sort of environment at roughly the same time, was to complain afterward that it was a tight and orderly little world which had almost no relation to the chaotic forces in the universe outside — and he was to translate his querulousness into great literature. But in Holmes's case the sense of security, which might have acted as an inhibition, gave his energies release and made his purposes unerring. Karl Llewellyn has remarked that Holmes should have been born an Adams. But we can find the best of the New England world more clearly exposed in him than in Henry Adams, in whom it flowered differently, with a hothouse intensity as in the gardens of Rappacini's daughter in Hawthorne's tale. In Holmes's life there is a wholeness which the New England aristocracy at its best produced.

His father, Oliver Wendell Holmes, was not only the poet, wit, and "Autocrat of the Breakfast Table," but a physician and medical researcher not without a place in the history of the fight against disease. Among Holmes's ancestors, who traced their stock back to early colonial times, the religious intensity of an earlier Calvinism had been transmuted into a sense of public service, and the concern with intellectual values led by an easy transition to a concern for intellectual freedom and civil liberties; just as in the English aristocracy the energy that earlier went into the Wars of the Roses went later into Parliament and the civil service. Holmes took a frank pride in his ancestry. "All my three names," he wrote in his autobiograph-

[1] For a discussion of the sources on which I have drawn in this biographical sketch, see the NOTE ON THE HOLMES LITERATURE at the end of this book.

ical sketch for the Harvard Class Album, "designate families from which I am descended." At another point in this sketch of himself he says, "I don't believe in gushing much in these college biographies." It is important both that he felt this sentiment and that he felt also the need to repress it.

Holmes was born March 8, 1841, in Boston. His father, in a letter the next day, wrote that someone who might in the future be addressed as President of the United States was at the moment "content with scratching his face and sucking his forefinger." Boston at that time, despite a population of less than 100,000, was the commercial capital of New England and the intellectual capital of America. The New England of which it formed part had passed the peak of its preoccupation with trading, shipbuilding and shipping. Textile mills were springing up to which the younger people were increasingly to turn. It was a New England in which the roots of a deep religious feeling still persisted; a New England which had produced the self-reliant militancy of Emerson and Thoreau, in which Hawthorne was writing his dark guilt-laden tales, and to which Melville was soon to return to digest his South Seas odyssey. Abolitionism, feminism, transcendentalism and Fourierism were churning the consciences of men and women, reform movements jostled the genteel tradition, and the swarming wharves lay dreaming of their past side by side with the rising squalor of the new mill towns.

In this New England and this Boston young Holmes grew up. His father's rising fame as what Parrington has called "the Beacon Street wit" meant that the boy had access to some of the best table conversation in Boston — that is to say, in America. Doctor Holmes was at the heart of the salon and literary club life of Boston. Theodore Parker and Wendell Phillips, central figures in the religious and social enlightenment of the time, the secular Savonarolas of Boston, were friends of the family and without doubt influenced the boy's thinking. Ralph Waldo Emerson was also a visitor, and to the boy he was "Uncle Waldo." Holmes's father scarcely shared the radicalism of either Parker or Emerson. His strictures on his society inflicted scratches but drew no blood. His novel, *Elsie Venner,* set Boston parlors aflutter because it pricked a whole variety of reformist intellectual bubbles. He was a conservative in all his social views except religion, in which he had sharpened himself into a Unitarian knife dedicated to hollowing out the darkness of Calvinism. He blasted with his wit the millennial and crochety doctrines of the social reformers of his day. Young Holmes was thus held secure in a haven of social orthodoxy without being wholly shut off from the tumult of innovation.

But I do not mean to imply that his boyhood was overly intellectual. He was active in all the boyhood sports, learning something of the aspects of Boston which were a closed book to his elders, spending delightful vacation months in the Holmes summer house near Pittsfield, on land which once belonged to Jacob Wendell, one of his ancestors. The impression of the Lenox meadows and the Berkshire Hills was to stay with Holmes as an enduring image of New England beauty. "I love granite rocks and barberry bushes," he was to write sixty years later, "because with them were my earliest joys that reach back through the past eternity of my life." And the boy also bought himself some etching tools and as an amateur developed a taste for art which was to be one of his abiding preoccupations.

Holmes's education was that of an intellectual aristocrat. Like others of the gentility he attended Mr. Dixwell's Latin School. The skeptical mind will go back to the chapters of Thorstein Veblen's *Theory of the Leisure Class* dealing with the place of dead languages in the education of live young men. But Holmes, for all his bantering disbelief in the classics, made these languages a living instrument in his later writing, and he drew, as those earlier realists Machiavelli and Montesquieu had drawn, upon the culture from which the languages came for some of his insights into his own culture. He was to draw upon this source also for the spirit of the Roman stoics that informed him.

Following his family tradition he went to Harvard, and entered in the fall of 1857 with the class of 1861. With him at

Harvard were the elite of New England, and a sprinkling of the Southern aristocracy as well. Harvard was at that time the best university in the country. It was awakening to the dawning world of American science, and it was preparing men to fill the strategic posts both in the maintenance of wealth and power in this world and the propitiation of the gods of the world beyond. The Harvard of Holmes's day stood midway between what Van Wyck Brooks has called the "flowering" of New England, and its "Indian summer." New England's flowering had taken place largely in the intellectual group outside of the college; its Indian summer was to be focused largely on the group inside the college. Between these two eras the Harvard of Holmes's time was a place through which the winds of contemporary doctrine did not blow very strongly. Holmes was interested in ideas, but except for some flurries about Abolition he had little of the radicalism of youth about contemporary issues. He had a talent for friendship, a capacity for vivid talk, and a gusto for life which made him an outstanding member of the class. He was absorbed with literature, philosophy and art. He belonged to the private clubs, the honor societies, the "liberal" Christian Union. He edited the literary magazine and wrote a prize essay on Plato. He continued with his interest in etchings, publishing in the college magazine an article on Albrecht Dürer.

But despite the placid and sheltered life he led, there were conflicts of ideas and clashes of social forces outside that were to affect him deeply, and to which to a degree he responded. Darwin published his *Origin of Species* while Holmes was in college, and his theories of the struggle for existence and the survival of the fittest were beginning to form the staple of debate. And before Darwin was Malthus, giving a similar sense of the cramped environment which, as Holmes was later to put it, pushed many lives always and inevitably down the deadline. Holmes's thought was thus early nurtured on death and conflict, and his later absorption with both may be traced to these early influences. And outside the walls of Harvard there were the growing tensions of what was being termed the "ir-

HOLMES: A PERSONAL HISTORY xxi

repressible conflict" between the North and South, between two economies and two conceptions of life. The men of Holmes's class, like those of the classes of our own decade, felt the shadow of the impending war and sought to pierce in their troubled way the darkness that stretched beyond it. Thirty years after the war, in his speech "The Soldier's Faith," Holmes thought he had caught a glimpse of its meaning — that "combat and pain still are the portion of man," that "the struggle for life is the order of the world, at which it is vain to repine."

2

The war came — came even before the class could graduate, so that Holmes, who like his father before him had been chosen Class Poet, had to compose his poem while training with his regiment. But since the regiment remained near Boston for a while, Holmes was able to graduate with his class. War proved to be Holmes's real college and testing ground.

It left a deep mark on him. He knew, as he later put it, that he had to "share the passion and action of his time at peril of being judged not to have lived." He learned on the battlefields of the Civil War what the realities of life were like. He enlisted in the Infantry, joining finally the Twentieth Massachusetts, a regiment which saw ample fighting through the war, with five eighths of its men either killed or wounded. Just before it moved from its training field in Massachusetts to the front, Holmes was commissioned First Lieutenant. "One day," Elizabeth Shepley Sergeant tells us, "as he was walking down Beacon Hill with Hobbes's *Leviathan* in his hand," Holmes learned of his commission. "So the young officer whom we may see in his uniform at Langdell Hall, at the Harvard Law School, with his visored cap on his knee, in one of those touching little faded photographs which were a sop to parental love — a mere lad trusting and vulnerable, like all lads who have fought all the great wars — went forth to a baptism that he has never forgotten." At the Battle of Ball's Bluff, on October 21, 1861, he received a wound in the region of the breast which at the time seemed likely to end fatally, but it proved finally to have missed both the heart and the lung. Home on leave, he is described in one of his father's letters as receiving visitors *"en grand seigneur*. I envy my white Othello with a semicircle of young Desdemonas about him listening to the often told story which they will have over again."

As soon as he was well, Holmes returned to the front. At the Battle of Antietam, on September 17, 1862, the Twentieth Infantry found itself outflanked by the Confederates and had to retreat with great casualties. Holmes, now a captain, was again wounded, this time through the neck. His father received the news by telegraph, and immediately set out to Maryland to find him. In an *Atlantic Monthly* article, "My Hunt After the Captain," he later told of how he searched along the road to Antietam which was clogged with stragglers and wounded, searched through hospitals and houses, until finally he traced him to a train leaving from Hagerstown for Philadelphia. He went through the cars until he found him, the captain, "my first-born whom I had sought through many cities." And thus for Holmes it was Boston again and another period of convalescence.

Holmes came back to the fighting in November 1862, only to be stricken with an undignified attack of dysentery. When he was well enough to be back in the ranks, he lived through the disaster of Fredericksburg under General Burnside in December 1862. On May 3, 1863, the Union forces under General Hooker fought a second battle near Fredericksburg, at Marye's Hill. There, while his company was seeking to capture a position, Holmes was struck in the heel by a piece of shrapnel, the bone splintered and the ligaments torn. The third of his wounds, it sent Holmes again to Boston, and for some time there was fear that he would lose his leg, but it healed excellently. When he returned to the army in January 1864, it was as aide-de-camp to a general; then he became a provost marshal. When he was mustered out of service on July 17, 1864, it was as Lieutenant-Colonel.

He had fought in some of the great battles of the war, although he missed Gettysburg and the battles at the close. He had seen his closest friends killed by his side. He had learned that "as long as man dwells upon the globe, his destiny is battle, and he has to take the chances of war." And with that recognition there had come a faith in the purposes, even though not fully known, for which men are called to fight, and in the strategy, even though not fully understood, that governs the campaign. Holmes never forgot these experiences. He had gone into the war a sensitive boy with nerves delicately organized and with an imagination, which does not often serve a soldier well. He had a hunger for adventure and distinction. He had had his chance at both, and at twenty-three had already "shared the incommunicable experience of war," lived through the most moving destiny that was given to his generation.

3

When he came back from the war, he turned to the problem of a career. His interest in philosophy was not the stuff of which professional philosophers are made. He had tried etching but did not think he was good enough. A literary career was more likely to be a by-product than a matter of direct purpose. Holmes decided that his new battleground would be the law. It was a barren ground and an unyielding one. To extract from it something great and enduring required both work and faith. Holmes was ready to offer both in full measure. It is not beyond our scope to guess that in Holmes's choice of the law rather than literature or philosophy or art, there was some buried Puritan tropism which made him turn where his strength and imagination would be most far-reachingly called upon.

The Harvard Law School, when Holmes entered it in the fall of 1864, was not yet in its great period. There were several teachers whom Holmes enjoyed. But it was not yet the day of Langdell and Ames, and the case method had not yet been introduced into Harvard. The returned soldier studied hard, so hard that his friends grew worried about him. But he knew also how to "slay the dust of pleading by certain sprinklings" which he "managed to contrive" with his friends. He took his degree in January 1866, and then set off for a visit to England armed with some letters of introduction from his father's friend John Lothrop Motley to John Stuart Mill and to Thomas Hughes, the author of the Tom Brown books. But the person he saw most of was Leslie Stephen, with whom he had already struck an acquaintance in Boston on one of those visits of recuperation from the battlefield. Holmes went on walking tours in England, joined the Alpine Club and climbed mountains in Switzerland with Stephen.

He came back to America, to be admitted to the bar in 1867. He joined a law firm and lived in a room on the top floor of his father's house on Beacon Street, overlooking the Charles River. For three years he worked hard as an apprentice in the firm, but after that his rise was rapid. His success was like an irresistible force. In 1870, before he was yet thirty, he became a lecturer in constitutional law at Harvard. In the same year, he assumed the editorship of the *American Law Journal,* which he held for three years and which gave him the chance to read widely in both the Anglo-American and Continental legal literature. Also, by compelling him to write comments on current cases, it gave his legal studies a sharpness of focus. In 1873, he edited the twelfth edition of Kent's *Commentaries on American Law,* in four volumes, with a considerable body of notes from his own pen. The year before, in 1872, Holmes married Miss Fanny Dixwell, the daughter of the principal of the Latin School he had attended, a high-spirited girl with a capacity for wit and raillery and a mind of her own. In 1874 he made a second trip to England, taking Mrs. Holmes along. There they met another recently married pair, Frederick Pollock and his wife. Both young men were interested in law and legal history, each found in the other a kinship of taste and outlook. Thus began the friendship of almost sixty years which was to be renewed by transatlantic trips and to be sustained by the now famous exchange of letters.

Holmes had to work hard for success, but he was so situated that success responded to his work. He seemed to have all the gifts the gods could offer. He had a handsome presence, a sharp and nimble mind, a great family tradition, a gift for flashing phrase, an elegance of language, a brilliant war record, a "grand tour" in Europe, a smattering of philosophy, a sense of self-sufficiency and of his own destiny, and just enough irresponsibility to set off his more substantial qualities. He taught in the classroom, he wrote editorials and articles, he read his fill of the English yearbooks, he had a chance to ponder the vistas of legal history and the relation of legal systems to their cultures.

Thus passed the decade of the '70's. It was a decade which was already under the shadow of a grasping and predatory industrialism. The onward march of American capitalist enterprise was opening up a continent and rifling as well as organizing its treasures. The legal profession was in this march a camp follower. Some of his later speeches to law students indicate that Holmes was through these years saddened at the sordid commercialism he saw, both among industrialists and among lawyers. Yet he managed to keep from being tainted by it. He had a strong enough stomach to confront it and yet the vision to look beyond to the more distant perspectives that opened up the meaning and even heroism of law.

The beginning of the '80's found Holmes moving forward in his chosen profession of legal teaching and scholarship and commentary. In 1880 he was asked to deliver a course of Lowell Lectures, and chose "The Common Law" as his topic. The lectures had ease, learning, and grace, and yet along with these there was a tough technical sense which impressed the young men who heard them as much as the delicacy of phrasing delighted them. Holmes worked hard preparing his lectures for the press, often late into the night after a day of work devoted to other duties. The book appeared in 1881 and came close to opening something of a new era in Anglo-American jurisprudence. It led to a professorship at Harvard Law School in 1882. He taught only a term, because hard on the heels of the Harvard appointment came the offer of a seat on the Supreme Judicial Court of Massachusetts. It was a dramatic moment, as

Holmes tells of it in a later speech, when "Shattuck came out and told me that in one hour the Governor would submit my name to the council for a judgeship, if notified of my assent. It was a stroke of lightning which changed the whole course of my life."

Holmes could hardly have hesitated seriously between the two appointments. He had already stipulated in accepting the professorship that he should be free to accept a judgeship. After consulting with his partner, Shattuck, he took the Court. Nor had the appointment come wholly as a surprise. He had already some years earlier had his eye on judicial office, and had been fluttered by the rumor that he might get a Federal District Court judgeship, which had finally gone to another man. While legal practice and writing and teaching would have suited his ambitions well enough, he wanted to have a hand more directly in shaping law. His grandfather on his mother's side, Charles Jackson, had also been a member of the Massachusetts Supreme Judicial Court. His father was delighted with the news. "To think of it," he wrote a friend, " — my little boy a Judge and able to send me to jail if I don't behave myself."

4

Holmes's appointment to the Court came in December 1882, when he was forty-one. In the group pictures of the Court that have come down to us, Holmes as the most recent member sits at the extreme left, looking almost a stripling in comparison with the rest. It was a Court of rather old men, and during the decade following Holmes's appointment it had a turnover of six or seven members. Holmes had a genius for friendship and a respect for the quality of a man even when his views were greatly divergent from his own. On the deaths of his colleagues Holmes was in several instances called upon to deliver a memorial speech, which he did with both taste and insight. In fact, one suspects that one or two of these commemorative speeches may outlast the work of their subjects.

There is not much detail available, outside of the Law Reports, about the Holmes of this period. He lived at the center of a lively group of friends, and he continued his father's tradition of good talk and zestful living. But he was careful also of the judicial decencies. Owen Wister tells of Holmes's tactful but firm refusal to accompany him to a bar for a drink because "I don't somehow cotton to the notion of our judges hobnobbing in hotel bars and saloons." We get a picture of Holmes at forty-five, strikingly handsome, "lean as a race-horse," with hair turning gray, talking colorfully through an evening under the stimulus of "two brilliant listeners — handsome ladies both." He made further trips to England in 1882, 1889, 1896, 1898, and 1901. During this period, within a brief span of time, Holmes lost his mother, brother, and sister by death. His father was left alone, and the Justice and his wife moved into the old house with him, remaining as companions until his death in 1894. In 1899 the death of Chief Justice Walbridge A. Field led to the appointment of Holmes to the chief-justiceship, which he held until he went to Washington.

If Holmes's tenure on the Massachusetts Court from 1882 to 1902 is one of the least known periods of his life, it was also one of the most important. It included the two decades from the age of forty to sixty when most men have already laid down the shaping lines of their thought and done their creative work. In the nation's history these were years of industrial development, political turmoil, cultural crudeness. They were the years during which business enterprise crystallized into a structure of corporate monopoly, years of labor's awakening, of Republican domination and Populist and Socialist stirrings; years of laissez faire and of the emergence of an industrial elite; years of the "robber barons" and of the consolidation of capitalist power; years of materialist values.

Holmes was aware of some of these things, although both by inclination and judicial duty he kept shy of them. He was particularly sensitive to the coarseness of the cultural tone of the nation. In several of his Memorial Day addresses delivered during this period he speaks, with a note almost of despair, of the crass values of the men of wealth and those of the legal profession who devoted themselves to the pursuit of wealth. But Holmes saw other things as well. Unlike the liberals of the Godkin and *Nation* school he did not regard the growth of business and labor organizations as an unrelieved evil. He accepted both as part of the laws of social development.

What remedies, then, did he see for the social struggles of the day and for the slackening of the national fiber? On the whole his were the views of an aristocratic conservative who did not care much either for business values or for the talk of reformers and the millennial dreams of the humanitarians. Holmes watched Populism, trade unions, socialism as they developed and spread. He had enough curiosity to read their literature, enough good sense not to be frightened as others were by these threats to his world. As an economist he clung to the conviction that most of the reform movements were based not upon economic reasoning but upon dramatic simplification. But as a judge he thought it no business of his to interpose obstacles in the path of legislative experiments with the new ideas. Hence his famous dissenting opinions in the trade-union cases of *Vegelahn* v. *Guntner* and *Plant* v. *Woods*. Hence also his dissents from the judicial prohibition of municipal ownership of coal and wood yards and local option for women suffrage. Holmes relied ultimately on the strength of the American tradition, the self-balancing tendencies within social experiment and the competition of ideas, and the inner cogency of the qualities which he loosely called "race."

His few public utterances on these qualities and on the need for maintaining unslackened the great military tradition of the nation laid him open to attack. The *Nation* group called one of his speeches in 1895 "sentimental jingoism." Holmes's comment in his letters to Pollock was withering but in public he said nothing. Similarly he was attacked as a "Communist" (the memory of the Paris Commune was still close enough to shape the epithet) for his dissents in the labor cases and the cases involving local autonomy. But except among the fanatics his prestige was steadily growing. Although his famous opinions were in the constitutional area, the bulk of his day-by-day work was in the fields outside of it — tort, agency, contract, criminal law. His decisions were increasingly cited by other courts. Several articles on him appeared in the legal periodicals — an unusual tribute for a judge on a state court. We do not know whether he was impatient about speaking from a restricted forum. We only know that these were years of training and discipline for him, when he tested his judicial notions and his philosophy against the hard material of the cases that came his way and against the deeply ingrained notions of his colleagues.

5

In 1902 Justice Horace Gray of the United States Supreme Court retired from the Court. Since Gray was a Massachusetts man, it was natural for President Theodore Roosevelt to turn to another Massachusetts man to replace him. Roosevelt at once thought of Holmes. He was attracted by the combination of the scholar with a distinguished military career, and the statesman with a literary and historical bent: after all, he found in himself the confirmation that such a blend was a good one. He was attracted also by Holmes's high reputation for legal ability and learning. And as for the dissents which Holmes had returned in the labor cases and which had brought down upon him the contumely of the men of substance, Roosevelt was not one to balk at that. In fact, he probably saw that he could turn it to advantage. The temper of the country was far more radical than any of the Republican Presidents had been able to understand. Roosevelt was getting into the swing of his trust-busting phase. He knew, deeply conservative as he was, that his social order could be preserved not by turning his back on the storm but by riding and commanding it.

The hitch lay in one speech that Holmes had made — the one on John Marshall.[2] It was undoubtedly one of Holmes's great utterances and one of his justest judgments of a man's

[2] See p. 382.

talent and his place in history. But to Roosevelt it seemed ominous. Roosevelt liked Marshall's broad interpretation of the national power. He saw him as the very archetype of the judge, "a constitutional statesman believing in great party principles, and willing to continue the Constitution so that the nation can develop on the broadest lines." Roosevelt knew that Holmes was a nationalist, and had long before written ecstatically to Lodge about Holmes's fervid 1895 speech celebrating the martial qualities. But his comments on the Federalist Chief Justice bothered Roosevelt. Holmes had preferred to view Marshall not so much as the single hero but rather as "a great ganglion in the nerves of society, or, to vary the figure, a strategic point in the campaign of history, and part of his greatness consists in his being *there*."

What Roosevelt did not want on the Court, his letter to Lodge continued, was a Taney who was "a curse to our national life because he belonged to the wrong party." What he wanted was "a statesman of the national type," "a constructive statesman, constantly keeping in mind . . . his relations with his fellow statesmen who in other branches of the government are striving . . . to advance the ends of government." Roosevelt wanted assurances. "I should like to know that Judge Holmes was in entire sympathy with our views, that is with your views and mine and Judge Gray's, for instance." To select a man "who was not absolutely sane and sound on the great national policies" would be "an irreparable wrong to the nation." Roosevelt instructed Lodge to show his letter to Holmes "if it became necessary." There is no indication that he did: Lodge's answer must have been reassuring enough to appease Roosevelt's doubts. The President probably made more inquiries during the month that followed Gray's resignation. Finally, having obtained the *imprimatur* of Senator Hoar of Massachusetts, he announced Holmes's appointment in August 1902. It went to the Senate early in December, the Senate acted on it in very short order, and Holmes became a member of the United States Supreme Court on December 6, 1902.

For a while all went well between the President and his new

Associate Justice. Roosevelt liked artistic and literary men around him, and made Holmes part of the group of "Roosevelt Familiars" which at one time or another included Lodge, Beveridge, John Hay, Saint-Gaudens, Owen Wister, and Jules Jusserand, with Lincoln Steffens and Finley Peter Dunne on the margin. He seems to have warmed to Holmes with his background of Civil War battles, his wit, his epigrams, his talk of books and etchings. The Holmeses, who had settled in Washington in 1903 and bought the house on I Street in which they were to live to the end, were often at the White House entertainments. But Holmes made no commitments, whether outer or inner, whether political or intellectual. The honeymoon was doomed to be short-lived and in a little more than a year it was rudely shattered. What shattered it was Holmes's dissent in Roosevelt's great trust-busting case, involving the Northern Securities Company, commented on at some length in the body of this book. Despite the hopes Roosevelt pinned on him, Holmes voted against the Government, writing one of the two dissenting opinions in the case. Roosevelt was furious. "I could carve out of a banana," he is reported (perhaps apocryphally) to have cried, "a justice with more backbone than that."

He was wrong. Holmes had enough backbone to stand up against the man who had appointed him only a short while before, and who had showered on him the lavishness of his warmth and personality. Roosevelt was so single-minded in his determination to have his way in the *Northern Securities* matter that he was obtuse in his judgment of what made Holmes tick.

Nevertheless the whole Roosevelt-Holmes relationship — including the President's letter to Lodge, his doubts, his final decision to appoint Holmes, and his fury at Holmes's dissent — deserves some analysis. It involves questions that cut deep into the nature of the American governmental system and into the personality of both principles in the affair. The commentators have tended to deal too harshly with Roosevelt. The curious thing is that among those most vehement in condemning him have been the liberals. At the same time that they assert that a Peckham or a Sutherland reads his economic views into the Constitution, they condemn Roosevelt for having acted on a similar assumption. It is time that we stripped ourselves of the latent hypocrisy in this. Present-day constitutional writers pretty generally recognize that Presidents do tend to appoint justices whose thinking runs along their own grooves, and that justices cannot wholly escape reading their social views into their opinions. If both these propositions are without truth, then a quarter-century of constitutional commentary has been either wasted or misunderstood.

There were, however, extraordinary items in this instance which must qualify the propositions just stated. One was Roosevelt's brashness. He had the temerity to take the assumption on which his predecessors had acted implicitly, at least since John Adams appointed John Marshall to the Court, and to put it quite explicitly in his letter to Lodge. Roosevelt thought of himself as a good deal of an iconoclast. The man who said that he could not show J. P. Morgan or Carnegie or Hill the same regard he had for Peary the explorer, or Bury and Rhodes the historians — the man who brought cowboys and prize fighters and big-game hunters into the White House much as his kinsman-successor brings movie stars — was not a man to balk at putting down on paper the hidden assumptions on which his predecessors had acted. He was writing to Henry Cabot Lodge, as one man of the world to another. He was at that time in earnest about his antitrust crusade. He knew that there was lined up against him on the Court a minority that might easily be turned into a potential majority, and he was determined that he would not willingly appoint to the Court a judge who might consciously turn the tide against him.[3] As Charles Beard has pointed out, Roosevelt wanted to see the harshness of corporation law tempered by a humanistic jurisprudence. Unless a President believes in government by deadlock, which he is not likely to do, he must appoint to the

[3] Roosevelt wrote Lodge a similar letter in 1906, on the appointment of Justice Lurton. See *Selections from the Correspondence of Theodore Roosevelt and Henry Cabot Lodge* (1925) 1 : 517–519 for Holmes, and 2 : 228–229 for the striking letter on Lurton.

Court judges who are roughly of his own persuasion — not necessarily from his own political party but within the ambit of his own world-view. Only thus can he keep the various parts of his Administration moving together as an Administration. In our own time we have had a dramatic illustration of this in the New Deal constitutional crisis and in the Court appointments following it. Franklin D. Roosevelt found out that justices with a world-view reaching back decades before the era of depression and the fascist threat were able to burke the whole meaning of his Administration.

The second item was that Holmes was not the ordinary judge, any more than Theodore Roosevelt was the ordinary President. Holmes had a firmly developed judicial method to a greater degree than any other judge of that day. He had already shown this quality on the state court, as the President might easily have discovered if he had studied his opinions. He had shown an impassioned indifference to the "hydraulic pressures" that converge on "great cases," a meticulous regard for the strict legal profile of a case, an inclination to let the legislature have its way, a sophistication that prevented him from projecting his economic philosophy and calling it the Constitution — and that in an era when it would have been easy enough to identify his views with the welfare of the nation.

But this did not mean that Holmes was all compact of austerity, a god who had pierced beyond the human impulses in him. If Roosevelt had relied on Holmes to give the Sherman Act full sway because he had practised judicial *laissez faire* toward other legislative acts, he failed to reckon with the fact that Holmes was not an Olympian but a philosopher — which is a wholly different matter. His judicial philosophy of leaving the legislature alone came from a deeper philosophy of leaving the cosmos alone. And when the strict meaning of restraint of trade at the common law coincided with this philosophy, Holmes was clad in a double armor of conviction. Roosevelt might have anticipated Holmes's *Northern Securities* dissent if he had studied Holmes's Massachusetts labor dissents. Taking into account Holmes's Darwinism and the sense of accepting the limits that the universe imposed upon him, they might well have given warning to any President hell-bent on antitrust enforcement. I shall discuss in my comment on the case the lack of economic realism in Holmes's opinion. But it was natural for Holmes, who approached the case without a feeling for the realities of economic power involved, to accept monopolies as well as trade unions as part of the laws of the organization and the equilibrium of life. Holmes's reasoning from the history of the common-law doctrine of restraint of trade unions was learned and subtle. But the real logic of his *Northern Securities* dissent was poles apart from the logic of Justices White, Fuller, and Peckham, who made up the rest of the minority, or from the logic of Roosevelt. These dissenting justices acted from an image of an economic universe. Roosevelt acted from an image of a political universe. Holmes acted from the image of a philosophic universe. And because he had so firm a nucleus of conviction, he was unperturbed by Roosevelt's lashings and his concentrated fury.

6

The appointment to the United States Supreme Court was for Holmes the culminating opportunity in a career of thought and effort. Behind him was a long row of cases — thousands of them; before him stretched thousands more. Each case required courage of heart, sharpness of mind, wisdom of judgment, cunning of hand in contriving the right words.

It was because Holmes felt thus that he was troubled at the comments in the press that greeted his appointment. The appointment itself went through the Senate smoothly enough. But when Holmes's name was first announced, he was irritated at the quality of the "stacks of notices." "The immense majority of them," he wrote to Pollock, "seem devoid of personal discrimination or courage. They are so favorable that they make my nomination a popular success but they have the flabbiness of American ignorance."[4] They generally mentioned

[4] See p. 437.

Holmes's *Vegelahn* dissent, and insinuated that its author "has partial views, is brilliant but not very sound." And then there follows in Holmes's letter one of the rare instances of a *cri du cœur:* "It makes one sick when he has broken his heart in trying to make every word living and real to see a lot of duffers . . . talking with the sanctity of print in a way that at once discloses to the knowing eye that literally they don't know anything about it." Thus Holmes had his taste of running the gantlet of lay opinion on a national scale. It was not a severe ordeal as such things go. Chief Justice Taney before him went through a far worse one when his nomination came to the Senate and an outcry arose that he had been Andrew Jackson's "pliant instrument" in the Bank controversy. Justice Brandeis was to have an even bitterer cup to drink when the corporate powers and their spokesmen in the Bar Association sought in a protracted Senate fight in 1916 to block his appointment. For Holmes's sensitive spirit either of these major attacks would have been a catastrophe, but his own minor one was sufficiently galling.

Holmes was not a young man when he took his place on the Court. He was sixty-one. Two members of the Court, Justices White and McKenna, were younger than he. Of the rest, there was no one as much as ten years his senior. It was not a brilliant Court nor an enlightened one. The two great justices who had made judicial history in the last decade of the century — Justices Miller and Field — were both gone. Those who were left were not even half-gods. Chief Justice Fuller was a nonentity. Of the rest, only Justices White, Harlan, H. B. Brown, and McKenna had more than average ability, and of these only White and Harlan had real stature. All of them, with the exception of Harlan, were deeply conservative, if not reactionary in their social outlook. The main outlines of judicial strategy had already been laid down — first, in the battle over the interpretation of "due process" between the cohorts led by Field and those led by Miller up to the middle of the 1880's, and then by the sequence of decisions in the 1890's breathing a bleak laissez-faire philosophy. It was clear that the whole duty of a Supreme Court Justice lay in filling in the outlines of these decisions and in using constitutional law as a way of entrenching the system of economic power.

Holmes refused to live up to the rules of the game so conceived. He had no intention of conscripting the legal Constitution as he saw it to the uses of the economic Constitution, any more than he would conscript it to the uses of a political program. If he disappointed President Roosevelt in the *Northern Securities* case, he had many more disappointments in store for those on the other side of the fence. His first opinion in 1903 (*Otis* v. *Parker*) showed clearly his intention to give state legislative action a broad margin of tolerance, even if it implied a system of state regulation of economic activity. But it was not until 1905, in the *Lochner* case, that Holmes found his real stride on the Supreme Court.

7

There were three important turning points in Holmes's career on the Supreme Court. One was the *Lochner* dissent in 1905, the second was the coming of Justice Brandeis to the Court in 1916, the third was America's entrance into the war soon after, bringing in its wake a group of civil liberties cases which were to occupy Holmes from 1917 for almost a decade. Each of these is worth more than passing mention.

With the *Lochner* case Holmes really began firing his big judicial guns. Up to that time no really great issue had arisen, although Holmes had given distress to the camp followers of both sides. The *Lochner* dissent marked a turning point. It had every index of having been painfully thought out. It had the clarity of a trumpet call after which there could be no retreat. There have been those who have read Holmes's dissent as mainly an exercise in satire. Charles Beard, for example, speaks of Holmes "allowing his genial wit to melt the frosty verbalism of the law." "Genial" is a curious adjective to apply in this case. Similarly when Thorstein Veblen a few years earlier published his *Theory of the Leisure Class* the critics viewed it as an elaborate literary satire. Like Veblen, but in his very different way, Holmes was very much in earnest. He had not entirely forgotten the military strategy of his Civil War experience. He knew that the thrust at the enemy must be sudden and sharp, with all your might. "When you strike at a king," Emerson had told him long before, "you must kill him." Holmes was striking not only at Justice Peckham's majority opinion in the *Lochner* case but at the whole dark and intolerant judicial tradition which Peckham was expressing.

While Holmes's motivations were those of a legal craftsman determined not to see his craft distorted, the consequences of his opinions reached to the living standards of the common man and his struggles for dignity. The *Lochner* dissent did not stand alone. In the quarter-century of judicial labors that remained to him, Holmes fought for the right of the legislature to promote equality of bargaining power for workers, for the right of social experiment, for state and federal social legislation, for the right of the people to develop an effective tax administration, for adequate governmental power in peace and war. He fought with courage and with subtlety. Where by yielding ground slightly he could get the rest of the Court to go along with him, he did so. But where no compromise was possible, he continued to speak forth, with a magisterial manner and a summary brevity which infuriated his opponents just as much as it delighted his followers.

And followers he did have. For the young lawyers and the students still in the law schools, looking about them for some figure who rose above the deadening plains of legal commercialism and judicial complacency, some veteran who could give them hope that they would not become the mercenaries of a corporate economy, Holmes became a symbol. His opinions were caught up by the law journals, which were just becoming a force. Those who fought to temper the harshness of corporate power and those who, whatever their views, sought in law a vitality that he restored to it, combined in homage to him. They read him avidly, they quoted the Holmesian nuggets they discovered, they wrote about him. Holmes was deeply pleased and yet he was basically unmoved. The real motivation came from deep within, from his craftsman's conception of the judicial power, his philosophy of its place in a limited universe, his unflagging sense of being part of a long campaign of history.

8

But it was a lonely fight. I shall have something to say later, in the prefatory note on Holmes as Supreme Court judge, about his friendships and associations with the other justices.[5] For a decade and a half, aside from occasional support from Harlan and then from Charles Evans Hughes, Holmes stood pretty much alone. But in 1916 with the appointment of Louis D. Brandeis to the Court, this was changed.

The relationship between Holmes and Brandeis was a complex one. Brandeis brought to the Court a first-rate legal mind, an arduous education in social realities, and a fund of economic knowledge. He brought a seriousness of intent and an unwavering will. While there can be no question that Brandeis exercised a substantial influence over Holmes, we must remember that not only the contours of Holmes's mind but also its basic propulsions had already become fixed by the time Brandeis came to the Court. The influence was vastly overestimated by men like Chief Justice Taft, who allowed his judgment to be swayed by his fear and prejudice. When he said in a letter that Holmes enabled Brandeis to cast two votes instead of one, it was a peevish utterance and he was unjust to both men.

They had known each other in Boston when Brandeis was a young lawyer just out of Harvard, and Holmes a state court judge interested in the affairs of the school and its graduates. But after that, except for Brandeis' appearances before the Court in Washington as a counsel, they had little contact until Brandeis became a colleague. There can be no question that Holmes was struck by Brandeis' complete integrity as well as by his vast knowledge, by his ethical sense, by his almost agonizing

[5] See pp. 131-133.

determination to do the right thing. "There goes a *good* man," he would say to Mrs. Holmes when Brandeis left their home. But the differences between the two were profound. Brandeis was an economist where Holmes was a philosopher. He was austere where Holmes, except when he was deeply aroused, tended to be whimsical, paradoxical and gay. Holmes was the author of *The Common Law,* "The Soldier's Faith," and numerous delightful and discursive letters to Pollock and others. Brandeis was the author of *Other People's Money,* and when he wrote letters they were like communiqués from a battlefield, with the rattle of artillery sounding in their one-two-three memorandum sequence. Holmes thought in terms of a finite universe of which man was only an infinitesimal part, and was skeptical of any sort of moral imperialism, including social reform. Brandeis saw the emergence of a concentrated corporate power within the commonwealth, of a state within a state, and bent every effort toward making real his dream of a Periclean democracy on the American plains. Brandeis was Holmes's conscience, and Holmes still had enough of the Puritan in him to have a slumbering conscience that could be awakened and fortified. But while Brandeis, as a conscience, bolstered Holmes's legal views and strengthened his more liberal impulses, he could not change Holmes in essentials. Despite all his proddings, Holmes could never read any of the economic treatises Brandeis urged on him. They were "improving" — an epithet Holmes applied to anything that disturbed his sense of a limited universe. Brandeis he considered one of the "onward and upward" fellows. The tastes of his friend, Sir Frederick Pollock, although not nearly so deep a person as Brandeis, were nearer his own.

9

With the outbreak of the World War, the Court was confronted by new problems. Holmes had never been an antimilitarist. He had always seen peace as "a little space of calm in the midst of the tempestuous untamed streaming of the world." "High and dangerous action," he had said, "teaches us to believe as right beyond dispute things for which our doubting minds are slow to find words of proof." If Holmes had been less of a philosopher, he would have come close to being something of a fire-eater. He had been increasingly troubled by noting among the young secretaries who came to him from the Harvard Law School, part of whose job was to read aloud to him and with whom he discussed life as well as law, an increasing skepticism of patriotic values. He had scant belief in this "experimenting in negations." And yet it is characteristic of him that while with the outbreak of the war he had far fewer words to eat and fewer attitudes to erase than anyone else, he did not go as far as others in uncritical glorifications of the war. This was partly because his whole method was to proceed by continuities rather than by mutations, partly because his critical mind sought always to balance the excesses he saw around him. It was also characteristic of Holmes that one who all his life had had a fighting faith should now be so moderate in trumpeting it and so wary of its abuse.

He had always liked the English without being an Anglophile. In England's moments of greatest danger during the war Holmes in his letters to Pollock rejoiced with the English victories, expressed concern at the reverses and the bombing raids on London, shared Pollock's impatience with President Wilson's conduct of foreign affairs in the years before America's entrance into the war, and would probably have preferred his former colleague Hughes in the Presidency after 1916. He was, to be sure, civilized enough not to let the war wipe out his feeling of esteem for the German legal scholars and historians whom he had known. But when the hour of decision came for America, Holmes had no hesitation. "Between two groups that want to make inconsistent kinds of a world, I see no remedy except force."

Holmes did not idealize the actual experience of war. He had learned what it was like. But he knew long before our own discovery of it the slackness of individual social will out of which the pacifist impulses grow. Philosophically he accepted war as part of his universe. He had, moreover, a belief in the toughening effect of warlike sports and pursuits ("a price well paid for the breeding of a race fit for leadership and command"). To most of us today such words will seem dangerously close to imperialism. But Holmes was more concerned with national cohesion than with conquest. He thought that the war experience gave the individual once more a sense of being part of "an unimaginable whole." If this is mysticism it is the sort that the recent experiences of Britain, Russia, and America tend to validate. These quotations have been from the Holmes of the 1890's. But as late as 1913, in his speech on "Law and the Court," he expressed "an old man's apprehension" that "competition from new races will cut deeper than working men's disputes and will test whether we can hang together or can fight."

Because of these convictions the war, when it came to the Supreme Court, did not catch Holmes intellectually unprepared. As a judge there were two principal problems he would have to face. The first was the question of the positive powers of a wartime democracy. For all his relativism, Holmes saw the war as a struggle on our side for our conception of civilized values. He could not see, therefore, how the network of government regulation of industry and the daily lives of people fell outside the Constitution or was a prohibitive price to pay for the survival of these values. The opinion which best expresses this belief is in *Missouri* v. *Holland,* the migratory bird treaty case, and in *Block* v. *Hirsh,* the leading Emergency Rent Law case.[6] That Holmes would have extended the same logic from the Congressional power to the Presidential war power follows from the analogy of his reasoning about the governor's power in *Moyer* v. *Peabody*. And it is likely that the present Supreme Court will similarly uphold the current working conception of adequate war powers in a democracy.

A more difficult problem that came before Holmes and the Court was that of civil liberties in wartime. I shall discuss this at some length in my prefaces to Holmes's civil liberties opin-

[6] For *Block* v. *Hirsh* see p. 278; for *Missouri* v. *Holland* see p. 273.

ions.[7] As a Massachusetts judge, Holmes had dealt with the regular run of civil liberties cases and in one, *Commonwealth v. Davis,* had written a legal opinion which was much cited later by those wishing to restrict by municipal ordinance the right to use public property as a forum for discussion. It was by no means a foregone conclusion, therefore, that Holmes would, with the World War cases, become a champion of civil liberties.

That he did may be traced to several strands of influence. One was Holmes's sense of critical balance and his dislike for the excesses committed by wartime patrioteers. A second was his admiration for the civil liberties of the English tradition, and for the temperate manner in which they handled problems of intellectual freedom. A third was the influence of Brandeis, who brought to the Court a fierce determination that nothing should destroy the right of criticism upon which democratic change depends. One may guess that in this association Brandeis helped enrich Holmes's grasp of the social values of the problem, and Holmes's contribution was to give the conception sharpness of legal contour and his unique gift of form. And finally there was Holmes's growing sense that men could do little by repression to divert the movement of events. This comes out most sharply in 1925 in the closing paragraph of his dissent in *Gitlow* v. *New York:* "If in the long run the beliefs expressed in proletarian dictatorship are destined to be accepted by the dominant forces of the community, the only meaning of free speech is that they should be given their chance and have their way." Here he sees free speech as the core of the succession of political power in a democracy, and the larger function of government to give expression to the struggle of life.

To these factors must be added Holmes's sense of legal craftsmanship and his devotion to legal values. That this was a real devotion is clear not only from the great personal reluctance he felt about his opinion in the *Debs* case, but even more from his brief memorandum on refusing a stay of execution for Sacco and Vanzetti in 1927. There is very little that Holmes added to the philosophical conception of intellectual freedom in a de-

[7] See p. 289.

mocracy, although he gave it a literary sharpness. His creative work lay in reducing the nebulousness of philosophical concepts to usable legal standards. In the *Schenck* case, and after that in the *Abrams* and *Gitlow* dissents, Holmes worked out the tests of clear and present danger and of actual intent which may serve as a point of departure for Supreme Court action in this area.

The philosophical concepts of intellectual freedom have been relatively constant from Milton to Mill, and from Bagehot to Holmes and Brandeis. The legal concepts have been given greater precision. But the social framework within which these philosophical and legal criteria are to be applied has changed drastically from the England of Milton's day to the America of our own, from the licensing acts which represented the dangers to intellectual freedom in the time of the Stuarts to the obscene scribblings of Coughlin and Pelley or the divisionist articles in the Chicago *Tribune* which represent the danger in the time of the Nazi thrust for world empire. Rarely have the contours of an intellectual and political problem shifted so drastically as in the decades between the prosecutions of Debs and Pelley, between the Post Office order against Berger's Milwaukee *Leader* and that against Coughlin's *Social Justice*. Neither the national sedition laws nor the state criminal syndicalism laws, which were chiefly relied on in the period of the first World War, seem adapted to the present social situation. Professor Herbert Wechsler has expressed this change with remarkable incisiveness: "The enemies of American democracy, whoever they are, are not advocating its violent overthrow. In the field of speech, they are talking about the vices of England, or of the Jews, or the folly of war or the advantages of trading with a victorious Germany. In the field of action, their eye is not on the overthrow of the government but on retarding production for defense. . . . The legislation which speaks in terms of advocacy of violent overthrow . . . represents an uncritical acceptance of a formula devised during the days when the Communist manifesto represented the technique of revolution; when revolutionaries operated by declaring rather than disguising their principles." And Dean Mark Howe has re-enforced this viewpoint in a notable review of Chafee's *Free Speech in the United States*.[8]

But all this has to do not so much with Holmes's own position as with the controversy over the present-day applications of it. It is a tribute to the mark that Holmes has left on us that in much of the current controversy over free speech in wartime the fires of doctrine should rage over how Holmes would have interpreted the problem and what he would say if he were alive today.

As he grew older, Holmes liked to joke about his being an old man. Yet behind the jest there was a serious concern lest he outstay his competence on the Court, as others before him had done. To the end of his tenure, however, there was no sign of declining powers. He had, of course, increasingly to conserve his strength, particularly after a major operation he had to undergo in 1922. In 1929 his wife died. Life was drawing to a close for him. In 1931, on the occasion of his ninetieth birthday, honors and tributes were heaped upon him from all sides. On January 12, 1932, he retired from the Court. He felt like a schoolboy released from his duties. He could no longer write letters by his own hand, but he continued with the aid of his secretary to read and keep in touch with the new figures on the intellectual horizon. With his zest for life scarcely diminished, he waited serenely for death. It came on March 6, 1935. Two days later he would have been ninety-four.

10

Is the influence he left a transitory one? And are we in danger of accepting him too uncritically? We have had warnings lately, from Walton Hamilton and others, against the development of a Holmes cult. And yet, if the materials for a cult are there, the warnings will do little good. Despite the strictures on

---

[8] 55 HLR 695, 698, 699 (1942). For further discussion of these issues of civil liberties, see the prefaces and cases in the section below on "State Power and Free Trade in Ideas," pp. 289 ff.

Holmes and the skepticism about him from skeptical minds, there will be in every generation young men to read Holmes's words who will not read the words of warning about him. And their minds will be captured not alone by the words but by the personal image of Holmes that emerges from them. What is this image? Borrowing the notion of a guardian genius, one might say that Holmes was watched over by one of those grave-gay deities of the Greeks with his Apollonian serenity and his irrepressible high spirits. What disappoints many about Holmes is the absence of passion and of a feeling of dedication, the lack of the pattern of torture and complexity such as the generations following Dostoevski and Nietzsche have come to expect of the modern hero. To use Nietzsche's dualism, there was very much of the Apollonian in Holmes and very little of the darker urges of the Dionysian.

He had a serenity even in his moments of anger or near-despair, an assurance even in the midst of skepticism. It is a chastening thing to read his writings over the span of his life — to see how slow has been the movement toward a workable democracy, how many obstructions have been placed in its path, how unmalleable have been the interpretations placed on the fundamental laws by the dominant judicial caste, how spirit-breaking the efforts to fight against complacency and blindness. But if it is chastening, it is also heartening, particularly today when the young men need to be heartened about the future of a militant democracy: heartening to see how at the high tide of capitalist materialism there were still those who stood by their faith in social reason and in the competition of ideas, their belief in the steady, if slow, march of social progress. Holmes was one of these. He was at once buoyant and unfooled. The most striking thing about him was that he refused to live in a closed universe. He was a great spokesman of our Constitutional tradition because he was a great enough conservative to stretch the framework of the past to accommodate at least some of the needs of the present. He saw himself as part of the army of historic movement, whose "black spearheads" he saw "stretching away against the unattainable sky."

That is different, however, from saying that he was a conscious militant in the armies of social change. To lay violent siege to history was as little in his temperament as to shake his fist at the cosmos. He accepted the limits both of history and of nature and within those limits he found his freedom in a free world. He was part of no movement. What he said and wrote did not grow out of the current social experience or the emerging cultural forces. They were rather the reaping of past experience and the extraction of its full implications by a man who was content enough with life, but who did not feel God enough to hem in those whose passion for change was greater than his.

In every culture the core of its existence has been a poetic attitude toward the world. This attitude has often been better expressed by the symbols of literature and art than by the urgencies of political or economic doctrine. For the poet can often distill into his symbols even the experiences of which he has not been a direct part, particularly if he have in him a sense of the past and a sensitiveness to the mood around him. Many have wondered how an aristocrat like Holmes, who lived the life almost of a recluse, who would have nothing to do with the mechanical gadgets of American life, who refused to read the newspapers and identified himself with none of the political or economic movements of his time, was nevertheless able to distill into his writings the sense of American libertarian democracy. One may as well ask how John Keats, despite his limited experience, was able to put into his poetry both the power and pain of his Europe. I venture the belief that the son of Dr. Holmes turned out to be more of a poet than his father, if by poet we mean someone who pierces the appearances of life and expresses his vision in moving symbols. And if this sheds some light on Holmes, it should be not without meaning for his age that one of its poets should have had to work in the intractable material of legal technics.

Despite this — better, because of this — Holmes has had a great impact on our Constitutional development and national history. For a time it seemed that his work, however gallant, would prove frustrate. The Supreme Court majority continued to show a glacial hostility to his basic constitutional attitudes, and the country as a whole showed an indifference to his fighting faith. If Holmes had to wait for his vindication on the latter until Dunkirk and Pearl Harbor, his victory with respect to the former came earlier, only a year or two after his death. The constitutional crisis of the New Deal and the struggle over the Court reorganization plan of another Roosevelt cleared the way for the complete adoption of Holmes's views on constitutional law. The new doctrinal directions of the present Supreme Court spell more than anything else a return to Holmes. Chief Justice Stone was his faithful companion in dissents, Justice Frankfurter his devoted disciple, and all but one or two of the others have studied him and caught his spirit. While they may disagree as to what Holmes's meaning is for today, they carry on much of their work in his shadow.

Thus Holmes has created the means for his vindication. But his vindication in turn will tend to reduce that sense of wonder upon which a man's *éclat* in history depends. Holmes wrote in his essay on Montesquieu that "because his book was a work of science and epoch-making, it is as dead as the classics." Similarly in some of his letters to Pollock on the difficulty today of reading the classics, he points out that what has been borrowed from them and built into the structure of our own thought, strips them of the sense of newness and surprise. That may well happen to Holmes in the next few generations. And yet, despite what familiarity may do to his thought, there is beyond the thought the imprint of a unique personality and of a poetic image.

There are those who compare Holmes with John Marshall. The comparison is unjust to both men. Unlike Marshall, Holmes is a great man regardless of whether he was a great justice. He will probably leave a greater effect on English style and on what the young men dream and want than upon American constitutional law. Marshall's reputation stands or falls with the vested interests he defended and with the viability of the system of economic relations that leans heavily on his constitutional interpretations. The greatness of Holmes will survive the vested interests and their constitutional bolstering. It will stand up as long as the English language stands up, as long as men find life complex and exciting, and law a part of life, and the sharp blade of thought powerful to cleave both.

PART I

Campaigns of Life and Law

1. A Fighting Faith: the Civil War
2. Law as Calling, Life as Art
3. Law as Civilization
4. Law as Judgment: Some Massachusetts Judicial Opinions

Campaigns of Life and Law

The selections in Part I extend from the Holmes who was a boy just out of college in 1861 to the Holmes who in 1902, when he was sixty-one, left the Supreme Judicial Court of Massachusetts to become a member of the United States Supreme Court. In the case of only one selection have I gone beyond this period — to the fiftieth anniversary speech on the Class of 1861, delivered in 1911, which belongs among the memories of the Civil War.[1] This was the period of Holmes's preparation, and of the flowering of that maturity whose fruits were to be plucked in Holmes's tenure on the United States Supreme Court.

There are varied strains in each of us which it is the task of growth to reconcile and integrate. In Holmes those strains were three — literature and philosophy; war; and law. All three are mentioned in the concluding passage of his Class Book statement in 1861: "The tendencies of the family and of myself have a strong natural bent to literature, etc.; at present I am trying for a commission in one of the Massachusetts Regiments, however, and hope to go south before very long. If I survive the war I expect to study law as my profession or at least for a starting point."[2]

It will be clear from this that Holmes was at the time undecided about his main professional interest. He was not certain, as he was to reveal in some of his later speeches, whether he could quite stomach law as a profession: it seemed narrow and arid.[3] Did he possibly at the start consider it as a way of maintaining himself while he gave his principal energies to literature? We know only once entered on a study of law he turned into its channels the main flow of his energies.

Before this career could be realized, the Civil War interposed itself, and young Holmes spent the four years of the war in the field, in hospitals, and at home convalescing. As Holmes looked back at his war experience later, there was a unity in his life as a soldier and his

[1] See "Parts of the Unimaginable Whole," the Class of '61: Fiftieth Anniversary (1911), p. 25.
[2] See p. 8.
[3] See "A Man and the Universe," p. 35.

life as a lawyer. Both were equally campaigns, both dealt with the risks of life and with its discipline, both involved an area of freedom and passion within a framework of rigor, both were windows opening on wider but crucial perspectives.

There were three aspects of law that interested him primarily, and these I have indicated by the subheadings of sections two, three and four in Part I. Law was a calling, with exacting vocational demands upon the practising lawyer; law was a cultural study — one of the social sciences — and as such it was one way of approaching the complex of civilization; and law, in judicial terms, was a form of judgment, of adjusting the conflicting claims, decrees, power thrusts in a society.

1. A Fighting Faith: the Civil War

"Through our great good fortune," writes Holmes in one of the speeches that follows, "in our youth our hearts were touched with fire. It was given to us to learn at the outset that life is a profound and passionate thing." The experience of the Civil War was the maturing force in Holmes's life. From it derive four of the great elements in his thinking: that life is risk, that our fates depend often on a throw of the dice, and that law must embody this aleatory quality; that life is battle, and the best meaning of effort comes out under fire; that one must be a good soldier with "a splendid carelessness for life" in a cause; and that one must have a fighting faith — that "to act with enthusiasm and faith is the condition of acting greatly."

The first selection shows Holmes still as student. Despite the deliberate and clipped dryness of this Class Book sketch, it reveals a pride of ancestry all the more effective because it is not stuffy. And when the student turned soldier and faced an uncertain future, it was with a quiet conviction of duty done, as the last line of his Class Poem runs, "We do in silence what the world shall sing."

Holmes's speeches on the Civil War, characterized by grace and restrained warmth and a felicity of phrase, contain some of the best of his writing. They are all occasional, yet they fulfill the requirements of the formal occasion without any stiffness. Their theme is the heroic and the ideal — what men can believe when they surrender themselves to something beyond themselves, and what they can do when they stretch their capacities to the breaking-point. Holmes is thus always in these speeches skirting the edges of the unutterable. If now and then he spills over into the sentimental and slightly mawkish ("Such hearts — ah me, how many — were stilled twenty years ago," or the passage in the 1884 Memorial Day speech on the women who waited at home) his literary skill is, on the whole, much greater than that of any man who was called upon in the 1880's to make commemorative speeches on the Civil War.

One finds in these speeches — especially in The Soldier's Faith — *an idealization of war which runs a nimble gantlet between militarist and humanist values. "I do not know what is true. I do not know* the meaning of the universe. But in the midst of doubt, in the collapse of creeds, there is one thing I do not doubt . . . and that is that the faith is true and adorable which leads a soldier to throw away his life in obedience to a blindly accepted duty, in a cause which he little understands, in a plan of campaign of which he has no notion, under tactics of which he does not see the use." Here is a sense of blind obedience which approaches the religious credo quia absurdum. A decade ago the American reader might have said it runs too close to the militarist. But a generation that has seen democracies go down through pacifism and passivity, through the smug materialism of wealth and the denigration of both fighting and faith, has learned to take this phase of Holmes seriously.[1]

In his later years Holmes found the memory of the Civil War so painful that he preferred not to read or talk about it. Yet he never lost a wholeness of view about the war — a recognition that in its daily grimy details it was an unromantic affair ("the reality was to pass a night on the ground in the rain with your bowels out of order, and after no particular breakfast to attack the enemy"), along with a persistent belief that in its essence it was a good antidote to the easy materialism of an industrial culture, and a healthy form of participation in the "unimaginable whole" of the collective world.

AUTOBIOGRAPHICAL SKETCH [2]

I, Oliver Wendell Holmes, Jr., was born March 8, 1841, in Boston. My father was born in Cambridge, graduated at Harvard, studied medicine in Paris and returning to Boston practised as a physician there a number of years. Giving this up, however, he has since supported himself by acting as a professor of the Medical School of Harvard College, by lecturing and by writing a number of books. In 1840 he married Amelia Lee Jackson, daughter of Judge Jackson of Boston, where he has since resided. All my three names designate families from which I am descended. A long pedigree of Olivers and

---

[1] For an interesting commentary on this phase of Holmes, showing how a pragmatist squares his pragmatism with the absolutes of a fighting faith, see T. V. Smith, *The Democratic Tradition in America* (1941), ch. iv, "Judicial Personalization of the Tradition: Justice Oliver Wendell Holmes."

[2] From Album of the Harvard College class of 1861, Number 1, p. 12, cited in *Preparation of an American Aristocrat*, by Frederick C. Fiechter, Jr. 6 *New England Quarterly* (1933), 3, 4.

A FIGHTING FAITH: THE CIVIL WAR 7

Wendells may be found in the book called *Memorials of the Dead in Boston. — King's Chapel Burying Ground*, pp. 144 and 234-5-6-7-8. Of my grandfather Abiel Holmes, an account may be found in the biographical dictionaries. (He was the author of the *Annals of America*, etc.) as also of my other grandfather Charles Jackson — (See, for instance, *Appleton's New American Cyclopedia* where the account of Judge Jackson was written by my father.) I think it better thus to give a few satisfactory references than to write an account which is half so. Some of my ancestors have fought in the Revolution; among the great-grandmothers of the family were Dorothy Quincy and Anne Bradstreet ("the tenth Muse"); and so on; but these things can be picked up from other sources I have indicated. My Grandfather A. Holmes was graduated from Yale in 1783 and in 1792 was "gradu honorario donatur" at Harvard. Various Olivers and Wendells will be found in the triennial, as also various Jacksons; including my grandfather. Our family has been in the habit of receiving a college education and I came of course in my turn, as my grandfathers, fathers, and uncles had been before me. I've always lived in Boston and went first to a woman's school there, then to Rev. T. R. Sullivan's, then to E. S. Dixwell's (Private Latin School) and thence to College. I never had any business but that of a student before coming to College; which I did with the majority of our class in July, entering without conditions. I was, while in College, a member and editor of the Institute (had somewhat to do with our two private clubs), of the Hasty Pudding, the Porcellian, the ΦBK and the "Christian Union"; not that I considered my life justified belonging to the latter, but because I wished to bear testimony in favor of a Religious society founded on liberal principles in distinction to the more "orthodox" and sectarian platform of the "Xtian Brethren." I was editor in the Senior year of the *Harvard Magazine* (the chief piece I wrote in it being on "Albert Durer"). I was author of an article on Plato which took the prize as the best article by an undergraduate (for the first year of its existence) in the *University Quarterly*. The only College prize I have tried for was the Greek which was divided between one of the Juniors and me. When the war broke out I joined the "4th Battalion of Infantry" and went down to Fort Independence expecting when drilled to go south (as a private). While at the Fort and after we were ordered up I had to patch up a Class Poem as quickly and as well as I could under the circumstances, since I had been elected to that office before going (2nd term Senior). We stayed about a month at the Fort and then I came to Boston and on classday (a week and a half ago) I delivered my poem side by side with my friend Hallowell who was orator and who had also been at the Fort. The tendencies of the family and of myself have a strong natural bent to literature, etc., at present I am trying for a commission in one of the Massachusetts Regiments, however, and hope to go south before very long. If I survive the war I expect to study law as my profession or at least for a starting point.

(in haste)

O. W. HOLMES, JR.,
July 2nd, 1861

[*and then in pencil*]

(N.B. I may say I don't believe in gushing much in these College Biog's and think a dry statement much fitter. Also I am too busy now to say more if I would.)

THE CLASS OF *1861*: A POEM [1]

How fought our brothers, and how died, the story
You bid me tell, who shared with them the praise,
Who sought with them the martyr's crown of glory,
The bloody birthright of heroic days.

But, all untuned amid the din of battle,
Not to our lyrics the inspiring strains belong;
The cannon's roar, the musket's deadly rattle
Have drowned the music, and have stilled the song.

Let others celebrate our high endeavor
When peace once more her starry flag shall fling
Wide o'er the land our arms made free forever;
We do in silence what the world shall sing.

---

[1] Delivered by Holmes at a class dinner at "Young's" in Boston, July 20, 1864. Reprinted in Silas Bent, *Justice Oliver Wendell Holmes, a Biography* (1932).

MEMORIAL DAY[1]

Not long ago I heard a young man ask why people still kept up Memorial Day, and it set me thinking of the answer. Not the answer that you and I should give to each other, — not the expression of those feelings that, so long as you and I live, will make this day sacred to memories of love and grief and heroic youth, — but an answer which should command the assent of those who do not share our memories, and in which we of the North and our brethren of the South could join in perfect accord.

So far as this last is concerned, to be sure, there is no trouble. The soldiers who were doing their best to kill one another felt less of personal hostility, I am very certain, than some who were not imperilled by their mutual endeavors. I have heard more than one of those who had been gallant and distinguished officers on the Confederate side say that they had had no such feeling. I know that I and those whom I knew best had not. We believed that it was most desirable that the North should win; we believed in the principle that the Union is indissoluble; we, or many of us at least, also believed that the conflict was inevitable, and that slavery had lasted long enough. But we equally believed that those who stood against us held just as sacred convictions that were the opposite of ours, and we respected them as every man with a heart must respect those who give all for their belief. The experience of battle soon taught its lesson even to those who came into the field more bitterly disposed. You could not stand up day after day in those indecisive contests where overwhelming victory was impossible because neither side would run as they ought when beaten, without getting at last something of the same brotherhood for the enemy that the north pole of a magnet has for the south, — each working in an opposite sense to the other, but each unable to get along without the other. As it was then, it is now. The soldiers of the war need no explanations; they can join in commemorating a soldier's death with feelings not different in kind, whether he fell toward them or by their side.

But Memorial Day may and ought to have a meaning also for those who do not share our memories. When men have instinctively agreed to celebrate an anniversary, it will be found that there is

---

[1] An address delivered May 30, 1884, at Keene, N. H., before John Sedgwick Post No. 4, Grand Army of the Republic. *Speeches* (1913), 11–12.

some thought or feeling behind it which is too large to be dependent upon associations alone. The Fourth of July, for instance, has still its serious aspect, although we no longer should think of rejoicing like children that we have escaped from an outgrown control, although we have achieved not only our national but our moral independence and know it far too profoundly to make a talk about it, and although an Englishman can join in the celebration without a scruple. For, stripped of the temporary associations which gave rise to it, it is now the moment when by common consent we pause to become conscious of our national life and to rejoice in it, to recall what our country has done for each of us, and to ask ourselves what we can do for our country in return.

So to the indifferent inquirer who asks why Memorial Day is still kept up we may answer, It celebrates and solemnly reaffirms from year to year a national act of enthusiasm and faith. It embodies in the most impressive form our belief that to act with enthusiasm and faith is the condition of acting greatly. To fight out a war, you must believe something and want something with all your might. So must you do to carry anything else to an end worth reaching. More than that, you must be willing to commit yourself to a course, perhaps a long and hard one, without being able to foresee exactly where you will come out. All that is required of you is that you should go somewhither as hard as ever you can. The rest belongs to fate. One may fall, — at the beginning of the charge or at the top of the earthworks; but in no other way can he reach the rewards of victory.

When it was felt so deeply as it was on both sides that a man ought to take part in the war unless some conscientious scruple or strong practical reason made it impossible, was that feeling simply the requirement of a local majority that their neighbors should agree with them? I think not: I think the feeling was right, — in the South as in the North. I think that, as life is action and passion, it is required of a man that he should share the passion and action of his time at peril of being judged not to have lived.

If this be so, the use of this day is obvious. It is true that I cannot argue a man into a desire. If he says to me, Why should I wish to know the secrets of philosophy? Why seek to decipher the hidden laws of creation that are graven upon the tablets of the rocks, or to unravel the history of civilization that is woven in the tissue of our jurisprudence, or to do any great work, either of speculation or of practical affairs? I cannot answer him; or at least my answer is as little worth making for any effect it will have upon his wishes as if he asked why should I eat this, or drink that. You must begin by wanting to. But although desire cannot be imparted by argument, it can be by contagion. Feeling begets feeling, and great feeling begets great feeling. We can hardly share the emotions that make this day to us the most sacred day of the year, and embody them in ceremonial pomp, without in some degree imparting them to those who come after us. I believe from the bottom of my heart that our memorial halls and statues and tablets, the tattered flags of our regiments gathered in the Statehouses, and this day with its funeral march and decorated graves, are worth more to our young men by way of chastening and inspiration than the monuments of another hundred years of peaceful life could be.

But even if I am wrong, even if those who come after us are to forget all that we hold dear, and the future is to teach and kindle its children in ways as yet unrevealed, it is enough for us that to us this day is dear and sacred.

Accidents may call up the events of the war. You see a battery of guns go by at a trot, and for a moment you are back at White Oak Swamp, or Antietam, or on the Jerusalem Road. You hear a few shots fired in the distance, and for an instant your heart stops as you say to yourself, The skirmishers are at it, and listen for the long roll of fire from the main line. You meet an old comrade after many years of absence; he recalls the moment when you were nearly surrounded by the enemy, and again there comes up to you that swift and cunning thinking on which once hung life or freedom — Shall I stand the best chance if I try the pistol or the sabre on that man who means to stop me? Will he get his carbine free before I reach him, or can I kill him first? These and the thousand other events we have known are called up, I say, by accident, and, apart from accident, they lie forgotten.

But as surely as this day comes round we are in the presence of the dead. For one hour, twice a year at least, — at the regimental dinner, where the ghosts sit at table more numerous than the living, and on this day when we decorate their graves, — the dead come back and live with us.

I see them now, more than I can number, as once I saw them on this earth. They are the same bright figures, or their counterparts, that come also before your eyes; and when I speak of those who were my brothers, the same words describe yours.

I see a fair-haired lad, a lieutenant, and a captain on whom life had begun somewhat to tell, but still young, sitting by the long mess-table in camp before the regiment left the State, and wondering how many of those who gathered in our tent could hope to see the end of what was then beginning. For neither of them was that destiny reserved. I remember, as I awoke from my first long stupor in the hospital after the battle of Ball's Bluff, I heard the doctor say, "He was a beautiful boy," and I knew that one of those two speakers was no more. The other, after passing harmless through all the previous battles, went into Fredericksburg with strange premonition of the end, and there met his fate.

I see another youthful lieutenant as I saw him in the Seven Days, when I looked down the line at Glendale. The officers were at the head of their companies. The companies' advance was beginning. We caught each other's eye and saluted. When next I looked, he was gone.

I see the brother of the last, — the flame of genius and daring in his face, — as he rode before us into the wood of Antietam, out of which came only dead and deadly wounded men. So, a little later, he rode to his death at the head of his cavalry in the Valley.

In the portraits of some of those who fell in the civil wars of England, Vandyke has fixed on canvas the type of those who stand before my memory. Young and gracious figures, somewhat remote and proud, but with a melancholy and sweet kindness. There is upon their faces the shadow of approaching fate, and the glory of generous acceptance of it. I may say of them, as I once heard it said of two Frenchmen, relics of the *ancien régime,* "They were very gentle. They cared nothing for their lives." High breeding, romantic chivalry — we who have seen these men can never believe that the power of money or the enervation of pleasure has put an end to them. We know that life may still be lifted into poetry and lit with spiritual charm.

But the men not less, perhaps even more, characteristic of New England, were the Puritans of our day. For the Puritan still lives in New England, thank God! and will live there so long as New England lives and keeps her old renown. New England is not dead yet. She still is mother of a race of conquerors, — stern men, little given to the expression of their feelings, sometimes careless of the graces, but fertile, tenacious, and knowing only duty. Each of you, as I do, thinks of a hundred such that he has known. I see one — grandson of a hard rider of the Revolution and bearer of his historic name — who was with us at Fair Oaks, and afterwards for five days and nights in front of the enemy the only sleep that he would take was what he could snatch sitting erect in his uniform and resting his back against a hut. He fell at Gettysburg.

His brother, a surgeon, who rode, as our surgeons so often did, wherever the troops would go, I saw kneeling in ministration to a wounded man just in rear of our line at Antietam, his horse's bridle round his arm, — the next moment his ministrations were ended. His senior associate survived all the wounds and perils of the war, but, not yet through with duty as he understood it, fell in helping the helpless poor who were dying of cholera in a Western city.

I see another quiet figure, of virtuous life and silent ways, not much heard of until our left was turned at Petersburg. He was in command of the regiment as he saw our comrades driven in. He threw back his left wing, and the advancing tide of defeat was shattered against his iron wall. He saved an army corps from disaster, and then a round shot ended all for him.

There is one who on this day is always present to my mind. He entered the army at nineteen, a second lieutenant. In the Wilderness, already at the head of his regiment, he fell, using the moment that was left him of life to give all his little fortune to his soldiers. I saw him in camp, on the march, in action. I crossed debatable land with him when we were rejoining the army together. I observed him in every kind of duty, and never in all the time that I knew him did I see him fail to choose that alternative of conduct which was most disagreeable to himself. He was indeed a Puritan in all his virtues, without the Puritan austerity; for, when duty was at an end, he who had been the master and leader became the chosen companion in every pleasure that a man might honestly enjoy. In action he was sublime. His few surviving companions will never forget the awful spectacle of his advance alone with his company in the streets of Fredericksburg. In less than sixty seconds he would become the focus of a hidden and annihilating fire from a semicircle of houses. His first platoon had vanished under it in an instant, ten men falling dead by his side. He had quietly turned back to where the other half of his company was waiting, had given the order, "Second platoon, forward!" and was again moving on, in obedience to superior command, to certain and useless death, when the order he was obeying was countermanded. The end was distant only a few seconds; but if you had seen him with his indifferent carriage, and sword swinging from his finger like a cane, you never would have suspected that he was doing more than conducting a company drill on the camp parade ground. He was little more than a boy, but the grizzled corps commanders knew and admired him; and for us, who not only admired, but loved, his death seemed to end a portion of our life also.

There is one grave and commanding presence that you all would recognize, for his life has become a part of our common history. Who does not remember the leader of the assault at the mine of Petersburg? The solitary horseman in front of Port Hudson, whom a foeman worthy of him bade his soldiers spare, from love and admiration of such gallant bearing? Who does not still hear the echo of those eloquent lips after the war, teaching reconciliation and peace? I may not do more than allude to his death, fit ending of his life. All that the world has a right to know has been told by a beloved friend in a book wherein friendship has found no need to exaggerate facts that speak for themselves. I knew him, and I may even say I knew him well; yet, until that book appeared, I had not known the governing motive of his soul. I had admired him as a hero. When I read, I learned to revere him as a saint. His strength was not in honor alone, but in religion; and those who do not share his creed must see that it was on the wings of religious faith that he mounted above even valiant deeds into an empyrean of ideal life.

I have spoken of some of the men who were near to me among others very near and dear, not because their lives have become historic, but because their lives are the type of what every soldier has known and seen in his own company. In the great democracy of self-devotion private and general stand side by side. Unmarshalled save by their own deeds, the armies of the dead sweep before us, "wearing their wounds like stars." It is not because the men whom I have mentioned were my friends that I have spoken of them, but, I repeat, because they are types. I speak of those whom I have seen. But you all have known such; you, too, remember!

It is not of the dead alone that we think on this day. There are those still living whose sex forbade them to offer their lives, but who gave instead their happiness. Which of us has not been lifted above himself by the sight of one of those lovely, lonely women, around whom the wand of sorrow has traced its excluding circle, — set apart, even when surrounded by loving friends who would fain bring back joy to their lives? I think of one whom the poor of a great city know as their benefactress and friend. I think of one who has lived not less greatly in the midst of her children, to whom she has taught such lessons as may not be heard elsewhere from mortal lips. The story of these and of their sisters we must pass in reverent silence. All that may be said has been said by one of their own sex: —

> But when the days of golden dreams had perished,
> And even despair was powerless to destroy,
> Then did I learn how existence could be cherished,
> Strengthened, and fed without the aid of joy.
>
> Then did I check the tears of useless passion,
> Weaned my young soul from yearning after thine,
> Sternly denied its burning wish to hasten
> Down to that tomb already more than mine.

Comrades, some of the associations of this day are not only triumphant, but joyful. Not all of those with whom we once stood shoulder to shoulder — not all of those whom we once loved and revered — are gone. On this day we still meet our companions in the freezing winter bivouacs and in those dreadful summer marches where every faculty of the soul seemed to depart one after another, leaving only a dumb animal power to set the teeth and to persist — a blind belief that somewhere and at last there was rest and water. On this day, at least, we still meet and rejoice in the closest tie which is possible between men — a tie which suffering has made indissoluble for better, for worse.

When we meet thus, when we do honor to the dead in terms that must sometimes embrace the living, we do not deceive ourselves. We attribute no special merit to a man for having served when all were serving. We know that, if the armies of our war did anything worth remembering, the credit belongs not mainly to the individuals who did it, but to average human nature. We also know very well that we cannot live in associations with the past alone, and we admit that, if we would be worthy of the past, we must find new fields for action or thought, and make for ourselves new careers.

But, nevertheless, the generation that carried on the war has been set apart by its experience. Through our great good fortune, in our youth our hearts were touched with fire. It was given to us to learn at the outset that life is a profound and passionate thing. While we are permitted to scorn nothing but indifference, and do not pretend to undervalue the worldly rewards of ambition, we have seen with our own eyes, beyond and above the gold fields, the snowy heights of honor, and it is for us to bear the report to those who come after us. But, above all, we have learned that whether a man accepts from Fortune her spade, and will look downward and dig, or from Aspiration her axe and cord, and will scale the ice, the one and only success which it is his to command is to bring to his work a mighty heart.

Such hearts — ah me, how many! — were stilled twenty years ago; and to us who remain behind is left this day of memories. Every year, — in the full tide of spring, at the height of the symphony of flowers and love and life, — there comes a pause, and through the silence we hear the lonely pipe of death. Year after year lovers wandering under the apple boughs and through the clover and deep grass are surprised with sudden tears as they see black veiled figures stealing through the morning to a soldier's grave. Year after year the comrades of the dead follow, with public honor, procession and commemorative flags and funeral march — honor and grief from us who stand almost alone, and have seen the best and noblest of our generation pass away.

But grief is not the end of all. I seem to hear the funeral march become a pæan. I see beyond the forest the moving banners of a hidden column. Our dead brothers still live for us, and bid us think of life, not death, — of life to which in their youth they lent the passion and glory of the spring. As I listen, the great chorus of life and joy begins again, and amid the awful orchestra of seen and unseen powers and destinies of good and evil our trumpets sound once more a note of daring, hope, and will.

HARVARD COLLEGE IN THE WAR[1]

MR. PRESIDENT AND GENTLEMEN OF THE ALUMNI:—

Another day than this has been consecrated to the memories of the war. On that day we think not of the children of the University or the city, hardly even of the children whom the State has lost, but of a mighty brotherhood whose parent was our common country. To-day the College is the center of all our feeling, and if we refer to the war it is in connection with the College, and not for its own sake, that we do so. What, then, did the College do to justify our speaking of the war now? She sent a few gentlemen into the field, who died there becomingly. I know of nothing more. The great forces which insured the North success would have been at work even if those men had been absent. Our means of raising money and troops would not have been less, I dare say. The great qualities of the race, too, would still have been there. The greatest qualities, after all, are those of a man, not those of a gentleman, and neither North nor South needed colleges to learn them. And yet — and yet I think we all feel that to us at least the war would seem less beautiful and inspiring if those few gentlemen had not died as they did. Look at yonder portrait and yonder bust,[2] and tell me if stories such as they commemorate do not add a glory to the bare fact that the strongest legions prevailed. So it has been since wars began. After history has done its best to fix men's thoughts upon strategy and finance, their eyes have turned and rested on some single romantic figure, — some Sidney, some Falkland, some Wolfe, some Montcalm, some Shaw. This is that little touch of the superfluous which is necessary. Necessary as art is necessary, and knowledge which serves no mechanical end. Superfluous only as glory is superfluous, or a bit of red ribbon that a man would die to win.

It has been one merit of Harvard College that it has never quite sunk to believing that its only function was to carry a body of

[1] Answer to a toast at Harvard University Commencement, June 25, 1884. *Speeches* (1913), 13–15.
[2] The portrait referred to is that of Colonel Robert Gould Shaw, killed at Fort Wagner, South Carolina, July 18, 1863, in command of the Fifty-fourth Massachusetts Regiment (colored). The bust is that of Brigadier-General Charles Russell Lowell, died, October 20, 1864, of wounds received at Cedar Creek, Virginia, October 19.

specialists through the first stage of their preparation. About these halls there has always been an aroma of high feeling, not to be found or lost in science or Greek, — not to be fixed, yet all-pervading. And the warrant of Harvard College for writing the names of its dead graduates upon its tablets is not in the mathematics, the chemistry, the political economy, which it taught them, but that in ways not to be discovered, by traditions not to be written down, it helped men of lofty natures to make good their faculties. I hope and I believe that it long will give such help to its children. I hope and I believe that, long after we and our tears for the dead have been forgotten, this monument to their memory still will give such help to generations to whom it is only a symbol, — a symbol of man's destiny and power for duty, but a symbol also of that something more by which duty is swallowed up in generosity, that something more which led men like Shaw to toss life and hope like a flower before the feet of their country and their cause.

THE SOLDIER'S FAITH [1]

Any day in Washington Street, when the throng is greatest and busiest, you may see a blind man playing a flute. I suppose that someone hears him. Perhaps also my pipe may reach the heart of some passer in the crowd.

I once heard a man say, "Where Vanderbilt sits, there is the head of the table. I teach my son to be rich." He said what many think. For although the generation born about 1840, and now governing the world, has fought two at least of the greatest wars in history, and has witnessed others, war is out of fashion, and the man who commands the attention of his fellows is the man of wealth. Commerce is the great power. The aspirations of the world are those of commerce. Moralists and philosophers, following its lead, declare that war is wicked, foolish, and soon to disappear.

The society for which many philanthropists, labor reformers, and men of fashion unite in longing is one in which they may be comfortable and may shine without much trouble or any danger. The unfortunately growing hatred of the poor for the rich seems to me to rest on the belief that money is the main thing (a belief in which

[1] An address delivered on Memorial Day, May 30, 1895, at a meeting called by the graduating class of Harvard University. *Speeches* (1913), 56–66.

A FIGHTING FAITH: THE CIVIL WAR 19

the poor have been encouraged by the rich), more than on any grievance. Most of my hearers would rather that their daughters or their sisters should marry a son of one of the great rich families than a regular army officer, were he as beautiful, brave, and gifted as Sir William Napier. I have heard the question asked whether our war was worth fighting, after all. There are many, poor and rich, who think that love of country is an old wife's tale, to be replaced by interest in a labor union, or, under the name of cosmopolitanism, by a rootless self-seeking search for a place where the most enjoyment may be had at the least cost.

Meantime we have learned the doctrine that evil means pain, and the revolt against pain in all its forms has grown more and more marked. From societies for the prevention of cruelty to animals up to socialism, we express in numberless ways the notion that suffering is a wrong which can be and ought to be prevented, and a whole literature of sympathy has sprung into being which points out in story and in verse how hard it is to be wounded in the battle of life, how terrible, how unjust it is that any one should fail.

Even science has had its part in the tendencies which we observe. It has shaken established religion in the minds of very many. It has pursued analysis until at last this thrilling world of colors and sounds and passions has seemed fatally to resolve itself into one vast network of vibrations endlessly weaving an aimless web, and the rainbow flush of cathedral windows, which once to enraptured eyes appeared the very smile of God, fades slowly out into the pale irony of the void.

And yet from vast orchestras still comes the music of mighty symphonies. Our painters even now are spreading along the walls of our Library glowing symbols of mysteries still real, and the hardly silenced cannon of the East proclaim once more that combat and pain still are the portion of man. For my own part, I believe that the struggle for life is the order of the world, at which it is vain to repine. I can imagine the burden changed in the way in which it is to be borne, but I cannot imagine that it ever will be lifted from men's backs. I can imagine a future in which science shall have passed from the combative to the dogmatic stage, and shall have gained such catholic acceptance that it shall take control of life, and condemn at once with instant execution what now is left for nature to destroy. But we are far from such a future, and we cannot stop to amuse or to terrify ourselves with dreams. Now, at least, and perhaps as long as man dwells upon the globe, his destiny is battle, and he has to take the chances of war. If it is our business to fight, the book for the army is a war-song, not a hospital-sketch. It is not well for soldiers to think much about wounds. Sooner or later we shall fall; but meantime it is for us to fix our eyes upon the point to be stormed, and to get there if we can.

Behind every scheme to make the world over, lies the question, What kind of world do you want? The ideals of the past for men have been drawn from war, as those for women have been drawn from motherhood. For all our prophecies, I doubt if we are ready to give up our inheritance. Who is there who would not like to be thought a gentleman? Yet what has that name been built on but the soldier's choice of honor rather than life? To be a soldier or descended from soldiers, in time of peace to be ready to give one's life rather than to suffer disgrace, that is what the world has meant; and if we try to claim it at less cost than a splendid carelessness for life, we are trying to steal the good will without the responsibilities of the place. We will not dispute about tastes. The man of the future may want something different. But who of us could endure a world, although cut up into five-acre lots and having no man upon it who was not well fed and well housed, without the divine folly of honor, without the senseless passion for knowledge outreaching the flaming bounds of the possible, without ideals the essence of which is that they never can be achieved? I do not know what is true. I do not know the meaning of the universe. But in the midst of doubt, in the collapse of creeds, there is one thing I do not doubt, that no man who lives in the same world with most of us can doubt, and that is that the faith is true and adorable which leads a soldier to throw away his life in obedience to a blindly accepted duty, in a cause which he little understands, in a plan of campaign of which he has no notion, under tactics of which he does not see the use.

Most men who know battle know the cynic force with which the thoughts of common sense will assail them in times of stress; but they know that in their greatest moments faith has trampled those thoughts under foot. If you have been in line, suppose on Tremont Street Mall, ordered simply to wait and to do nothing, and have watched the enemy bring their guns to bear upon you down a gentle slope like that from Beacon Street, have seen the puff of the firing, have felt the burst of the spherical case-shot as it came toward you, have heard and seen the shrieking fragments go tearing through your company, and have known that the next or the next shot carries your fate; if you have advanced in line and have seen ahead of you the spot which you must pass where the rifle bullets are striking; if you have ridden by night at a walk toward the blue line of fire at the dead angle of Spottsylvania, where for twenty-four hours the soldiers were fighting on the two sides of an earthwork, and in the morning the dead and dying lay piled in a row six deep, and as you rode have heard the bullets splashing in the mud and earth about you; if you have been on the picketline at night in a black and unknown wood, have heard the spat of the bullets upon the trees, and as you moved have felt your foot slip upon a dead man's body; if you have had a blind fierce gallop against the enemy, with your blood up and a pace that left no time for fear — if, in short, as some, I hope many, who hear me, have known, you have known the vicissitudes of terror and of triumph in war, you know that there is such a thing as the faith I spoke of. You know your own weakness and are modest; but you know that man has in him that unspeakable somewhat which makes him capable of miracle, able to lift himself by the might of his own soul, unaided, able to face annihilation for a blind belief.

From the beginning, to us, children of the North, life has seemed a place hung about by dark mists, out of which come the pale shine of dragon's scales, and the cry of fighting men, and the sound of swords. Beowulf, Milton, Dürer, Rembrandt, Schopenhauer, Turner, Tennyson, from the first war-song of our race to the stall-fed poetry of modern English drawing-rooms, all have had the same vision, and all have had a glimpse of a light to be followed. "The end of worldly life awaits us all. Let him who may, gain honor ere death. That is best for a warrior when he is dead." So spoke Beowulf a thousand years ago.

> Not of the sunlight,
> Not of the moonlight,
> Not of the starlight!
> O young Mariner,
> Down to the haven,
> Call your companions,
> Launch your vessel,
> And crowd your canvas,

> And, ere it vanishes
> Over the margin,
> After it, follow it,
> Follow The Gleam.

So sang Tennyson in the voice of the dying Merlin.

When I went to the war I thought that soldiers were old men. I remembered a picture of the revolutionary soldier which some of you may have seen, representing a white-haired man with his flintlock slung across his back. I remembered one or two living examples of revolutionary soldiers whom I had met, and I took no account of the lapse of time. It was not until long after, in winter quarters, as I was listening to some of the sentimental songs in vogue, such as —

> Farewell, Mother, you may never
> See your darling boy again,

that it came over me that the army was made up of what I now should call very young men. I dare say that my illusion has been shared by some of those now present, as they have looked at us upon whose heads the white shadows have begun to fall. But the truth is that war is the business of youth and early middle age. You who called this assemblage together, not we, would be the soldiers of another war, if we should have one, and we speak to you as the dying Merlin did in the verse which I just quoted. Would that the blind man's pipe might be transfigured by Merlin's magic, to make you hear the bugles as once we heard them beneath the morning stars! For you it is that now is sung the Song of the Sword: —

> The War-Thing, the Comrade,
> Father of honor
> And giver of kingship,
> The fame-smith, the song master.
>
> . . . .
>
> *Priest* (saith the Lord)
> *Of his marriage with victory.*
>
> . . . .
>
> Clear singing, clean slicing;
> Sweet spoken, soft finishing;
> Making death beautiful,

A FIGHTING FAITH: THE CIVIL WAR 23

Life but a coin
To be staked in the pastime
Whose playing is more
Than the transfer of being;
Arch-anarch, chief builder,
Prince and evangelist,
I am the Will of God:
I am the Sword.

War, when you are at it, is horrible and dull. It is only when time has passed that you see that its message was divine. I hope it may be long before we are called again to sit at that master's feet. But some teacher of the kind we all need. In this snug, over-safe corner of the world we need it, that we may realize that our comfortable routine is no eternal necessity of things, but merely a little space of calm in the midst of the tempestuous untamed streaming of the world, and in order that we may be ready for danger. We need it in this time of individualist negations, with its literature of French and American humor, revolting at discipline, loving fleshpots, and denying that anything is worthy of reverence, — in order that we may remember all that buffoons forget. We need it everywhere and at all times. For high and dangerous action teaches us to believe as right beyond dispute things for which our doubting minds are slow to find words of proof. Out of heroism grows faith in the worth of heroism. The proof comes later, and even may never come. Therefore I rejoice at every dangerous sport which I see pursued. The students at Heidelberg, with their sword-slashed faces, inspire me with sincere respect. I gaze with delight upon our poloplayers. If once in a while in our rough riding a neck is broken, I regard it, not as a waste, but as a price well paid for the breeding of a race fit for headship and command.

We do not save our traditions, in this country. The regiments whose battle-flags were not large enough to hold the names of the battles they had fought, vanished with the surrender of Lee, although their memories inherited would have made heroes for a century. It is the more necessary to learn the lesson afresh from perils newly sought, and perhaps it is not vain for us to tell the new generation what we learned in our day, and what we still believe. That the joy of life is living, is to put out all one's powers as far as they will go; that the measure of power is obstacles overcome; to ride boldly at what is in front of you, be it fence or enemy; to pray, not for comfort, but for combat; to keep the soldier's faith against the doubts of civil life, more besetting and harder to overcome than all the misgivings of the battle-field, and to remember that duty is not to be proved in the evil day, but then to be obeyed unquestioning; to love glory more than the temptations of wallowing ease, but to know that one's final judge and only rival is oneself — with all our failures in act and thought, these things we learned from noble enemies in Virginia or Georgia or on the Mississippi, thirty years ago; these things we believe to be true.

> "Life is not lost," said she, "for which is bought
> Endlesse renown."

We learned also, and we still believe, that love of country is not yet an idle name.

> Deare countrey! O how dearely deare
> Ought thy remembraunce, and perpetuall band
> Be to thy foster-child, that from thy hand
> Did commun breath and nouriture receave!
> How brutish is it not to understand
> How much to her we owe, that all us gave;
> That gave unto us all, whatever good we have!

As for us, our days of combat are over. Our swords are rust. Our guns will thunder no more. The vultures that once wheeled over our heads are buried with their prey. Whatever of glory yet remains for us to win must be won in the council or the closet, never again in the field. I do not repine. We have shared the incommunicable experience of war; we have felt, we still feel, the passion of life to its top.

Three years ago died the old colonel of my regiment, the Twentieth Massachusetts. He gave our regiment its soul. No man could falter who heard his "Forward, Twentieth!" I went to his funeral. From a side door of the church a body of little choir-boys came in like a flight of careless doves. At the same time the doors opened at the front, and up the main aisle advanced his coffin, followed by the few gray heads who stood for the men of the Twentieth, the rank and file whom he had loved, and whom he led for the last time. The church was empty. No one remembered the old man whom we were burying, no one save those next to him, and us. And I said to

A FIGHTING FAITH: THE CIVIL WAR 25

myself, The Twentieth has shrunk to a skeleton, a ghost, a memory, a forgotten name which we other old men alone keep in our hearts. And then I thought: It is right. It is as the colonel would have had it. This also is part of the soldier's faith: Having known great things, to be content with silence. Just then there fell into my hands a little song sung by a warlike people on the Danube, which seemed to me fit for a soldier's last word, another song of the sword, but a song of the sword in its scabbard, a song of oblivion and peace.

A soldier has been buried on the battle-field.

>And when the wind in the tree-tops roared,
>The soldier asked from the deep dark grave:
> "Did the banner flutter then?"
>"Not so, my hero," the wind replied,
>"The fight is done, but the banner won,
>Thy comrades of old have borne it hence,
> Have borne it in triumph hence."
>Then the soldier spake from the deep dark grave:
> "I am content."
>
>. . . . .
>
>Then he heareth the lovers laughing pass,
> And the soldier asks once more:
>"Are these not the voices of them that love,
> That love — and remember me?"
>"Not so, my hero," the lovers say,
>"We are those that remember not;
>For the spring has come and the earth has smiled,
> And the dead must be forgot."
>Then the soldier spake from the deep dark grave:
> "I am content."

"PARTS OF THE UNIMAGINABLE WHOLE"[1]

Mr. President and Brethren of the Alumni: —

One of the recurring sights of Alaska, I believe, is when a section of the great glacier cracks and drops into the sea. The last time that I remember witnessing the periodic semi-centennial plunge of

[1] "The Class of '61": Fiftieth Anniversary Reunion (June 28, 1911). *Speeches* (1913), 95–97.

a college class was when I heard Longfellow say "Morituri salutamus." If I should repeat that phrase of the gladiators soon to die, it would be from knowledge and reason, not from feeling, for I own that I am apt to wonder whether I do not dream that I have lived, and may not wake to find that all that I thought done is still to be accomplished and that life is all ahead. — But we have had our warning. Even within the last three months Henry Bowditch, the world-known physiologist, and Frank Emmons, the world-known geologist, have dropped from the class, leaving only the shadow of great names.

I like to think that they were types of '61, not only in their deeds, but in their noble silence. It has been my fortune to belong to two bodies that seemed to me somewhat alike — the 20th Massachusetts Regiment and the class of '61. The 20th never wrote about itself to the newspapers, but for its killed and wounded in battle it stood in the first half-dozen of all the regiments of the north. This little class never talked much about itself, but graduating just as the war of secession began, out of its eighty-one members it had fifty-one under arms, the largest proportion that any class sent to that war.

One learns from time an amiable latitude with regard to beliefs and tastes. Life is painting a picture, not doing a sum. As twenty men of genius looking out of the same window will paint twenty canvases, each unlike all the others, and every one great, so, one comes to think, men may be pardoned for the defects of their qualities if they have the qualities of their defects. But, after all, we all of us have our notions of what is best. I learned in the regiment and in the class the conclusion, at least, of what I think the best service that we can do for our country and for ourselves: To see so far as one may, and to feel, the great forces that are behind every detail — for that makes all the difference between philosophy and gossip, between great action and small; the least wavelet of the Atlantic Ocean is mightier than one of Buzzard's Bay — to hammer out as compact and solid a piece of work as one can, to try to make it first rate, and to leave it unadvertised.

It was a good thing for us in our college days, as Moorfield Storey pointed out a few years ago in an excellent address, that we were all poor. At least we lived as if we were. It seems to me that the training at West Point is better fitted to make a man than for a youth to have all the luxuries of life poured into a trough

A FIGHTING FAITH: THE CIVIL WAR 27

for him at twenty. We had something of that discipline, and before it was over many of us were in barracks learning the school of the soldier. Man is born a predestined idealist, for he is born to act. To act is to affirm the worth of an end, and to persist in affirming the worth of an end is to make an ideal. The stern experience of our youth helped to accomplish the destiny of fate. It left us feeling through life that pleasures do not make happiness and that the root of joy as of duty is to put out all one's powers toward some great end.

When one listens from above to the roar of a great city, there comes to one's ears — almost indistinguishable, but there — the sound of church bells, chiming the hours, or offering a pause in the rush, a moment for withdrawal and prayer. Commerce has outsoared the steeples that once looked down upon the marts, but still their note makes music of the din. For those of us who are not churchmen the symbol still lives. Life is a roar of bargain and battle, but in the very heart of it there rises a mystic spiritual tone that gives meaning to the whole. It transmutes the dull details into romance. It reminds us that our only but wholly adequate significance is as parts of the unimaginable whole. It suggests that even while we think that we are egotists we are living to ends outside ourselves.

2. Law as Calling, Life as Art

Before the mores of the United States Supreme Court cut him off from public utterance, Holmes was greatly in demand as an after-dinner speaker, and several times he spoke upon receiving an honorary degree. Holmes was never merely graceful on these occasions. He used his grace to bring home to his audiences of lawyers by the precept of his words what he was already showing by the example of his life: that the legal profession could be pursued for not ignoble ends and in a philosophic spirit. He admitted to having once had his doubts whether the narrowing effects of the law could be avoided. But he had stayed to discover "that a man may live greatly in the law as well as elsewhere; . . . that there as well as elsewhere he may wreak himself upon life, may drink the bitter cup of heroism, may wear his heart out after the unattainable."

It is a safe appraisal to say that no greater or more moving celebration of the legal profession is to be found anywhere in the Anglo-American literature than that in these speeches. The thread that runs through them all is a strong and bold one: that law is an exacting goddess, demanding of her votaries an intellectual and moral discipline.

But in one respect Holmes's task in these speeches was more difficult than that of his forerunners who had sought to invest the calling of the law with nobility. Those who understand the context of corporate capitalism in which the legal profession has had to operate will understand why Holmes pleaded so anxiously against the acquisitive spirit among lawyers;[1] but they will understand too that Holmes was waging a losing battle. A quarter-century after these speeches Woodrow Wilson did an analysis of the social position of the lawyers that had far more bite and pessimism than Holmes's Bar Association speeches had.[2] At the same time a contemporary of Wilson's, Louis D. Brandeis, renewed Holmes's struggle to break down the narrow bounds of the legal profession: but where Holmes

---

[1] In addition to the speeches in this section, see in the following section the speech on "The Path of the Law," pp. 71–89. See also the Introductory Essay, "Holmes: A Personal History," pp. xxv–xxvii.

[2] "The Lawyer and the Community," 192 *North American Review* (1910), 604–622.

had spoken of philosophy, Brandeis spoke of service to the nation; where Holmes talked abstractly of battle, Brandeis talked pragmatically of reform; where Holmes fashioned graceful phrases, Brandeis quarried in the hard rock of social reality. Perhaps by the very fact of his indirections and his lesser urgency Holmes may ironically prove the more enduring voice.

"OUR MISTRESS, THE LAW" [1]

Mr. Chairman and Gentlemen of the Bar: —

The Court and the Bar are too old acquaintances to speak much to each other of themselves, or of their mutual relations. I hope I may say we are too old friends to need to do it. If you did not believe it already, it would be useless for me to affirm that, in the judges' half of our common work, the will at least is not wanting to do every duty of their noble office; that every interest, every faculty, every energy, almost every waking hour, is filled with their work; that they give their lives to it, more than which they cannot do. But if not of the Bench, shall I speak of the Bar? Shall I ask what a court would be, unaided? The law is made by the Bar, even more than by the Bench; yet do I need to speak of the learning and varied gifts that have given the Bar of this State a reputation throughout the whole domain of the common law? I think I need not, nor of its high and scrupulous honor. The world has its fling at lawyers sometimes, but its very denial is an admission. It feels, what I believe to be the truth, that of all secular professions this has the highest standards.

And what a profession it is! No doubt everything is interesting when it is understood and seen in its connection with the rest of things. Every calling is great when greatly pursued. But what other gives such scope to realize the spontaneous energy of one's soul? In what other does one plunge so deep in the stream of life — so share its passions, its battles, its despair, its triumphs, both as witness and actor?

But that is not all. What a subject is this in which we are united — this abstraction called the Law, wherein, as in a magic mirror, we see reflected, not only our own lives, but the lives of all men that

[1] "The Law," Suffolk Bar Association Dinner, February 5, 1885. *Speeches* (1913), 16–18.

have been! When I think on this majestic theme, my eyes dazzle. If we are to speak of the law as our mistress, we who are here know that she is a mistress only to be wooed with sustained and lonely passion — only to be won by straining all the faculties by which man is likest to a god. Those who, having begun the pursuit, turn away uncharmed, do so either because they have not been vouchsafed the sight of her divine figure, or because they have not the heart for so great a struggle. To the lover of the law, how small a thing seem the novelist's tales of the loves and fates of Daphnis and Chloë! How pale a phantom even the Circe of poetry, transforming mankind with intoxicating dreams of fiery ether, and the foam of summer seas, and glowing greensward, and the white arms of women! For him no less a history will suffice than that of the moral life of his race. For him every text that he deciphers, every doubt that he resolves, adds a new feature to the unfolding panorama of man's destiny upon this earth. Nor will his task be done until, by the farthest stretch of human imagination, he has seen as with his eyes the birth and growth of society, and by the farthest stretch of reason he has understood the philosophy of its being. When I think thus of the law, I see a princess mightier than she who once wrought at Bayeux, eternally weaving into her web dim figures of the ever-lengthening past — figures too dim to be noticed by the idle, too symbolic to be interpreted except by her pupils, but to the discerning eye disclosing every painful step and every world-shaking contest by which mankind has worked and fought its way from savage isolation to organic social life.

But we who are here know the Law even better in another aspect. We see her daily, not as anthropologists, not as students and philosophers, but as actors in a drama of which she is the providence and overruling power. When I think of the Law as we know her in the courthouse and the market, she seems to me a woman sitting by the wayside, beneath whose overshadowing hood every man shall see the countenance of his deserts or needs. The timid and overborne gain heart from her protecting smile. Fair combatants, manfully standing to their rights, see her keeping the lists with the stern and discriminating eye of even justice. The wretch who has defied her most sacred commands, and has thought to creep through ways where she was not, finds that his path ends with her, and beholds beneath her hood the inexorable face of death.

Gentlemen, I shall say no more. This is not the moment for disquisitions. But when for the first time I was called to speak on such an occasion as this, the only thought that could come into my mind, the only feeling that could fill my heart, the only words that could spring to my lips, were a hymn to her in whose name we are met here to-night — to our mistress, the Law.

"YOUR BUSINESS AS THINKERS"[1]

And now, perhaps, I ought to have done. But I know that some spirit of fire will feel that his main question has not been answered. He will ask, What is all this to my soul? You do not bid me sell my birthright for a mess of pottage; what have you said to show that I can reach my own spiritual possibilities through such a door as this? How can the laborious study of a dry and technical system, the greedy watch for clients and practice of shopkeepers' arts, the mannerless conflicts over often sordid interests, make out a life? Gentlemen, I admit at once that these questions are not futile, that they may prove unanswerable, that they have often seemed to me unanswerable. And yet I believe there is an answer. They are the same questions that meet you in any form of practical life. If a man has the soul of Sancho Panza, the world to him will be Sancho Panza's world; but if he has the soul of an idealist, he will make — I do not say find — his world ideal. Of course, the law is not the place for the artist or the poet. The law is the calling of thinkers. But to those who believe with me that not the least godlike of man's activities is the large survey of causes, that to know is not less than to feel, I say — and I say no longer with any doubt — that a man may live greatly in the law as well as elsewhere; that there as well as elsewhere his thought may find its unity in an infinite perspective; that there as well as elsewhere he may wreak himself upon life, may drink the bitter cup of heroism, may wear his heart out after the unattainable. All that life offers any man from which to start his thinking or his striving is a fact. And if this universe is one universe, if it is so far thinkable that you can pass in reason from one part of it to another, it does not matter very much what that fact is. For every fact leads to every other by the path of the air. Only men do not yet see how, always. And your business as thinkers is to make plainer the way

[1] "The Profession of the Law": Conclusion of a lecture delivered to undergraduates of Harvard University, on February 17, 1886. *Speeches* (1913), 22–25.

from some thing to the whole of things; to show the rational connection between your fact and the frame of the universe. If your subject is law, the roads are plain to anthropology, the science of man, to political economy, the theory of legislation, ethics, and thus by several paths to your final view of life. It would be equally true of any subject. The only difference is in the ease of seeing the way. To be master of any branch of knowledge, you must master those which lie next to it; and thus to know anything you must know all.

Perhaps I speak too much the language of intellectual ambition. I cannot but think that the scope for intellectual, as for physical adventure, is narrowing. I look for a future in which the ideal will be content and dignified acceptance of life, rather than aspiration and the passion for achievement. I see already that surveys and railroads have set limits to our intellectual wilderness — that the lion and the bison are disappearing from them, as from Africa and the no longer boundless West. But that undelightful day which I anticipate has not yet come. The human race has not changed, I imagine, so much between my generation and yours but that you still have the barbaric thirst for conquest, and there is still something left to conquer. There are fields still open for occupation in the law, and there are roads from them that will lead you where you will.

But do not think I am pointing you to flowery paths and beds of roses — to a place where brilliant results attend your work, which shall be at once easy and new. No result is easy which is worth having. Your education begins when what is called your education is over — when you no longer are stringing together the pregnant thoughts, the "jewels five-words-long," which great men have given their lives to cut from the raw material, but have begun yourselves to work upon the raw material for results which you do not see, cannot predict, and which may be long in coming — when you take the fact which life offers you for your appointed task. No man has earned the right to intellectual ambition until he has learned to lay his course by a star which he has never seen — to dig by the divining rod for springs which he may never reach. In saying this, I point to that which will make your study heroic. For I say to you in all sadness of conviction, that to think great thoughts you must be heroes as well as idealists. Only when you have worked alone — when you have felt around you a black gulf of solitude more isolating than that which surrounds the dying man, and in hope and in despair have trusted to your own unshaken will — then only will you have achieved. Thus only can you gain the secret isolated joy of the thinker, who knows that, a hundred years after he is dead and forgotten, men who never heard of him will be moving to the measure of his thought — the subtile rapture of a postponed power, which the world knows not because it has no external trappings, but which to his prophetic vision is more real than that which commands an army. And if this joy should not be yours, still it is only thus that you can know that you have done what it lay in you to do — can say that you have lived, and be ready for the end.

"THE LOVE OF HONOR"[1]

MR. PRESIDENT AND GENTLEMEN: —

I know of no mark of honor which this country has to offer that I should value so highly as this which you have conferred upon me. I accept it proudly as an accolade, like the little blow upon the shoulder from the sword of a master of war which in ancient days adjudged that a soldier had won his spurs and pledged his life to decline no combat in the future.

The power of honor to bind men's lives is not less now than it was in the Middle Ages. Now as then it is the breath of our nostrils; it is that for which we live, for which, if need be, we are willing to die. It is that which makes the man whose gift is the power to gain riches sacrifice health and even life to the pursuit. It is that which makes the scholar feel that he cannot afford to be rich.

One would sometimes think, from the speech of young men, that things had changed recently, and that indifference was now the virtue to be cultivated. I never heard any one profess indifference to a boat race. Why should you row a boat race? Why endure long months of pain in preparation for a fierce half-hour that will leave you all but dead? Does any one ask the question? Is there any one who would not go through all its costs, and more, for the moment when anguish breaks into triumph — or even for the glory of having nobly lost? Is life less than a boat race? If a man will give all the blood in his body to win the one, will he not spend all the might of his soul to prevail in the other?

I know, Mr. President, that there is a motive above even honor

[1] "On Receiving the Degree of Doctor of Laws," Yale University Commencement, June 30, 1886, *Speeches* (1913), 26–27.

which may govern men's lives. I know that there are some rare spirits who find the inspiration of every moment, the aim of every act, in holiness. I am enough of a Puritan, I think, to conceive the exalted joy of those who look upon themselves only as instruments in the hands of a higher power to work out its designs. But I think that most men do and must reach the same result under the illusion of self-seeking. If the love of honor is a form of that illusion, it is no ignoble one. If it does not lift a man on wings to the sky, at least it carries him above the earth and teaches him those high and secret pathways across the branches of the forest the travellers on which are only less than winged.

Not the least service of this great University and its sister from which I come is, that by their separate teaching and by their mutual rivalry they have fostered that lofty feeling among their graduates. You have done all that a university can do to fan the spark in me. I will try to maintain the honor you have bestowed.

THE BLACK SPEARHEADS OF CHANGE[1]

MR. PRESIDENT AND GENTLEMEN OF THE ASSOCIATION: —

As most of those here have graduated from the Law School within the last twenty-five years, I know that I am in the presence of very learned men. For my own part, lately my thoughts have been turned to

>   old, unhappy, far-off things,
>   And battles long ago;

and when once the ghosts of the dead fifers of thirty years since begin to play in my head, the laws are silent. And yet as I look around me, I think to myself, like Correggio, "I too am, or at least have been, a pedagogue." And as such I will venture a reflection.

Learning, my learned brethren, is a very good thing. I should be the last to undervalue it, having done my share of quotation from the Year Books. But it is liable to lead us astray. The law, so far as it depends on learning, is indeed, as it has been called, the government of the living by the dead. To a very considerable extent no

---

[1] "Learning and Science": speech at a dinner of the Harvard Law School Association in honor of Professor C. C. Langdell, June 25, 1895. *Speeches* (1913), 67–69.

doubt it is inevitable that the living should be so governed. The past gives us our vocabulary and fixes the limits of our imagination; we cannot get away from it. There is, too, a peculiar logical pleasure in making manifest the continuity between what we are doing and what has been done before. But the present has a right to govern itself so far as it can; and it ought always to be remembered that historic continuity with the past is not a duty, it is only a necessity.

I hope that the time is coming when this thought will bear fruit. An ideal system of law should draw its postulates and its legislative justification from science. As it is now, we rely upon tradition, or vague sentiment, or the fact that we never thought of any other way of doing things, as our only warrant for rules which we enforce with as much confidence as if they embodied revealed wisdom. Who here can give reasons of any different kind for believing that half the criminal law does not do more harm than good? Our forms of contract, instead of being made once for all, like a yacht, on lines of least resistance, are accidental relics of early notions, concerning which the learned dispute. How much has reason had to do in deciding how far, if at all, it is expedient for the State to meddle with the domestic relations? And so I might go on through the whole law.

The Italians have begun to work upon the notion that the foundations of the law ought to be scientific, and, if our civilization does not collapse, I feel pretty sure that the regiment or division that follows us will carry that flag. Our own word seems the last always; yet the change of emphasis from an argument in Plowden to one in the time of Lord Ellenborough, or even from that to one in our own day, is as marked as the difference between Cowley's poetry and Shelley's. Other changes as great will happen. And so the eternal procession moves on, we in the front for the moment; and, stretching away against the unattainable sky, the black spearheads of the army that has been passing in unbroken line already for near a thousand years.

A MAN AND THE UNIVERSE[1]

A university is a place from which men start for the Eternal City. In the university are pictured the ideals which abide in the City of God. Many roads lead to that haven, and those who are here have

[1] Speech at Brown University Commencement, 1897. CLP (1920), 164–166.

traveled by different paths towards the goal. I do not know what better the travelers can do at a gathering like this, where for a moment the university becomes conscious of itself and of its meaning, than to report to those about to start something of their experiences and to give a hint of what is to be expected on the way.

My way has been by the ocean of the law. On that I have learned a part of the great lesson, the lesson not of law but of life. There were few of the charts and lights for which one longed when I began. One found oneself plunged in a thick fog of details — in a black and frozen night, in which were no flowers, no spring, no easy joys. Voices of authority warned that in the crush of that ice any craft might sink. One heard Burke saying that law sharpens the mind by narrowing it. One heard in Thackeray of a lawyer bending all the powers of a great mind to a mean profession. One saw that artists and poets shrank from it as from an alien world. One doubted oneself how it could be worthy of the interest of an intelligent mind. And yet, one said to oneself, law is human — it is a part of man, and of one world with all the rest. There must be a drift, if one will go prepared and have patience, which will bring one out to daylight and a worthy end. You all have read or heard the story of Nansen and see the parallel which I use. Most men of the college-bred type in some form or other have to go through that experience of sailing for the ice and letting themselves be frozen in. In the first stage one has companions, cold and black though it be, and if he sticks to it, he finds at last that there is a drift as was foretold. When he has found that he has learned the first part of his lesson, that one is safe in trusting to courage and to time. But he has not yet learned all. So far his trials have been those of his companions. But if he is a man of high ambitions he must leave even his fellow-adventurers and go forth into a deeper solitude and greater trials. He must start for the pole. In plain words he must face the loneliness of original work. No one can cut out new paths in company. He does that alone.

When he has done that and has turned misgiving into success he is master of himself and knows the secret of achievement. He has learned the second part of his lesson and is ready for the consummation of the whole. For he has gained another knowledge more fruitful than success. He knows now what he had divined at the outset, that one part of the universe yields the same teaching as any other if only it is mastered, that the difference between the great way of taking things and the small — between philosophy and gossip — is only the difference between realizing the part as a part of a whole and looking at it in its isolation as if it really stood apart. The consummation to which I referred comes when he applies this knowledge to himself. He may put it in the theological form of justification by faith or in the philosophical one of the continuity of the universe. I care not very much for the form if in some way he has learned that he cannot set himself over against the universe as a rival god, to criticize it, or to shake his fist at the skies, but that his meaning is its meaning, his only worth is as a part of it, as a humble instrument of the universal power. It seems to me that this is the key to intellectual salvation, as the key to happiness is to accept a like faith in one's heart, and to be not merely a necessary but a willing instrument in working out the inscrutable end.

"THE TEST IS BATTLE": GEORGE OTIS SHATTUCK [1]

GENTLEMEN OF THE BAR: —

I owe Mr. Shattuck more than I ever have owed any one else in the world, outside my immediate family. From the time when I was a student in his office until he died, he was my dear and intimate friend. He taught me unrepeatable lessons. He did me unnumbered kindnesses. To live while still young in daily contact with his sweeping, all-compelling force, his might of temperament, his swiftness (rarely found with such might), his insight, tact, and subtlety, was to receive an imprint never to be effaced. My education would have been but a thin and poor thing had I missed that great experience. The things he did for me in other practical ways even gratitude cannot enumerate or remember. It seemed to me that he could not find any one near him without interesting himself in his fortunes and his fate.

You cannot expect, then, from me a critical analysis and estimate. I could not sit coldly down to measure and weigh his qualities, or "peep and botanize" upon his grave. He was my dear and honored friend. I can do little more than repeat that.

Some of his qualities, however, were manifest to any one who

[1] Answer to resolutions of the Bar, Boston, May 29, 1897. *Speeches* (1913), 70–74.

knew him well. He needed the excitement of advocacy or of some practical end to awaken his insight, but when it was awakened there was no depth of speculation or research which he was not ready and more than able to sound. His work may not always have had the neatness of smaller minds, but it brought out deeply hidden truths by some invisible radiance that searched things to their bones.

He seemed to like to take great burdens upon himself, — not merely when there was a corresponding reward, but when his feelings were touched, as well. He was a model in his bearing with clients. How often have I seen men come to him borne down by troubles which they found too great to support, and depart with light step, having left their weight upon stronger shoulders. But while his calm manner made such things seem trifles, he took them a good deal on his nerves. I saw the ends of his fingers twitch as he quietly listened and advised. He never shunned anxiety, and anxiety is what kills.

His swiftness and tact, which I have mentioned, made him great in cross-examination, the command of which the late Mr. Durant used to call the highest gift of a lawyer. A large part of the cross-examination which I hear, even from able men, seems to me to waste time and often to hurt their case. Mr. Shattuck, while he was in the habit of trying cases, rarely made a mistake. He saw the bearing of every answer on every part of the evidence. If by any chance he got an unexpected reply, he adjusted himself to it in a flash, and met it by a new approach from some remote side. He could bring out the prejudices that unfitted a witness for just this case, and yet leave his general value and his personal feelings untouched, with a delicacy, clearness, and force that left me simply astounded.

At the time to which I refer, when I first knew him, and while he still tried many cases, he was a great man with the jury in every way. His addresses carried everything before them like a victorious cavalry charge, sometimes, as it seemed to me, sweeping the judge along with the rest in the rout. Latterly his most successful appearances were in arguments of law. He had learned the all too rarely learned lesson of pointed brevity. In a few luminous words he went to the bottom of his question, and then took his seat. In short, I know of no form of forensic effort in which at some time in his career he had not reached as high a point as I personally ever have seen attained.

He was no less eminent in his work out of court. He was one of the wisest and most far-seeing of advisers. I know of splendidly victorious men who have said that but for his help when the battle was turning against them they would have gone down in the fight.

But that great vitality found only a partial outlet and expression in the law. He liked to ride and drive and sail and farm, and at times to talk. His fondness for farming was a noticeable feature. I think he had a sympathy with the great, quiet forces which he saw at work, and a sympathy with the animals of the farm. Also the visible return which the earth makes for labor pleased him. It made him realize that he was adding to the world's stores.

I have had much delight in his companionship. Whether driving over the sandy roads of the Cape, or sailing in his yacht, or dining at his house, or at some later and less regular entertainment in the garret in which I used to live, he had a kind of benevolent beaming in his face and heart which gave unction to enjoyment.

People often speak of correcting the judgment of the time by that of posterity. I think it is quite as true to say that we must correct the judgment of posterity by that of the time. A small man may be remembered for some little felicity which enabled him to write a successful lyric, or in some way to charm the senses or emotions of a world always readier with its rewards for pleasures than for great thoughts or deeds. But I know of no true measure of men except the total of human energy which they embody — counting everything, with due allowance for quality, from Nansen's power to digest blubber or to resist cold, up to his courage, or to Wordsworth's power to express the unutterable, or to Kant's speculative reach. The final test of this energy is battle in some form — actual war — the crush of Arctic ice — the fight for mastery in the market or the court. Many of those who are remembered have spared themselves this supreme trial, and have fostered a faculty at the expense of their total life. It is one thing to utter a happy phrase from a protected cloister; another to think under fire — to think for action upon which great interests depend. The most powerful men are apt to go into the mêlée and fall or come out generals. The great problems are questions of here and now. Questions of here and now occupy nine hundred and ninety-nine thousandths of the ability of the world; and when the now has passed and has given place to another now, the heads and hands that built the organic structure of society are forgotten from the speech of their fellows, and live only in the tissue of their work.

Such may be the fate of the man whom to-day we remember and honor. But remembered or forgotten, few indeed, I believe, of those whom I have seen have counted for as much in the hardest work of the day. I do not regret that it should be known by few. What is any remembrance of men to our high ambition? Sooner or later the race of men will die; but we demand an eternal record. We have it. What we have done is woven forever into the great vibrating web of the world. The eye that can read the import of its motion can decipher the story of all our deeds, of all our thoughts. To that eye I am content to leave the recognition and the memory of this great head and heart.

LIFE AS JOY, DUTY, END[1]

Gentlemen of the Suffolk Bar: —

The kindness of this reception almost unmans me, and it shakes me the more when taken with a kind of seriousness which the moment has for me. As with a drowning man, the past is telescoped into a minute, and the stages are all here at once in my mind. The day before yesterday I was at the law school, fresh from the army, arguing cases in a little club with Goulding and Beaman and Peter Olney, and laying the dust of pleading by certain sprinklings which Huntington Jackson, another ex-soldier, and I managed to contrive together. A little later in the day, in Bob Morse's office, I saw a real writ, acquired a practical conviction of the difference between assumpsit and trover, and marvelled open-mouthed at the swift certainty with which a master of his business turned it off.

Yesterday I was at the law school again, in the chair instead of on the benches, when my dear partner, Shattuck, came out and told me that in one hour the Governor would submit my name to the council for a judgeship, if notified of my assent. It was a stroke of lightning which changed the whole course of my life.

And the day before yesterday, gentlemen, was thirty-five years, and yesterday was more than eighteen years, ago. I have gone on feeling young, but I have noticed that I met fewer of the old to whom to show my deference, and recently I was startled by being told that ours is an old bench. Well, I accept the fact, although I

[1] Speech at a dinner given to Chief Justice Holmes by the Bar Association of Boston on March 7, 1900. *Speeches* (1913), 82–86.

find it hard to realize, and I ask myself, what is there to show for this half lifetime that has passed? I look into my book in which I keep a docket of the decisions of the full court which fall to me to write, and find about a thousand cases. A thousand cases, many of them upon trifling or transitory matters, to represent nearly half a lifetime! A thousand cases, when one would have liked to study to the bottom and to say his say on every question which the law ever has presented, and then to go on and invent new problems which should be the test of doctrine, and then to generalize it all and write it in continuous, logical, philosophic exposition, setting forth the whole corpus with its roots in history and its justifications of expedience real or supposed!

Alas, gentlemen, that is life. I often imagine Shakespeare or Napoleon summing himself up and thinking: "Yes, I have written five thousand lines of solid gold and a good deal of padding — I, who would have covered the milky way with words that outshone the stars!" "Yes, I beat the Austrians in Italy and elsewhere: I made a few brilliant campaigns, and I ended in middle life in a *cul-de-sac* — I, who had dreamed of a world monarchy and Asiatic power." We cannot live our dreams. We are lucky enough if we can give a sample of our best, and if in our hearts we can feel that it has been nobly done.

Some changes come about in the process, changes not necessarily so much in the nature as in the emphasis of our interest. I do not mean in our wish to make a living and to succeed — of course, we all want those things — but I mean in our ulterior intellectual or spiritual interest, in the ideal part, without which we are but snails or tigers.

One begins with a search for a general point of view. After a time he finds one, and then for a while he is absorbed in testing it, trying to satisfy himself whether it is true. But after many experiments or investigations all have come out one way, and his theory is confirmed and settled in his mind, he knows in advance that the next case will be but another verification, and the stimulus of anxious curiosity is gone. He realizes that his branch of knowledge only presents more illustrations of the universal principle; he sees it all as another case of the same old *ennui,* or the same sublime mystery — for it does not matter what epithets you apply to the whole of things, they are merely judgments of yourself. At this stage the pleasure is no less, perhaps, but it is the pure pleasure of doing the work, irrespective of further aims, and when you reach that stage you reach, as it seems to me, the triune formula of the joy, the duty, and the end of life.

It was of this that Malebranche was thinking when he said that, if God held in one hand truth, and in the other the pursuit of truth, he would say: "Lord, the truth is for thee alone; give me the pursuit." The joy of life is to put out one's power in some natural and useful or harmless way. There is no other. And the real misery is not to do this. The hell of the old world's literature is to be taxed beyond one's powers. This country has expressed in story — I suppose because it has experienced it in life — a deeper abyss, of intellectual asphyxia or vital *ennui,* when powers conscious of themselves are denied their chance.

The rule of joy and the law of duty seem to me all one. I confess that altruistic and cynically selfish talk seem to me about equally unreal. With all humility, I think "Whatsoever thy hand findeth to do, do it with thy might" infinitely more important than the vain attempt to love one's neighbor as one's self. If you want to hit a bird on the wing, you must have all your will in a focus, you must not be thinking about yourself, and, equally, you must not be thinking about your neighbor; you must be living in your eye on that bird. Every achievement is a bird on the wing.

The joy, the duty, and, I venture to add, the end of life. I speak only of this world, of course, and of the teachings of this world. I do not seek to trench upon the province of spiritual guides. But from the point of view of the world the end of life is life. Life is action, the use of one's powers. As to use them to their height is our joy and duty, so it is the one end that justifies itself. Until lately the best thing that I was able to think of in favor of civilization, apart from blind acceptance of the order of the universe, was that it made possible the artist, the poet, the philosopher, and the man of science. But I think that is not the greatest thing. Now I believe that the greatest thing is a matter that comes directly home to us all. When it is said that we are too much occupied with the means of living to live, I answer that the chief worth of civilization is just that it makes the means of living more complex; that it calls for great and combined intellectual efforts, instead of simple, uncoordinated ones, in order that the crowd may be fed and clothed and housed and moved from place to place. Because more complex and intense intellectual efforts mean a fuller and richer life. They mean more life. Life is an end in itself, and the only question as to whether it is worth living is whether you have enough of it.

I will add but a word. We all are very near despair. The sheathing that floats us over its waves is compounded of hope, faith in the unexplainable worth and sure issue of effort, and the deep, subconscious content which comes from the exercise of our powers. In the words of a touching Negro song —

> Sometimes I's up, sometimes I's down,
> Sometimes I's almost to the groun';

but these thoughts have carried me, as I hope they will carry the young men who hear me, through long years of doubt, self-distrust, and solitude. They do now, for, although it might seem that the day of trial was over, in fact it is renewed each day. The kindness which you have shown me makes me bold in happy moments to believe that the long and passionate struggle has not been quite in vain.

3. Law as Civilization

These selections represent the growth of Holmes's thinking on the relation of law to social experience up to the time when his appointment to the United States Supreme Court turned the main stream of his energy away from legal commentary. As distinguished from the selections in the previous section, which contain Holmes's more formal and occasional utterances on the law as a vocation, this section comprises his scholarly writings during this period.

While he was a young lawyer, Holmes served an apprenticeship to legal philosophy as an active editor of the American Law Review, *where he read and commented on the recent cases and the new books, stored up a vast deal of learning, sharpened his mind against the great minds of the legal literature, and fashioned a working philosophy of law. Out of this period emerged his edition of Chancellor Kent's* Commentaries; *a series of legal essays of which several are here reprinted; and a book of lectures,* The Common Law, *which ranks with the great writings of Henry Sumner Maine and others in the tradition of legal analysis by the historical method.*

Holmes's perspective of law as civilization was that of a generation which had sat at the feet of Charles Darwin, Herbert Spencer, Walter Bagehot. Life was a struggle for existence, and Holmes had a healthy respect for the survivors, whether men or institutions. Life was a matter of social law, and Holmes was skeptical of the reformist tinkering with what was an inherent part of human society. Life was a clash of power, and law in the main was the rationalization of the interests of the dominant group. Thus there is a blend in Holmes of a gentlemanly Darwinism (society is a jungle, but men have ideals as well as appetites), a reluctant economic interpretation (classes do exist — the masters and the men), and a deep institutionalism (the coating of custom is baked hard, and only a strong thrust from below can break it).

All these themes will be found implicit in the remarkable case note that Holmes, still a young lawyer of thirty-eight, wrote on the Gas-Stokers *case for the* American Law Review. *The note is interesting also because it contains a criticism of Herbert Spencer's static theory which he later alluded to in the* Lochner *opinion. But the main interest lies in the revelation of Holmes as a "tough" legal theorist, who sees human sympathy as setting the bounds rather than the conditions of realistic legal action, and who — anticipating Pareto by many years — sees legal systems as the outer vestments of the power of a dominant (although always changing) elite.*

There was another element in Holmes's perspective of law as civilization, related and equally "tough," yet separable. That was the sense that law, like society, is careful of the species, careless of the individual fate; that it must serve the uses of the generality of men, even though it entail hardship for the particular person. It was this sense that formed the source of the doctrine of the "external standard" for liability, which was first developed by Holmes in his Common Law, which was more fully developed in "Privilege, Malice, and Intent"[1] and in his liability decisions on the Massachusetts Court, and which keeps cropping up in the Holmes-Pollock correspondence as one of the legal convictions the two men had in common. It was this sense also which underlay several of Holmes's "Draconian" decisions that have been much criticized, particularly the "poisoned pool"[2] decision and the railroad-crossing decision.[3]

This does not mean that Holmes did not have in him a basic humanism. He did. Holmes usually upheld social legislation on the doctrine of the not unreasonable legislator. But note the similarity between this doctrine and that of the external standard. In both instances Holmes is refusing to go into the subjective question of motivation. In both instances he avoids the imposition of moral patterns on the flux of law. In both instances he leaves the basic decision to the common sense of the community, externalized in a standard of liability according to consequences rather than motive, or in the choice of representatives to determine the direction of public policy. But when these standards clashed with humanitarianism in the sense of sympathy for particular individuals, Holmes did not hesitate to override the latter. In fact, one may guess that he even took some satisfaction in the sense that he was subordinating

---

[1] For reasons of space I have not included this. It will be found in 8 ALR (1894), and reprinted in CLP, 117–137.
[2] *United Zinc and Chemical Company v. Britt*, 258 U.S. 268 (1922). See below, p. 201.
[3] *Baltimore and Ohio R.R. Co. v. Goodman*, 27 U.S. 66 (1927). See below, p. 205.

merely humanitarian considerations for the more arduous and exacting demands of "our mistress, the Law."

For Holmes, it was no small part of the "spirit of the common law" that it was common and not individual. This did not mean that he ceased to be basically a capitalist or that he became a collectivist. But it did mean that he was impatient of the attempts to extend capitalist entrenchment through the sheer logic of individualism. As he puts it on the first page of The Common Law — "The life of the law has not been logic: it has been experience." Part of his deep feeling for the common law was his feeling for the sheer accumulation of experience that was invested in it. Logic was not excluded: it could not be. But experience was the starting point where logic began; and where different logics clashed, experience was used as a touchstone for the selection of the relevant logic. The experience, moreover, was that which was common to all the people, and which therefore pointed to the social interest. That was why Holmes always regarded the notion of copyright at common law as nonsense; for it maximized the individual benefit at the expense of common experience.

Despite the technical character of Holmes's Common Law, I have included excerpts from it in the selections that follow. This is the only book Holmes ever wrote. Even if he had never written anything else, it would have given him a high rank among Anglo-American legal historians and theorists. It is at once ambitious in scope, learned in the mass of scholarly and often recondite material it draws upon, connected in its basic hypothesis, and at the same time not too difficult to read even for the layman. It was written at a time when legal scholars in Germany and England were beginning to view law as anthropologists might view it — as an organic part of the culture within which it grew up.

Holmes accordingly makes use of comparative material from ethnology and philology. One review of the book at the time [4] gives as Holmes's main arguments the following: that the common law has been deeply influenced by the tendency to be found in every primitive culture toward the fictitious personification of things and animals; that it embodies similarly a fictitious transfer of status by succession; and that it is deeply pervaded by the notion that only limited remedies shall be allowed for wrongs, thus leading to a system of limited legal rights. It will thus be readily clear that Holmes's

[4] "Holmes's Common Law," 32 Nation, 464–465.

book was as much an essay in anthropology and cultural history as in law. It sought to trace how the primitive conceptions of the northern European peoples left their impress on the common law, and how they account for the archaic and anomalous traits which still survive in the common law of today.

But Holmes was not only concerned in the Common Law *with the anthropological phase of legal history. He was also concerned with legal philosophy. The review I have cited was impatient of Holmes's "long philosophical discussions of intent and the like," which to the reviewer "give a tediously discursive and aimless air to the book." Nevertheless, later generations have found these philosophical portions anything but aimless and tedious, and I have taken the selections that follow mainly from these passages. Holmes was concerned to show that life was a perilous matter, and that law could not be less perilous and more secure than the intrinsic nature of life itself. If his book has a dry quality of deflation in it, it is not because Holmes seeks to deflate the importance of his subject, but because he is skeptical of the possibility of finding absolute and secure answers to the problems that life poses for law. The tone of the book is anti-moralistic. Holmes insists that there can be no absolute ethics which the law embodies. Whenever the juristic minds shape the law they do so out of the customs of the culture, and they must shape it consciously by weighing considerations of public policy.*

Perhaps the best statement — luminous, graceful, on the plane of the lay mind — that Holmes ever wrote on his whole conception of the nature and inner spirit of law is the long lecture-essay included at the end of this section, "The Path of the Law." The reader may possibly find it helpful to start the section with this, and then go on to the more difficult (although earlier) selections. Holmes was in his middle fifties when he wrote it. He was talking to students who stood on the threshold of a legal career. In it he speaks with something approaching tenderness yet without condescension. The essay presents an interesting and on the whole successful blend of the two Holmeses — the "tough" legal historian and critic, and the craftsman and reformer in the law — who did not always live on good terms with each other.

"MASTERS AND MEN": THE GAS-STOKERS' STRIKE[1]

The famous strike of the gas-stokers in December last, by which all London was plunged for several nights into partial darkness, at last found its way into the courts. The company prosecuted five men for conspiracy. The trial lasted only one day; the facts were simple and undisputed, substantially as follows: The stokers are hired by the company under special contracts, which require a certain notice to be given of an intention to leave work; the time of this notice varies in the contracts of different classes of workmen, ranging from one week to thirty days. Most of the stokers were combined together into a trade-union association. One of them, a member of the association, was discharged by the company, for what cause did not appear; but it was not claimed that the discharge was in violation of the contract. His fellow-members of the association demanded his reinstatement, but in vain. They thereupon, on the second of December, refused altogether to go to work unless their demand was complied with. There was no violence towards officers of the company; but there was some violence, accompanied by a good deal of threatening, towards members of the association who had not been advised of the intention of the conspirators, and who at first hesitated to fall in with the design. The court charged the jury that the defendants had a perfect right to form a trade-union, and that the fact that their action was in restraint of trade, which would have made it an offense at common law, could not be considered in this action; but that the company alleged that the defendants "either agreed to do an unlawful act or to do a lawful act by unlawful means; and he asked the jury whether there was a combination between the defendants either to hinder or prevent the company from carrying on their business by means of the men simultaneously breaking the contract of service they had entered into with the company. This was an illegal act, and, what was more, a criminal act. If they did agree to interfere with their employers' business, by simultaneously breaking such contracts, they were then agreeing to do that which would bring them within the definition of conspiracy."

The jury were out only twenty minutes, and then brought in a

[1] 7ALR 582 (1873). This first appeared as a commentary on a case of current interest to lawyers.

verdict of guilty, but with a recommendation to mercy. This, however, the court disregarded, and sentenced the accused to imprisonment for one year. In imposing the sentence the judge said that he had told the jury that "on the question whether they were to find the defendants guilty or not, they ought not to be influenced by the suggestion that what they were attempting to do would be dangerous to the public. But it did seem to him now, when he was called on to consider what kind of conspiracy they had been guilty of, that he could not throw aside what was one of the obvious results of the conspiracy into which they entered, and what must have been in their minds; and he could not doubt that the obvious result was great danger to the public of this metropolis; that that danger was present to their minds; and it was by the acting on that knowledge and on the effect they thought it would have upon their masters' minds, and trading upon their knowledge of the danger, that they entered into this conspiracy, in order to force their masters to follow their will. . . .

"The prisoners were the principals — the chief actors; two of them were delegates chosen by the men, and therefore evidently men to whom they looked up. They took a leading part in the conspiracy. Therefore, notwithstanding their good character they had unfortunately put themselves into the position of being properly convicted of a dangerous and wicked conspiracy. The time had come when a serious punishment, and not nominal or a light one, must be inflicted — a punishment that would teach men in their position that, although without offence they might be members of a trade-union, or might agree to go into an employment, or to leave it without committing any offence, yet that they must take care when they agreed together that they must not agree to do it by illegal means. If they did that they were guilty of conspiracy, and if they misled others they were guilty of a wicked conspiracy."

Those who are interested in the immediate social aspects of this case, and who wish to hear the other side of this resort to the courts, as a move in the game between masters and men, will do well to read an able article on Class Legislation in the *Fortnightly Review* for February last, which combines much sense with some unsound notions of law.[2] The aspect of the various instances of class

---

[2] The article Holmes refers to is "Class Legislation," by Henry Crompton, 13 *Fortnightly Review*, n.s. (1873), 205–217. In the same issue is an article by A. V. Dicey, and in the following month's issue one by Holmes's friend, Leslie Stephen.

legislation there collected to which we would call attention, is their relation to such essays on the theory of legislation as Mr. Herbert Spencer publishes from time to time. It has always seemed to us a singular anomaly that believers in the theory of evolution and in the natural development of institutions by successive adaptations to the environment, should be found laying down a theory of government intended to establish its limits once for all by a logical deduction from axioms. But the objection which we wish to express at the present time is, that this presupposes an identity of interest between the different parts of a community which does not exist in fact. Consistently with his views, however, Mr. Spencer is forever putting cases to show that the reaction of legislation is equal to its action. By changing the law, he argues, you do not get rid of any burden, but only change the mode of bearing it; and if the change does not make it easier to bear for society, considered as a whole, legislation is inexpedient. This tacit assumption of the solidarity of the interests of society is very common, but seems to us to be false. The struggle for life, undoubtedly, is constantly putting the interests of men at variance with those of the lower animals. And the struggle does not stop in the ascending scale with the monkeys, but is equally the law of human existence. Outside of legislation this is undeniable. It is mitigated by sympathy, prudence, and all the social and moral qualities. But in the last resort a man rightly prefers his own interest to that of his neighbors. And this is as true in legislation as in any other form of corporate action. All that can be expected from modern improvements is that legislation should easily and quickly, yet not too quickly, modify itself in accordance with the will of the *de facto* supreme power in the community, and that the spread of an educated sympathy should reduce the sacrifice of minorities to a minimum. But whatever body may possess the supreme power for the moment is certain to have interests inconsistent with others which have competed unsuccessfully.

The more powerful interests must be more or less reflected in legislation; which, like every other device of man or beast, must tend in the long run to aid the survival of the fittest. The objection to class legislation is not that it favors a class, but either that it fails to benefit the legislators, or that it is dangerous to them because a competing class has gained in power, or that it transcends the limits of self-preference which are imposed by sympathy. Interference with contracts by usury laws and the like is open to the first objection, that it only makes the burden of borrowers heavier. The law brought to bear upon the gas-stokers is perhaps open to the second, that it requires to be backed by a more unquestioned power than is now possessed by the favored class; and some English statutes are also very probably open to the third. But it is no sufficient condemnation of legislation that it favors one class at the expense of another; for much or all legislation does that; and none the less when the *bona fide* object is the greatest good of the greatest number. Why should the greatest number be preferred? Why not the greatest good of the most intelligent and most highly developed? The greatest good of a minority of our generation may be the greatest good of the greatest number in the long run. But if the welfare of all future ages is to be considered, legislation may as well be abandoned for the present. If the welfare of the living majority is paramount, it can only be on the ground that the majority have the power in their hands. The fact is that legislation in this country, as well as elsewhere, is empirical. It is necessarily made a means by which a body, having the power, put burdens which are disagreeable to them on the shoulders of somebody else. Communism would no more get rid of the difficulty than any other system, unless it limited or put a stop to the propagation of the species. And it may be doubted whether that solution would not be as disagreeable as any other.

SELECTIONS FROM THE COMMON LAW [1]

(1) LIABILITY AND REVENGE [2]

The object of this book is to present a general view of the Common Law. To accomplish the task, other tools are needed besides logic. It is something to show that the consistency of a system requires a particular result, but it is not all. The life of the law has not been logic: it has been experience. The felt necessities of the

[1] Holmes's book *The Common Law* was a series of lectures originally delivered in Boston. The selections that follow are from the first four lectures. About a quarter of the material from these lectures is here included. I have chiefly left out further illustrative material and scholarly references to authorities. I have sought only to preserve the essential frame of the argument.
[2] This selection is from Lecture I, "Early Forms of Liability."

time, the prevalent moral and political theories, intuitions of public policy, avowed or unconscious, even the prejudices which judges share with their fellow-men, have had a good deal more to do than the syllogism in determining the rules by which men should be governed. The law embodies the story of a nation's development through many centuries, and it cannot be dealt with as if it contained only the axioms and corollaries of a book of mathematics. In order to know what it is, we must know what it has been, and what it tends to become. We must alternately consult history and existing theories of legislation. But the most difficult labor will be to understand the combination of the two into new products at every stage. The substance of the law at any given time pretty nearly corresponds, so far as it goes, with what is then understood to be convenient; but its form and machinery, and the degree to which it is able to work out desired results, depend very much upon its past.

In Massachusetts to-day, while, on the one hand, there are a great many rules which are quite sufficiently accounted for by their manifest good sense, on the other, there are some which can only be understood by reference to the infancy of procedure among the German tribes, or to the social condition of Rome under the Decemvirs. . . .

The first subject to be discussed is the general theory of liability civil and criminal. . . . It is commonly known that the early forms of legal procedure were grounded in vengeance. . . . Vengeance imports a feeling of blame, and an opinion, however distorted by passion, that a wrong has been done. It can hardly go very far beyond the case of a harm intentionally inflicted: even a dog distinguishes between being stumbled over and being kicked.

Whether for this cause or another, the early English appeals for personal violence seem to have been confined to intentional wrongs. . . . Our system of private liability for the consequences of a man's own acts, that is, for his trespasses, started from the notion of actual intent and actual personal culpability.

The original principles of liability for harm inflicted by another person or thing have been less carefully considered hitherto than those which governed trespass, and I shall therefore devote the rest of this Lecture to discussing them. I shall try to show that this liability also had its root in the passion of revenge, and to point out the changes by which it reached its present form. But I shall not

LAW AS CIVILIZATION

confine myself strictly to what is needful for that purpose, because it is not only most interesting to trace the transformation throughout its whole extent, but the story will also afford an instructive example of the mode in which the law has grown, without a break, from barbarism to civilization. . . .

A very common phenomenon, and one very familiar to the student of history, is this. The customs, beliefs, or needs of a primitive time establish a rule or a formula. In the course of centuries the custom, belief, or necessity disappears, but the rule remains. The reason which gave rise to the rule has been forgotten, and ingenious minds set themselves to inquire how it is to be accounted for. Some ground of policy is thought of, which seems to explain it and to reconcile it with the present state of things; and then the rule adapts itself to the new reasons which have been found for it, and enters on a new career. The old form receives a new content, and in time even the form modifies itself to fit the meaning which it has received. The subject under consideration illustrates this course of events very clearly.

* * * *

We have now followed the development of the chief forms of liability in modern law for anything other than the immediate and manifest consequences of a man's own acts. We have seen the parallel course of events in the two parents, — the Roman law and the German customs, — and in the offspring of those two on English soil with regard to servants, animals, and inanimate things. We have seen a single germ multiplying and branching into products as different from each other as the flower from the root. It hardly remains to ask what that germ was. We have seen that it was the desire of retaliation against the offending thing itself. Undoubtedly, it might be argued that many of the rules stated were derived from a seizure of the offending thing as security for reparation, at first, perhaps, outside the law. That explanation, as well as the one offered here, would show that modern views of responsibility had not yet been attained, as the owner of the thing might very well not have been the person in fault. But such has not been the view of those most competent to judge. A consideration of the earliest instances will show, as might have been expected, that vengeance, not compensation, and vengeance on the offending thing, was the original object. The ox in Exodus was to be stoned. The axe in the Athenian law was to be banished. The tree, in Mr. Tylor's instance, was to be chopped to pieces. The slave under all the systems was to be surrendered to the relatives of the slain man, that they might do with him what they liked. The deodand was an accursed thing. The original limitation of liability to surrender, when the owner was before the court, could not be accounted for if it was his liability, and not that of his property, which was in question. Even where, as in some of the cases, expiation seems to be intended rather than vengeance, the object is equally remote from an extrajudicial distress.

The foregoing history, apart from the purposes for which it has been given, well illustrates the paradox of form and substance in the development of law. In form its growth is logical. The official theory is that each new decision follows syllogistically from existing precedents. But just as the clavicle in the cat only tells of the existence of some earlier creature to which a collar-bone was useful, precedents survive in the law long after the use they once served is at an end and the reason for them has been forgotten. The result of following them must often be failure and confusion from the merely logical point of view.

On the other hand, in substance the growth of the law is legislative. And this in a deeper sense than that what the courts declare to have always been the law is in fact new. It is legislative in its grounds. The very considerations which judges most rarely mention, and always with an apology, are the secret root from which the law draws all the juices of life. I mean, of course, considerations of what is expedient for the community concerned. Every important principle which is developed by litigation is in fact and at bottom the result of more or less definitely understood views of public policy; most generally, to be sure, under our practice and traditions, the unconscious result of instinctive preferences and inarticulate convictions, but none the less traceable to views of public policy in the last analysis. And as the law is administered by able and experienced men, who know too much to sacrifice good sense to a syllogism, it will be found that, when ancient rules maintain themselves in the way that has been and will be shown in this book, new reasons more fitted to the time have been found for them, and that they gradually receive a new content, and at last a new form, from the grounds to which they have been transplanted.

But hitherto this process has been largely unconscious. It is important, on that account, to bring to mind what the actual course of events has been. If it were only to insist on a more conscious recognition of the legislative function of the courts, as just explained, it would be useful, as we shall see more clearly further on.

What has been said will explain the failure of all theories which consider the law only from its formal side, whether they attempt to deduce the *corpus* from *a priori* postulates, or fall into the humbler error of supposing the science of the law to reside in the *elegantia juris*, or logical cohesion of part with part. The truth is, that the law is always approaching, and never reaching, consistency. It is forever adopting new principles from life at one end, and it always retains old ones from history at the other, which have not yet been absorbed or sloughed off. It will become entirely consistent only when it ceases to grow.

The study upon which we have been engaged is necessary both for the knowledge and for the revision of the law.

However much we may codify the law into a series of seemingly self-sufficient propositions, those propositions will be but a phase in a continuous growth. To understand their scope fully, to know how they will be dealt with by judges trained in the past which the law embodies, we must ourselves know something of that past. The history of what the law has been is necessary to the knowledge of what the law is.

Again, the process which I have described has involved the attempt to follow precedents, as well as to give a good reason for them. When we find that in large and important branches of the law the various grounds of policy on which the various rules have been justified are later inventions to account for what are in fact survivals from more primitive times, we have a right to reconsider the popular reasons, and, taking a broader view of the field, to decide anew whether those reasons are satisfactory. They may be, notwithstanding the manner of their appearance. If truth were not often suggested by error, if old implements could not be adjusted to new uses, human progress would be slow. But scrutiny and revision are justified.

But none of the foregoing considerations, nor the purpose of showing the materials for anthropology contained in the history of the law, are the immediate object here. My aim and purpose have been to show that the various forms of liability known to modern law spring from the common ground of revenge. In the sphere of contract the fact will hardly be material outside the cases which have been stated in this Lecture. But in the criminal law and the law of torts it is of the first importance. It shows that they have started from a moral basis, from the thought that someone was to blame.

It remains to be proved that, while the terminology of morals is still retained, and while the law does still and always, in a certain sense, measure legal liability by moral standards, it nevertheless, by the very necessity of its nature, is continually transmuting those moral standards into external or objective ones, from which the actual guilt of the party concerned is wholly eliminated.

(2) Punishment, Morals and the External Standard [1]

The desire for vengeance imports an opinion that its object is actually and personally to blame. It takes an internal standard, not an objective or external one, and condemns its victim by that. The question is whether such a standard is still accepted either in this primitive form, or in some more refined development, as is commonly supposed, and as seems not impossible, considering the relative slowness with which the criminal law has improved.

It certainly may be argued, with some force, that it has never ceased to be one object of punishment to satisfy the desire for vengeance. The argument will be made plain by considering those instances in which, for one reason or another, compensation for a wrong is out of the question.

Thus an act may be of such a kind as to make indemnity impossible by putting an end to the principal sufferer, as in the case of murder or manslaughter.

Again, these and other crimes, like forgery, although directed against an individual, tend to make others feel unsafe, and this general insecurity does not admit of being paid for.

Again, there are cases where there are no means of enforcing indemnity. In Macaulay's draft of the Indian Penal Code, breaches of contract for the carriage of passengers were made criminal. The palanquin-bearers of India were too poor to pay damages, and yet had to be trusted to carry unprotected women and children through wild and desolate tracts, where their desertion would have placed those under their charge in great danger.

[1] This selection is from Lecture II, "The Criminal Law."

LAW AS CIVILIZATION

In all these cases punishment remains as an alternative. A pain can be inflicted upon the wrong-doer, of a sort which does not restore the injured party to his former situation, or to another equally good, but which is inflicted for the very purpose of causing pain. And so far as this punishment takes the place of compensation, whether on account of the death of the person to whom the wrong was done, the indefinite number of persons affected, the impossibility of estimating the worth of the suffering in money, or the poverty of the criminal, it may be said that one of its objects is to gratify the desire for vengeance. The prisoner pays with his body.

The statement may be made stronger still, and it may be said, not only that the law does, but that it ought to, make the gratification of revenge an object. This is the opinion, at any rate, of two authorities so great, and so opposed in other views, as Bishop Butler and Jeremy Bentham.[2] Sir James Stephen says, "The criminal law stands to the passion of revenge in much the same relation as marriage to the sexual appetite."[3]

The first requirement of a sound body of law is, that it should correspond with the actual feelings and demands of the community, whether right or wrong. If people would gratify the passion of revenge outside of the law, if the law did not help them, the law has no choice but to satisfy the craving itself, and thus avoid the greater evil of private retribution. At the same time, this passion is not one which we encourage, either as private individuals or as law-makers. Moreover, it does not cover the whole ground. There are crimes which do not excite it, and we should naturally expect that the most important purposes of punishment would be coextensive with the whole field of its application. It remains to be discovered whether such a general purpose exists, and if so what it is. Different theories still divide opinion upon the subject.

It has been thought that the purpose of punishment is to reform the criminal; that it is to deter the criminal and others from committing similar crimes; and that it is retribution. Few would now maintain that the first of these purposes was the only one. If it were, every prisoner should be released as soon as it appears clear that he will never repeat his offence, and if he is incurable he

---

[2] Butler, Sermons, VIII. Bentham, "Theory of Legislation" (*Principles of Penal Code*, Part 2, ch. 16), Hildreth's tr., p. 309.
[3] *General View of the Criminal Law of England*, p. 99.

should not be punished at all. Of course it would be hard to reconcile the punishment of death with this doctrine.

The main struggle lies between the other two. On the one side is the notion that there is a mystic bond between wrong and punishment; on the other, that the infliction of pain is only a means to an end. Hegel, one of the great expounders of the former view, puts it, in his quasi mathematical form, that, wrong being the negation of right, punishment is the negation of that negation, or retribution. Thus the punishment must be equal, in the sense of proportionate to the crime, because its only function is to destroy it. Others, without this logical apparatus, are content to rely upon a felt necessity that suffering should follow wrong-doing.

It is objected that the preventive theory is immoral, because it overlooks the ill-desert of wrong-doing, and furnishes no measure of the amount of punishment, except the lawgiver's subjective opinion in regard to the sufficiency of the amount of preventive suffering. In the language of Kant, it treats man as a thing, not as a person; as a means, not as an end in himself. It is said to conflict with the sense of justice, and to violate the fundamental principle of all free communities, that the members of such communities have equal rights to life, liberty, and personal security.

In spite of all this, probably most English-speaking lawyers would accept the preventive theory without hesitation. As to the violation of equal rights which is charged, it may be replied that the dogma of equality makes an equation between individuals only, not between an individual and the community. No society has ever admitted that it could not sacrifice individual welfare to its own existence. If conscripts are necessary for its army, it seizes them, and marches them, with bayonets in their rear, to death. It runs highways and railroads through old family places in spite of the owner's protest, paying in this instance the market value, to be sure, because no civilized government sacrifices the citizen more than it can help, but still sacrificing his will and his welfare to that of the rest.[4]

If it were necessary to trench further upon the field of morals, it might be suggested that the dogma of equality applied even to individuals only within the limits of ordinary dealings in the common run of affairs. You cannot argue with your neighbor, except

[4] Even the law recognizes that this is a sacrifice. *Commonwealth* v. *Sawin*, 2 Pick. (Mass.), 547, 549.

LAW AS CIVILIZATION

on the admission for the moment that he is as wise as you, although you may by no means believe it. In the same way, you cannot deal with him, where both are free to choose, except on the footing of equal treatment, and the same rules for both. The ever-growing value set upon peace and the social relations tends to give the law of social being the appearance of the law of all being. But it seems to me clear that the *ultima ratio,* not only *regum,* but of private persons, is force, and that at the bottom of all private relations, however tempered by sympathy and all the social feelings, is a justifiable self-preference. If a man is on a plank in the deep sea which will only float one, and a stranger lays hold of it, he will thrust him off if he can. When the state finds itself in a similar position, it does the same thing.

The considerations which answer the argument of equal rights also answer the objections to treating man as a thing, and the like. If a man lives in society, he is liable to find himself so treated. The degree of civilization which a people has reached, no doubt, is marked by their anxiety to do as they would be done by. It may be the destiny of man that the social instincts shall grow to control his actions absolutely, even in anti-social situations. But they have not yet done so, and as the rules of law are or should be based upon a morality which is generally accepted, no rule founded on a theory of absolute unselfishness can be laid down without a breach between law and working beliefs.

If it be true, as I shall presently try to show, that the general principles of criminal and civil liability are the same, it will follow from that alone that theory and fact agree in frequently punishing those who have been guilty of no moral wrong, and who could not be condemned by any standard that did not avowedly disregard the personal peculiarities of the individuals concerned. If punishment stood on the moral grounds which are proposed for it, the first thing to be considered would be those limitations in the capacity for choosing rightly which arise from abnormal instincts, want of education, lack of intelligence, and all the other defects which are most marked in the criminal classes. I do not say that they should not be, or at least I do not need to for my argument. I do not say that the criminal law does more good than harm. I only say that it is not enacted or administered on that theory.

There remains to be mentioned the affirmative argument in

favor of the theory of retribution, to the effect that the fitness of punishment following wrong-doing is axiomatic, and is instinctively recognized by unperverted minds. I think that it will be seen, on self-inspection, that this feeling of fitness is absolute and unconditional only in the case of our neighbors. It does not seem to me that any one who has satisfied himself that an act of his was wrong, and that he will never do it again, would feel the least need or propriety, as between himself and an earthly punishing power alone, of his being made to suffer for what he had done, although, when third persons were introduced, he might, as a philosopher, admit the necessity of hurting him to frighten others. But when our neighbors do wrong, we sometimes feel the fitness of making them smart for it, whether they have repented or not. The feeling of fitness seems to me to be only vengeance in disguise, and I have already admitted that vengeance was an element, though not the chief element, of punishment.

But, again, the supposed intuition of fitness does not seem to me to be coextensive with the thing to be accounted for. The lesser punishments are just as fit for the lesser crimes as the greater for the greater. The demand that crime should be followed by its punishment should therefore be equal and absolute in both. Again, a *malum prohibitum* is just as much a crime as a *malum in se*. If there is any general ground for punishment, it must apply to one case as much as to the other. But it will hardly be said that, if the wrong in the case just supposed consisted of a breach of the revenue laws, and the government had been indemnified for the loss, we should feel any internal necessity that a man who had thoroughly repented of his wrong should be punished for it, except on the ground that his act was known to others. If it was known, the law would have to verify its threats in order that others might believe and tremble. But if the fact was a secret between the sovereign and the subject, the sovereign, if wholly free from passion, would undoubtedly see that punishment in such a case was wholly without justification.

On the other hand, there can be no case in which the law-maker makes certain conduct criminal without his thereby showing a wish and purpose to prevent that conduct. Prevention would accordingly seem to be the chief and only universal purpose of punishment. The law threatens certain pains if you do certain things, intending thereby to give you a new motive for not doing them. If you persist in doing them, it has to inflict the pains in order that its threats may continue to be believed.

If this is a true account of the law as it stands, the law does undoubtedly treat the individual as a means to an end, and uses him as a tool to increase the general welfare at his own expense. It has been suggested above, that this course is perfectly proper; but even if it is wrong, our criminal law follows it, and the theory of our criminal law must be shaped accordingly.

Further evidence that our law exceeds the limits of retribution, and subordinates consideration of the individual to that of the public well-being, will be found in some doctrines which cannot be satisfactorily explained on any other ground.

The first of these is, that even the deliberate taking of life will not be punished when it is the only way of saving one's own. This principle is not so clearly established as that next to be mentioned; but it has the support of very great authority.[5] If that is the law, it must go on one of two grounds, either that self-preference is proper in the case supposed, or that, even if it is improper, the law cannot prevent it by punishment, because a threat of death at some future time can never be a sufficiently powerful motive to make a man choose death now in order to avoid the threat. If the former ground is adopted, it admits that a single person may sacrifice another to himself, and *a fortiori* that a people may. If the latter view is taken, by abandoning punishment when it can no longer be expected to prevent an act, the law abandons the retributive and adopts the preventive theory.

The next doctrine leads to still clearer conclusions. Ignorance of the law is no excuse for breaking it. This substantive principle is sometimes put in the form of a rule of evidence, that every one is presumed to know the law. It has accordingly been defended by Austin and others, on the ground of difficulty of proof. If justice requires the fact to be ascertained, the difficulty of doing so is no ground for refusing to try. But every one must feel that ignorance of the law could never be admitted as an excuse, even if the fact could be proved by sight and hearing in every case. Furthermore, now that parties can testify, it may be doubted whether a man's knowledge of the law is any harder to investigate than many questions which are gone into. The difficulty, such as it is, would be met

---

[5] Cf. 1 East, P. C. 294; *United States* v. *Holmes,* 1 Wall, Jr. 1; 1 Bishop, Crim. Law, §§ 347–349, 845 (6th ed.); 4 Bl. Comm. 31.

by throwing the burden of proving ignorance on the law-breaker.

The principle cannot be explained by saying that we are not only commanded to abstain from certain acts, but also to find out that we are commanded. For if there were such a second command, it is very clear that the guilt of failing to obey it would bear no proportion to that of disobeying the principal command if known, yet the failure to know would receive the same punishment as the failure to obey the principal law.

The true explanation of the rule is the same as that which accounts for the law's indifference to a man's particular temperament, faculties, and so forth. Public policy sacrifices the individual to the general good. It is desirable that the burden of all should be equal, but it is still more desirable to put an end to robbery and murder. It is no doubt true that there are many cases in which the criminal could not have known that he was breaking the law, but to admit the excuse at all would be to encourage ignorance where the law-maker has determined to make men know and obey, and justice to the individual is rightly outweighed by the larger interests on the other side of the scales.

If the foregoing arguments are sound, it is already manifest that liability to punishment cannot be finally and absolutely determined by considering the actual personal unworthiness of the criminal alone. That consideration will govern only so far as the public welfare permits or demands. And if we take into account the general result which the criminal law is intended to bring about, we shall see that the actual state of mind accompanying a criminal act plays a different part from what is commonly supposed.

For the most part, the purpose of the criminal law is only to induce external conformity to rule. All law is directed to conditions of things manifest to the senses. And whether it brings those conditions to pass immediately by the use of force, as when it protects a house from a mob by soldiers, or appropriates private property to public use, or hangs a man in pursuance of a judicial sentence, or whether it brings them about mediately through men's fears, its object is equally an external result. In directing itself against robbery or murder, for instance, its purpose is to put a stop to the actual physical taking and keeping of other men's goods, or the actual poisoning, shooting, stabbing, and otherwise putting to death of other men. If those things are not done, the law forbidding them is equally satisfied, whatever the motive.

Considering this purely external purpose of the law together with the fact that it is ready to sacrifice the individual so far as necessary in order to accomplish that purpose, we can see more readily than before that the actual degree of personal guilt involved in any particular transgression cannot be the only element, if it is an element at all, in the liability incurred. So far from its being true, as is often assumed, that the condition of a man's heart or conscience ought to be more considered in determining criminal than civil liability, it might almost be said that it is the very opposite of truth. For civil liability, in its immediate working, is simply a redistribution of an existing loss between two individuals; and it will be argued in the next Lecture that sound policy lets losses lie where they fall, except where a special reason can be shown for interference. The most frequent of such reasons is, that the party who is charged has been to blame.

It is not intended to deny that criminal liability, as well as civil, is founded on blameworthiness. Such a denial would shock the moral sense of any civilized community; or, to put it another way, a law which punished conduct which would not be blameworthy in the average member of the community would be too severe for that community to bear. It is only intended to point out that, when we are dealing with that part of the law which aims more directly than any other at establishing standards of conduct, we should expect there more than elsewhere to find that the tests of liability are external, and independent of the degree of evil in the particular person's motives or intentions. The conclusion follows directly from the nature of the standards to which conformity is required. These are not only external, as was shown above, but they are of general application. They do not merely require that every man should get as near as he can to the best conduct possible for him. They require him at his own peril to come up to a certain height. They take no account of incapacities, unless the weakness is so marked as to fall into well-known exceptions, such as infancy or madness. They assume that every man is as able as every other to behave as they command. If they fall on any one class harder than on another, it is on the weakest. For it is precisely to those who are most likely to err by temperament, ignorance, or folly, that the threats of the law are the most dangerous.

The reconciliation of the doctrine that liability is founded on blameworthiness with the existence of liability where the party is not to blame, will be worked out more fully in the next Lecture. It is found in the conception of the average man, the man of ordinary intelligence and reasonable prudence. Liability is said to arise out of such conduct as would be blameworthy in him. But he is an ideal being, represented by the jury when they are appealed to, and his conduct is an external or objective standard when applied to any given individual. That individual may be morally without stain, because he has less than ordinary intelligence or prudence. But he is required to have those qualities at his peril. If he has them, he will not, as a general rule, incur liability without blameworthiness.

(3) Torts and Social Experience [1]

The object of the next two Lectures is to discover whether there is any common ground at the bottom of all liability in tort, and if so, what that ground is. Supposing the attempt to succeed, it will reveal the general principle of civil liability at common law. The liabilities incurred by way of contract are more or less expressly fixed by the agreement of the parties concerned, but those arising from a tort are independent of any previous consent of the wrong-doer to bear the loss occasioned by his act. . . . When A assaults or slanders his neighbor, or converts his neighbor's property, he does a harm which he has never consented to bear, and if the law makes him pay for it, the reason for doing so must be found in some general view of the conduct which every one may fairly expect and demand from every other, whether that other has agreed to it or not.

Such a general view is very hard to find. The law did not begin with a theory. It has never worked one out. The point from which it started and that at which I shall try to show that it has arrived are on different planes. In the progress from one to the other, it is to be expected that its course should not be straight and its direction not always visible. All that can be done is to point out a tendency, and to justify it. The tendency, which is our main concern, is a matter of fact to be gathered from the cases. But the difficulty of showing it is much enhanced by the circumstance that, until lately, the substantive law has been approached only through

[1] This selection is from Lecture III, "Torts — Trespass and Negligence"; also Lecture IV, "The Theory of Torts."

LAW AS CIVILIZATION

the categories of the forms of action. Discussions of legislative principle have been darkened by arguments on the limits between trespass and case, or on the scope of a general issue. In place of a theory of tort, we have a theory of trespass. And even within that narrower limit, precedents of the time of the assize and *jurata* have been applied without a thought of their connection with a long forgotten procedure.

Since the ancient forms of action have disappeared, a broader treatment of the subject ought to be possible. Ignorance is the best of law reformers. People are glad to discuss a question on general principles, when they have forgotten the special knowledge necessary for technical reasoning. But the present willingness to generalize is founded on more than merely negative grounds. The philosophical habit of the day, the frequency of legislation, and the ease with which the law may be changed to meet the opinions and wishes of the public, all make it natural and unavoidable that judges as well as others should openly discuss the legislative principles upon which their decisions must always rest in the end, and should base their judgments upon broad considerations of policy to which the traditions of the bench would hardly have tolerated a reference fifty years ago.

The business of the law of torts is to fix the dividing lines between those cases in which a man is liable for harm which he has done, and those in which he is not. But it cannot enable him to predict with certainty whether a given act under given circumstances will make him liable, because an act will rarely have that effect unless followed by damage, and for the most part, if not always, the consequences of an act are not known, but only guessed at as more or less probable. All the rules that the law can lay down beforehand are rules for determining the conduct which will be followed by liability if it is followed by harm — that is, the conduct which a man pursues at his peril. The only guide for the future to be drawn from a decision against a defendant in an action of tort is that similar acts, under circumstances which cannot be distinguished except by the result from those of the defendant, are done at the peril of the actor; that if he escapes liability, it is simply because by good fortune no harm comes of his conduct in the particular event.

If, therefore, there is any common ground for all liability in tort, we shall best find it by eliminating the event as it actually turns out, and by considering only the principles on which the peril of his conduct is thrown upon the actor. We are to ask what are the elements, on the defendant's side, which must all be present before liability is possible, and the presence of which will commonly make him liable if damage follows.

The law of torts abounds in moral phraseology. It has much to say of wrongs, of malice, fraud, intent, and negligence. Hence it may naturally be supposed that the risk of a man's conduct is thrown upon him as the result of some moral shortcoming. But while this notion has been entertained, the extreme opposite will be found to have been a far more popular opinion; — I mean the notion that a man is answerable for all the consequences of his acts, or, in other words, that he acts at his peril always, and wholly irrespective of the state of his consciousness upon the matter.

Be the exceptions more or less numerous, the general purpose of the law of torts is to secure a man indemnity against certain forms of harm to person, reputation, or estate, at the hands of his neighbors, not because they are wrong, but because they are harms. The true explanation of the reference of liability to a moral standard, in the sense which has been explained, is not that it is for the purpose of improving men's hearts, but that it is to give a man a fair chance to avoid doing the harm before he is held responsible for it. It is intended to reconcile the policy of letting accidents lie where they fall, and the reasonable freedom of others with the protection of the individual from injury.

But the law does not even seek to indemnify a man from all harms. An unrestricted enjoyment of all his possibilities would interfere with other equally important enjoyments on the part of his neighbors. There are certain things which the law allows a man to do, notwithstanding the fact that he foresees that harm to another will follow from them. He may charge a man with crime if the charge is true. He may establish himself in business where he foresees that the effect of his competition will be to diminish the custom of another shopkeeper, perhaps to ruin him. He may erect a building which cuts another off from a beautiful prospect, or he may drain subterranean waters and thereby drain another's well; and many other cases might be put.

As any of these things may be done with foresight of their evil consequences, it would seem that they might be done with intent, and even with malevolent intent, to produce them. The whole argument of this Lecture and the preceding tends to this conclusion. If the aim of liability is simply to prevent or indemnify from harm so far as is consistent with avoiding the extreme of making a man answer for accident, when the law permits the harm to be knowingly inflicted it would be a strong thing if the presence of malice made any difference in its decisions. That might happen, to be sure, without affecting the general views maintained here, but it is not to be expected, and the weight of authority is against it.

As the law, on the one hand, allows certain harms to be inflicted irrespective of the moral condition of him who inflicts them, so, at the other extreme, it may on grounds of policy throw the absolute risk of certain transactions on the person engaging in them, irrespective of blameworthiness in any sense.

Most liabilities in tort lie between these two extremes, and are founded on the infliction of harm which the defendant had a reasonable opportunity to avoid at the time of the acts or omissions which were its proximate cause. But as fast as specific rules are worked out in place of the vague reference to the conduct of the average man, they range themselves alongside of other specific rules based on public policy, and the grounds from which they spring cease to be manifest. So that, as will be seen directly, rules which seem to lie outside of culpability in any sense have sometimes been referred to remote fault, while others which started from the general notion of negligence may with equal ease be referred to some extrinsic ground of policy.

Apart from the extremes just mentioned, it is now easy to see how the point at which a man's conduct begins to be at his own peril is generally fixed. When the principle is understood on which that point is determined by the law of torts, we possess a common ground of classification, and a key to the whole subject, so far as tradition has not swerved the law from a consistent theory. It has been made pretty clear, from what precedes, that I find that ground in knowledge of circumstances accompanying an act or conduct indifferent but for those circumstances.

But it is worth remarking, before that criterion is discussed, that a possible common ground is reached at the preceding step in the descent from malice through intent and foresight. Foresight is a possible common denominator of wrongs at the two extremes of malice and negligence. The purpose of the law is to prevent or secure a man indemnity from harm at the hands of his neighbors, so far as consistent with other considerations which have been mentioned, and excepting, of course, such harm as it permits to be intentionally inflicted. When a man foresees that harm will result from his conduct, the principle which exonerates him from accident no longer applies, and he is liable. But, as has been shown, he is bound to foresee whatever a prudent and intelligent man would have foreseen, and therefore he is liable for conduct from which such a man would have foreseen that harm was liable to follow.

Accordingly, it would be possible to state all cases of negligence in terms of imputed or presumed foresight. It would be possible even to press the presumption further, applying the very inaccurate maxim, that every man is presumed to intend the natural consequences of his own acts; and this mode of expression will, in fact, be found to have been occasionally used, more especially in the criminal law, where the notion of intent has a stronger foothold. The latter fiction is more remote and less philosophical than the former; but, after all, both are equally fictions. Negligence is not foresight, but precisely the want of it; and if foresight were presumed, the ground of the presumption, and therefore the essential element, would be the knowledge of facts which made foresight possible.

Taking knowledge, then, as the true starting-point, the next question is how to determine the circumstances necessary to be known in any given case in order to make a man liable for the consequences of his act. They must be such as would have led a prudent man to perceive danger, although not necessarily to foresee the specific harm. But this is a vague test. How is it decided what those circumstances are? The answer must be, by experience.

But there is one point which has been left ambiguous in the preceding Lecture and here, and which must be touched upon. It has been assumed that conduct which the man of ordinary intelligence would perceive to be dangerous under the circumstances, would be blameworthy if pursued by him. It might not be so, however. Suppose that, acting under the threats of twelve armed men, which put him in fear of his life, a man enters another's close and takes a horse. In such a case, he actually contemplates and chooses harm to another as the consequence of his act. Yet the act is neither blameworthy nor punishable. But it might be actionable, and Rolle, C. J. ruled that it was so in *Gilbert* v. *Stone*.[2] If this be law, it goes the full length of deciding that it is enough if the defendant has had a

[2] Aleyn, 35; Style, 72; A. D. 1648.

chance to avoid inflicting the harm complained of. And it may well be argued that, although he does wisely to ransom his life as he best may, there is no reason why he should be allowed to intentionally and permanently transfer his misfortunes to the shoulders of his neighbors.

It cannot be inferred, from the mere circumstance that certain conduct is made actionable, that therefore the law regards it as wrong, or seeks to prevent it. Under our mill acts a man has to pay for flowing his neighbor's lands, in the same way that he has to pay in trover for converting his neighbor's goods. Yet the law approves and encourages the flowing of lands for the erection of mills.

Moral predilections must not be allowed to influence our minds in settling legal distinctions. If we accept the test of the liability alone, how do we distinguish between trover and the mill acts? or between conduct which is prohibited, and that which is merely taxed? The only distinction which I can see is in the difference of the collateral consequences attached to the two classes of conduct. In the one, the maxim *in pari delicto potior est conditio defendentis,* and the invalidity of contracts contemplating it, show that the conduct is outside the protection of the law. In the other, it is otherwise.[3] This opinion is confirmed by the fact, that almost the only cases in which the distinction between prohibition and taxation comes up concern the application of these maxims.

* * * *

I therefore repeat, that experience is the test by which it is decided whether the degree of danger attending given conduct under certain known circumstances is sufficient to throw the risk upon the party pursuing it.

For instance, experience shows that a good many guns supposed to be unloaded go off and hurt people. The ordinarily intelligent and prudent member of the community would foresee the possibility of danger from pointing a gun which he had not inspected into a crowd, and pulling the trigger, although it was said to be unloaded. Hence, it may very properly be held that a man who does such a thing does it at his peril, and that, if damage ensues, he is answerable for it. The co-ordinated acts necessary to point a gun and pull a trigger, and the intent and knowledge shown by the co-ordination of those acts, are all consistent with entire blamelessness. They

[3] 1 Kent (12th ed.), 467, n. 1; 6 ALR 723–725; 7 *id.* 652.

threaten harm to no one without further facts. But the one additional circumstance of a man in the line and within range of the piece makes the conduct manifestly dangerous to any one who knows the fact. There is no longer any need to refer to the prudent man, or general experience. The facts have taught their lesson, and have generated a concrete and external rule of liability. He who snaps a cap upon a gun pointed in the direction of another person, known by him to be present, is answerable for the consequences.

The question what a prudent man would do under given circumstances is then equivalent to the question what are the teachings of experience as to the dangerous character of this or that conduct under these or those circumstances; and as the teachings of experience are matters of fact, it is easy to see why the jury should be consulted with regard to them. They are, however, facts of a special and peculiar function. Their only bearing is on the question, what ought to have been done or omitted under the circumstances of the case, not on what was done. Their function is to suggest a rule of conduct.

* * * *

The theory of torts may be summed up very simply. At the two extremes of the law are rules determined by policy without reference to any kind of morality. Certain harms a man may inflict even wickedly; for certain others he must answer, although his conduct has been prudent and beneficial to the community.

But in the main the law started from those intentional wrongs, which are the simplest and most pronounced cases, as well as the nearest to the feeling of revenge which leads to self-redress. It thus naturally adopted the vocabulary and in some degree the tests, of morals. But as the law has grown, even when its standards have continued to model themselves upon those of morality, they have necessarily become external, because they have considered, not the actual condition of the particular defendant, but whether his conduct would have been wrong in the fair average member of the community, whom he is expected to equal at his peril.

In general, this question will be determined by considering the degree of danger attending the act or conduct under the known circumstances. If there is danger that harm to another will follow, the act is generally wrong in the sense of the law.

But in some cases the defendant's conduct may not have been morally wrong, and yet he may have chosen to inflict the harm, as where he has acted in fear of his life. In such cases he will be liable, or not, according as the law makes moral blameworthiness, within the limits explained above, the ground of liability, or deems it sufficient if the defendant has had reasonable warning of danger before acting. This distinction, however, is generally unimportant, and the known tendency of the act under the known circumstances to do harm may be accepted as the general test of conduct.

The tendency of a given act to cause harm under given circumstances must be determined by experience. And experience either at first hand or through the voice of the jury is continually working out concrete rules, which in form are still more external and still more remote from a reference to the moral condition of the defendant, than even the test of the prudent man which makes the first stage of the division between law and morals. It does this in the domain of wrongs described as intentional, as systematically as in those styled unintentional or negligent.

But while the law is thus continually adding to its specific rules, it does not adopt the coarse and impolitic principle that a man acts always at his peril. On the contrary, its concrete rules, as well as the general questions addressed to the jury, show that the defendant must have had at least a fair chance of avoiding the infliction of harm before he becomes answerable for such a consequence of his conduct. And it is certainly arguable that even a fair chance to avoid bringing harm to pass is not sufficient to throw upon a person the peril of his conduct, unless, judged by average standards, he is also to blame for what he does.

THE PATH OF THE LAW [1]

When we study law we are not studying a mystery but a well-known profession. We are studying what we shall want in order to appear before judges, or to advise people in such a way as to keep them out of court. The reason why it is a profession, why people will pay lawyers to argue for them or to advise them, is that in societies like ours the command of the public force is intrusted to the judges in certain cases, and the whole power of the state will be put

[1] An Address delivered at the dedication of the new hall of the Boston University School of Law, on January 8, 1897. First published in 10 HLR (1897), 457-478.

forth, if necessary, to carry out their judgments and decrees. People want to know under what circumstances and how far they will run the risk of coming against what is so much stronger than themselves, and hence it becomes a business to find out when this danger is to be feared. The object of our study, then, is prediction, the prediction of the incidence of the public force through the instrumentality of the courts.

The means of the study are a body of reports, of treatises, and of statutes, in this country and in England, extending back for six hundred years, and now increasing annually by hundreds. In these sibylline leaves are gathered the scattered prophecies of the past upon the cases in which the axe will fall. These are what properly have been called the oracles of the law. Far the most important and pretty nearly the whole meaning of every new effort of legal thought is to make these prophecies more precise, and to generalize them into a thoroughly connected system. The process is one, from a lawyer's statement of a case, eliminating as it does all the dramatic elements with which his client's story has clothed it, and retaining only the facts of legal import, up to the final analyses and abstract universals of theoretic jurisprudence. The reason why a lawyer does not mention that his client wore a white hat when he made a contract, while Mrs. Quickly would be sure to dwell upon it along with the parcel gilt goblet and the sea-coal fire, is that he foresees that the public force will act in the same way whatever his client had upon his head. It is to make the prophecies easier to be remembered and to be understood that the teachings of the decisions of the past are put into general propositions and gathered into text-books, or that statutes are passed in a general form. The primary rights and duties with which jurisprudence busies itself again are nothing but prophecies. One of the many evil effects of the confusion between legal and moral ideas, about which I shall have something to say in a moment, is that theory is apt to get the cart before the horse, and to consider the right or the duty as something existing apart from and independent of the consequences of its breach, to which certain sanctions are added afterward. But, as I shall try to show, a legal duty so called is nothing but a prediction that if a man does or omits certain things he will be made to suffer in this or that way by judgment of the court; — and so of a legal right.

The number of our predictions when generalized and reduced to a system is not unmanageably large. They present themselves as a finite body of dogma which may be mastered within a reasonable time. It is a great mistake to be frightened by the ever-increasing number of reports. The reports of a given jurisdiction in the course of a generation take up pretty much the whole body of the law, and restate it from the present point of view. We could reconstruct the corpus from them if all that went before were burned. The use of the earlier reports is mainly historical, a use about which I shall have something to say before I have finished.

I wish, if I can, to lay down some first principles for the study of this body of dogma or systematized prediction which we call the law, for men who want to use it as the instrument of their business to enable them to prophesy in their turn, and, as bearing upon the study, I wish to point out an ideal which as yet our law has not attained.

The first thing for a business-like understanding of the matter is to understand its limits, and therefore I think it desirable at once to point out and dispel a confusion between morality and law, which sometimes rises to the height of conscious theory, and more often and indeed constantly is making trouble in detail without reaching the point of consciousness. You can see very plainly that a bad man has as much reason as a good one for wishing to avoid an encounter with the public force, and therefore you can see the practical importance of the distinction between morality and law. A man who cares nothing for an ethical rule which is believed and practised by his neighbors is likely nevertheless to care a good deal to avoid being made to pay money, and will want to keep out of jail if he can.

I take it for granted that no hearer of mine will misinterpret what I have to say as the language of cynicism. The law is the witness and external deposit of our moral life. Its history is the history of the moral development of the race. The practice of it, in spite of popular jests, tends to make good citizens and good men. When I emphasize the difference between law and morals I do so with reference to a single end, that of learning and understanding the law. For that purpose you must definitely master its specific marks, and it is for that I ask you for the moment to imagine yourselves indifferent to other and greater things.

I do not say that there is not a wider point of view from which the distinction between law and morals becomes of secondary or no importance, as all mathematical distinctions vanish in presence of the infinite. But I do say that that distinction is of the first importance for the object which we are here to consider, — a right study and mastery of the law as a business with well understood limits, a body of dogma enclosed within definite lines. I have just shown the practical reason for saying so. If you want to know the law and nothing else, you must look at it as a bad man, who cares only for the material consequences which such knowledge enables him to predict, not as a good one, who finds his reasons for conduct, whether inside the law or outside of it, in the vaguer sanctions of conscience. The theoretical importance of the distinction is no less, if you would reason on your subject aright. The law is full of phraseology drawn from morals, and by the mere force of language continually invites us to pass from one domain to the other without perceiving it, as we are sure to do unless we have the boundary constantly before our minds. The law talks about rights, and duties, and malice, and intent, and negligence, and so forth, and nothing is easier, or, I may say, more common in legal reasoning, than to take these words in their moral sense, at some stage of the argument, and so to drop into fallacy. For instance, when we speak of the rights of man in a moral sense, we mean to mark the limits of interference with individual freedom which we think are prescribed by conscience, or by our ideal, however reached. Yet it is certain that many laws have been enforced in the past, and it is likely that some are enforced now, which are condemned by the most enlightened opinion of the time, or which at all events pass the limit of interference as many consciences would draw it. Manifestly, therefore, nothing but confusion of thought can result from assuming that the rights of man in a moral sense are equally rights in the sense of the Constitution and the law. No doubt simple and extreme cases can be put of imaginable laws which the statute-making power would not dare to enact, even in the absence of written constitutional prohibitions, because the community would rise in rebellion and fight; and this gives some plausibility to the proposition that the law, if not a part of morality, is limited by it. But this limit of power is not coextensive with any system of morals. For the most part it falls far within the lines of any such system, and in some cases may extend beyond them, for reasons drawn from the habits of a particular people at a particular time. I once heard the late Professor Agassiz say that a German population would rise if you added two cents to the price of a glass of beer. A statute in such a case would be empty words, not because it was wrong, but because it could not be enforced. No one will deny that

LAW AS CIVILIZATION

wrong statutes can be and are enforced, and we should not all agree as to which were the wrong ones.

The confusion with which I am dealing besets confessedly legal conceptions. Take the fundamental question, What constitutes the law? You will find some text writers telling you that it is something different from what is decided by the courts of Massachusetts or England, that it is a system of reason, that it is a deduction from principles of ethics or admitted axioms or what not, which may or may not coincide with the decisions. But if we take the view of our friend the bad man we shall find that he does not care two straws for the axioms or deductions, but that he does want to know what the Massachusetts or English courts are likely to do in fact. I am much of his mind. The prophecies of what the courts will do in fact, and nothing more pretentious, are what I mean by the law.

Take again a notion which as popularly understood is the widest conception which the law contains — the notion of legal duty, to which already I have referred. We fill the word with all the content which we draw from morals. But what does it mean to a bad man? Mainly, and in the first place, a prophecy that if he does certain things he will be subjected to disagreeable consequences by way of imprisonment or compulsory payment of money. But from his point of view, what is the difference between being fined and being taxed a certain sum for doing a certain thing? That his point of view is the test of legal principles is shown by the many discussions which have arisen in the courts on the very question whether a given statutory liability is a penalty or a tax. On the answer to this question depends the decision whether conduct is legally wrong or right, and also whether a man is under compulsion or free. Leaving the criminal law on one side, what is the difference between the liability under the mill acts or statutes authorizing a taking by eminent domain and the liability for what we call a wrongful conversion of property where restoration is out of the question? In both cases the party taking another man's property has to pay its fair value as assessed by a jury, and no more. What significance is there in calling one taking right and another wrong from the point of view of the law? It does not matter, so far as the given consequence, the compulsory payment, is concerned, whether the act to which it is attached is described in terms of praise or in terms of blame, or whether the law purports to prohibit it or to allow it. If it matters at all, still speaking from the bad man's point of view, it must be because in one case and not in the other some further disadvantages, or at least some further consequences, are attached to the act by the law. The only other disadvantages thus attached to it which I ever have been able to think of are to be found in two somewhat insignificant legal doctrines, both of which might be abolished without disturbance. One is, that a contract to do a prohibited act is unlawful, and the other, that, if one of two or more joint wrongdoers has to pay all the damages, he cannot recover contribution from his fellows. And that I believe is all. You see how the vague circumference of the notion of duty shrinks and at the same time grows more precise when we wash it with cynical acid and expel everything except the object of our study, the operations of the law.

Nowhere is the confusion between legal and moral ideas more manifest than in the law of contract. Among other things, here again the so called primary rights and duties are invested with a mystic significance beyond what can be assigned and explained. The duty to keep a contract at common law means a prediction that you must pay damages if you do not keep it — and nothing else. If you commit a tort, you are liable to pay a compensatory sum. If you commit a contract, you are liable to pay a compensatory sum unless the promised event comes to pass, and that is all the difference. But such a mode of looking at the matter stinks in the nostrils of those who think it advantageous to get as much ethics into the law as they can. It was good enough for Lord Coke, however, and here, as in many other cases, I am content to abide with him. In *Bromage* v. *Genning*,[2] a prohibition was sought in the King's Bench against a suit in the marches of Wales for the specific performance of a covenant to grant a lease, and Coke said that it would subvert the intention of the covenantor, since he intends it to be at his election either to lose the damages or to make the lease. Sergeant Harris for the plaintiff confessed that he moved the matter against his conscience, and a prohibition was granted. This goes further than we should go now, but it shows what I venture to say has been the common law point of view from the beginning, although Mr. Harriman, in his very able little book upon Contracts, has been misled, as I humbly think, to a different conclusion.

I have spoken only of the common law, because there are some cases in which a logical justification can be found for speaking of

[2] Roll. Rep. 368.

LAW AS CIVILIZATION

civil liabilities as imposing duties in an intelligible sense. These are the relatively few in which equity will grant an injunction, and will enforce it by putting the defendant in prison or otherwise punishing him unless he complies with the order of the court. But I hardly think it advisable to shape general theory from the exception, and I think it would be better to cease troubling ourselves about primary rights and sanctions altogether, than to describe our prophecies concerning the liabilities commonly imposed by the law in those inappropriate terms.

I mentioned, as other examples of the use by the law of words drawn from morals, malice, intent, and negligence. It is enough to take malice as it is used in the law of civil liability for wrongs — what we lawyers call the law of torts — to show that it means something different in law from what it means in morals, and also to show how the difference has been obscured by giving to principles which have little or nothing to do with each other the same name. Three hundred years ago a parson preached a sermon and told a story out of Foxe's *Book of Martyrs* of a man who had assisted at the torture of one of the saints, and afterward died, suffering compensatory inward torment. It happened that Foxe was wrong. The man was alive and chanced to hear the sermon, and thereupon he sued the parson. Chief Justice Wray instructed the jury that the defendant was not liable, because the story was told innocently, without malice. He took malice in the moral sense, as importing a malevolent motive. But nowadays no one doubts that a man may be liable, without any malevolent motive at all, for false statements manifestly calculated to inflict temporal damage. In stating the case in pleading, we still should call the defendant's conduct malicious; but, in my opinion at least, the word means nothing about motives, or even about the defendant's attitude toward the future, but only signifies that the tendency of his conduct under the known circumstances was very plainly to cause the plaintiff temporal harm.[3]

In the law of contract the use of moral phraseology has led to equal confusion, as I have shown in part already, but only in part. Morals deal with the actual internal state of the individual's mind, what he actually intends. From the time of the Romans down to now, this mode of dealing has affected the language of the law as to contract, and the language used has reacted upon the thought. We talk about a contract as a meeting of the minds of the parties,

[3] See *Hanson* v. *Globe Newspaper Co.*, 159 Mass. 293, 302. See also below, p. 96.

and thence it is inferred in various cases that there is no contract because their minds have not met; that is, because they have intended different things or because one party has not known of the assent of the other. Yet nothing is more certain than that parties may be bound by a contract to things which neither of them intended, and when one does not know of the other's assent. Suppose a contract is executed in due form and in writing to deliver a lecture, mentioning no time. One of the parties thinks that the promise will be construed to mean at once, within a week. The other thinks that it means when he is ready. The court says that it means within a reasonable time. The parties are bound by the contract as it is interpreted by the court, yet neither of them meant what the court declares that they have said. In my opinion no one will understand the true theory of contract or be able even to discuss some fundamental questions intelligently until he has understood that all contracts are formal, that the making of a contract depends not on the agreement of two minds in one intention, but on the agreement of two sets of external signs — not on the parties' having *meant* the same things but on their having *said* the same thing. Furthermore, as the signs may be addressed to one sense or another — to sight or to hearing — on the nature of the sign will depend the moment when the contract is made. If the sign is tangible, for instance, a letter, the contract is made when the letter of acceptance is delivered. If it is necessary that the minds of the parties meet, there will be no contract until the acceptance can be read — none, for example, if the acceptance be snatched from the hand of the offerer by a third person.

This is not the time to work out a theory in detail, or to answer many obvious doubts and questions which are suggested by these general views. I know of none which are not easy to answer, but what I am trying to do now is only by a series of hints to throw some light on the narrow path of legal doctrine, and upon two pitfalls which, as it seems to me, lie perilously near to it. Of the first of these I have said enough. I hope that my illustrations have shown the danger, both to speculation and to practice, of confounding morality with law, and the trap which legal language lays for us on that side of our way. For my own part, I often doubt whether it would not be a gain if every word of moral significance could be banished from the law altogether, and other words adopted which should convey legal ideas uncolored by anything outside the law. We should lose

LAW AS CIVILIZATION

the fossil records of a good deal of history and the majesty got from ethical associations, but by ridding ourselves of an unnecessary confusion we should gain very much in the clearness of our thought.

So much for the limits of the law. The next thing which I wish to consider is what are the forces which determine its content and its growth. You may assume, with Hobbes and Bentham and Austin, that all law emanates from the sovereign, even when the first human beings to enunciate it are the judges, or you may think that law is the voice of the Zeitgeist, or what you like. It is all one to my present purpose. Even if every decision required the sanction of an emperor with despotic power and a whimsical turn of mind, we should be interested none the less, still with a view to prediction, in discovering some order, some rational explanation, and some principle of growth for the rules which he laid down. In every system there are such explanations and principles to be found. It is with regard to them that a second fallacy comes in, which I think it important to expose.

The fallacy to which I refer is the notion that the only force at work in the development of the law is logic. In the broadest sense, indeed, that notion would be true. The postulate on which we think about the universe is that there is a fixed quantitative relation between every phenomenon and its antecedents and consequents. If there is such a thing as a phenomenon without these fixed quantitative relations, it is a miracle. It is outside the law of cause and effect, and as such transcends our power of thought, or at least is something to or from which we cannot reason. The condition of our thinking about the universe is that it is capable of being thought about rationally, or, in other words, that every part of it is effect and cause in the same sense in which those parts are with which we are most familiar. So in the broadest sense it is true that the law is a logical development, like everything else. The danger of which I speak is not the admission that the principles governing other phenomena also govern the law, but the notion that a given system, ours, for instance, can be worked out like mathematics from some general axioms of conduct. This is the natural error of the schools, but it is not confined to them. I once heard a very eminent judge say that he never let a decision go until he was absolutely sure that it was right. So judicial dissent often is blamed, as if it meant simply that one side or the other were not doing their sums right, and, if they would take more trouble, agreement inevitably would come.

This mode of thinking is entirely natural. The training of lawyers is a training in logic. The processes of analogy, discrimination, and deduction are those in which they are most at home. The language of judicial decision is mainly the language of logic. And the logical method and form flatter that longing for certainty and for repose which is in every human mind. But certainty generally is illusion, and repose is not the destiny of man. Behind the logical form lies a judgment as to the relative worth and importance of competing legislative grounds, often an inarticulate and unconscious judgment, it is true, and yet the very root and nerve of the whole proceeding. You can give any conclusion a logical form. You always can imply a condition in a contract. But why do you imply it? It is because of some belief as to the practice of the community or of a class, or because of some opinion as to policy, or, in short, because of some attitude of yours upon a matter not capable of exact quantitative measurement, and therefore not capable of founding exact logical conclusions. Such matters really are battle grounds where the means do not exist for determinations that shall be good for all time, and where the decision can do no more than embody the preference of a given body in a given time and place. We do not realize how large a part of our law is open to reconsideration upon a slight change in the habit of the public mind. No concrete proposition is self-evident, no matter how ready we may be to accept it, not even Mr. Herbert Spencer's "Every man has a right to do what he wills, provided he interferes not with a like right on the part of his neighbors."

Why is a false and injurious statement privileged, if it is made honestly in giving information about a servant? It is because it has been thought more important that information should be given freely, than that a man should be protected from what under other circumstances would be an actionable wrong. Why is a man at liberty to set up a business which he knows will ruin his neighbor? It is because the public good is supposed to be best subserved by free competition. Obviously such judgments of relative importance may vary in different times and places. Why does a judge instruct a jury that an employer is not liable to an employee for an injury received in the course of his employment unless he is negligent, and why do the jury generally find for the plaintiff if the case is allowed to go to them? It is because the traditional policy of our law is to confine liability to cases where a prudent man might have foreseen the injury, or at least the danger, while the inclination of a very large part of the community is to make certain classes of persons insure the safety of those with whom they deal. Since the last words were written, I have seen the requirement of such insurance put forth as part of the programme of one of the best known labor organizations. There is a concealed, half conscious battle on the question of legislative policy, and if any one thinks that it can be settled deductively, or once for all, I only can say that I think he is theoretically wrong, and that I am certain that his conclusion will not be accepted in practice *semper ubique et ab omnibus*.

Indeed, I think that even now our theory upon this matter is open to reconsideration, although I am not prepared to say how I should decide if a reconsideration were proposed. Our law of torts comes from the old days of isolated, ungeneralized wrongs, assaults, slanders, and the like, where the damages might be taken to lie where they fell by legal judgment. But the torts with which our courts are kept busy to-day are mainly the incidents of certain well-known businesses. They are injuries to person or property by railroads, factories, and the like. The liability for them is estimated, and sooner or later goes into the price paid by the public. The public really pays the damages, and the question of liability, if pressed far enough, is really the question how far it is desirable that the public should insure the safety of those whose work it uses. It might be said that in such cases the chance of a jury finding for the defendant is merely a chance, once in a while rather arbitrarily interrupting the regular course of recovery, most likely in the case of an unusually conscientious plaintiff, and therefore better done away with. On the other hand, the economic value even of a life to the community can be estimated, and no recovery, it may be said, ought to go beyond that amount. It is conceivable that some day in certain cases we may find ourselves imitating, on a higher plane, the tariff for life and limb which we see in the *Leges Barbarorum*.

I think that the judges themselves have failed adequately to recognize their duty of weighing considerations of social advantage. The duty is inevitable, and the result of the often proclaimed judicial aversion to deal with such considerations is simply to leave the very ground and foundation of judgments inarticulate, and often unconscious, as I have said. When socialism first began to be talked about, the comfortable classes of the community were a good deal frightened. I suspect that this fear has influenced judicial action both here and in England, yet it is certain that it is not a conscious factor in the decisions to which I refer. I think that something similar has led people who no longer hope to control the legislatures to look to the courts as expounders of the Constitutions, and that in some courts new principles have been discovered outside the bodies of those instruments, which may be generalized into acceptance of the economic doctrines which prevailed about fifty years ago, and a wholesale prohibition of what a tribunal of lawyers does not think about right. I cannot but believe that if the training of lawyers led them habitually to consider more definitely and explicitly the social advantage on which the rule they lay down must be justified, they sometimes would hesitate where now they are confident, and see that really they were taking sides upon debatable and often burning questions.

So much for the fallacy of logical form. Now let us consider the present condition of the law as a subject for study, and the ideal toward which it tends. We still are far from the point of view which I desire to see reached. No one has reached it or can reach it as yet. We are only at the beginning of a philosophical reaction, and of a reconsideration of the worth of doctrines which for the most part still are taken for granted without any deliberate, conscious, and systematic questioning of their grounds. The development of our law has gone on for nearly a thousand years, like the development of a plant, each generation taking the inevitable next step, mind, like matter, simply obeying a law of spontaneous growth. It is perfectly natural and right that it should have been so. Imitation is a necessity of human nature, as has been illustrated by a remarkable French writer, M. Tarde, in an admirable book, *Les Lois de l'Imitation*. Most of the things we do, we do for no better reason than that our fathers have done them or that our neighbors do them, and the same is true of a larger part than we suspect of what we think. The reason is a good one, because our short life gives us no time for a better, but it is not the best. It does not follow, because we all are compelled to take on faith at second hand most of the rules on which we base our action and our thought, that each of us may not try to set some corner of his world in the order of reason, or that all of us collectively should not aspire to carry reason as far as it will go throughout the whole domain. In regard to the law, it is true, no doubt, that an evolutionist will hesitate to affirm universal validity for his social ideals, or for the principles which he thinks should be embodied in legislation. He is content if he can prove them best for here and now. He may be ready to admit that he knows nothing about an absolute best in the cosmos, and even that he knows next to nothing about a permanent best for men. Still it is true that a body of law is more rational and more civilized when every rule it contains is referred articulately and definitely to an end which it subserves, and when the grounds for desiring that end are stated or are ready to be stated in words.

At present, in very many cases, if we want to know why a rule of law has taken its particular shape, and more or less if we want to know why it exists at all, we go to tradition. We follow it into the Year Books, and perhaps beyond them to the customs of the Salian Franks, and somewhere in the past, in the German forests, in the needs of Norman kings, in the assumptions of a dominant class, in the absence of generalized ideas, we find out the practical motive for what now best is justified by the mere fact of its acceptance and that men are accustomed to it. The rational study of law is still to a large extent the study of history. History must be a part of the study, because without it we cannot know the precise scope of rules which it is our business to know. It is a part of the rational study, because it is the first step toward an enlightened scepticism, that is, towards a deliberate reconsideration of the worth of those rules. When you get the dragon out of his cave on to the plain and in the daylight, you can count his teeth and claws, and see just what is his strength. But to get him out is only the first step. The next is either to kill him, or to tame him and make him a useful animal. For the rational study of the law the black-letter man may be the man of the present, but the man of the future is the man of statistics and the master of economics. It is revolting to have no better reason for a rule of law than that so it was laid down in the time of Henry IV. It is still more revolting if the grounds upon which it was laid down have vanished long since, and the rule simply persists from blind imitation of the past. I am thinking of the technical rule as to trespass *ab initio,* as it is called, which I attempted to explain in a recent Massachusetts case.[4]

Let me take an illustration, which can be stated in a few words, to show how the social end which is aimed at by a rule of law is obscured and only partially attained in consequence of the fact that the rule owes its form to a gradual historical development, instead of being reshaped as a whole, with conscious articulate reference to the end in view. We think it desirable to prevent one man's property being misappropriated by another, and so we make larceny a crime. The evil is the same whether the misappropriation is made by a man into whose hands the owner has put the property, or by one who wrongfully takes it away. But primitive law in its weakness did not get much beyond an effort to prevent violence, and very naturally made a wrongful taking, a trespass, part of its definition of the crime. In modern times the judges enlarged the definition a little by holding that, if the wrong-doer gets possession by a trick or device, the crime is committed. This really was giving up the requirement of a trespass, and it would have been more logical, as well as truer to the present object of the law, to abandon the requirement altogether. That, however, would have seemed too bold, and was left to statute. Statutes were passed making embezzlement a crime. But the force of tradition caused the crime of embezzlement to be regarded as so far distinct from larceny that to this day, in some jurisdictions at least, a slip corner is kept open for thieves to contend, if indicted for larceny, that they should have been indicted for embezzlement, and if indicted for embezzlement, that they should have been indicted for larceny, and to escape on that ground.

Far more fundamental questions still await a better answer than that we do as our fathers have done. What have we better than a blind guess to show that the criminal law in its present form does more good than harm? I do not stop to refer to the effect which it has had in degrading prisoners and in plunging them further into crime, or to the question whether fine and imprisonment do not fall more heavily on a criminal's wife and children than on himself. I have in mind more far-reaching questions. Does punishment deter? Do we deal with criminals on proper principles? A modern school of Continental criminalists plumes itself on the formula, first suggested, it is said, by Gall, that we must consider the

[4] *Commonwealth* v. *Rubin,* 165 Mass. 453.

criminal rather than the crime. The formula does not carry us very far, but the inquiries which have been started look toward an answer of my questions based on science for the first time. If the typical criminal is a degenerate, bound to swindle or to murder by as deep seated an organic necessity as that which makes the rattlesnake bite, it is idle to talk of deterring him by the classical method of imprisonment. He must be got rid of; he cannot be improved, or frightened out of his structural reaction. If, on the other hand, crime, like normal human conduct, is mainly a matter of imitation, punishment fairly may be expected to help to keep it out of fashion. The study of criminals has been thought by some well known men of science to sustain the former hypothesis. The statistics of the relative increase of crime in crowded places like large cities, where example has the greatest chance to work, and in less populated parts, where the contagion spreads more slowly, have been used with great force in favor of the latter view. But there is weighty authority for the belief that, however this may be, "not the nature of the crime, but the dangerousness of the criminal, constitutes the only reasonable legal criterion to guide the inevitable social reaction against the criminal." [5]

* * * *

Perhaps I have said enough to show the part which the study of history necessarily plays in the intelligent study of the law as it is to-day. In the teaching of this school and at Cambridge it is in no danger of being undervalued. Mr. Bigelow here and Mr. Ames and Mr. Thayer there have made important contributions which will not be forgotten, and in England the recent history of early English law by Sir Frederick Pollock and Mr. Maitland has lent the subject an almost deceptive charm. We must beware of the pitfall of antiquarianism, and must remember that for our purposes our only interest in the past is for the light it throws upon the present. I look forward to a time when the part played by history in the explanation of dogma shall be very small, and instead of ingenious research we shall spend our energy on a study of the ends sought to be attained and the reasons for desiring them. As a step toward that ideal it seems to me that every lawyer ought to seek an understanding of economics. The present divorce

[5] Havelock Ellis, *The Criminal*, 41, citing Garofalo. See also Ferri, *Sociologie Criminelle, passim.* Compare Tarde, *La Philosophie Pénale.*

between the schools of political economy and law seems to me an evidence of how much progress in philosophical study still remains to be made. In the present state of political economy, indeed, we come again upon history on a larger scale, but there we are called on to consider and weigh the ends of legislation, the means of attaining them, and the cost. We learn that for everything we have we give up something else, and we are taught to set the advantage we gain against the other advantage we lose, and to know what we are doing when we elect.

There is another study which sometimes is undervalued by the practical minded, for which I wish to say a good word, although I think a good deal of pretty poor stuff goes under that name. I mean the study of what is called jurisprudence. Jurisprudence, as I look at it, is simply law in its most generalized part. Every effort to reduce a case to a rule is an effort of jurisprudence, although the name as used in English is confined to the broadest rules and most fundamental conceptions. One mark of a great lawyer is that he sees the application of the broadest rules. There is a story of a Vermont justice of the peace before whom a suit was brought by one farmer against another for breaking a churn. The justice took time to consider, and then said that he had looked through the statutes and could find nothing about churns, and gave judgment for the defendant. The same state of mind is shown in all our common digests and text-books. Applications of rudimentary rules of contract or tort are tucked away under the head of Railroads or Telegraphs or go to swell treatises on historical subdivisions, such as Shipping or Equity, or are gathered under an arbitrary title which is thought likely to appeal to the practical mind, such as Mercantile Law. If a man goes into law it pays to be a master of it, and to be a master of it means to look straight through all the dramatic incidents and to discern the true basis for prophecy. Therefore, it is well to have an accurate notion of what you mean by law, by a right, by a duty, by malice, intent, and negligence, by ownership, by possession, and so forth. I have in my mind cases in which the highest courts seem to me to have floundered because they had no clear ideas on some of these themes. I have illustrated their importance already. If a further illustration is wished, it may be found by reading the Appendix to Sir James Stephen's *Criminal Law* on the subject of possession, and then turning to Pollock and Wright's enlightened book. Sir James Stephen is not the only writer whose attempts to analyze legal ideas have been confused by striving for a useless quintessence of all systems, instead of an accurate anatomy of one. The trouble with Austin was that he did not know enough English law. But still it is a practical advantage to master Austin, and his predecessors, Hobbes and Bentham, and his worthy successors, Holland and Pollock. Sir Frederick Pollock's recent little book is touched with the felicity which marks all his works, and is wholly free from the perverting influence of Roman models.

The advice of the elders to young men is very apt to be as unreal as a list of the hundred best books. At least in my day I had my share of such counsels, and high among the unrealities I place the recommendation to study the Roman law. I assume that such advice means more than collecting a few Latin maxims with which to ornament the discourse — the purpose for which Lord Coke recommended Bracton. If that is all that is wanted, the title *De Regulis Juris Antiqui* can be read in an hour. I assume that, if it is well to study the Roman law, it is well to study it as a working system. That means mastering a set of technicalities more difficult and less understood than our own, and studying another course of history by which even more than our own the Roman law must be explained. If any one doubts me, let him read Keller's *Der Römische Civil Process und die Actionen,* a treatise on the praetor's edict, Muirhead's most interesting *Historical Introduction to the Private Law of Rome,* and, to give him the best chance, Sohm's admirable *Institutes.* No. The way to gain a liberal view of your subject is not to read something else, but to get to the bottom of the subject itself. The means of doing that are, in the first place, to follow the existing body of dogma into its highest generalizations by the help of jurisprudence; next, to discover from history how it has come to be what it is; and, finally, so far as you can, to consider the ends which the several rules seek to accomplish, the reasons why those ends are desired, what is given up to gain them, and whether they are worth the price.

I have been speaking about the study of the law, and I have said next to nothing of what commonly is talked about in that connection — text-books and the case system, and all the machinery with which a student comes most immediately in contact. Nor shall I say anything about them. Theory is my subject, not practical details. The modes of teaching have been improved since my time, no doubt, but ability and industry will master the raw material with any mode. Theory is the most important part of the dogma of the law, as the architect is the most important man who takes part in the building of a house. The most important improvements of the last twenty-five years are improvements in theory. It is not to be feared as unpractical, for, to the competent, it simply means going to the bottom of the subject. For the incompetent, it sometimes is true, as has been said, that an interest in general ideas means an absence of particular knowledge. I remember in army days reading of a youth who, being examined for the lowest grade and being asked a question about squadron drill, answered that he never had considered the evolutions of less than ten thousand men. But the weak and foolish must be left to their folly. The danger is that the able and practical-minded should look with indifference or distrust upon ideas the connection of which with their business is remote. I heard a story, the other day, of a man who had a valet to whom he paid high wages, subject to deduction for faults. One of his deductions was, "For lack of imagination, five dollars." The lack is not confined to valets. The object of ambition, power, generally presents itself nowadays in the form of money alone. Money is the most immediate form, and is a proper object of desire. "The fortune," said Rachel, "is the measure of the intelligence." That is a good text to waken people out of a fool's paradise. But, as Hegel says,[6] "It is in the end not the appetite, but the opinion, which has to be satisfied." To an imagination of any scope the most far-reaching form of power is not money, it is the command of ideas. If you want great examples, read Mr. Leslie Stephen's *History of English Thought in the Eighteenth Century*, and see how a hundred years after his death the abstract speculations of Descartes had become a practical force controlling the conduct of men. Read the works of the great German jurists, and see how much more the world is governed to-day by Kant than by Bonaparte. We cannot all be Descartes or Kant, but we all want happiness. And happiness, I am sure from having known many successful men, cannot be won simply by being counsel for great corporations and having an income of fifty thousand dollars. An intellect great enough to win the prize needs other food besides

[6] *Phil. des Rechts,* § 190.

success. The remoter and more general aspects of the law are those which give it universal interest. It is through them that you not only become a great master in your calling, but connect your subject with the universe and catch an echo of the infinite, a glimpse of its unfathomable process, a hint of the universal law.

4. Law as Judgment: Some Massachusetts Judicial Opinions

Holmes served on the Supreme Judicial Court of Massachusetts for two decades. They were the decades in which he was forced to think most deeply about the function of law in society — about such matters as the liability of administrative officers, the area of discretion in administrative determination, the limits of judicial tolerance of legislative action, the scope of the police power, the relations of labor and capital, the nature and basis of liability in tort, the safeguards of criminal procedure. These are the themes of the cases that follow. The selection is in one sense far from representative: most of the cases are concerned with questions of public law, whereas the great bulk of Judge Holmes's opinions on the Massachusetts Court dealt with matters of litigation under private law. Yet the dividing line between the two is a difficult one, as witness the labor cases, which start as problems of individual liability but end as problems of collective power. I have for the most part in the following selections picked the better-known Holmes Massachusetts Court opinions;[1] *and they are known largely because, in the area of Constitutional law and power relations, they dealt with the same issues that Holmes was later to deal with and foreshadowed his later and more famous opinions on the United States Supreme Court.*

It has often been said of Holmes, as of Justice Cardozo, that even if he had remained on the state bench and had never reached the national, he would still have been a first-rate figure. However this may be, there can be little question that Holmes belongs with the half-dozen most important figures in the state judicial history of America.

He had a chance as a state judge to apply the already characteristic body of principles that he had developed as a legal student and writer during the years he edited the American Law Review *and contributed to the* Harvard Law Review. *Or what is even truer,*

---

[1] For a convenient selection of the state decisions, the student of Holmes is indebted to H. C. Shriver, *Judicial Opinions of Oliver Wendell Holmes* (1940).

since he had in him so much of the empiricist, he brought to his judicial duties a bundle of hypotheses about law and its social basis, which he tested in the action of the courts. This bundle included the famous Holmesian doctrine of the external standard as the test of liability; the doctrine that differences in legal responsibility are differences in degree and that the problem of the judge is — despite the element of arbitrariness involved — to draw the line somewhere at roughly the right point; the doctrine of legislative reasonableness as demarking the scope of judicial review. In general his approach was that of a judicial innovator working within the limits of the social conservative. He saw legal truth as a series of "can't helps" and was willing to let a doctrine stand rather than disturb it; but if the imperatives of social experience demanded that it be disturbed, he was judicial craftsman enough to dare to fashion new doctrine closer to those imperatives. Thus with his opinions on the external standard of liability, on municipal socialism and local option in the matter of women's suffrage, and particularly on the questions of picketing and the closed shop. Yet it must be remembered — and the decisions that follow will bear this out — that even when Holmes was most the legal innovator, he remained the social conservative.

For perhaps the fullest statement of Holmes's theory of judicial decision while he was on the Massachusetts Court, the reader should turn back to "The Path of the Law," in the previous section.[2] Here Holmes warned the law students he was addressing against the pitfalls of a mechanical logic and an arid historicism on the one hand, and on the other of moralism and softmindedness. He saw himself as an "evolutionist" who takes the long historical growths of the law, stunted and distorted by the dead weight of imitation of the past, and shapes them closer to the rational social ends that they must subserve, not for "the absolute best in the cosmos" but "for here and now." Much later, in the 1920's,[3] he was to feel that the social reformers had too great a passion for equality and paid too much attention to tinkering with property and too little to the quality of the race. But in the 1890's he was fighting the lethargic rather than the zealous. "I think," he told his audience, "that the judges themselves have failed adequately to recognize their duty of weighing considerations of social advantage."

[2] See p. 71.
[3] See "Law and Social Reform," p. 399.

How shall we reconcile this with the often repeated statements in the opinions below that as a judge he was not concerned with the wisdom of the social policy involved in the legislative act? The question reaches to the heart of Holmes's rôle as a judge. Holmes knew that judges as well as legislators made law. But he wanted them to confine their lawmaking to the common law, where they shaped and reshaped social experience into legal rules. When the community spoke consciously and deliberately through legislatures, it was the job of the judge not to impose his own view of policy upon the community's. But — and here is the nub of the matter — this did not mean that even in this area the judge was not to have a view of policy. It was better for him to make it articulate, but to know when to use and when not to use it. "The result of the often proclaimed judicial aversion to deal with such considerations (of social policy) is simply to leave the very ground and foundation of judgments inarticulate, and often unconscious. . . ." The fear of socialism, he continued, "has influenced judicial action both here and in England. Yet it is certain that it is not a conscious factor in the decisions to which I refer. . . . I cannot but believe that if the training of lawyers led them habitually to consider more definitely and explicitly the social advantage on which the rule they lay down must be justified, they sometimes would hesitate where now they are confident, and see that really they were taking sides upon debatable and often burning questions." [4]

Thus the Holmes who was a state judge was able to reconcile his judicial tolerance of legislative policy with a strong sense of the pitfalls that lurked for the judge in leaving his basic social premises inarticulate.

THE LEGISLATURE AND THE WEAVERS

Commonwealth v. Perry
155 Mass. 117, 123 (1891)

Commonwealth v. Perry *was Justice Holmes's first blow for the Massachusetts trade unions and one of his infrequent dissents while he was on the state court. The Massachusetts*

[4] See p. 82. For a somewhat similarly phrased statement in one of Holmes's state court opinions, see his dissent in *Vegelahn v. Guntner,* p. 109.

legislature had passed a law to protect weavers, saying that the employer could not withhold any portion of his workers' wages because of imperfections in the work. The Court held that it violated the state constitution, citing Article I of the Declaration of Rights on the inalienable right "of acquiring, possessing, and protecting property," which (Justice Knowlton wrote) "includes the right to make reasonable contracts." In his dissent Justice Holmes strikes the note that was to pervade his later constitutional opinions: that he was not sitting in judgment as a political economist on the social validity of the legislation, but was a judge trying to determine whether the matter was outside the scope of legislative action, however wise or foolish.

It is worth noting that Justice Knowlton's reliance on the doctrine of contract as a property right reflected the views of the faction of the United States Supreme Court, headed by Justice Field, which had by this time become a triumphant majority; and that Holmes's view is closer to that of Justice Miller, whose opinion in the Slaughter-House *cases*[1] *Holmes cited at the end.*

Holmes's language is restrained, and without flash of phrase; but it is already apparent in the dry clipped sentences that the fifty-year-old Justice has come to maturity and knows with a quiet sureness what he means to say.

Holmes, J., dissenting:

I have the misfortune to disagree with my brethren. I have submitted my views to them at length, and, considering the importance of the question, feel bound to make public a brief statement, notwithstanding the respect and deference I feel for the judgment of those with whom I disagree.

In the first place, if the statute is unconstitutional, as construed by the majority, I think it should be construed more narrowly and literally, so as to save it.

Taking it literally, it is not infringed, and there is no withholding of wages, when the employer only promises to pay a reasonable price for imperfect work, or a price less than the price paid for perfect work, and does pay that price in fact.

[1] For a discussion of the Field-Miller feud, see my "Supreme Court and American Capitalism" in *Ideas Are Weapons*, pp. 449–453, also Charles Fairman's *Mr. Justice Miller and the Supreme Court* (1939).

But I agree that the act should be construed more broadly, and should be taken to prohibit palpable evasions, because I am of opinion that even so construed it is constitutional, so far as any argument goes which I have heard.

The prohibition, if any, must be found in the words of the Constitution, either expressed or implied, upon a fair and historical construction. What words of the United States or State constitution are relied on? The statute cannot be said to impair the obligation of contracts made after it went into effect. . . . So far as has been pointed out to me, I do not see that it interferes with the right of acquiring, possessing, and protecting property any more than the laws against usury or gaming. In truth, I do not think that that clause of the Bill of Rights has any application. It might be urged, perhaps, that the power to make reasonable laws impliedly prohibits the making of unreasonable ones, and that this law is unreasonable. If I assume that this construction of the constitution is correct, and that, speaking as a political economist, I should agree in condemning the law, still I should not be willing or think myself authorized to overturn legislation on that ground, unless I thought that an honest difference of opinion was impossible, or pretty nearly so.

But if the statute did no more than to abolish contracts for a *quantum meruit,* and recoupment for defective quality not amounting to a failure of consideration, I suppose that it only would put an end to what are, relatively speaking, innovations in the common law, and I know of nothing to hinder it. . . . I do not confine myself to technical considerations. I suppose that this act was passed because the operatives, or some of them, thought that they were often cheated out of a part of their wages under a false pretense that the work done by them was imperfect, and persuaded the Legislature that their view was true. If their view was true, I cannot doubt that the Legislature had the right to deprive the employers of an honest tool which they were using for a dishonest purpose, and I cannot pronounce the legislation void, as based on a false assumption, since I know nothing about the matter one way or the other. The statute, however construed, leaves the employers their remedy for imperfect work by action. I doubt if we are at liberty to consider the objection that this remedy is practically worthless; but if we are, then the same objection is equally true, although for different reasons, if the workmen are left to their remedy for wages wrongfully withheld. My view seems to me to be favored by *Hancock* v. *Yaden,* 121 Ind. 366, and *Slaughter-House* cases, 16 Wall. 36, 80, 81.

"COMMUNISM" IN WOOD AND COAL

Advisory Opinion of the Justices
155 Mass. 598, 607 (1892)

"I must not write long," runs a letter from Judge Holmes to Frederick Pollock in 1892, "for this morning I must prepare to give my opinion to the legislature whether they can authorize municipal wood and coal yards — a step towards Communism. I am likely to be in the minority and to think that they can, but I may come out the other way or the rest of the 7 may agree with me." [1] *They did not; five of the justices advising that the act was unconstitutional, and the sixth concurring in part; and Holmes's dissent is all the starker for its brevity.*

The act in question, on whose constitutionality the judges were asked to pass in an advisory opinion, was one "to enable Cities and Towns to purchase, sell and distribute Fuel" through municipal yards. Eleven years later, in 1903 — when Holmes had left the bench — the Court was still defending the Commonwealth from municipal socialism.[2] *On that occasion a commentator in the* Harvard Law Review *spoke of "the continued and vigorous opposition of the court to radical extension of the doctrine of municipal ownership. The growing popularity of that doctrine has been attested by recent municipal elections."* [3] *Holmes was later to refer to the "vague terror" of the word "socialism" which swept the country around this time.*[4]

The legal question involved was whether the tax required

---

[1] H–P, 1:142 (April 15, 1892). It is interesting to note that Holmes as a state court judge felt himself free in his letters to comment on pending cases to an extent far beyond his later reticence as a judge on the national bench.
[2] Opinion of the Justices, 182 Mass. 605. There was not a single member of the Court in this case who took Holmes's view.
[3] 16 HLR 585 (1903).
[4] See p. 390.

to raise the money would be for a public purpose.⁵ *Holmes's opinion is a clear-cut expression of his doctrine of judicial tolerance of legislative policy.*

Holmes, J., dissenting:

I am of opinion that when money is taken to enable a public body to offer to the public without discrimination an article of general necessity, the purpose is no less public when that article is wood or coal than when it is water, or gas, or electricity, or education, to say nothing of cases like the support of paupers or the taking of land for railroads or public markets.

I see no ground for denying the power of the Legislature to enact the laws mentioned in the questions proposed. The need or expediency of such legislation is not for us to consider.

PUBLICATION AT PERIL

Hadley P. Hanson v. Globe Newspaper Company
159 Mass. 293, 299 (1893)

"Whatever a man publishes," wrote Lord Mansfield in a decision in 1774, "he publishes at his peril." Almost a century and a quarter later Holmes restated and applied the doctrine in his famous dissent in the present case.

The Boston Globe *had reported the drunkenness and arrest of an H. P. Hanson, a South Boston real estate and insurance broker. The man actually involved had been A. P. H. Hanson. But unfortunately there was also an H. P. Hanson who corresponded both to the residence and vocation given. This Hanson sued the* Globe *for libel. The Court majority held there was none, on the ground that the words of the article were not intended to refer to the real H. P. Hanson, and the facts were well known to the public anyway. Writing to Pollock thirty-two years later, in 1925, Holmes recalled this decision: "I thought the majority failed to grasp the first principles of liability in tort."* [1] *His own tendency was to apply to defamation the principle of absolute liability.*

⁵ For a review of the general subject, see McAllister, "Public Purpose in Taxation," *Selected Essays on Constitutional Law* (1938), Vol. 5, pp. 1–24.
[1] H–P, II:155 (Feb. 20, 1925).

LAW AS JUDGMENT

Holmes's dissent followed the logic of his doctrine of the external standard — that "the publication is so manifestly detrimental that the defendant publishes it at the peril of being able to justify it, in the sense in which the public will understand it." Two other justices joined in the dissent. A comment in the Harvard Law Review *has called it "the first clearly enunciated" objective standard for libel cases.*[2] *Pollock, writing to Holmes with approval, had a whimsical sense that the Zeitgeist might be with them all too much: "But Nemesis is upon us. The reasonable man and the 'external standard' have filtered down to the common examination candidate, who is beginning to write horrible nonsense about them."*[3] *Two years later, in 1895, a California court followed Holmes's doctrine.*[4] *In 1909 Holmes had the sastifaction, in* Peck v. Tribune Co., *of writing the opinion of the Supreme Court in a similar case.*[5] *In 1919 he had the 'inward satisfaction' of reading an English libel case,* Hulton v. Jones, *and noting that his 1893 dissent, "though rather too long, does not suffer by comparison."*[6] *The reader will probably agree that it carries its erudition none too heavily, and winds its way skillfully through the intricacies of reasoning.*

Holmes, J., dissenting:

I am unable to agree with the decision of the majority of the court, and as the question is of some importance in its bearing on legal principles, and as I am not alone in my views, I think it proper to state the considerations which have occurred to me.

The first thing to determine is what question is presented. If we were to stop with the words in which the conclusion of the report is couched there would be no question at all. "The court found as a fact that the alleged libel declared on by the plaintiff was not published by the defendant of or concerning the plaintiff." But it is not to be supposed that a justice of the Superior Court would send a report to this court in which he did not intend to present a question of law. The so-called finding either is a ruling on the effect of the facts previously found, or at least, putting it in the

[2] 38 HLR 1100 (1925).
[3] H–P, I:46 (Aug. 31, 1893).
[4] *Taylor* v. *Hearst*, 107 Cal. 262 (1895).
[5] See below, p. 353.
[6] H–P, II:29 (Nov. 6, 1919).

most favorable way for the defendant, is a conclusion drawn from those facts alone. Whether the conclusion be one of fact or of law, the question is whether it is justified by the facts set forth, without other facts or evidence.

The facts are that libellous matter was published in an article by the defendant about "H. P. Hanson, a real estate and insurance broker of South Boston," that the plaintiff bore that name and description, and, so far as appears, that no one else did, but that the defendant did not know of his existence, and intended to state some facts about one Andrew P. H. Hanson, also a real estate and insurance broker of South Boston, concerning whom the article was substantially true.

The article described the subject of it as a prisoner in the criminal dock, and states that he was fined, and this makes it possible to speak of the article as one describing the conduct of a prisoner. But this mode of characterization seems to me misleading. In form it describes the plight and conduct of "H. P. Hanson, a real estate and insurance broker of South Boston." The statement is, "H. P. Hanson, a real estate and insurance broker of South Boston, emerged from the seething mass of humanity that filled the dock," etc. In order to give it any different subject, or to give the subject any further qualifications or description, you have to resort to the predicate, to the very libellous matter itself. It is not necessary to say that this never can be done, but it must be done with great caution. The very substance of the libel complained of is the statement that the plaintiff was a prisoner in the criminal dock, and was fined. The object of the article, which is a newspaper criminal court report, is to make that statement. The rest of it amounts to nothing, and is merely an attempt to make the statement amusing. If an article should allege falsely that A. murdered B. with a knife, it would not be a satisfactory answer to an action by A. that it was a description of the conduct of the murderer of B., and was true concerning him. The public, or all except the few who may have been in court on the day in question, or who consult the criminal records, have no way of telling who was the prisoner except by what is stated in the article, and the article states that it was "H. P. Hanson, a real estate and insurance broker of South Boston."

If I am right so far, the words last quoted, and those words alone, describe the subject of the allegation, in substance as well as in form. Those words also describe the plaintiff, and no one else. The only ground, then, on which the matters alleged of and concerning the subject can be found not to be alleged of and concerning the plaintiff, is that the defendant did not intend them to apply to him, and the question is narrowed to whether such a want of intention is enough to warrant the finding, or to constitute a defence, when the inevitable consequence of the defendant's acts is that the public, or that part of it which knows the plaintiff, will suppose that the defendant did use its language about him.

On general principles of tort, the private intent of the defendant would not exonerate it. It knew that it was publishing statements purporting to be serious, which would be hurtful to a man if applied to him. It knew that it was using as the subject of those statements words which purported to designate a particular man, and would be understood by its readers to designate one. In fact, the words purported to designate, and would be understood by its readers to designate, the plaintiff. If the defendant had supposed that there was no such person, and had intended simply to write an amusing fiction, that would not be a defence, at least unless its belief was justifiable. Without special reason, it would have no right to assume that there was no one within the sphere of its influence to whom the description answered. The case would be very like firing a gun into a street, and, when a man falls, setting up that no one was known to be there. *Commonwealth* v. *Pierce,* 138 Mass. 165,178. *Hull's case,* Kelyng, 40. *Rex* v. *Burton,* 1 Strange, 481. *Rigmaidon's case,* 1 Lewin, 180. *Regina* v. *Desmond,* Steph. Cr. Law, 146. So, when the description which points out the plaintiff is supposed by the defendant to point out another man whom in fact it does not describe, the defendant is equally liable as when the description is supposed to point out nobody. On the general principles of tort, the publication is so manifestly detrimental that the defendant publishes it at the peril of being able to justify it in the sense in which the public will understand it.

But in view of the unfortunate use of the word "malice" in connection with libel and slander, a doubt may be felt whether actions for these causes are governed by general principles. The earliest forms of the common law known to me treat slander like any other tort, and say nothing about malice. 4 Seld. Soc. Pub. 40, 48, 61. Probably the word was borrowed at a later, but still early date, from the *malitia* of the canon law. By the canon law, one who maliciously charged another with a grave sin incurred excommunication, *ipso facto.* Lyndw., Provinciale, lib. 5, tit. 17 (*De Sent Excomm.* c. 1, *Auctoritate Dei*). Oughton, *Ordo Judiciorum,* tit. 261. Naturally *malitia* was defined as *cogitatio malae mentis,* coming near to conscious malevolence. Lyndw., *ubi supra,* note f. Naturally also for a time the common law followed its leader. Three centuries ago it seems to have regarded the malice alleged in slander and libel as meaning the malice of ethics and the spiritual law.

In the famous case where a parson in a sermon repeated, out of Foxe's *Book of Martyrs,* the story "that one Greenwood, being a perjured person, and a great persecutor, had great plagues inflicted upon him, and was killed by the hand of God, whereas in truth he never was so plagued, and was himself present at that sermon," and afterwards sued the parson for the slander, Chief Justice Wray instructed the jury "that, it being delivered but as a story, and not with any malice or intention to slander any, he was not guilty of the words maliciously; and so was found not guilty. . . ."

But that case is no longer law. . . . The law constantly is tending towards consistency of theory. For a long time it has been held that the malice alleged in an action of libel means no more than it does in other actions of tort. . . . Indeed, one of the earliest cases to state modern views was a case of libel. . . . Accordingly, it was recently laid down by this court that the liability was the usual liability in tort for the natural consequences of a manifestly injurious act. A man may be liable civilly, and formerly, at least by the common law of England, even criminally, for publishing a libel without knowing it. . . . And it seems he might be liable civilly for publishing it by mistake, intending to publish another paper. . . . So, when by mistake the name of the plaintiff's firm was inserted under the head "First Meetings under the Bankruptcy Act," instead of under "Dissolution of Partnerships.". . . So a man will be liable for a slander spoken in jest, if the bystanders reasonably understand it to be a serious charge. . . . Of course it does not matter that the defendant did not intend to injure the plaintiff, it lies upon him "only to show that this construction, which they've put in the paper, is such as the generality of readers must take it in, according to the obvious and natural sense of it." . . . In *Smith* v. *Ashley,* 11 Met. 367, the jury were instructed that the publisher of a newspaper article written by another, and supposed and still asserted by the defendant to be fiction, was not liable if he believed it to be so. Under the circumstances of the case, "believed" meant "reasonably believed." Even so qualified, it is questioned by Mr. Odgers if the ruling would be followed in England. . . . But it has no application to this case, as here the defendant's agent wrote the article, and there is no evidence that he or the defendant had any reason to believe that H. P. Hanson meant any one but the plaintiff.

The foregoing decisions show that slander and libel now, as in the beginning, are governed by the general principles of the law of tort, and, if that be so, the defendant's ignorance that the words which it published identified the plaintiff is no more an excuse, than ignorance of any other fact about which the defendant has been put on inquiry. To hold that a man publishes such words at his peril, when they are supposed to describe a different man, is hardly a severer application of the law, than when they are uttered about a man believed on the strongest grounds to be dead, and thus not capable of being the subject of a tort. It has been seen that by the common law of England such a belief would not be an excuse. . . .

I feel some difficulty in putting my finger on the precise point of difference between the minority and majority of the court. I understand, however, that a somewhat unwilling assent is yielded to the general views which I have endeavored to justify, and I should gather that the exact issue was to be found in the statement that the article was one describing the conduct of a prisoner brought before the Municipal Court of Boston, coupled with the later statement that the language, taken in connection with the publicly known circumstances under which it was written, showed at once that the article referred to A. P. H. Hanson, and that the name of H. P. Hanson was used by mistake. I have shown why it seems to me that these statements are misleading. I only will add, on this point, that I do not know what the publicly known circumstances are. I think it is a mistake of fact to suppose that the public generally know who was before the Municipal Criminal Court on a given day. I think it is a mistake of law to say that, because a small part of the public have that knowledge, the plaintiff cannot recover for the harm done him in the eyes of the greater part of the public, probably including all his acquaintances who are ignorant about the matter, and I also think it no sufficient answer to say that they might consult the criminal records, and find out that probably there was some error. . . . If the case should proceed further on the facts, it might appear that, in view of the plaintiff's character and circumstances, all who knew him would assume that there was a mistake, that the harm to him was merely nominal, and that he had been too hasty in resorting to an action to vindicate himself. But that question is not before us.

With reference to the suggestion that, if the article, in addition to what was true concerning A. P. H. Hanson, had contained matter which was false and libellous as to him, he might have maintained an action, it is unnecessary to express an opinion. I think the proposition less obvious than that the plaintiff can maintain one. If an article should describe the subject of its statements by two sets of marks, one of which identified one man and one of which identified another, and a part of the public naturally and reasonably were led by the one set to apply the statements to one plaintiff, and another part were led in the same way by the other set to apply them to another, I see no absurdity in allowing two actions to be maintained. But that is not this case.

Even if the plaintiff and A. P. H. Hanson had borne the same name, and the article identified its subject only by a proper name, very possibly that would not be enough to raise the question. For, as every one knows, a proper name always purports to designate one person and no other, and although, through the imperfection of our system of naming, the same combination of letters and sounds may be applied to two or more, the name of each, in theory of law, is distinct, although there is no way of finding out which person was named but by inquiring which was meant. *"Licet idem sit nomen, tamen diversum est propter diversitatem personae."*. . .

Mr. Justice Morton and Mr. Justice Barker agree with this opinion.

THE REFERENDUM AND THE WOMAN VOTER

Advisory Opinion of the Justices
160 Mass. 586, 593 (1894)

It is difficult for us to think ourselves back to a time when a proposal like the referendum seemed revolutionary. Yet that is the context in which the Massachusetts Court approached the question whether it would consider constitutional a legislative act granting women the right to vote in town and city elections — throughout the state if approved by a state-wide referendum, or in particular cities or towns if endorsed by local option. Four of the judges declared that the act would run counter to the basic principles of American constitutionalism and representative government: Massachusetts was not a pure democracy, and the legislative power lay not with the people but with the legislature, or General Court.

That they were less troubled by the dangers of woman suffrage than by the dangers of the referendum is fairly clear, and is strengthened by some sentences in a letter from Holmes to Pollock: "The last two or three years I have found myself separated from my brethren on some important constitutional questions; the last a few days ago on the power of the legislature to pass an act subject to approval of the people by vote (the referendum of Switzerland about which the workingmen here are beginning to make a row). My brethren deny it and I affirm it, and among the respectable there are some who regard me as a dangerous radical! If I had seen fit to clothe my views in different language I dare say I could have been a pet of the proletariat — whereas they care nothing for me and some of the others distrust me." [1] In a letter to Pollock the previous year Holmes had described a visit he had made to a labor leader, whom he had asked what he would like if he could have it. "Organization, the 8 hour law, and the Swiss referendum seem to be his particular objects." [2]

In this context Holmes's opinion stands out both for the courage of its position and its sharp limitation to the constitu-

[1] H–P, I:50 (April 2, 1894).
[2] H–P, I:44 (Jan. 20, 1893).

tional issue. His characterization of the Massachusetts Constitution as "a frame of government for men of opposite opinions and for the future" marks the maturing of the constitutional views he was to express on the Supreme Court. His references to Hobbes are particularly apt; it is worth noting that he had been reading the Leviathan *during the past year.*[3]

Holmes, J.:

If the questions proposed to the justices came before us as a court and I found myself unable to agree with my brethren, I should defer to their opinion without any intimation of dissent. But the understanding always has been that questions like the present are addressed to us as individuals and require an individual answer.

It is assumed in the questions that the Legislature has power to grant women the right to vote in town and city elections. I see no reason to doubt that it has that power.

1. I admit that the Constitution establishes a representative government, not a pure democracy. It establishes a General Court which is to be the law-making power. But the question is whether it puts a limit upon the power of that body to make laws. In my opinion the Legislature has the whole law-making power except so far as the words of the Constitution expressly or impliedly withhold it, and I think that in construing the Constitution we should remember that it is a frame of government for men of opposite opinions and for the future, and therefore not hastily import into it our own views, or unexpressed limitations derived merely from the practice of the past. I ask myself, as the only question, what words express or imply that a power to pass a law subject to rejection by the people is withheld? I find none which do so. The question is not whether the people of their own motion could pass a law without any act of the Legislature. That no doubt, whether valid or not, would be outside the Constitution. So perhaps might be a statute purporting to confer the power of making laws upon them. But the question, put in a form to raise the fewest technical objections, is whether an act of the Legislature is made unconstitutional by a proviso that, if rejected by the people, it shall not go into effect. If it does go into effect, it does so by the express enactment of the representative body. I see no evidence in the instrument that this question ever occurred to the framers of the Constitution. It is but

[3] H-P, *ibid.*

a short step further to say that the Constitution does not forbid such a law. I agree that the discretion of the Legislature is intended to be exercised. I agree that confidence is put in it as an agent. But I think that so much confidence is put in it that it is allowed to exercise its discretion by taking the opinion of its principal if it thinks that course to be wise. It has been asked whether the Legislature could pass an act subject to the approval of a single man. I am not clear that it could not. The objection, if sound, would seem to have equal force against all forms of local option. But I will consider the question when it arises. The difference is plain between that case and one where the approval required is that of the sovereign body. The contrary view seems to me an echo of Hobbes's theory that the surrender of sovereignty by the people was final. I notice that the case from which most of the reasoning against the power of the Legislature has been taken by later decisions states that theory in language which almost is borrowed from the *Leviathan. Rice v. Foster,* 4 Harringt. (Del.) 479, 488. Hobbes urged his notion in the interest of the absolute power of King Charles I., and one of the objects of the Constitution of Massachusetts was to deny it. I answer the first question, Yes. I may add, that, while the tendency of judicial decision seems to be in the other direction, such able judges as Chief Justices Parker of Massachusetts, Dixon of Wisconsin, Redfield of Vermont, and Cooley of Michigan, have expressed opinions like mine.

2. If the foregoing view of the power of the Legislature is right, I am of opinion that the second question also should be answered, Yes. I find nothing which forbids the Legislature to establish a local option upon this point any more than with regard to the liquor laws. Under the circumstances, I do not argue this or the following question at length.

3. The act suggested by the third question is open to the seeming objection that it might take a part of their power out of the hands of the present possessors without their assent except as given by their representatives. But if, as I believe, the Legislature could give to women the right to vote if they accepted it by a preliminary vote, and could impose as a second condition that the grant should not be rejected by the voters of the Commonwealth, I do not see why it might not combine the two conditions into one, although as a result the grant might become a law against the will of a majority of the male voters. I answer this question, also, Yes.

SPEAKING WITHOUT A PERMIT

Commonwealth v. Davis
162 Mass. 510 (1895)

To those who regard Justice Holmes as an invariable champion of civil liberties as against any other social consideration the present case is recommended — as also the Schenck and Debs opinions in the U. S. Supreme Court section.[1] Here Holmes upheld a Boston ordinance which provided that no one could make a speech on the Boston Common without a permit from the mayor. He denied that the right of free speech or of assembly was involved, seeing the ordinance rather as "directed toward the modes in which the Boston Common may be used." Our generation is familiar, as perhaps Holmes's was not, with the attempts of labor-hating mayors to use for antilabor purposes just such a distinction between the suppression of the right of assembly and the use of public property. The United States Supreme Court has dealt realistically with a case of this sort in Hague v. CIO.[2]

It is possible that the reason why Holmes took the narrower view in the present case was that he was writing in a relatively less turbulent social context, when no concrete issues of freedom of speech had arisen, and he was loath to launch on the broad sea of social philosophy. It is worth noting that his decision was affirmed several years later by the U. S. Supreme Court speaking through Justice White, who wrote that the Fourteenth Amendment "does not have the effect of creating a particular and personal right in the citizen to use public property in defiance of the constitution and laws of the

---

[1] See pp. 292–304.

[2] 307 U.S. 496 (1939). It is worth noting that in his dissent in the *Hague* case Justice Butler insists there is no difference between it and the present case as affirmed by the Supreme Court (see note 3). But the rest of the Court either saw a distinction or chose silently to ignore Holmes's opinion. The American Bar Association, through its Bill of Rights Committee headed by Grenville Clarke, filed a brief as friends of the Court. A summary of that brief, and a discussion of the place of Justice Holmes's views against the whole background of the literature of the right of assembly, will be found in Chafee, *Free Speech in the United States* (1941) 409–435. It is difficult to read this without concluding that the Court in the *Hague* case was wise not to follow the social and legal logic of Holmes's opinion.

state." [3] *In a series of cases, centering chiefly around the power of the state or local area to regulate the activities of the Jehovah's Witnesses sect, including the already famous flag-salute case,*[4] *the United States Supreme Court has taken a similar view on the broad issue.*

Holmes, J., for the Court:

The only question raised by these exceptions which was not decided in the former case of *Commonwealth* v. *Davis,* 140 Mass. 485, is one concerning the construction of the present ordinance. That such an ordinance is constitutional is implied by the former decision, and does not appear to us open to doubt. To say that it is unconstitutional means that, even if the Legislature has purported to authorize it, the attempt was vain. The argument to that effect involves the same kind of fallacy that was dealt with in *McAuliffe* v. *New Bedford,* 155 Mass. 216. It assumes that the ordinance is directed against free speech generally, (as in *Des Plaines* v. *Poyer,* 123 Ill. 348, the ordinance held void was directed against public picnics and open-air dances generally,) whereas in fact it is directed toward the modes in which Boston Common may be used. There is no evidence before us to show that the power of the Legislature over the Common is less than its power over any other park dedicated to the use of the public, or over public streets the legal title to which is in a city or town. *Lincoln* v. *Boston,* 148 Mass. 578, 580. As representative of the public, it may and does exercise control over the use which the public may make of such places, and it may, and does, delegate more or less of such control to the city or town immediately concerned. For the Legislature absolutely or conditionally to forbid public speaking in a highway or public park is no more an infringement of the rights of a member of the public than for the owner of a private house to forbid it in his house. When no proprietary right interferes, the Legislature may end the right of the public to enter upon the public place by putting an end to

[3] *Davis* v. *Mass.,* 167 U.S. 43 (1897).

[4] *Minersville School District* v. *Gobitis* 310 U.S. 586 (1940); opinion of the Court by Justice Frankfurter. But see *Schneider* v. *New Jersey,* 308 U.S. 147 (1939), holding anti-street-littering ordinances invalid on the ground that the prohibition of the distribution of handbills in these cases violated the basic right to impart information. A 1942 case, however, *Jones* v. *City of Opelika,* 62 S. C. Reporter (1942), 1231, continued to hold as in the *Gobitis* case that local ordinances (in this case, a licensing tax on book canvassers) may be valid even if one of their consequences may be to regulate the dissemination of knowledge. The opinion was written by Justice Reed.

the dedication to public uses. So it may take the lesser step of limiting the public use to certain purposes. See Dillon, Mun. Corp. (4th ed.) secs. 393, 407, 651, 656, 666; *Brooklyn Park Commissioners* v. *Armstrong,* 45 N. Y. 234, 243, 244.

If the Legislature had power under the Constitution to pass a law in the form of the present ordinance, there is no doubt that it could authorize the city of Boston to pass the ordinance, and it is settled by the former decision that it has done so. As matter of history we suppose there is no doubt that the town, and after it the city, has always regulated the use of the Common except so far as restrained by statute.[5] It is settled also that the prohibition in such an ordinance, which would be binding if absolute, is not made invalid by the fact that it may be removed in a particular case by a license from a city officer, or a less numerous body than the one which enacts the prohibition. *Commonwealth* v. *Ellis,* 158 Mass. 555, 557, and cases cited. It is argued that the ordinance really is directed especially against free preaching of the Gospel in public places, as certain Western ordinances seemingly general have been held to be directed against the Chinese. But we have no reason to believe, and do not believe, that this ordinance was passed for any other than its ostensible purpose, namely, as a proper regulation of the use of public grounds.

It follows that, as we said at the outset, the only question open is the construction of the present ordinance. We are of opinion that the words "No person shall . . . make any public address," in the Revised Ordinances of 1892, c. 43, sec. 66, have as broad a meaning as the words "No person shall . . . deliver a sermon, lecture, address, or discourse," in the Revised Ordinances of 1883, c. 37, sec. 11, under which *Commonwealth* v. *Davis,* 140 Mass. 485, was decided. See Rev. Ord. 1885, c. 42, sec. 11. Whether lecture, political discourse, or sermon, a speech on the Common addressed to all persons who choose to draw near and listen is a public address, and the omission of the superfluous words in the last revision is only a matter of style and the abridgment properly sought for in codification.

Exceptions overruled.

[5] In addition to St. 1854, c. 448, sec. 35, which appears in the opinion in *Commonwealth* v. *Davis,* 140 Mass. 485, the government in the present case called the attention of the court to sec. 39 of the same statute, which confers upon the city council the care and management of the public buildings and of all the property of the city.

LABOR IN THE STRUGGLE FOR LIFE

Vegelahn v. Guntner
167 Mass. 92, 104 (1896)

This is one of the great Holmes opinions, and contains the germ of much of what followed in his thinking both on economic topics and on civil liberties. The majority, through Justice Allen, upheld an injunction which prohibited even peaceful picketing by strikers, on the ground that threats of violence might be implied as well as actual, and that there was such a thing as moral intimidation and constraint which were outside of allowable competition.[1] Chief Justice Field and Holmes each wrote a dissenting opinion.

Holmes's dissent is one of the best examples of his capacity to fuse rigorous legal reasoning with realistic social thought. He cuts through the argument that peaceful picketing inflicts damage by pointing out that all business competition does, and that a legal system is unjust which allows combinations of businessmen for competitive purposes, but denies the privilege of effective action by combinations of labor. To the objection that the worker–employer relations are not "free competition," Holmes answers that if the term is too narrow to include it, let us change the term to "free struggle for life." This struggle he sees throughout our economic system; as part of it there is "the ever-increasing might and scope of combination," which is leading to "the organization of the world";[2] and he adds that it is "futile to set our faces against this tendency," which he regards both as beneficial and inevitable.[3]

[1] Holmes, sitting alone on the injunction, had previously rendered an interlocutory decree against it. Then the case came before the full Court for the final decree.

[2] "Organization of the world" is exactly the phrase he had used two years before in his article, *Privilege, Malice, and Intent.* 8 HLR 1–14 (1894), reprinted in CLP, 117–137.

[3] It is interesting in this connection that Melville M. Bigelow, in a book, *Centralization and the Law* (1906), which he wrote along with Brooks Adams and others, commented with some acuteness on Holmes's opinion in this case. He approved of it highly but thought that in the conflict between Holmes and the Court majority in the whole group of labor cases, Holmes was necessarily on the losing side, and his efforts were bound to prove frustrate because the great social energy of the time was that of capitalist monopoly and "the tendency

And yet, whatever his views on economic direction, Holmes was aware that he was taking what was temporarily the less popular view of the law. A comment on the case in the Harvard Law Review the same year remarked that "most of the public, outside of the trade unions, have a sufficient prejudice against anything that could be called 'picketing' to approve without hesitation the sweeping injunction" [4] of Vegelahn v. Guntner. One need not premise a pro-labor bias on Holmes's part to explain his opinion. While in terms of his doctrine of the external standard in liability for harm one might have expected him to uphold the injunction, he saw peaceful picketing as coming squarely within the privileged area because it was an inherent part of the competitive system and the battle of life. One gets here the tougher strain of his thinking. His reference to the inevitable trend of organization was reminiscent of his remarks on the Gas-Stokers' case almost two decades before.[5]

It will not do to interpret this strain as "liberal," since exactly the same reasoning led Holmes to write the pro-monopoly dissent in the Northern Securities case which so enraged the trust-busting side of Theodore Roosevelt. For Holmes saw, as did few others, that "free competition" in the economic system actually meant having freedom for combination in order to have a competitive chance. It became a question of degree as to how far the process of combination could be pushed before it suppressed competition wholly. There can be little quarrel now with Holmes's stand that peaceful picketing does not mean pushing it too far. As to whether a railroad holding company means pushing it too far is another matter, and one which will be discussed later.[6] There is a suggestion in this opin-

---

of the social equilibrium was steadily the other way" from that of Holmes (op. cit. p. 12). Holmes and Pollock had an exchange of letters on this book, one of Holmes's letters being included below, p. 438. Bigelow was a more thoroughgoing believer in the economic interpretation of the law than either of them had any use for, and they carried on a mild common feud with him. Nevertheless his views on the whole line of Massachusetts labor decisions, in which Holmes was in the minority, have stood the test of time well. The history of American legal thought has not yet done justice to either Bigelow or Brooks Adams.

[4] 10 HLR 301 (1896).
[5] See p. 48, and my comment, p. 44.
[6] See my comment on the Northern Securities opinion, p. 217.

ion as to the crucial standard for the limits of combination — the point at which an equality of bargaining power has been reached.[7] I submit that the application of this standard by Holmes in the Northern Securities opinion might have saved him from a blunder in social and economic realism.

Holmes's opinion did not escape criticism from the narrower conservatives of his day. Word spread about that he was an "unsound" man and on the labor side — which caused some comment when he was named to the United States Supreme Court some six years later.

In the early history of the struggle over the labor injunction, Holmes's opinion ranks with that of Chief Justice Shaw of Massachusetts in Commonwealth v. Hunt.[8] Two years later in Allen v. Flood, the English House of Lords had to deal with a similar situation, and the majority followed substantially Holmes's view. Pollock, writing to Holmes about the opinions in this case, says "Macnaghten's is the judgment which posterity, if it be wise, will study side by side with yours . . . Only the organs of extreme capitalism (not having the wit to see that the contrary decision would have cut both ways) have expressed any dissatisfaction."[9] Holmes's confident prophecy, in the next to last paragraph of his opinion, that peaceful picketing would come to be recognized by economists and legislators, has been fulfilled.

Holmes, J., dissenting:

In a case like the present, it seems to me that, whatever the true result may be, it will be of advantage to sound thinking to have the less popular view of the law stated, and therefore, although when I have been unable to bring my brethren to share my con-

[7] See p. 115, the important paragraph beginning, "One of the eternal conflicts out of which life is made up," especially the phrase, "if the battle is to be carried on in a fair and equal way."

[8] 4 Met. 111 (Mass. 1842). For a discussion of this and other early cases in legal and economic history, see Witte, *Early American Labor Cases*, 35 YLJ 825 (1926).

[9] H–P, I:81. Dec. 28, 1897. It was acute of Pollock to see at the time that the logic of an intransigeant opposition to the organization of labor could be turned against the organization of capital as well. The linking of combinations of labor and capital as equally injurious to the public welfare has a long history in legal and economic thought, Thurman Arnold's administration of the antitrust laws being only the latest instance. No critical study of this doctrine has yet been made.

victions my almost invariable practice is to defer to them in silence, I depart from that practice in this case, notwithstanding my unwillingness to do so in support of an already rendered judgment of my own.

In the first place, a word or two should be said as to the meaning of the report. I assume that my brethren construe it as I meant it to be construed, and that, if they were not prepared to do so, they would give an opportunity to the defendants to have it amended in accordance with what I state my meaning to be. There was no proof of any threat or danger of a patrol exceeding two men, and as of course an injunction is not granted except with reference to what there is reason to expect in its absence, the question on that point is whether a patrol of two men should be enjoined. Again, the defendants are enjoined by the final decree from intimidating by threats, express or implied, of physical harm to body or property, any person who may be desirous of entering into the employment of the plaintiff so far as to prevent him from entering the same. In order to test the correctness of the refusal to go further, it must be assumed that the defendants obey the express prohibition of the decree. If they do not, they fall within the injunction as it now stands, and are liable to summary punishment. The important difference between the preliminary and the final injunction is that the former goes further, and forbids the defendants to interfere with the plaintiff's business "by any scheme . . . organized for the purpose of . . . preventing any person or persons who now are or may hereafter be . . . desirous of entering the [plaintiff's employment] from entering it." I quote only a part, and the part which seems to me most objectionable. This includes refusal of social intercourse, and even organized persuasion or argument, although free from any threat of violence, either express or implied. And this is with reference to persons who have a legal right to contract or not to contract with the plaintiff, as they may see fit. Interference with existing contracts is forbidden by the final decree. I wish to insist a little that the only point of difference which involves a difference of principle between the final decree and the preliminary injunction which it is proposed to restore, is what I have mentioned, in order that it may be seen exactly what we are to discuss. It appears to me that the judgment of the majority turns in part on the assumption that the patrol necessarily carries with it a threat of bodily harm. That assumption I think unwarranted,

LAW AS JUDGMENT

for the reasons which I have given. Furthermore, it cannot be said, I think, that two men, walking together up and down a sidewalk and speaking to those who enter a certain shop, do necessarily and always thereby convey a threat of force. I do not think it possible to discriminate, and to say that two workmen, or even two representatives of an organization of workmen, do — especially when they are, and are known to be, under the injunction of this court not to do so. See Stimson, *Labor Law,* 60, especially pages 290, 298–300; *Reg.* v. *Shepherd,* 11 Cox, Cr. Cas. 325. I may add, that I think the more intelligent workingmen believe as fully as I do that they no more can be permitted to usurp the State's prerogative of force than can their opponents in their controversies. But if I am wrong, then the decree as it stands reaches the patrol, since it applies to all threats of force. With this I pass to the real difference between the interlocutory and the final decree.

I agree, whatever may be the law in the case of a single defendant, *Rice* v. *Albee,* 164 Mass. 88, that when a plaintiff proves that several persons have combined and conspired to injure his business, and have done acts producing that effect, he shows temporal damage and a cause of action, unless the facts disclose, or the defendants prove, some ground of excuse or justification. And I take it to be settled, and rightly settled, that doing that damage by combined persuasion is actionable, as well as doing it by falsehood or by force. *Walter* v. *Cronin,* 107 Mass. 55.

Nevertheless, in numberless instances the law warrants the intentional infliction of temporal damage because it regards it as justified. It is on the question of what shall amount to a justification, and more especially on the nature of the considerations which really determine or ought to determine the answer to that question, that judicial reasoning seems to me often to be inadequate. The true grounds of decision are considerations of policy and of social advantage, and it is vain to suppose that solutions can be attained merely by logic and the general propositions of law which nobody disputes. Propositions as to public policy rarely are unanimously accepted, and still more rarely, if ever, are capable of unanswerable proof. They require a special training to enable anyone even to form an intelligent opinion about them. In the early stages of law, at least, they generally are acted on rather as inarticulate instincts than as definite ideas for which a rational defence is ready.

To illustrate what I have said in the last paragraph — it has been the law for centuries that a man may set up a business in a small country town too small to support more than one, although thereby he expects and intends to ruin someone already there, and succeeds in his intent. In such a case he is not held to act "unlawfully and without justifiable cause," as was alleged in *Walker* v. *Cronin* and *Rice* v. *Albee*. The reason, of course, is that the doctrine generally has been accepted that free competition is worth more to society than it costs, and that on this ground the infliction of the damage is privileged. *Commonwealth* v. *Hunt,* 4 Met. 111, 134. Yet even this proposition nowadays is disputed by a considerable body of persons, including many whose intelligence is not to be denied, little as we may agree with them.

I have chosen this illustration partly with reference to what I have to say next. It shows without the need of further authority that the policy of allowing free competition justifies the intentional inflicting of temporal damage, including the damage of interference with a man's business by some means, when the damage is done not for its own sake, but as an instrumentality in reaching the end of victory in the battle of trade. In such a case it cannot matter whether the plaintiff is the only rival of the defendant, and so is aimed at specifically, or is one of a class all of whom are hit. The only debatable ground is the nature of the means by which such damage may be inflicted. We all agree that it cannot be done by force or threats of force. We all agree, I presume, that it may be done by persuasion to leave a rival's shop and come to the defendant's. It may be done by the refusal or withdrawal of various pecuniary advantages which, apart from this consequence, are within the defendant's lawful control. It may be done by the withdrawal of, or threat to withdraw, such advantages from third persons who have a right to deal or not to deal with the plaintiff, as a means of inducing them not to deal with him either as customers or servants. *Bowen* v. *Matheson,* 14 Allen, 499 . . . *Mogul Steamship Co.* v. *McGregor* [1892] A.C. 25.

I pause here to remark that the word "threats" often is used as if, when it appeared that threats had been made, it appeared that unlawful conduct had begun. But it depends on what you threaten. As a general rule, even if subject to some exceptions, what you may do in a certain event you may threaten to do, that is, give warning of your intention to do in that event, and thus allow the other person the chance of avoiding the consequence. So as to

LAW AS JUDGMENT 115

"compulsion," it depends on how you "compel." . . . So as to "annoyance" or "intimidation." . . . In *Sherry* v. *Perkins*, 147 Mass. 212, it was found as a fact that the display of banners which was enjoined was part of a scheme to prevent workmen from entering or remaining in the plaintiff's employment, "by threats and intimidation." The context showed that the words as there used meant threats of personal violence, and intimidation by causing fear of it.

I have seen the suggestion made that the conflict between employers and employed was not competition. But I venture to assume that none of my brethren would rely on that suggestion. If the policy on which our law is founded is too narrowly expressed in the term free competition, we may substitute free struggle for life. Certainly, the policy is not limited to struggles between persons of the same class, competing for the same end. It applies to all conflicts of temporal interests.

So far, I suppose, we are agreed. But there is a notion, which latterly has been insisted on a good deal, that a combination of persons to do what any one of them lawfully might do by himself will make the otherwise lawful conduct unlawful. It would be rash to say that some as yet unformulated truth may not be hidden under this proposition. But in the general form in which it has been presented and accepted by many courts, I think it plainly untrue, both on authority and principle. . . . There was combination of the most flagrant and dominant kind in *Bowen* v. *Matheson* [14 Allen, 499] and in the *Mogul Steamship Co. Case* [(1892) App. Cas. 25], and combination was essential to the success achieved. But it is not necessary to cite cases; it is plain from the slightest consideration of practical affairs, or the most superficial reading of industrial history, that free competition means combination, and that the organization of the world, now going on so fast, means an ever-increasing might and scope of combination. It seems to me futile to set our faces against this tendency. Whether beneficial on the whole, as I think it, or detrimental, it is inevitable, unless the fundamental axioms of society, and even the fundamental conditions of life, are to be changed.

One of the eternal conflicts out of which life is made up is that between the effort of every man to get the most he can for his services, and that of society, disguised under the name of capital, to get his services for the least possible return. Combination on the one side is patent and powerful. Combination on the other is the necessary and desirable counterpart, if the battle is to be carried on in a fair and equal way. I am unable to reconcile *Temperton* v. *Russell* (1893) 1 Q. B. 715, and the cases which follow it, with the *Steamship Co. Case*. But *Temperton* v. *Russell* is not a binding authority here, and therefore I do not think it necessary to discuss it.

If it be true that workingmen may combine with a view, among other things, to getting as much as they can for their labor, just as capital may combine with a view to getting the greatest possible return, it must be true that when combined they have the same liberty that combined capital has to support their interests by argument, persuasion, and the bestowal or refusal of those advantages which they otherwise lawfully control. I can remember when many people thought that, apart from violence or breach of contract, strikes were wicked, as organized refusals to work. I suppose that intelligent economists and legislators have given up that notion today. I feel pretty confident that they equally will abandon the idea that an organized refusal by workmen of social intercourse with a man who shall enter their antagonist's employ is wrong, if it is dissociated from any threat of violence, and is made for the sole object of prevailing if possible in a contest with their employer about the rate of wages. The fact, that the immediate object of the act by which the benefit to themselves is to be gained is to injure their antagonist, does not necessarily make it unlawful, any more than when a great house lowers the price of goods for the purpose, and with the effect of driving a smaller antagonist from the business. Indeed, the question seems to have been decided as long ago as 1842 by the good sense of Chief Justice Shaw, in *Com.* v. *Hunt,* 4 Metc. (Mass.) 111. I repeat, at the end, as I said at the beginning, that this is the point of difference in principle, and the only one, between the interlocutory and final decree. . . .

The general question of the propriety of dealing with this kind of case by injunction I say nothing about, because I understand that the defendants have no objection to the final decree if it goes no further, and that both parties wish a decision upon the matters which I have discussed.

THE CLOSED SHOP AND THE WAGE FUND

Plant v. Woods
176 Mass. 492, 504 (1900)

This is a case of an injunction against the threatened use of the strike and boycott weapons to enforce a closed shop. It is curiously premonitory of the current jurisdictional struggles between rival unions, but the main economic issue is that of the closed shop. The defendants were members of a local union of painters in Springfield, Mass., which was affiliated with a national union at Baltimore. They had been suddenly faced by the desertion from their ranks of painters and decorators who set up a rival union attached to a national organization in Indiana. To protect their existence, the old union men besought their employers to turn the turncoats back into their organization or turn them out of their jobs. And they "did not deny" that they might use the strike or boycott if their demand for the closed shop were not met. No acts of violence were committed, and there was no injury to property. The plaintiffs, belonging to the new union, asked for the injunction. It was granted in a decree by the Court below, and the grant was affirmed by the Supreme Court majority, speaking through Justice Hammond.

Holmes in his dissenting opinion packs a good deal of legal and economic reasoning into three paragraphs. The legal problem involved was one of whether the threatened harm, for which liability would ordinarily lie, was privileged. It thus lay squarely in the path of the problem passed on in Vegelahn v. Guntner *and discussed at length in Holmes's article on "Privilege, Malice, and Intent."* [1] *In his dissent Holmes rejoices that instead of following the majority opinion in* Vegelahn v. Guntner *the Court has here chosen to follow the general reasoning of his dissent in that case. Where he disagreed was on the Court's evaluation of the motive of the defendants. Holmes faced the issue of motive squarely. He was willing to assume that the defendants had actually gone so far as to*

[1] 8 HLR 1–14 (1894), reprinted CLP, 117–137.

threaten a strike and boycott, instead of merely "not denying" that they might use it. And he held that the act was privileged because the intent embraced a legitimate object, that of bargaining and struggling for higher wages and better working conditions. The demand for a closed shop, as he saw it, was concerned with this at one remove. It was an attempt "to strengthen the defendants' society as a preliminary and means" to the ultimate purpose.

Holmes adds significantly, "I think that unity of organization is necessary to make the contest of labor effectual, and that societies of laborers lawfully may employ in their preparation the means which they might use in the final contest." Thus he goes beyond the legal question itself to its economic base — the conditions and methods necessary to give the legal right meaning and to save it from futility. Thus he rejects the subtle (and perhaps unwitting) establishment by his colleagues of one law for the masters and one for the men. For the boycott had often been upheld by the courts when used by business rivals to close a market by economic pressure, but had been fairly consistently held illegal when used by the workers to unionize a shop.[2]

Holmes had established his own position on these matters in his 1894 Harvard Law Review article. "You know my mind is made up," he wrote Pollock in 1902, "in accord with (my) article . . . I think that in some cases which should be approached from the point of view of privilege — the temporal damage being foreseen or even intended — the nature of the motive may make all the difference. . . . Plant v. Woods followed the line of thought in my article although I dissented on a difference of degree."[3] Holmes had said in his article, "The time has gone by when the law is only an unconscious embodiment of the common will. It has become a conscious reaction upon itself of organized society knowingly seeking to determine its own destinies."[4] In fact, the power of collective bargaining seemed to Holmes not only a phase of "the organization of the world which is taking place so fast,"

[2] See W. D. Lewis, "The Closed Market, the Union Shop, and the Common Law," 18 HLR 444, 447 (1905).
[3] H–P, I:110 (Dec. 28, 1902).
[4] 8 HLR 9 (1894).

but also a condition of the old common law ideal of freedom of contract which his colleagues thought of as being threatened by the trade unions. "A man," *he wrote in his comment on the English case of the Mogul Steamship Company,* "is hardly free in his abstaining" *from making a contract* "unless he can state the terms or conditions upon which he intends to abstain." [5]

Some part of the interest of Holmes's dissenting opinion in Plant v. Woods lies in his anxiety to dissociate himself from what he regarded as radical economic doctrine. "I think it well to add that I cherish no illusions as to the meaning and effect of strikes." And he goes on to state the wage-fund doctrine of the impossibility of increasing through labor action the total amount of income available for distribution as wages. Thus the judge becomes in this opinion explicitly the economist, as in the Vegelahn opinion he had become explicitly the sociologist and had written a discourse on the struggle for life. If one seeks to connect the two discourses one gets a curious result: every group by the laws of life must seek to better itself — but labor's effort is doomed by some iron law mechanism; nevertheless the law will not deny to the individual workers the arid satisfaction of a struggle among themselves for larger portions of the rigidly restricted total. Thus by following the economic orthodoxy of the wage-fund theory Holmes undoes a good deal of the realism underlying his comment on the Gas-Stokers' case or his dissent in the Vegelahn case. Justice Frankfurter has pointed to the present case as an instance of Holmes's capacity to "transcend personal predilections and private notions of social policy, and become truly the impersonal voice of the Constitution." [6] That may be so. But in this instance Holmes achieved his impersonality only by leaping over the gap between his legal realism and his economic orthodoxy.[7]

---

[5] 8 HLR 8 (1894).

[6] *Mr. Justice Holmes and the Supreme Court,* 44–45 (1938).

[7] I may perhaps be doing Holmes an injustice by calling his position the wage-fund doctrine. He does not say, as the doctrine does characteristically, that there is a separate fund reserved out of the national income for wages that cannot be increased. But he does say that with slight deductions for luxuries the whole "annual product" goes to "consumption by the multitude" — and that therefore the economic effect of the strike is to increase the income of organized labor not at the expense of the employer but at the expense of unorganized labor. From the "iron law of wages" doctrine to the "wage fund" doctrine, this has been the contention of conservative wage theorists. Holmes arrives at the con-

Holmes's dissent failed to arrest the anti-labor judicial trends which were at the time becoming firmly established. The proposition that a strike for a closed shop is illegal became formalized and was known as the "Massachusetts rule." [8] *As such it spread to other states as well, including Pennsylvania, New Jersey, Oregon, and Texas. But Holmes's dissent here and in analogous cases later became the judicial spearhead of the movement which has in the legislative field resulted in the National Labor Relations Act and other first steps toward the protection of union organization.*

Holmes, C. J.:

When a question has been decided by the court, I think it proper, as a general rule, that a dissenting judge, however strong his convictions may be, should thereafter accept the law from the majority and leave the remedy to the Legislature, if that body sees fit to interfere. If the decision in the present case simply had relied upon *Vegelahn* v. *Guntner,* 167 Mass. 92, I should have hesitated to say anything, although I might have stated that my personal opinion had not been weakened by the substantial agreement with my views to be found in the judgments of the majority of the House of Lords in *Allen* v. *Flood,* A. C. 1. But much to my satisfaction, if I may say so, the court has seen fit to adopt the mode of approaching the question which I believe to be the correct one, and to open an issue which otherwise I might have thought closed. The difference between my brethren and me now seems to be a difference of degree, and the line of reasoning followed makes it proper for me to explain where the difference lies.

I agree that the conduct of the defendants is actionable unless justified. *May* v. *Wood,* 172 Mass. 11, 14, and cases cited. I agree that the presence or absence of justification may depend upon the

---

clusion by his own route. For a fuller statement, see below "Law and the Court," p. 387 and also "Economic Elements," CLP, 279. For a discussion of the history of the wage-fund doctrine, published only four years before the present opinion, see Taussig, *Wages and Capital* (1896).

[8] There is a good summary and analysis of the whole sequence of Massachusetts labor decisions, from *Walker* v. *Cronin,* 107 Mass. 555 (1871) to *Berry* v. *Donovan,* 188 Mass. 353 (1905), in M. M. Bigelow, ed., *Centralization and the Law* (1906) 9–12. It includes a discussion of the four great cases in which Holmes wrote dissents — *Vegelahn* v. *Guntner* (see above); *Rice* v. *Albee,* 164 Mass. 88 (1895); *May* v. *Wood,* 172 Mass. 11 (1898); and the present case. See also ch. 1 of Frankfurter and Greene, *The Labor Injunction* (1930).

object of their conduct, that is, upon the motive with which they acted. *Vegelahn* v. *Guntner,* 167 Mass. 92, 105, 106. I agree, for instance, that if a boycott or a strike is intended to override the jurisdiction of the courts by the action of a private association, it may be illegal. *Weston* v. *Barnicoat,* 175 Mass. 454. On the other hand, I infer that a majority of my brethren would admit that a boycott or strike intended to raise wages directly might be lawful, if it did not embrace in its scheme or intent violence, breach of contract, or other conduct unlawful on grounds independent of the mere fact that the action of the defendants was combined. A sensible workingman would not contend that the courts should sanction a combination for the purpose of inflicting or threatening violence or the infraction of admitted rights. To come directly to the point, the issue is narrowed to the question whether, assuming that some purposes would be a justification, the purpose in this case of the threatened boycotts and strikes was such as to justify the threats. That purpose was not directly concerned with wages. It was one degree more remote. The immediate object and motive was to strengthen the defendants' society as a preliminary and means to enable it to make a better fight on questions of wages or other matters of clashing interests. I differ from my brethren in thinking that the threats were as lawful for this preliminary purpose as for the final one to which strengthening the union was a means. I think that unity of organization is necessary to make the contest of labor effectual, and that societies of laborers lawfully may employ in their preparation the means which they might use in the final contest.

Although this is not the place for extended economic discussion, and although the law may not always reach ultimate economic conceptions, I think it well to add that I cherish no illusions as to the meaning and effect of strikes. While I think the strike a lawful instrument in the universal struggle of life, I think it pure phantasy to suppose that there is a body of capital of which labor as a whole secures a larger share by that means. The annual product, subject to an infinitesimal deduction for the luxuries of the few, is directed to consumption by the multitude, and is consumed by the multitude, always. Organization and strikes may get a larger share for the members of an organization, but, if they do, they get it at the expense of the less organized and less powerful portion of the laboring mass. They do not create something out of nothing.

It is only by divesting our minds of questions of ownership and other machinery of distribution, and by looking solely at the question of consumption, — asking ourselves what is the annual product, who consumes it, and what changes would or could we make, — that we can keep in the world of realities. But, subject to the qualifications which I have expressed, I think it lawful for a body of workmen to try by combination to get more than they now are getting, although they do it at the expense of their fellows, and to that end to strengthen their union by the boycott and the strike.

DEATH BY MOLAR OR MOLECULAR MOTION

Storti v. *Commonwealth*
178 Mass. 549 (1901)

The Storti *case came up before the Massachusetts Supreme Court several times, Storti's lawyer being adept at the art of judicial delay through procedural appeal. The present appeal was on the constitutional question of cruel and unusual punishment. Storti was the first person to be sentenced to death under the 1898 Massachusetts statute which substituted electrocution for hanging. Holmes's opinion is notable not only for the brilliance with which it cleaves through verbal cobwebs to get at the operative realities, but also for the dry irony by which he shows how insubstantial these cobwebs are.*

Holmes, C. J., for the Court:

. . . [1] Taking all the preliminaries most favorably for the prisoner, we are clearly of opinion that the Constitution is not contravened by the act, and we render our opinion at once that we may avoid delaying the course of the law and raising false hopes in his mind. The answer to the whole argument which has been presented is that there is but a single punishment, death. It is not contended that if this is true the statute is invalid, but it is said that it is not true, and that you cannot separate the means from the end in considering what the punishment is, any more when the means is a current of electricity than when it is a slow fire. We

[1] The first two paragraphs of the opinion have been omitted.

should have thought that the distinction was plain. In the latter case the means is adopted not solely for the purpose of accomplishing the end of death but for the purpose of causing other pain to the person concerned. The so-called means is also an end of the same kind as the death itself, or in other words is intended to be a part of the punishment. But when, as here, the means adopted are chosen with just the contrary intent, and are devised for the purpose of reaching the end proposed as swiftly and painlessly as possible, we are of opinion that they are not forbidden by the Constitution although they should be discoveries of recent science and never should have been heard of before. Not only is the prohibition addressed to what in a proper sense may be called the punishment but, further, the word "unusual" must be construed with the word "cruel" and cannot be taken so broadly as to prohibit every humane improvement not previously known in Massachusetts. *People* v. *Durston,* 119 N. Y. 569; S. C. *In re Kemmler,* 136 U. S. 436.

The suggestion that the punishment of death, in order not to be unusual, must be accomplished by molar rather than by molecular motion seems to us a fancy unwarranted by the Constitution.

No doubt a means might be adopted which, although adopted only as a means, practically would be part of the punishment and would have to be considered as such. But such a case is not presented by a means chosen precisely because it is instantaneous. There was a hint at an argument based on mental suffering, but the suffering is due not to its being more horrible to be struck by lightning than to be hanged with the chance of slowly strangling, but to the general fear of death. The suffering due to that fear the law does not seek to spare. It means that it shall be felt. . . .[2]

Judgment to stand; writ of habeas corpus denied.

[2] The last two paragraphs have been omitted.

PART II

Supreme Court Justice

1. America as a Going Concern
2. State Power and Free Trade in Ideas

Supreme Court Justice

For thirty years, from 1902 to 1932, Holmes sat on the United States Supreme Court as Associate Justice. He served longer on the Court than any Justice in its history, except Marshall and Field. He played so important a part in its struggles and in the shaping of its working conceptions that without him any history of the Court during this period would lose a major part of its meaning. And in the course of these three decades he developed both a characteristic method of judicial interpretation and a unique style in expressing that method.

His method — or better, his outlook on constitutional law — was composed of several elements. One was a broad judicial tolerance of legislative and executive action, which might be called judicial laissez faire. Holmes was not one of those justices who regarded judicial review as the crux of the American governmental process. "I do not think," he was to say in one of his greatest speeches, "the United States would come to an end if we lost our power to declare an Act of Congress void. I do think the Union would be imperiled if we could not make that declaration as to the laws of the several States." [1] *Accordingly, he favored exercising the judicial power only where there was an obvious abuse of national power or an encroachment of function by the national government or one of its branches, and (with respect to the states) only when there was a real danger of the serious dislocation of the federal system.*

This attitude was particularly significant during a time when the Supreme Court majority was actively engaged in concept-creation. The two notable creations of the Court during this period were the related concepts of due process of law and liberty of contract. When I say "creations" I do not, of course, mean that the judges created the concepts themselves and certainly not the phrases. I mean that they poured a new and arbitrary meaning into the old moulds.

Justice Holmes fought at first urbanely but with increasing although magisterial bitterness against both concepts. Many of the cases in the area of conflict, as the following selections will show,

[1] "Law and the Court" (1913), see p. 387.

had to do with state regulatory legislation, particularly of prices and the labor contract. The states formed the focal centers of judicial struggle for two reasons: first, because the successive national administrations were under the secure control of the Republican Party, with its deeply rooted preference for uncontrolled industrial activity; and second, because the uneven economic development in the various states and regions had left some of them, particularly in the West, under the sway of Populist and agrarian feeling, while elsewhere in the Eastern industrial centers it had created a workers' group which was increasingly using the legislative machinery in the fight for living standards. The Supreme Court majority interpreted the Constitutional provisions of "due process" and "liberty" so as to set distinct limits to this regulatory activity.

Holmes's attitude toward such state legislation was a compound of what I have called "judicial tolerance" along with judicial restraint and judicial relativism. By "tolerance" I mean his willingness to give the states the benefit of the doubt, and to assume the validity of their legislation except where it was clearly (that is, to a reasonable man) out of bounds. By "restraint" I mean his belief that, in interpreting the Constitution as distinguished from the common law, the judges had no concern with social policy, which was not theirs to fashion. And by "relativism" I mean his belief that it was best for the Court to avoid all absolute concepts: "General propositions," he said in the Lochner dissent, "do not decide specific cases." Only where the state act was "manifestly absurd" did it, in his view, come within judicial control.

This strain in Holmes's judicial thinking is a notable one and has been often noted. What has not been so clear about it is its motivation and its impulsions. There are some who have seen Holmes as achieving a heroic and almost Olympian detachment, as of a god above the petty and contending mortals. I have called this elsewhere the "austerity theory" of Holmes's judicial behavior.[2] My own inclination is to say that Holmes was human enough but that his whole conception of the function of law dictated the qualities of detachment I have cited. He was a legal craftsman with a sense of the limits of his craft. He did not believe that law should, or even could, hem the life of the community within its bounds. He

[2] See my "Holmes, Frankfurter, and the Austerity Theory" in *Ideas Are Weapons* (1939), p. 64. I fear, however, that I took too extreme a position in that essay, and in what follows I have sought to modify it.

saw turbulent forces at work in any social system as in nature, and was content as a judge to let them work themselves out without too much interference, not because he preferred to stay out but because his whole naturalistic view taught him it would be futile to intervene.

This brings us to a second great element in Holmes's outlook. He had a distaste for any vacuum in governmental power. It was difficult for him to conceive that the framers of the Constitution should have intended the Government to lack power to deal with the problems which all civilized nations face in common. This is most sharply expressed in his dissent in Hammer v. Dagenhart [3] *with respect to the question of child labor, and in* Block v. Hirsh [4] *with respect to the question of war-emergency rent regulation; but it will be found by implication in many of the other opinions as well.*

A third element was Holmes's preference for viewing constitutional law as part of a larger whole — in the context of America as a going concern, and that in turn in the context of Western civilization as a going concern. He was well aware both that no perfection was to be found in any political body, and also that any healthy organism would tend to correct many of its errors and outgrow many of its difficulties. He did not seek in the law a certitude which could not be achieved in life. He felt that in law, as in life, one had to face the risk, and one learned both through experiment and experience.[5] *He saw America as a large enough going concern to contain room both for new methods of developing our resources and also for new legislative controls of these methods.*

More than anyone before him in the history of the Supreme Court, Holmes brought to his task a large philosophic view and broad intellectual and literary interests. To be sure, he was only an amateur philosopher. In his youth he had often crossed intellectual swords with William James. In early manhood he had argued long and earnestly with Brooks Adams on the pros and cons of materialism in history. As he found more time, he read deeply in Bradley, Santayana, Dewey. His exchange of letters with Pollock is an exchange between two men who were curious about

---

[3] See p. 165.
[4] See p. 278.
[5] See, for example, his dissent in *Abrams* v. *U. S.*, p. 304 below: "It [the Constitution] is an experiment, as all life is an experiment."

how things hung together or did not hang together in the cosmos. But despite his distaste for metaphysics, Holmes has perhaps come closer than anyone we have had in American history to the philosopher become king. Only Justice Cardozo after him had anything like the same breadth of interest or the same grasp of philosophical problems.

The routine of Holmes's life as a member of the Supreme Court was, of course, as usual with Supreme Court justices, a stable and pleasant one. He worked steadily — if not as hard as he often professed in his letters [6] — at cases before the Court. He read a considerable body of literature, rarely in law or public affairs, but mainly in philosophy, social theory, or fiction.[7] He saw a few friends. His main energies went into his work, and yet it could not be said of him — as it might be said of Marshall, Taney, Miller, or Hughes — that he had little intellectual life outside of his work. His judicial opinions, to be sure, furnished the focus of his energies. But the real drama of his life remained the internal drama of a mind which noted and absorbed the paradoxes and the universals in life, and which saw the law as only one form of their expression.

Such a mind struck hard against the flint of the social attitudes held by Justice Holmes's colleagues, and when it did, there were certain to be sparks. The practice of the Court is, after discussing a case, to have the Chief Justice assign the writing of the opinion of the Court, and to print the draft opinions thus written and circulate them among the other justices before the final opinions are written. Holmes's draft opinions not infrequently came back with sharp and sometimes shocked comments from his brothers.[8] They felt often that his language was too strong. "The boys," he wrote Pollock in *1918*, apropos the draft opinions, "generally cut one of the genitals out of mine, in the form of some expression that they think too free." [9] One suspects that Holmes knew this before-

---

[6] For some doubts cast entertainingly on these professions see Walton Hamilton's review of the *Holmes–Pollock* letters, "On Dating Mr. Justice Holmes," in the *University of Chicago Law Review*, Vol. 9, 1–29 (1941).

[7] His reading lists are contained in the famous "Black Book" or literary log which he kept, and which his literary executors would do us a service to publish.

[8] Through the courtesy of Justice Frankfurter I have seen a sampling of these — enough to know how illuminating they will prove when published.

[9] H–P, I:258 (January 24, 1918).

hand, and that with a shrewd Yankee eye for the weaknesses of his colleagues he often put in things that were "calculated to give the brethren pain," so that in the end he could retain what he had all along intended. In 1930 he again wrote Pollock, with a mixture of gaiety and rue, "I am on most friendly terms with all the judges, but I suspect that if I should be gathered to Abraham's bosom some of them would think it an advantage to the law, even if they missed a friend." [10] At times Holmes could be nettled by his colleagues' comments. "I am hard at work," he wrote, " . . . preparing small diamonds for people of limited intellectual means." [11]

Although Holmes was friendly with every member of the Court, there were only a few for whom he expressed his admiration. One of these was Chief Justice White, whom Holmes regarded as longwinded in his opinions and often tortuous in his arguments, but whom he nevertheless called "profound," "especially in the legislative direction which we don't recognize as a judicial requirement but which is so, especially in our Court." [12] Holmes was generous in desiring the chief-justiceship for White rather than for himself. "I always have assumed absolutely that I should not be regarded as possible. . . . I think I should be a better administrator than White, but he would be more politic." [13] About Harlan, who was White's senior, Holmes writes with mixed feelings. "That sage, although a man of real power, did not shine either in analysis or generalization and I never troubled myself much when he shied. I used to say that he had a powerful vise the jaws of which couldn't be got nearer than two inches to each other." [14] Justice Brewer, who was on the Court with Holmes for eight years and until his death in 1910, was "a very pleasant man in private, but he had the itch for public speaking and writing and made me shudder many times. . . . Altogether I think he was rather an enfant terrible." [15] Justice Hughes was on the Court with Holmes from 1910 until his resignation in 1916 to run for the Presidency. "I shall miss him consumedly, for he is not only a good fellow, experienced and wise,

[10] H-P, II:268 (June 9, 1930).
[11] H-P, II:173 (Dec. 1, 1925).
[12] H-P, I:170 (September 24, 1910).
[13] *Id.*
[14] H-P, II:7-8 (April 5, 1919).
[15] H-P, I:160 (April 1, 1910).

but funny, and with doubts that open vistas through the wall of a nonconformist conscience." [16]

As President, Taft evidently consulted Holmes in 1910 with respect to two pending appointments.[17] Holmes cared more for him in the Presidency than he did for Theodore Roosevelt, but it was as a colleague on the Court that Holmes valued him most: "Perhaps the main question as to a C. J. is his way of disposing of executive details, and Taft seems likely to take them easily and get through them without friction." [18] And several months later: "We are very happy with the present Chief . . . he is good-humored, laughs readily, not quite rapid enough, but keeping things moving pleasantly." [19] And Taft in turn had a deep affection for Holmes. His biographer relates that he and Holmes went to Court together almost daily, "until 1926 on foot and after that by motor." [20] At the beginning Taft thought Holmes too old to carry on his work, but he was to change his mind. "Association with Justice Holmes is a delight. He is feebler physically, but I cannot see that the acuteness of his mind has been affected at all. . . . In many ways he is the life of the court, and it is a great comfort to have such a well of pure common law undefiled immediately next one so that one can drink and be sure one is getting the pure article." But in 1926 he veered again about Holmes: "He is, in my judgment, a very poor constitutional lawyer. . . . He lacks the experience of affairs in government that would keep him straight on constitutional questions."

Undoubtedly Taft soured on Holmes as the years went on because of the latter's association with Brandeis. "I am very fond of the old gentleman," he wrote in 1928, "but he is so completely under the control of Brother Brandeis that it gives to Brandeis two votes instead of one. He has more interest in, and gives more attention to, his dissents than he does to the opinions he writes for the court, which are very short and not very helpful." Taft attributed this influence partly to Holmes's age: "I think perhaps his age makes him a little more subordinate or yielding to Brandeis,

[16] H–P, I:237 (July 12, 1916).
[17] H–P, I:170 (September 24, 1910).
[18] H–P, II:79 (October 2, 1921).
[19] H–P, II:96 (May 21, 1922).
[20] This and the following quotations from Chief Justice Taft will be found in Henry F. Pringle's *The Life and Times of William Howard Taft* (1939) 969.

who is his constant companion, than he would have been in his prime." But Taft was not a detached observer, particularly since Holmes and Brandeis together represented the new jurisprudence which had come to challenge what Taft and some of his colleagues stood for. Theirs was a world of ideas and values which lay beyond the comprehension of the genial and yet stubbornly narrow-visioned Chief Justice.

The relation between Holmes and Brandeis was a deep and striking one. Here was a patrician, with his background of Emerson's Boston, and, on the other hand, a son of a Bohemian immigrant family, with the background of the Continental liberalism of the *1848* revolutions. The stream of influence which ran between them was not wholly a one-way affair. Brandeis was deeply moved and impressed by Holmes's generous perspectives, and by the brilliance of his insights. Holmes in turn was impressed by Brandeis' learning and the loftiness of his outlook: "I think he has done great work and I believe with high motives." [21] They found themselves in agreement in a surprisingly large number of cases. "We are so apt to agree," Holmes wrote on an occasion when they were on different sides, "that I am glad he dissents from the only opinion I have to deliver." [22]

Holmes had an exacting conception of his job on the Court. If, as Taft complained, his opinions were often too short, it was not because of indolence but because, for the purpose he had in mind — for the puncturing of doctrinal errors too long indulged in by the Court — a short opinion was often more effective. He never dissented for the sake of dissenting but only when, like Luther, he could "do no other." He did not relish justices who intruded their differences into the deliberations of the Court. He noted "the disappearance of men with the habit of some of our older generation, that regarded a difference of opinion as a cockfight and often left a good deal to be desired in point of manners." [23] But this sense of restraint did not keep him silent when silence would have been a betrayal of his whole method of constitutional interpretation. It was this method that Holmes cared about, and it is this method which has now triumphed.

[21] H–P, II:191 (Oct. 31, 1926).
[22] H–P, II:215 (Feb. 17, 1928). For further discussion of the common ground and the divergences of Holmes and Brandeis, see the Introduction above, pp. xl–xli.
[23] H–P, II:114 (Feb. 24, 1923).

1. America as a Going Concern

It is hard to find a unifying thread to tie together those decisions by Holmes which fall outside of the civil liberties area.[1] I have fixed upon the notion of America as a going concern because it is a broad enough tent-covering to include rather loosely related cases, and yet it corresponds to one of the deeper phases of Holmes's thinking.

The cases I have included fall broadly into five groups: first, the state police-power cases, generally touching on matters of social legislation and involving the canons of due process of law and freedom of contract; second, the cases involving two other conceptions — that of industry affected with a public interest, and that of a federal common law; third, the tort and copyright cases — not of great importance but touching on one of Holmes's continuing interests; fourth, the cases involving economic organization and power, including antitrust action, government control of prices and standards, and taxation; and fifth, executive power and war power.

In grouping the decisions I have sought roughly to follow the sequence above, and within each division I have arranged the cases chronologically. It will be apparent that these divisions are neither wholly doctrinal nor wholly economic and political, but a crisscross between the two. I have felt it better to leave it thus than to make the effort of finding wholly logical divisions which might run counter to some of the realities of Holmes's thinking.

The cases themselves have been selected partly for their legal importance, partly for their role in American history, and partly for their sheer readability. One result has been that there are many cases omitted which were more important than some of those that have been included — more important but much less readable. On the whole, however, I have sought to include most of the important cases, and have omitted others equally important only when their value was wholly a technical one.

This is not the place for a discussion of Holmes's economic and

[1] For the civil liberties cases see the next section, "State Power and Free Trade in Ideas," p. 289.

*political thinking,*² *but the reader may find several matters worth noting before he goes on to the cases themselves.*

Holmes as economist does not play an important role in these decisions. To be sure, the decision in the Arizona Employers' Liability *cases* ³ *is based on a theory of a shifting of the incidence of social insurance payments; the* Victor Herbert *v.* Shanley Co. *decision* ⁴ *is based on a theory of joint costs; the* Dr. Miles Medical Co. *opinion* ⁵ *is based on a marginal utility theory of price. But Holmes was not always at his best when he was an economist. And the whole nature of his judicial method minimized the part that his economic doctrines played in his decisions.*

It is worth noting that, conservative as he was in his explicit economic doctrines, a strain of economic realism persistently finds its way into his opinions. His discussion of the depositors' banking fund in Noble State Bank *v.* Haskell ⁶ *is an instance; similarly, his discussion of commerce as* a continuum *in the* Swift *case,*⁷ *and most of all, his statement in the* Coppage *v.* Kansas *decision that there must be an "equality of position between the parties in which liberty of contract begins."* ⁸ *Holmes shows here as well as anywhere else the insights that went beyond the abstraction of individual freedom and that revealed its relation to the realities of economic and political power.*

Running through the cases there is a pervasive dislike for the doctrinal — a dislike that does not prevent Holmes from using a doctrine himself, but which lends a cutting edge to the rapier sentences which demolish a doctrine when he sees fit to demolish it. His analyses of the concept of "public interest" in Tyson Brothers *v.* Banton,⁹ *of "liberty of contract" in* Adkins *v.* Children's Hospital ¹⁰ *and of a federal common law in the* Black *and* White Taxicab Co.¹¹ *have become classic. This does not mean that Holmes used wholly rule-of-thumb methods. His sense of the common law*

---

² A more extensive discussion will be found in the introduction to this volume, pp. xxix–xlix.
³ See p. 160.
⁴ See p. 216.
⁵ See p. 239.
⁶ See p. 179.
⁷ See p. 231.
⁸ See p. 152.
⁹ See p. 170.
¹⁰ See p. 172.
¹¹ See p. 193.

tradition is demonstrated time and again in the cases, and his approach thus tends often to be an historical one. And since he approaches the cases as an historian, he recognizes and allows for the continuing expansion of social control through the process of experiment.

This does not proceed from any liking for governmental power as against private power, but simply from the proposition that the needs which the legislatures sense and express are not the fanatical inventions of unreasonable men. Holmes had an eye for the realities of the legislative and administrative processes. In spite of his decision in the Myers *case,*[12] *he usually kept in mind the need for not complicating too greatly the task of the administrator. And this same administrative realism was linked with another strain in Holmes's thought — an understanding that where "great public needs" exist, the constitutional interpretation which allows for the power to meet them is to be preferred to that which denies such power. This is the meaning not only of* Noble State Bank v. Haskell *but also of* Moyer v. Peabody,[13] *involving the executive power in a time of emergency, and* Block v. Hirsh,[14] *involving wartime housing legislation. It is a tribute to Holmes's conception of America as a going concern that it should be as useful in our present time of great public danger as in the lesser urgencies of peace.*

THE FIRST SUPREME COURT CASE

Otis v. *Parker*
187 U. S. 606 (1903)

Holmes took his seat on the United States Supreme Court on December 8, 1902. Otis v. Parker *was argued before the Court on December 11 and 12 and decided on January 5, 1903. It was thus the first decision of the Court in which Holmes participated.* "Here I am," *he wrote to Pollock on December 28, 1902,*[1] "and more absorbed, interested and impressed than ever I had dreamed I might be. The work of the past seems a finished book — locked up far away, and a

---
[12] See p. 285.
[13] See p. 268.
[14] See p. 278.
[1] H–P, I:109.

new and solemn volume opens. The variety and novelty to me of the questions, the remote spaces from which they come, the amount of work they require, all help the effect." Otis v. Parker *is followed in the reports by two others in which Holmes wrote the opinion of the Court — one,* Diamond Glue Co. v. U. S. Glue Co., *187 U. S. 611, upholding a Wisconsin statute, and the others,* Hanley v. Kansas City R. R. Co. *187 U. S. 617, upsetting an Arkansas regulation of railroad rates on the ground of the commerce clause.*

The opinion itself, while the first that Holmes wrote, already contains full-grown several of the principal elements in his conception of judicial tolerance of legislative policy as the essence of the judicial process. This conception was at its clearest and best on questions of the Fourteenth Amendment and the state police power. The issue here was whether a section on the California Constitution, providing that contracts for the sale of mining stock on margin or for future delivery should be unenforceable, violated the Fourteenth Amendment. Holmes, while conceding by implication that freedom of contract comes under the due process protection of the Fourteenth Amendment, answered that in this case there was no violation. But in giving his answer he traversed ground that included the following positions which he afterward was to make familiar: that a case cannot be decided on the basis of "general propositions"; that the judges must not read into the Constitution "a particular set of ethical or economical opinions, which by no means are held semper ubique et ab omnibus"; *that the judges must defer to the judgment of the legislature on social policy, and hold its action within the police power unless they are willing to declare it to have been "wholly without foundation"; that "we cannot say that there might not be conditions to warrant the prohibition"; and that "the deep-seated conviction" of the people of California was "entitled to great respect," and was not unreasonable in the context of the state's history. As for the issue that was raised of the denial of equal protection of the laws, Holmes makes short work of it.*

Holmes wrote for the majority here, with Justices Brewer and Peckham dissenting without opinion. His language is restrained, yet it has some flashing passages, of which the sen-

tence with reference to Bentham is characteristic both of his intellectual and of his literary methods.

Holmes, J., for the Court:
This is an action in three counts, for money had and received, for money paid and promised to be repaid, and for margins paid to the defendants as stock brokers on contracts to buy and sell mining stocks, respectively. The answers to the first two counts are general denials and other matters now immaterial. The answer to the third count, beside a general denial, sets up that the count is based upon a provision in Article IV, § 26, of the constitution of California, that that provision is contrary to the first section of the Fourteenth Amendment of the Constitution of the United States. . . .

The provision of the state constitution is as follows: "All contracts for the sales of shares of the capital stock of any corporation or association, on margin, or to be delivered at a future day, shall be void, and any money paid on such contracts may be recovered by the party paying it by suit in any court of competent jurisdiction." There was some suggestion that these words might be narrowed by construction to contracts not contemplating a *bona fide* acquisition of the stock, but intended to cover only a wager or contemplated settlement of differences. Of course, if they were construed in that sense there would be no doubt of their validity. *Booth* v. *Illinois*, 184 U. S. 425. But while the Supreme Court of California says in this case that it "will always see that legitimate business transactions are not brought under the ban," in the same sentence it leaves open the hypothesis that the provision "fails to distinguish between *bona fide* contracts and gambling contracts," and sustains it as a proper police regulation, even if it does fail as supposed. Therefore it may be held hereafter that ordinary contracts for the sale of stocks on margin are not legitimate transactions, and it would not be safe for us to take the words in any other than their literal meaning, or to assume in advance of a decision that they will be taken in a narrow sense. In this case the jury were instructed broadly to find for the plaintiff if he had paid any money to the defendants as a margin for the purchase of stock of a corporation, and this instruction was sustained.

The objection urged against the provision in its literal sense is that this prohibition of all sales on margin bears no reasonable relation to the evil sought to be cured, and therefore falls within the first section of the Fourteenth Amendment. It is said that it unduly limits the liberty of adult persons in making contracts which concern only themselves, and cuts down the value of a class of property that often must be disposed of under contracts of the prohibited kind if it is to be disposed of to advantage, thus depriving persons of liberty and property without due process of law, and that it unjustifiably discriminates against property of that class, while other familiar objects of speculation, such as cotton or grain, are not touched, thus depriving persons of the equal protection of the laws.

It is true, no doubt, that neither a state legislature nor a state constitution can interfere arbitrarily with private business or transactions, and that the mere fact that an enactment purports to be for the protection of public safety, health or morals, is not conclusive upon the courts. *Mugler* v. *Kansas,* 123 U. S. 623, 661; *Lawton* v. *Steele,* 152 U. S. 133, 137. But general propositions do not carry us far. While the courts must exercise a judgment of their own, it by no means is true that every law is void which may seem to the judges who pass upon it excessive, unsuited to its ostensible end, or based upon conceptions of morality with which they disagree. Considerable latitude must be allowed for differences of view, as well as for possible peculiar conditions which this court can know but imperfectly, if at all. Otherwise a constitution, instead of embodying only relatively fundamental rules of right, as generally understood by all English-speaking communities, would become the partisan of a particular set of ethical or economical opinions, which by no means are held *semper ubique et ab omnibus.*

Even if the provision before us should seem to us not to have been justified by the circumstances locally existing in California at the time when it was passed, it is shown by its adoption to have expressed a deep-seated conviction on the part of the people concerned as to what that policy required. Such a deep-seated conviction is entitled to great respect. If the State thinks that an admitted evil cannot be prevented except by prohibiting a calling or transaction not in itself necessarily objectionable, the courts cannot interfere, unless, in looking at the substance of the matter, they can see that it "is a clear, unmistakable infringement of rights secured by the fundamental law." *Booth* v. *Illinois,* 184 U. S. 425, 429. No court would declare a usury law unconstitutional, even if every member of it believed that Jeremy Bentham had said the last word on that subject, and had shown for all time that such laws did more harm than good. The Sunday laws, no doubt, would be sustained by a bench of judges, even if every one of them thought it superstitious to make any day holy. Or, to take cases where opinion has moved in the opposite direction, wagers may be declared illegal without the aid of statute, or lotteries forbidden by express enactment, although at an earlier day they were thought pardonable at least. The case would not be decided differently if lotteries had been lawful when the Fourteenth Amendment became law, as indeed they were in some civilized States. See *Ballock* v. *State,* 73 Maryland, 1.

We cannot say that there might not be conditions of public delirium in which at least a temporary prohibition of sales on margins would be a salutary thing. Still less can we say that there might not be conditions in which it reasonably might be thought a salutary thing, even if we disagreed with the opinion. Of course, if a man can buy on margin he can launch into a much more extended venture than where he must pay the whole price at once. If he pays the whole price he gets the purchased article, whatever its worth may turn out to be. But if he buys stocks on margin he may put all his property into the venture, and being unable to keep his margins good if the stock market goes down, a slight fall leaves him penniless, with nothing to represent his outlay, except that he has had the chances of a bet. There is no doubt that purchases on margin may be and frequently are used as a means of gambling for a great gain or a loss of all one has. It is said that in California, when the constitution was adopted, the whole people were buying mining stocks in this way with the result of infinite disaster. *Cashman* v. *Root,* 89 California, 373, 382, 383. If at that time the provision of the constitution, instead of being put there, had been embodied in a temporary act, probably no one would have questioned it, and it would be hard to take a distinction solely on the ground of its more permanent form. Inserting the provision in the constitution showed, as we have said, the conviction of the people at large that prohibition was a proper means of stopping the evil. And as was said with regard to a prohibition of option contracts in *Booth* v. *Illinois,* 184 U. S. 425, 431, we are unwilling to declare the judgment to have been wholly without foundation.

With regard to the objection that this provision strikes at only some, not all, of the objects of possible speculation, it is enough to say that probably in California the evil sought to be stopped was confined in the main to stocks in corporations. California is a mining State, and mines offer the most striking temptations to people in a hurry to get rich. Mines generally are represented by stocks. Stock is convenient for purposes of speculation, because of the ease with which it is transferred from hand to hand, as well as for other reasons. If stopping the purchase and sale of stocks on margin would stop the gambling which it was desired to prevent, it was proper for the people of California to go no farther in what they forbade. The circumstances disclose a reasonable ground for the classification, and thus distinguish the case from *Connolly* v. *Union Sewer Pipe Co.*, 184 U. S. 540. We cannot say that treating stocks of corporations as a class subject to special restrictions was unjust discrimination or the denial of the equal protection of the laws.

Judgment affirmed.

ALLOWING PLAY FOR THE JOINTS

Missouri, Kansas, and Tennessee Railroad v. *May*
194 U. S. 267 (1904)

This is the "Johnson grass" case. Again the problem is one of the state police power — the area in which a state can invade the property realm because of its protective function. The central question involved in it is that of improper "classification" — whether the railroads were singled out for regulation and thereby deprived of the constitutional guarantee of the equal protection of the laws. It does not add much to Otis v. Parker *on legal grounds. But it further clarifies Holmes's intellectual method. I refer first to the concept of a shadowy but a pragmatic "line which has to be worked out between cases differing only in degree"; second, to Holmes's technique of saying "for all that we know" as a way by which the Court may accept the legislature's view of the problem to be met; and third, to the caution to the Court that it tread*

softly in administering constitutional prohibitions, and that it allow "play for the joints of the machine."
In this case Holmes spoke for the whole Court.

Holmes, J., for the Court:

This is an action to recover a penalty of $25, brought by the owner of a farm contiguous to the railroad of the plaintiff in error, on the ground that the latter has allowed Johnson grass to mature and go to seed upon its road. The penalty is given to contiguous owners by a Texas statute of 1901, chap. 117, directed solely against railroad companies for permitting such grass or Russian thistle to go to seed upon their right of way, subject, however, to the condition that the plaintiff has not done the same thing. The case is brought here on the ground that the statute is contrary to the Fourteenth Amendment of the Constitution of the United States.

It is admitted that Johnson grass is a menace to crops, that it is propagated only by seed, and that a general regulation of it for the protection of farming would be valid. It is admitted also that legislation may be directed against a class when any fair ground for the discrimination exists. But it is said that this particular subjection of railroad companies to a liability not imposed on other owners of land on which Johnson grass may grow is so arbitrary as to amount to a denial of the equal protection of the laws. There is no dispute about general principles. The question is whether this case lies on one side or the other of a line which has to be worked out between cases differing only in degree. With regard to the manner in which such a question should be approached, it is obvious that the legislature is the only judge of the policy of a proposed discrimination. The principle is similar to that which is established with regard to a decision of Congress that certain means are necessary and proper to carry out one of its express powers. *McCulloch* v. *Maryland,* 4 Wheat. 316, 4 L. ed. 579. When a state legislature has declared that, in its opinion, policy requires a certain measure, its action should not be disturbed by the courts under the 14th Amendment, unless they can see clearly that there is no fair reason for the law that would not require with equal force its extension to others whom it leaves untouched.

Approaching the question in this way we feel unable to say that the law before us may not have been justified by local conditions.

It would have been more obviously fair to extend the regulation at least to highways. But it may have been found, for all that we know, that the seed of Johnson grass is dropped from the cars in such quantities as to cause special trouble. It may be that the neglected strips occupied by railroads afford a ground where noxious weeds especially flourish, and that whereas self-interest leads the owners of farms to keep down pests, the railroad companies have done nothing in a matter which concerns their neighbors only. Other reasons may be imagined. Great constitutional provisions must be administered with caution. Some play must be allowed for the joints of the machine, and it must be remembered that legislatures are ultimate guardians of the liberties and welfare of the people in quite as great a degree as the courts.

Judgment affirmed.

HERBERT SPENCER IN NEW YORK BAKERIES

Lochner v. New York
198 U. S. (1905) 45, 74

Few things that Holmes wrote have become more famous or called forth more comment than his dissent in the Lochner *case. A generation of progressives just waking up to the harshness of a laissez-faire capitalism and the need for state action, and a generation of legal students discovering the dim outlines of a sociological jurisprudence, hailed his championship of their cause. He had been a relatively unknown quantity on the Court. His first dissent in the* Northern Securities *case*[1] *had not been one to reassure the progressives. Now, with the* Lochner *dissent, he emerged almost overnight as the leader of liberal jurisprudence in America.*

The New York statute in question was one of a number in the country seeking to soften the impact of an acquisitive economy upon the workers. The currents of feeling that President Theodore Roosevelt was expressing in the national government were being expressed by state legislatures widely enough to bother the spokesmen and guardians of capitalist power.

[1] See p. 217.

It was the era of the Muckrakers, who were applying new techniques of journalistic investigation to social problems, and were making the people aware that all was not well with the commonwealth. New York passed an act which included, among several provisions directly relating to the health of the bakery workers, a provision for a ten-hour day and sixty-hour week in that industry.

The Supreme Court divided on it five to four. Justice Peckham wrote the majority opinion invalidating the law on the ground that liberty of contract, guaranteed by the Fourteenth Amendment, had to be protected by the Court; that the bakery industry was not more dangerous to the health of the workers than many others; that hours of labor bore only a very indirect relation to such health; that to appeal to the police power to validate this provision of the Act would mean that "no trade, no occupation, no mode of earning one's living, could escape this all-pervading power, and the acts of the legislature in limiting the hours of labor in all employments would be valid, although such limitation might seriously cripple the ability of the laborer to support himself and his family"; and that "the real object and purpose" of the Act were not to protect health, but "to regulate the hours of labor between the master and his employees." It was, writes Walton Hamilton (in The Constitution Reconsidered, *ed. Conyers Read, 1938, p. 186), "an apostolic letter to the many legislatures in the land, appointing limits to their police power and laying a ban upon social legislation."*

With all its legal fundamentalism and economic primitivism there are few opinions in constitutional law as worthy of study as Justice Peckham's.[2] *It is, first of all, a study in con-*

---

[2] 198 U. S. 45. Peckham, while on the New York Court of Appeals, had written in *Budd* v. *N. Y.*, of a statute setting rates for grain elevators, that it was "vicious in its nature, communistic in its tendency." 117 N. Y. I (1889) 47. The opinion, some forty pages long, was written with a scarcely controlled passion. Its citations of Stanley Jevons's *The State in Relation to Labor* furnish an interesting pendent to Holmes's remark on Herbert Spencer in the *Lochner* dissent. Speaking of the rule of *Munn* v. *Illinois*, Peckham implies rather broadly that Lord Hale's "paternalism" in economics is of a piece with his belief in witchcraft. Louis Boudin in his *Government by Judiciary* (1932), II, 433-434, believes that Peckham's opinion in the *Budd* case is better, bolder and franker than his opinion in the *Lochner* case; and that the latter by no means contains the well-considered economic theory which Holmes imputes to it. One may

cept-creation. "Liberty of contract" is nowhere to be found in the Fourteenth Amendment, but is a creation of the judges. Holmes himself was to trace something of its history in his dissent in the Adkins case a decade and a half later.[3] It was advanced in the eighteen-seventies, by Justice Bradley in his dissent in the Slaughter-House cases,[4] as the liberty to pursue one's calling; it somehow took on some of the afflatus of the very different doctrine of the sanctity of contract, as guaranteed by the "obligation of contracts" clause; it reappeared as the Court's object of guardianship in the majority opinion by Peckham in the Allgeyer case [5] in the eighteen-nineties; and it was now treated by Peckham as established and indefeasible, stretching beyond the liberty to pursue one's calling so far as to mean a vested property interest in the employer-employee relationship as against any regulatory action on the part of the government.

Second, Justice Peckham's opinion is a good study in judicial policy-making. To be sure, he starts by saying that "this is not a question of substituting the judgment of the court for that of the legislature." But he goes on to say that "we do not believe in the soundness of the views which uphold this law." Thus he ends, after all, by effecting the substitution he had professed to avoid. And he does so by seeking to act as an expert on a question for which the judiciary has no expert training — whether in the bakery industry there is a relation between hours of work and health. As Sir Frederick Pollock remarked, "The legal weakness of this reasoning is that no credit seems to be given to the state legislature for knowing its own business, and it is treated like an inferior court which has to give proof of its competence." [6]

Third, the Peckham opinion is worth study as an inquiry into legislative motive. It asserts that the health objective is

---

answer, however, that Holmes's whole point is that the economic theory is there by implication and is not made articulate. Nevertheless, Boudin's discussion of the *Lochner* case, Vol. II, 433–441, is worth reading.

[3] See p. 172. For a good brief account of the doctrine's history, see Walton Hamilton's article "Freedom of Contract" in the *Encyclopedia of the Social Sciences*, Vol. 6 (1931), 450–455.
[4] 16 Wallace 36 (1873).
[5] *Allgeyer* v. *Louisiana*, 165 U. S. 578 (1897).
[6] 3 *Law Quarterly Review*, 211 (1905).

only a screen; that statutes such as that under review have become numerous; and that their "real object and purpose" is the regulation of labor relations. Chief Justice Taney used to insist that the Court was not concerned with questions of motive but only with questions of power. One need only add that there are no sure external standards for judging legislative motive: and that once such an inquiry is admitted, the Court is on the high seas of subjectivism with not a port in sight.

There were two dissenting opinions — one by Justice Harlan, in which Justices White and Day concurred, and a separate dissent by Holmes. Justice Harlan sought to answer Peckham point for point, paying particular attention to the factual question of the relation of hours of labor to health in bakery establishments. He quotes the New York Bureau of Labor Statistics; he cites a treatise on Diseases of the Workers; and he insists that, whatever the views of the judges, "a legislative enactment . . . is never to be . . . held invalid unless it be, beyond question, plainly and palpably in excess of legislative power." Thus the two opinions, while starting from the same general principles of constitutional interpretation, clash mainly because Justice Peckham puts the burden of proof upon the statute, to fight its way into the domain of the police power; and Justice Harlan puts the burden of proof upon those challenging it, to fight their way into the domain of liberty of contract.

What then remained for Holmes, and why did he write a separate opinion instead of concurring in Harlan's painstaking dissent? It was mainly because Harlan's opinion, like Peckham's, seemed too close to the surface of legal rationalization and failed to lay bare the economic preconceptions ("a judgment or intuition more subtle than any articulate major premise") on which the Peckham decision was in reality based. Like an archaeologist Holmes digs into the subsoil to reveal the buried intellectual cities beneath Peckham's legal language. What he sees is "an economic theory which a large part of the country does not entertain" — an economic theory that is irrelevant to the interpretation of the Fourteenth Amendment, because "a constitution is not intended to embody a particular economic theory, whether of paternalism and the organic relation of the citizen to the State or of laissez faire. It is made for *people of fundamentally differing views." This is the heart of his dissent. The famous sentence, "The Fourteenth Amendment does not enact Mr. Herbert Spencer's* Social Statics,*" gets its effect because it makes the general position concrete.*

There is a note of impatience here and a magisterial tone which had not previously (Holmes wrote this in 1905) cropped up in his Supreme Court opinions, even in the dissents. How explain it? It was partly that Holmes had found his place on the Court, had measured himself against the others, and had a sense of assurance. Even more, it was because the majority opinion was so flagrant an instance of indifference to Holmes's crucial principle of judicial tolerance of reasonable legislative action. It was not only that Justice Peckham's legal reasoning diverged from Holmes's: the intellectual universes of the two men were completely at variance. Also, 1905 was the year in which Holmes was reading Karl Pearson's Grammar of Science: *with the pseudo-scientism demanded by Peckham and supplied by Harlan, someone like Holmes could have little patience ("It does not need research to show . . ."). Holmes was reading Santayana's* Life of Reason; *how outrageous, then, must have appeared the unwillingness of the majority to consider as anything but "unreasonable," "arbitrary," and "meddlesome" the honest attempts of a legislature to find a legal method of humanizing the toil of men in a bakery. Holmes was in his letters defining truth as what one "can't help believing." He was in a mood to deflate all moral imperialisms; and what stood more in need of deflation than the moral imperialism of five Supreme Court justices who imposed their own nineteenth-century notions of economic "soundness" on the attempts of the majority in a community to lead their own lives in their own way? Out of the internal tension of this clash of universes came the restrained intellectual passion which gives the* Lochner *dissent its greatness.*[7]

The Lochner *case left a scar upon the consciousness of its time. Liberal opinion was jolted, and the dissatisfaction with judicial supremacy (dormant since the Income Tax cases) was reawakened. The Holmes dissent served to polarize the*

---

[7] Hamilton (*op. cit.,* p. 186) calls it "the most famous dissent in all legal history." If a case could be made for any other claimants, it would be for Holmes's dissent in the *Abrams* case or for Justice Curtis's in the *Dred Scott* case.

forces of a newer jurisprudence. Writing only four years later, in 1909, Roscoe Pound saw the Holmes dissent as "the best exposition we have" of "the sociological movement in jurisprudence, the movement for pragmatism as a philosophy of law, the movement for the adjustment of principles and doctrines to the human conditions they are to govern rather than to assumed first principles, the movement for putting the human factor in the central place and relegating logic to its true position as an instrument."[8] The decision itself was generally believed overruled. Muller v. Oregon[9] upheld a ten-hour law for women, the fact of sex being the basis on which the Court distinguished it from the Lochner case. But even this distinction was wiped out in Bunting v. Oregon[10] where a ten-hour law for men and women alike was upheld. In both, however, there were exhaustive "Brandeis briefs" showing the relation between hours of work and health. Thus Holmes's *"it does not need research to show"* was disregarded. In other respects too, while the Holmes view triumphed, the ghost of Peckham's intellectual universe was not wholly laid. Just as everyone believed his opinion was dead, the Court decision in the Adkins *case cited it as authority as late as 1922.*

Holmes, J., dissenting:

I regret sincerely that I am unable to agree with the judgment in this case and that I think it my duty to express my dissent.

This case is decided upon an economic theory which a large part of the country does not entertain. If it were a question whether I agreed with that theory, I should desire to study it further and long before making up my mind. But I do not conceive that to be my duty, because I strongly believe that my agreement or disagreement has nothing to do with the right of a majority to embody their opinions in law. It is settled by various decisions of this Court that State constitutions and State laws may regulate life in many ways which we as legislators might think as injudicious or, if you

[8] 18 YLJ 454. "Liberty of Contract" (1909). It is nevertheless worth noting that the *Harvard Law Review,* in its case note on the *Lochner* decision 18 HLR 619 (1905), made no mention at all of Holmes's dissent, although it commented on Harlan's. Its comment on the majority decision was that it checked the "prevalent legislative tendency to enact labor laws," and that it was therefore "likely to increase trade-union activity to enable workmen to obtain benefits unaided by paternal legislation."
[9] 248 U. S. 412 (1908).
[10] 243 U. S. 426 (1917).

like, as tyrannical as this, and which equally with this interfere with the liberty to contract. Sunday laws and usury laws are ancient examples. A more modern one is the prohibition of lotteries. The liberty of the citizen to do as he likes so long as he does not interfere with the liberty of others to do the same, which has been a shibboleth for some well-known writers, is interfered with by school laws, by the Post Office, by every State or municipal institution which takes his money for purposes thought desirable, whether he likes it or not. The Fourteenth Amendment does not enact Mr. Herbert Spencer's *Social Statics*. The other day we sustained the Massachusetts vaccination law. *Jacobson* v. *Massachusetts,* 197 U. S. 11. United States and State statutes and decisions cutting down the liberty to contract by way of combination are familiar to this Court. *Northern Securities Co.* v. *United States,* 193 U. S. 197. Two years ago we upheld the prohibition of sales of stock on margins or for future delivery in the constitution of California. *Otis* v. *Parker,* 187 U. S. 606. The decision sustaining an eight-hour law for miners is still recent. *Holden* v. *Hardy,* 169 U. S. 366. Some of these laws embody convictions or prejudices which judges are likely to share. Some may not. But a constitution is not intended to embody a particular economic theory, whether of paternalism and the organic relation of the citizen to the State or of laissez faire. It is made for people of fundamentally differing views, and the accident of our finding certain opinions natural and familiar or novel and even shocking ought not to conclude our judgment upon the question whether statutes embodying them conflict with the Constitution of the United States.

General propositions do not decide concrete cases. The decision will depend on a judgment or intuition more subtle than any articulate major premise. But I think that the proposition just stated, if it is accepted, will carry us far toward the end. Every opinion tends to become a law. I think that the word liberty in the Fourteenth Amendment is perverted when it is held to prevent the natural outcome of a dominant opinion, unless it can be said that a rational and fair man necessarily would admit that the statute proposed would infringe fundamental principles as they have been understood by the traditions of our people and our law. It does not need research to show that no such sweeping condemnation can be passed upon the statute before us. A reasonable man might think it a proper measure on the score of health. Men whom I certainly could not pronounce unreasonable would uphold it as a first instalment of a general regulation of the hours of work. Whether in the latter aspect it would be open to the charge of inequality I think it unnecessary to discuss.

LIBERTY AND THE "YELLOW DOG" CONTRACT

Adair v. U. S.
208 U. S. 161, 190 (1908)

After the Lochner *decision the "liberty of contract" doctrine continued its sway over the Court majority. Three years later, in the* Adair *case, the doctrine was transferred in its application from the Fourteenth to the Fifth Amendment and used to invalidate a federal railroad labor statute. Curiously, the Justice who wrote the Court's opinion against the law in the* Adair *case, basing it on the liberty of contract doctrine, was Justice Harlan, who had written a long dissent in the* Lochner *case.*[1]

The statute in this case was the Erdman Act, drawn by Richard Olney,[2] *sponsored by President Cleveland, and passed in 1898, providing among other things that it was criminal for a railroad company to discharge or otherwise discriminate against a worker on the ground of his membership in a union. It thus prohibited making a "yellow dog" contract a condition of continued employment. Its purpose, as Holmes implies, was to prevent a repetition of the Pullman strikes that had been agitating the country. It contained the seeds of the modern mediation machinery of the Railway Labor Board. What was at issue in the present case, however, was not a "yellow dog" contract in itself, but the act of Adair, as agent for the Louisville and Nashville Railroad, in discharging O. B. Coppage because of his membership in the Order of Locomotive firemen.*

Justice Harlan's majority opinion invalidating the Act was based on two arguments: it diminished the freedom of contract both of the employer and of the worker, and was thus a viola-

---

[1] Justice Harlan had in most of his other opinions a fairly consistent record in defending human rights. There is a good biography of Harlan by R. E. Cushman in the *Dictionary of American Biography*.

[2] Olney later wrote a criticism of the Court's decision, *Discrimination Against Union Labor — Legal?* 42 ALR 161 (1908).

tion of the liberty protected against the federal Government in the Fifth Amendment; and it could not be brought within the commerce power of Congress because labor relations had no "real or substantial connection" with commerce. Justice McKenna wrote a dissent.

Holmes dissented separately. The crux of his opinion is that freedom of contract is not an absolute. He expresses the belief that the concept "has been stretched to its extreme by the decisions," but that, even so, there is still room in the doctrine for a restraint of individual liberty in the public interest; and that it is not unreasonable for Congress to believe that the provision, by helping labor relations, would further its general policy with respect to the railroads and interstate commerce — especially since the connection of labor with the transportation industry "is at least as intimate and important as that of safety couplers."

Holmes, J., dissenting:

I also think that the statute is constitutional, and but for the decision of my brethren I should have felt pretty clear about it.

As we all know, there are special labor unions of men engaged in the service of carriers. These unions exercise a direct influence upon the employment of labor in that business, upon the terms of such employment and upon the business itself. Their very existence is directed specifically to the business, and their connection with it is at least as intimate and important as that of safety couplers and, I should think, as the liability of master to servant — matters which it is admitted Congress might regulate so far as they concern commerce among the States. I suppose that it hardly would be denied that some of the relations of railroads with unions of railroad employees are closely enough connected with commerce to justify legislation by Congress. If so, legislation to prevent the exclusion of such unions from employment is sufficiently near.

The ground on which this particular law is held bad is not so much that it deals with matters remote from commerce among the States as that it interferes with the paramount individual rights, secured by the Fifth Amendment. The section is, in substance, a very limited interference with freedom of contract, no more. It does not require the carriers to employ anyone. It does not forbid them to refuse to employ anyone, for any reason they deem good, even where the notion of a choice of persons is a fiction and wholesale employment is necessary upon general principles that it might be proper to control. The section simply prohibits the more powerful party to exact certain undertakings or to threaten dismissal or unjustly discriminate on certain grounds against those already employed. I hardly can suppose that the grounds on which a contract lawfully may be made to end are less open to regulation than other terms. So I turn to the general question whether the employment can be regulated at all. I confess that I think that the right to make contracts at will that has been derived from the word liberty in the Amendments has been stretched to its extreme by the decisions; but they agree that sometimes the right may be restrained. Where there is, or generally is believed to be, an important ground of public policy for restraint, the Constitution does not forbid it, whether this Court agrees or disagrees with the policy pursued. It cannot be doubted that to prevent strikes and, so far as possible, to foster its scheme of arbitration, might be deemed by Congress an important point of policy, and I think it impossible to say that Congress might not reasonably think that the provision in question would help a good deal to carry its policy along. But suppose the only effect really were to tend to bring about the complete unionizing of such railroad laborers as Congress can deal with, I think that object alone would justify the act. I quite agree that the question what and how much good labor unions do is one on which intelligent people may differ — I think that laboring men sometimes attribute to them advantages, as many attribute to combinations of capital disadvantages, that are really due to economic conditions of a far wider and deeper kind — but I could not pronounce it unwarranted if Congress should decide that to foster a strong union was for the best interest, not only of the men, but of the railroads and the country at large.

EQUAL BARGAINING POWER FOR WORKERS

Coppage v. *Kansas*
236 U. S. 1, 28 (1915)

This opinion should be read with the opinion in the Adair *case, for* Coppage *is the sequel to* Adair. *There was a similar* law here against "yellow dog" labor contracts, except that this time a state instead of a federal law was involved, and this law was somewhat broader in scope, making it a criminal offense for an employer to make nonmembership in a union a condition of continued or prospective employment. Justice Pitney wrote the opinion of the majority, in a six-to-three decision. He argues earnestly that Kansas exceeded its police power in passing the law; that while the Court does not "question the legitimacy" of labor unions, it calls the right of the employer and employee each to contract freely a sacred property right; and then it asks, "Granted the equal freedom of both parties to the contract of employment, has not each party the right to stipulate upon what terms only he will consent to the inception, or the continuance, of that relationship?" Pitney bases his reasoning mainly on the Adair decision. The result was thus that neither the federal nor the state government could constitutionally act to protect trade-union membership in the unequal bargaining struggle between employers and workers. Curiously this decision was handed down during a period when the Court was considered to be in one of its "progressive" phases.

There was a long dissent by Justice Day, concurred in by Justice Hughes. They sought to distinguish this from the Adair case on the ground of the different nature of the statutes, and argued long and earnestly that the Act did not on its face violate the employers' freedom. In reply to Justice Pitney's charge that its real purpose was that of "levelling the inequalities of fortune" rather than the promotion of general welfare, they said that it was not for the Court to inquire into the motive behind the Act.[1]

Holmes's dissent is one of his most famous, as it is one of his briefest. To borrow a phrase from The Sun Also Rises, "it is not brilliant: it is only perfect." In it he has whittled away everything but the essentials, and the bareness of his analysis reveals the outlines of his judicial method. He comes back once more to his concept of judicial tolerance of the not un-

---

[1] A comment in 28 HLR 496, 498 (1915) made the shrewd observation that Pitney "presupposes a major premise, which is deduced from the nature of things, that no statute which makes the 'levelling of the inequalities of fortune' an end in itself can reasonably tend to promote the public welfare."

reasonable legislative act, which in this case expresses the conviction of the not unreasonable worker that he has something to gain by protecting his membership in a trade union. Once again he insists that whether legislature and worker are right in their conviction is not his concern nor relevant to the Court's function. And once again he hits at the "liberty of contract" cases, and this time, instead of saying that the precedents still offer room for retreat, he says baldly that Lochner *and* Adair *are bad law and should be overruled. And there is an interesting reference, compounded at once of pride and a sense of sadness, to the continuity of his own thinking on trade-union organization and legislative discretion ever since* Vegelahn v. Guntner *and his early days on the Massachusetts Court.*

That Holmes was not merely rhetorical when he dissociated his own views from the views of labor is evidenced by passages in two of his letters to Pollock. One goes back to 1911, three years before Coppage. *"While I believe the economic advantage is on the side of the organization of capital over against the organization of labor, labor sees it mainly against — and labor has the votes. Hence it is inclined to destroy as an antagonist what is really the most powerful co-operative force."* [2] *The other is a year after* Coppage: *"I have been philosophizing anew on emotional weather and its independence of what might be expected to be the causes, e.g., workingmen oppressed before the French Revolution, yet seemingly gay (Restif de la Bretonne), workingmen now in the saddle, yet groaning and grunting and seeming to be having a worse time than ever."* [3]

The crux of Holmes's Coppage *opinion is to be found in the clause, "to establish the equality of position between the parties in which liberty of contract begins." Holmes had been for some time on the verge of saying exactly this in his "liberty of contract" dissents, but it never emerges so clearly as here. It is the culmination of the line of cases from* Vegelahn *on. It represents a flashing insight into the whole relationship between the trade-union movement and the libertarian tradition. Holmes saw here that the employers had the economic advantage; that the meaning of freedom for the worker was*

[2] H–P, I:186 (Aug. 21, 1911).
[3] H–P, I:229 (Dec. 29, 1915).

therefore restricted; that freedom could not become real until the bargaining positions were equalized by allowing the worker to become part of his own organization; that labor legislation, instead of restricting the area of individual freedom for the worker, enlarged it; that political power on the part of the legislature was brought in to equalize economic power, so that contractual liberty could have some meaning. All these are the implications we may laboriously draw. Holmes's phrase had the greatness of simplicity.

One of the results of the Coppage decision was to outlaw twelve other state laws of a similar tenor. In *1917*, in Hitchman Coal and Coke Co. v. Mitchell, 245 U. S. 229 (*1917*), the Court, voting six to three, sustained an injunction forbidding union officials to organize workers who were bound by "yellow dog" contracts. Holmes wrote two drafts of a dissenting opinion, but he finally decided not to submit them.[4] Eventually, however, the Supreme Court came back to the Holmes position, in the decisions in the NLRB cases. History, which has its ironies, has also its compensations. Justice Hughes, who had concurred in the Day dissent in Coppage, later as Chief Justice wrote the NLRB decisions.

Holmes, J., dissenting:

I think the judgment should be affirmed. In present conditions a workman not unnaturally may believe that only by belonging to a union can he secure a contract that shall be fair to him. *Holden* v. *Hardy,* 169 U. S. 366, 397. *Chicago, Burlington & Quincy R. R.* v. *McGuire,* 219 U. S. 549, 570. If that belief, whether right or wrong, may be held by a reasonable man, it seems to me that it may be enforced by law in order to establish the equality of position between the parties in which liberty of contract begins. Whether in the long run it is wise for the workingmen to enact legislation of this sort is not my concern, but I am strongly of opinion that there is nothing in the Constitution of the United States to prevent it, and that *Adair* v. *United States* and *Lochner* v. *New York* should be overruled. I have stated my grounds in those cases and think it unnecessary to add others that I think exist. See further *Vegelahn*

[4] The Holmes drafts are now at the Harvard Law School Library. It is interesting to note here that the Court decided the *Hitchman* case on common-law grounds, and according to its own notions of common law, as in *Swift* v. *Tyson.*

v. *Guntner,* 167 Mass. 92, 104, 108. *Plant* v. *Woods,* 176 Mass. 492, 505. I still entertain the opinions expressed by me in Massachusetts.

"EXPERIMENTS IN INSULATED CHAMBERS"

Truax v. *Corrigan*
257 U. S. 312, 343 (1921)

There was in the period just before the World War a growing feeling that court injunctions in labor disputes were being used to break strikes. In *1913* Arizona enacted a statute providing that no injunctions be issued against peaceful picketing unless to prevent injuries for which there was no remedy at law. This was almost identical with the wording of Section 20 of the Clayton Act, passed by Congress in *1914* for a similar purpose. There was a strike in a restaurant in Bisbee, Arizona; and Truax, the owner, asked for an injunction, claiming that the picketing by the strikers had drastically diminished his business and adversely affected his property. The Arizona Supreme Court refused to issue the injunction, holding the Act constitutional and the picketing peaceful. In a five-to-four decision the Supreme Court overruled the state court and held the law unconstitutional.

The majority opinion by Chief Justice Taft reasoned that even peaceful picketing might be unlawful and might therefore be enjoined; that the injunctive remedy was denied in labor disputes only; that acts which would be illegal if done by Truax's competitors were by the law in question allowed when done by the union; that this was a discriminatory classification, and that it therefore violated the equal protection guarantee of the Fourteenth Amendment; that it legalized acts inherently unlawful, and therefore violated the due process clause.[1]

---

[1] Professor Thomas Reed Powell points out, in "The Supreme Court's Control over the Issuance of Injunctions in Labor Disputes," 13 *Proceedings of Academy of Political Science* (1928) 37 (reprinted in *Selected Essays,* II:733, 754), that the Court's reasoning as it stands is absurd; but that it would be on better (if still shaky) ground if it held that to deny relief by injunction against coercive picketing is to close all effective remedies and therefore to deny due process of law.

This reasoning of Taft's is an almost classic example of the sort of judicial philosophy which caused what Justice Hughes once called the Court's "self-inflicted wounds." Professor Felix Frankfurter wrote at the time in a New Republic editorial that "this decision of the Supreme Court is . . . fraught with more evil than any which it has rendered in a generation. . . . For all the regard that the Chief Justice of the United States pays to the facts of industrial life, he might as well have written this opinion as Chief Justice of the Fiji Islands." *The article went on to point out that the history of the labor injunction was only a little over thirty years old. But for the Chief Justice "there never was a time when injunctive relief was not the law of nature. For him the world never was without it, and therefore the foundations of the world are involved in its withdrawal."* [2]

There were three dissenting opinions. Justice Pitney, with Justice Clarke concurring, made a cogent legal analysis; Justice Brandeis wrote a long and equally cogent economic and historical analysis; and Holmes wrote a brief dissent, at once semantic, procedural, and philosophical. Turning to the majority opinion's argument that Truax was denied equal protection because the injunction was denied him only against labor rather than against everyone, Justice Pitney suggests that the result is "to transform the provision of the Fourteenth Amendment from a guarantee of the 'protection of equal laws' into an insistence upon laws complete, perfect, symmetrical"; and he argues that, even without the injunctive remedy, Truax still had common law action to redress any wrongs committed against him. Within broad limits, he urged, it was for the states themselves to determine "their respective conditions of law and order, and what kind of civilization they shall have as a result."

The dissenting opinion by Justice Brandeis was one of his most massive. It used the method of historical relativism: in a long survey of English, American and Australian experience with the legislative and judicial treatment of

---

[2] "The Same Mr. Taft," 27 *New Republic* (1921) 230–231, reprinted in Felix Frankfurter, *Law and Politics* (1939) 41–47. See also the previous chapter in the book, "Taft and the Supreme Court," 37–40.

labor disputes he showed how the conceptions of both had slowly changed under trial and error. Answering the contention that the Act invaded property rights, Brandeis urged that the labor injunction had generally been used not to protect property but to make it "dominant over men"; that through it the state had thrown its power over to the employer; that the denial of the injunction helped equalize the struggle; "and that, pending the ascertainment of new principles to govern industry, it was wiser for the state not to interfere in industrial struggles by the issuance of an injunction."

Holmes's dissent tends somewhat toward looseness of construction. But in detail it is sharp, profound and aphoristic. He had used the phrase "delusive exactness" with reference to the Court's conception of the Fourteenth Amendment, and he now returns to it to develop what is a little essay in the semantics of the word "property," and our tendency to reify it. "You cannot give it definiteness of contour by calling it a thing. It is a course of conduct," and therefore "subject to substantial modification." He thus demolishes the argument from "due process" with respect to property rights. As for the classification argument used by Taft, he answers "Legislation may begin where an evil begins." And he ends with his famous comment on social experiment that is all the more striking because Justices Taft and Brandeis had also referred to experiment. Justice Taft wrote: "The Constitution was intended — its very purpose was — to prevent experimentation with the fundamental rights of the individual." Justice Brandeis wrote of the labor-employer struggle, "The rules governing the contest necessarily change from time to time. For conditions change, and . . . the rules evolved, being merely experiments in government, must be discarded when they prove to be failures." These two quotations furnish a context for Holmes's phrase about "the making of social experiments that an important part of the community desires, in the insulated chambers afforded by the several states."

After this decision, and after some others which in the same year whittled away what little meaning Congress may have intended to give the Clayton Act on the score of the *labor injunction, Congress in 1932 passed the Norris-La Guardia Anti-Injunction Act, "to restore," as Justice Frankfurter has put it, "the broad purpose which Congress thought it had formulated in the Clayton Act but which was frustrated, so Congress believed, by unduly restrictive judicial construction."* [3] *The Act has stood the tests of constitutionality. The experiment in the insulated chamber of Arizona did, after all, prove fruitful.*

Holmes, J., dissenting:

The dangers of a delusive exactness in the application of the Fourteenth Amendment have been adverted to before now. *Louisville & Nashville R. R. Co.* v. *Barber Asphalt Paving Co.,* 197 U. S. 430, 434. Delusive exactness is a source of fallacy throughout the law. By calling a business "property" you make it seem like land, and lead up to the conclusion that a statute cannot substantially cut down the advantages of ownership existing before the statute was passed. An established business no doubt may have pecuniary value and commonly is protected by law against various unjustified injuries. But you cannot give it definiteness of contour by calling it a thing. It is a course of conduct and like other conduct is subject to substantial modification according to time and circumstances both in itself and in regard to what shall justify doing it a harm. I cannot understand the notion that it would be unconstitutional to authorize boycotts and the like in the aid of the employees' or the employers' interest by statute when the same result has been reached constitutionally without statute by courts with whom I agree. See *The Hamilton,* 207 U. S. 398, 404. In this case it does not even appear that the business was not created under the laws as they now are. *Denny* v. *Bennett,* 128 U. S. 489.

I think further that the selection of the class of employers and employees for special treatment, dealing with both sides alike, is beyond criticism on principles often asserted by this Court. And especially I think that without legalizing the conduct complained of the extraordinary relief by injunction may be denied to the class. Legislation may begin where an evil begins. If, as many intelligent people believe, there is more danger that the injunction will be abused in labor cases than elsewhere, I can feel no doubt of the power of the legislature to deny it in such cases. I refer to two

[3] *U. S.* v. *Hutcheson,* 312 U. S. (1941) 219, 236.

160   THE MIND AND FAITH OF JUSTICE HOLMES

decisions in which I have stated what I understand to be the law sanctioned by many other decisions. *Carroll v. Greenwich Insurance Co.*, 199 U. S. 401, 411, and *Quong Wing v. Kirkendall*, 223 U. S. 59.

In a matter like this I dislike to turn attention to anything but the fundamental question of the merits, but *Connolly v. Union Sewer Pipe Co.*, 184 U. S. 540, raises at least a doubt in my mind of another sort. The exception and the rule as to granting injunctions are both part of the same code, enacted at the same time. If the exception fails, according to the *Connolly Case* the statute is bad as a whole. It is true that here the exception came in later than the rule, but after they had been amalgamated in a single act I cannot know that the later legislature would have kept the rule if the exception could not be allowed. If labor had the ascendancy that the exceptions seem to indicate, I think that probably it would have declined to allow injunctions in any case if that was the only way of reaching its end. But this is a matter upon which the State court has the last word, and if it takes this view its decision must prevail. I need not press further the difficulty of requiring a State court to issue an injunction that it never has been empowered to issue by the quasi-sovereign that created the Court.

I must add one general consideration. There is nothing I more deprecate than the use of the Fourteenth Amendment beyond the absolute compulsion of its words to prevent the making of social experiments that an important part of the community desires, in the insulated chambers afforded by the several States, even though the experiments may seem futile or even noxious to me and to those whose judgment I most respect. I agree with the more elaborate expositions of my brothers Pitney and Brandeis and in their conclusion that the judgment should be affirmed.

PAYING FOR PAIN AND MUTILATION

Arizona Employers' Liability Cases
250 U. S. 400, 431 (1919)

It was rarely that Holmes expressed harsh judgments of his colleagues on the Court. A case therefore in which, in a letter to Pollock, he called the Court's opinion "flabby" and the dissent "amazing" must have contained some provocative legal and social issues.

During the second decade of the century there was a widespread movement for state workmen's compensation laws which would shift the burden of payment primarily to the employer. The New York Court of Appeals invalidated such a law in *1911* but by the end of the decade most of the states had passed it. The test of constitutionality in the Arizona cases was therefore crucial. Arizona's law was passed in *1913*.[1] It provided that in certain hazardous industries all the risks of damage to employees were to be thrown on the employers. The Court considered together five cases under it, and held it constitutional by a five-to-four decision. "To my wonder," wrote Holmes to Pollock, "four were the other way, and my opinion was thought too strong by some of the majority, so that Pitney spoke for the Court and I concurred with what I had to say — Brandeis and Clarke only with me." On reading the opinions, Pollock wrote, "It is amazing to my English mind that four judges of your Court should be found to assert a constitutional right not to be held liable in a civil action without actual fault . . . I like your short opinion better than the larger one." To which Holmes replied, "I agree with you on all points. I thought the dissent amazing and that the opinion, which I agreed to make the opinion of the Court in order to get something that could be called that, was but a flabby performance."[2]

Justice Pitney's decision was long and cautious. It is reasonable, he argued, for the burden to be borne by the employer "because he takes the gross receipts of the common enterprise, and by reason of his position of control can make such adjustments as ought to be . . . made, in the way of reducing wages and increasing the selling price of the product." Holmes's con-

---

[1] This was in accordance with a mandatory provision in the State Constitution. The common law rule of liability was expressly changed in the State Constitution so as to exclude the "fellow servant" defense and leave those of "assumption of risk" and "contributory negligence" as questions of fact to the jury. The employee was given a choice between an action at common law under these terms with no limitation on recovery, and (in dangerous occupations) resort either to the employers' liability law or the compulsory compensation law, in which recovery was limited. All five of the cases considered together in Holmes's opinion arose in the copper industry.

[2] H–P, II:15, 21, 22.

curring opinion goes first straight at the legal problem. He shows that the rule of no liability without fault is not a legal absolute. Pollock's letters to Holmes furnished him substantiation of this from the lore of Pollock's knowledge of the common law; and Holmes's citations of precedent were by one who had himself had a not inconsiderable role as a state court judge in shaping the doctrine of liability both in torts and in criminal law [3] according to the principle of the external standard. Secondly, Holmes insists that as a matter of social policy the provisions of the Act are not an unreasonable means to the end sought. "Accidents," says Holmes, "probably will happen a good deal less often when the employer knows that he must answer for them if they do." And as for the cost, its incidence is shifted by the employer to the public. "It is reasonable that the public should pay the whole cost of producing what it wants and a part of the cost is the pain and mutilation incident to production." [4]

There were two dissenting opinions, one by Justice McKenna and one by Justice McReynolds, with Chief Justice White and Justice Van Devanter joining in each. There was a bitterness in the comment of Justice McReynolds: "As a measure to stifle enterprise, produce discontent, strife, idleness, and pauperism the outlook for the enactment seems much too good." Justice McKenna also foresaw dire results from the validating of the Act. "I hope it is something more than timidity, dread of the new that makes me fear that it is a step from the deck to the sea — the metaphor suggests a peril in the consequences." "It seems to me," he continued, "to be of the very foundation of right — of the essence of liberty as it is of morals — to be free from liability if one is free from fault. . . . Consider what the employer does: he invests his money in productive enterprise . . . he engages employees at their request and pays them the wages they demand, he takes all the risks of the adventure. Now there is put upon him an immeasurable element that may make disaster inevitable. I find it difficult to answer the argument

---

[3] See *Hanson v. Globe Co.*, p. 96. Also see *Commonwealth v. Pierce*, 138 Mass. (1884) in which Holmes upheld a manslaughter conviction for a medical practitioner who had swathed a patient in cloths soaked in kerosene, causing death.

[4] For an earlier formulation of this reaction by Holmes, see "The Path of the Law," above, p. 71.

advanced to support or palliate this effect. . . . *It is a certain impeachment of some rights to assume that they need justification and a betrayal of them to make them a matter of controversy. There are precepts of constitutional law as there are precepts of moral law that reach the conviction of aphorisms."* There are few more striking examples in the judicial literature of the relation between a mystical absolutism of natural rights and the practice of *laissez* faire.

Holmes, J., concurring:

The plaintiff (the defendant in error) was employed in the defendant's mine, was hurt in the eye in consequence of opening a compressed air valve and brought the present suit. The injury was found to have been due to risks inherent to the business and so was within the Employers' Liability Law of Arizona, Rev. Stats. 1913, Title 14, c. 6. By that law as construed the employer is liable to damages for injuries due to such risks in specified hazardous employments when guilty of no negligence. Par. 3158. There was a verdict for the plaintiff, judgment was affirmed by the Supreme Court of the State, 19 Arizona, 151, and the case comes here on the single question whether, consistently with the Fourteenth Amendment, such liability can be imposed. It is taken to exclude "speculative, exemplary and punitive damages," but to include all loss to the employee caused by the accident, not merely in the way of earning capacity, but of disfigurement and bodily or mental pain. See *Arizona Copper Co.* v. *Burciaga,* 177 Pac. Rep. 29, 33.

There is some argument made for the general proposition that immunity from liability when not in fault is a right inherent in free government and the *obiter dicta* of Mr. Justice Miller in *Citizens' Savings & Loan Association* v. *Topeka,* 20 Wall. 655 are referred to. But if it is thought to be public policy to put certain voluntary conduct at the peril of those pursuing it, whether in the interest of safety or upon economic or other grounds, I know nothing to hinder. A man employs a servant at the peril of what that servant may do in the course of his employment and there is nothing in the Constitution to limit the principle to that instance. . . . There are cases in which even the criminal law requires a man to know facts at his peril. Indeed, the criterion which is thought to be free from constitutional objection, the criterion of fault, is the application of an external standard, the conduct of a prudent man in the known circumstances, that is, in doubtful cases, the opinion of the jury, which the defendant has to satisfy at his peril and which he may miss after giving the matter his best thought. . . . Without further amplification so much may be taken to be established by the decisions. *New York Central R. R. Co.* v. *White,* 243 U. S. 188, 198, 204. *Mountain Timber Co.* v. *Washington,* 243 U. S. 219, 336.

I do not perceive how the validity of the law is affected by the fact that the employee is a party to the venture. There is no more certain way of securing attention to the safety of the men, an unquestionably constitutional object of legislation, than by holding the employer liable for accidents. Like the crimes to which I have referred they probably will happen a good deal less often when the employer knows that he must answer for them if they do. I pass, therefore, to the other objection urged and most strongly pressed. It is that the damages are governed by the rules governing in action of tort — that is, as we have said, that they may include disfigurement and bodily or mental pain. Natural observations are made on the tendency of juries when such elements are allowed. But if it is proper to allow them of course no objection can be founded on the supposed foibles of the tribunal that the Constitution of the United States and the States have established. Why then, is it not proper to allow them? It is said that the pain cannot be shifted to another. Neither can the loss of a leg. But one can be paid for as well as the other. It is said that these elements do not constitute an economic loss, in the sense of diminished power to produce. They may. *Ball* v. *William Hunt & Sons, Ltd.,* [1912], A. C. 496. But whether they do or not they are as much part of the workman's loss as the loss of a limb. The legislature may have reasoned thus. If a business is unsuccessful it means that the public does not care enough for it to make it pay. If it is successful the public pays its expenses and something more. It is reasonable that the public should pay the whole cost of producing what it wants and a part of that cost is the pain and mutilation incident to production. By throwing that loss upon the employer in the first instance we throw it upon the public in the long run and that is just. If a legislature should reason in this way and act accordingly it seems to me that it is within constitutional bounds, *Erickson* v. *Preuss,* 223 N. Y. 365. It is said that the liability is unlimited, but this is not true. It is limited to a conscientious valuation of the loss suffered. Apart from the control exercised by the judge it is to be hoped that juries would realize that unreasonable verdicts would tend to make the business impossible and thus to injure those whom they might wish to help. But whatever they may do we must accept the tribunal, as I have said, and are bound to assume that they will act rightly and confine themselves to the proper scope of the law.

It is not urged that the provision allowing twelve percent interest on the amount of the judgment from the date of filing the suit, in case of an unsuccessful appeal, is void. . . .

Mr. Justice Brandeis and Mr. Justice Clarke concur in this statement of additional reasons that lead me to agree with the opinion just delivered by my brother Pitney.

"THE PRODUCT OF RUINED LIVES"

Hammer v. Dagenhart
247 U. S. 251, 277 (1918)

Of all Holmes's opinions one of the most moving from a humanitarian standpoint, as well as most cogent from a legal standpoint, is his dissent in what is known as the First Child Labor *case. Of his dissents in this and the* Toledo Newspaper [1] *case Holmes wrote to Pollock: "I imagine the majority thought them ill-timed and regrettable as I thought the decisions."* [2]

The attempt to deal with the evil of child labor in America, arduous as it has been, has yielded relatively little result. Before the turn of the century what state laws were passed were casual and not very seriously enforced. After 1903, however, the states began to pass eight-hour laws for children, which are today in force in most states, although some still exempt the canning industries and all of them exempt the industrialized agriculture that Carey McWilliams has called "factories in the field." The difficulty with relying on state regulation has been that it has put a premium on backwardness, since mills and factories have moved to the states where they could get cheap

---
[1] See p. 332.
[2] H–P, I:267 (June 14, 1918).

child labor. Recognizing the need for uniformity and spurred largely by the social consciousness awakened by some of the Muckrakers and by the able work of Florence Kelley and the National Consumers' League, Congress finally acted. In 1906 bills were introduced by Senators Beveridge and Lodge, but failed to pass. In 1916 the Keating-Owen Act was passed, prohibiting the transportation in interstate commerce of any products from factories in which children were employed, under the conditions described in Holmes's opinion. The Act became effective in 1917, a Child Labor Division under Grace Abbott was set up in the Children's Bureau, which was headed by Julia Lathrop, and almost immediately a test of the law was made in North Carolina.

Dagenhart had two sons, one under fourteen and one between fourteen and sixteen, working in a North Carolina textile mill, who would have been allowed to work under the state law (forbidding child labor under twelve) but who were affected by the federal ban. He sued for an injunction against the United States District Attorney, Hammer, to prevent him from enforcing the law. The district court held the law unconstitutional and the Supreme Court affirmed the judgment, by a five-to-four decision, with Justice Day writing the majority opinion, and Justice Holmes, joined by Justices McKenna, Brandeis, and Clarke, writing a dissent.

In his decision Justice Day[3] held that the Act sought not to regulate commerce but to ban child labor; that it was therefore an attempt to regulate manufacturing, which was a state concern reserved to the states under the Tenth Amendment; that Congress had no power to equalize competitive conditions as between states with and without child-labor laws; and that however desirable the banning of child labor might be, Congress did not have the constitutional power to exclude goods from interstate commerce unless they were themselves intrinsically harmful.

Holmes's opinion is one of his most powerful, both in its

---

[3] Justice Day's opinion has been one of the Supreme Court decisions most severely criticized by constitutional commentators. For a thoroughgoing dissection of its legal reasoning the reader may consult E. S. Corwin's *Twilight of the Supreme Court* (1934) pp. 26–37. For a good contemporary comment, see T. M. Gordon, "The Child Labor Law Case," 32 HLR 45–67 (1918).

analysis of the distribution of powers under the federal system and in his marshaling of precedent.[4] *His contention that regulation of commerce may include prohibition is well buttressed by the decisions; his "if there were no Constitution" argument is both fresh and sharp; and his clinching point is that Congress has traditionally been allowed to regulate commerce even when the secondary effects of that regulation trenched on the internal affairs of the states. In every respect this must be considered one of the masterpieces in the literature of American governmental power.*

Holmes shows himself here, like Chief Justice Marshall before him, a champion of adequate national power. Yet he never pushed this at the expense of state power. As the larger portion of the decisions included in this book show, he was as doughty a champion of state legislative, executive, and judicial power as any member of the majority in this case. In fact, the very line of reasoning used by the majority here had led them and like-minded judges in other cases to invalidate state as well as national efforts to deal with admitted social problems such as child labor. Thus a "no man's land" was created between state and federal limitations. The operative ideology in such reasoning as that of Justice Day was not states'-rights but laissez-faire economics and the right of industry to be free of child labor regulation.

There is an interesting sequel to this case. Frustrated by the Court in this effort, Congress made another effort to deal with the child labor evil several years later. This time it passed a law using its taxing power against what Holmes here calls "the product of ruined lives." But in 1922, in the Second Child Labor case,[5] Chief Justice Taft wrote a decision declaring that unconstitutional as well. The continued efforts to pass a Child Labor Amendment have been unsuccessful. Finally, in

---

[4] "I flatter myself," he wrote Pollock, "that I showed a lot of precedent and also the grounds in reason." H–P, I:267 (June 14, 1918).

[5] *Bailey* v. *Drexel Furniture Co.*, 259 U. S. 20 (1922). Holmes did not dissent here. Henry F. Pringle, in his *Life and Times of William Howard Taft* (1939) II:1012, says that the Chief Justice was instrumental in winning over both Holmes and Brandeis to his view. For a discussion of the prospects for the fight against child labor after the 1922 decision, see Frankfurter, *Law and Politics* (1939), "Child Labor and the Court," 206–210. For the whole field see R. G. Fuller, *Child Labor and the Constitution* (1923).

1941, the Supreme Court expressly overruled its previous decision.[6] *It was clear that the Supreme Court had once again been forced to return to Holmes: one lawyer, as the decision was read, was overheard to remark that he thought he heard a peal of mellow laughter from the sky. Amidst the expressions of approval from the press came a not irrelevant letter from Edith Abbott, of the University of Chicago, asking how the Court could make up for the "stunted minds and broken lives" of the children whom it had surrendered to exploitation in the years since 1918.*[7]

Holmes, J., dissenting:

The single question in this case is whether Congress has power to prohibit the shipment in interstate or foreign commerce of any product of a cotton mill situated in the United States, in which within thirty days before the removal of the product children under fourteen have been employed, or children between fourteen and sixteen have been employed more than eight hours in a day, or more than six days in any week, or between seven in the evening and six in the morning. The objection urged against the power is that the States have exclusive control over their methods of production and that Congress cannot meddle with them, and taking the proposition in the sense of direct intermeddling I agree to it and suppose that no one denies it. But if an act is within the powers specifically conferred upon Congress, it seems to me that it is not made any less constitutional because of the indirect effects that it may have, however obvious it may be that it will have those effects, and that we are not at liberty upon such grounds to hold it void.

The first step in my argument is to make plain what no one is likely to dispute — that the statute in question is within the power expressly given to Congress if considered only as to its immediate effects and that if invalid it is so only upon some collateral ground. The statute confines itself to prohibiting the carriage of certain goods in interstate or foreign commerce. Congress is given power

---

[6] The legislation under review was the federal Fair Labor Standards Act of 1938. This contained a provision that the head of the Children's Division can prohibit the shipment in interstate commerce of goods in which oppressive child labor has been employed. The Act was upheld in *U. S. v. Darby,* 312 U. S. 100 (1941), by a unanimous Court speaking through Justice Stone.

[7] 104 *New Republic* (1941), 408.

to regulate such commerce in unqualified terms. It would not be argued today that the power to regulate does not include the power to prohibit. Regulation means the prohibition of something, and when interstate commerce is the matter to be regulated, I cannot doubt that the regulation may prohibit any part of such commerce that Congress sees fit to forbid. At all events it is established by the *Lottery Case* and others that have followed it that a law is not beyond the regulative power of Congress merely because it prohibits certain transportation out and out. *Champion* v. *Ames,* 188 U. S. 321, 355, 359, *et seq.* So I repeat that this statute in its immediate operation is clearly within the Congress's constitutional power.

The question then is narrowed to whether the exercise of its otherwise constitutional power by Congress can be pronounced unconstitutional because of its possible reaction upon the conduct of the States in a matter upon which I have admitted that they are free from direct control. I should have thought that that matter had been disposed of so fully as to leave no room for doubt. I should have thought that the most conspicuous decisions of this Court had made it clear that the power to regulate commerce and other constitutional powers could not be cut down or qualified by the fact that it might interfere with the carrying out of the domestic policy of any State.

The manufacture of oleomargarine is as much a matter of State regulation as the manufacture of cotton cloth. Congress levied a tax upon the compound, when colored so as to resemble butter, that was so great as obviously to prohibit the manufacture and sale. In a very elaborate discussion the present Chief Justice excluded any inquiry into the purpose of an act which apart from that purpose was within the power of Congress. *McCray* v. *United States,* 195 U. S. 27. Fifty years ago a tax on state banks, the obvious purpose and actual effect of which was to drive them, or at least their circulation, out of existence, was sustained, although the result was one that Congress had no constitutional power to require. The Court made short work of the argument as to the purpose of the act. "The judicial cannot prescribe to the legislative department of the Government limitations upon the exercise of its acknowledged powers." *Veazie Bank* v. *Fenno,* 8 Wall. 533. So it well might have been argued that the corporation tax was intended under the guise of a revenue measure to secure a control not otherwise belonging to Congress, but the tax was sustained, and the objection so far as noticed was disposed of by citing *McCray* v. *United States. Flint* v. *Stone Tracy Co.,* 220 U. S. 107. And to come to cases upon interstate commerce, notwithstanding *United States* v. *E. C. Knight Co.,* 156 U. S. 1, the Sherman Act has been made an instrument for the breaking up of combinations in restraint of trade and monopolies, using the power to regulate commerce as a foothold, but not proceeding because that commerce was the end actually in mind. The objection that the control of the States over production was interfered with was urged again and again but always in vain. *Standard Oil Co.* v. *United States,* 221 U. S. 1, 68, 69. *United States* v. *American Tobacco Co.,* 221 U. S. 106, 184. *Hoke* v. *United States,* 227 U. S. 308, 321, 322. See finally and especially *Seven Cases of Eckman's Alterative* v. *United States,* 239 U. S. 510, 514, 515.

The Pure Food and Drug Act, which was sustained with the intimation that "no trade can be carried on between the States to which it does not extend," applies not merely to articles that the changing opinion of the time condemns as intrinsically harmful but to others innocent in themselves, simply on the ground that the order for them was induced by a preliminary fraud. *Weeks* v. *United States,* 245 U. S. 618. It does not matter whether the supposed evil precedes or follows the transportation. It is enough that in the opinion of Congress the transportation encourages the evil. I may add that in the cases on the so-called White Slave Act it was established that the means adopted by Congress as convenient to the exercise of its power might have the character of police regulations. *Hoke* v. *United States,* 227 U. S. 308, 323. *Caminetti* v. *United States,* 242 U. S. 470, 492. In *Clark Distilling Co.* v. *Western Maryland Ry. Co.,* 242 U. S. 311, 328, *Leisy* v. *Hardin,* 135 U. S. 100, 108, is quoted with seeming approval to the effect that "a subject-matter which has been confided exclusively to Congress by the Constitution is not within the jurisdiction of the police power of the State, unless placed there by congressional action." I see no reason for that proposition not applying here.

The notion that prohibition is any less prohibition when applied to things now thought evil I do not understand. But if there is any matter upon which civilized countries have agreed — far more unanimously than they have with regard to intoxicants and some other matters over which this country is now emotionally aroused — it is the evil of premature and excessive child labor. I should have thought that if we were to introduce our own moral conceptions where in my opinion they do not belong, this was pre-eminently a case for upholding the exercise of all its powers by the United States.

But I had thought that the propriety of the exercise of a power admitted to exist in some cases was for the consideration of Congress alone and that this Court always had disavowed the right to intrude its judgment upon questions of policy or morals. It is not for this Court to pronounce when prohibition is necessary to regulation if it ever may be necessary — to say that it is permissible as against strong drink but not as against the product of ruined lives.

The Act does not meddle with anything belonging to the States. They may regulate their internal affairs and their domestic commerce as they like. But when they seek to send their products across the state line they are no longer within their rights. If there were no Constitution and no Congress their power to cross the line would depend upon their neighbors. Under the Constitution such commerce belongs not to the States but to Congress to regulate. It may carry out its views of public policy whatever indirect effect they may have upon the activities of the States. Instead of being encountered by a prohibitive tariff at her boundaries the State encounters the public policy of the United States which it is for Congress to express. The public policy of the United States is shaped with a view to the benefit of the nation as a whole. If, as has been the case within the memory of men still living, a State should take a different view of the propriety of sustaining a lottery from that which generally prevails, I cannot believe that the fact would require a different decision from that reached in *Champion* v. *Ames*, 188 U. S. 321. Yet in that case it would be said with quite as much force as in this that Congress was attempting to intermeddle with the State's domestic affairs. The national welfare as understood by Congress may require a different attitude within its sphere from that of some self-seeking State. It seems to me entirely constitutional for Congress to enforce its understanding by all the means at its command.

A DOGMA AMONG SCRUBWOMEN

Adkins v. Children's Hospital
261 U. S. 525, 567 (1923)

After the favorable decisions in the state hours-of-labor cases,[1] there seemed some hope that the Court, leaving behind a quarter-century of laissez-faire doctrine, had entered on a new liberal phase. When Oregon had passed a minimum wage law, there had been much general optimism about it. The Supreme Court passed on it in 1917 and, with Justice Brandeis not sitting because of having been associated with the case, upheld the law by a four-to-four tie.[2] But while the tie settled the question of the Oregon statute, it left still open the question of the constitutionality of minimum wage legislation. Several other states passed similar laws, all of them upheld by their state Supreme Courts. Professor Powell, in an interesting statistical summary,[3] has shown that outside the United States Supreme Court the judicial score was for affirmation by a vote of twenty-seven judges to two.

In this context Congress passed a law setting up a board to determine minimum wages for women in the District of Columbia. To carry out the analogy with the state police power, this was fortified in the Act by reference to the relation between wages and the health and morals of women. The Children's Hospital of Washington, employing a number of women workers — among them some scrubwomen — at less than the minimum, brought suit to prevent Adkins and other Board members from enforcing the wage orders. The District of Columbia Court of Appeals voted two to one for the Act, but when a judge who had been sick returned to the bench the case was reheard and the decision went two to one against the Act. The case came before the Supreme Court, with Professor (later Justice) Frankfurter submitting the sort of "Bran-

---

[1] *Muller v. Oregon*, 208 U. S. 412 (1908), and *Bunting v. Oregon*, 243 U. S. 246 (1917).
[2] *Stettler v. O'Hara*, 243 U. S. 269 (1917).
[3] T. R. Powell, "The Judiciality of Minimum Wage Legislation," 37 HLR 545 (1924), reprinted in *Selected Essays*, I:553–560, II:716–732.

deis brief" he had submitted in the Bunting case. But in the period that had intervened since Bunting, the Court had been undergoing a change of viewpoint reflected in such decisions adverse to social legislation as Hammer v. Dagenhart (*1918*), Truax v. Corrigan (*1921*) and Bailey v. Drexel Furniture Co. (*1922*) — a change which itself perhaps reflected the changed social climate after Wilson's first administration. By the time the Adkins case came to the Supreme Court in *1923*, Justices Day, Pitney, and Clarke had been replaced by Justices Butler, Sanford, and Sutherland, two of whom voted against the Act. It was declared unconstitutional by a vote of five judges, with three dissenting, and with Justice Brandeis — by a perhaps overrefined sense of scruple, since he was technically eligible — not sitting.

The opinion that Justice Sutherland wrote for the majority was the exact antithesis, in the intellectual universe that it implied, from the dissent of Justice Holmes. Justice Sutherland was just starting his work on the Court: he was to be during his tenure the judicial wheelhorse of the conservative majority, writing his prim and derivative constitutional essays in a schoolmasterish way. His opinion is based on the liberty of contract doctrine; it rests for precedent on the Lochner, Adair, and Coppage decisions; it holds that the liberty of the employer to make a contract for the purchase of the labor commodity is infringed by the Act. "In principle, there can be no difference between the case of selling labor and the case of selling goods. . . . The shopkeeper, having dealt fairly and honestly . . . is not concerned . . . with the question of his customer's necessities." Thus, by treating the labor contract like any commodity purchase-and-sale, he bears out the contention of Marx that under capitalism labor has become a mere commodity on the market, and he makes legal thinking part of the "*fetishism of the commodity*" of which Marx spoke.[4]

When confronted by the cases in which the Court had up-

[4] It is worth noting that in a letter to Holmes putting himself on the side of the dissenting opinions, Sir Frederick Pollock took issue with this. "The power of disposing of one's own bodily or mental activity," he writes, "is very different from the power of dealing with money or corporeal chattels: and a contract for work and labour is not either in common sense or in the Common Law a subspecies of the contract of sale." H–P, II:117 (June 5, 1923).

held restraints of liberty of contract, Sutherland answers that "freedom of contract is . . . the general rule and restraint the exception." Just where he got this general rule, or even where he got the doctrine, he does not make clear. On the troublesome question of Muller v. Oregon, he makes the distinction that it is legal to regulate hours but not wages: since hours may have some relation to health, but "morality rests upon other considerations than wages." Chief Justice Taft, who had written the conservative opinions in the Truax case and the Second Child Labor case, found all this too much. He did not join with Holmes, however, since he could not agree "with some general observations in the forcible opinion" of Holmes; so he dissented separately, with Justice Sanford joining him. It was not the Court's job, he wrote — and an echo of earlier Holmesian opinions could be heard in his words — "to hold congressional acts invalid simply because they are passed to carry out economic views which the Court believes to be unwise or unsound."

The Holmes dissent contains the best of his discussions of liberty of contract, which had started as an "innocuous generality" of the liberty to pursue the ordinary callings, and had ended as a "dogma." There follows the familiar Holmes method of listing the many legal precedents in which the absolute in the dogmas had been qualified away by restraints on it. Of Sutherland's attempt to brush aside Muller v. Oregon by the distinction between regulating hours and regulating wages, his answer is characteristically sharp: "The bargain is equally affected whichever half you regulate." Of the question whether women's wages present more of a problem than men's, on the score of health and morals: "It will need more than the Nineteenth Amendment to convince me that there are no differences between men and women." And he goes on, again, to thrust his own views out of the picture. The problem is whether the view of Congress as to the relation of living standards for women to their "ill health, immorality, and the deterioration of the race," is a view that cannot be held by reasonable men. And whereas Justice Sutherland had dismissed the Frankfurter brief as "proper enough for the consideration of lawmaking bodies," saying that the judicial question "cannot be aided by adding heads,"

Holmes upholds its relevance as an index of legislative reasonableness: although he himself has doubts about the Act because of its "interstitial" costs.

There is a wild element of chance attaching to the whole history of the case. If, as Professor Powell points out, Justice Brandeis had sat on the Oregon minimum wage case and made a clear majority; or if the Appeals Court judge had not been sick, so that the Adkins *case had come to the Supreme Court in the previous term of Court, the Act would probably have been upheld. "In the words of the poet," writes Powell, "it was not the Constitution but 'a measureless malfeasance which obscurely willed it thus' — the malfeasance of chance and of the calendar." Whatever the malfeasance, the effect of the decision was that for a decade, until the wage structure was completely broken down by the Great Depression, there was no minimum wage fixing to speak of in America.*[5]

Nevertheless the Holmes dissent and the controversy over the case had their effect upon legal thinking. When finally in 1936 a New York minimum wage statute, carefully drawn with the Adkins *decision in mind, came before the Court and was again held unconstitutional by a five-to-four vote,*[6] *the result was a strong wave of feeling against the Court, and even the Republican Convention declared against the decision. Of the five judges who made up the* Adkins *majority in 1923 four were still on the Court in 1936 and all of them voted against the New York statute — Justices Van Devanter, Mc-Reynolds, Sutherland, and Butler. Chief Justice Hughes dissented, and a sentence in the dissent of Justice Stone might have been part of Holmes's* Adkins *opinion about the Washington scrubwomen: "There is a grim irony in speaking of the*

---

[5] The storm of protest against the decision of the Court was intense, both in lay circles and among constitutional commentators. See Professor Powell's article, already cited; also Boudin, *Government by Judiciary* (1932) II:477–499; also a collection of comments gathered by the National Consumers' League, *The Supreme Court and Minimum Wage Legislation* (1925), including articles by Pound, Powell, Haines, Sayre, Parkinson, Corwin, Wormser.

[6] *Morehead* v. *Tipaldo,* 298 U. S. 587 (1936). The practical effect of the decision was to hold the statute unconstitutional. In legal terms, however, the Court held only that the attempt of the New York legislature to draw an Act that could be distinguished from that condemned in the Adkins case was unsuccessful. The difference, as Professor Mark Howe has pointed out, is slight but not without significance to the politics of adjudication.

freedom of contract of those who, because of their economic necessities, give their services for less than is needful to keep body and soul together."

In 1937, however, one of the first fruits of the new orientation of the Court was the decision in West Coast Hotel Co. v. Parrish [7] *upholding a minimum wage law of the state of Washington very similar to that of New York. In his decision Chief Justice Hughes expressly overruled the* Adkins *case, and almost paraphrased the earlier Holmes dissent on the questions of freedom of contract and on judicial tolerance of legislative policy. In 1939 there were minimum wage laws in twenty-five states. In 1938 Congress passed a Fair Labor Standards Act, providing for minimum wages, and it was upheld by the Supreme Court in 1941.*[8] *Thus there came to an end an exciting effort to better one phase of American life, marked by the changes and chances of the judicial process in which Holmes played an honorable and important part.*

Holmes, J., dissenting:

The question in this case is the broad one, Whether Congress can establish minimum rates of wages for women in the District of Columbia with due provision for special circumstances, or whether we must say that Congress has no power to meddle with the matter at all. To me, notwithstanding the deference due to the prevailing judgment of the Court, the power of Congress seems absolutely free from doubt. The end, to remove conditions leading to ill health, immorality and the deterioration of the race, no one would deny to be within the scope of constitutional legislation. The means are means that have the approval of Congress, of many States, and of those governments from which we have learned our greatest lessons. When so many intelligent persons, who have studied the matter more than any of us can, have thought that the means are effective and are worth the price, it seems to me impossible to deny that the belief reasonably may be held by reasonable men. If the law encountered no other objection than that the means bore no relation to the end or that they cost too much I do not suppose that anyone would venture to say that it was bad. I agree, of course, that a law answering the foregoing require-

[7] *West Coast Hotel Co. v. Parrish*, 300 U. S. 379 (1937).
[8] *U. S. v. Darby*, 312 U. S. (1914) 100.

AMERICA AS A GOING CONCERN

ments might be invalidated by specific provisions of the Constitution. For instance, it might take private property without just compensation. But in the present instance the only objection that can be urged is found within the vague contours of the Fifth Amendment, prohibiting the depriving any person of liberty or property without due process of law. To that I turn.

The earlier decisions upon the same words in the Fourteenth Amendment began within our memory and went no farther than an unpretentious assertion of the liberty to follow the ordinary callings. Later that innocuous generality was expanded into the dogma, Liberty of Contract. Contract is not specially mentioned in the text that we have to construe. It is merely an example of doing what you want to do, embodied in the word liberty. But pretty much all law consists in forbidding men to do some things they want to do, and contract is no more exempt from law than other acts. Without enumerating all the restrictive laws that have been upheld I will mention a few that seem to me to have interfered with liberty of contract quite as seriously and directly as the one before us. Usury laws prohibit contracts by which a man receives more than so much interest for the money that he lends. Statutes of frauds restrict many contracts to certain forms. Some Sunday laws prohibit practically all contracts during one-seventh of our whole life. Insurance rates may be regulated. *German Alliance Insurance Co. v. Lewis,* 233 U. S. 389. (I concurred in that decision without regard to the public interest with which insurance was said to be clothed. It seemed to me that the principle was general.) Contracts may be forced upon the companies. *National Union Fire Insurance Co. v. Wanberg,* 260 U. S. 71. Employers of miners may be required to pay for coal by weight before screening. *McLean v. Arkansas,* 211 U. S. 539. Employers generally may be required to redeem in cash store orders accepted by their employees in payment. *Knoxville Iron Co. v. Harbison,* 183 U. S. 13. Payment of sailors in advance may be forbidden. *Patterson v. Bark Eudora,* 190 U. S. 169. The size of a loaf of bread may be established. *Schmidinger v. Chicago,* 226 U. S. 578. The responsibility of employers to their employees may be profoundly modified. *New York Central R. R. Co. v. White,* 243 U. S. 188. *Arizona Employers Liability Cases,* 250 U. S. 400. Finally women's hours of labor may be fixed; *Muller v. Oregon,* 208 U. S. 412 . . . ; and the principle was extended to men with the allowance of a limited overtime to be paid for "at the rate of time and one-half of the regular wage," in *Bunting* v. *Oregon,* 243 U. S. 426.

I confess that I do not understand the principle on which the power to fix a minimum for the wages of women can be denied by those who admit the power to fix a maximum for their hours of work. I fully assent to the proposition that here as elsewhere the distinctions of the law are distinctions of degree, but I perceive no difference in the kind or degree of interference with liberty, the only matter with which we have any concern, between the one case and the other. The bargain is equally affected whichever half you regulate. *Muller* v. *Oregon,* I take it, is as good law today as it was in 1908. It will need more than the Nineteenth Amendment to convince me that there are no differences between men and women, or that legislation cannot take those differences into account. I should not hesitate to take them into account if I thought it necessary to sustain this act. *Quong Wing* v. *Kirkendall,* 223 U. S. 59, 63. But after *Bunting* v. *Oregon,* 243 U. S. 426, I had supposed that it was not necessary, and that *Lochner* v. *New York,* 198 U. S. 45, would be allowed a deserved repose.

This statute does not compel anybody to pay anything. It simply forbids employment at rates below those fixed as the minimum requirement of health and right living. It is safe to assume that women will not be employed at even the lowest wages allowed unless they earn them, or unless the employer's business can sustain the burden. In short, the law in its character and operation is like hundreds of so-called police laws that have been upheld. I see no greater objection to using a Board to apply the standard fixed by the act than there is to the other commissions with which we have become familiar, or than there is to the requirement of a license in other cases. The fact that the statute warrants classification, which like all classifications may bear hard upon some individuals, or in exceptional cases, notwithstanding the power given to the Board to issue a special license, is no greater infirmity than is incident to all law. But the ground on which the law is held to fail is fundamental and therefore it is unnecessary to consider matters of detail.

The criterion of constitutionality is not whether we believe the law to be for the public good. We certainly cannot be prepared to deny that a reasonable man reasonably might have that belief in view of the legislation of Great Britain, Victoria and a number of States of this Union. The belief is fortified by a very remarkable collection of documents submitted on behalf of the appellants, material here, I conceive, only as showing that the belief reasonably may be held. In Australia the power to fix a minimum for wages in the case of industrial disputes extending beyond the limits of any one State was given to a court, and its President wrote a most interesting account of its operation, 29 *Harvard Law Review* 13. If a legislature should adopt what he thinks the doctrine of modern economists of all schools, that "freedom of contract is a misnomer as applied to a contract between an employer and an ordinary individual employee" *ibid.* 25, I could not pronounce an opinion with which I agree impossible to be entertained by reasonable men. If the same legislature should accept his further opinion that industrial peace was best obtained by the device of a court having the above powers, I should not feel myself able to contradict it, or to deny that the end justified restrictive legislation quite as adequately as beliefs concerning Sunday or exploded theories about usury. I should have my doubts, as I have them about this statute — but they would be whether the bill that has to be paid for every gain, although hidden as interstitial detriments, was not greater than the gain was worth: a matter that it is not for me to decide.

I am of opinion that the statute is valid and that the decree should be reversed.

THE STATE AND THE GREAT PUBLIC NEEDS

Noble State Bank v. *Haskell*
219 U. S. 104 and 575 (1911)

Because of the impact of the Panic of 1907, Oklahoma passed an Act setting up a fund for the guarantee of bank deposits. Speaking for a unanimous Court, Holmes held that the Act did not violate the due process provision of the Fourteenth Amendment. In doing so he wrote one of the great Supreme Court decisions on the police power. It is not one of his aphoristic opinions; and one may presume that he was slightly bored with the details of the banking business. But it is argued with a beautiful clarity. Its conception of the police power is as broad as any in the decisions of the Court. Instead of the conventional formula that the police power allows a state to act for the public health, safety, or morals, Holmes asserts that the police power "extends to all the great public needs." To be sure, he limits this in a later paragraph by referring again to his pragmatic test: "Lines are pricked out by the gradual approach and contact of decisions on the opposing sides." And he agrees that the state cannot enter on large-scale subsidies of business. Yet even with these qualifications, the permissive aspects of the decision are broad enough to allow for an experimental range in state economic control.

It was this aspect of the decision that led Harold Laski to call it "the modern charter of the federal state," "a license to experiment with the unknown, a right to sail one's ship upon the rocks."[1] It took great courage, for one whose views of economic policy were as conservative as Holmes's were, to face the implications of state power under the Constitution. And it is interesting that even here Holmes refuses the role of innovator, and professes to give only "an interpretation of what has taken place in the past." The judge as economist is excluded, to make way for the judge as historian.

While largely technical in subject matter, the decision is also notable for its manner. There is in it a combination of candor about the tentative nature of the judicial process ("the analysis of the police power, whether correct or not") with a clipped and magisterial quality in brushing aside pedantic and hypothetical questions. ("The last is a futile question, and we will answer the others when they arise.") This combination of a hard factualness with the grand manner makes the great judicial tradition as Holmes practised it.

The decision has been criticized for the breadth of its definition of the police power,[2] and for not distinguishing clearly between questions of fact and questions of law. But while many would agree that Holmes's language "opens a Pandora box from which may proceed dangerous economic

---

[1] *Mr. Justice Holmes*, edited by Felix Frankfurter, 144–145 (1931).

[2] George W. Wickersham, "The Police Power, a Product of the Rule of Reason," 27 HLR 297, 312 (1914).

heresies, which demagogues and political quacks will seek to make effective in legislation," they will also agree that *"logically there seems to be no escape" from Holmes's reasoning.*[3] *Time has upheld its wisdom. The decision served as a precedent for state acts in the field of social legislation, particularly workmen's compensation acts, providing a pooled fund from enforced contributions without equalizing burdens or benefits.*[4] *And a similar technique was used in the Glass-Steagall Banking Act of 1933, in setting up the Federal Deposit Insurance Corporation.*

Holmes, J., for the Court:

This is a proceeding against the Governor of the State of Oklahoma and other officials who constitute the State Banking Board, to prevent them from levying and collecting an assessment from the plaintiff under an Act approved December 17, 1907. This Act creates the Board and directs it to levy upon every bank existing under the laws of the State an assessment of one percent of the bank's average daily deposits, with certain deductions, for the purpose of creating a Depositors' Guaranty Fund. There are provisos for keeping up the fund, and by an Act passed March 11, 1909, since the suit was begun, the assessment is to be five percent. The purpose of the fund is shown by its name. It is to secure the full repayment of deposits. When a bank becomes insolvent and goes into the hands of the Bank Commissioner, if its cash immediately available is not enough to pay depositors in full, the Banking Board is to draw from the Depositors' Guaranty Fund (and from additional assessments if required) the amount needed to make up the deficiency. A lien is reserved upon the assets of the failing bank to make good the sum thus taken from the fund. The plaintiff says that it is solvent and does not want the help of the Guaranty Fund, and that it cannot be called upon to contribute toward securing or paying the depositors in other banks consistently with Article I, § 10, and the Fourteenth Amendment of the Constitution of the United States. The petition was dismissed on demurrer by the Supreme Court of the State, 22 Oklahoma, 48.

[3] Both quotations are from Edgar Watkins, "The Law and the Profits," 2 *Selected Essays*, 459, 464.
[4] Ray A. Brown, "Police Power — Legislation for Health and Personal Safety," 42 HLR 866, 895 (1929).

The reference to Article I, § 10, does not strengthen the plaintiff's bill. The only contract that it relies upon is its charter. That is subject to alteration or repeal, as usual, so that the obligation hardly could be said to be impaired by the Act of 1907 before us, unless that statute deprives the plaintiff of liberty or property without due process of law. See *Sherman* v. *Smith*, 1 Black, 587. Whether it does so or not is the only question in the case.

In answering that question we must be cautious about pressing the broad words of the Fourteenth Amendment to a drily logical extreme. Many laws which it would be vain to ask the Court to overthrow could be shown, easily enough, to transgress a scholastic interpretation of one or another of the great guaranties in the Bill of Rights. They more or less limit the liberty of the individual or they diminish property to a certain extent. We have few scientifically certain criteria of legislation, and as it often is difficult to mark the line where what is called the police power of the States is limited by the Constitution of the United States, judges should be slow to read into the latter a *nolumus mutare* as against the law-making power.

The substance of the plaintiff's argument is that the assessment takes private property for private use without compensation. And while we should assume that the plaintiff would retain a reversionary interest in its contribution to the fund so as to be entitled to a return of what remained of it if the purpose were given up (see *Receiver of Danby Bank* v. *State Treasurer*, 39 Vermont, 92, 98), still there is no denying that by this law a portion of its property might be taken without return to pay debts of a failing rival in business. Nevertheless, notwithstanding the logical form of the objection, there are more powerful considerations on the other side. In the first place it is established by a series of cases that an ulterior public advantage may justify a comparatively insignificant taking of private property for what, in its immediate purpose, is a private use. *Clark* v. *Nash*, 198 U. S. 361. *Strickley* v. *Highland Boy Mining Co.*, 200 U. S. 527, 531. *Offield* v. *New York, New Haven & Hartford R. R. Co.*, 203 U. S. 372. *Bacon* v. *Walker*, 204 U. S. 311, 315. And in the next, it would seem that there may be other cases beside the every day one of taxation, in which the share of each party in the benefit of a scheme of mutual protection is sufficient compensation for a correlative burden that it is compelled to assume. See *Ohio Oil Co.* v. *Indiana*, 177 U. S. 190. At

AMERICA AS A GOING CONCERN

least, if we have a case within the reasonable exercise of the police power as above explained, no more need be said.

It may be said in a general way that the police power extends to all the great public needs, *Canfield v. U. S.*, 167 U. S. 518. It may be put forth in aid of what is sanctioned by usage, or held by the prevailing morality or strong and preponderant opinion to be greatly and immediately necessary to the public welfare. Among matters of that sort probably few would doubt that both usage and preponderant opinion give their sanction to enforcing the primary conditions of successful commerce. One of those conditions at the present time is the possibility of payment by checks drawn against bank deposits, to such an extent do checks replace currency in daily business. If then the legislature of the State thinks that the public welfare requires the measure under consideration, analogy and principle are in favor of the power to enact it. Even the primary object of the required assessment is not a private benefit as it was in the cases above cited of a ditch for irrigation or a railway to a mine, but it is to make the currency of checks secure, and by the same stroke to make safe the almost compulsory resort of depositors to banks as the only available means of keeping money on hand. The priority of claim given to depositors is incidental to the same object and is justified in the same way. The power to restrict liberty fixing a minimum of capital required of those who would engage in banking is not denied. The power to restrict investments to securities regarded as relatively safe seems equally plain. It has been held, we do not doubt rightly, that inspections may be required and the cost thrown on the bank. See *Charlotte, Columbia & Augusta R. R. Co. v. Gibbes,* 142 U. S. 386. The power to compel, beforehand, co-operation, and thus, it is believed, to make a failure unlikely and a general panic almost impossible, must be recognized, if government is to do its proper work, unless we can say that the means have no reasonable relation to the end. *Gundling v. U. S.,* 177 U. S. 183, 188. So far is that from being the case that the device is a familiar one. It was adopted by some States the better part of a century ago, and seems never to have been questioned until now. . . . Recent cases going not less far are *Lemieux v. Young,* 211 U. S. 489, 496. *Kidd, Dater & Price Co. v. Musselman Grocer Co.,* 217 U. S. 461.

It is asked whether the State could require all corporations or all grocers to help to guarantee each other's solvency, and where we are going to draw the line. But the last is a futile question, and we will answer the others when they arise. With regard to the police power, as elsewhere in the law, lines are pricked out by the gradual approach and contact of decisions on the opposing sides. *Hudson County Water Co.* v. *McCarter,* 209 U. S. 349, 355. It will serve as a datum on this side, that in our opinion the statute before us is well within the State's constitutional power, while the use of the public credit on a large scale to help individuals in business has been held to be beyond the line. *Loan Association* v. *Topeka,* 20 Wall. 655. *Lowell* v. *Boston,* 111 Mass. 454.

The question that we have decided is not much helped by propounding the further one, whether the right to engage in banking is or can be made a franchise. But as the latter question has some bearing on the former and as it will have to be considered in the following cases, if not here, we will dispose of it now. It is not answered by citing authorities for the existence of the right at common law. There are many things that a man might do at common law that the States may forbid. He might embezzle until a statute cut down his liberty. We cannot say that the public interests to which we have averted, and others, are not sufficient to warrant the State in taking the whole business of banking under its control. On the contrary we are of opinion that it may go on from regulation to prohibition except upon such conditions as it may prescribe. In short, when the Oklahoma legislature declares by implication that free banking is a public danger, and that incorporation, inspection and the above-described co-operation are necessary safeguards, this Court certainly cannot say that it is wrong. . . . [*Here a series of state court decisions are cited.*] Some further details might be mentioned, but we deem them unnecessary. Of course objections under the State constitution are not open here.

Judgment affirmed.

Leave to file application for rehearing is asked in this case. We see no reason to grant it, but, as the judgment delivered seems to have conveyed a wrong impression of the opinion of the Court in some details, we add a few words to what was said when the case was decided. We fully understand the practical importance of the question and the very powerful argument that can be made against the wisdom of the legislation, but on that point we have nothing to say, as it is not our concern. *Clark* v. *Nash,* 198 U. S. 361,

Strickley v. *Highland Boy Mining Co.,* 200 U. S. 527, etc., were cited to establish, not that property might be taken for a private use, but that among the public uses for which it might be taken were some which, if looked at only in their immediate aspect, according to the proximate effect of the taking, might seem to be private. This case, in our opinion, is of that sort. The analysis of the police power, whether correct or not, was intended to indicate an interpretation of what has taken place in the past, not to give a new or wider scope to the power. The propositions with regard to it, however, in any form, are rather in the nature of preliminaries. For in this case there is no out and out unconditional taking at all. The payment can be avoided by going out of the banking business, and is required only as a condition for keeping on, from corporations created by the State. We have given what we deem sufficient reasons for holding that such a condition may be imposed.

Leave to file petition denied.

WHERE POLICE POWER ENDS
Pennsylvania Coal Co. v. *Mahon*
260 U. S. 393 (1922)

Holmes fought so often on the side of construing the Fourteenth Amendment narrowly and the state police power broadly that he seemed to many to lay himself open to the charge that he gave the legislatures carte blanche *and drew no constitutional bounds around public policy. The present opinion, in which he calls a halt to the police power and insists that property rights are being violated, points in the other direction. He wrote it as the opinion of the Court. As such, he had some trouble with it in the conference with his colleagues when the preliminary draft was discussed. Everyone, he wrote Pollock, seemed to have misgivings about it. But he believed it "to be a compact statement of the real facts of the law and as such sure to rouse opposition for want of the customary soft phrases. But as I couldn't get at what the trouble was, or rather troubles were, for different men had different difficulties, I told them I would put my head under my wing and go to sleep until somebody wrote something."* [1] *He must have been*

[1] H-P, II: 106 (Nov. 26, 1922).

pleased with his finished product, for he writes later to Pollock, enclosing the opinion, so that he "may judge whether there is any falling off"; and adds, "it was unpopular in Pennsylvania, of course." [2]

It is unusual to have Holmes saying, as he does in this case, "We are in danger of forgetting that a strong public desire to improve the public condition is not enough to warrant achieving the desire by a shorter cut than the constitutional way of paying for the change" — particularly since the Supreme Court majority with which Holmes was in this case aligned was scarcely in danger of forgetting it. Brandeis wrote an earnest dissent arguing among other things that where a property right was restricted to protect the public safety it was not taking property without compensation; and that the Supreme Court should yield to the better knowledge of Pennsylvania conditions that the state court possessed.[3] It is a dissent worth reading, as is also Holmes's reaction to it in a letter to Pollock.[4]

Holmes, J., for the Court:

This is a bill in equity brought by the defendants in error to prevent the Pennsylvania Coal Company from mining under their property in such way as to remove the supports and cause a subsidence of the surface and of their house. The bill sets out a deed executed by the Coal Company in 1878, under which the plaintiffs claim. The deed conveys the surface, but in express terms reserves the right to remove all the coal under the same, and the grantee takes the premises with the risk, and waives all claims for damages that may arise from mining out the coal. But the plaintiffs say that whatever may have been the Coal Company's rights, they were taken away by an Act of Pennsylvania, approved May 27, 1921, commonly

---

[2] H–P, II: 109 (Dec. 31, 1922).

[3] At one point the Brandeis dissent sounds merely rhetorical — when he says that "the property so restricted remains in the possession of its owner," which is a doubtful consolation, as Professor Powell remarks, when you cannot mine your coal and yet have to pay taxes on it. Otherwise the dissent is persuasive today. The differences between Holmes and Brandeis turned on the varying estimates of the public danger involved and the property damage suffered.

[4] H–P, II:108–9. Pollock was on Holmes's side writing to him "that if Brandeis' dissent were right, the Fourteenth Amendment would be eviscerated: and your opinion exposes the fallacy of stretching police power to that extent in a very convincing fashion." H–P, II:111.

known there as the Kohler Act. The Court of Common Pleas found that if not restrained the defendant would cause the damage to prevent which the bill was brought, but denied an injunction, holding that the statute if applied to this case would be unconstitutional. On appeal the Supreme Court of the State agreed that the defendant had contract and property rights protected by the Constitution of the United States, but held that the statute was a legitimate exercise of the police power and directed a decree for the plaintiffs. A writ of error was granted bringing the case to this Court.

The statute forbids the mining of anthracite coal in such way as to cause the subsidence of, among other things, any structure used as a human habitation, with certain exceptions, including among them land where the surface is owned by the owner of the underlying coal and is distant more than 150 feet from any improved property belonging to any other person. As applied to this case the statute is admitted to destroy previously existing rights of property and contract. The question is whether the police power can be stretched so far.

Government hardly could go on if to some extent values incident to property could not be diminished without paying for every such change in the general law. As long recognized, some values are enjoyed under an implied limitation and must yield to the police power. But obviously the implied limitation must have its limits, or the contract and due process clauses are gone. One fact for consideration in determining such limits is the extent of the diminution. When it reaches a certain magnitude, in most if not in all cases there must be an exercise of eminent domain and compensation to sustain the act. So the question depends upon the particular facts. The greatest weight is given to the judgment of the legislature, but it always is open to interested parties to contend that the legislature has gone beyond its constitutional power.

This is the case of a single private house. No doubt there is a public interest even in this, as there is in every purchase and sale and in all that happens within the commonwealth. Some existing rights may be modified even in such a case. *Rideout* v. *Knox,* 148 Mass. 368. But usually in ordinary private affairs the public interest does not warrant much of this kind of interference. A source of damage to such a house is not a public nuisance even if similar damage is inflicted on others in different places. The damage is not common or public. . . . The extent of the public interest is shown by the statute to be limited, since the statute ordinarily does not apply to land when the surface is owned by the owner of the coal. Furthermore, it is not justified as a protection of personal safety. That could be provided for by notice. Indeed the very foundation of this bill is that the defendant gave timely notice of its intent to mine under the house. On the other hand the extent of the taking is great. It purports to abolish what is recognized in Pennsylvania as an estate in land — a very valuable estate — and what is declared by the court below to be a contract hitherto binding the plaintiffs. If we were called upon to deal with the plaintiff's position alone, we should think it clear that the statute does not disclose a public interest sufficient to warrant so extensive a destruction of the defendant's constitutionally protected rights.

But the case has been treated as one in which the general validity of the act should be discussed. The Attorney General of the State, the City of Scranton, and the representatives of other extensive interests were allowed to take part in the argument below and have submitted their contentions here. It seems, therefore, to be our duty to go farther in the statement of our opinion, in order that it may be known at once, and that further suits should not be brought in vain.

It is our opinion that the act cannot be sustained as an exercise of the police power, so far as it affects the mining of coal under streets or cities in places where the right to mine such coal has been reserved. As said in a Pennsylvania case, "For practical purposes, the right to coal consists in the right to mine it." *Com. ex. rel. Keator* v. *Clearview Coal Co.,* 256 Pa. 328, 331. What makes the right to mine coal valuable is that it can be exercised with profit. To make it commercially impracticable to mine certain coal has very nearly the same effect for constitutional purposes as appropriating or destroying it. This we think that we are warranted in assuming that the statute does.

It is true that in *Plymouth Coal Co.* v. *Pennsylvania,* 232 U. S. 531, it was held competent for the legislature to require a pillar of coal to be left along the line of adjoining property, that, with the pillar on the other side of the line, would be a barrier sufficient for the safety of the employees of either mine in case the other should be abandoned and allowed to fill with water. But that was a requirement for the safety of the employees invited into the mine, and secured an average reciprocity of advantage that has been recognized as a justification of various laws.

The rights of the public in a street purchased or laid out by eminent domain are those that it has paid for. If in any case its representatives have been so short sighted as to acquire only surface rights without the right of support, we see no more authority for supplying the latter without compensation than there was for taking the right of way in the first place and refusing to pay for it because the public wanted it very much. The protection of private property in the 5th Amendment presupposes that it is wanted for public use, but provides that it shall not be taken for such use without compensation. A similar assumption is made in the decisions upon the 14th Amendment. *Hairston* v. *Danville & U. R. Co.*, 208 U. S. 598, 605. When this seemingly absolute protection is found to be qualified by the police power, the natural tendency of human nature is to extend the qualification more and more until at last private property disappears. But that cannot be accomplished in this way under the Constitution of the United States.

The general rule at least is, that while property may be regulated to a certain extent, if regulation goes too far it will be recognized as a taking. It may be doubted how far exceptional cases, like the blowing up of a house to stop a conflagration, go — and if they go beyond the general rule, whether they do not stand as much upon tradition as upon principle. *Bowditch* v. *Boston*, 101 U. S. 16, 25 L ed. 980. In general it is not plain that a man's misfortunes or necessities will justify his shifting the damages to his neighbor's shoulders. *Spade* v. *Lynn & B. R. Co.*, 172 Mass. 488, 489. We are in danger of forgetting that a strong public desire to improve the public condition is not enough to warrant achieving the desire by a shorter cut than the constitutional way of paying for the change. As we have already said, this is a question of degree — and therefore cannot be disposed of by general propositions. But we regard this as going beyond any of the cases decided by this Court. The late decisions upon laws dealing with the congestion of Washington and New York, caused by the war, dealt with laws intended to meet a temporary emergency and providing for compensation determined to be reasonable by an impartial board. They went to the verge of the law but fell far short of the present act. *Block* v. *Hirsch,* 256

U. S. 135, *Marcus Brown Holding Co.* v. *Feldman*, 256 U. S. 170, *Edgar A. Levy Leasing Co.* v. *Siegel*, 258 U. S. 242.

We assume, of course, that the statute was passed upon the conviction that an exigency existed that would warrant it, and we assume that an exigency exists that would warrant the exercise of eminent domain. But the question at bottom is upon whom the loss of the changes desired should fall. So far as private persons or communities have seen fit to take the risk of acquiring only surface rights, we cannot see that the fact that their risk has become a danger warrants the giving to them greater rights than they bought.

Decree reversed.

DOCTRINAL FICTIONS AND STATE POWER

Tyson Bros. v. *Banton*
273 U. S. 418, 445 (1927)

All law is in a sense a set of fictions which we have to act out as the price of civilization. There are many hints in Holmes to indicate that he saw this. But he saw also that law is power, and he urged strongly that judges should not abuse that power by converting their doctrinal fictions into irrefragable facts. He warned them against obstructing the sweep of legislative policy and under the guise of legal doctrines substituting their own notions of policy. Four years before the Tyson case, in his Adkins dissent in 1923,[1] Holmes made a frontal assault on the judicial doctrine of "liberty of contract." In the present case he delivers a similar assault on the doctrine of "public interest" as delimiting with precision the instances where state regulation of prices will be allowed. He sees both doctrines as a form of apologetic for something that needs no apology — the recognition that power to regulate life does inhere in state sovereignty where it is not expressly forbidden by the Constitution.

In pursuing this theme Holmes's opinion presents as forthright a statement of state legislative power as is to be found in the judicial literature of American constitutional law: "Subject

[1] See above, p. 172.

to compensation when compensation is due, the legislature may forbid or restrict any business when it has a sufficient force of public opinion behind it." More clearly than anywhere else Holmes presents here his conviction that law, including constitutional law, is crystallized public opinion. He is seeking to get at the dynamic of legal history. He is not indulging in liberal platitudes about the need for law to embody public opinion, but is saying as an anthropologist that in every society there is actually some energy behind law, and in ours — despite all the efforts of his brethren on the Court — it is the felt needs of the people.

In the present case what was involved was a New York law setting a fifty-cent limit for the mark-up of theater ticket prices by the agencies. The majority, speaking through Justice Sutherland, held the law unconstitutional under the due process clause of the Fourteenth Amendment, on the ground that it was a taking of property without due process, and that the industry was not clothed with a "public interest" and therefore could not be excepted from the prohibition. There were dissenting opinions by Justices Holmes, Stone, and Sanford; Holmes joined in that of Stone, and Brandeis joined in that of both Holmes and Stone.

Holmes's opinion in the present case is at once weighty in substance and light in tone. In a famous phrase Holmes disposes of fifty years of the doctrine of public interest (since Munn v. Illinois) by calling the doctrine "a fiction intended to beautify what is disagreeable to the sufferers." And he sees this resort to fictions as part of the judges' unwillingness "to grant power" and "to recognize it when it exists." He speaks of the regulation of lotteries and wine as instances analogous to control of the theater, in which states have actually exercised power. And he adds as an afterthought the consideration that the theater is as important as any other phase of our life, on the ground that "the superfluous is the necessary." He might also have added that by economic theory and practice today every price is affected with a public interest, since it is part of an interrelated price structure.

There is a brilliant treatment by Walton Hamilton [2] of the way in which a chance phrase, "affected with a public interest,"

[2] "Affectation with a Public Interest," 39 YLJ 1089 (1930).

set down in a treatise on "the Ports of the Sea" by Sir Matthew Hale, "Britain's Chief Justice . . . of a quarter-millennium ago," has set the rule which we use as one of the legal tests for the regulation of our economy.[3] Holmes did as much as any other legal thinker to blast the authority of this dogma.

Holmes, J., dissenting:

We fear to grant power and are unwilling to recognize it when it exists. The states very generally have stripped jury trials of one of their most important characteristics by forbidding judges to advise the jury upon the facts (*Graham v. United States*, 231 U. S. 474, 480), and when legislatures are held to be authorized to do anything considerably affecting public welfare it is covered by apologetic phrases like the police power, or the statement that the business concerned has been dedicated to a public use. The former expression is convenient, to be sure, to conciliate the mind to something that needs explanation: the fact that the constitutional requirement of compensation when property is taken cannot be pressed to its grammatical extreme; that property rights may be taken for public purposes without pay if you do not take too much; that some play must be allowed to the joints if the machine is to work. But police power often is used in a wide sense to cover and, as I said, apologize for the general power of the legislature to make a part of the community uncomfortable by a change.

I do not believe in such apologies. I think the proper course is to recognize that a State legislature can do whatever it sees fit to do unless it is restrained by some express prohibition in the Constitution of the United States or of the State, and that courts should be careful not to extend such prohibitions beyond their obvious meaning by reading into them conceptions of public policy that the particular court may happen to entertain. Coming down to the case before us I think, as I intimated in *Adkins* v. *Children's Hospital*, that the notion that a business is clothed with a public interest and

[3] The doctrine came into American law chiefly through Chief Justice Waite's opinion in *Munn* v. *Illinois* in 1876, but Waite had no inkling of the uses to which it would later be put. See the discussion of Waite in Frankfurter, *The Commerce Clause under Marshall, Taney, and Waite* (1937) 83–91. Holmes was probably right in his dismissal of the doctrine, given its later history. But I tend to agree with a recent writer that Chief Justice Waite did have in mind something both valid and profound, but that later decisions distorted it. See Boudin, *Government by Judiciary* (1932) II:388–392.

has been devoted to the public use is little more than a fiction intended to beautify what is disagreeable to the sufferers. The truth seems to me to be that, subject to compensation when compensation is due, the legislature may forbid or restrict any business when it has a sufficient force of public opinion behind it. Lotteries were thought useful adjuncts of the State a century or so ago; now they are believed to be immoral and they have been stopped. Wine has been thought good for man from the time of the Apostles until recent years. But when public opinion changed it did not need the Eighteenth Amendment, notwithstanding the Fourteenth, to enable a State to say that the business should end. *Mugler* v. *Kansas,* 123 U. S. 623. What has happened to lotteries and wine might happen to theaters in some moral storm of the future, not because theaters were devoted to a public use, but because people had come to think that way.

But if we are to yield to fashionable conventions, it seems to me that theaters are as much devoted to public use as anything well can be. We have not that respect for art that is one of the glories of France. But to many people the superfluous is the necessary, and it seems to me that government does not go beyond its sphere in attempting to make life livable for them. I am far from saying that I think this particular law a wise and rational provision. That is not my affair. If the people of the State of New York speaking by the authorized voice say that they want it, I see nothing in the Constitution of the United States to prevent their having their will.

"PURE USURPATION AND SUBTLE FALLACY"

Black and White Taxicab Co. v. Brown and Yellow Taxicab Co.
276 U. S. 518, 532 (1928)

Not the least of Holmes's achievements as a judge was the part he played in the overthrow of the doctrine of Swift v. Tyson, *established by Justice Story's decision in 1842. That case*[1] *was the beginning of one of the most dramatic struggles*

---

[1] 16 Peters 1 (1842). Justice Robert H. Jackson has told the story in his article, "The Rise and Fall of *Swift* v. *Tyson:* a Dramatic Episode," in the *Am. Bar Assn. Journal,* Vol. 24 (Aug. 1938) 609; he has a shorter account in his *Struggle for Judicial Supremacy* (1941) 272–283.

in American legal history. Holmes had a major hand in the struggle, although he did not live to witness its ending.

The Constitution gave the federal courts jurisdiction over suits between citizens of different states. But the courts were faced with the problem of what law they would apply. In Swift v. Tyson *Justice Story held that on matters of commercial law the decisions of the state courts were not binding on the federal courts, and in the absence of statute the latter could use their own judgment in interpreting the rules of the common law that were to be applied. The result was the building up of what has sometimes been called a "federal common law" used by the federal courts. But the result was also a conflict between decisions on non-statutory matters by the state courts and decisions by the federal courts on the same matters and often in the same states. As Justice Jackson puts it, "the independence of the federal courts created conflict in the name of uniformity." With the rise of the powerful corporations the problem took on an increased economic meaning. As Professor (now Justice) Frankfurter once emphasized, a corporation chartered in a state other than where it was sued could on the ground of diversity of citizenship remove cases to the federal courts where the expenses of trial were more onerous or where the "federal common law" doctrine was more favorable.*[2] *And there was an implication also for political power: in matters like insurance, where the Court denied Congress the right to legislate, it was itself legislating by building up a body of federal common law.*

Holmes made his first attack on the doctrine of Swift v. Tyson *in a dissenting opinion in* Kuhn v. Fairmont Coal Co.[3]

I have just dissented in a case [he writes Pollock in 1910] where four judges to three have decided that the United States Courts were not bound to follow a State decision as [to] the effect of a deed of coal in the State. They follow an established though very fishy principle started by Story, that in general commercial law the U. S. Courts would follow their own judgment, *non obstant* decisions of the State as to

[2] Felix Frankfurter, "Distribution of Judicial Power between United States and State Courts," 13 *Cornell Law Quarterly* 499, 525.
[3] 215 U. S. 349, 370 (1910).

transactions within it. . . . They say we must use our independent judgment. I reply, as to what? The State law. But the State judges and the State legislatures make the State law — we don't — and . . . we have had to recognize in other cases the law-making functions of the judges. I think I punched a hole in their bottom, though a very keen man might require a little further analysis than I thought expedient to go into as against old Harlan who simply rolled off the cases.[4]

In that case Holmes spoke bluntly of "the uncertainty and vacillation of the theory upon which Swift v. Tyson *and the later extensions of its doctrine, have proceeded," and ended by urging that the doctrine stop "when we come to a kind of case that, by nature and necessity, is peculiarly local." Justices White and McKenna joined him in his dissent.*

In 1917 Holmes got another chance to press the somewhat analogous question of state jurisdiction as against the admiralty jurisdiction of the Supreme Court. What was involved was a case of death by injury on a gangplank between pier and vessel — Southern Pacific Co. v. Jensen.[5] *New York sought to apply its workmen's compensation law, but Justice McReynolds's opinion held that the federal Courts had admiralty jurisdiction, which excluded the state law. Holmes dissented vigorously. Maritime law, he said, is "a very limited body of customs and ordinances of the sea. . . . I recognize without hesitation that judges do and must legislate, but they can do so only interstitially; they are confined from molar to molecular motions." And he goes on: "From the often repeated statement that there is no common law of the United States . . . the natural inference is that in the silence of Congress this court has believed the very limited law of the sea to be supplemented here as in England by the common law, and that here that means, by the common law of the state. . . . The common law is not a brooding omnipresence in the sky, but the articulate voice of some sovereign or quasi-sovereign that can be identified; although some decisions with which I have disagreed seem to me to have forgotten that fact." And this time Holmes*

[4] H-P, I:157–158 (Jan. 7, 1910).
[5] 244 U. S. 205, 222 (1917).

found joining him three other justices — Pitney, Brandeis, and Clarke — in his dissent.

In 1927 came the Black and White Taxicab *case, with an unusually flagrant instance of the resort to federal diversity jurisdiction to avoid established state law. The Kentucky decisions made exclusive taxi concessions at railroad stations invalid on grounds of public policy. The owners of the Brown and Yellow Taxicab Company had therefore dissolved it as a Kentucky corporation, reincorporated it in Tennessee, and got a new contract for the concession. They sued the Black and White Company to prevent interference with their contract and were upheld by the courts. Justice Butler, speaking for the majority, not only stuck to* Swift v. Tyson *but expanded its application to areas where it had not earlier been applied. Holmes again dissented, this time joined by Justices Brandeis and Stone. Over the course of years he had done something to influence a number of Justices — White, McKenna, Pitney, Clarke, Brandeis, Stone — to his view, but of these only the last-named two were on the Court in 1928.*

There is an interesting exchange of correspondence between Holmes and Pollock on this case, which should be consulted in full in the Holmes–Pollock Letters.[6] *Here there is space for only a few passages. Holmes writes Pollock first how excited he is about the case and explains the prevailing doctrine.*

> I say that this is a pure usurpation founded on a subtle fallacy. They say the question is a question of the common law and that they must decide what the common law is. I hit this once in a dissent by saying that the common law is not a brooding omnipresence in the sky. The question of what is the law of Massachusetts or of Louisiana is a matter that Mass. or La. has a right to determine for itself, and that being so, the voice of the state should be obeyed as well when it speaks through its Supreme Court as it would if it spoke through its Legislature. It all comes from Story in *Swift* v. *Tyson* . . . The decision was unjustifiable in theory but did no great harm when confined to what Story dealt with, but under the influence of Bradley, Harlan, et al. it now has assumed the form that upon questions of the general law the

[6] H–P, II:214–217.

U. S. courts must decide for themselves — of course expressing a desire to follow the state courts if they can. I doubt if I can carry a majority, for the tradition is old, and some ex-circuit judges will not have forgotten the arrogant assumption to which they have been accustomed. This of course strictly between ourselves. . . .

> It would be interesting to seek the sources for Holmes's strong convictions on this score. He was interested in the workings of the federal system, and was probably irritated at the wasteful, confused way in which one of the most delicate problems of federal-state adjustments was handled. There is some evidence that Holmes's view on this matter goes back with consistency to the notes in his edition of Kent's Commentaries *in the early 1870's*. Moreover he had a strong sense of localism and a feeling for organic continuities. There is, for example, an interesting passage in his opinion in Jackman v. Rosenbaum Co.[7] where there was a question of invalidating the rule of a state court on party walls: "The Fourteenth Amendment, itself a historical product, did not destroy history for the states and substitute mechanical compartments of law all exactly alike. . . . In a case involving local history . . . we should be slow to overrule the decision of Courts steeped in the local tradition." Moreover, as one who had himself been a state Supreme Court judge he resented the "arrogant assumption" behind the rule of Swift v. Tyson; and as one who preached and practised judicial tolerance of state action, he was as loath to override a state judiciary as a state legislature. But beyond all these considerations was the fact that Holmes's whole conception of law — as nothing more pretentious than the prediction, or record, of what courts do in fact — made him object to the notion of a transcendent body of common law hanging in the federal air.
>
> Like his best opinions generally, the one below seems therefore to have come from his deepest convictions, and is written with candor and fire. No great humanitarian issues had been involved: but Holmes's whole sense of legal craftsmanship had been invoked. Emerson had once told him in his youth, "When you strike at a king, you must kill him." Swift v. Tyson

[7] 260 U. S. 22 (1922).

had a regal position in American law. *Holmes struck hard. He did not kill it, but the wounds he inflicted weakened it crucially.* Ten years after the Black and White Taxi *case, the Supreme Court, in* Erie R. R. Co. v. Tompkins,[8] *speaking through Justice Brandeis, deliberately and clearly overruled* Swift v. Tyson *and its century of established doctrine.*

This has not, however, entirely resolved the problem. While the federal courts can no longer fall back on the concept of a federal common law, the state courts have by no means a clear guide to their own common law. State judges often profess to respect their own precedents but actually ignore them by the familiar process of differentiating them. Professor Thomas Reed Powell has raised the question whether the federal courts should not, in reviewing state court opinions, analyze the validity of the instances of differentiation and sift the valid from the invalid.

Holmes, J., dissenting:

This is a suit brought by the respondent, the Brown and Yellow Taxicab and Transfer Company, as plaintiff to prevent the petitioner, the Black and White Taxicab and Transfer Company, from interfering with the carrying out of a contract between the plaintiff and the other defendant, the Louisville and Nashville Railroad Company. The plaintiff is a corporation of Tennessee. It had a predecessor of the same name which was a corporation of Kentucky. Knowing that the courts of Kentucky held contracts of the kind in question invalid and that the courts of the United States maintained them as valid, a family that owned the Kentucky corporation procured the incorporation of the plaintiff and caused the other to be dissolved after conveying all the corporate property to the plaintiff. The new Tennessee corporation then proceeded to make with the Louisville and Nashville Railroad Company the contract above-mentioned, by which the railroad company gave to it exclusive privileges in the station grounds, and two months later the Tennessee corporation brought this suit. The Circuit Court of Appeals, affirming a decree of the District Court, granted an injunction and upheld this contract. It expressly recognized that the decisions of the Kentucky courts held that in Kentucky a railroad company could not grant such rights, but this being a question

[8] 304 U. S. 64 (1938).

AMERICA AS A GOING CONCERN

of general law, it went its own way regardless of the Courts of this State. 15 F. (2d) 509.

The Circuit Court of Appeals had so considerable a tradition behind it in deciding as it did, that if I did not regard the case as exceptional I should not feel warranted in presenting my own convictions again after having stated them in *Kuhn v. Fairmont Coal Co.*, 215 U. S. 349. But the question is important and in my opinion the prevailing doctrine has been accepted upon a subtle fallacy that never has been analyzed. If I am right the fallacy has resulted in an unconstitutional assumption of powers by the courts of the United States which no lapse of time or respectable array of opinion should make us hesitate to correct. Therefore I think it proper to state what I think the fallacy is. — The often repeated proposition of this and the lower courts is that the parties are entitled to independent judgment on matters of general law. By that phrase is meant matters that are not governed by any law of the United States or by any statute of the State — matters that in States other than Louisiana are governed in most respects by what is called the common law. It is through this phrase that what I think the fallacy comes in.

Books written about any branch of the common law treat it as a unit, cite cases from this Court, from the Circuit Court of Appeals, from the State Courts, from England and the Colonies of England indiscriminately, and criticize them as right or wrong according to the writer's notions of a single theory. It is very hard to resist the impression that there is one august corpus, to understand which clearly is the only task of any court concerned. If there were such a transcendental body of law outside of any particular State but obligatory within it unless and until changed by statute, the Courts of the United States might be right in using their independent judgment as to what it was. But there is no such body of law. The fallacy and illusion that I think exist consist in supposing that there is this outside thing to be found. Law is a word used with different meanings, but law in the sense in which courts speak of it today does not exist without some definite authority behind it. The common law so far as it is enforced in a State, whether called common law or not, is not the common law generally but the law of that State existing by the authority of that State without regard to what it may have been in England or anywhere else. It may be adopted by statute in place of another system previously in force. *Boquillas Cattle Co. v. Curtis,* 213 U. S. 339, 345. But a general adoption of it does not prevent the State courts from refusing to follow the English decisions upon a matter where local conditions are different. *Wear v. Kansas,* 245 U. S. 154, 156, 157. It may be changed by statute, *Baltimore & Ohio R. R. Co. v. Baugh,* 149 U. S. 368, 378, as is done every day. It may be departed from deliberately by judicial decisions, as with regard to water rights, in States where the common law generally prevails. Louisiana is a living proof that it need not be adopted at all. (I do not know whether under the prevailing doctrine we should regard ourselves as authorities upon the general law of Louisiana superior to those trained in the system.) Whether and how far and in what sense a rule shall be adopted whether called common law or Kentucky law is for the State alone to decide.

If within the limits of the Constitution a State should declare one of the disputed rules of general law by statute there would be no doubt of the duty of all courts to bow, whatever their private opinions might be. *Mason v. United States,* 260 U. S. 545, 555. *Gulf Refining Co. v. United States,* 269 U. S. 125, 137. I see no reason why it should have less effect when it speaks by its other voice. See *Benedict v. Ratner,* 268 U. S. 353, *Sim v. Edenborn,* 242 U.S. 131. If a State Constitution should declare that on all matters of general law the decisions of the highest Court should establish the law until modified by statute or by a later decision of the same Court, I do not perceive how it would be possible for a Court of the United States to refuse to follow what the State Court decided in that domain. But when the constitution of a State establishes a Supreme Court it by implication does make that declaration as clearly as if it had said it in express words, so far as it is not interfered with by the superior power of the United States. The Supreme Court of a State does something more than make a scientific inquiry into a fact outside of and independent of it. It says with an authority that no one denies, except when a citizen of another State is able to invoke an exceptional jurisdiction, that thus the law is and shall be. Whether it be said to make or to declare the law, it deals with the law of the State with equal authority however its function may be described.

Mr. Justice Story in *Swift v. Tyson,* 16 Peters 1, evidently under the tacit domination of the fallacy to which I have referred, devotes some energy to showing that § 34 of the Judiciary Act of 1789, c.20, refers only to statutes when it provides that except as excepted the laws of the several States shall be regarded as rules of decision in trials at common law in Courts of the United States. An examination of the original document by a most competent hand has shown that Mr. Justice Story probably was wrong if anyone is interested to inquire what the framers of the instrument meant. 37 *Harvard Law Review,* 49 at pp. 81–88. But this question is deeper than that; it is a question of the authority by which certain particular acts, here the grant of exclusive privileges in a railroad station, are governed. In my opinion the authority and the only authority is the State, and if that be so, the voice adopted by the State as its own should utter the last word. I should leave *Swift* v. *Tyson* undisturbed, as I indicated in *Kuhn* v. *Fairmont Coal Co.,* but I would not allow it to spread the assumed dominion into new fields.

In view of what I have said it is not necessary for me to give subordinate or narrower reasons for my opinion that the decision below should be reversed. But there are adequate reasons short of what I think should be recognized. This is a question concerning the lawful use of land in Kentucky by a corporation chartered by Kentucky. The policy of Kentucky with regard to it has been settled in Kentucky for more than thirty-five years. *McConnell* v. *Pedigo,* 92 Ky. 465. (1892.) Even under the rule that I combat, it has been recognized that a settled line of State decisions was conclusive to establish a rule of property or the public policy of the State. *Hartford Fire Insurance Co.* v. *Chicago, Milwaukee & St. Paul Ry. Co.,* 175 U. S. 91, 100. I should have supposed that what arrangements could or could not be made for the use of a piece of land was a purely local question, on which, if on anything, the State should have its own way and the State courts should be taken to declare what the State wills. See especially *Smith Middlings Purifier Co.* v. *McGroarty,* 136 U. S. 237, 241.

THE CASE OF THE POISONED POOL

United Zinc Co. v. *Britt*
258 U. S. 268 (1922)

Holmes's opinion in this case has stirred considerable criticism. The controversy has turned on the question of whether, in pursuit of one of his favorite doctrines of liability, Holmes did not wind up with an unsocial result. The case falls in the category of "attractive nuisance" cases. Two children, aged eight and eleven, died of swimming in a pool of water which had become poisoned with sulphuric acid. The pool was on the defendant's land, and he knew of the state of the pool. Holmes wrote the opinion of the Court, holding the defendant not liable.

There was a dissenting opinion by Justice Clarke, in which Chief Justice Taft and Justice Day joined. The dissent charges Holmes with substituting for the "humane" doctrine of the federal courts the "hard" or "Draconian" doctrine of the Massachusetts courts. Justice Clarke emphasized that it was a hot summer day, that the pool looked clear and attractive, that there was no fence around it and several paths leading to it, and that there was a highway near by. He leaned heavily upon the two leading cases in the field, generally known as the "turntable cases" — the Stout case and the McDonald case,[1] both of which Holmes mentions and seeks to distinguish from the present case. Justice Clarke argued that a doctrine which put the risks upon adult trespassers did not apply here, and that allowance had to be made for the "instincts and habitual conduct of children of tender years."

While Holmes professes in this opinion not to overrule the turntable cases, there can be little question that he modifies the earlier doctrine considerably. The earlier doctrine used as a standard for liability the question whether the children's presence and injury were foreseeable. Holmes insists that this doctrine must be very cautiously applied, and holds that under the present facts there was no implied license or invitation for the children to enter the pool. His decision pleased his friend Pollock, who wrote that it "gave a timely check to the persistent attempts made through a long course of years to deny, in effect, that a child below the age of discretion can in any circumstances be a trespasser."[2] It is difficult, however, not to agree with a law-review comment on the case, that "this substitution

---

[1] For comment on these cases, as also on the present case, see Manley O. Hudson, "The Turntable Cases in the Federal Courts," 36 HLR 826–857 (1923). An earlier survey of these cases by Jeremiah Smith, "Liability of Landowners to Children Entering without Permission," 11 HLR (1898) 349–434, has frequent references to Holmes's earlier article on "Privilege, Malice, and Liability," and on the whole points in the direction that Holmes took.

[2] 44 HLR (1931) 695.

AMERICA AS A GOING CONCERN

of rigidity for flexibility . . . seems a retrogression in the humanization of the law of torts."[3]

"I fired off a decision," Holmes wrote to Pollock about this case, "cutting the turn table cases (children hurt when playing on them) down to somewhat more precise limits. My brother Clarke uttered a larmoyant dissent that seemed to me more sentiment and rhetoric than reasoning, but the C. J. and Day agreed with him. I cannot but suspect, on reasoning of their own." [4] Holmes shows here the characteristic detachment from "humanitarian" considerations on which he prided himself. One need not quarrel with him on that score. Nevertheless he is open to two serious criticisms quite apart from the question of humanitarianism. He himself often stated that in borderline cases under the common law the function of the judge was to make articulate the social values on which his decision turned. In this case Holmes leaned toward the protection of the property owner as a social value, rather than toward the interest which the community has in protecting the children in their free and natural impulses toward play. The second criticism is that even in technical legal terms Holmes was not right. Although he often protested against the idea of a "general" common law superior to the doctrine held by the Supreme Court of the particular state, he here overturned the ruling of the Kansas courts and substituted for it the common-law ruling associated with the Massachusetts courts.

Holmes, J., for the Court:

This is a suit brought by the respondents against the petitioner to recover for the death of two children, sons of the respondents. The facts that for the purposes of decision we shall assume to have been proved are these. The petitioner owned a tract of about twenty acres in the outskirts of the town of Iola, Kansas. Formerly it had there a plant for the making of sulphuric acid and zinc spelter. In 1910 it tore the buildings down but left a basement and cellar, in which in July, 1916, water was accumulated, clear in appearance but in fact dangerously poisoned by sulphuric acid and zinc sulphate that had come in one way or another from the petitioner's works, as the petitioner knew. The

[3] 36 HLR (1922) 113. This seems today to represent the trend of commentary.
[4] H-P, II:92 (March 29, 1922).

respondents had been travelling, and encamped at some distance from this place. A travelled way passed within 120 or 100 feet of it. On July 27, 1916, the children, who were eight and eleven years old, came upon the petitioner's land, went into the water, were poisoned and died. The petitioner saved the question whether it could be held liable. At the trial the judge instructed the jury that if the water looked clear but in fact was poisonous and thus the children were allured to it the petitioner was liable. The respondents got a verdict and judgment, which was affirmed by the Circuit Court of Appeals. . . .

Union Pacific Ry. Co. v. McDonald, 152 U. S. 262, and kindred cases, were relied upon as leading to the result, and perhaps there is language in that and in *Sioux City and Pacific Ry. Co. v. Stout,* 17 Wall, 657, that might seem to justify it; but the doctrine needs very careful statement not to make an unjust and impracticable requirement. If the children had been adults they would have had no case. They would have been trespassers and the owner of the land would have owed no duty to remove even hidden danger; it would have been entitled to assume that they would obey the law and not trespass. The liability for spring guns and mantraps arises from the fact that the defendant has not rested on that assumption, but on the contrary has expected the trespasser and prepared an injury that is no more justified than if he had held the gun and fired it. . . . Infants have no greater right to go upon other people's land than adults, and the mere fact that they are infants imposes no duty upon the landowners to expect them and to prepare for their safety. On the other hand the duty of one who invites another upon his land not to lead him into a trap is well settled, and while it is very plain that temptation is not invitation, it may be held that knowingly to establish and expose, unfenced, to children of an age when they follow a bait as mechanically as a fish, something that is certain to attract them, has the legal effect of an invitation to them although not to an adult. But the principle if accepted must be very cautiously applied.

In *Railroad Co. v. Stout,* 17 Wall. 657, the well-known case of a boy injured on a turntable, it appeared that children had played there before to the knowledge of employees of the railroad, and, in view of that fact and the situation of the turntable near a road without visible separation, it seems to have been assumed without much discussion that the railroad owed a duty to the boy. Perhaps this was as strong a case as would be likely to occur of maintaining a known temptation, where temptation takes the place of invitation. A license was implied and liability for a danger not manifest to a child was declared in the very similar case of *Cooke* v. *Midland Great Western Ry. of Ireland* [1909], A.C. 229.

In the case at bar it is at least doubtful whether the water could be seen from any place where the children lawfully were and there is no evidence that it was what led them to enter the land. But that is necessary to start the supposed duty. There can be no general duty on the part of a landowner to keep his land safe for children, or even free from hidden dangers, if he has not directly or by implication invited or licensed them to come there. The difficulties in the way of implying a license are adverted to in *Chenery* v. *Fitchburg R.R. Co.*, 160 Mass. 211, 212, but need not be considered here. It does not appear that children were in the habit of going to the place; so that foundation also fails.

Union Pacific Ry. Co. v. *McDonald*, 152 U. S. 262, is less in point. There a boy was burned by falling into burning coal slack close by the side of a path on which he was running homeward from other boys who had frightened him. It hardly appears that he was a trespasser and the path suggests an invitation; at all events boys habitually resorted to the place where he was. Also the defendant was under a statutory duty to fence the place sufficiently to keep out cattle. The decision is very far from establishing that the petitioner is liable for poisoned water not bordering a road, not shown to have been the inducement that led the children to trespass, if in any event the law would deem it sufficient to excuse their going there, and not shown to have been the indirect inducement because known to the children to be frequented by others. It is suggested that the roads across the place were invitations. A road is not an invitation to leave it elsewhere than at its end.

DEATH AT A RAILROAD CROSSING

Baltimore and Ohio Railroad Co. v. *Goodman*
275 U. S. 66 (1927)

Here is another instance, as in the "poison pool" case, in which Holmes has been severely criticized for introducing his own notions of the common law as part of a "general" common law. It is a fairly typical railroad crossing case, bringing up the issue of contributory negligence by the deceased, whose widow was suing the railroad. While many commentators have questioned the actual decision at which Holmes arrived, it is even more striking that the Court should have reviewed the case at all, since it involved no federal right. One can scarcely escape the conclusion that Holmes was seeking to lay down a rule for future cases — a rule which was quite uncompromising in the standard of care which it imposed on the motorist at a railroad crossing, since he had to stop, get out of the car, look around, get back into the car, and drive on. Judge Cuthbert Pound has remarked that this is a burdensome standard to impose on a "reasonable man," [1] *and this is all the more serious as Holmes usually sought to base his general rules not on legal logic but on current experience.*

Another aspect of the case is of interest. Holmes usually hesitated about laying down rigid standards for future conduct, and preferred to let the succession of cases "prick out a line." Yet here, although he admits that questions of due care should generally be left to the jury, he insists that "we are dealing with a standard of conduct, and when it is clear it should be laid down once for all by the courts." He was following here some earlier notions expressed in his book, The Common Law,[2] *that mixed questions of law and fact could be formulated as definite standards. Nevertheless here too the weight of legal opinion regards this as unduly inflexible.*

The decision aroused considerable discussion not only in the legal press but in the lay newspapers as well,[3] *and a debate ensued as to what the effects would be both on crossing accidents and on motoring. Holmes, of course, cared nothing for such discussion. But if he thought that his decision would have any appreciable effect on the rulings of either the federal or state courts, he was doomed to disappointment. The states refused to follow the new federal rule, either flatly or by distinguishing it. Thus the reason usually advanced for the creation of a "gen-*

---

[1] Book Review 14 HLR (1931) 1303–1304.
[2] *The Common Law* (1881), 122–125.
[3] See for example, the New York *Times,* Nov. 1, 1927, p. 1, p. 26, and Feb. 25, 1928, p. 8.

eral" common law by the federal courts — that it makes for uniformity throughout the nation — did not hold here.[4]

Amidst the chorus of criticism, there was at least one voice of praise — that of Pollock. "The man," he wrote Holmes, "ran into the train at least as much as the train ran into the man."[5] And he commented later that the decision would "remind every man who drives or walks over a grade crossing that he must stop for the train, not the train for him. . . . Why this decision surprised anyone I cannot understand."[6] The surprise, of course, flows not so much from Holmes's actual decision as from his enunciation of a rigid rule where it was not necessary, and especially from his willingness to overrule the state court and convert into federal common law a social logic so vague that it came close to being a "brooding omnipresence in the sky."

Holmes, J., for the Court:

This is a suit brought by the widow and administratrix of Nathan Goodman against the petitioner for causing his death by running him down at a grade crossing. The defence is that Goodman's own negligence caused the death. At the trial the defendant asked the Court to direct a verdict for it, but the request and others looking to the same direction were refused, and the plaintiff got a verdict and a judgment which was affirmed by the Circuit Court of Appeals.

Goodman was driving an automobile truck in an easterly direction and was killed by a train running southwesterly across the road at a rate of not less than 60 miles an hour. The line was straight but it is said by the respondent that Goodman "had no practical view" beyond a section house 243 feet north of the crossing until he was about 20 feet from the first rail, or, as the respondent argues, 12 feet from danger, and that then the engine was still obscured by the section house. He had been driving at the rate of 10 or 12 miles an hour, but had cut down his rate to 5 or 6 miles at about 40 feet from the crossing. It is thought that there was an

---

[4] For an excellent review of the state decisions and legislation after Holmes's opinion, see the Note in 43 HLR (1930) 126–132. This is sharply critical of Holmes's whole opinion and associates it with the rule in *Swift* v. *Tyson,* a suggestion which probably horrified him if he read it.

[5] H–P, II:211 (Jan. 12, 1928).

[6] 44 HLR (1931) 695.

emergency in which, so far as appears, Goodman did all that he could.

We do not go into further details as to Goodman's precise situation, beyond mentioning that it was daylight and that he was familiar with the crossing, for it appears to us plain that nothing is suggested by the evidence to relieve Goodman from responsibility for his own death. When a man goes upon a railroad track he knows that he goes to a place where he will be killed if a train comes upon him before he is clear of the track. He knows that he must stop for the train not the train stop for him. In such circumstances it seems to us that if a driver cannot be sure otherwise whether a train is dangerously near he must stop and get out of his vehicle, although obviously he will not often be required to do more than to stop and look. It seems to us that if he relies upon not hearing the train or any signal and takes no further precaution he does so at his own risk. If at the last moment Goodman found himself in an emergency it was his own fault that he did not reduce his speed earlier or come to a stop. It is true as said in *Flannelly* v. *Delaware and Hudson Co.* 225 U. S. 597, 603, that the question of due care very generally is left to the jury. But we are dealing with a standard of conduct, and when the standard is clear it should be laid down once for all by the Courts. See *Southern Pacific Co.* v. *Berkshire*, 254 U. S. 415, 417 419.

CIRCUS LITHOGRAPHS AND ORIGINALITY

Bleistein v. *Donaldson Lithographing Company*
188 U. S. 239 (1903)

Holmes's opinions on copyright are among his most interesting, even though not of world-shaking importance. It was probably because, among the various types of property that it was the function of the law to protect, he cared most deeply about the property in which a man had most directly fused his effort and creativeness. Nevertheless, he understood also the tyranny over society that a copyright might represent.

The Bleistein *case is of interest chiefly because it gave Holmes a chance to write on a subject very close to his heart — lithography. As a student at Harvard he had written a prize* essay on *Albrecht Dürer;* and from *1917* on there are frequent references in his letters to his habit of picking up etchings cheaply whenever he could: for Holmes was a collector of sorts. The relish with which in the Bleistein case he refers to the etchings of Rembrandt and Goya and quotes from Ruskin on drawing is an expression of his lifelong interest.

But the decision goes beyond that personal absorption. The ground for overruling the lower court in the present case is that it had construed originality in art too narrowly.[1] From Holmes's viewpoint, this made the court vulnerable on two scores: it had arrogated to itself the function of judgment in a field in which it was not competent; and it had denied artistic merit to cheap circus lithographs merely because they were intended for mass consumption. Along with his often expressed sense of the loneliness of the task of the creative worker, Holmes did not make the mistake of thinking of art only as related to an elite. Thus in this decision he was able to fuse his principles of judicial tolerance and self-restraint with his conception of the nature and sources of art.

Holmes, J., for the Court:

This case comes here from the United States circuit court of appeals for the sixth circuit by writ of error . . . It is an action brought by the plaintiffs in error to recover the penalties prescribed for infringements of copyrights. . . . The alleged infringements consisted in the copying in reduced form of three chromolithographs prepared by employees of the plaintiffs for advertisements of a circus owned by one Wallace. Each of the three contained a portrait of Wallace in the corner, and lettering bearing some slight relation to the scheme of decoration, indicating the subject of the design and the fact that the reality was to be seen at the circus. One of the designs was of an ordinary ballet, one of a number of men and women, described as the Stirk family, performing on bicycles, and one of groups of men and women whitened to represent statues. The circuit court directed a verdict for the defendant on the ground that the chromolithographs were

---

[1] Justice Harlan wrote a dissent upholding the lower court, in which Justice McKenna joined. The purpose of the copyright power — to promote the progress of science and useful arts — did not, to them, "embrace a mere advertisement of a circus."

not within the protection of the copyright law, and this ruling was sustained by the circuit court of appeals. *Courier Lithographing Co. v. Donaldson Lithographing Co.,* 44 C. C. A. 296.

There was evidence warranting the inference that the designs belonged to the plaintiffs, they having been produced by persons employed and paid by the plaintiffs in their establishment to make those very things. . . . It fairly might be found, also, that the copyrights were taken out in the proper names. One of them was taken out in the name of the Courier Lithographing Company. The former was the name of an incorporated joint-stock association formed under the laws of New York (Laws of 1894, chap. 235), and made up of that name. . . .

Finally, there was evidence that the pictures were copyrighted before publication. There may be a question whether the use by the defendant for Wallace was not lawful within the terms of the contract with Wallace, or a more general one as to what rights the plaintiff reserved. But we cannot pass upon these questions as matter of law; they will be for the jury when the case is tried again, and therefore we come at once to the ground of decision in the courts below. That ground was not found in any variance between pleading and proof, such as was put forward in argument, but in the nature and purpose of the designs.

We shall do no more than mention the suggestion that painting and engraving, unless for a mechanical end, are not among the useful arts, the progress of which Congress is empowered by the Constitution to promote. The Constitution does not limit the useful to that which satisfies immediate bodily needs. *Burrow-Giles Lithographing Co. v. Sarony,* 111 U. S. 53. It is obvious also that the plaintiff's case is not affected by the fact, if it be one, that the pictures represent actual groups — visible things. They seem from the testimony to have been composed from hints or description, not from sight of a performance. But even if they had been drawn from the life, that fact would not deprive them of protection. The opposite proposition would mean that a portrait by Velasquez or Whistler was common property because others might try their hand on the same face. Others are free to copy the original. They are not free to copy the copy. . . . The copy is the personal reaction of an individual upon nature. Personality always contains something unique. It expresses its singularity even in handwriting, and a very modest grade of art has in it something irreducible, which is one man's alone. That something he may copyright unless there is a restriction in the words of the act.

If there is a restriction it is not to be found in the limited pretensions of these particular works. The least pretentious picture has more originality in it than directories and the like, which may be copyrighted. Drone, *Copyright,* 153. See *Henderson* v. *Tompkins,* 60 Fed. 758, 765. The amount of training required for humbler efforts than those before us is well indicated by Ruskin. "If any young person after being taught what is, in polite circles, called 'drawing,' will try to copy the commonest piece of real *work,*— suppose a lithograph on the title page of a new opera air, or a woodcut in the cheapest illustrated newspaper of the day,— they will find themselves entirely beaten." *Elements of Drawing,* first ed. 3. There is no reason to doubt all their details, in their design and particular combinations of figures, lines, and colors, are the original work of the plaintiffs' designer. If it be necessary, there is express testimony to that effect. It would be pressing the defendant's right to the verge, if not beyond, to leave the question of originality to the jury upon the evidence in this case, as was done in *Hegeman* v. *Springer,* 49 C. C. A. 86, 110 Fed. 374.

We assume that the construction of the Rev. Stat. pp. 4952 (U. S. Comp. Stat., 1901, p. 3406), allowing a copyright to the "author, designer, or proprietor . . . of any engraving, cut, print . . . (or) chromo" is affected by the act of 1874 (18 Stat. at L. 78, 79, chap. 301, pp. 3, U. S. Comp. Stat.), "in the construction of this act, the words 'engraving,' 'cut,' and 'print' shall be applied only to pictorial illustrations or works connected with the fine arts." We see no reason for taking the words "connected with the fine arts" as qualifying anything except the word "works," but it would not change our decision if we should assume further that they also qualified "pictorial illustrations," as the defendant contends.

These chromolithographs are "pictorial illustrations." The word "illustrations" does not mean that they must illustrate the text of a book, and that the etchings of Rembrandt or Muller's engraving of the Madonna di San Sisto could not be protected today if any man were able to produce them. Again, the act, however construed, does not mean that ordinary posters are not good enough to be considered within its scope. The antithesis to "illustrations or works connected with the fine arts" is not works of little merit or of humbler degree, or illustrations addressed to the less educated classes; it is "prints or labels designed to be used for any other articles of manufacture." Certainly works are not the less connected with the fine arts because their pictorial quality attracts the crowd, and therefore gives them real use, — if use means to increase trade and to help to make money. A picture is none the less a picture and none the less a subject of a copyright, that it is used for an advertisement. And if pictures may be used to advertise soap, or the theatre, or monthly magazines, as they are, they may be used to advertise a circus. Of course, the ballet is as legitimate a subject for illustration as any other. A rule cannot be laid down that would excommunicate the painting of Degas.

Finally, the special adaptation of these pictures to the advertisement of the Wallace shows does not prevent a copyright. That may be a circumstance for the jury to consider in determining the extent of Mr. Wallace's rights, but it is not a bar. Moreover, on the evidence, such prints are used by less pretentious exhibitions when those for whom they were prepared have given them up.

It would be a dangerous undertaking for persons trained only to the law to constitute themselves final judges of the worth of pictorial illustrations, outside of the narrowest and most obvious limits. At one extreme, some works of genius would be sure to miss appreciation. Their very novelty would make them repulsive until the public had learned the new language in which their author spoke. It may be more than doubted, for instance, whether the etchings of Goya or the paintings of Manet would have been sure of protection when seen for the first time. At the other end, copyright would be denied to pictures which appealed to a public less educated than the judge. Yet if they command the interest of any public, they have a commercial value — and the taste of any public is not to be treated with contempt. It is an ultimate fact for the moment, whatever may be our hopes for a change. That these pictures had their worth and their success is sufficiently shown by the desire to reproduce them without regard to the plaintiffs' rights. See *Henderson* v. *Tompkins,* 60 Fed. 758, 765. We are of opinion that there was evidence that the plaintiffs have rights entitled to the protection of the law.

The judgment of the Circuit Court of Appeals is reversed; the judgment of the Circuit Court is also reversed and the cause re-

manded to that court with directions to set aside the verdict and grant a new trial.

"A PAGE ON COPYRIGHT"

White-Smith Music Co. v. Apollo Co.
209 U. S. 1, 18 (1908)

"*A patent,*" Holmes wrote in an early letter to Pollock, "*is property carried to the highest degree of abstraction — a right in rem to exclude, without a physical object or content.*" And he adds, "*I have often thought of writing about a page on copyright. The notion that such a right could exist at common law or be worked out by it seems to me imbecility. It would be intolerable if not limited in time and I think it would be hard to state a basis for the notion which would not lead one far afield. Non obstant the long-winded judgments in the old cases.*" [1]

Holmes had his chance to write his "*page on copyright*" in the White-Smith Music Co. *case. It will be apparent how much his opinion borrows not only in general conception but even in direct language from his casual remarks in the letter to Pollock. Fourteen years intervened between the two, and no doubt Holmes had no copy of his letter, but was dipping again into the deep-flowing stream of his thought. It is a striking illustration of the continuity of that stream.*

The case itself was a difficult one for him. All his impulses were to dissent; yet the facts of the statute and the precedents kept him from doing anything more protestant than writing a separate concurring opinion. The plaintiff company had published as sheet music two compositions called "Little Cotton Dolly" and "Kentucky Babe"; the defendant company sold player-pianos ("pianolas," as they were known at the time) and perforated rolls of music, including the two above. The plaintiff invoked the Copyright Act, but failed in the New York Circuit Court, in the Circuit Court of Appeals, and finally in the Supreme Court. Justice Day, speaking for the majority, held that Congress had not intended by the

[1] H–P, I:53 (June 26, 1894).

Copyright Act to include perforated music rolls. The Act included "any . . . musical composition," to be sure, and gave the creator of it "the sole liberty of printing, reprinting, publishing, completing, copying, executing, finishing and vending the same." But Justice Day held that, broad as the existing law seemed, it could not apply beyond reproductions that could be visible to the eye. The opinion as a whole is static in character. Underlying it is the unexpressed assumption that Congress could not have meant to include perforated music rolls within the copyright protection because when the term "musical composition" was first placed in the copyright statutes in *1831* perforated music was unknown. Although Day admits that the Supreme Court is not bound under the rule of stare decisis by the decisions of lower federal courts until they are reviewed by the Supreme Court, he nevertheless relies on the uniformity with which the lower court decisions had held such perforated rolls outside the Copyright Act, and cites the English precedents to similar effect.

Holmes was evidently impressed by all this, and felt that he could not fly in the face of what seemed the prevailing judicial sentiment. Nevertheless his essay on the legal and social meaning of copyright is a gem of analysis, and its reasoning should have led him to a dissent. The issue was not without some economic importance at the time, since, as Justice Day pointed out, there were in *1902* some *75,000* pianolas in the United States, and in that year from a million to a million-and-a-half perforated rolls were manufactured. To a generation that thinks in terms of ASCAP and the omnipresent juke-box these may be small figures; yet the analogy is not wholly without point.

Holmes, J., concurring:

In view of the facts and opinions in this country and abroad to which my brother Day has called attention I do not feel justified in dissenting from the judgment of the court, but the result is to give to copyright less scope than its rational significance and the ground on which it is granted seem to me to demand. Therefore I desire to add a few words to what he has said.

The notion of property starts, I suppose, from confirmed possession of a tangible object and consists in the right to exclude others from interference with the more or less free doing with it as one wills. But in copyright property has reached a more abstract expression. The right to exclude is not directed to an object in possession or owned, but is *in vacuo,* so to speak. It restrains the spontaneity of men where but for it there would be nothing of any kind to hinder their doing as they saw fit. It is a prohibition of conduct remote from the persons or tangibles of the party having the right. It may be infringed a thousand miles from the owner and without his ever becoming aware of the wrong. It is a right which could not be recognized or endured for more than a limited time, and therefore, I may remark in passing, it is one which hardly can be conceived except as a product of statute, as the authorities now agree.

The ground of this extraordinary right is that the person to whom it is given has invented some new collocation of visible or audible points — of lines, colors, sounds, or words. The restraint is directed against reproducing this collocation, although but for the invention and the statute anyone would be free to combine the contents of the dictionary, the elements of the spectrum, or the notes of the gamut in any way that he had the wit to devise. The restriction is confined to the specific form, to the collocation devised, of course, but one would expect that, if it was to be protected at all, that collocation would be protected according to what was its essence. One would expect the protection to be co-extensive not only with the invention, which, though free to all, only one had the ability to achieve, but with the possibility of reproducing the result which gives to the invention its meaning and worth. A musical composition is a rational collocation of sounds apart from concepts, reduced to a tangible expression from which the collocation can be reproduced either with or without continuous human intervention. On principle anything that mechanically reproduces that collocation of sounds ought to be held a copy, or if the statute is too narrow ought to be made so by a further act, except so far as some extraneous consideration of policy may oppose. What license may be implied from a sale of the copyrighted article is a different and harder question, but I leave it untouched, as license is not relied upon as a ground for the judgment of the court.

MUSIC WITH MEALS

Herbert v. Shanley Co.
242 U. S. 591 (1917)

When Holmes had another chance to protect the copyright of the creators of musical compositions, he did so — undeterred by the fact that the music had somehow gotten mixed up with a meal and was difficult to separate.

Holmes, J., for the Court:

These two cases present the same question: whether the performance of a copyrighted musical composition in a restaurant or hotel without charge for admission to hear it infringes the exclusive right of the owner of the copyright to perform the work publicly for profit. Act of March 4, 1909, chap. 320, § 1 (e), 35 Stat. 1075. The last-numbered case was decided before the other and may be stated first. The plaintiff owns the copyright of a lyric comedy in which is a march called "From Maine to Oregon." It took out a separate copyright for the march and published it separately. The defendant hotel company caused this march to be performed in the dining room of the Vanderbilt Hotel for the entertainment of guests during meal times, in the way now common, by an orchestra employed and paid by the company. It was held by the Circuit Court of Appeals, reversing the decision of the District Court, that this was not a performance for profit within the meaning of the act. 136 C. C. A. 639, 221 Fed. 229.

The other case is similar so far as the present discussion is concerned. The plaintiffs were the composers and owners of a comic opera entitled "Sweethearts," containing a song of the same title as a leading feature in the performance. There is a copyright for the opera and also one for the song which is published and sold separately. This the Shanley Company caused to be sung by professional singers, upon a stage in its restaurant on Broadway, accompanied by an orchestra. The district court, after holding that by the separate publication the plaintiffs' rights were limited to those conferred by the separate copyright, a matter that it will not be necessary to discuss, followed the decision in 136 C. C. A. 639, 221 Fed. 229, as to public performance for profit. 222 Fed. Rep. 344.

The decree was affirmed by the circuit court of appeals. 143 C. C. A. 460, 229 Fed. 340.

If the rights under the copyright are infringed only by a performance where money is taken at the door, they are very imperfectly protected. Performances not different in kind from those of the defendants could be given that might compete with and even destroy the success of the monopoly that the law intends the plaintiffs to have. It is enough to say that there is no need to construe the statute so narrowly. The defendants' performances are not eleemosynary. They are part of a total for which the public pays, and the fact that the price of the whole is attributed to a particular item which those present are expected to order, is not important. It is true that the music is not the sole object, but neither is the food, which probably could be got cheaper elsewhere. The object is a repast in surroundings that to people having limited powers of conversation or disliking the rival noise give a luxurious pleasure not to be had from eating a silent meal. If music did not pay it would be given up. If it pays it pays out of the public's pocket. Whether it pays or not the purpose of employing it is profit and that is enough.

A GREAT CASE AND BAD LAW

Northern Securities Company v. *U. S.*
193 U. S. 197, 400 (1904)

Holmes's liberal eulogists have not said much about the Northern Securities *case, except to note how in it Holmes disappointed President Theodore Roosevelt's expectations. The story* [1] *lights up the intricate relationships in general of Presidential leadership, economic interests, and the judicial process. But it has very specific meaning for the* Northern Securities *affair. When Roosevelt was looking about for a*

[1] I have told the story in the Introduction, pp. xxxi–xxxvi. It can be pieced together from the exchange of letters between President Roosevelt and Henry Cabot Lodge: *Selections from the Correspondence of Theodore Roosevelt and Henry Cabot Lodge,* Vol. I:517–519 (1925). For a comment see Felix Frankfurter, *Law and Politics* (1939) p. 66. See also, for a discussion of the general question, the chapter on "Personality and Judicial Review" in Robert K. Carr, *The Supreme Court and Judicial Review* (1942).

judge to take Gray's place on the Supreme Court, he was already in the midst of his "trust-busting" campaign, and he knew that the Supreme Court's stand would be crucial in the campaign. He thought that four of the Justices — Fuller, White, Peckham and Brewer — were already pretty well set against his trust policies. The next appointee might therefore prove the odd-man holding the balance of power on the Court. The great constitutional issue as he saw it was that of finding in the Constitution power for the national Government adequate to deal with problems of national scope. He was to call this in 1912 the "New Nationalism."

And so Roosevelt asked his friend, Henry Cabot Lodge, whether Holmes could be trusted. What assurances about Holmes's views Roosevelt may have received from Lodge, or on what Lodge may have based these assurances, we cannot know. But when the crucial Northern Securities case came before the Court, involving the holding company that J. P. Morgan and James J. Hill had formed in order to merge the control of the Northern Pacific and Great Northern Railroads, Holmes voted against the national power to dissolve it. In a later letter in 1921 Holmes writes about Roosevelt and the Northern Securities incident, "It broke up our incipient friendship . . . as he looked on my dissent to the Northern Securities case as a political departure (or, I suspect more truly, couldn't forgive anyone who stood in his way)." [2]

The Northern Securities case was the focus of considerable public attention. It was argued before the Supreme Court in December 1903 by distinguished counsel, including Francis Lynde Stetson for the Morgan partners, and Attorney General Knox for the Government. The Court upheld the Government by a five-to-four decision. In his dissent Holmes lined up with the conservative wing of the Court — with Fuller, White, and Peckham. He wrote an opinion much superior to White's dissent, which talked principally of the commerce clause, and a fit counterblast to Harlan's majority opinion. It is, given its basic premises, powerfully reasoned, with logical acuteness and felicity of illustration. The conservative forces might well have rejoiced at the prospect of getting so doughty a legal champion.

[2] See below, p. 445.

How shall we explain Holmes's attitude? There are some things we can only guess at. He had an ascetic conception of the judicial process; and the very fact that he had reason to suspect that the man who had appointed him expected a certain decision from him in the case would have caused him to lean backward.

Moreover, Holmes had formulated a clear philosophy on combinations — a philosophy most strikingly stated in his Massachusetts opinions in Vegelahn v. Guntner *and* Plant v. Woods.[3] *He spoke in the first case of "the ever-increasing might and scope of combinations," which was leading to "the organization of the world," and which he accepted not only as inevitable but not without some relish for its Darwinian implications. He had in those opinions expressly dissociated himself from the trade-union philosophy, and had rested his own views on the common law and these more basic "laws of life." Holmes held a view which in its own fashion cut both ways: a view of the inevitability and desirability of combinations, whether of labor or capital. He was thus partly pushed into his* Northern Securities *opinion by the "hydraulic pressure" of his own past opinions and his deeply ingrained naturalist philosophy. One difference may, however, be noted between his* Vegelahn *opinion and this one. In the earlier case the "law of life" coincided with the trend of the laws of the land and the newly emerging forces of democratic power, to which Holmes was usually sensitive. The "law of life" was, in short, also the law of the democratic will. In the present case the Sherman Act and the democratic will were on the other side.*

Another element that entered into the fashioning of the opinion was Holmes's ingrained sense of the common law. He was immersed in its spirit, he had done his most ambitious single work on it, he felt himself as expert in it as anyone on the Court. When he approached the interpretation of the Sherman Act, it was primarily as a common-law lawyer. And the Sherman Act in its phrasing lent itself to such an approach. It embodied the strongly felt, although imperfectly formulated, purpose of fighting trusts. But it had at the same time to work

---

[3] For these cases see pp. 109–122.

within the medium of the Constitution. It attached itself therefore to the commerce power of Congress. This fact, along with the ideology of the competitive system, led its framers to place the principal emphasis upon "restraint of trade," a concept with a long history at common law and a very precise meaning there.

The men seeking to regulate an economic system at the turn of the twentieth century in America were thus prisoners not only of the language and ideology of the eighteenth-century Constitution, but also of the language of a common law that stretched back into English history for centuries, and that carried with it the freightage of the early attempts to regulate the petty economy of England. It is worth noting that of the two dissenting opinions in the present case, that of Justice White attacks the Government's position from the side of constitutional phraseology, denying that the dissolution of a holding company comes within the commerce power of Congress; and that of Holmes attacks it from the side of the common law, denying that the history of the concept of "restraint of trade" can be made to include combinations that are willingly entered into by the parties and that do not exclude from trade a third party not a partner to the combination. "We must read the words before us," writes Holmes, "as if the question were whether two small exporting grocers shall go to jail." This is crucial. For by becoming the historian of the common law at this point, Holmes goes beyond what any of the Congressional laymen who framed the Sherman Act or the people who accepted it could have known of the meaning and usage of the common-law concept. And he carries over, perhaps unconsciously, the context of the economic system existing at the time the common-law concept was formulated.

What Holmes fails to take account of is that the people wanted trusts prevented, and sought the means most opportunely at hand. Judging from the great popular response that Theodore Roosevelt's campaign against the Northern Securities Company evoked, they did think of this huge holding company as a trust within the meaning of the Sherman Act and did regard it as a menace. Holmes should have known that the "hydraulic pressure" of popular opinion could not in this instance be ignored, on the same grounds that he had always invoked such data to indicate that a legislative position was not manifestly absurd. While the people and the legislators were uncertain whether they would or could restore the competitive system, they were very clear about their fear of monopolies. What they feared was the fact itself of the concentration of vast economic power because of the economic and political consequences of that concentration. Holmes speaks, at the beginning, of "great cases" making "bad law," and of avoiding the influence of "some accident of immediate overwhelming interest." But to call the movement for antitrust reform an "accident" was very like playing with words. It was the major attempt of the day to counteract the forces which men believed to be defeating democracy. While James J. Hill was quoted after the decision as saying that he cared little about its outcome — that now he would merely have to sign two certificates instead of one — the fact is that the antitrust forces were heartened by the majority decision.

Thus Holmes was caught. He did not wish to push his own theory of economic organization, and he must have known that his doctrines of judicial self-restraint were against him here. But he could not accept the theory of Congress, mainly because of his knowledge of the common law and his notions about the inevitability of combination. And so he fell back, a bit rhetorically, on a plea for "reading English intelligently," and on an arduous and ascetic interpretation of the literal common-law meaning of "restraint of trade."

One other consideration against Holmes's view: the effectiveness of the antitrust laws depended upon a view of the scope of the commerce power, which Holmes generally interpreted broadly. In this case he takes the narrower view. "I can see no part of the conduct of life with which on similar principles Congress might not interfere." This is un-Holmesian. Ordinarily his own answer to such a comment would be that there is a pragmatic line that has to be pricked out between what Congress can and cannot do, and that the Court will meet the extreme hypothetical cases as they arise. Holmes here took a position that was against the logic of American development and against the emerging law of the future, which was to be a law built around a national power increasing to deal with problems of national scope. It is worth noting that just a year *later Holmes gave a signal illustration of the broad view of the commerce power in* Swift v. U. S.[4]

Nevertheless one thing may be said in defense of Holmes's consistency. It must be remembered that he was primarily a legal craftsman. Technically the present case turned on the statutory construction of the Sherman Act. In construing a statute the tradition is to give words their common-law meaning, to demand that innovations be made explicit, to assume that Congress can still have recourse to redrafting the statute. Holmes was exacting in construing a statute and latitudinarian in construing powers under the Constitution. He often said that there was nothing in the Constitution that prevented the country from going to hell if it chose to. But once a statute was clearly constitutional and it became a matter of construing it, Holmes put on his most scrupulous spectacles.

Holmes, J., dissenting:

I am unable to agree with the judgment of the majority of the Court, and although I think it useless and undesirable, as a rule, to express dissent, I feel bound to do so in this case and to give my reasons for it.

Great cases like hard cases make bad law. For great cases are called great not by reason of their real importance in shaping the law of the future but because of some accident of immediate overwhelming interest which appeals to the feelings and distorts the judgment. These immediate interests exercise a kind of hydraulic

---

[4] See below, p. 231. One interesting subject of speculation is of the possible relation between Holmes's opinion in this case and Pollock's views. Pollock paid a visit to America in the fall of 1903, and it is not too conjectural to conjecture that he and Holmes had some discussion of the problem of restraint of trade (which was so much in the air then), particularly in relation to the common law they both loved so. When Pollock returned to England, he wrote an article for the *Harvard Law Review* (17, 150 — January, 1904) on the United States Circuit Court decision in the *Northern Securities* case, in which his position as to the meaning of restraint of trade was roughly similar to the one Holmes was to take. The case was argued before the Supreme Court December 14 and 15, 1903. On January 2, 1904, there is a letter from Holmes to Pollock saying, "I will keep my eyes peeled for your remarks on Restraint of Trade," and adding, quite properly, that he could not discuss the case then before this Court. The letter referred to Pollock's article, which appeared in the January issue of the *Review*. On March 14 the case was decided. Pollock diverged from Holmes in one respect: he went beyond the legal form of the holding company agreement to the question of where the actual control lay, and concluded that if the agreement was only a convenient device for a new monopoly unit it was in restraint of trade.

pressure which makes what previously was clear seem doubtful, and before which even well-settled principles of law will bend. What we have to do in this case is to find the meaning of some not very difficult words. We must try, I have tried, to do it with the same freedom of natural and spontaneous interpretation that one would be sure of if the same question arose upon an indictment for a similar act which excited no public attention and was of importance only to a prisoner before the court. Furthermore, while at times judges need for their work the training of economists or statesmen, and must act in view of their foresight of consequences, yet when their task is to interpret and apply the words of a statute, their function is merely academic to begin with — to read English intelligently — and a consideration of consequences comes into play, if at all, only when the meaning of the words used is open to reasonable doubt.

The question to be decided is whether under the Act of July 2, 1890, c. 647, 26 Stat. 209, it is unlawful, at any stage of the process, if several men unite to form a corporation for the purpose of buying more than half the stock of each of two competing interstate railroad companies, if they form the corporation, and the corporation buys the stock. I will suppose further that every step is taken from the beginning with the single intent of ending competition between the companies. I make this addition not because it may not be and is not disputed but because, as I shall try to show, it is totally unimportant under any part of the statute with which we have to deal.

The statute of which we have to find the meaning is a criminal statute. The two sections on which the Government relies both make certain acts crimes. That is their immediate purpose and that is what they say. It is vain to insist that this is not a criminal proceeding. The words cannot be read one way in a suit which is to end in fine and imprisonment and another way in one which seeks an injunction. The construction which is adopted in this case must be adopted in one of the other sort. I am no friend of artificial interpretations because a statute is of one kind rather than another, but all agree that before a statute is to be taken to punish that which always has been lawful it must express its intent in clear words. So I say we must read the words before us as if the question were whether two small exporting grocers shall go to jail.

Again, the statute is of a very sweeping and general character.

It hits "every" contract or combination of the prohibited sort, great or small, and "every" person who shall monopolize or attempt to monopolize, in the sense of the act, "any part" of the trade or commerce among the several States. There is a natural inclination to assume that it was directed against certain great combinations and to read it in that light. It does not say so. On the contrary, it says "every" and "any part." Still less was it directed specially against railroads. There even was a reasonable doubt whether it included railroads until the point was decided by this court.

Finally, the statute must be construed in such a way as not merely to save its constitutionality but, so far as is consistent with a fair interpretation, not to raise grave doubts on that score. I assume for purposes of discussion, although it would be a great and serious step to take, that in some case that seemed to it to need heroic measures Congress might regulate not only commerce but instruments of commerce or contracts the bearing of which upon commerce would be only indirect. But it is clear that the mere fact of an indirect effect upon commerce not shown to be certain and very great would not justify such a law. The point decided in *United States* v. *E. C. Knight Co.,* 156 U. S. 1, 17, was that "the fact that trade or commerce might be indirectly affected was not enough to entitle complainants to a decree." Commerce depends upon population, but Congress could not, on that ground, undertake to regulate marriage and divorce. If the act before us is to be carried out according to what seems to me the logic of the argument for the Government, which I do not believe that it will be, I can see no part of the conduct of life with which on similar principles Congress might not interfere.

This act is construed by the Government to affect the purchasers of shares in two railroad companies because of the effect it may have or, if you like, is certain to have upon the competition of these roads. If such a remote result of the exercise of an ordinary incident of property and personal freedom is enough to make that exercise unlawful, there is hardly any transaction concerning commerce between the States that may not be made a crime by the finding of a jury or a court. The personal ascendancy of one man may be such that it would give to his advice the effect of a command if he owned but a single share in each road. The tendency of his presence in the stockholders' meetings might be certain to prevent competition, and thus his advice, if not his mere existence, become a crime.

I state these general considerations as matters which I should have to take into account before I could agree to affirm the decree appealed from, but I do not need them for my own opinion, because when I read the act I cannot feel sufficient doubt as to the meaning of the words to need to fortify my conclusion by any generalities. Their meaning seems to me plain on their face.

The first section makes "every contract, combination in the form of trust or otherwise, or conspiracy in restraint of trade or commerce among the several States, or with foreign nations," a misdemeanor punishable by fine, imprisonment or both. Much trouble is made by substituting other phrases assumed to be equivalent, which then are reasoned from as if they were in the act. The court below argued as if maintaining competition were the expressed object of the act. The act says nothing about competition. I stick to the exact words used. The words hit two classes of cases, and only two — Contracts in restraint of trade and combinations or conspiracies in restraint of trade, and we have to consider what these respectively are. Contracts in restraint of trade are dealt with and defined by the common law. They are contracts with a stranger to the contractor's business (although in some cases carrying on a similar one) which wholly or partially restrict the freedom of the contractor in carrying on that business as otherwise he would. The objection of the common law to them was primarily on the contractor's own account. The notion of monopoly did not come in unless the contract covered the whole of England. *Mitchel* v. *Reynolds,* 1 P. Wms. 181. Of course this objection did not apply to partnerships or other forms, if there were any, of substituting a community of interest where there had been competition. There was no objection to such combinations merely as in restraint of trade or otherwise unless they amounted to a monopoly. Contracts in restraint of trade, I repeat, were contracts with strangers to the contractor's business, and the trade restrained was the contractor's own.

Combinations or conspiracies in restraint of trade, on the other hand, were combinations to keep strangers to the agreement out of the business. The objection to them was not an objection to their effect upon the parties making the contract, the members of the combination or firm, but an objection to their intended effect upon strangers to the firm and their supposed consequent effect upon the public at large. In other words, they were regarded as contrary to public policy because they monopolized or attempted to monopolize some portion of the trade or commerce of the realm. See *United States* v. *E. C. Knight Co.*, 156 U. S. 1. All that is added to the first section by § 2 is that like penalties are imposed upon every single person who, without combination, monopolizes, or attempts to monopolize, commerce among the States; and that the liability is extended to attempting to monopolize any part of such trade or commerce. It is more important as an aid to the construction of § 1 than it is on its own account. It shows that whatever is criminal when done by way of combination is equally criminal if done by a single man. That I am right in my interpretation of the words of § 1 is shown by the words "in the form of a trust or otherwise." The prohibition was suggested by the trusts, the objection to which, as everyone knows, was not the union of former competitors but the sinister power exercised or supposed to be exercised by the combination in keeping rivals out of the business and ruining those who already were in. It was the ferocious extreme of competition with others, not the cessation of competition among the partners, that was the evil feared. Further proof is to be found in § 7, giving an action to any person injured in his business or property by the forbidden conduct. This cannot refer to the parties of the agreement and plainly means that outsiders who are injured in their attempt to compete with a trust or other similar combination may recover for it. *Montague & Co.* v. *Lowry*, 193 U. S. 38. How effective the section may be or how far it goes is not material to my point. My general summary of the two classes of cases which the act affects is confirmed by the title, "An Act to protect Trade and Commerce against unlawful Restraints and Monopolies."

What I now ask is under which of the foregoing classes this case is supposed to come; and that question must be answered as definitely and precisely as if we were dealing with the indictments which logically ought to follow this decision. The provision of the statute against contracts in restraint of trade has been held to apply to contracts between railroads, otherwise remaining independent, by which they restricted their respective freedom as to rates. This restriction by contract with a stranger to the contractor's business is the ground of the decision in *United States* v. *Joint*

Traffic Association, 171 U. S. 505, following and affirming *United States* v. *Trans-Missouri Freight Association,* 166 U. S. 290. I accept those decisions absolutely, not only as binding upon me but as decisions which I have no desire to criticize or abridge. But the provision has not been decided and, it seems to me, could not be decided without a perversion of plain language to apply to an arrangement by which competition is ended through community of interest — an arrangement which leaves the parties without external restriction. That provision, taken alone, does not require that all existing competitions shall be maintained. It does not look primarily, if at all, to competition. It simply requires that a party's freedom in trade between the States shall not be cut down by contract with a stranger. So far as that phrase goes, it is lawful to abolish competition by any form of union. It would seem to me impossible to say that the words "every contract in restraint of trade is a crime punishable with imprisonment" would send the members of a partnership between, or a consolidation of, two trading corporations to prison — still more impossible to say that it forbade one man or corporation to purchase as much stock as he liked in both. Yet those words would have that effect if this clause of § 1 applies to the defendants here. For it cannot be too carefully remembered that that clause applies to "every" contract of the forbidden kind — a consideration which was the turning point of the *Trans-Missouri Freight Association's* case.

If the statute applies to this case it must be because the parties, or some of them, have formed, or because the Northern Securities Company is, a combination in restraint of trade among the States, or, what comes to the same thing in my opinion, because the defendants or some one of them are monopolizing or attempting to monopolize some part of the commerce between the States. But the mere reading of those words shows that they are used in a limited and accurate sense. According to popular speech, every concern monopolizes whatever business it does, and if that business is trade between two States it monopolizes a part of the trade among the States. Of course the statute does not forbid that. It does not mean that all business must cease. A single railroad down a narrow valley or through a mountain gorge monopolizes all the railroad transportation through that valley or gorge. Indeed, every railroad monopolizes, in a popular sense, the trade of some area. Yet I suppose no one would say that the statute forbids a combination of men into a corporation to build and run such a railroad between the States.

I assume that the Minnesota charter of the Great Northern and the Wisconsin charter of the Northern Pacific both are valid. Suppose that, before either road was built, Minnesota, as part of the system of transportation between the States, had created a railroad company authorized singly to build all the lines in the States now actually built, owned and controlled by either of the two existing companies. I take it that that charter would have been just as good as the present one, even if the statutes which we are considering had been in force. In whatever sense it would have created a monopoly the present charter does. It would have been a large one, but the act of Congress makes no discrimination according to size. Size has nothing to do with the matter. A monopoly of "any part" of commerce among the States is unlawful. The supposed company would have owned lines that might have been competing — probably the present one does. But the act of Congress will not be construed to mean the universal disintegration of society into single men, each at war with all the rest, or even the prevention of all further combinations for a common end.

There is a natural feeling that somehow or other the statute meant to strike at combinations great enough to cause just anxiety on the part of those who love their country more than money, while it viewed such little ones as I have supposed with just indifference. This notion, it may be said, somehow breathes from the pores of the act, although it seems to be contradicted in every way by the words in detail. And it has occurred to me that it might be that when a combination reached a certain size it might have attributed to it more of the character of a monopoly merely by virtue of its size than would be attributed to a smaller one. I am quite clear that it is only in connection with monopolies that size could play any part. But my answer has been indicated already. In the first place, size in the case of railroads is an inevitable incident and if it were an objection under the act, the Great Northern and the Northern Pacific already were too great and encountered the law. In the next place in the case of railroads it is evident that the size of the combination is reached for other ends than those which would make them monopolies. The combinations are not formed for the purpose of excluding others from the field. Finally, even a small railroad will have the same tendency to exclude others from

AMERICA AS A GOING CONCERN

its narrow area that great ones have to exclude others from the greater one, and the statute attacks the small monopolies as well as the great. The very words of the act make such a distinction impossible in this case and it has not been attempted in express terms.

If the charter which I have imagined above would have been good notwithstanding the monopoly, in a popular sense, which it created, one next is led to ask whether and why a combination or consolidation of existing roads, although in actual competition, into one company of exactly the same powers and extent, would be any more obnoxious to the law. Although it was decided . . . that since the statute, as before, the States have the power to regulate the matter, it was said in the argument that such a consolidation would be unlawful, and it seems to me that the Attorney General was compelled to say so in order to maintain his case. But I think that logic would not let him stop there or short of denying the power of a State at the present time to authorize one company to construct and own two parallel lines that might compete. The monopoly would be the same as if the roads were consolidated after they had begun to compete — and it is on the footing of monopoly that I now am supposing the objection made.

But to meet the objection to the prevention of competition at the same time, I will suppose that three parties apply to a State for charters; one for each of two new and possibly competing lines respectively, and one for both of these lines, and that the charter is granted to the last. I think that charter would be good and I think the whole argument to the contrary rests on a popular instead of an accurate and legal conception of what the word "monopolize" in the statute means.

I repeat, that in my opinion there is no attempt to monopolize, and what, I have said, in my judgment amounts to the same thing, that there is no combination in restraint of trade, until something is done with the intent to exclude strangers to the combination from competing with it in some part of the business which it carries on.

Unless I am entirely wrong in my understanding of what a "combination in restraint of trade" means, then the same monopoly may be attempted and effected by an individual and is made equally illegal in that case by § 2. But I do not expect to hear it maintained that Mr. Morgan could be sent to prison for buying as many shares as he liked of the Great Northern and the Northern Pacific, even if he bought them both at the same time and got more than half the stock of each road.

There is much that was mentioned in argument which I pass by. But in view of the great importance attached by both sides to the supposed attempt to suppress competition, I must say a word more about that. I said at the outset that I should assume, and I do assume, that one purpose of the purchase was to suppress competition between the two roads. I appreciate the force of the argument that there are independent stockholders in each; that it cannot be presumed that the respective boards of directors will propose any illegal act; that if they should they could be restrained, and that all that has been done as yet is too remote from the illegal result to be classed even as an attempt. Not every act done in furtherance of an unlawful end is an attempt or contrary to the law. There must be a certain nearness to the result. It is a question of proximity and degree. *Commonwealth* v. *Peaslee,* 177 Massachusetts, 267, 272. So, as I have said, is the amenability of acts in furtherance of interference with commerce among the States to legislation by Congress. So, according to the intimation of this court, is the question of liability under the present statute. . . . But I assume further, for the purposes of discussion, that what has been done is near enough to the result to fall under the law, if the law prohibits that result, although that assumption very nearly if not quite contradicts the decision in *United States* v. *E. C. Knight Co.,* 156 U. S. 1. But I said that the law does not prohibit the result. If it does it must be because there is some further meaning than I have yet discovered in the words "combinations in restraint of trade." I think that I have exhausted the meaning of those words in what I already have said. But they certainly do not require all existing competitions to be kept on foot, and, on the principle of the *Trans-Missouri Freight Association's* case, invalidate the continuance of old contracts by which former competitors united in the past.

A partnership is not a contract or combination in restraint of trade between the partners unless the well-known words are to be given a new meaning invented for the purposes of this act. It is true that the suppression of competition was referred to in *United States* v. *Trans-Missouri Freight Association,* 166 U. S. 290, but, as I have said, that was in connection with a contract with a stranger to the defendant's business — a true contract in restraint of trade.

To suppress competition in that way is one thing, to suppress it by fusion is another. The law, I repeat, says nothing about competition and only prevents its suppression by contracts or combinations in restraint of trade, and such contracts or combinations derive their character as restraining trade from other features than the suppression of competition alone. To see whether I am wrong, the illustrations put in the argument are of use. If I am, then a partnership between two stage drivers who had been competitors in driving across a state line, or two merchants once engaged in rival commerce among the States, whether made after or before the act, if now continued, is a crime. For, again I repeat, if the restraint on the freedom of the members of a combination caused by their entering into partnership is a restraint of trade, every such combination, as well the small as the great, is within the act.

In view of my interpretation of the statute I do not go further into the question of the power of Congress. That has been dealt with by my brother White and I concur in the main with his views. I am happy to know that only a minority of my brethren adopt an interpretation of the law which in my opinion would make eternal the *bellum omnium contra omnes* and disintegrate society so far as it could into individual atoms. If that were its intent I should regard calling such a law a regulation of commerce as a mere pretense. It would be an attempt to reconstruct society. I am not concerned with the wisdom of such an attempt but I believe that Congress was not entrusted by the Constitution with the power to make it and I am deeply persuaded that it has not tried.

I am authorized to say that the Chief Justice, Mr. Justice White and Mr. Justice Peckham concur in this dissent.

COMMERCE AS A CONTINUUM

Swift and Co. v. U. S.
196 U. S. 375 (1905)

A year after his dissent in the Northern Securities *case, in which he had taken a narrow view of the operation of the national power under the commerce clause to deal with monopoly problems of national scope, Holmes wrote the unanimous opinion in the* Swift *case, containing as broad a view of the commerce power as the Court had yet taken. This must not be regarded wholly as a retreat from Holmes's earlier position. The railroads were a natural monopoly; meat packing was not. In the earlier case there was no claim that third parties were being shut out of the market by the combination between the two railroads; here they were. In the earlier case the problem was one of defining restraint of trade; here it was one of defining interstate commerce. Technically, therefore, Holmes could make intellectual ends meet. Yet the fact is that he is much more comfortable here, in his broad view of the constitutional power.*

There were about thirty firms in Chicago, Omaha, St. Joseph, Kansas City, East St. Louis, and St. Paul engaged in the meat industries: buying livestock in their stockyards, slaughtering it and preparing it as meat in their packing plants, selling and shipping the meat beyond state lines. The Roosevelt administration proceeded against them under the Sherman Act on the charge of collusive bidding, price-fixing, and restricting supply in order to push up prices.[1] *Several elements in the intellectual climate at the time made such a suit possible. The Report of the Industrial Commission (1904), then in progress, revealed the facts of monopoly conditions in the industry; and the work of the Muckrakers, particularly that of Upton Sinclair in his novel,* The Jungle, *published in 1906, directed the public attention to conditions in the meat industries.*

The defendants in the case relied principally on the Sugar Trust *case, in which the Sherman Act had got off to a bad start when the Court drew a line between doing something about stock ownership and doing something about restraint of trade. The* Addyston Pipe *case*[2] *qualified the* Sugar Trust *case somewhat. But the* Swift *case virtually overruled it. Holmes, to be sure, is careful not to do so explicitly, but rather to distinguish the two situations on the ground that the acts*

---

[1] This was one of the two suits which the government instituted under the Sherman Act in 1902; the other was the *Northern Securities* suit. See Walton Hamilton and Irene Till, *Antitrust in Action*, TNEC Monograph 16 (1940) Appendix G. The same monograph gives an excellent description of the whole pattern of antitrust enforcement, and of the difficulties of enforcement in the early years.

[2] *Addyston Pipe & Steel Co.* v. *U. S.*, 175 U. S. 211 (1899). The sugar case was *U. S.* v. *E. C. Knight Co.*, 156 U. S. 1 (1895).

complained of in the Sugar Trust *case were those of manufacture, while here they are those of sale. Nevertheless, the* Swift *decision makes exactly the point the* Knight *decision strove not to make: that commerce is to be seen as part of the broad movement of economic life; that even acts which are in themselves individually intrastate in character and therefore subject to state control may — as parts of a more general framework — be interstate in character and therefore subject to Congressional control; and that commerce is in fact, like all modern business, "a continuum in which its local phases have become submerged."* [3]

Chief Justice Taft was later to call Swift v. U. S. *a "milestone in the interpretation of the commerce clause";*[4] *and in a letter to Pollock in 1922 Holmes anticipated the compliment by saying of Taft's decision in* Stafford v. Wallace [5] *that it "expressed the movement of interstate commerce in a large and rather masterly way."* [6] *In that case Taft upheld the Packers and Stockyards Act. Holmes's 1905 opinion in the* Swift *case prepared the ground for the enactment of that and other legislation. But the problem of monopoly in meat packing still remained a concern of the antitrust laws. In 1920 a consent decree was entered in another suit against Swift and Co. and the other packers. Litigation continued from 1920 to 1932 while the packers sought to have the decree vacated or modified. The case reached the Supreme Court twice more — in 1928 and 1931.*

Holmes, J., for the Court:

This is an appeal from a decree of the Circuit Court, on demurrer, granting an injunction against the appellants' commission of alleged violations of the Act of July 2, 1890, c. 647, 26 Stat. 209, "to protect trade and commerce against unlawful restraints and monopolies . . ." [7] . . . To sum up the bill more shortly, it charges a com-

---

[3] I use Corwin's words here as a good description of the doctrine of the case, *The Twilight of the Supreme Court* (1937), 43.
[4] *Board of Trade of the City of Chicago* v. *Olsen,* 262 U. S. 1, 35 (1923).
[5] 258 U. S. 495 (1922).
[6] H–P, II:96 (May 21, 1922).
[7] The parts of the opinion recounting the ten sections of the indictment are omitted as too detailed. For a factual summary see my prefatory note to this case.

bination of a dominant proportion of the dealers in fresh meat throughout the United States not to bid against each other in the live stock markets of the different States, to bid up prices for a few days in order to induce the cattle men to send their stock to the stock yards, to fix prices at which they will sell, and to that end to restrict shipments of meat when necessary, to establish a uniform rule of credit to dealers and to keep a black list, to make uniform and improper charges for cartage, and finally, to get less than lawful rates from the railroads to the exclusion of competitors. It is true that the last charge is not clearly stated to be a part of the combination. But as it is alleged that the defendants have each and all made arrangements with the railroads, that they were exclusively to enjoy the unlawful advantage, and that their intent in what they did was to monopolize the commerce and to prevent competition, and in view of the general allegation to which we shall refer, we think that we have stated correctly the purport of the bill. . . . After all the specific charges there is a general allegation that the defendants are conspiring with one another, the railroads and others, to monopolize the supply and distribution of fresh meats throughout the United States, &c., as has been stated above, and it seems to us that this general allegation of intent colors and applies to all the specific charges of the bill. Whatever may be thought concerning the proper construction of the statute, a bill in equity is not to be read and construed as an indictment would have been read and construed a hundred years ago, but it is to be taken to mean what it fairly conveys to a dispassionate reader by a fairly exact use of English speech. Thus read this bill seems to us intended to allege successive elements of a single connected scheme. . . .

The general objection is urged that the bill does not set forth sufficient definite or specific facts. This objection is serious, but it seems to us inherent in the nature of the case. The scheme alleged is so vast that it presents a new problem in pleading. If, as we must assume, the scheme is entertained, it is, of course, contrary to the very words of the statute. Its size makes the violation of the law more conspicuous, and yet the same thing makes it impossible to fasten the principal fact to a certain time and place. The elements, too, are so numerous and shifting, even the constituent parts alleged are and from their nature must be so extensive in time and space, that something of the same impossibility applies to them.

The law has been upheld, and therefore we are bound to enforce it notwithstanding these difficulties. On the other hand, we equally are bound by the first principles of justice not to sanction a decree so vague as to put the whole conduct of the defendants' business at the peril of a summons for contempt. We cannot issue a general injunction against all possible breaches of the law. We must steer between these opposite difficulties as best we can.

The scheme as a whole seems to us to be within reach of the law. The constituent elements, as we have stated them, are enough to give to the scheme a body and, for all that we can say, to accomplish it. Moreover, whatever we may think of them separately when we take them up as distinct charges, they are alleged sufficiently as elements of the scheme. It is suggested that the several acts charged are lawful and that intent can make no difference. But they are bound together as the parts of a single plan. The plan may make the parts unlawful. *Aikens* v. *Wisconsin*, 195 U. S. 194, 206. The statute gives this proceeding against combinations in restraint of commerce among the States and against attempts to monopolize the same. Intent is almost essential to such a combination and is essential to such an attempt. Where acts are not sufficient in themselves to produce a result which the law seeks to prevent — for instance, the monopoly — but require further acts in addition to the mere forces of nature to bring that result to pass, an intent to bring it to pass is necessary in order to produce a dangerous probability that it will happen. *Commonwealth* v. *Peaslee*, 177 Mass. 267, 272. But when that intent and the consequent dangerous probability exist, this statute, like many others and like the common law in some cases, directs itself against that dangerous probability as well as against the completed result. What we have said disposes incidentally of the objection to the bill as multifarious. The unity of the plan embraces all the parts.

One further observation should be made. Although the combination alleged embraces restraint and monopoly of trade within a single State, its effect upon commerce among the States is not accidental, secondary, remote or merely probable. On the allegations of the bill the latter commerce no less, perhaps even more, than commerce within a single State is an object of attack. See *Leloup* v. *Port of Mobile*, 127 U. S. 640, 647; *Crutcher* v. *Kentucky*, 141 U. S. 47, 59; *Allen* v. *Pullman Co.*, 191 U. S. 171, 179, 180. Moreover, it is a direct object, it is that for the sake of which the several specific acts and courses of conduct are done and adopted. Therefore the case is not like *United States* v. *E. C. Knight Co.,* 156 U. S. 1, where the subject-matter of the combination was manufacture and the direct object monopoly of manufacture within a State. However likely monopoly of commerce among the States in the article manufactured was to follow the agreement it was not a necessary consequence nor a primary end. Here the subject-matter is sales and the very point of the combination is to restrain and monopolize commerce among the States in respect to such sales. The two cases are near to each other, as sooner or later always must happen where lines are to be drawn, but the line between them is distinct. *Montague & Co.* v. *Lowry,* 193 U. S. 38.

So, again, the line is distinct between this case and *Hopkins* v. *United States,* 171 U. S. 578. All that was decided there was that the local business of commission brokers was not commerce among the States, even if what the brokers were employed to sell was an object of such commerce. The brokers were not like the defendants before us, themselves the buyers and sellers. They only furnished certain facilities for the sales. Therefore, there again the effects of the combination of brokers upon the commerce was only indirect and not within the Act. Whether the case would have been different if the combination had resulted in exorbitant charges, was left open. In *Anderson* v. *United States,* 171 U. S. 604, the defendants were buyers and sellers at the stock yards, but their agreement was merely not to employ brokers, or to recognize yard-traders, who were not members of their association. Any yard-trader could become a member of the association on complying with the conditions, and there was said to be no feature of monopoly in the case. It was held that the combination did not directly regulate commerce between the States, and, being formed with a different intent, was not within the Act. The present case is more like *Montague & Co.* v. *Lowry,* 193 U. S. 38.

For the foregoing reasons we are of opinion that the carrying out of the scheme alleged, by the means set forth, properly may be enjoined, and that the bill cannot be dismissed.

So far it has not been necessary to consider whether the facts charged in any single paragraph constitute commerce among the States or show an interference with it. There can be no doubt, we apprehend, as to the collective effect of all the facts, if true, and if the defendants entertain the intent alleged. We pass now to the particulars, and will consider the corresponding parts of the injunction at the same time. The first question arises on the sixth section. That charges a combination of independent dealers to restrict the competition of their agents when purchasing stock for them in the stock yards. The purchasers and their slaughtering establishments are largely in different States from those of the stock yards, and the sellers of the cattle, perhaps it is not too much to assume, largely in different States from either. The intent of the combination is not merely to restrict competition among the parties, but, as we have said, by force of the general allegation at the end of the bill, to aid in an attempt to monopolize commerce among the States.

It is said that this charge is too vague and that it does not set forth a case of commerce among the States. Taking up the latter objection first, commerce among the States is not a technical legal conception, but a practical one, drawn from the course of business. When cattle are sent for sale from a place in one State, with the expectation that they will end their transit, after purchase, in another, and when in effect they do so, with only the interruption necessary to find a purchaser at the stock yards, and when this is a typical, constantly recurring course, the current thus existing is a current of commerce among the States, and the purchase of the cattle is a part and incident of such commerce. What we say is true at least of such a purchase by residents in another State from that of the seller and of the cattle. And we need not trouble ourselves at this time as to whether the statute could be escaped by any arrangement as to the place where the sale in point of law was consummated. See *Norfolk & Western Ry.* v. *Sims,* 191 U. S. 441. But the sixth section of the bill charges an interference with such sales, a restraint of the parties by mutual contract and a combination not to compete in order to monopolize. It is immaterial if the section also embraces domestic transactions.

It should be added that the cattle in the stock yard are not at rest even to the extent that was held sufficient to warrant taxation in *American Steel & Wire Co.* v. *Speed,* 192 U. S. 500. But it may be that the question of taxation does not depend upon whether the article taxed may or may not be said to be in the course of commerce between the States, but depends upon whether the tax so far affects that commerce as to amount to a regulation of it. The injunction against taking part in a combination, the effect of which will be a restraint of trade among the States by directing the defendants' agents to refrain from bidding against one another at the sales of live stock, is justified so far as the subject-matter is concerned.

The injunction, however, refers not to trade among the States in cattle, concerning which there can be no question of original packages, but to trade in fresh meats, as the trade forbidden to be restrained, and it is objected that the trade in fresh meats described in the second and third sections of the bill is not commerce among the States, because the meat is sold at the slaughtering places, or when sold elsewhere may be sold in less than the original packages. But the allegations of the second section, even if they import a technical passing of title at the slaughtering places, also import that the sales are to persons in other States, and that the shipments to other States are part of the transaction — "pursuant to such sales" — and the third section imports that the same things which are sent to agents are sold by them, and sufficiently indicates that some at least of the sales are of the original packages. Moreover, the sales are by persons in one State to persons in another. But we do not mean to imply that the rule which marks the point at which State taxation or regulation becomes permissible necessarily is beyond the scope of interference by Congress in cases where such interference is deemed necessary for the protection of commerce among the States. Nor do we mean to intimate that the statute under consideration is limited to that point. Beyond what we have said above, we leave those questions as we find them. They were touched upon in the *Northern Securities Company Case*, 139 U. S. 197.

We are of opinion, further, that the charge in the sixth section is not too vague. The charge is not of a single agreement but of a course of conduct intended to be continued. Under the Act it is the duty of the Court, when applied to, to stop the conduct. The thing done and intended to be done is perfectly definite: with the purpose mentioned, directing the defendants' agents and inducing each other to refrain from competition in bids. The defendants cannot be ordered to compete, but they properly can be forbidden to give directions or to make agreements not to compete. See *Addyston Pipe & Steel Co.* v. *United States*, 175 U. S. 211. The injunction follows the charge. No objection was made on the ground that it is not confined to the places specified in the bill. It seems to us, however, that it ought to set forth more exactly the transactions in which such directions and agreements are forbidden. The trade in fresh meat referred to should be defined somewhat as it is in the bill, and the sales of stock should be confined to sales of stock at the stock yards named, which stock is sent from other States to the stock yards for sale or is bought at those yards for transport to another State.[8]

SOCIAL DESIRES AND DR. MILES'S MEDICINES

Dr. Miles Medical Co. v. Park and Sons Co.
220 U. S. 373, 409 (1911)

Several times in Holmes one finds a combination of vigorous legal analysis with dubious economic reasoning. The Dr. Miles Medical Co. *case is perhaps the best instance.*

The Miles Company had worked out a very careful plan for resale price maintenance. All jobbers buying its medicines agreed to act as its agents and to sell the products to retailers and other wholesalers only at a price fixed by the company, and only by making a second set of resale price maintenance contracts in turn with them. The defendant company had bought large supplies from the agents of the Miles Company and had entered into the contract, but had then broken the price terms of the contracts, reselling the medicines to other wholesalers and to retailers to be sold at cut-rates, as what we should today call "loss-leaders."

The majority of the Court, through Justice Hughes, held that the price-maintenance scheme could not be enforced through an injunction, and that the second set of contracts (with the retailers) were in restraint of trade and were illegal both at common law and under the Sherman Antitrust Act. In a long opinion Hughes reasoned that the second set of contracts were not between the company and its agents — although the term "retail agency contracts" was used — but between the company and all prospective purchasers. Thus the restraint which was purely internal in the first set of contracts now became external and, since they were made with

---

[8] The remainder of the opinion is omitted.

"most of the jobbers and wholesale druggists and a majority of the retail druggists of the country," and had as their purpose "the control of the entire trade," they clearly affected the market. The essence of the common-law conception of restraint of trade, Hughes went on, is harm to the public interest. "Agreements or combinations between dealers, having for their sole purpose the destruction of competition and the fixing of prices, are injurious to the public interest and void. They are not saved by the advantage that the participants expect to derive from the enhanced price to the consumer."

Holmes was the sole dissenter.[1] After disposing of some technical preliminaries, he took several lines of attack. By agreeing that the first set of contracts were enforceable, Hughes had left himself vulnerable, and Holmes made directly for the opening in his armor. "By a slight change in the form of contract the plaintiff can accomplish the result. . . . If it should make the retail dealers also agents in law as well as in name and retain the title until the goods left their hands I cannot conceive that even the present enthusiasm for regulating the prices to be charged by other people would deny that the owner was acting within his rights."

But the second line of attack was more fundamental: that "we greatly exaggerate the value and importance to the public of competition in the production or distribution of an article . . . as fixing a fair price. What really fixes that is the competition of conflicting desire. . . . The point of most profitable returns marks the equilibrium of social desires and determines

[1] Justice Lurton took no part in the decision of the case, but it is clear he would have voted with the majority. He had decided the same case in the same way while on the Circuit Court of Appeals, and Justice Hughes adopted much of his reasoning and language. For a detailed discussion of the legal history of resale price maintenance contracts, see Seligman and Love, *Price Cutting and Price Maintenance* (1932), 42–89. The present case has generally been considered the decisive one in the whole sequence. While the Hughes opinion leaves much to be desired and is technical and narrow in its legal grounds, it has been followed by the Courts. They have, however, held that the manufacturer can refuse to sell to the retailers who cut prices, but even here they have kept him from using this refusal as a threat. Where the manufacturer makes the distributor his agent he may give him instructions on price. The principal cases after the present one are *Bauer and Cie v. O'Donnell*, 229 U. S. 1 (1913); *U. S. v. Colgate and Co.*, 250 U. S. 300 (1919); *F. T. C. v. Beech-Nut Packing Co.*, 257 U. S. 441 (1922); *U. S. v. General Electric Co.*, 272 U. S. 476 (1926).

the fair price in the only sense in which I can find meaning in those words." One could not ask a better statement of the subjective or marginal-utility school of value theory in economics. Holmes rejects the idea of price as determined by the cost curve or even by the distributive competition of the market, but assigns the determining role to the competitive play of desires in our minds.

Holmes was no technical economist as he was a technical lawyer, and though he was a brilliant amateur at anything he turned his mind to — whether metaphysics or Greek tragedy or the history of etchings or economic theory — he did not have the discipline or the competence to support the magisterial assurance with which in this field he made and destroyed theories. Someone might have answered his opinion by reminding him that the common law did not enact Eugen von Böhm-Bawerk's Positive Theory of Capital. In a previous Massachusetts opinion, Plant v. Woods, he had similarly and brilliantly stated his belief in the wage-fund doctrine.[2] But there he had done so as an aside, making it clear that what economic theory of wages you held was irrelevant to the decision. Here his theory is quite central to his own decision, and he also sees the Court's decision as based on a theory of price as determined by competitive production and distribution.

One may say in his defense that he was seeking to follow out his general doctrine of judicial laissez faire. He does not see the Sherman Act as applying directly. In the absence of a statute, which might have covered the case and might have been based on a not unreasonable — even if invalid — economic theory, he prefers to leave the play of economic forces as it is, and not interfere with Dr. Miles's contracts. The difficulty, of course, is that Holmes conceives of a natural economic system which functions for Peter but does not function for Paul. If, regardless of Dr. Miles's contracts, fair price will be determined by the equilibrium of social desires, then the same ought to hold also regardless of the Park Company's breaking of those contracts. The action of the Miles Company in making its prices what we should today call "sticky," in

---

[2] See p. 117.

taking them out of the market mechanism and making them "administered prices," is no part of a natural economic order, but is just as man-made as the Sherman Act or the decision by Justice Hughes.

In reality the Court was faced with a choice between economic strategies in determining prices: whether to use the strategy of the resale price-maintenance contract, enforced by the Court, or that of the Sherman Act, also enforced by the Court. In the first case the prices are subject to the economic power of the producing company, backed by the judicial process; in the second case they are made subject to the economic power of the strategically large wholesalers or retailers, using the product as a pawn in their competitive struggle, and again backed by the judicial process. In the first case the producer achieves some security and maximizes his profits; in the second case the consumer gets the benefit of lower prices, but may have to make up for it on other commodities. Thus the economic issue was by no means as clear as either Justice Hughes or Justice Holmes seemed to make it. Because of the confused economic situation of which the Miles case was an expression, Congress in *1914* passed the Federal Trade Commission Act. But as the judicial history of that act and the current controversies over such state legislation as the Feld-Crawford Act in New York were to show, the economic problem is still with us.[3]

In one respect Holmes was thoroughly consistent here. Ordinarily judges act as economists in their decisions but will not admit it. Their economics is part of what Holmes called their "inarticulate major premise." Holmes here made his economics articulate and candid. Where he got it we shall

---

[3] The considerations of policy usually advanced for resale price maintenance are that without it the product may become part of retail price wars and lose its prestige; that the manufacturer has created a market for his brand by national advertising and has a vested interest in the maintenance of the market; that price-cutting reduces the number of retail outlets; and that a brand is a form of copyright or patent, and carries with it exclusive rights and corresponding control. For a critical discussion of the last point with respect to patents as a whole, see Walton Hamilton, *Patents and Free Enterprise,* TNEC Monograph 31 (1941). The Federal Trade Commission held two elaborate investigations of the whole problem in 1929 and 1931 and published reports. Under the NRA, when antitrust restrictions were relaxed, some of the codes permitted resale price maintenance. The present tendency of federal legislation is to give a limited sanction to resale price-fixing of branded and trade-marked goods.

AMERICA AS A GOING CONCERN

not know until an adequate biography tells us what his economic reading was at college and after, and what influences shaped his economic thinking. There are some notations in his letters to Pollock at about the time of this decision, indicating that he was reading the second edition of Ely's Principles of Economics *(which leans in the direction of marginal-utility theory), and that he had Alfred Marshall's famous* Principles of Economics *with him, whether he ever read them at this time or not. "I have been excusing myself," he writes a few months after the* Miles *case, "from reading your Marshall of whom I had thought, and instead at this moment am full of Fairfax's Tasso."* [4] *But it is a bit futile to argue much either way from notations like this. Holmes did not willingly read technical economics. His thinking on this score was the distillation of the ideas he had picked up rather early, mulled over during the course of years and fitted into his other philosophical views.*[5]

Holmes, J. dissenting:

This is a bill to restrain the defendant from inducing, by corruption and fraud, agents of the plaintiff and purchasers from it to break their contracts not to sell its goods below a certain price. There are two contracts concerned. The first is that of the jobber or wholesale agent to whom the plaintiff consigns its goods, and I will say a few words about that, although it is not this branch of the case that induces me to speak. That they are agents and not buyers I understand to be conceded, and I do not see how it can be denied. We have nothing before us but the form and the alleged effect of the written instrument, and they both are express that the title to the goods is to remain in the plaintiff until actual sale as permitted by the contract. So far as this contract limits the authority of the agents as agents I do not understand its validity to be disputed. But it is construed also to permit the purchase of medicine by consignees from other consignees, and to make the specification of prices applicable to goods so purchased as well

[4] H-P, I:183 (July 28, 1911).
[5] Pollock, incidentally, felt as strongly as Holmes about the legal aspects of the case. "Either your dissenting opinion . . . is right or much of our recent authority here is wrong. . . . It seems to me that the majority of your Honourable Court are being led into an archaic reaction by their anti-monopolist zeal . . . *A ma entente ceo est merveillous ley.*" H-P, I:178 (May 3, 1911).

as to goods consigned. Hence when the bill alleges that the defendant has obtained medicine from these agents by inducing them to break their contracts, the allegation does not require proof of breach of trust by an agent, but would be satisfied by proving a breach of promise in respect of goods that the consignee had bought and owned. This reasoning would have been conclusive in the days of Saunders if the construction of the contract is right, as I suppose that it is. But the contract as to goods purchased is at least in the background and obscure; it is not the main undertaking that the instrument is intended to express. I should have thought that the bill ought to be read as charging the defendant with inducing a breach of the ordinary duty of consignees as such (*Swift* v. *United States,* 196 U. S. 375, 395), and, therefore, as entitling the plaintiff to relief. *Angle* v. *Chicago, St. Paul, Minneapolis & Omaha Ry. Co.,* 151 U. S. 1.

The second contract is that of the retail agents, so called, being really the first purchasers, fixing the price below which they will not sell to the public. There is no attempt to attach a contract or condition to the goods, as in *Bobbs-Merrill Co.* v. *Straus,* 210 U. S. 330, or in any way to restrict dealings with them after they leave the hands of the retail men. The sale to the retailers is made by the plaintiff, and the only question is whether the law forbids a purchaser to contract with his vendor that he will not sell below a certain price. This is the important question in this case. I suppose that in the case of a single object such as a painting or a statue the right of the artist to make such a stipulation hardly would be denied. In other words, I suppose that the reason why the contract is held bad is that it is part of a scheme embracing other similar contracts each of which applies to a number of similar things, with the object of fixing a general market price. This reason seems to me inadequate in the case before the Court. In the first place by a slight change in the form of the contract the plaintiff can accomplish the result in a way that would be beyond successful attack. If it should make the retail dealers also agents in law as well as in name and retain the title until the goods left their hands I cannot conceive that even the present enthusiasm for regulating the prices to be charged by other people would deny that the owner was acting within his rights. It seems to me that this consideration by itself ought to give us pause.

But I go farther. There is no statute covering the case; there is no body of precedent that by ineluctable logic requires the conclusion to which the Court has come. The conclusion is reached by extending a certain conception of public policy to a new sphere. On such matters we are in perilous country. I think that, at least, it is safe to say that the most enlightened judicial policy is to let people manage their own business in their own way, unless the ground for interference is very clear. What then is the ground upon which we interfere in the present case? Of course, it is not the interest of the producer. No one, I judge, cares for that. It hardly can be the interest of subordinate vendors, as there seems to be no particular reason for preferring them to the originator and first vendor of the product. Perhaps it may be assumed to be the interest of the consumers and the public. On that point I confess that I am in a minority as to larger issues than are concerned here. I think that we greatly exaggerate the value and importance to the public of competition in the production or distribution of an article (here it is only distribution), as fixing a fair price. What really fixes that is the competition of conflicting desires. We, none of us, can have as much as we want of all the things that we want. Therefore, we have to choose. As soon as the price of something that we want goes above the point at which we are willing to give up other things to have that, we cease to buy it and buy something else. Of course, I am speaking of things that we can get along without. There may be necessaries that sooner or later must be dealt with like short rations in a shipwreck, but they are not Dr. Miles' medicines. With regard to things like the latter it seems to me that the point of most profitable returns marks the equilibrium of social desires and determines the fair price in the only sense in which I can find meaning in those words. The Dr. Miles Medical Company knows better than we do what will enable it to do the best business. We must assume its retail price to be reasonable, for it is so alleged and the case is here on demurrer; so I see nothing to warrant my assuming that the public will not be served best by the company being allowed to carry out its plan. I cannot believe that in the long run the public will profit by this Court permitting knaves to cut reasonable prices for some ulterior purpose of their own and thus to impair, if not to destroy, the production and sale of articles which it is assumed to be desirable that the public should be able to get.

The conduct of the defendant falls within a general prohibition of the law. It is fraudulent and has no merits of its own to recommend it to the favor of the Court. An injunction against the defendant's dealing in non-transferable round-trip reduced rate tickets has been granted to a railroad company upon the general principles of the law protecting contracts, and the demoralization of rates has been referred to as a special circumstance in addition to the general grounds. *Bitterman* v. *Louisville & Nashville R. R. Co.,* 207 U. S. 205, 222, 223, 224. The general and special considerations equally apply here, and we ought not to disregard them, unless the evil effect of the contract is very plain. The analogy relied upon to establish that evil effect is that of combinations in restraint of trade. I believe that we have some superstitions on that head, as I have said; but those combinations are entered into with intent to exclude others from a business naturally open to them, and we unhappily have become familiar with the methods by which they are carried out. I venture to say that there is no likeness between them and this case. *Jayne* v. *Loder,* 149 Fed. Rep. 21, 27; and I think that my view prevails in England. *Elliman, Sons & Co.* v. *Carrington & Son, Limited* [1901], 2 Ch. 275. See *Garst* v. *Harris,* 177 Massachusetts, 72; *Garst* v. *Charles,* 187 Massachusetts, 144. I think also that the importance of the question and the popularity of what I deem mistaken notions make it my duty to express my view in this dissent.

FREE TRADE IN INDUSTRIAL INFORMATION

American Column and Lumber Co. v. *U. S.*
257 U. S. 377, 412 (1921)

"I think I still have my teeth in that way," wrote Holmes to Pollock in 1921, at eighty, with respect to "firing off an opinion." One of the opinions he had recently written was his dissent in the present case: it was one of the "brisk differences, amiable but marked," that characterized the 1921 term of Court.[1]

This case is known generally as "the Hardwood *case." It is one of four decided by the Court from 1921–1925 on the*

[1] H–P, II:88 (Jan. 23, 1922).

legality of what is known as "open price reporting" as a method used by trade associations in achieving price uniformity. After the "rule of reason" decision in the Standard Oil case *(1911)*[2] *the way to legality seemed open to "good" combinations, that were not oppressive of competitors and aimed at constructive social results. The method of exchanging price and other industrial information among the members of a trade association was accordingly developed, and during the first World War seemed to have the encouragement of the Government.*

After the war, however, the Government sued the Hardwood Association, pointed to the high lumber prices in 1919, and ascribed them to the collusive price practices of what had come to be known as "the new competition." In a six-to-three opinion the Court, speaking through Justice Clarke, held that the association had violated the antitrust laws by what might in effect be called an "open conspiracy." There was certainly evidence that the association, which controlled about a third of the production of hardwood, had employed a secretary who on a rising market noted the increasing demand, urged limitation of output, and gave publicity to the production levels of individual members. But the dissenting opinions – there were two, one by Holmes and one by Brandeis in which McKenna joined – held this to be a legally valid attempt to exchange industrial information, and economically justified because whatever reduction in competition was achieved was for the purpose of industrial order.

Holmes's dissent is not one of his best, as that of Brandeis is. The two were based on rather different social values. Brandeis was concerned with the "curse of bigness." He feared that if small independent producers who had banded together into a trade association were not allowed to act together reasonably for common economic ends, they would "be led to enter the inviting field of consolidation," and the result would be a "huge trust" with all of its consequences in concen-

---

[2] *Standard Oil Co. v. U. S.* 1 (1911); see also *U. S. v. American Tobacco Co.,* 221 U. S. 106 (1911). In these cases the Supreme Court held that the Sherman Anti-Trust Act prohibits not all restraints of trade but only the unreasonable ones. The Court left the determination of reasonableness to itself. Brooks Adams wrote that in so doing the Court was taking over the authority of the mediaeval church to "grant indulgences for reasonable causes."

tration of power. Holmes, since he did not share Brandeis' fear of the big trusts, could scarcely restrict himself to this reasoning, although by concurring in Brandeis' "more elaborate discussion" he showed he was not wholly at variance with it. Brandeis' reasoning was tactical: it was part of his strategy for equalizing the position of the small producers as against the big ones, and organizing industrial order. Holmes's reasoning again, as in the Dr. Miles *case,* assumed a naturally functioning economic norm to which some adjustments had to be made. He saw the action of the Hardwood Association not as "an attempt to override normal market conditions" but as "an attempt to conform to them."

Caught thus between the assumptions of Brandeis and his own, Holmes's dissent lacks the force that his decisions generally get from their singleness of intellectual conception. As a result the opinion runs off into the problem of guaranteeing free speech and maximizing knowledge and education — values that are desirable but a discussion of which seems irrelevant in dealing with a problem whose solution must come from economic analysis and economic strategy.

The Hardwood *decision and the one of similar tenor that followed it, the* Linseed Oil *decision,*[3] *were never overruled by the Court. Yet in 1925, in the* Maple Flooring *case*[4] *and the* Cement *case*[5] *— both instances of open price reporting by trade associations — the Court did pronounce an essentially similar procedure to be reasonable.*

Holmes, J., dissenting:

When there are competing sellers of a class of goods, knowledge of the total stock on hand, of the probable total demand and of the prices paid of course will tend to equalize the prices asked. But I should have supposed that the Sherman Act did not set itself against knowledge — did not aim at a transitory cheapness unprofitable to the community as a whole because not corresponding to the actual conditions of the country. I should have thought that the ideal of commerce was an intelligent interchange made with full knowledge of the facts as a basis for a forecast of the

[3] *U. S.* v. *American Linseed Oil Co.,* 262 U. S. 371 (1923).
[4] *Maple Flooring Manufacturers' Association* v. *U. S.,* 268 U. S. 563 (1925).
[5] *Cement Manufacturers' Protective Association* v. *U. S.,* 268 U. S. 588 (1925).

future on both sides. A combination to get and distribute such knowledge, notwithstanding its tendency to equalize, not necessarily to raise, prices, is very far from a combination in unreasonable restraint of trade. It is true that it is a combination of sellers only, but the knowledge acquired is not secret, it is public, and the buyers, I think I may assume, are not less active in their efforts to know the facts. A combination in unreasonable restraint of trade imports an attempt to override normal market conditions. An attempt to conform to them seems to me the most reasonable thing in the world. I see nothing in the conduct of the appellants that binds the members even by merely social sanctions to anything that would not be practised, if we can imagine it, by an all-wise socialistic government acting for the benefit of the community as a whole. The parties to the combination are free to do as they will.

I must add that the decree as it stands seems to me surprising in a country of free speech that affects to regard education and knowledge as desirable. It prohibits the distribution of stock, production or sales reports, the discussion of prices at association meetings, and the exchange of predictions of high prices. It is true that these acts are the main evidence of the supposed conspiracy, but that to my mind only shows the weakness of the Government's case. I cannot believe that the fact, if it be assumed, that the acts have been done with a sinister purpose, justifies excluding mills in the backwoods from information, in order to enable centralized purchasers to take advantage of their ignorance of the facts.

I agree with the more elaborate discussion of the case by my brother Brandeis.

SHODDY AND THE MANIFESTLY ABSURD

Weaver v. *Palmer Bros. Co.*
270 U. S. 402, 415 (1926)

The State of Pennsylvania, because of a fear of unsterilized shoddy, passed an act in 1923 prohibiting the use of shoddy in bedding. The Supreme Court, speaking through Justice Butler, held it unconstitutional under the due process clause of the Fourteenth Amendment. Holmes wrote a dissent in which Justices Brandeis and Stone joined. It is one of his briefer and more peremptory dissents, with a not wholly restrained fire breaking through. It begins by asking whether the Pennsylvania legislature's view of social policy was so extreme as to be "manifestly absurd"; and it ends by warning the majority that it is "pressing the Fourteenth Amendment too far."

There were two basic clashes between the majority and Holmes. One was the question of whether the Court should independently review the facts as well as the law. Justice Butler did so, holding there was no evidence on the record below that the shoddy spread disease, and also that if the shoddy were properly sterilized any danger to health would be removed. Holmes's view on the other hand was that unless the legislature's opinion on the facts was completely untenable, the Court had to assume it was true. Here Holmes was following the doctrine of Powell v. Pennsylvania,[1] where Justice Harlan had laid down a doctrine of judicial restraint in conducting independent investigations of fact. The Supreme Court increasingly departed from that doctrine in the 1920's.

The second issue was one of classification: on the assumption that some shoddy might be unsterilized, did the legislature have the right to prevent the use of all shoddy in bedding? Or, more important, why aim only at shoddy when disease might be spread by other materials as well? Behind Holmes's reply was the reasoning that the difficulty of distinguishing between sterilized and unsterilized shoddy in bedding made it not unreasonable for the legislature to pass a general prohibition rather than enter on a cumbersome plan of inspection and regulation. His reference at the end to Schlesinger v. Wisconsin is significant: for there too he contends for allowing the legislature a margin of tolerance: "the law allows a penumbra to be embraced that goes beyond the outline of its object in order that the object may be secured."[2]

If Holmes's tone is more abrupt in this case than in some of his earlier ones, we must remember that he was eighty-five, had been fighting on the Court for almost a quarter-century for a tolerant construction of the Fourteenth Amendment,

[1] 127 U. S. 678 (1888).
[2] See p. 258.

AMERICA AS A GOING CONCERN

and could not help feeling that he was not making much of a dent. In a letter to Pollock written a few months before this decision he writes, "I am very hard at work again as we are sitting, but in good shape and enjoying it, preparing small diamonds for people of limited intellectual means." [3]

Holmes, J., dissenting:

If the Legislature of Pennsylvania was of opinion that disease is likely to be spread by the use of unsterilized shoddy in comfortables I do not suppose that this Court would pronounce the opinion so manifestly absurd that it could not be acted upon. If we should not, then I think that we ought to assume the opinion to be right for the purpose of testing the law. The Legislature may have been of opinion further that the actual practice of filling comfortables with unsterilized shoddy gathered from filthy floors was widespread, and this again we must assume to be true. It is admitted to be impossible to distinguish the innocent from the infected product in any practicable way, when it is made up into comfortables. On these premises, if the Legislature regarded the danger as very great and inspection and tagging as inadequate remedies, it seems to me that in order to prevent the spread of disease it constitutionally could forbid any use of shoddy for bedding and upholstery. Notwithstanding the broad statement in *Schlesinger* v. *Wisconsin* the other day I do not suppose that it was intended to overrule *Purity Extract and Tonic Co.* v. *Lynch,* 226 U. S. 192 and the other cases to which I referred there.

It is said that there was unjustifiable discrimination. A classification is not to be pronounced arbitrary because it goes on practical grounds and attacks only those objects that exhibit or foster an evil on a large scale. It is not required to be mathematically precise and to embrace every case that theoretically is capable of doing the same harm. "If the law presumably hits the evil where it is most felt, it is not to be overthrown because there are other instances to which it might have been applied." *Miller* v. *Wilson,* 236 U. S. 373, 384. In this case, as in *Schlesinger* v. *Wisconsin,* I think we are pressing the Fourteenth Amendment too far.

[3] H–P, II: 173 (Dec. 1, 1925).

ON LEGISLATIVE MOTIVE

Frost v. California
271 U. S. 583, 600 (1926)

This case represents another incident in Holmes's fight for state legislative discretion. California, faced by the growth of commercial truck and bus traffic, tried by legislative act to bring the traffic under the regulation of the state railroad commission. The case turned on the question of whether the state Act was in reality for the conservation of the highways, or for some other purpose. Holmes clashed here with Justice Sutherland, who wrote the majority opinion invalidating the Act.

In his dissent (joined in by Justice Brandeis, with a separate dissent by Justice McReynolds), Holmes insisted that the Court could not review legislative motive. His position in all these cases of state power usually was that the purposes which impel a state legislature to pass an act are relevant, because the Court must determine whether they are clearly unreasonable purposes. It must then determine whether the means to be used bear a reasonable relation to the ends. But it cannot go beyond that. He says of "the reasons that may have induced the Legislature" that "if a warrant can be found in those reasons, they must be presumed to have been the ground."

Justice Sutherland's contention was that the real motive lay not in protecting and conserving the highways, but in protecting the railroads "by controlling competitive conditions."

Holmes, J., dissenting:

The question is whether a state may require all corporations or persons, with immaterial exceptions, who operate automobiles, etc., for the transportation of persons or property over a regular route and between fixed termini on the public highways of the State, for compensation, to obtain a certificate from the railroad commission that public necessity and convenience require such operation. A fee has to be paid for this certificate and transportation companies are made subject to the power of the railroad commission to regulate their rates, accounts and service. The provisions on this last point are immaterial here, as the case arises upon an order of the commission under section 5 that the plaintiffs in error desist from transportation of property as above unless and until they obtain the certificate required, and by the terms of the statute every section and claim in it is independent of the validity of all the rest. Section 10. Whatever the Supreme Court of California may have intimated, the only point that is decided, because that was the only question before it, was that the order of the commission should stand.

This portion of the act is to be considered with reference to the reasons that may have induced the Legislature to pass it, for if a warrant can be found in such reasons they must be presumed to have been the ground. I agree, of course, with the cases cited by my brother Sutherland, to which may be added *American Bank & Trust Co. v. Federal Reserve Bank*, 256 U. S. 350, 358, that even generally lawful acts or conditions may become unlawful when done or imposed to accomplish an unlawful end. But that is only the converse of the proposition that acts in other circumstances unlawful may be justified by the purpose for which they are done. This applies to acts of the Legislatures as well as to the doings of private parties. The only valuable significance of the much abused phrase police power is this power of the State to limit what otherwise would be rights having a pecuniary value, when a predominant public interest requires the restraint. The power of the State is limited in its turn by the constitutional guaranties of private rights, and it often is a delicate matter to decide which interest preponderates and how far the State may go without making compensation. The line cannot be drawn by generalities, but successive points in it must be fixed by weighing the particular facts. Extreme cases on the one side and on the other are *Edgar A. Levy Leasing Co. v. Siegel*, 258 U. S. 242, and *Pennsylvania Coal Co. v. Mahon*, 260 U. S. 393.

The point before us seems to me well within the legislative power. We all know what serious problems the automobile has introduced. The difficulties of keeping the streets reasonably clear for travel and for traffic are very great. If a State speaking through its Legislature should think that, in order to make its highways most useful, the business traffic upon them must be controlled, I suppose that no one would doubt that it constitutionally could, as, I presume, most States or cities do, exercise some such control. The only question is how far it can go. I see nothing to prevent its going to the point of requiring a license and bringing the whole business under the control of a railroad commission so far as to determine the number, character and conduct of transportation companies and so to prevent the streets from being made useless and dangerous by the number and lawlessness of those who seek to use them. I see nothing in this act that would require private carriers to become common carriers, but if there were such requirement, it, like the provisions concerning rates and accounts, would not be before us now, since, as I have said, the statute makes every section independent and declares that if valid it shall stand even if all the others fall. As to what is before us, I see no great difference between requiring a certificate and requiring a bond as in *Packard* v. *Banton,* 264 U. S. 140, and although, as I have said, I do not get much help from general propositions in a case of this sort, I cannot forbear quoting what seems to me applicable here. Distinguishing between activities that may be engaged in as a matter of right and those like the use of the streets that are carried on by government permission, it is said: "In the latter case the power to exclude altogether generally includes the lesser power to condition and may justify a degree of regulation not admissible in the former." 264 U. S. 145. I think that the judgment should be affirmed.

ABSENTEE CONTROL IN DRUGSTORES

Louis K. Liggett Co. v. *Baldridge*
271 U. S. 105, 114 (1928)

The question in this case was whether Pennsylvania's efforts to organize the local conditions of its economic system would be allowed by the Supreme Court. The Court's answer was negative, and again Holmes dissented. There was a 1927 Pennsylvania law, presumably aimed against chain drugstores, providing that all drugstores should be owned only by licensed pharmacists; and that if a corporation was the owner, all mem-

bers of the corporation had to meet the requirements, corporations already in existence and owning drugstores at the time of the passage of the Act being exempted. The Liggett Company, a Massachusetts corporation, fell within the exemption, but it bought two more stores after the passage of the Act, and the Pennsylvania Board of Pharmacy refused it a permit.

Justice Sutherland, in the majority opinion, held that the law violated the due process and equal protection provisions of the Fourteenth Amendment; that as a foreign corporation the Liggett Company could not be held subject to Pennsylvania statutes in conflict with the Constitution; that the Act bore no reasonable or direct relation to health, since there were other health provisions in effect; that it was therefore not justified under the police power of the state. He dismissed as resting on "conjecture" the legislative claim that there was a relation between the ownership of drugstores by pharmacists and the health of the people.

Holmes's dissent, in which Justice Brandeis joined, goes as usual directly to the heart of the matter. In his reference to the evil of "the divorce between the power of control and knowledge," there is a note almost reminiscent of Thorstein Veblen's concept of "absentee ownership." And there is again the Holmesian insistence that an act must not necessarily be an adequate social remedy in order to be constitutional.

The issue of social control that the Pennsylvania law raises is a vexed one. There is much to be said for chain stores on the score of efficiency and economy, just as there is a good deal to be said for the small-enterprise unit on the score of personal concern and a direct neighborhood relation. It is interesting that Holmes rather than Brandeis wrote the dissent in this case: Brandeis' views about the curse of bigness might have led him more deeply into the economic and social aspects of the case. Certainly the advantages of the fusion of technical knowledge and business control are maximized in the case of drugstores. While in immediate terms Sutherland may have been right in saying that health was protected by existing regulation, it would take more than his rather cavalier dismissal of the health phase to settle the issue of the relation between, let us say, the growth of chain stores in the drug business and the relegation of the pharmaceutical aspects of the drugstore to a subsidiary place in what has become a sort of department store. Justice Sutherland's subjective method here was a poor substitute for either the Brandeis method of factual research or the Holmes method of judicial tolerance.

For the heart of Holmes's dissent lies in his sentence, "*The Constitution does not make it a condition of preventive legislation that it should work a perfect cure.*" We should generally agree today that the problem of which chain stores are an expression is not solved by anti-chain-store legislation. But that, Holmes contended, is not the business of the Supreme Court. And time has upheld him.

Holmes, J., dissenting:

A standing criticism of the use of corporations in business is that it causes such business to be owned by people who do not know anything about it. Argument has not been supposed to be necessary in order to show that the divorce between the powers of control and knowledge is an evil. The selling of drugs and poisons calls for knowledge in a high degree, and Pennsylvania after enacting a series of other safeguards has provided that in that matter the divorce shall not be allowed. Of course, notwithstanding the requirement that in corporations hereafter formed all the stockholders shall be licensed pharmacists, it still would be possible for a stockholder to content himself with drawing dividends and to take no hand in the company's affairs. But obviously he would be more likely to observe the business with an intelligent eye than a casual investor who looked only to the standing of the stock in the market. The Constitution does not make it a condition of preventive legislation that it should work a perfect cure. It is enough if the questioned act has a manifest tendency to cure or at least make the evil less. It has been recognized by the professions, by statutes and by decisions, that a corporation offering professional services is not placed beyond legislative control by the fact that all the services in question are rendered by qualified members of the profession. . . .

But for decisions to which I bow I should not think any conciliatory phrase necessary to justify what seems to me one of the incidents of legislative power. I think, however, that the police power, as that term has been defined and explained, clearly extends to a law like this, whatever I may think of its wisdom, and that the decree should be affirmed.

Of course the appellant cannot complain of the exception in its favor that allows it to continue to own and conduct the drugstores that it now owns. The Fourteenth Amendment does not forbid statutes and statutory changes to have a beginning and thus to discriminate between the rights of an earlier and those of a later time. *Sperry & Hutchinson Co.* v. *Rhodes,* 220 U. S. 502, 505.

TAX LAW AND THE PENUMBRA

Schlesinger v. *Wisconsin*
270 U. S. 230, 241 (1925)

Holmes's tax decisions are numerous and important for the law of taxation: [1] *but they are also technical, and I have thought it desirable to reprint in this volume only a few. The present one is interesting principally because, by giving expression to Holmes's well-known doctrine of the penumbra, it goes beyond tax law to the whole body of Constitutional law.*

A Wisconsin law provided that when gifts were made within six years of death, there was to be an absolute presumption, for the purpose of the inheritance tax, that they were made in contemplation of death. In this case gifts of five million dollars were made, and the executors of the estate pleaded the unconstitutionality of the law under the Fourteenth Amendment. The Supreme Court majority held that the statutory presumption represented a denial of due process of law.

Justice Holmes dissented. He argues that the necessities of tax law administration and the difficulty of proving actual intent warrant making some sort of presumption absolute; that it becomes a question of degree as to how far in time that can be stretched; that there will undoubtedly be cases in which an injustice is done; but that "the law allows a penumbra to be embraced that goes beyond the outline of its object in order that the object may be secured." Thus we find here, as in the "unsterilized shoddy" case,[2] *Holmes thinking in very modern*

---

[1] In addition to this and the cases that follow, I may mention especially his dissent in *Towne* v. *Eisner,* 245 U. S. 418 (1918), where the question was whether a stock dividend was income.

[2] See above, p. 249.

terms of allowing an area of discretion for the difficulties of administrative process.

Holmes, J., dissenting:

If the Fourteenth Amendment were now before us for the first time I should think it ought to be construed more narrowly than it has been construed in the past. But even now it seems to me not too late to urge that in dealing with State legislation upon matters of substantive law we should avoid with great caution attempts to substitute our judgment for that of the body whose business it is in the first place with regard to questions of domestic policy that are fairly open to debate.

The present seems to me one of those questions. I leave aside the broader issues that might be considered and take the statute as it is written, putting the tax on the ground of an absolute presumption that gifts of a material part of the donor's estate made within six years of his death were made in contemplation of death. If the time were six months instead of six years I hardly think that the power of the State to pass the law would be denied, as the difficulty of proof would warrant making the presumption absolute; and while I should not dream of asking where the line can be drawn, since the great body of the law consists in drawing such lines, yet when you realize that you are dealing with a matter of degree you must realize that reasonable men may differ widely as to the place where the line should fall. I think that our discussion should end if we admit, what I certainly believe, that reasonable men might regard six years as not too remote. Of course many gifts will be hit by the tax that were made with no contemplation of death. But the law allows a penumbra to be embraced that goes beyond the outline of its object in order that the object may be secured. A typical instance is the prohibition of the sale of unintoxicating malt liquors in order to make effective a prohibition of the sale of beer. The power "is not to be denied simply because some innocent articles or transactions may be found within the proscribed class." *Purity Extract & Tonic Co.* v. *Lynch*, 226 U. S. 192, 201, 204. *Jacob Ruppert* v. *Caffey*, 251 U. S. 264, 283. In such cases (and they are familiar) the Fourteenth Amendment is invoked in vain. Later cases following the principle of *Purity Extract & Tonic Co.* v. *Lynch* are *Hebe Co.* v. *Shaw*, 248 U. S. 297, 303;

Pierce Oil Co. v. *Hope*, 248 U. S. 498, 500. See further *Capital City Dairy Co.* v. *Ohio*, 183 U. S. 238, 246.

I am not prepared to say that the Legislature of Wisconsin, which is better able to judge than I am, might not believe, as the Supreme Court of the State confidently affirms, that by far the larger proportion of gifts coming under the statute actually were made in contemplation of death. I am not prepared to say that if the Legislature held that belief, it might not extend the tax to gifts made within six years of death in order to make sure that its policy of taxation should not be escaped. I think that with the States as with Congress, when the means are not prohibited and are calculated to effect the object, we ought not to inquire into the degree of the necessity for resorting to them. *James Everard's Breweries* v. *Day*, 265 U. S. 545, 559.

It may be worth noticing that the gifts of millions taxed in this case were made from about four years before death to a little over one year. The statute is not called upon in its full force in order to justify this tax. If I thought it necessary I should ask myself whether it should not be construed as intending to get as near to six years as it constitutionally could, and whether it would be bad for a year and a month.

"A LINE THERE MUST BE"

Louisville Gas Co. v. *Coleman*
277 U. S. 32, 41 (1928)

> *This is a tax case that turns on the question of classification. Because the Fourteenth Amendment guarantees to the people of each state the equal protection of its laws, cases arise in which the question is whether a legislative distinction drawn between groups of classes of citizens violates this guarantee. A Kentucky law laid a recording tax, on mortgages, of twenty cents for each hundred dollars, but it exempted from the operation of the tax any mortgage that was to mature within five years. The Court majority held, in an opinion by Justice Sutherland, that this was an arbitrary classification and violated the equal protection provision. After all, Justice Sutherland reasoned, "the only difference well may be that one*

[*mortgage*] *is payable in sixty months and the other in fifty-nine months."*

Holmes's dissent, in which Justices Brandeis, Sanford, and Stone joined, cuts through the elaborate reasoning of the majority opinion. Holmes asserts again his often repeated doctrine that, while all differences in law are differences of degree, a line must be drawn somewhere. And since there can be no absolute logical precision in drawing the line, the legislative line must be accepted unless it is clearly unreasonable.

But Holmes also finds in this case a factual basis for the line. The reader may wish to refer to Justice Brandeis' long and painstaking dissent in this case, in which he goes into the factual background of the law to which Holmes only alludes. While it arrives at the same conclusion, it is an interesting contrast to Holmes's two-paragraph dissent, couched in very general terms.

Holmes, J., dissenting:

When a legal distinction is determined, as no one doubts that it may be, between night and day, childhood and maturity, or any other extremes, a point has to be fixed or a line has to be drawn, or gradually picked out by successive decisions, to mark where the change takes place. Looked at by itself without regard to the necessity behind it, the line or point seems arbitrary. It might as well or might nearly as well be a little more to the one side or the other. But when it is seen that a line or point there must be, and that there is no mathematical or logical way of fixing it precisely, the decision of the legislature must be accepted unless we can say that it is very wide of any reasonable mark.

There is a plain distinction between large loans secured by negotiable bonds and mortgages that easily escape taxation, and small ones to needy borrowers for which they give their personal note for a short term and a mortgage of their house. I hardly think it would be denied that the large transactions of the money market reasonably may be subjected to a tax from which small ones for private need are exempted. The Legislature of Kentucky after careful consideration has decided that the distinction is clearly marked when the loan is for so long a term as five years. Whatever doubt I may feel, I certainly cannot say that it is wrong. If it is right as to the run of cases a possible exception here and there would not make the law bad. All taxes have to be laid by general rules.

I think the judgment should be affirmed.

NO LIMIT BUT THE SKY

Baldwin v. Missouri
281 U. S. 586, 595 (1930)

When President Roosevelt held his now famous press conference after the Schechter decision, in 1935, the opinion to which he kept referring as an example of the doctrinal road the Court might have taken but did not was Holmes's dissent in Baldwin v. Missouri. Similarly he comes back to it in the introductory essay to the 1935 volume of his State Papers. What made the opinion strikingly useful to the President was that it characterized sharply the extension of judicial legislation and the nullification of state action as having "hardly any limit but the sky." The logic of the New Deal constitutional impasse was already implicit in this case, five years before.

The opinion has another distinction. It was Holmes's last dissent. And it is characteristic of his vigor that his last dissent was also one of his sharpest dissents. Holmes does not hesitate to thrust some barbs at his colleagues. If they were to continue on their course of judicial legislation they had no guide (he reminds them) but their own discretion. And after listing the precedents that the Court was disregarding, he speaks jibingly of their being "on the Index Expurgatorius." "But," *he adds,* "we need an authoritative list."

The present case relates to the problem of extra-territorial taxation. An Illinois resident died owning intangible property situated in Missouri, on which Missouri imposed a transfer tax, although Illinois had already levied an inheritance tax. The Missouri Supreme Court upheld the transfer tax on the authority of Blackstone v. Miller. *On appeal the decision was reversed by the United States Supreme Court, in an opinion by Justice McReynolds.*[1] *Holmes was joined in his dissent by Justices*

---

[1] Holmes wrote Pollock that the opinion by Justice McReynolds, like previous ones by the same justice, "overruled decisions written by me and others, when I thought authority, logic and settled practice authorized the tax." H–P, II:268 (June 9, 1930).

Brandeis and Stone. Justice Stone also wrote a separate dissent.

Until the early years of the present century double taxation by the states had been held not invalid by the Supreme Court. Holmes himself wrote the Court decision in the principal case, Blackstone v. Miller, in *1903* [2] with only Justice White dissenting. But starting in *1905* [3] the Court began to diverge from this stand. From then on the Court became extremely critical of multiple taxation of every sort. The first step in the new direction was taken in the Union Refrigerator *case,* in which the Court held that tangible personal property which was permanently situated outside the state of domicil could not be taxed. The second step was taken when the ruling was extended to inheritance taxation, again as far as tangibles were concerned, in Frick v. Pennsylvania.[4] The third step was taken in two decisions — the Farmers Loan and Trust Co. v. Minnesota,[5] and in the present case, both of them holding that the state of domicil alone could levy an inheritance tax on the transfer of credits. In the first case Justice McReynolds wrote the Court opinion, Justice Stone wrote a concurring opinion reaching the same result on different grounds, and Justice Holmes wrote a dissent in which Justice Brandeis joined. But his dissent was less sharp than in the present case, which was his climactic one in this line of decisions. Before Holmes left the bench the Court majority extended the doctrine to a transfer of stock at death, in the First National Bank of Boston v. Maine.[6] *Justice Stone, who had sought to follow the majority as far as possible, and who had written a concurring opinion in the* Farmers Loan *case, wrote a dissenting opinion in which Holmes and Brandeis joined.*

It should be noted that through this whole line of cases the

[2] 188 U. S. 189 (1903).
[3] *Union Refrigerator Transit Co.* v. *Kentucky,* 199 U. S. 194, 211 (1905). Holmes wrote a brief concurring opinion, in which White joined, expressing doubt as to the Court's course.
[4] 268 U. S. 473 (1925).
[5] 280 U. S. 204 (1930).
[6] 284 U. S. 312 (1932). For an acute legal discussion of the whole field as it stood after this case, see Charles L. B. Lowndes, "The Passing of Situs — Jurisdiction to Tax Shares of Corporate Stock," 45 HLR (1932) 777–792. See also Robert C. Brown, "Multiple Taxation by the States — What is Left of It?" 48 HLR (1935) 407–432.

AMERICA AS A GOING CONCERN

Court spoke in vague terms of jurisdiction to tax and of the situs of intangibles, but it did not dare at any point to say that double taxation was in itself unconstitutional. Nevertheless, the effect of the decisions was to outlaw it. While it may be expected that the new Supreme Court will not take a similar view, its direction is not yet wholly clear.

Holmes, J., dissenting:

Although this decision hardly can be called a surprise after *Farmers' Loan & Trust Co.* v. *Minnesota* 280 U. S. 204, and *Safe Deposit & Trust Co.* v. *Virginia*, 280 U. S. 83, and although I stated my views in those cases, still as the term is not over I think it legitimate to add one or two reflections to what I have said before. I have not yet adequately expressed the more than anxiety that I feel at the ever increasing scope given to the Fourteenth Amendment in cutting down what I believe to be the constitutional rights of the States. As the decisions now stand, I see hardly any limit but the sky to the invalidating of those rights if they happen to strike a majority of this Court as for any reason undesirable. I cannot believe that the Amendment was intended to give us *carte blanche* to embody our economic or moral beliefs in its prohibitions. Yet I can think of no narrower reason that seems to me to justify the present and the earlier decisions to which I have referred. Of course the words "due process of law" if taken in their literal meaning have no application to this case; and while it is too late to deny that they have been given a much more extended and artificial signification, still we ought to remember the great caution shown by the Constitution in limiting the power of the States, and should be slow to construe the clause in the Fourteenth Amendment as committing to the Court, with no guide but the Court's own discretion, the validity of whatever laws the States may pass. In this case the bonds, notes and bank accounts were within the power and received the protection of the State of Missouri; the notes so far as appears were within the considerations that I offered in the earlier decisions mentioned, so that logically Missouri was justified in demanding a *quid pro quo;* the practice of taxation in such circumstances I think has been ancient and widespread, and the tax was warranted by decisions of this Court, *Liverpool and L. and G. Ins. Co.* v. *Board of Assessors,* 221 U. S. 346, *Wheeler* v. *Sohmer*, 233 U. S. 434. (I suppose that these cases and many others now join

Blackstone v. *Miller,* 188 U. S. 189, on the *Index Expurgatorius* — but we need an authoritative list.) It seems to me to be exceeding our powers to declare such a tax a denial of due process of law.

And what are the grounds? Simply, so far as I can see, that it is disagreeable to a bond owner to be taxed in two places. Very probably it might be good policy to restrict taxation to a single place, and perhaps the technical conception of domicil may be the best determinant. But it seems to me that if that result is to be reached it should be reached through understanding among the States, by uniform legislation or otherwise, not by evoking a constitutional prohibition from the void of "due process of law" when logic, tradition and authority have united to declare the right of the State to lay the now prohibited tax.

Mr. Justice Brandeis and Mr. Justice Stone agree with this opinion.

JUDGES AS A PRIVILEGED CLASS

Evans v. *Gore*
253 U. S. 245, 264 (1920)

This is not a case of either great economic or political consequence, but it does Holmes honor. A federal judge in Kentucky contended that the Revenue Act of 1919, passed after the Income Tax Amendment, could not tax his salary as a judge: for, he contended, the Constitution provides that the compensation of judges shall not be diminished during their continuance in office. By a seven-to-two vote the Court upheld the contention. Justice Van Devanter, in the majority opinion, argued that "the primary purpose of the prohibition against diminution was not to benefit the judges, but . . . to attract good and competent men to the bench and to promote that independence of action and judgment which is essential" for judges. "Obviously, diminution may be effected in more ways than one. . . . Of what avail to him [Evans] was the part which was paid with one hand and taken back with the other?" It is a long opinion, and many will find in it weasel words. Justice Van Devanter said that the constitutional limitation was "to be construed not as a private grant, but as a limitation in the public interest." On which Professor (now Judge) Henry W. Edgerton comments, "It seems clear that the only interests which the decision served were those of the judges of the U. S. Courts, including the Supreme Court, in escaping taxation."[1]

Justice Holmes wrote a dissent in which Justice Brandeis joined. His crucial point is the distinction between "preventing attempts to deal with a judge's salary as such" and "exonerating him from the ordinary duties of a citizen," thus making the judges "a privileged class free from bearing their share of the cost of institutions upon which their well-being if not their life depends." This is reminiscent of the comment Holmes was fond of making about his own taxes — that they were the price he paid for civilization.

The case has an interesting sequel. The question next arose before the Court whether judges whose term of office had begun after the income tax was in effect could claim a similar tax immunity, and in Miles v. Graham[2] the Court replied yes. Congress then took the step of providing expressly that the salaries of newly appointed judges should be subject to income tax. By this time there was a new Supreme Court, following new doctrinal directions. In O'Malley v. Woodrough,[3] Justice Frankfurter, speaking for the majority, not only upheld this action of Congress, but reopened the issue of Evans v. Gore and overruled it. "To suggest that it [the tax] makes inroads upon the independence of judges . . . is to trivialize the great historic experience on which the framers based the safeguards of Article III, par. 1." Justice Butler, dissenting, said that "another landmark has been removed."

There is a letter from Holmes to Pollock in which he mentions an amusing personal aspect of Evans v. Gore. "As a result of a decision from which I dissented it turned out that I, in common with other U. S. judges, had paid considerably too large an income tax. The U. S. now actually has refunded it and I celebrated the fact by buying a few prints out of the odd

---

[1] *The Incidence of Judicial Control over Congress,* 22 *Cornell Law Quarterly* 299 (1937).
[2] 268 U. S. 501 (1925).
[3] 307 U. S. 277 (1938).

hundreds of dollars received. . . . So I am an aesthete for the moment."[4] *That must be set down as the only social gain on the credit side of the Court decision in* Evans v. Gore.

Holmes, J., dissenting:

This is an action brought by the plaintiff in error against an acting Collector of Internal Revenue to recover a portion of income tax paid by the former. The ground of the suit is that the plaintiff is entitled to deduct from the total of his net income six thousand dollars, being the amount of his salary as a judge of the District Court of the United States. The Act of February 24, 1919, c. 18, § 210, 40 Stat. 1057, 1062, taxes the net income of every individual, and § 213, p. 1065, requires the compensation received by the judges of the United States to be included in the gross income from which the net income is to be computed. This was done by the plaintiff in error and the tax was paid under protest. He contends that the requirement mentioned and the tax, to the extent that it was enhanced by consideration of the plaintiff's salary, are contrary to Article III, § 1, of the Constitution, which provides that the compensation of judges shall not be diminished during their continuance in office. Upon demurrer judgment was entered for the defendant, and the case comes here upon the single question of the validity of the above-mentioned provisions of the act.

The decision below seems to me to have been right for two distinct reasons: that this tax would have been valid under the original Constitution, and that if not so, it was made lawful by the Sixteenth Amendment. In the first place, I think that the clause protecting the compensation of judges has no reference to a case like this. The exemption of salaries from diminution is intended to secure the independence of the judges on the ground, as it was put by Hamilton in the *Federalist* (No. 79) that "a power over a man's subsistence amounts to a power over his will." That is a very good reason for preventing attempts to deal with a judge's salary as such, but it seems to me no reason for exonerating him from the ordinary duties of a citizen, which he shares with all others. To require a man to pay the taxes that all other men have to pay cannot possibly be made an instrument to attack his independence as a judge. I see nothing in the purpose of this clause of the Constitution to indicate that the judges were to be a privileged class free

[4] H-P, II:90 (Feb. 26, 1922).

AMERICA AS A GOING CONCERN

from bearing their share of the cost of the institutions upon which their well-being if not their life depends.

I see equally little in the letter of the clause to indicate the intent supposed. The tax on net incomes is a tax on the balance of a mutual account in which there always are some and may be many items on both sides. It seems to me that it cannot be affected by an inquiry into the source from which the items more or less remotely are derived. Obviously there is some point at which the immunity of a judge's salary stops, or to put it in the language of the clause, a point at which it could not be said that his compensation was diminished by a charge. If he bought a house the fact that a part or the whole of the price had been paid from his compensation as judge would not exempt the house. So if he bought bonds. Yet in such cases the advantages of his salary would be diminished. Even if the house or bonds were bought with other money the same would be true, since the money would not have been free for such an application if he had not used his salary to satisfy other more peremptory needs. At some point, I repeat, money received as salary loses its specific character as such. Money held in trust loses its identity by being mingled with the general funds of the owner. I see no reason why the same should not be true of a salary. But I do not think that the result could be avoided by keeping the salary distinct. I think that the moment the salary is received, whether kept distinct or not, it becomes part of the general income of the owner and is mingled with the rest, in theory of law, as an item in the mutual account with the United States. I see no greater reason for exempting the recipients while they still have the income as income than when they have invested it in a house or bond.

The decisions heretofore reached by this Court seem to me to justify my conclusion. In *Peck & Co. v. Lowe,* 247 U. S. 165, a tax was levied by Congress upon the income of the plaintiff corporation. More than two-thirds of the income were derived from exports and the Constitution in terms prohibits any tax on articles exported from any State. By construction it had been held to create "a freedom from any tax which directly burdens the exportation." *Fairbank* v. *United States,* 181 U. S. 283, 293. The prohibition was unequivocal and express, not merely an inference as in the present case. Yet it was held unanimously that the tax was valid. "It is not laid on income from exportation . . . in a discriminative way, but just as it is laid on other income. . . . There is no discrimination.

At most, exportation is affected only indirectly and remotely. The tax is levied . . . after the recipient of the income is free to use it as he chooses. Thus what is taxed — the net income — is as far removed from exportation as are articles intended for export before the exportation begins." 247 U. S. 174, 175. All this applies with even greater force when, as I have observed, the Constitution has no words that forbid a tax. In *United States Glue Co. v. Oak Creek*, 247 U. S. 321, 329, the same principle was affirmed as to interstate commerce and it was said that if there was no discrimination against such commerce the tax constituted one of the ordinary burdens of government from which parties were not exempted because they happened to be engaged in commerce among the States.

A second and independent reason why this tax appears to me valid is that, even if I am wrong as to the scope of the original document, the Sixteenth Amendment justifies the tax, whatever would have been the law before it was applied. By that Amendment, Congress is given power to "collect taxes on incomes, from whatever source derived." It is true that it goes on "without apportionment among the several States, and without regard to any census or enumeration," and this shows the particular difficulty that led to it. But the only cause of that difficulty was an attempt to trace income to its source, and it seems to me that the Amendment was intended to put an end to the cause and not merely to obviate a single result. I do not see how judges can claim an abatement of their income tax on the ground that an item in their gross income is salary, when the power is given expressly to tax incomes from whatever source derived.

THE GOVERNOR AND THE LABOR LEADER

Moyer v. Peabody
212 U. S. 78 (1909)

There was a tough-minded strain in Holmes's thinking that comes out clearly in the Moyer *case. Charles Moyer was head of the Western Federation of Miners, a militant union with syndicalist tendencies which was the center of much labor-capital violence in the Western states during this period. He* had been tried, with Big Bill Haywood and others, in a sensational murder trial and eventually freed.[1] Martial law, on which the present case turns, was frequently invoked, and not infrequently used through the pressure of the mining companies as an anti-union weapon. But it was also true that the Federation was thoroughly soaked in the ideology of the class struggle, and as ready to use violence as any American labor movement has been.

Holmes's opinion is one of the leading constitutional cases on the relation of the executive power to martial rule.[2] Moyer was arrested as a preventive measure and held without trial for ten weeks, without any charge being brought against him. He sued the Governor for having deprived him of his liberty without due process of law. Holmes upheld the Governor.

There are three basic steps in his reasoning: as a general proposition, the executive process may be substituted for the judicial in time of public danger; the Governor had the power, within his executive discretion, to declare a state of insurrection, call out the troops and order them to kill — and, since the larger power includes the lesser, he had the power to detain Moyer; although the detention proved to be "without sufficient reason," it was "in good faith." The implication is that, in the context of the necessities of the situation, good faith is all that the Court can require of the executive without crippling his power and therefore the survival power of the state.

It is clear that Holmes wanted a going governmental system, whether in time of social peace or of grave danger to the state. And he was willing to pay the price for the necessary executive power by the risks of the invasion of individual liberties. The difficulty of the opinion does not lie here. It lies in Holmes's failure to set any bounds, except those of good faith, to the power of the executive in suppressing disorder. In a later case, Sterling v. Constantin,[3] Chief Justice Hughes

---

[1] The defendants were charged with the murder of Steunenberg, former Governor of Idaho, in 1905. The trial was a *cause célèbre*. It ended in acquittal. The events leading to the present case had taken place two years before.

[2] The present case was the first case on martial law to reach the Supreme Court since the famous decision in *Ex parte Milligan*.

[3] 287 U. S. 378 (1932). For a discussion of this case, and incidentally of the present case, see Charles Fairman, *The Law of Martial Rule and the National*

pointed out the need to provide for court review of the question whether a danger actually existed such as to warrant martial rule.

Holmes was stretching his position a bit farther than he needed because he was fearful of any sentimentalism about liberty which would make effective government impossible in an emergency. "Every society," he was fond of saying, "is founded upon the death of men." If, as a result of the era of world troubles, the United States ever finds itself again as a constitutional government on the verge of civil conflict, Holmes's opinion will not only be invoked in putting down local insurrection, but by analogy the same reasoning will be transferred to the Presidential power.

Holmes, J., for the Court:

This is an action brought by the plaintiff in error against the former Governor of the State of Colorado, the former Adjutant General of the National Guard of the same State, and a captain of a company of the National Guard, for an imprisonment of the plaintiff by them while in office. The complaint was dismissed on demurrer, and the case comes here on a certificate that the demurrer was sustained solely on the ground that there was no jurisdiction in the Circuit Court. 148 Fed. Rep. 870.

The complaint alleges that the imprisonment was continued from the morning of March 30, 1904, to the afternoon of June 15, and that the defendants justified under the constitution of Colorado making the Governor commander-in-chief of the State forces, and giving him power to call them out to execute laws, suppress insurrection and repel invasion. It alleges that his imprisonment was without probable cause, that no complaint was filed against plaintiff, and that (in that sense) he was prevented from having access to the courts of the State, although they were open during the whole time; but it sets out proceedings on *habeas corpus,* instituted by him before the Supreme Court of the State, in which that court refused to admit him to bail and ultimately discharged the writ. *In re Moyer,* 35 Colorado, 154 and 159. In those proceedings it appeared that the Governor had declared a county to be in a state

---

Emergency, 55 HLR 1253 (1942). See also Robert S. Rankin, *When Civil Law Fails* (1939).

of insurrection, had called out troops to put down the trouble, and had ordered that the plaintiff should be arrested as a leader of the outbreak, and should be detained until he could be discharged with safety, and that then he should be delivered to the civil authorities to be dealt with according to law.

The jurisdiction of the Circuit Court, if it exists, is under Rev. Stat. § 629, Sixteenth. That clause gives original jurisdiction "of all suits authorized by law to be brought by any person to redress the deprivation, under color of any law, statute, ordinance, regulation, custom, or usage of any State, of any right, privilege, or immunity, secured by the Constitution of the United States, or of any right secured by any law providing for equal rights of citizens of the United States, or of all persons within the jurisdiction of the United States." The complaint purports to be founded upon the Constitution and on Rev. Stat. § 1979, which authorizes suit to be brought for such deprivation as above described. Therefore the question whether the complaint states a case upon the merits under § 1979 in this instance is another aspect of the question whether it states a case within the jurisdiction of the court under § 629, cl. 16. Taken either way, the question is whether this is a suit authorized by law, that is, by § 1979, or the Constitution, or both.

The plaintiff's position, stated in a few words, is that the action of the Governor, sanctioned to the extent that it was by the decision of the Supreme Court, was the action of the State and therefore within the Fourteenth Amendment; but that if that action was unconstitutional the Governor got no protection from personal liability for his unconstitutional interference with the plaintiff's rights. It is admitted, as it must be, that the Governor's declaration that a state of insurrection existed is conclusive of that fact. It seems to be admitted also that the arrest alone would not necessarily have given a right to bring this suit. *Luther* v. *Borden,* 7 How. 1, 45, 46. But it is said that a detention for so many days, alleged to be without probable cause, at a time when the courts were open, without an attempt to bring the plaintiff before them, makes a case on which he has a right to have a jury pass.

We shall not consider all of the questions that the facts suggest, but shall confine ourselves to stating what we regard as a sufficient answer to the complaint, without implying that there are not others equally good. Of course the plaintiff's position is that he has been deprived of his liberty without due process of law.

But it is familiar that what is due process of law depends on circumstances. It varies with the subject-matter and the necessities of the situation. Thus summary proceedings suffice for taxes, and executive decisions for exclusion from the country. *Murray* v. *Hoboken Land & Improvement Co.,* 18 How. 272; *United States* v. *Ju Toy,* 198 U. S. 253, 263. What, then, are the circumstances of this case? By agreement the record of the proceedings upon *habeas corpus* was made part of the complaint, but that did not make the averments of the petition for the writ averments of the complaint. The facts that we are to assume are that a state of insurrection existed and that the Governor, without sufficient reason but in good faith, in the course of putting the insurrection down, held the plaintiff until he thought that he safely could release him.

It would seem to be admitted by the plaintiff that he was president of the Western Federation of Miners, and that, whoever was to blame, trouble was apprehended with the members of that organization. We mention these facts not as material, but simply to put in more definite form the nature of the occasion on which the Governor felt called upon to act. In such a situation we must assume that he had a right under the State constitution and laws to call out troops, as was held by the Supreme Court of the State. The constitution is supplemented by an Act providing that "when an invasion of or an insurrection in the State is made or threatened the Governor shall order the National Guard to repel or suppress the same." Laws of 1897, c. 63, Art. 7, § 2, p. 204. That means that he shall make the ordinary use of soldiers to that end; that he may kill persons who resist and, of course, that he may use the milder measure of seizing the bodies of those whom he considers to stand in the way of restoring peace. Such arrests are not necessarily for punishment, but are by way of precaution to prevent the exercise of hostile power. So long as such arrests are made in good faith and in the honest belief that they are needed in order to head the insurrection off, the Governor is the final judge and cannot be subjected to an action after he is out of office on the ground that he had not reasonable ground for his belief. If we suppose a Governor with a very long term of office, it may be that a case could be imagined in which the length of the imprisonment would raise a different question. But there is nothing in the duration of the plaintiff's detention or in the allegations of the complaint that would warrant submitting the judgment of the Governor to revision by a jury. It is not alleged that his judgment was not honest, if that be material, or that the plaintiff was detained after fears of the insurrection were at an end.

No doubt there are cases where the expert on the spot may be called upon to justify his conduct later in court, notwithstanding the fact that he had sole command at the time and acted to the best of his knowledge. That is the position of the captain of a ship. But even in that case great weight is given to his determination and the matter is to be judged on the facts as they appear then and not merely in the light of the event. *Lawrence* v. *Minturn,* 17 How. 100, 110; *The Star of Hope,* 9 Wall 203; *The Germanic,* 196 U. S. 589, 594, 595. When it comes to a decision by the head of the State upon a matter involving its life, the ordinary rights of individuals must yield to what he deems the necessities of the moment. Public danger warrants the substitution of executive process for judicial process. See *Keely* v. *Sanders,* 90 U. S. 441, 446. This was admitted with regard to killing men in the actual clash of arms, and we think it obvious, although it was disputed, that the same is true of temporary detention to prevent apprehended harm. As no one would deny that there was immunity for ordering a company to fire upon a mob in insurrection, and that a State law authorizing the Governor to deprive citizens of life under such circumstances was consistent with the Fourteenth Amendment, we are of opinion that the same is true of a law authorizing by implication what was done in this case. As we have said already, it is unnecessary to consider whether there are other reasons why the Circuit Court was right in its conclusion. It is enough that in our opinion the declaration does not disclose a "suit authorized by law to be brought to redress the deprivation of any right secured by the Constitution of the United States." See *Dow* v. *Johnson,* 100 U. S. 158.

Judgment affirmed.

THEY CREATED A NATION, NOT A DOCUMENT

Missouri v. Holland
252 U. S. 416 (1920)

After all the learned words that have been written about the treaty-making power and about the place of this crucial decision in it, Holmes's own words retain a daring simplicity that needs little commentary. We had entered into a treaty with Great Britain by which the United States and Canada were each to enact laws for the protection of migratory birds. Congress passed an enforcing statute which Missouri challenged on the ground that the regulation of the killing of migratory birds was a state rather than a national matter, being part of the powers reserved to the states under the Tenth Amendment, and that the national power cannot effect by treaty what it could not effect by legislation. There was in Holmes an impatience with all forms of dwarfing pettiness which never wholly slumbered, and which was most summary when the crippling views were sought to be applied to the national power and majesty in war or international relations. "It is not lightly to be assumed," he wrote in rejecting Missouri's contention and affirming the constitutionality of the Act, "that, in matters requiring national action, 'a power which must belong to and somewhere reside in every civilized government' is not to be found."

There is in this opinion more than a hint of John Marshall's manner and approach. My own belief is that even in Marshall's opinions one would have to search long to find as sharp and powerful an expression of the view that national survival is not only a political but also a constitutional imperative. Holmes's words bear repeating: "When we are dealing with words that also are a constituent act, like the Constitution of the United States, we must realize that they have called into life a being the development of which could not have been foreseen completely by the most gifted of its begetters. It was enough for them to realize or to hope that they had created an organism; it has taken a century and has cost their successors much sweat and blood to prove that they created a nation."

Such a view means, in its broadest terms, that Holmes saw constitutional law as far more than commentary on a document. He saw it as the relation between a document and the organic fact of American national life. And in this relation, instead of pruning American life to a stunting conception of the document, he preferred to infuse a largeness into the document which would make it measure up to the greatness of American life. "We must consider what this country has become instead of deciding what the Amendment has reserved."

Justices Van Devanter and Pitney dissented.

Holmes, J., for the Court:

This is a bill in equity brought by the State of Missouri to prevent a game warden of the United States from attempting to enforce the Migratory Bird Treaty Act of July 3, 1918, c. 128, 40 Stat. 755, and the regulations made by the Secretary of Agriculture in pursuance of the same. The ground of the bill is that the statute is an unconstitutional interference with the rights reserved to the States by the Tenth Amendment, and that the acts of the defendant done and threatened under that authority invade the sovereign right of the State and contravene its will manifested in statutes. The State also alleges a pecuniary interest, as owner of the wild birds within its borders and otherwise, admitted by the Government to be sufficient, but it is enough that the bill is a reasonable and proper means to assert the alleged quasi sovereign rights of a State. . . . A motion to dismiss was sustained by the District Court on the ground that the act of Congress is constitutional. 258 Fed. Rep. 479. . . . The State appeals.

On December 8, 1916, a treaty between the United States and Great Britain was proclaimed by the President. It recited that many species of birds in their annual migration traversed certain parts of the United States and of Canada, that they were of great value as a source of food and in destroying insects injurious to vegetation, but were in danger of extermination through lack of adequate protection. It therefore provided for specified closed seasons and protection in other forms, and agreed that the two powers would take or propose to their law-making bodies the necessary measures for carrying the treaty out. 39 Stat. 1702. The above mentioned Act of July 3, 1918, entitled an act to give effect to the convention, prohibited the killing, capturing or selling of any of the migratory birds included in the terms of the treaty except as permitted by regulations compatible with those terms, to be made by the Secretary of Agriculture. Regulations were proclaimed on July 31, and October 25, 1918. 40 Stat. 1812; 1863. It is unnecessary to go into any details, because, as we have said, the question raised is the general one whether the treaty and statute are void as an interference with the rights reserved to the States.

To answer this question it is not enough to refer to the Tenth

Amendment, reserving the powers not delegated to the United States, because by Article II, section 2, the power to make treaties is delegated expressly, and by Article VI treaties made under the authority of the United States, along with the Constitution and laws of the United States made in pursuance thereof, are declared the supreme law of the land. If the treaty is valid there can be no dispute about the validity of the statute under Article I, section 8, as a necessary and proper means to execute the powers of the Government. The language of the Constitution as to the supremacy of treaties being general, the question before us is narrowed to an inquiry into the ground upon which the present supposed exception is placed.

It is said that a treaty cannot be valid if it infringes the Constitution, that there are limits, therefore, to the treaty-making power, and that one such limit is that what an act of Congress could not do unaided, in derogation of the powers reserved to the States, a treaty cannot do. An earlier act of Congress that attempted by itself and not in pursuance of a treaty to regulate the killing of migratory birds within the States had been held bad in the District Court. *United States* v. *Shauver,* 214 Fed. Rep. 154. *United States* v. *McCullagh,* 221 Red. Rep. 288. Those decisions were supported by arguments that migratory birds were owned by the States in their sovereign capacity for the benefit of their people, and that under cases like *Geer* v. *Connecticut,* 161 U. S. 519, this control was one that Congress had no power to displace. The same argument is supposed to apply now with equal force.

Whether the two cases cited were decided rightly or not they cannot be accepted as a test of the treaty power. Acts of Congress are the supreme law of the land only when made in pursuance of the Constitution, while treaties are declared to be so when made under the authority of the United States. It is open to question whether the authority of the United States means more than the formal acts prescribed to make the convention. We do not mean to imply that there are no qualifications to the treaty-making power; but they must be ascertained in a different way. It is obvious that there may be matters of the sharpest exigency for the national well being that an act of Congress could not deal with but that a treaty followed by such an act could, and it is not lightly to be assumed that, in matters requiring national action, "a power which must belong to and somewhere reside in every civilized government" is not to be found. *Andrews* v. *Andrews,* 188 U. S. 14, 33. What was said in that case with regard to the powers of the States applies with equal force to the powers of the nation in cases where the States individually are incompetent to act. We are not yet discussing the particular case before us but only are considering the validity of the test proposed. With regard to that we may add that when we are dealing with words that also are a constituent act, like the Constitution of the United States, we must realize that they have called into life a being the development of which could not have been foreseen completely by the most gifted of its begetters. It was enough for them to realize or to hope that they had created an organism; it has taken a century and has cost their successors much sweat and blood to prove that they created a nation. The case before us must be considered in the light of our whole experience and not merely in that of what was said a hundred years ago. The treaty in question does not contravene any prohibitory words to be found in the Constitution. The only question is whether it is forbidden by some invisible radiation from the general terms of the Tenth Amendment. We must consider what this country has become in deciding what that Amendment has reserved.

The State as we have intimated founds its claim of exclusive authority upon an assertion of title to migratory birds, an assertion that is embodied in statute. No doubt it is true that as between a State and its inhabitants the State may regulate the killing and sale of such birds, but it does not follow that its authority is exclusive of paramount powers. To put the claim of the State upon title is to lean upon a slender reed. Wild birds are not in the possession of anyone; and possession is the beginning of ownership. The whole foundation of the State's rights is the presence within their jurisdiction of birds that yesterday had not arrived, tomorrow may be in another State and in a week a thousand miles away. If we are to be accurate we cannot put the case of the State upon higher ground than that the treaty deals with creatures that for the moment are within the State borders, that it must be carried out by officers of the United States within the same territory, and that but for the treaty the State would be free to regulate this subject itself.

As most of the laws of the United States are carried out within the States and as many of them deal with matters which in the silence of such laws the State might regulate, such general grounds are not enough to support Missouri's claim. Valid treaties of course "are as binding within the territorial limits of the States as they are elsewhere throughout the dominion of the United States." *Baldwin* v. *Franks,* 120 U. S. 678,683. No doubt the great body of private relations usually fall within the control of the State, but a treaty may override its power. We do not have to invoke the later developments of constitutional law for this proposition; it was recognized as early as *Hopkirk* v. *Bell,* 3 Cranch, 454, with regard to statutes of limitation, and even earlier, as to confiscation, in *Ware* v. *Hylton,* 3 Dall. 199. It was assumed by Chief Justice Marshall with regard to the escheat of land to the State in *Chirac* v. *Chirac,* 2 Wheat. 259,275. . . . So as to a limited jurisdiction of foreign consuls within a State. *Wildenhus's Case,* 120 U. S. 1. . . . Further illustration seems unnecessary, and it only remains to consider the application of established rules to the present case.

Here a national interest of very nearly the first magnitude is involved. It can be protected only by national action in concert with that of another power. The subject-matter is only transitorily within the State and has no permanent habitat therein. But for the treaty and the statute there soon might be no birds for any powers to deal with. We see nothing in the Constitution that compels the Government to sit by while a food supply is cut off and the protectors of our forests and our crops are destroyed. It is not sufficient to rely upon the States. The reliance is vain, and were it otherwise, the question is whether the United States is forbidden to act. We are of opinion that the treaty and statute must be upheld. *Carey* v. *South Dakota,* 250 U. S. 118.

Decree affirmed.

Mr. Justice Van Devanter and Mr. Justice Pitney dissent.

HOUSING IN WARTIME WASHINGTON

Block v. *Hirsh*

256 U. S. 135 (1921)

This is one of two emergency rent cases. Both were five-to-four decisions, and Holmes wrote the majority opinion in both.[1] *The present case has two aspects of importance. It deals*

---

[1] The second one, *Marcus Brown Co.* v. *Feldman,* 256 U. S. 170 (1921), is not reprinted because it adds nothing distinctive to what Holmes says here.

with the war power in a democracy; and it deals with the relation of property rights to the purposes of the state.

The war brought with it a scarcity of housing facilities in the administrative and industrial centers.[2] The situation in Washington, which was particularly acute, was dealt with by a Congressional Act for the District of Columbia that sought to prevent profiteering in rents, through methods given in the opinion; the situation in New York City was dealt with by a similar New York state law, as explained in the Marcus Brown case. A dissent by Justice McKenna, in which Chief Justice White and Justices Van Devanter and McReynolds joined, was entered in each case.

It urged in this case that the Congressional Act violated the Fifth Amendment by taking property without compensation; and that the Act as passed was not, as it claimed, for the regulation of health or the alleviation of administrative tension. "Of what concern is it to the public health or the operations of the Federal Government who shall occupy a cellar, and a room above it, for business purposes in the City of Washington?" The purpose was rather, Justice McKenna insisted, socialism. Have conditions arisen, he asked, "that are not amenable to passing palliatives, so that socialism, or some form of socialism, is the only permanent corrective or accommodation?" He preferred, he said, to abide by the "prohibitions" of the Constitution, which were "as absolute as axioms."

This joined issue squarely with Justice Holmes, who, as anxious as any of his colleagues to abide by the Constitution, did not consider any governmental concepts as absolutes. Property, among other social values, was not "exempt from legislative modification required from time to time in civilized life," although "the fact that tangible property is also visible tends to give a rigidity" to our notion of it. As to the reality of the need of legislation, "Congress stated a publicly notorious and almost world-wide fact."

But in validating the means that Congress used, Holmes seemed to vacillate between a very broad statement ("the

---

[2] For the evidence given at the hearings on emergency rent legislation, see the *Hearings . . . on H. R. 9642*, U. S. Congress, House, Committee on Labor, Feb. 11, 1918. See also E. L. Schaub, "The Regulation of Rentals during the War Period," 28 *Journal of Political Economy* 1 (1920), and A. A. Friedrich, "Rent Regulation," 13 *Encyclopedia of the Social Sciences*, 293 (1934).

question is whether Congress was incompetent to meet it [the need] in a way in which it has been met by most of the civilized countries of the world"), and a narrower appeal to the doctrine that "circumstances have clothed the letting of buildings in the District of Columbia with a public interest so great as to justify regulation by law." Holmes had always been reluctant to use the doctrine of industry "affected with a public interest," although he had done so in the Noble State Bank case; and he was to reject the doctrine completely in his dissent in Tyson v. Banton. In the present case he is in a transitional mood, paying some deference to the doctrine, but resting his position primarily on the broader ground of what was necessary for national survival.

For that is the real importance of the emergency rent cases — their recognition of the broad base of national power necessary for the effective waging of war. John Quincy Adams once said that while the peace power of the American Government was closely contained within the constitutional provisions, the war power *"is only limited by the usages of nations."* Holmes's remark on the competence of Congress to deal with the housing problem in the manner which other civilized nations have adopted is strikingly parallel to Adams' conception. And it is notable that even when he talks of the letting of houses as clothed with a public interest he does not do it in the static terms in which the doctrine was generally put, but makes it a dynamic matter: *"Circumstances may so change in time or so differ in space as to clothe with such an interest what at other times or in other places would be a matter of purely private concern."*[3] Here is a doctrine broad enough and flexible enough to meet fully the requirements of a democracy like ours in a world in which the techniques of total warfare have become imperatives.

One other thing is worth noting: that the minority in the rent cases, which insisted that property or contract rights

---

[3] A few years after this decision, in *Chastleman Corp* v. *Sinclair*, 264 U. S. 543 (1924) the Court implied that the validity of the rent regulation would not reach beyond the duration of the emergency. In the Second World War the Office of Price Administration, acting under the directives of a Presidential order, declared the existence of a housing emergency in a number of war industry centers all over the country, and was prepared to act to maintain rent ceilings.

AMERICA AS A GOING CONCERN

could not be thus abridged in a war emergency, and held the constitutional prohibitions "absolute as axioms," did not feel that way about other constitutional prohibitions when they voted with the majority in the freedom of speech cases arising out of the war. Holmes was far more consistent in his willingness, whether in Block v. Hirsh *or in the* Schenck *case, to recognize that neither property nor liberty is an absolute; but his hierarchy of values showed itself by his greater solicitude that a heavier burden of proof be placed on the abridgment of civil liberties.*

Holmes, J., for the Court:

This is a proceeding brought by the defendant in error, Hirsh, to recover possession of the cellar and first floor of a building on F Street in Washington which the plaintiff in error, Block, holds over after the expiration of a lease to him. Hirsh bought the building while the lease was running, and on December 15, 1919, notified Block that he should require possession on December 31, when the lease expired. Block declined to surrender the premises, relying upon the Act of October 22, 1919, c. 80, Title II — 'District of Columbia Rents'; especially § 109, 41 Stat. 297, 298, 301. That is also the ground of his defense in this Court, and the question is whether the statute is constitutional, or, as held by the Court of Appeals, an attempt to authorize the taking of property not for public use and without due process of law, and for this and other reasons void.

By § 109 of the act the right of a tenant to occupy any hotel (apartment, or 'rental property,' i.e., any building or part thereof, other than hotel or apartment, § 101), is to continue notwithstanding the expiration of his term, at the option of the tenant, subject to regulation by the Commission appointed by the act, so long as he pays the rent and performs the conditions as fixed by the lease or as modified by the Commission. It is provided in the same section that the owner shall have the right to possession 'for actual and bona fide occupancy by himself, or his wife, children, or dependents . . . upon giving thirty days' notice in writing.' According to his affidavit Hirsh wanted the premises for his own use, but he did not see fit to give thirty days' notice because he denied the validity of the act. The statute embodies a scheme or code which it is needless to set forth, but it should be stated that it ends with the declaration in § 122 that the provisions of Title II are made necessary by the emergencies growing out of the war, resulting in rental conditions in the District dangerous to the public health and burdensome to public officers, employees and accessories, and thereby embarrassing the Federal Government in the transaction of the public business. As emergency legislation the Title is to end in two years unless sooner repealed.

No doubt it is true that a legislative declaration of facts that are material only as the ground for enacting a rule of law, for instance, that a certain use is a public one, may not be held conclusive by the Courts. . . . But a declaration by a legislature concerning public conditions that by necessity and duty it must know, is entitled at least to great respect. In this instance Congress stated a publicly notorious and almost world-wide fact. That the emergency declared by the statute did exist must be assumed, and the question is whether Congress was incompetent to meet it in the way in which it has been met by most of the civilized countries of the world.

The general proposition to be maintained is that circumstances have clothed the letting of buildings in the District of Columbia with a public interest so great as to justify regulation by law. Plainly circumstances may so change in time or so differ in space as to clothe with such an interest what at other times or in other places would be a matter of purely private concern. It is enough to refer to the decisions as to insurance, in *German Alliance Insurance Co.* v. *Lewis,* 233 U. S. 389; irrigation, in *Clark* v. *Nash,* 198 U. S. 361; and mining, in *Strickley* v. *Highland Boy Gold Mining Co.,* 200 U. S. 527. They sufficiently illustrate what hardly would be denied. They illustrate also that the use by the public generally of each specific thing affected cannot be made the test of public interest, *Mt. Vernon-Woodberry Cotton Duck Co.* v. *Alabama Interstate Power Co.* 240 U. S. 30, 32, and that the public interest may extend to the use of land. They dispel the notion that what in its immediate aspect may be only a private transaction may not be raised by its class or character to a public affair. See, also, *Noble State Bank* v. *Haskell,* 219 U. S. 104, 110, 111.

The fact that tangible property is also visible tends to give a rigidity to our conception of our rights in it that we do not attach to others less concretely clothed. But the notion that the former are exempt from legislative modification required from time to time in civilized life is contradicted not only by the doctrine of eminent domain, under which what is taken is paid for, but by that of the police power in its proper sense, under which property rights may be cut down, and to that extent taken, without pay. Under the police power the right to erect buildings in a certain quarter of a city may be limited to from eighty to one hundred feet. *Welch* v. *Swasey,* 214 U. S. 91. Safe pillars may be required in coal mines. *Plymouth Coal Co.* v. *Pennsylvania,* 232 U. S. 531. Billboards in cities may be regulated. *St. Louis Poster Co.* v. *St. Louis,* 249 U. S. 269. Watersheds in the country may be kept clear. *Perley* v. *North Carolina,* 249 U. S. 511. These cases are enough to establish that a public exigency will justify the legislature in restricting property rights in land to a certain extent without compensation. But if to answer one need the legislature may limit height to answer another it may limit rent. We do not perceive any reason for denying the justification held good in the foregoing cases to a law limiting the property rights now in question if the public exigency requires that. The reasons are of a different nature but they certainly are not less pressing. Congress has stated the unquestionable embarrassment of Government and danger to the public health in the existing conditions of things. The space in Washington is necessarily monopolized in comparatively few hands, and letting portions of it is as much a business as any other. Housing is a necessary of life. All the elements of a public interest justifying some degree of public control are present. The only matter that seems to us open to debate is whether the statute goes too far. For just as there comes a point at which the police power ceases and leaves only that of eminent domain, it may be conceded that regulations of the present sort pressed to a certain height might amount to a taking without due process of law. *Martin* v. *District of Columbia,* 205 U. S. 135, 139.

Perhaps it would be too strict to deal with this case as concerning only the requirement of thirty days' notice. For although the plaintiff alleged that he wanted the premises for his own use the defendant denied it and might have prevailed upon that issue under the act. The general question to which we have adverted must be decided, if not in this then in the next case, and it should be disposed of now. The main point against the law is that tenants are allowed to remain in possession at the same rent that they have been paying, unless modified by the Commission established by the act, and that thus the use of the land and the right of the owner to do what he will with his own and to make what contracts he pleases are cut down. But if the public interest be established the regulation of rates is one of the first forms in which it is asserted, and the validity of such regulation has been settled since *Munn v. Illinois*, 94 U. S. 113. It is said that a grain elevator may go out of business whereas here the use is fastened upon the land. The power to go out of business, when it exists, is an illusory answer to gas companies and waterworks, but we need not stop at that. The regulation is put and justified only as a temporary measure. See *Wilson v. New*, 243 U. S. 332, 345, 346. *Fort Smith & Western R. R. Co. v. Mills*, 253 U. S. 206. A limit in time, to tide over a passing trouble, well may justify a law that could not be upheld as a permanent change.

Machinery is provided to secure to the landlord a reasonable rent. § 106. It may be assumed that the interpretation of "reasonable" will deprive him in part at least of the power of profiting by the sudden influx of people to Washington caused by the needs of Government and the war, and thus of a right usually incident to fortunately situated property — of a part of the value of his property as defined in *International Harvester Co. v. Kentucky*, 234 U. S. 222. *Southern Ry. Co. v. Greene*, 216 U. S. 400, 414. But while it is unjust to pursue such profits from a national misfortune with sweeping denunciations, the policy of restricting them has been embodied in taxation and is accepted. It goes little if at all farther than the restriction put upon the rights of the owner of money by the more debatable usury laws. The preference given to the tenant in possession is an almost necessary incident of the policy and is traditional in English law. If the tenant remained subject to the landlord's power to evict, the attempt to limit the landlord's demands would fail.

Assuming that the end in view otherwise justifies the means adopted by Congress, we have no concern of course with the question whether those means were the wisest, whether they may not cost more than they come to, or will effect the result desired. It is enough that we are not warranted in saying that legislation that has been resorted to for the same purpose all over the world, is futile or has no reasonable relation to the relief sought. *Chicago, Burlington & Quincy R. R. Co. v. McGuire*, 219 U. S. 549, 569.

The statute is objected to on the further ground that landlords and tenants are deprived by it of a trial by jury on the right to possession of the land. If the power of the Commission established by the statute to regulate the relation is established, as we think it is, by what we have said, this objection amounts to little. To regulate the relation and to decide the facts affecting it are hardly separable. While the act is in force there is little to decide except whether the rent allowed is reasonable, and upon that question the courts are given the last word. A part of the exigency is to secure a speedy and summary administration of the law and we are not prepared to say that the suspension of ordinary remedies was not a reasonable provision of a statute reasonable in its aim and intent. The plaintiff obtained a judgment on the ground that the statute was void, root and branch. That judgment must be reversed.

SPIDERWEBS AND PRESIDENTIAL POWER

Myers v. U. S.
272 U. S. 52, 177 (1926)

This case arose from the silence of the Constitution about the power of removal of appointed officials. For a hundred and thirty-five years the Supreme Court had avoided passing on the vexed question of whether Congress could stipulate that it should have a hand in it. The Myers *case was the first judicial test.*[1] *Myers was appointed by President Wilson to a first-class postmastership at Portland, Oregon, in 1917 and removed by him in 1920 before his term of four years was up. An 1876 Congressional statute stipulated that postmasters "shall be appointed and may be removed by the President by and with the advice and consent of the Senate and shall hold their offices for four years unless sooner removed or suspended according to law."*

The Supreme Court recognized the case to be difficult constitutionally. But its political implications were important. It was argued twice, once in December 1924 and once in the

---

[1] It was not, of course, the first time the question had come before the Supreme Court. But each time the Court had studiously evaded the issue. See Frankfurter and Hart, *The Business of the Supreme Court at October Term, 1934,* 49 HLR 68, 105.

spring of 1925, before the Court could reach a majority vote. On the rehearing Senator George Wharton Pepper appeared as amicus curiae *to present the views of the Senate. The Court finally divided six to three, holding the removal power provision of the 1876 statute invalid and upholding the exclusive removal power by the President. The opinions were among the longest in the history of the Court. The majority opinion of Chief Justice Taft was some 22,000 words, covering seventy-one pages in the Reports; the dissenting opinions of Justices McReynolds and Brandeis were not much shorter. Holmes wrote a dissent of three paragraphs.*

The Chief Justice's opinion was an exhaustive survey of the doctrinal history of the removal of power. His principal historical reliance was on three sources: what has been called the "decision of 1789" — the debate in the first House of Representatives in that year and the conclusion reached; President Jackson's Protest Message to Congress on the occasion of his removal of Duane, his Secretary of the Treasury, in 1834; and the debates over the Tenure of Office Act under President Johnson after the Civil War. Taft argued also that since the President was entrusted with the execution of the laws, he had not only the right but the duty of retaining complete control over the removal of those executive officials who might otherwise interfere with his fulfillment of this duty.

There was protest against this decision both from the right and left on the Court, as also in the country. And the weight of opinion today holds that Justices McReynolds and Brandeis had the better of the historical and constitutional arguments. Nevertheless, Taft would seem to have been writing from a clearer and more functional view of the problem of Presidential leadership in a democracy. While President, he had approached his problems from a judicial standpoint, because of his earlier conditioning as a judge; and while Chief Justice, he approached his problems from an administrative standpoint, because of his earlier conditioning as a President.

Holmes's dissent is difficult to reconcile with such realism about the executive process as he had shown in his Moyer *decision. He takes here a view of Presidential power that seems far too limited for our day. It could be shown historically that there has been a rough sequence in our conceptions of the fun-*

damental locus of our governmental power: first Congressional, then judicial, and latterly — with the growth of a vast administrative structure — Presidential. While Holmes is justified in calling most of Taft's reasoning "spiders' webs inadequate to control the dominant facts," his own conception of the dominant facts seems one-sided. For while it is true that the President can exercise his executive power only within the legislative framework set by Congress (even this is too summary: the President has a whole range of non-Congressionally conditioned functions, especially in the shaping of foreign policy), it is also true that once Congress passes a law, the President becomes an administrative chief with respect to it and needs scope for his leadership that will not be sabotaged by officials who will not follow that leadership.[2]

On this score the Myers case has a sequel. In Humphrey's Executor v. U. S.[3] the Supreme Court decided that there was a distinction between executive officers and those members of administrative agencies (Humphrey had been a member of the Federal Trade Commission, appointed by President Hoover and removed by President Roosevelt because he did not have "full confidence" in him) who fulfill quasi-legislative and quasi-judicial functions as well. Although Justice Sutherland insisted that he was overruling not the actual holding in the Myers case but only a dictum of Chief Justice Taft, there can be little doubt that the Humphrey case, in Professor Corwin's words, "goes a long way toward scrapping the Myers decision."[4] Since President Roosevelt acted on the basis of the Myers decision, some have felt, like Attorney General (now Justice) Jackson in his Struggle for Judicial Supremacy,[5] that it would have been more candid for the Court to admit it had changed its mind, rather than imply that the President had

---

[2] While I cannot follow Holmes in this case I must say, in justice to his position, that there is force in his contention that on the matter of the removal power, the Constitution is itself a blank; Holmes argues from this that Congress had therefore complete legislative control over it. My own approach would be to say that since the Constitution is a blank on this matter, one must reason from the nature of the functions that both Congress and the President have to perform in the Government.
[3] 295 U. S. 602 (1935).
[4] Corwin, Edward S., *The President: Office and Powers* (1940), 92.
[5] Jackson, Robert H., *The Struggle for Judicial Supremacy* (1941), 109.

sought to flout the Constitution.⁶ *In any event it is clear from Holmes's dissent in the* Myers *case that, like Justice Brandeis, he would have voted with the Court in the* Humphrey *case.*

Holmes, J., dissenting;

My brothers McReynolds and Brandeis have discussed the question before us with exhaustive research and I say a few words merely to emphasize my agreement with their conclusion.

The arguments drawn from the executive power of the President, and from his duty to appoint officers of the United States (when Congress does not vest the appointment elsewhere), to take care that the laws be faithfully executed, and to commission all officers of the United States, seem to me spiders' webs inadequate to control the dominant facts.

We have to deal with an office that owes its existence to Congress and that Congress may abolish tomorrow. Its duration and the pay attached to it while it lasts depend on Congress alone. Congress alone confers on the President the power to appoint to it and at any time may transfer the power to other hands. With such power over its own creation, I have no more trouble in believing that Congress has power to prescribe a term of life for it free from any interference than I have in accepting the undoubted power of Congress to decree its end. I have equally little trouble in accepting its power to prolong the tenure of an incumbent until Congress or the Senate shall have assented to his removal. The duty of the President to see that the laws be executed is a duty that does not go beyond the laws or require him to achieve more than Congress sees fit to leave within his power.

⁶ The *Myers* case had been decided after so long a deliberation and had focused so much attention that one must suspect Justice Sutherland of having been ingenuous in restricting the scope of its actual decision to "a postmaster of the first class." The whole context of Chief Justice Taft's opinion was such as to leave no doubt that he included the Federal Trade Commission in its scope.

2. State Power and Free Trade in Ideas

Holmes's opinions in the civil liberties cases gave occasion to some of his most moving utterances. In this area he was writing con amore *without the slight sense of inhibition such as that he had when confronted with technical economic problems. Here, in the relation of state power to individual intellectual freedom, was a subject on which Plato, Milton, Mill, Bagehot and others had expended their best energies — a subject which of all problems in the realm of state theory is at once the most difficult and the most challenging. If there was one task which this writer-philosopher-lawyer could best confront, by reason of both past preparation and his deepest nature, it was this. He brought to it on the one hand a solicitude for individual expression and also a toughness of mind which saw the survival of the state as a condition precedent to the creativeness of individuals within it.*

Unlike the cases in the previous section, Holmes's civil liberties opinions are not numerous, and it has been possible to include most of them. They fall roughly into three groups. The first concerns freedom of speech, thought, and political opposition. The second concerns the procedural safeguards which the Constitution throws around the individual, particularly in court. The third concerns the privacy — and, more broadly, the liberty — of the person. Within each of these groupings the cases are arranged roughly in chronological order.

But running through all three groups there are several persistent themes. For one thing, Holmes did not regard the Bill of Rights as embodying any absolute guarantees. Some limits had to be drawn around freedom. But where they were to be drawn depended upon the balance of social and individual values in the specific cases. In the cases involving procedural safeguards in court, this result was best achieved by protecting not only the forms but the realities of due procedure, even at the cost of ruffling judicial sensibilities or wounding localist feelings. With respect to the privacy and freedom of the person Holmes was willing to go far to safeguard them against legislative or administrative invasion, unless that invasion were clearly necessary for the welfare of the whole community. In the realm of speech, Holmes felt that the balance was best achieved by a reliance on the competition of ideas. But even this principle was subject to qualifications. Holmes sought to shape a usable test for thus limiting the competition of ideas — the test of the "clear and present danger" doctrine.

Holmes did not resolve the difficulties involved in the problem of state power and individual expression. There is much to criticize in the opinions that follow. There has been a tendency to think that he went too far in his Debs opinion, and that Debs's speech was probably not very different from the Gitlow manifesto in the directness of its relation to an immediate danger. Also his dissent in Meyer v. Nebraska, *upholding the right of the state to exclude teaching in any languages other than English from the primary schools, has been criticized as restricting cultural diversity too tightly by state uniformity.*

But beyond these criticisms of specific opinions, how about Holmes's broader doctrine of free trade in ideas? As a philosophical concept it has certain clear weaknesses. One phase of emphasis in it tends toward the "survival" theory of truth — the position that the idea which survives in the struggle of ideas is therefore the true one. This is a dangerous position in a time when the manipulation of symbols has become as highly organized as under the Nazi regime, and in the working of Nazi propaganda outside of Germany.[1] *Another phase of Holmes's concept leads in a quite different direction — not the pragmatic view that what survives is the truth, but the idealist view that what is true will survive. In this sense, Holmes is in a direct sequence of tradition from Milton's* Areopagitica *and Mill's* On Liberty.[2]

The analogy with economic organization that Holmes uses probably assumes too much. For one thing, is it ever possible actually

---

[1] On the theme of the survival theory of truth, see the exchange of letters between Holmes and Professor Max Otto of the University of Wisconsin, reprinted in the *Journal of Philosophy*, 38: 389-392 (1941).

[2] Milton's formulation was as follows: "And though all the winds of doctrine were let loose to play upon the earth, so Truth be in the field, we do injuriously by licensing and prohibiting to misdoubt her strength. Let her and Falsehood grapple; who ever knew Truth put to the worse, in a free and open encounter?" It will be clear that both Milton, when he spoke of "a free and open encounter," and Holmes, when he spoke of "free trade in ideas," assumed that the cards would not be stacked against any competing idea system. Whether that assumption is a tenable one today is open to doubt.

STATE POWER AND FREE TRADE IN IDEAS

to achieve free trade in ideas? It is far more likely that what we have in the intellectual sphere, as in the economic sphere, is not a competitive system but something that the economists call "imperfect competition." And assuming that one can get a situation roughly approximating the competition of ideas, the question is raised, here as in economics, whether that is possible without drastic government intervention in order to establish the conditions of competition.[3]

Comparing Holmes and Brandeis in the civil liberties area, one sees Brandeis as a more consistent champion of the widest possible scope of individual freedom and the narrowest possible limitation of that freedom by federal or state action. While not nearly so brilliant as Holmes in his phrasing, Brandeis had a simpler position. In Meyer v. Nebraska, *again, where Holmes voted to uphold the state act excluding teaching in languages other than English in the primary schools, Brandeis voted against the act. A possible lead which might uncover the impulsions behind Holmes's reasoning was that he was for restricting judicial review and letting the state legislature have its way except in those areas where the right of political opposition was directly involved. In the* Gitlow *case it was, and with it the whole mechanism by which present minorities could be translated into future majorities. In the* Meyer *case the issue was not one of political opposition but of cultural diversity and whether the state had the right to limit it in the interests of social cohesion. Here Brandeis, ever militant in his vigilance against anything that sought to repress individual freedom, placed his fears of state repression above his championing of state legislative power. Brandeis sought always to protect minorities. Holmes was willing to let majorities have their way unless they struck at the deep principles of democratic procedure.*[4]

[3] For a first-rate discussion of this and other issues touching on the cases in this section, see David Riesman, "Civil Liberties in a Period of Transition," a chapter in *Public Policy*, Vol. 3 (1942), 33–96.

[4] For a discussion of the influence of Holmes upon the civil liberties issues before the Supreme Court during the second World War, see the Introduction, pp. xlv–xlvi. See also his important decision in a civil liberties case while on the Massachusetts Court — *Commonwealth* v. *Davis*, p. 106.

CLEAR AND PRESENT DANGER

Schenck v. U. S.
249 U. S. 47 (1919)

The World War brought in its wake some knotty problems for judicial review in the area of civil liberties. This case and the two that follow constitute a great trinity of the sedition cases growing out of the war. Congress in June 1917 enacted an overall espionage and sedition statute, and followed it in May 1918 with an even more sweeping measure against disloyal or seditious utterances.[1] There was undoubtedly considerable popular demand for such action, and it has been argued that the additional provisions were necessary in order to forestall local vigilantism. The federal district courts handed down a number of convictions under the Act, of which six [2] were upheld by the Supreme Court. Of these the Schenck case shows the clearest intent to obstruct the draft.

Holmes wrote the unanimous opinion of the Court in this key decision of the cluster of modern cases that concerns the relation between freedom of utterance and the military dangers and needs of the country. It contains the first full formulation of what has come to be known as the "clear and present danger" doctrine. It uses, as the test of speech that falls outside the guarantees of the First Amendment, "whether the words are used in such circumstances and are of such a nature as to create a clear and present danger that they will bring about the substantive evils that Congress has a right to prevent." This means negatively that speech is not to be banned merely because the words are considered objectionable or because they may have some secondary consequences considered undesirable. There are three elements in the criteria set up:

---

[1] For the history of these Sedition Acts, as for other matters connected with wartime freedom of speech, see Z. Chafee, *Free Speech in the United States* (1941), to which I am deeply indebted even where I diverge from its interpretation. The 1918 Amendment was repealed in 1921, but the 1917 Act remained on the statute books and was used in the war prosecutions of the second World War.

[2] In addition to the *Schenck, Debs,* and *Abrams* cases, there were *Frohwerk* v. *U. S.,* 249 U. S. 204 (1919), *Schaefer* v. *U. S.,* 251 U. S. 468 (1920), and *Pierce* v. *U. S.,* 252 U. S. 239 (1920).

first, the words themselves must have a direct relation to the substantive evil (in this case, obstructing recruiting and spreading disaffection among the armed forces); second, the evil itself must be one on which Congress has power to legislate; third, the context or situation must be such that the speech results in a clear and immediate danger that the purposes of Congress will be frustrated. One must recall Holmes's long and rich experience in dealing with the common law: the doctrine of clear and present danger is obviously drawn from that which seeks to lay down a test for incitement under the common law, with the difference that the context here has been broadened to the scope of the military danger of a nation. Holmes steered a middle course between Judge Learned Hand's "objective standard," laid down in the Masses trial,[3] where the emphasis is placed on the words themselves and on the specific intent to incite a crime, rather than on the surrounding circumstances, and on the other hand the "dangerous tendency" doctrine.

What Holmes is saying in effect is that free speech is not an absolute value, to be guaranteed under every circumstance and at any social cost. We are not, as Holmes says, free to shout "Fire" in a crowded theater; similarly the fact of a nation at war may provide a context in which words are as dangerous as the acts to which they are an incitement. The concept of free speech becomes relative: the stress is put not on the words themselves, but on their relation to the context and circumstances in which they are used; but the words must bear a direct relation to that context. Thus Holmes presents what the philosophers might call an "operational" definition. Yet if he does not make an absolute out of free speech, neither does he give scope to an unrestricted war hysteria. One may say that in the act of sending Schenck to jail, Holmes enunciated a doctrine well calculated to safeguard the individual value and social need of intellectual freedom without unduly jeopardizing the strength of the state. The application of the doctrine is, of course, in every individual instance at the mercy of the administrative offices of the Attorney General and the

---

[3] *Masses Publishing Co. v. Patten*, 244 Fed. 535 (1917), reversed by the Circuit Court of Appeals, 246 Fed. 241 (1917), which used the "dangerous tendency" test.

Postmaster General, and the lower Federal Courts, and eventually of the Supreme Court. The personnel of all three were at the time not too well disposed toward freedom of utterance. Yet by putting the emphasis where he did, Holmes sought to minimize the scope of administrative and judicial arbitrariness.

From the standpoint of style, this is not one of the great Holmes opinions. He was writing the opinion of the Court, and whenever he did that he depersonalized his writing as far as he could, to secure something on which everyone would agree. There is some humor in the understatement with which he summarized the impassioned Socialist manifesto in the case. Otherwise his principal quality here is clarity and a grave deliberateness.

Holmes, J., for the Court:

This is an indictment in three counts. The first charges a conspiracy to violate the Espionage Act of June 15, 1917, c. 30, § 3, 40 Stat. 217, 219, by causing and attempting to cause insubordination, &c., in the military and naval forces of the United States, and to obstruct the recruiting and enlistment service of the United States, when the United States was at war with the German Empire, to-wit, that the defendants wilfully conspired to have printed and circulated to men who had been called and accepted for military service under the Act of May 18, 1917, a document set forth and alleged to be calculated to cause such insubordination and obstruction. The count alleges overt acts in pursuance of the conspiracy, ending in the distribution of the document set forth. The second count alleges a conspiracy to commit an offense against the United States, to-wit, to use the mails for transmission of matter declared to be non-mailable by Title XII, § 2, of the Act of June 15, 1917, to-wit, the above-mentioned document, with an averment of the same overt acts. The third count charges an unlawful use of the mails for the transmission of the same matter and otherwise as above. The defendants were found guilty on all the counts. They set up the First Amendment to the Constitution forbidding Congress to make any law abridging the freedom of speech, or of the press, and bringing the case here on that ground have argued some other points also of which we must dispose.

It is argued that the evidence, if admissible, was not sufficient to prove that the defendant Schenck was concerned in sending the documents. According to the testimony Schenck said he was general secretary of the Socialist Party and had charge of the Socialist headquarters from which the documents were sent. He identified a book found there as the minutes of the Executive Committee of the party. The book showed a resolution of August 13, 1917, that fifteen thousand leaflets should be printed on the other side of one of them in use, to be mailed to men who had passed exemption boards, and for distribution. Schenck personally attended to the printing. On August 20 the general secretary's report said, "Obtained new leaflets from printer and started work addressing envelopes," &c.; and there was a resolve that Comrade Schenck be allowed $125 for sending leaflets through the mail. He said that he had about fifteen or sixteen thousand printed. There were files of the circular in question in the inner office which he said were printed on the other side of the one-sided circular and were there for distribution. Other copies were proved to have been sent through the mails to drafted men. Without going into confirmatory details that were proved, no reasonable man could doubt that the defendant Schenck was largely instrumental in sending the circulars about. As to the defendant Baer, there was evidence that she was a member of the Executive Board and that the minutes of its transactions were hers. The argument as to the sufficiency of the evidence that the defendants conspired to send the documents only impairs the seriousness of the real defence.

It is objected that the documentary evidence was not admissible because obtained upon a search warrant, valid so far as appears. The contrary is established. *Adams* v. *New York*, 192 U. S. 585; *Weeks* v. *United States*, 232 U. S. 383, 395, 396. The search warrant did not issue against the defendant but against the Socialist headquarters at 1326 Arch Street and it would seem that the documents technically were not even in the defendant's possession. See *Johnson* v. *United States*, 288 U. S. 457. Notwithstanding some protest in argument the notion that evidence even directly proceeding from the defendant in a criminal proceeding is excluded in all cases by the Fifth Amendment is plainly unsound. *Holt* v. *United States*, 218 U. S. 245, 252, 253.

The document in question upon its first printed side recited the first section of the Thirteenth Amendment, said that the idea embodied in it was violated by the Conscription Act and that a conscript is little better than a convict. In impassioned language it intimated that conscription was despotism in its worst form and a monstrous wrong against humanity in the interest of Wall Street's chosen few. It said, "Do not submit to intimidation," but in form at least confined itself to peaceful measures such as a petition for the repeal of the Act. The other and later printed side of the sheet was headed, "Assert Your Rights." It stated reasons for alleging that anyone violated the Constitution when he refused to recognize "your right to assert your opposition to the draft," and went on, "If you do not assert and support your rights, you are helping to deny or disparage rights which it is the solemn duty of all citizens and residents of the United States to retain." It described the arguments on the other side as coming from cunning politicians and a mercenary capitalist press, and even silent assent to the conscription law as helping to support an infamous conspiracy. It denied the power to send our citizens away to foreign shores to shoot up the people of other lands, and added that words could not express the condemnation such cold-blooded ruthlessness deserves, &c., &c., winding up, "You must do your share to maintain, support and uphold the rights of the people of this country." Of course the document would not have been sent unless it had been intended to have some effect, and we do not see what effect it could be expected to have upon persons subject to the draft except to influence them to obstruct the carrying of it out. The defendants do not deny that the jury might find against them on this point.

But it is said, suppose that that was the tendency of this circular, it is protected by the First Amendment to the Constitution. Two of the strongest expressions are said to be quoted respectively from well-known public men. It well may be that the prohibition of laws abridging the freedom of speech is not confined to previous restraints, although to prevent them may have been the main purpose, as intimated in *Patterson* v. *Colorado,* 205 U. S. 454, 462. We admit that in many places and in ordinary times the defendants in saying all that was said in the circular would have been within their constitutional rights. But the character of every act depends upon the circumstances in which it is done. *Aikens* v. *Wisconsin,* 195 U. S. 194, 205, 206. The most stringent protection of free speech would not protect a man in falsely shouting fire in a theater and causing a panic. It does not even protect a man from an injunction against uttering words that may have all the effect of force. *Gompers* v. *Bucks Stove & Range Co.,* 221 U. S. 418, 439. The question in every case is whether the words used are used in such circumstances and are of such a nature as to create a clear and present danger that they will bring about the substantive evils that Congress has a right to prevent. It is a question of proximity and degree. When a nation is at war many things that might be said in time of peace are such a hindrance to its effort that their utterance will not be endured so long as men fight and that no court could regard them as protected by any constitutional right. It seems to be admitted that if an actual obstruction of the recruiting service were proved, liability for words that produced that effect might be enforced. The statute of 1917 in §4 punishes conspiracies to obstruct as well as actual obstruction. If the act (speaking, or circulating a paper), its tendency and the intent with which it is done are the same, we perceive no ground for saying that success alone warrants making the act a crime. *Goldman* v. *United States,* 245 U. S. 474, 477. Indeed that case might be said to dispose of the present contention if the precedent covers all *media concludendi.* But as the right to free speech was not referred to specially, we have thought fit to add a few words.

It was not argued that a conspiracy to obstruct the draft was not within the words of the Act of 1917. The words are "obstruct the recruiting or enlistment service," and it might be suggested that they refer only to making it hard to get volunteers. Recruiting heretofore usually having been accomplished by getting volunteers, the word is apt to call up that method only in our minds. But recruiting is gaining fresh supplies for the forces, as well by draft as otherwise. It is put as an alternative to enlistment or voluntary enrollment in this Act. The fact that the Act of 1917 was enlarged by the amending Act of May 16, 1918, c. 75, 40 Stat. 553, of course, does not affect the present indictment and would not, even if the former Act had been repealed. Rev. St. ¶ 13.

A SPEECH BY EUGENE DEBS

Debs v. *U. S.*
249 U. S. 211 (1919)

This is the most sharply criticized of any of Holmes's civil liberties opinions.[1] *It involves a speech made in Canton,*

[1] I am, of course, referring to the main trend of constitutional commentary. So violent a criticism as Wigmore's article on Holmes's *Abrams* dissent (see p.

Ohio, by Eugene V. Debs, the head of the American Socialist Party. Debs represented a militant and articulate opposition not only to the war policy of the Administration but to other aspects of its policy as well. The speech itself, as Holmes relates it, is uncompromising in its opposition to the war; but the problem was whether it was also an incitement against recruiting. Holmes wrote the unanimous opinion of the Court. He guesses in one of his letters that it was probably a strategic move of the Chief Justice to assign it to him, since Holmes was regarded as a champion of free speech.[2]

It is important that nowhere in the decision does Holmes refer to his own "clear and present danger" doctrine. The reason lies probably in the history of the case: the federal court that tried the case below had instructed the jury[3] to decide on "the natural tendency and reasonably probable effect" of the speech. Given the very broad scope of the Espionage Act, especially if not construed very strictly, Holmes could no doubt justify bringing the speech within the terms of the act. But the opinion unfortunately contains neither a careful examination of the constitutionality of an act thus broadly drawn, nor of the application to Debs's speech of the criteria Holmes laid down in the Schenck case.

But criticism of Holmes's position here should be tempered by an understanding of the problems of judicial strategy which, like other judges, he and his colleague Justice Brandeis had to consider. He was wise to speak for the unanimous Court in the Schenck and Frohwerk cases, especially the former, in which he had the opportunity to commit the Court to the general doctrine of clear and present danger. Many have believed that Debs's words referred far more to ultimate social change than to immediate obstruction of the war effort, and that Debs's direct intent to effect the latter was

---

306) must be placed in the area of war pathology. Among the more drastic criticisms are Ernst Freund, cited below, note 7; and Forrest R. Black, "Debs v. U. S.: a Judicial Milepost on the Road to Absolutism," 81 University of Pennsylvania Law Review (1932) 160.

[2] See below, p. 442.

[3] On the character of the jury, see Max Eastman's Liberator article, "The Trial of Eugene Debs" (November 1918), as quoted in Chafee, op. cit. 73. They were retired farmers and merchants, of an average age of seventy-two and an average wealth of fifty to sixty thousand dollars.

far more a matter of presumption than of evidence. Yet neither Holmes nor Brandeis felt that the case was clear enough to warrant a break with the Court majority such as they were later to make in the Abrams *case.*[4]

Holmes was not happy about the case. "*I am beginning to get stupid letters of protest,*" *he writes Pollock,* "*against a decision that Debs, a noted agitator, was rightly convicted of obstructing the recruiting service so far as the law was concerned. I wondered that the Government should press the case to a hearing before us, as the inevitable result was that fools, knaves, and ignorant persons were bound to say he was convicted because he was a dangerous agitator and that obstructing the draft was a pretence.*"[5]

Debs received a ten-year sentence. He was already an old and exhausted man when he went off to jail. He was bitter in his comment on the "coterie of begowned corporation lawyers in Washington." "Great issues are not decided by courts," he said, "but by the people." And from the steps of the railroad car he spoke to the people who had come to say farewell. "They can't stop the movement. You keep up on the outside and I'll keep up on the inside." The editorials in the New York newspapers almost unanimously depicted Debs as "not a martyr but a defeated fighter" (New York Times, March 12, 1919), and expressed admiration for his willingness to pay the price for his beliefs.

But in liberal and radical circles there was considerable protest. "Of course," writes Holmes to Pollock, "there were people who pitched into the Court for sending Debs to prison . . . but there was no doubt that the Jury was warranted in finding him guilty or that the act was Constitutional. Now I hope the President will pardon him and some other poor devils with whom I have more sympathy."[6] We may judge that Holmes was sensitive to some of this criticism. "The cause of the government has gained nothing," wrote Ernst Freund in the New Republic, "while the forces of discontent have been strengthened, and have been given an example of loose and arbitrary law which at some time may react against those

[4] Chafee points this out admirably, *op. cit.,* 86.
[5] See below, p. 442.
[6] H–P, II:11 (April 27, 1919).

who have set it." [7] *Even after the war Wilson remained unrelenting about a pardon for Debs. While in prison Debs ran for President in 1920 and received almost a million votes. He was pardoned in 1921 by President Harding, without restoration of citizenship.*

There is a sharply defined dramatic contrast between the two principal figures in this case: Debs, with his proletarian background and his record of unceasing struggle, a master of the earthy language of the people, in his own way of a mold having something of the heroic in it; and Holmes, the New England aristocrat, with an individual style and grace, at once profound and sophisticated. Debs was in dead earnest. Holmes was slightly contemptuous of the "poor fools whom I should have been inclined to pass over if I could. The greatest bores in the world are the come-outers who are cock-sure of a dozen nostrums. The dogmatism of a little education is hopeless." [8]

Holmes, J., for the Court:

This is an indictment under the Espionage Act of June 15, 1917, c. 30 § 3, 40 Stat. 217, 219, as amended by the Act of May 16, 1918, c. 75, § 1, 40 Stat. 553. It has been cut down to two counts, originally the third and fourth. The former of these alleges that on or about June 16, 1918, at Canton, Ohio, the defendant caused and incited and attempted to cause and incite insubordination, disloyalty, mutiny and refusal of duty in the military and naval forces of the United States and with intent so to do delivered, to an assembly of people, a public speech, set forth. The fourth count alleges that he obstructed and attempted to obstruct the recruiting and enlistment service of the United States and to that end and with that intent delivered the same speech, again set forth. There was a demurrer to the indictment on the ground that the statute is unconstitutional as interfering with free speech, contrary to the First Amendment, and to the several counts as insufficiently stating the supposed offense. This was overruled, subject to exception. There were other exceptions to the admission of evidence

---

[7] "The Debs Case and Freedom of Speech"; *New Republic*, Vol. 19, p. 13 (May 3, 1919). A little while after the appearance of this article there is the following passage in a letter to Pollock: "The spring here is enchanting . . . Really if a glance at the *New Republic* had not thrown the customary gloom over life it would seem fair once more." H–P, II:14 (May 26, 1919).

[8] H–P, II:11 (April 27, 1919).

STATE POWER AND FREE TRADE IN IDEAS

with which we shall deal. The defendant was found guilty and was sentenced to ten years' imprisonment on each of the two counts, the punishment to run concurrently on both.

The main theme of the speech was socialism, its growth, and a prophecy of its ultimate success. With that we have nothing to do, but if a part or the manifest intent of the more general utterances was to encourage those present to obstruct the recruiting service and if in passages such encouragement was directly given, the immunity of the general theme may not be enough to protect the speech. The speaker began by saying that he had just returned from a visit to the workhouse in the neighborhood where three of their most loyal comrades were paying the penalty for their devotion to the working class — these being Wagenknecht, Baker and Ruthenberg, who had been convicted of aiding and abetting another in failing to register for the draft. *Ruthenberg* v. *United States*, 245 U. S. 480. He said that he had to be prudent or might not be able to say all that he thought, thus intimating to his hearers that they might infer that he meant more, but he did say that those persons were paying the penalty for standing erect and for seeking to pave the way to better conditions for all mankind. Later he added further eulogies and said that he was proud of them. He then expressed opposition to Prussian militarism in a way that naturally might have been thought to be intended to include the mode of proceeding in the United States.

After considerable discourse that it is unnecessary to follow, he took up the case of Kate Richards O'Hare, convicted of obstructing the enlistment service, praised her for her loyalty to socialism and otherwise, and said that she was convicted on false testimony, under a ruling that would seem incredible to him if he had not had some experience with a Federal court. We mention this passage simply for its connection with evidence put in the trial. The defendant spoke of other cases, and then, after dealing with Russia, said that the master class has always declared the wars and the subject class has always fought the battles — that the subject class has had nothing to gain and all to lose, including their lives; that the working class who furnish the corpses have never yet had a voice in declaring war and have never yet had a voice in declaring peace. "You have your lives to lose; you certainly ought to have the right to declare war if you consider a war necessary." The defendant next mentioned Rose Pastor Stokes, convicted of attempting to cause insubordination and refusal of duty in the military forces of the United States and obstructing the recruiting service. He said that she went out to render her service to the cause in this day of crises, and they sent her to the penitentiary for ten years; that she had said no more than the speaker had said that afternoon; that if she was guilty so was he, and that he would not be cowardly enough to plead his innocence; but that her message that opened the eyes of the people must be suppressed, and so, after a mock trial before a packed jury and a corporation tool on the bench, she was sent to the penitentiary for ten years.

There followed personal experiences and illustrations of the growth of socialism, a glorification of minorities, and a prophecy of the success of the international socialist crusade, with the interjection that "you need to know that you are fit for something better than slavery and cannon fodder." The rest of the discourse had only the indirect though not necessarily ineffective bearing on the offenses alleged that is to be found in the usual contrasts between capitalists and laboring men, sneers at the advice to cultivate war gardens, attribution to plutocrats of the high price of coal, &c., with the implication running through it all that the working men are not concerned in the war, and a final exhortation, "Don't worry about the charge of treason to your masters; but be concerned about the treason that involves yourselves." The defendant addressed the jury himself, and while contending that his speech did not warrant the charges, said, "I have been accused of obstructing the war. I admit it. Gentlemen, I abhor war. I would oppose war if I stood alone." The statement was not necessary to warrant the jury in finding that one purpose of the speech, whether incidental or not does not matter, was to oppose not only war in general but this war, and that the opposition was so expressed that its natural and intended effect would be to obstruct recruiting. If that was intended and if, in all the circumstances, that would be its probable effect, it would not be protected by reason of its being part of a general program and expressions of a general and conscientious belief.

The chief defenses upon which the defendant seemed willing to rely were the denial that we have dealt with and that based upon the First Amendment to the Constitution, disposed of in *Schenck* v. *United States, ante,* 47. His counsel questioned the sufficiency of the indictment. It is sufficient in form. *Frohwerk* v. *United States,*

STATE POWER AND FREE TRADE IN IDEAS 303

ante, 204. The most important question that remains is raised by the admission in evidence of the record of the conviction of Ruthenberg, Wagenknecht and Baker, Rose Pastor Stokes, and Kate Richards O'Hare. The defendant purported to understand the grounds on which these persons were imprisoned and it was proper to show what those grounds were in order to show what he was talking about, to explain the true import of his expression of sympathy and to throw light on the intent of the address, so far as the present matter is concerned.

There was introduced also an "Anti-War Proclamation and Program" adopted at St. Louis in April, 1917, coupled with testimony that about an hour before his speech the defendant had stated that he approved of that platform in spirit and in substance. The defendant referred to it in his address to the jury, seemingly with satisfaction and willingness that it should be considered in evidence. But his counsel objected and has argued against its admissibility, at some length. This document contained the usual suggestion that capitalism was the cause of the war and that our entrance into it "was instigated by the predatory capitalists in the United States." It alleged that the war of the United States against Germany could not "be justified even on the plea that it is a war of defense of American rights or American 'honor.'" It said, "We brand the declaration of war by our Government as a crime against the people of the United States and against the nations of the world. In all modern history there has been no war more unjustifiable than the war in which we are about to engage." Its first recommendation was "continuous, active and public opposition to the war, through demonstrations, mass petitions, and all other means within our power." Evidence that the defendant accepted this view and this declaration of his duties at the time that he made his speech is evidence that if in that speech he used words tending to obstruct the recruiting service he meant that they should have that effect. The principle is too well established and too manifestly good sense to need citation of the books. We should add that the jury were most carefully instructed that they could not find the defendant guilty for advocacy of any of his opinions unless the words used had as their natural tendency and reasonable, probable effect to obstruct the recruiting service, &c., and unless the defendant had the specific intent to do so in his mind.

Without going into further particulars, we are of opinion that the verdict on the fourth count, for obstructing and attempting to obstruct the recruiting service of the United States, must be sustained. Therefore it is less important to consider whether that upon the third count, for causing and attempting to cause insubordination, &c., in the military and naval forces, is equally impregnable. The jury were instructed that for the purposes of the statute the persons designated by the Act of May 18, 1917, registered and enrolled under it, and thus subject to be called into the active service, were a part of the military forces of the United States. The Government presents a strong argument from the history of the statutes that the instruction was correct and in accordance with established legislative usage. We see no sufficient reason for differing from the conclusion but think it unnecessary to discuss the question in detail.

TWO LEAFLETS AND AN EXPERIMENT

Abrams v. *U. S.*
250 U. S. 616, 624 (1919)

This is the best-known of the cases under the Espionage Act and perhaps the greatest of Holmes's opinions. Jacob Abrams and several other Russian emigrants threw down some leaflets from the roof of a loft in the garment district of New York City. Abrams was tried under the Espionage Act, convicted, and sentenced to twenty years' imprisonment.[1] *The Supreme Court affirmed the conviction, the majority opinion being written by Justice Clarke.*[2] *Justice Brandeis joined in Holmes's dissent. They had both upheld the convictions in the previous five cases under the Espionage Act, but at this point they could not go along. Holmes's dissent is, in its implications, an eloquent proof that it was not they who had broken with the Court majority, but the majority that had broken with them and diverged from the criteria of the limits of free speech first laid down in the* Schenck *case.*

[1] For a good history and analysis of the case, with a bibliography of comments on it, see Chafee, *op. cit.*, 108–140.

[2] As a mildly liberal member of the Court, Justice Clarke may have been assigned the opinion by the same strategy which gave the *Schenck* and *Debs* opinions to Holmes.

The crux of the indictment was the fourth count, charging that Abrams and his associates had urged the curtailment of war production, "with intent by such curtailment to cripple or hinder the United States in the prosecution of the war." In legal terms the case turned on the meaning of "intent." Justice Clarke argued that while the defendants had only urged that the workers produce no arms for an attempt at American intervention in the Russian Revolution, and while America was not at war with Russia, the necessary consequence of their incitement would be to hamper the war with Germany; and that they were willing to cripple the German war if they could thereby also cripple intervention in Russia. As Professor Corwin has put it, in an article agreeing with the majority decision, "In law, as in ethics and in common sense, men must be held to intend, if not the usual consequences of their acts, certainly the necessary means to their objectives."[3] Holmes however argues that this was too indirect: that "the aim to produce" the consequence must be "the proximate motive of the specific act, although there may be some deeper motive behind."[4]

Holmes's second line of argument is that even if the intent were there, in the strict sense in which the statute meant it, there is in the context no clear and present danger in the words. "Nobody can suppose that the surreptitious publishing of a silly leaflet by an unknown man, without more, would present an immediate danger that its opinions would hinder the success of the government arms."

His third line of argument turns on the severity of the sentence. "Even if I am technically wrong and enough can be squeezed from these poor and puny anonymities to turn the

[3] "Freedom of Speech and Press under the First Amendment," 30 YLJ 48 (1920).
[4] One phase of the trial procedure in the federal district court, turning on the technical question of the admissibility of evidence, has however (as Professor Chafee points out) wider implications for the free speech cases. The defense offered to show, through the testimony of Raymond Robins and others, that the American intervention in Russia was not part of the war with Germany, but the trial judge excluded the evidence as irrelevant. Since the testimony did not bear on the overt acts of the defendants, the ruling was technically correct. But, in a trial taking place in a context of popular conviction that the Bolshevists were only German spies, the ruling gave an enormous advantage to the prosecution (Chafee, *op. cit.*, 117–121).

color of legal litmus paper . . . the most nominal punishment seems to me all that could possibly be inflicted,[5] *unless the defendants are to be made to suffer not for what the indictment alleges but for the creed that they avow."*

It is in pursuance of his belief that it is for their creed that the defendants are being punished that Holmes gives voice to the eloquent little essay on the competition of ideas with which the opinion closes. I can add little to what has been said in comment on Holmes's language. It has economy, grace, finality, and is the greatest utterance on intellectual freedom by an American, ranking in the English tongue with Milton and Mill.

But something may be said also of its quality as social thought. There are two grounds on which freedom of speech is generally considered an inherent part of democratic living. One is that there can be no dignity in the individual life without it. The other is that it gives survival value to a government. It is the second to which Holmes gives expression here. In the urgency of governing groups to have their own way they forget that "time has upset many fighting faiths." In the long run "truth is the only ground upon which their wishes safely can be carried out." For government is an experimental process. Even the Constitution "is an experiment, as all life is an experiment." And to make the experiment of government successful, room must be found for new ideas which will challenge the old. "The ultimate good desired is better reached by free trade in ideas." Where Milton in Areopagitica used the symbolism of a battle, Holmes uses the symbolism of his economic system. "The best test of truth is the power of the thought to get itself accepted in the competition of the market." It should be noted that this was only one strain in Holmes's thinking. In addition to the Miltonic strain, there was also a Darwinian one. "Truth," he said, on another occasion, "is the majority vote of that nation that can lick all the others."

As Holmes's Debs opinion had been attacked from the left, so his Abrams dissent was violently attacked from the right. Dean Wigmore wrote of the opinion: "It is shocking in its

---

[5] **Pollock** too thought the sentence "monstrously excessive" and "enough to make one astute in favour of the defence." H-P, II:31 (Dec. 1, 1919).

STATE POWER AND FREE TRADE IN IDEAS 307

obtuse indifference to the vital issues at stake in August, 1918, and it is ominous in its portent of like indifference to pending and coming issues. . . . You cannot argue with a state of mind. But you can point out its nature and portent. . . . I firmly believe that in these days the tender champions of freedom of speech are like Don Quixote, fighting giants and ogres who have long since been laid in the dust. . . . Hundreds of well-meaning citizens — "parlor bolsheviks" and "pink radicals," as the phrase goes — are showing a similar complaisance or good-natured tolerance to the licensing of the violence-propaganda. . . . In the transcendental realms of philosophic and historical discussion by closet jurists, these expressions ["The Constitution is an experiment" etc. . . .] might pass. But when found publicly recorded in an opinion of the Supreme Guardians of that Constitution, licensing propaganda which in the next case before the court may be directed against that Constitution itself, that language is ominous indeed." [6]

"Wigmore," wrote Holmes to Pollock, *"goes for me ex cathedra. . . . Wigmore's explosion struck me, (I only glanced at it), as sentiment rather than reasoning — and in short I thought it bosh. He has grown rather dogmatic in tone with success."* [7] And one of Pollock's letters furnishes an interesting footnote to the relative treatment of civil liberties issues in England and America: *"I believe there were many leaflets of much the same kind [as the Abrams leaflets] distributed in this country on which it was not thought useful to prosecute anyone."* [8]

Holmes, J., dissenting:

This indictment is founded wholly upon the publication of two leaflets which I shall describe in a moment. The first count charges a conspiracy pending the war with Germany to publish abusive language about the form of government of the United

---

[6] "Freedom of Speech and Freedom of Thuggery, in War-Time and Peace-Time," 14 *Illinois Law Review* 539 (1920).

[7] H–P, II:42 (April 25, 1920). Pollock answered, "I was sorry to see Wigmore carried away by the panic mongers. His reasons amounted to saying that it is wrong to criticize an indictment for murder because homicide is a very dangerous offense and many murderers are very wicked men." H–P, II:48 (Aug. 10, 1920).

[8] H–P, II:31–32 (Dec. 1, 1919).

States, laying the preparation and publishing of the first leaflet as overt acts. The second count charges a conspiracy pending the war to publish language intended to bring the form of government into contempt, laying the preparation and publishing of the two leaflets as overt acts. The third count alleges a conspiracy to encourage resistance to the United States in the same war and to attempt to effectuate the purpose by publishing the same leaflets. The fourth count lays a conspiracy to incite curtailment of production of things necessary to the prosecution of the war and to attempt to accomplish it by publishing the second leaflet to which I have referred.

The first of these leaflets says that the President's cowardly silence about the intervention in Russia reveals the hypocrisy of the plutocratic gang in Washington. It intimates that "German militarism combined with Allied capitalism to crush the Russian revolution," goes on that the tyrants of the world fight each other until they see a common enemy — working-class enlightenment — when they combine to crush it; and that now militarism and capitalism combined, though not openly, to crush the Russian revolution. It says that there is only one enemy of the workers of the world and that is capitalism; that it is a crime for workers of America, &c., to fight the workers' republic of Russia, and ends "Awake! Awake, you workers of the world!" Signed "Revolutionists." A note adds, "It is absurd to call us pro-German. We hate and despise German militarism more than do you hypocritical tyrants. We have more reasons for denouncing German militarism than has the coward of the White House."

The other leaflet, headed "Workers — Wake Up," with abusive language says that America together with the Allies will march for Russia to help the Czecho-Slovaks in their struggle against the Bolsheviki, and that this time the hypocrites shall not fool the Russian emigrants and friends of Russia in America. It tells the Russian emigrants that they now must spit in the face of false military propaganda by which their sympathy and help to the prosecution of the war have been called forth and says that with the money they have lent or are going to lend "they will make bullets not only for the Germans but also for the Workers' Soviets of Russia," and further, "Workers in the ammunition factories, you are producing bullets, bayonets, cannon, to murder not only the Germans but also your dearest, best, who are in Russia fighting

STATE POWER AND FREE TRADE IN IDEAS

for freedom." It then appeals to the same Russian emigrants at some length not to consent to the "inquisitionary expedition to Russia," and says that the destruction of the Russian revolution is "the politics of the march on Russia." The leaflet winds up by saying "Workers, our reply to this barbaric intervention has to be a general strike!" and after a few words on the spirit of revolution, exhortations not to be afraid, and some usual tall talk, ends "Woe unto those who will be in the way of progress. Let solidarity live! The Rebels."

No argument seems to me necessary to show that these pronunciamentos in no way attack the form of government of the United States, or that they do not support either of the first two counts. What little I have to say about the third count may be postponed until I have considered the fourth. With regard to that it seems too plain to be denied that the suggestion to workers in ammunition factories that they are producing bullets to murder their dearest, and the further advocacy of a general strike, both in the second leaflet, do urge curtailment of production of things necessary to the prosecution of the war within the meaning of the Act of May 16, 1918, c. 75, 40 Stat. 553, amending § 3 of the earlier Act of 1917. But to make the conduct criminal that statute requires that it should be "with intent by such curtailment to cripple or hinder the United States in the prosecution of the war." It seems to me that no such intent is proved.

I am aware of course that the word intent as vaguely used in ordinary legal discussion means no more than knowledge at the time of the act that the consequences said to be intended will ensue. Even less than that will satisfy the general principle of civil and criminal liability. A man may have to pay damages, may be sent to prison, at common law might be hanged, if at the time of his act he knew facts from which common experience showed that the consequences would follow, whether he individually could foresee them or not. But, when words are used exactly, a deed is not done with intent to produce a consequence unless that consequence is the aim of deed. It may be obvious, and obvious to the actor, that the consequence will follow, and he may be liable for it even if he forgets it, but he does not do the act with intent to produce it unless the aim to produce it is the proximate motive of the specific act, although there may be some deeper motive behind.

It seems to me that this statute must be taken to use its words in a strict and accurate sense. They would be absurd in any other. A patriot might think that we were wasting money on aeroplanes, or making more cannon of a certain kind than we needed, and might advocate curtailment with success, yet even if it turned out that the curtailment hindered and was thought by other minds to have been obviously likely to hinder the United States in the prosecution of the war, no one would hold such conduct a crime. I admit that my illustration does not answer all that might be said but it is enough to show what I think and to let me pass to a more important aspect of the case. I refer to the First Amendment to the Constitution that Congress shall make no law abridging the freedom of speech.

I never have seen any reason to doubt that the questions of law that alone were before this Court in the cases of *Schenck, Frohwerk* and *Debs,* were rightly decided. I do not doubt for a moment that by the same reasoning that would justify punishing persuasion to murder, the United States constitutionally may punish speech that produces or is intended to produce a clear and imminent danger that it will bring about forthwith certain substantive evils that the United States constitutionally may seek to prevent. The power undoubtedly is greater in time of war than in time of peace because war opens dangers that do not exist at other times.

But as against dangers peculiar to war, as against others, the principle of the right to free speech is always the same. It is only the present danger of immediate evil or an intent to bring it about that warrants Congress in setting a limit to the expression of opinion where private rights are not concerned. Congress certainly cannot forbid all effort to change the mind of the country. Now nobody can suppose that the surreptitious publishing of a silly leaflet by an unknown man, without more, would present any immediate danger that its opinions would hinder the success of the Government arms or have any appreciable tendency to do so. Publishing these opinions for the very purpose of obstructing, however, might indicate a greater danger and at any rate would have the quality of an attempt. So I assume that the second leaflet, if published for the purpose alleged in the fourth count, might be punishable. But it seems pretty clear to me that nothing less than that would bring these papers within the scope of this law. An actual intent in the sense that I have explained is necessary to constitute an attempt, where a further act of the same individual is required to complete the substantive crime, for reasons given in *Swift & Co. v. United States*, 196 U. S. 375, 396. It is necessary where the success of the attempt depends upon others, because if that intent is not present the actor's aim may be accomplished without bringing about the evils sought to be checked. An intent to prevent interference with the revolution in Russia might have been satisfied without any hindrance to carrying on the war in which we were engaged.

I do not see how anyone can find the intent required by the statute in any of the defendants' words. The second leaflet is the only one that affords even a foundation for the charge, and there, without invoking the hatred of German militarism expressed in the former one, it is evident from the beginning to the end that the only object of the paper is to help Russia and stop American intervention there against the popular government — not to impede the United States in the war that it was carrying on. To say that two phrases taken literally might import a suggestion of conduct that would have interference with the war as an indirected and probably undesired effect seems to me by no means enough to show an attempt to produce that effect.

I return for a moment to the third count. That charges an intent to provoke resistance to the United States in its war with Germany. Taking the clause in the statute that deals with that in connection with the other elaborate provisions of the Act, I think that resistance to the United States means some forcible act of opposition to some proceeding of the United States in pursuance of the war. I think the intent must be the specific intent that I have described and for the reasons that I have given. I think that no such intent was proved or existed in fact. I also think that there is no hint at resistance to the United States as I construe the phrase.

In this case sentences of twenty years' imprisonment have been imposed for the publishing of two leaflets that I believe the defendants had as much right to publish as the Government has to publish the Constitution of the United States now vainly invoked by them. Even if I am technically wrong and enough can be squeezed from these poor and puny anonymities to turn the color of legal litmus paper — I will add, even if what I think the necessary intent were shown — the most nominal punishment seems to me all that possibly could be inflicted, unless the defendants are to be made to suffer not for what the indictment alleges but for the creed that they avow — a creed that I believe to be the creed of ignorance and immaturity when honestly held, as I see no reason to doubt that it was held here, but which, although made the subject of examination at the trial, no one has a right even to consider in dealing with the charges before the Court.

Persecution for the expression of opinions seems to me perfectly logical. If you have no doubt of your premises or your power and want a certain result with all your heart you naturally express your wishes in law and sweep away all opposition. To allow opposition by speech seems to indicate that you think the speech impotent, as when a man says that he has squared the circle, or that you do not care wholeheartedly for the result, or that you doubt either your power or your premises. But when men have realized that time has upset many fighting faiths, they may come to believe even more than they believe the very foundations of their own conduct that the ultimate good desired is better reached by free trade in ideas — that the best test of truth is the power of the thought to get itself accepted in the competition of the market, and that truth is the only ground upon which their wishes safely can be carried out. That, at any rate, is the theory of our Constitution. It is an experiment, as all life is an experiment. Every year if not every day we have to wager our salvation upon some prophecy based upon imperfect knowledge. While that experiment is part of our system I think that we should be eternally vigilant against attempts to check the expression of opinions that we loathe and believe to be fraught with death, unless they so imminently threaten immediate interference with the lawful and pressing purposes of the law that an immediate check is required to save the country. I wholly disagree with the argument of the Government that the First Amendment left the common law as to seditious libel in force. History seems to me against the notion. I had conceived that the United States through many years had shown its repentance for the Sedition Act of 1798 by repaying fines that it imposed. Only the emergency that makes it immediately dangerous to leave the correction of evil counsels to time warrants making any exception to the sweeping command, "Congress shall make no law . . . abridging the freedom of speech." Of course I am speaking only of expressions of opinion and exhortations, which were all that were uttered here, but I regret that I cannot put into more impressive words my belief that in their conviction upon this indictment the defendants were deprived of their rights under the Constitution of the United States.

THE POSTMASTER GOES TO WAR

Milwaukee Social Democratic Publishing Co. v. Burleson
255 U. S. 407, 436 (1921)

Victor Berger, like Eugene Debs, was one of the militant antiwar leaders of the Socialist Party. In September 1917, shortly after the passage of the Espionage Act, Postmaster Burleson issued an order denying to Berger's paper, the Milwaukee Leader, *the use of the second-class mails. The Supreme Court upheld the Postmaster's order by a seven-to-two decision, Justice Clarke again writing the majority opinion as in the* Abrams *case. Justices Brandeis and Holmes wrote dissenting opinions.*[1]

The decision[2] *turned on the section of the Espionage Act of 1917 declaring that any matter in violation of the statute is "nonmailable matter and shall not be conveyed in the mails or delivered from any post office, or by any letter carrier." There is no question in any of the opinions that the Postmaster General could under the Act declare specific issues of a paper to be nonmailable. But the issue that was raised was whether this power extended to the power to exclude a publication in general from the second-class mail. Justice Clarke held that second-class rates, under the Mail Classification Act of 1879, were a privilege withdrawable when a publication failed to conform to the law. Since the* Leader *had in several issues*

---

[1] See the biographical sketch of Berger by Max and Edna Lerner in the *Dictionary of American Biography,* supplement volume. Berger was one of the signers of the St. Louis antiwar manifesto of the Socialist Party of April 14, 1917. The banning of his paper from the mails in September 1917 was followed in February 1918 by an indictment and trial of Berger himself under the Espionage Act. Before the trial and while the indictment was pending, Berger was elected to Congress on a Socialist antiwar platform. At the trial he was convicted and sentenced to a twenty-year prison term. Out on bail on appeal, he sought to take his seat in Congress, but although twice elected, he was twice rebuffed. In 1921 the Supreme Court reversed his conviction on the ground that Judge Landis, who had tried him, was disqualified by remarks made before the trial. The charges against him were finally dropped.

[2] For a full discussion of the case, see Chafee, *op. cit.,* 298–305.

published material that violated the Espionage Act, it was reasonable as an administrative matter to ban it until it showed evidence of good intention, rather than seeking to censor every issue in advance.

In dissenting, Justice Brandeis insisted that access to the second-class mail was not a privilege but a right; that to argue that third-class mail could be used was technical and frivolous; and that the effect of the Postmaster's order was to impose a heavy and punitive financial burden on the paper. There had been, he said, no conviction of Berger by court process but only the judgment of the Postmaster General. To give that official not only the power to exclude wholly from the mails specific issues of a paper under the Espionage Act, but also all future issues under the vague control of the second-class mailing privilege, was to establish a censorship of the Postmaster General with a "vague and absolute authority."

Holmes's reasoning is similar to that of Brandeis, but is characteristically sharper in its phrasing. On the legal issue his dissent turns on the proposition that the power of excluding from the mails is no different under the Espionage Act from what it is with respect to nonwar obscene matter — the power to pass on each specific issue of a paper.[3] On social grounds he points out that to refuse the second-class rates is to kill a newspaper, and that "such a practically despotic power" destroys free speech, since "the use of the mails is almost as much a part of free speech as the right to use our tongues." [4]

The Holmes-Brandeis view has seemed to liberal opinion a sound one in the context of the *1917* world. In the context of the second World War, however, it can no longer be applied with the same results. Then the Milwaukee *Leader* was one of the few papers opposing the war; now the rise of the Nazis to power has brought with it, as one of its crucial and principal instruments of warfare, a far-flung and

---

[3] Since this case Holmes's view has been strengthened on one score: in the *Near* v. *Minnesota* decision Justice Hughes held that a court injunction barring the publication of *future* as well as *current* issues of a paper ran counter to the Blackstone doctrine of "previous restraint" 283 U. S. 697 (1931). One may question the wisdom of trying to order social policy in a crucial area of state survival on principles drawn wholly from the common law of libel.

[4] The suspension of the *Leader* remained in force until Will H. Hays, who succeeded Burleson as Postmaster General, lifted it.

STATE POWER AND FREE TRADE IN IDEAS 315

highly organized propaganda machine operating as part of the Nazi campaign of terror and disintegration. In the years after 1935, hundreds of publications arose which were either directly connected with fascist movements, like Pelley's Silver Shirt paper and the Christian Front Social Justice, *or, like more powerful newspapers such as the* Chicago Tribune, *tended to coincide with the Nazi pattern out of anti-Administration bitterness. To take the position that only specific issues can be excluded from the mails and that there can be no suspension of the second-class mailing rights as a whole is clearly to deny to the government an indispensable weapon for fighting the enemy, and to leave the nation at the enemies' mercy on one of its most valuable fronts. The long siege of proto-fascist propaganda in the United States, before Pearl Harbor, had left substantial elements of public opinion in a receptive mind for the most vicious anti-democratic and anti-war writing in our recent history.*

In this context Attorney General Biddle in April 1942 asked the Postmaster General to deny the second-class mailing rights to Coughlin's newspaper, Social Justice. *He pointed out the clear Nazi pattern in the paper, the faithful following of the Goebbels line since 1938, and the persistence of this pattern after America's final entrance into the war. Biddle found himself in a difficult situation. An ardent admirer of Holmes, he probably wished to stand by the reasoning in his dissent in the* Milwaukee Leader *case. But he saw also that to do so would be tantamount to giving the newspaper allies of the enemy almost complete freedom of movement in America. In a letter of April 14, 1942, to the Postmaster General he therefore based his action on the majority opinion in the present case, not mentioning the dissents.*

There are, however, several elements of difference between the cases that are not without importance. First the Social Justice *action was not taken by Postmaster General Walker on his own judgment, but was initiated by Attorney General Biddle and based on careful and elaborate analysis of Supreme Court precedents. The element of arbitrary action on the part of the Postmaster General is thus removed or qualified. But more important, the nature of warfare as waged by the Nazis in 1942 is such as to take such publications out of the marginal realm and put them in the center of the obstruction of the war effort. The issue whether Justices Holmes and Brandeis, if alive today, would stand by their dissent in the present case, could be argued pro and con at protracted length. My own hesitant guess is that Brandeis might come out with a different result but that Holmes would probably stick to his guns. For Holmes was more the legal technologist, Brandeis more the social realist. And it is becoming increasingly clear that the government which waits until propaganda has reached the point of clearly threatening the immediate survival of the nation is likely to wait until it is too late, and will probably never have the strength to strike when the time comes.*[5]

Holmes, J., dissenting:

I have had the advantage of reading the judgment of my brother Brandeis in this case and I agree in substance with his view. At first it seemed to me that if a publisher should announce in terms that he proposed to print treason and should demand a second-class rate it must be that the Postmaster General would have authority to refuse it. But reflection has convinced me that I was wrong. The question of the rate has nothing to do with the question whether the matter is mailable, and I am satisfied that the Postmaster cannot determine in advance that a certain newspaper is going to be nonmailable and on that ground deny to it not the use of the mails but the rate of postage that the statute says shall be charged.

Of course the Postmaster may deny or revoke the second-class rate to a publication that does not comply with the conditions attached to it by statute, but as my brother Brandeis has pointed out, the conditions attached to the second-class rate by the statute cannot be made to justify the Postmaster's action except by a quibble. On the other hand the regulation of the right to use the mails by the Espionage Act has no peculiarities as a war measure but is

[5] See Riesman, *op. cit.*, 40: "The job of wise statesmanship would seem to be to eliminate unnecessary gambles in the realm of public policy; in government, as in medicine or law, progress in the art is measured by the extent to which preventive measures are adopted before the point is reached at which only curative remedies are left." I am increasingly convinced that a realistic legal policy would modify the "clear and present danger" doctrine in the direction of an "intellectual trading with the enemy" standard, which sought to find substantial propaganda connections with the enemy and the existence of an actual intent to play the enemies' propaganda game.

similar to that in earlier cases, such as obscene documents. Papers that violate the act are declared nonmailable and the use of the mails for the transmission of them is made criminal. But the only power given to the Postmaster is to refrain from forwarding the papers when received and to return them to the senders. Act of June 15, 1917, c. 30, Title XII, 40 Stat. 217, 230. Act of May 16, 1918, c. 75, 40 Stat. 553, 554. He could not issue a general order that a certain newspaper should not be carried because he thought it likely or certain that it would contain treasonable or obscene talk. The United States may give up the Post Office when it sees fit, but while it carries it on, the use of the mails is almost as much a part of free speech as the right to use our tongues, and it would take very strong language to convince me that Congress ever intended to give such a practically despotic power to any one man. There is no pretense that it has done so. Therefore I do not consider the limits of its constitutional power.

To refuse the second-class rate to a newspaper is to make its circulation impossible and has all the effect of the order that I have supposed. I repeat: when I observe that the only powers expressly given to the Postmaster General to prevent the carriage of unlawful matter of the present kind are to stop and to return papers already existing and posted, when I notice that the conditions expressly attached to the second-class rate look only to wholly different matters, and when I consider the ease with which the power claimed by the Postmaster could be used to interfere with very sacred rights, I am of opinion that the refusal to allow the relator the rate to which it was entitled whenever its newspaper was carried, on the ground that the paper ought not to have been carried at all, was unjustified by the statute and was a serious attack upon the liberties that not even the war induced Congress to infringe.

A COMMON TONGUE AND FREEDOM OF TEACHING

Meyer v. Nebraska
262 U. S. 390 (1923)
Bartels v. Iowa
262 U. S. 404, 412 (1923)

These two cases were considered together by the Court and both involve similar state laws. Nebraska, Iowa, and Ohio had passed laws shortly after the World War directed against the teaching of German in the primary schools. That in Ohio was specifically so phrased; the laws in the other two states forbade the use in teaching of any modern language except English. Meyer was convicted for teaching reading in German to a child of ten in a parochial school, in contravention of the Nebraska statute. Justice McReynolds, speaking for the majority, held the Acts unconstitutional as violations of the guarantee of liberty in the Fourteenth Amendment. Justice Holmes wrote a dissent covering all the cases, in which Justice Sutherland joined.

There have been some who have expressed surprise at Holmes's opinion in these cases, on the ground that his civil liberties views should have put him on the side of freedom of teaching, and therefore against the validity of the statutes, as his liberal colleague Justice Brandeis was. Yet I feel that Holmes had a consistent position. He believed in judicial tolerance of state legislative action, even when he disapproved of the state policies. The question here again, as in so many of the economic cases, was whether the end the state sought to achieve was legitimate, and whether the means were not unreasonably related to the end. The end, as he saw it, was to further national cohesion by aiming at a common language in childhood, especially where (to use the words of the majority decision) "certain communities commonly use foreign words, follow foreign leaders, move in a foreign atmosphere." And the means (except in the case of the Ohio statute, which narrowly excluded only German) were not unreasonable.

The majority opinion by Justice McReynolds, on the other hand, follows much the same pattern as the freedom of contract cases.[1] It construes the guarantees of the Fourteenth Amendment very broadly and makes them almost conclusive, even where the questions involved are primarily those of policy. Justice McReynolds seems to have feared a trend toward state control of education which would not stop short of communism. He refers to Plato's *Republic* with its proposal "that the wives of our guardians are to be common, and their children are to be common, and no parent is to know his own

---

[1] It is significant that he relies almost wholly on these cases for his citation of authority.

child, nor any child his parent." From the Iowa and Nebraska of the postwar years to Platonic communism seems a far cry: yet it may serve to set the framework for Justice McReynolds' reasoning.

In this case there are two pairs of doctrines involved that had to be balanced. One is the need for autonomy of the mechanism by which the truth is spread, as against the community's interest in the rearing of its young and the transmission of its cultural heritage. The second is the doctrine of the power of judicial review as against the doctrine of state legislative power. Of the first pair, Holmes is willing to recognize either as a valid social end. But once the state has chosen to emphasize the value of achieving cohesion through "a common tongue," Holmes's respect for state legislative power and his disinclination toward judicial encroachment lead him to accept a not unreasonable means toward that end.

The extent of state control of education that will be allowed under Holmes's principle is not easy to determine. It is not difficult to find in state regulatory or prohibitive legislation a legitimate end. The difficulty lies in estimating the reasonableness of the means. That Holmes drew a line somewhere was shown by his failure to dissent from the Court's opinion in Pierce v. Society of Sisters,[2] invalidating an Oregon law compelling attendance of all children at public primary schools. One cannot help wondering how he would have felt about the recent but already famous flag salute case, Minersville School District v. Gobitis,[3] in which Justice Frankfurter for the Court upheld a school regulation making the pledge of allegiance to the flag compulsory, even as applying to groups with conscientious religious scruples. My own feeling is that the Court's decision on the whole follows the legal logic of Holmes's dissent in the present case, while Justice Stone's dissent in the Gobitis case follows the legal logic of Justice McReynolds' majority opinion in the present case, although its social logic and its mood are far from Justice McReynolds and come closer to the reasons that led Justice Brandeis to join in the Court's opinion. I admit, however, that I have had real difficulty in reaching this conclusion because of three diver-

[2] 268 U. S. 510 (1925).
[3] 310 U. S. 586 (1940).

gences between the two cases: first, the salute to the flag, however important its symbolic value, seems substantially a good deal less important as a means to social cohesiveness than the exclusive use of English in teaching in the schools; second, the value subordinated in the Gobitis *case — the complete freedom of conscience — seems considerably more important than the right to have a child taught in German in the schools. Third, the instances of mob violence against members of the Jehovah's Witnesses sect that followed the* Gobitis *decision indicated that the need for protecting them as a minority was a real one.*[4] *Nevertheless, the general reasoning of Holmes in the* Meyer *case still seems relevant in* Gobitis.

A word on style. Amidst a tangled set of issues there is a striking simplicity of language here which those who have followed Holmes on the Court have sweated for but have not achieved.

Holmes, J., dissenting:

We all agree, I take it, that it is desirable that all the citizens of the United States should speak a common tongue, and therefore that the end aimed at by the statute is a lawful and proper one. The only question is whether the means adopted deprive teachers of the liberty secured to them by the Fourteenth Amendment. It is with hesitation and unwillingness that I differ from my brethren with regard to a law like this but I cannot bring my mind to believe that in some circumstances, and circumstances existing it is said in Nebraska, the statute might not be regarded as a reasonable or even necessary method of reaching the desired result. The part of the act with which we are concerned deals with the teaching of young children. Youth is the time when familiarity with a language is established and if there are sections in the State where a child would hear only Polish or French or German spoken at home I am not prepared to say that it is unreasonable to provide that in his early years he shall hear and speak only English at school. But if it is reasonable it is not an undue restriction of the liberty either of teacher or scholar. No one would doubt that a teacher might be

---

[4] I may add, for what it may be worth, that I do not like the result reached in the *Gobitis* case; but that Justice Frankfurter's approach, in his attempt to balance social and legal values and his refusal to make religious liberty an absolute controlling consideration, seems to me sound.

forbidden to teach many things, and the only criterion of his liberty under the Constitution that I can think of is "whether, considering the end in view, the statute passes the bounds of reason and assumes the character of a merely arbitrary fiat." *Purity Extract & Tonic Co. v. Lynch,* 226 U. S. 192, 204. *Hebe Co. v. Shaw,* 248 U. S. 297, 303. *Jacob Ruppert v. Caffey,* 251 U. S. 264. I think I appreciate the objection to the law but it appears to me to present a question upon which men reasonably might differ and therefore I am unable to say that the Constitution of the United States prevents the experiment being tried.

I agree with the Court as to the special proviso against the German language contained in the statute dealt with in *Bohning v. Ohio.*

"EVERY IDEA IS AN INCITEMENT"

Gitlow v. N. Y.
268 U. S. 652, 672 (1925)

As a result of the excitement connected with the assassination of President McKinley by a supposed anarchist, the state of New York enacted a Criminal Anarchy Act in 1902. Seventeen years later, in 1919, as a result of the excitement connected with the World War and the Russian Revolution, Benjamin Gitlow was arrested and convicted under this Act for writing a Socialist pamphlet called The Left Wing Manifesto. *Gitlow was a former member of the New York Assembly and one of the leaders of the left wing of the Socialist Party which the following year split off and became the Communist Party. The manifesto was the typical statement of the creed of revolutionary socialism, written in the most pedantic neo-Marxian jargon, attacking the Social Democrats for their moderation, and advocating nonparliamentary political and economic methods. It ended, "The proletarian revolution and the Communist reconstruction of society — the struggle for these — is now indispensable. . . . The Communist International calls the proletariat of the world to the final struggle!" Gitlow's arrest and conviction, like his pamphlet, were part of the climate of opinion of the time. There was a widespread* wave of antiradicalism, both in the state and federal governments.[1] *In New York the joint legislative committee of both Houses under Senator Lusk gathered volumes of supposedly inflammatory material, conducted illegal raids, and whipped up an antiradical hysteria in the press. At its incitement five Socialist members of the New York legislature were deprived of their seats. Given this context it was not surprising that the newly formed Communist Party started its career by going underground.*

The Supreme Court affirmed the conviction, Justice Sanford writing a long majority opinion which made three points: that freedom of speech, as guaranteed by the First Amendment, was part of the "liberty" of the Fourteenth Amendment; that an academic essay or philosophical abstraction would not come under the terms of the state act; but that Gitlow's words had been no mere abstraction but "the language of direct incitement."

Justice Holmes wrote a dissent in which Justice Brandeis joined. On the first point he agreed with the majority. This unanimity on the inclusion of freedom of speech in the protections of the Fourteenth Amendment makes this case, regardless of its specific outcome, one of the important steps in the history of the absorption of the First Amendment in the Fourteenth. Actually the first important step toward including freedom of speech within the protection of the Fourteenth Amendment was taken in Gilbert v. Minnesota *(254 U. S. 325 [1920]), in which Justice McKenna hesitatingly groped toward such a view, and Justice Brandeis in his dissent unhesitatingly affirmed it (see Chafee, op. cit., 285–298).*[2] *In 1923 Justice*

---

[1] For a good recent review of the criminal syndicalism laws, see E. F. Dowell, *A History of Criminal Syndicalism Legislation in the U. S.* (1939). The term "criminal syndicalism" as used by the statutes meant in essence advocacy of acts of violence for accomplishing economic or political change, but in the application of the statutes the term came to mean almost any criticism of the existing power structure. About a third of the states passed criminal syndicalism acts between 1917 and 1920. The American Civil Liberties Union took part in fighting the present case, Gitlow's counsel being Walter Nelles, Walter Pollak, and Albert De Silver. The case was twice argued in 1923, and not decided until two years later.

[2] Justice Sanford mentions the case of *Prudential Insurance Co.* v. *Cheek* in which, as late as 1922, the Court had considered that freedom of speech was not part of the Amendment, but says that the "incidental statement" there was not "determinative of this question."

McReynolds in Meyer v. Nebraska *had included freedom of following the occupation of teaching within the Amendment. But in the* Gitlow *case, jurisdiction of the Supreme Court to review state freedom of speech cases was first deliberately announced. The first state law invalidated under this rule was in* Near v. Minnesota (*1931*).[3] *Since that time many other guarantees of the Bill of Rights have been read into the "liberty" of the Fourteenth Amendment.*[4] *There were some who, like Charles Warren in a 1926 legal article, viewed this Gitlow doctrine with "some apprehension" because they foresaw a new "field of interference with state legislation." Holmes, however, accepted the principle, even though he differed from the majority on its application to this case. If "liberty" in the Fourteenth Amendment was to be interpreted broadly enough to allow for an almost absolute view of property it might as well be interpreted broadly enough to include the primary social value of liberty of discussion.*

His quarrel with the majority turned on the application of the clear and present danger doctrine to Gitlow's pamphlet. "Every idea is an incitement," he says, answering Justice Sanford's description of Gitlow's Manifesto. But this one "had no chance of starting a present conflagration." And then follows a sentence in which Justice Holmes, like Jefferson before him, recognizes that changes of power by majority will are part of our institutions: "If in the long run the beliefs expressed in proletarian dictatorship are destined to be accepted by the dominant forces in the community, the only meaning of free speech is that they should be given their chance and have their way." [5]

[3] Earlier, in *Fiske* v. *Kansas,* 274 U. S. 380 (1927), the Court had reversed a conviction for distributing I. W. W. literature.

[4] For a recent summary of the status of the Bill of Rights guarantees with respect to the Fourteenth Amendment, see Justice Cardozo's decision in *Palko* v. *Connecticut,* 302 U. S. 319 (1937).

[5] In later freedom of speech cases under state criminal syndicalism statutes the Supreme Court under the leadership of Chief Justice Hughes moved away from the majority position in the Gitlow case toward Holmes's dissent in the same case and toward Justice Brandeis' magnificent dissent in *Whitney* v. *California,* 274 U. S. 357 (1927). The important cases here were *Stromberg* v. *California,* invalidating the "red flag" section of a state sedition law; *De Jonge* v. *Oregon,* 299 U. S. 353 (1937), which read the right of assembly and petition into the "liberty" of the Fourteenth Amendment despite an Oregon criminal syndicalism statute; and *Herndon* v. *Lowry,* 301 U. S. 242 (1937), which held that

Gitlow's personal history was not without interest. The leader of the left wing at the time was James P. Cannon, and the little group was rent with factional quarrels between him and Gitlow and others. In his autobiography, *I Confess*, Gitlow writes that he was "so involved in factional squabbles" that he was "too swamped to give the matter of my personal fate or the significance of this decision any thought at all." He implies that because of their personal enmity to him the decision was welcomed by Cannon, Foster and other Communist leaders. Gitlow was pardoned by Governor Smith after he had been returned to Sing Sing by the Supreme Court. He later broke away from the Communist Party and became one of its bitterest critics.

Holmes, J., dissenting:

Mr. Justice Brandeis and I are of opinion that this judgment should be reversed. The general principle of free speech, it seems to me, must be taken to be included in the Fourteenth Amendment, in view of the scope that has been given to the word "liberty" as there used, although perhaps it may be accepted with a somewhat larger latitude of interpretation than is allowed to Congress by the sweeping language that governs or ought to govern the laws of the United States. If I am right, then I think that the criterion sanctioned by the full Court in *Schenck* v. *United States*, 249 U. S. 47, 52, applies, "The question in every case is whether the words used are used in such circumstances and are of such a nature as to create a clear and present danger that will bring about the substantive evils that [the State] has a right to prevent." It is true that in my opinion this criterion was departed from in *Abrams* v. *United States*, 250 U. S. 616, but the convictions that I expressed in that case are too deep for it to be possible for me as yet to believe that it and *Schaefer* v. *United States*, 251, U. S. 466, have settled the law. If what I think the correct test is applied, it is manifest that there was no present danger of an attempt to overthrow the government by force on the part of the admittedly small minority who shared the defendant's views. It is said that this manifesto is more than a theory, that it was an incitement. Every idea is an incitement. It offers itself for

---

an old and hitherto unenforced Georgia insurrection statute was inapplicable to a Communist organizer, and that the violence advocated was too distant to represent a present danger.

belief and if believed it is acted on unless some other belief outweighs it or some failure of energy stifles the movement at its birth. The only difference between the expression of an opinion and an incitement in the narrower sense is the speaker's enthusiasm for the result. Eloquence may set fire to reason. But whatever may be thought of the redundant discourse before us it had no chance of starting a present conflagration. If in the long run the beliefs expressed in proletarian dictatorship are destined to be accepted by the dominant forces of the community, the only meaning of free speech is that they should be given their chance and have their way.

If the publication of this document had been laid as an attempt to induce an uprising against government at once and not at some indefinite time in the future, it would have presented a different question. The object would have been one with which the law might deal, subject to the doubt whether there was any danger that the publication could produce any result, or in other words, whether it was not futile and too remote from possible consequences. But the indictment alleges the publication and nothing more.

"FREEDOM FOR THE THOUGHT THAT WE HATE"

U. S. v. Schwimmer
279 U. S. 644, 653 (1928)

In this case Holmes, himself a vigorous anti-pacifist, sought to uphold the right of a pacifist to become naturalized as an American citizen. Rosika Schwimmer was of Hungarian-Jewish descent: she had, incidentally, come into the public eye during the World War when she had persuaded Henry Ford to embark on his Peace Ship expedition. Her application for citizenship had been denied by the federal district court, which was reversed by the Circuit Court of Appeals, on the ground that her refusal to bear arms was immaterial since women were incapable of bearing arms. The Supreme Court upheld the original denial of application, by a vote of six to three. Justice Butler wrote the majority opinion; Justice Holmes wrote a dissent, in which Justice Brandeis joined; Justice Sanford indicated in a dissent that he agreed with the Circuit Court reasoning.

Holmes had never cared much for pacifism. "I agree with your condemnation of armchair pacifists," he wrote Pollock, "on the general ground that until the world has got farther along war is not only not absurd but is inevitable and rational — though of course I would make great sacrifices to avoid one."[1] Nevertheless, he saw the Schwimmer decision as an attempt to use the national power over naturalization as a punitive measure against unpopular opinion, and he therefore wrote his dissent, urging "not free thought for those who agree with us but freedom for the thought that we hate." This was the last dissent that Holmes wrote in a free speech case.

The majority decision was widely criticized on its legal reasoning. Ernst Freund wrote that it "should make a stronger appeal to militant patriots than to careful lawyers."[2] But in 1931 the Supreme Court followed it up in U. S. v. Macintosh, 283 U. S. 605, in which Justice Sutherland for the majority of five denied citizenship to a Yale Professor of Divinity on the ground of pacifism. Justice Holmes again was on the dissenting side, joining with Justices Brandeis and Stone in the dissent of Chief Justice Hughes, who, in Max Radin's words, "noticed the Schwimmer case only with the consecrated phrase with which courts administer euthanasia to their non-viable progeny: he said it stood on its own facts."[3] It was of the Sutherland opinion that Pollock wrote to Holmes, "it rather shocks me to learn . . . how great are the ravages, even in your Court, of the post-war State jingoism mania"; and he adds that in England it never occurred to the Home Secretary "to ask an applicant whether he (let alone she) had scruples of conscience about bearing arms for the defense of the realm."[4]

Holmes, J., dissenting:

The applicant seems to be a woman of superior character and intelligence, obviously more than ordinarily desirable as a citizen of the United States. It is agreed that she is qualified for citizen-

---

[1] H–P, II:230 (Sept. 20, 1928).
[2] 7 New York University Law Quarterly Review 157.
[3] 6 St. John's Law Quarterly Review 45.
[4] H–P, II:299–300 (Dec. 10, 1931).

STATE POWER AND FREE TRADE IN IDEAS 327

ship except so far as the views set forth in a statement of facts "may show that the applicant is not attached to the principles of the Constitution of the United States and well disposed to the good order and happiness of the same, and except in so far as the same may show that she cannot take the oath of allegiance without a mental reservation." The views referred to are an extreme opinion in favor of pacifism and a statement that she would not bear arms to defend the Constitution. So far as the adequacy of her oath is concerned, I hardly can see how it is affected by the statement, inasmuch as she is a woman over fifty years of age, and would not be allowed to bear arms if she wanted to. And as to the opinion the whole examination of the applicant shows that she holds none of the now-dreaded creeds, but thoroughly believes in organized government and prefers that of the United States to any other in the world. Surely it cannot show lack of attachment to the principles of the Constitution that she thinks it can be improved. I suppose that most intelligent people think that it might be. Her particular improvement looking to the abolition of war seems to me not materially different in its bearing on this case from a wish to establish cabinet government as in England, or a single house, or one term of seven years for the President. To touch a more burning question, only a judge mad with partisanship would exclude because the applicant thought that the Eighteenth Amendment should be repealed.

Of course the fear is that if a war came the applicant would exert activities such as were dealt with in *Schenck* v. *United States,* 249 U. S. 47. But that seems to me unfounded. Her position and motives are wholly different from those of Schenck. She is an optimist and states in strong and, I do not doubt, sincere words her belief that war will disappear and that the impending destiny of mankind is to unite in peaceful leagues. I do not share that optimism nor do I think that a philosophic view of the world would regard war as absurd. But most people who have known it regard it with horror, as a last resort, and, even if not yet ready for cosmopolitan efforts, would welcome any practicable combination that would increase the power on the side of peace. The notion that the applicant's optimistic anticipations would make her a worse citizen is sufficiently answered by her examination, which seems to me a better argument for her admission than any I can offer. Some of her answers might excite popular prejudice, but if there is any principle of the Constitution that more imperatively calls for attachment than any other it is the principle of free thought — not free thought for those who agree with us but freedom for the thought that we hate. I think that we should adhere to that principle with regard to admission into, as well as to life within, this country. And, recurring to the opinion that bars this applicant's way, I would suggest that the Quakers have done their share to make the country what it is, that many citizens agree with the applicant's belief, and that I had not supposed hitherto that we regretted our inability to expel them because they believe more than some of us do in the teachings of the Sermon on the Mount.

NEGRO DISFRANCHISEMENT IN TEXAS

Nixon v. Herndon
273 U. S. 536 (1927)

The history of Negro disfranchisement in the South [1] furnishes the context of this case. The white garrison population after the Civil War felt compelled to resort to a variety of methods to retain its political domination.[2] The Ku Klux Klan period was followed by educational voting tests, poll taxes and "grandfather clauses" in the eighties and nineties. The objective was to achieve a "lily-white" political party, and counsel in this case actually argued that Negroes were not deprived of their freedom because they could organize their own political parties. Behind racial prejudice lay a fear of "black government" by the "newly captured savages"; and especially a fear that voting by Negroes would give them a balance-of-power position between parties and party factions, thus forcing the parties to resort to bribery and to build up rival Negro political machines. "Thus is presented the strange picture of one race disfranchising another to save itself from the consequences of its own vices."[3] Ordinarily Texas, like some ten other Southern states, had relied on the Democratic county executive committees to accomplish the primary disfranchisement quietly

---

[1] I am indebted for much of what follows to an excellent unsigned note on *Nixon v. Condon*, in 41 YLJ, 1212–1220 (1932).
[2] For these methods see Paul Lewinson, *Race, Class, and Party* (1932) Ch. VI and VII.
[3] YLJ note, cited above.

through the non-statutory "white primaries": and, of course, since (given one-party domination) primaries are the effective elections in Texas, primary disfranchisement meant electoral disfranchisement. But the danger that party factions might break this gentlemen's agreement led to the passing of a statute in 1923 prohibiting Negroes from voting in Democratic primaries.[4]

Nixon, an El Paso Negro, brought suit to test its constitutionality. Counsel on both sides in the original trial argued on the basis of the Fifteenth Amendment, which had guaranteed the Negroes against discrimination on account of their race with respect to suffrage. The Supreme Court might have determined the question whether a primary was an election and thus within the protection of the Amendment. But Justice Holmes, writing the unanimous opinion of the Court, refused to pass on the Fifteenth Amendment, on the ground that "it seems hard to imagine a more direct and obvious infringement of the Fourteenth," which was intended primarily to protect Negro rights. He skirted close to the question he sought to avoid: "The primary," he said, "may determine the final result." One may guess that he steered away from the vexed question of the Fifteenth Amendment for reasons of strategy in getting a united court. Perhaps he felt that the judicial process would not in any event, whether under Fourteenth or Fifteenth Amendment, avail the Negroes. When, at the Court session, he had finished reading his opinion, he is reported to have added as an aside, "I know that our good brethren, the Negroes of Texas, will now rejoice that they possess at the primary the rights which heretofore they have enjoyed at the general election."

He was right in his doubts. His decision in Nixon v. Herndon caused a "wave of dismay" to pass through the South. "It was widely felt . . . that the white primary bulwark of white supremacy, was gravely imperiled."[5] But there was a

---

[4] The law grew out of an intraparty fight between two Democratic candidates for district attorney in a county which admitted some Negroes to the primary. To weaken his rival's county machine the defeated candidate started a move for a state-wide statute barring Negroes from the primaries. The law was passed through the support of the Negrophobe counties which had barred Negroes under a party rule. See Lewinson, op. cit., 113.

[5] Lewinson, op. cit., 113.

loophole. "Color," Justice Holmes had written at the end of his opinion, "cannot be made the basis of a statutory classification." But what if it were non-statutory? The Texas legislature accordingly repealed the offending statute in 1927 and passed another, vesting power in the party executive committees to determine the requirements for membership in the party, and therefore for primary voting. The Democratic party passed a resolution that "all white Democrats . . . and none other" be admitted, Nixon again sued, and was again upheld by the Supreme Court on the ground that the party resolution was adopted as a result of the statute, and was therefore the act of a state agency.[6] The Texas legislature again repealed the statute, and the Democratic state convention in 1932 adopted a resolution giving the right to vote in primaries to "all white citizens." This was upheld in Grovey v. Townsend[7] on the ground that the party is a private body, and there was no state legislation which might give its resolution the character of a state act. Thus Holmes's opinion in Nixon v. Herndon proved eventually futile. The problem of the relation of primary laws to the "equal protection" clause of the Fourteenth Amendment has not yet been wholly resolved. But in the recent case of U. S. v. Classic[8] the Court held that, particularly under the circumstances offered by Southern states with their dominant-party system, a primary election is an integral part of the election process and the citizen has the right to a primary free from fraud. This paves the way for reversing Grovey v. Townsend and actually goes farther than Holmes was willing explicitly to go.

Holmes, J., for the Court:

This is an action against the judges of elections for refusing to permit the plaintiff to vote at a primary election in Texas. It lays the damages at five thousand dollars. The petition alleges that the

[6] *Nixon* v. *Condon*, 286 U. S. 73 (1932). Justice Cardozo wrote the opinion in a 5-4 decision, Justice McReynolds writing the dissent. On the *Nixon* cases, in addition to the YLJ citation in note 1, see 32 Columbia Law Review (1932) 1069 and 48 HLR (1935) 1436.

[7] 295 U. S. 45 (1935). Justice Roberts wrote the unanimous opinion of the Court. Holmes was by that time off the bench.

[8] 313 U. S. 299 (1941). For comment see 41 Columbia Law Review (1941) 1101. On recent related cases in the area of Negro civil liberties, see Riesman, *op. cit.*, 84–86.

STATE POWER AND FREE TRADE IN IDEAS 331

plaintiff is a negro, a citizen of the United States and of Texas and a resident of El Paso, and in every way qualified to vote, as set forth in detail, except that the statute to be mentioned interferes with his right; that on July 26, 1924, a primary election was held at El Paso for the nomination of candidates for a senator and representatives in Congress and state and other offices, upon the Democratic ticket; that the plaintiff, being a member of the Democratic party, sought to vote, but was denied the right by defendants; that the denial was based upon a statute of Texas enacted in May, 1923, and designated article 3093a, by the words of which "in no event shall a negro be eligible to participate in a Democratic party primary election held in the state of Texas," &c., and that this statute is contrary to the Fourteenth and Fifteenth Amendments to the Constitution of the United States. The defendants moved to dismiss upon the ground that the subject-matter of the suit was political and not within the jurisdiction of the court and that no violation of the Amendments was shown. The suit was dismissed and a writ of error was taken directly to this Court. Here no argument was made on behalf of the defendants but a brief was allowed to be filed by the attorney general of the state.

The objection that the subject-matter of the suit is political is little more than a play upon words. Of course the petition concerns political action, but it alleges and seeks to recover for private damage. That private damage may be caused by such political action and may be recovered for in a suit at law hardly has been doubted for over two hundred years, since *Ashby* v. *White*, 2 Ld. Raym. 938, 3 *id.* 320, and has been recognized by this Court. *Wiley* v. *Sinkler*, 179 U. S. 58, 64, 65. *Giles* v. *Harris*, 189 U. S. 475, 485. See also Judicial Code, § 24 (11), (12), (14). Act of March 3, 1911, c. 231, 36 Stat. 1087, 1092. If the defendants' conduct was a wrong to the plaintiff the same reasons that allow a recovery for denying the plaintiff a vote at a final election allow it for denying a vote at the primary election that may determine the final result.

The important question is whether the statute can be sustained. But although we state it as a question the answer does not seem to us open to a doubt. We find it unnecessary to consider the Fifteenth Amendment, because it seems to us hard to imagine a more direct and obvious infringement of the Fourteenth. That Amendment, while it applies to all, was passed, as we know, with a special intent to protect the blacks from discrimination against them. *Slaughter-House Cases,* 16 Wall. 36. *Strauder* v. *West Virginia,* 100 U. S. 303. That Amendment "not only gave citizenship and the privileges of citizenship to persons of color, but it denied to any state the power to withhold from them the equal protection of the laws. . . . What is this but declaring that the law in the states shall be the same for the black as for the white; that all persons whether colored or white, shall stand equal before the laws of the states, and, in regard to the colored race, for whose protection the Amendment was primarily designed, that no discrimination shall be made against them by law because of their color?" Quoted from the last case in *Buchanan* v. *Warley,* 245 U. S. 60, 77. See *Yick Wo* v. *Hopkins,* 118 U. S. 356, 374. The statute of Texas in the teeth of the prohibitions referred to, assumes to forbid negroes to take part in a primary election the importance of which we have indicated, discriminating against them by the distinction of color alone. States may do a good deal of classifying that it is difficult to believe rational, but there are limits, and it is too clear for extended argument that color cannot be made the basis of a statutory classification affecting the right set up in this case.

Judgment reversed.

THE JUDGE AND THE EDITOR

Toledo Newspaper Co. v. *U. S.*
247 U. S. 402, 422 (1918)

This was one of the cases[1] *in which Holmes wrote dissents "that I imagine the majority thought ill-timed and regrettable as I thought the decisions." The newspaper involved was the* Toledo *News-Bee. Chief Justice White, for the majority, upheld the proceeding against the editor. Freedom of the press, he said, does not imply "the right to frustrate and defeat the discharge of those governmental duties upon the performance of which the freedom of all, including that of the press, depends." The Court vote was five to two, Justices Day and Clarke not sitting because of their relation with the judge.*

[1] See the prefatory note to *Hammer* v. *Dagenhart,* p. 165.

STATE POWER AND FREE TRADE IN IDEAS

Justice Holmes was joined in his dissent by Justice Brandeis. Although Holmes never liked newspapers, rarely read them, and detested the style that reporters had come to adopt, he saw their function in the community as an important one. But even more he was averse to the adoption by judges of a sacrosanct attitude about themselves. He could not find in what was said in the Toledo newspaper "anything that would have affected a mind of reasonable fortitude"; but even if there was ground for contempt proceedings, there was no such immediate obstruction of justice as to warrant a summary trial by the judge without a jury. Here, as in Evans v. Gore, *Holmes shows that he did not want to see the creation of a judicial caste separated from the rest of the citizenry. "I thought the performance wholly unwarranted," he writes Pollock, "and the last thing that could maintain respect for the Courts."* [2]

Like so many of his other dissents, Holmes's view in the Toledo Newspaper Co. *has been adopted by the Supreme Court as the prevailing doctrine on contempt of court trials. In* Nye v. U. S., *313 U. S. 33 (1941), Justice Douglas wrote a six-to-three opinion of the Court, leaning heavily upon Holmes's doctrine, but moving beyond it so as explicitly to construe the necessary "nearness" to the court of the act of contempt in geographical rather than in causal terms. And in* Bridges v. California, *62 SC 190 (1941), the Supreme Court went even farther in reversing a citation for contempt resulting from an utterance critical of a Court. Justice Black, speaking for the majority, measured the freedom of such utterance by the "clear and present danger" standard, and the balancing of the social values involved.*

Holmes, J., dissenting:

One of the usual controversies between a street railway and the city that it served had been going on for years and had culminated in an ordinance establishing three cent fares that was to go into effect on March 28th, 1914. In January of that year the people who were operating the road began a suit for an injunction on the

---

[2] H–P, I:267 (June 14, 1918). It must be added, however, that the present case was one involving interpretation of a federal statute dealing with contempts, rather than one of constitutional interpretation.

ground that the ordinance was confiscatory. The plaintiffs in error, a newspaper and its editor, had long been on the popular side and had furnished news and comment to sustain it; and when, on March 24, a motion was made for a temporary injunction in the suit, they published a cartoon representing the road as a moribund man in bed with its friends at the bedside and one of them saying, "Guess we'd better call in Doc Killits." Thereafter pending the controversy they published news, comment and cartoons as before. The injunction was issued on September 12. The Judge (Killits) who was referred to took no steps until September 29, when he directed an information to be filed covering publications from March 24 through September 17. This was done on October 28. In December the case was tried summarily without a jury by the judge who thought his authority contemned, and in the following year he imposed a considerable fine. The question is whether he acted within his powers under the statutes of the United States.

The statute in force at the time of the alleged contempts confined the power of Courts in cases of this sort to where there had been "misbehavior of any person in their presence, or so near thereto as to obstruct the administration of justice." Before the trial took place an act was passed giving a trial by jury upon demand of the accused in all but the above mentioned instances, October 14, 1914. In England, I believe, the usual course is to proceed by the regular way by indictment. I mention this fact and the later statute only for their bearing upon the meaning of the exception in our law. When it is considered how contrary it is to our practice and ways of thinking for the same person to be accuser and sole judge in a matter which, if he be sensitive, may involve strong personal feeling, I should expect the power to be limited by the necessities of the case "to insure order and decorum in their presence" as it is stated in *Ex parte Robinson*, 19 Wall. 505. See Prynne, Plea for the Lords, 309, cited in McIlwain, The High Court of Parliament and its Supremacy, 191. And when the words of the statute are read it seems to me that the limit is too plain to be construed away. To my mind they point and point only to the present protection of the Court from actual interference, and not to postponed retribution for lack of respect for its dignity — not to moving to vindicate its independence after enduring the newspaper's attacks for nearly six months as the court did in this case. Without invoking the rule of strict

STATE POWER AND FREE TRADE IN IDEAS

construction I think that "so near as to obstruct" means so near as actually to obstruct — and not merely near enough to threaten a possible obstruction. "So near as to" refers to an accomplished fact, and the word "misbehavior" strengthens the construction I adopt. Misbehavior means something more than adverse comment or disrespect.

But suppose that an imminent possibility of obstruction is sufficient. Still I think that only immediate and necessary action is contemplated, and that no case for summary proceedings is made out if after the event publications are brought to the attention of the judge that might have led to an obstruction although they did not. So far as appears that is the present case. But I will go a step farther. The order for the information recites that from time to time sundry numbers of the paper have come to the attention of the judge as a daily reader of it, and I will assume, from that and the opinion, that he read them as they came out, and I will assume further that he was entitled to rely upon his private knowledge without a statement in open court. But a judge of the United States is expected to be a man of ordinary firmness of character, and I find it impossible to believe that such a judge could have found in anything that was printed even a tendency to prevent his performing his sworn duty. I am not considering whether there was a technical contempt at common law but whether what was done falls within the words of an act intended and admitted to limit the power of the Courts.

The chief thing done was to print statements of a widespread public intent to board the cars and refuse to pay more than three cents even if the judge condemned the ordinance, statements favoring the course, if you like, and mention of the city officials who intended to back it up. This popular movement was met on the part of the railroad by directing its conductors not to accept three cent fares, but to carry passengers free who refused to pay more; so that all danger of violence on that score was avoided, even if it was a danger that in any way concerned the Court. The newspaper further gave one or two premature but ultimately correct intimations of what the judge was going to do, made one mistaken statement of a ruling which it criticized indirectly, uttered a few expressions that implied that the judge did not have the last word and that no doubt contained innuendoes not flattering to his personality. Later there was an account of a local Socialist meeting at which a member, one Quinlivan, spoke in such a way that the judge attached him for contempt and thereupon, on the same day that the decree was entered in the principal case, the paper reported as the grounds for the attachment that Quinlivan had pronounced Judge Killits to have shown from the first that he was favorable to the railroad, had criticized somewhat ignorantly a ruling said to put the burden of proof on the city, and had said that Killits and his press were unfair to the people, winding up "impeach Killits." I confess that I cannot find in all this or in the evidence in the case anything that would have affected a mind of reasonable fortitude, and still less can I find there anything that obstructed the administration of justice in any sense that I possibly can give to those words.

In the elaborate opinion that was delivered by Judge Killits to justify the judgment it is said "In this matter the record shows that the court endured the *News-Bee's* attacks upon suitors before it and upon the court itself, and carried all the embarrassment inevitable from these publications, for nearly six months before moving to vindicate its independence." It appears to me that this statement is enough to show that there was no emergency, that there was nothing that warranted a finding that the administration of justice was obstructed, or a resort to this summary proceeding, but that on the contrary when the matter was over, the judge thought that the "consistently unfriendly attitude against the court" and the fact that the publications tended "to arouse distrust and dislike of the court," were sufficient to justify this information and a heavy fine. They may have been, but not, I think, in this form of trial. I would go as far as any man in favor of the sharpest and most summary enforcement of order in Court and obedience to decrees, but when there is no need for immediate action contempts are like any other breach of law and should be dealt with as the law deals with other illegal acts. Action like the present in my opinion is wholly unwarranted by even color of law.

PEONAGE IN ALABAMA

Bailey v. *Alabama*
219 U. S. 219, 245 (1911)

For those who still cling to a lingering belief that Holmes was a humanitarian liberal in his impulses, the "Alabama peonage" case should be required reading. Lonzo Bailey was an Alabama Negro working as a farm hand for one of the farms of the Riverside Company. In 1907 he received fifteen dollars from the company, and in return he signed a written contract to work for it for a year for twelve dollars a month, of which he was to receive $10.75 a month and the rest was to count against the cash advance of fifteen dollars. He stayed on his job a little over a month, then stopped work without refunding the advance. There was an Alabama statute, passed in 1896 and amended in 1903 and 1907, providing for just such a contingency. Its terms were that anyone who "with intent to injure or defraud his employer" does what Bailey did shall be subject to fine; and that his failure to refund the money shall be "prima facie *evidence of the intent to injure . . . or defraud.*"

Bailey's case came before the Supreme Court on two occasions. In the first — Bailey v. Alabama, 211 U. S. 452 (1908) — Holmes wrote the opinion of the Court saying that "the trouble with the whole case is that it is brought here prematurely by an attempt to take a short cut," and the case was sent back for trial in the Alabama courts. Justices Harlan and Day dissented. On trial Bailey was found guilty, fined thirty dollars and costs, and in default of payment, sentenced to twenty days of hard prison labor for the fine and 116 days for the costs. He appealed on the ground that the statute, by making non-payment of the debt prima-facie evidence of intent to defraud, deprived him of his liberty under the Fourteenth Amendment, and led to involuntary servitude for a debt within the meaning of the Thirteenth Amendment. The Supreme Court reversed the opinion of the Alabama Supreme Court and held the statute unconstitutional under the Thirteenth Amendment. The opinion of the Court was written by Justice Hughes; Holmes wrote the present dissent, in which Justice Lurton concurred.

Justice Hughes points out in his majority opinion that the act of Congress passed in 1867 for the enforcement of the Thirteenth Amendment contains a provision against "voluntary or involuntary service or labor of any persons as peons, in liquidation of any debt or obligation"; and that the term "involuntary servitude" was understood historically to have "a *larger meaning than slavery." "A peon," he continues, "is one who is compelled to work for his creditor until his debt is paid . . . there is no more important concern than to safeguard the freedom of labor upon which alone can enduring prosperity be based. The provision designed to secure it would soon become a barren frame if it were possible to . . . hold over the heads of laborers the threat of punishment for crime, under the name of fraud, but merely upon evidence of failure to work out their debts."*

Holmes's dissent has struck many commentators as legalistic in the worst sense of legalism. While he goes through a rigorous train of reasoning (as, in his own way, Justice Hughes does also), it is of the sort which pays homage to the forms without going beyond them to the social reality. Holmes's insistence that the prima-facie assumption of intent to defraud need not be the determining factor with a jury has a hollow sound in the known context of class and race relations in the South; and his reliance on the "men of the world" who compose such a jury has an element of unconscious humor. By the same sort of reasoning the Court opinion in Frank v. Mangum,[1] *from which Holmes dissented, would have been justified; and his opinion in* Moore v. Dempsey[2] *would have been impossible. In the latter case Holmes insists that procedural justice is more than a formal mask. One may suggest that the same consideration if applied here should have led Holmes to agree with Justice Hughes. Holmes undoubtedly sought here to lean backward in his anxiety not to write a "humanitarian" opinion, but the result was that he wrote one which cannot stand up as good law.*

Holmes, J., dissenting:

We all agree that this case is to be considered and decided in the same way as if it arose in Idaho or New York. Neither public document nor evidence discloses a law which by its administration is made something different from what it appears on its face, and therefore the fact that in Alabama it mainly concerns the blacks does not matter. *Yick* v. *Hopkins,* 118 U. S. 356, does not apply. I shall begin then by assuming for the moment what I think is not

[1] See below, p. 342.
[2] See below, p. 347.

STATE POWER AND FREE TRADE IN IDEAS 339

true and shall try to show not to be true, that this statute punishes the mere refusal to labor according to contract as a crime, and shall inquire whether there would be anything contrary to the 13th Amendment or the statute if it did, supposing it to have been enacted in the State of New York. I cannot believe it. The 13th Amendment does not outlaw contracts for labor. That would be at least as great a misfortune for the laborer as for the man that employed him. For it certainly would affect the terms of the bargain unfavorably for the laboring man if it were understood that the employer could do nothing in case the laborer saw fit to break his word. But any legal liability for breach of a contract is a disagreeable consequence which tends to make the contractor do as he said he would. Liability to an action for damages has that tendency as well as a fine. If the mere imposition of such consequences as tend to make a man keep to his promise is the creation of peonage when the contract happens to be for labor, I do not see why the allowance of a civil action is not, as well as an indictment ending in fine. Peonage is service to a private master at which a man is kept by bodily compulsion against his will. But the creation of the ordinary legal motives for right conduct does not produce it. Breach of a legal contract without excuse is wrong conduct, even if the contract is for labor, and if a State adds to civil liability a criminal liability to fine, it simply intensifies the legal motive for doing right, it does not make the laborer a slave.

But if a fine may be imposed, imprisonment may be imposed in case of a failure to pay it. Nor does it matter if labor is added to the imprisonment. Imprisonment with hard labor is not stricken from the statute books. On the contrary, involuntary servitude as a punishment for crime is excepted from the prohibition of the 13th Amendment in so many words. Also the power of the States to make breach of contract a crime is not done away with by the abolition of slavery. But if breach of contract may be made a crime at all, it may be made a crime with all the consequences usually attached to crime. There is produced a sort of illusion if a contract to labor ends in compulsory labor in prison. But compulsory work for no private master in a jail is not peonage. If work in a jail is not condemned in itself, without regard to what the conduct is it punishes, it may be made a consequence of any conduct that the State has power to punish at all. I do not blink the fact that the liability to imprisonment may work as a motive when a fine without it would not, and that it may induce the laborer to keep on when he would like to leave. But it does not strike me as an objection to a law that it is effective. If the contract is one that ought not to be made, prohibit it. But if it is a perfectly fair and proper contract, I can see no reason why the State should not throw its weight on the side of performance. There is no relation between its doing so in the manner supposed and allowing a private master to use private force upon a laborer who wishes to leave.

But all that I have said so far goes beyond the needs of the case as I understand it. I think it a mistake to say that this statute attaches its punishment to the mere breach of a contract to labor. It does not purport to do so; what it purports to punish is fraudulently obtaining money by a false pretense of an intent to keep the written contract in consideration of which the money is advanced. (It is not necessary to cite cases to show that such an intent may be the subject of a material false representation.) But the import of the statute is supposed to be changed by the provision that a refusal to perform, coupled with a failure to return the money advanced, shall be *prima facie* evidence of fraudulent intent, I agree that if the statute created a conclusive presumption, it might be held to make a disguised change in the substantive law. *Keller* v. *United States,* 213 U. S. 138, 150. But it only makes the conduct *prima facie* evidence, a very different matter. Is it not evidence that a man had a fraudulent intent if he receives an advance upon a contract over night and leaves in the morning? I should have thought that it very plainly was. Of course the statute is in general terms and applies to a departure at any time without excuse or repayment, but that does no harm except on a tacit assumption that this law is not administered as it would be in New York, and that juries will act with prejudice against the laboring man. For *prima facie* evidence is only evidence, and as such may be held by the jury insufficient to make out guilt. 161 Ala. 78. This was decided by the Supreme Court of Alabama in this case, and we should be bound by their construction of the statute, even if we thought it wrong. But I venture to add that I think it entirely right. *State* v. *Intoxicating Liquors,* 80 Me. 57. This being so, I take it that a fair jury would acquit, if the only evidence were a departure after eleven months' work, and if it received no color from some special well-known course of events. But the matter well may be left to a jury, because their experience as men of the world may teach them that in certain conditions it is so common for laborers to remain during a part of the season, receiving advances, and then to depart at the period of need in the hope of greater wages at a neighboring plantation, that when a laborer follows that course there is a fair inference of fact that he intended it from the beginning. The Alabama statute, as construed by the state court and as we must take it, merely says, as a court might say, that the prosecution may go to the jury. This means, and means only that the court cannot say, from its knowledge of the ordinary course of events, that the jury could not be justified by its knowledge in drawing the inference from the facts proved. In my opinion the statute embodies little if anything more than what I should have told the jury was the law without it. The right of the State to regulate laws of evidence is admitted and the statute does not go much beyond the common law. *Com. v. Rubin,* 165 Mass. 453.

I do not see how the result that I have reached thus far is affected by the rule laid down by the court, but not contained in the statute, that the prisoner cannot testify to his uncommunicated intentions, and therefore, it is assumed, would not be permitted to offer a naked denial of an intent to defraud. If there is an excuse for breaking the contract it will be found in external circumstances, and can be proved. So the sum of the wrong supposed to be inflicted is that the intent to go off without repaying may be put further back than it would otherwise. But if there is a wrong it lies in leaving the evidence to the jury, a wrong that is not affected by the letting in or keeping out an item of evidence on the other side. I have stated why I think it was not a wrong.

To sum up, I think that obtaining money by fraud may be made a crime as well as murder or theft; that a false representation, expressed or implied, at the time of making a contract of labor, that one intends to perform it, and thereby obtaining an advance, may be declared a case of fraudulently obtaining money as well as any other; that if made a crime it may be punished like any other crime, and that an unjustified departure from the promised service without repayment may be declared a sufficient case to go to the jury for their judgment; all without in any way infringing the 13th Amendment of the statutes of the United States.

TRIAL BY MOB

Frank v. Mangum
237 U. S. 309, 345 (1915)

The trial of Leo Frank was one of the American causes célèbres of the prewar years. Frank was a young New Yorker who had come to Atlanta, Georgia, and become manager of a pencil factory owned by his uncle. In 1913 he was tried and convicted of the murder of a girl who worked in the plant, in a trial which achieved national prominence because it was conducted in an atmosphere in which intense anti-Semitism was fused with the Southern hatred of "foreigners" from New York. After unsuccessful appeals to the Georgia Supreme Court, Frank applied to the District Court for a writ of habeas corpus, alleging mob domination of the trial. The Georgia Supreme Court had determined the question of the fairness of the trial, and the District Court refused to intervene on the ground that procedural due process had been complied with. The hearing before the Supreme Court attracted national attention, with Louis Marshall appearing for Frank. The Supreme Court, in a long and learned majority opinion by Justice Pitney, upheld the District Court.

Justice Holmes wrote a dissent in which Justice Hughes joined, holding that the District Court should have proceeded to try the facts of the case. The crux of the dissent was that mob domination of a trial may be a fact despite procedural correctness and despite the fact that the official trial record showed no flaw. "This is not a matter for polite presumptions; we must look facts in the face. Any judge who has sat with juries knows that in spite of forms they are extremely likely to be impregnated by the environing atmosphere." And in his recital of the alleged circumstances of the trial, Holmes emphasized that even the judge had not thought it safe, in the event of an acquittal or a "hung" jury, for either the prisoner or his counsel to be present at the jury polling.

Holmes's opinion is thus a study in the contrast of form and substance. It was a problem that reached deep to his philosophic conviction that form had no reality apart from

STATE POWER AND FREE TRADE IN IDEAS 343

substance. "*The only use of the forms,*" he wrote to his Chinese friend John Wu, "*is to present their contents, just as the only use of a pint pot is to present the beer . . . and infinite meditation upon the pot never will give you the beer.*"[1] A tragic substantiation of Holmes's views on the fact of mob domination was given by what later happened to Frank. Before his execution could take place, under guard from one prison to another, he was taken from the State prison farm by a mob and lynched.

Frank v. Mangum *did not remain court doctrine long. In 1923 it was in effect overruled by* Moore v. Dempsey.[2]

Holmes, J., dissenting:

Mr. Justice Hughes and I are of opinion that the judgment should be reversed. The only question before us is whether the petition shows on its face that the writ of *habeas corpus* should be denied, or whether the District Court should have proceeded to try the facts. The allegations that appear to us material are these. The trial began on July 28, 1913, at Atlanta, and was carried on in a court packed with spectators and surrounded by a crowd outside, all strongly hostile to the petitioner. On Saturday, August 23, this hostility was sufficient to lead the judge to confer in the presence of the jury with the Chief of Police of Atlanta and the Colonel of the Fifth Georgia Regiment stationed in that city, both of whom were known to the jury. On the same day, the evidence seemingly having been closed, the public press, apprehending danger, united in a request to the Court that the proceedings should not continue on that evening. Thereupon the Court adjourned until Monday morning. On that morning when the Solicitor General entered the court he was greeted with applause, stamping of feet and clapping of hands, and the judge before beginning his charge had a private conversation with the petitioner's counsel in which he expressed the opinion that there would be "probable danger of

[1] See H. C. Shriver, *Book Notices and Uncollected Letters and Papers of Holmes* (1936) 167. Pollock, in expressing his agreement with Holmes in one of his letters, went to the heart of the issue. "I should expect you to hold the final judgment in the State court conclusive as to all matters of form and local procedure, but not as to . . . the fundamental conditions of justice . . . a question whether the jury was in fact intimidated was extraneous to the record. . . ." H–P, I:226 (May 19, 1915).

[2] See p. 347.

violence" if there should be an acquittal or disagreement, and that it would be safer for not only the petitioner but his counsel to be absent from Court when the verdict was brought in. At the judge's request they agreed that the petitioner and they should be absent, and they kept their word. When the verdict was rendered, and before more than one of the jurymen had been polled there was such a roar of applause that the polling could not go on till order was restored. The noise outside was such that it was difficult for the judge to hear the answers of the jurors although he was only ten feet from them. With these specifications of fact, the petitioner alleges that the trial was dominated by a hostile mob and was nothing but an empty form.

We lay on one side the question whether the petitioner could or did waive his right to be present at the polling of the jury. That question was apparent in the form of the trial and was raised by the application for a writ of error; and although after application to the full Court we thought that the writ ought to be granted, we never have been impressed by the argument that the presence of the prisoner was required by the Constitution of the United States. But *habeas corpus* cuts through all forms and goes to the very tissue of the structure. It comes in from the outside, not in subordination to the proceedings, and although every form may have been preserved opens the inquiry whether they have been more than an empty shell.

The argument for the appellee in substance is that the trial was in a court of competent jurisdiction, that it retains jurisdiction although, in fact, it may be dominated by a mob, and that the rulings of the state court as to the fact of such domination cannot be reviewed. But the argument seems to us inconclusive. Whatever disagreement there may be as to the scope of the phrase "due process of law," there can be no doubt that it embraces the fundamental conception of a fair trial, with opportunity to be heard. Mob law does not become due process of law by securing the assent of a terrorized jury. We are not speaking of mere disorder, or mere irregularities in procedure, but of a case where the processes of justice are actually subverted. In such a case, the Federal court has jurisdiction to issue the writ. The fact that the state court still has its general jurisdiction and is otherwise a competent court does not make it impossible to find that a jury has been subjected to intimidation in a particular case. The loss of jurisdiction is not

STATE POWER AND FREE TRADE IN IDEAS 345

general but particular, and proceeds from the control of a hostile influence.

When such a case is presented, it cannot be said, in our view, that the State court decision makes the matter *res judicata*. The State acts when by its agency it finds the prisoner guilty and condemns him. We have held in a civil case that it is no defense to the assertion of the Federal right in the Federal court that the State has corrective procedure of its own — that still less does such a procedure draw to itself the final determination of the Federal question. *Simon* v. *Southern Ry.,* 236 U. S. 115, 122, 123. We see no reason for a less liberal rule in a matter of life and death. When the decision of the question of fact is so interwoven with the decision of the question of constitutional right that the one necessarily involves the other, the Federal court must examine the facts. *Kansas Southern Ry.* v. *C. H. Albers Commission Co.,* 223 U. S. 573, 591. *Nor. & West. Ry.* v. *Conley,* March 8, 1915, 236 U. S. 605. Otherwise, the right will be a barren one. It is significant that the argument for the State does not go so far as to say that in no case would it be permissible on application for *habeas corpus* to override the findings of fact by the state courts. It would indeed be a most serious thing if this Court were so to hold, for we could not but regard it as a removal of what is perhaps the most important guaranty of the Federal Constitution. If, however, the argument stops short of this, the whole structure built upon the State procedure and decisions falls to the ground.

To put an extreme case and show what we mean, if the trial and the later hearings before the Supreme Court had taken place in the presence of an armed force known to be ready to shoot if the result was not the one desired, we do not suppose that this Court would allow itself to be silenced by the suggestion that the record showed no flaw. To go one step further, suppose that the trial had taken place under such intimidation that the Supreme Court of the State on writ of error had discovered no error in the record, we still imagine that this court would find a sufficient one outside of the record, and that it would not be disturbed in its conclusion by anything that the Supreme Court of the State might have said. We therefore lay the suggestion that the Supreme Court of the State has disposed of the present question by its judgment on one side along with the question of the appellant's right to be present. If the petition discloses facts that amount to a loss of jurisdiction in the trial court, jurisdiction could not be restored by any decision above. And notwithstanding the principle of comity and convenience (for in our opinion it is nothing more, *United States v. Sing Tuck,* 194 U. S. 161, 168) that calls for a resort to the local appellate tribunal before coming to the courts of the United States for a writ of *habeas corpus,* when, as here, that resort has been had in vain, the power to secure fundamental rights that had existed at every stage becomes a duty and must be put forth.

The single question in our minds is whether a petition alleging that the trial took place in the midst of a mob savagely and manifestly intent on a single result, is shown on its face unwarranted by the specifications, which may be presumed to set forth the strongest indications of the fact at the petitioner's command. This is not a matter for polite presumptions; we must look facts in the face. Any judge who has sat with juries knows that in spite of forms they are extremely likely to be impregnated by the environing atmosphere. And when we find the judgment of the expert on the spot, of the judge whose business it was to preserve not only form but substance, to have been that if one juryman yielded to the reasonable doubt that he himself later expressed in court as the result of most anxious deliberation, neither prisoner nor counsel would be safe from the rage of the crowd, we think the presumption overwhelming that the jury responded to the passions of the mob. Of course we are speaking only of the case made by the petition, and whether it ought to be heard. Upon allegations of this gravity in our opinion it ought to be heard, whatever the decision of the state court may have been, and it did not need to set forth contradictory evidence, or matter of rebuttal, or to explain why the motions for a new trial and to set aside the verdict were overruled by the state court. There is no reason to fear an impairment of the authority of the State to punish the guilty. We do not think it impracticable in any part of this country to have trials free from outside control. But to maintain this immunity it may be necessary that the supremacy of the law and of the Federal Constitution should be vindicated in a case like this. It may be that on a hearing a different complexion would be given to the judge's alleged request and expression of fear. But supposing the alleged facts to be true, we are of opinion that if they were before the Supreme Court it sanctioned a situation upon which the Courts of the United States should act, and if for any reason they were not before the Supreme

Court, it is our duty to act upon them now and to declare lynch law as little valid when practiced by a regularly drawn jury as when administered by one elected by a mob intent on death.

JUSTICE AS A MASK

Moore v. Dempsey
261 U. S. 86 (1923)

Eight years after Frank v. Mangum *the Supreme Court in effect overruled it. The case involved the Elaine race riots in Arkansas. Great importance was attached to it, and Moorfield Storey, the President of the National Association for the Advancement of Colored People, appeared as one of the counsel for the Negroes. Storey had also taken part in two earlier important Negro cases —* Guinn v. U. S. *(the Grandfather's Clause case)* [1] *and* Buchanan v. Warley *(the Louisville Segregation case),* [2] *and through the NAACP he brought the present case to the Supreme Court.* [3] *Justice Holmes's reasoning in his earlier dissent in the* Frank *case became the doctrine of the majority here — that the fact of mob domination of a trial in a state court represents denial of due process, even though procedural correctives have been applied. Holmes's recital, in his opinion, of the circumstances of the case is a masterpiece of narrative. One gets from it rapid glimpses of the entire pattern of power and opinion in the sharecropping South: the attempts to organize in the face of landowner terrorism, the meeting in the Negro church, the armed attack, the manhunt by vigilantes, the lynching mob, the Committee of Seven, the torturing of witnesses, the intimidation of counsel, the skeleton trial, the resolutions by the American Legion and the Rotary and Lions Clubs, the attempts to appease the mob spirit by hastening execution. "The whole proceeding," he writes, "is a mask."*

In a letter to Pollock, before the decision was announced, Holmes wrote that his opinion "may go over for one of the

[1] 238 U. S. 347 (1915).
[2] 245 U. S. 60 (1917).
[3] See M. A. DeWolfe Howe, *Portrait of an Independent: Moorfield Storey* (1932), pp. 250–257.

JJ. or two, to consider whether it shall be swallowed according to the majority or whether, as a child put it, they will swallow up." [4] In a dissent, in which Justice Sutherland joined, Justice McReynolds stood by the doctrine of Frank v. Mangum. (It will be noted that Holmes, while not overruling that doctrine, made no particular attempt to distinguish the two cases.) "I cannot agree now," wrote Justice McReynolds, "to put it aside and substitute the view expressed by the minority of the court in that cause. . . . The fact that petitioners are poor and ignorant and black naturally arouses sympathy; but that does not release us from enforcing principles. . . ."

Subsequent Supreme Court decisions on due process in the trial of Negroes in the South are worth noting. In the spirit of the Holmes opinions the Court held in Powell v. Alabama [5] that due process had been withheld because the seven Negroes sentenced to death for rape had been denied adequate counsel; in Norris v. Alabama [6] because the exclusion of Negroes from the jury panel was in the context a denial of due process; in Brown v. Mississippi [7] because three Negroes were sentenced to death for murder on confessions exacted by third-degree methods; and in Chambers v. Florida,[8] for a similar reason in the case of four young Negroes.

Holmes, J., for the Court:

This is an appeal from an order of the district court for the eastern district of Arkansas, dismissing a writ of *habeas corpus* upon demurrer, the presiding judge certifying that there was probable cause for allowing the appeal. There were two cases originally, but by agreement they were consolidated into one. The appellants are five negroes, who were convicted of murder in the first degree and sentenced to death by the court of the State of Arkansas. The ground of the petition for the writ is that the proceedings in the state court, although a trial in form, were only a form, and that the appellants were hurried to conviction under the

[4] H-P, II:110 (Jan. 25, 1923).
[5] The first Scottsboro case, 287 U. S. 45 (1932).
[6] The second Scottsboro case, 294 U. S. 587 (1935).
[7] 297 U. S. 278 (1936).
[8] 309 U. S. 227 (1940).

STATE POWER AND FREE TRADE IN IDEAS

pressure of a mob, without any regard for their rights, and without according to them due process of law.

The case stated by the petition is as follows, and it will be understood that while we put it in narrative form, we are not affirming the facts to be as stated but only what we must take them to be, as they are admitted by the demurrer: On the night of September 30, 1919, a number of colored people, assembled in their church, were attacked and fired upon by a body of white men, and, in the disturbance that followed, a white man was killed. The report of the killing caused great excitement and was followed by the hunting down and shooting of many negroes, and also by the killing, on October 1, of one Clinton Lee, a white man, for whose murder the petitioners were indicted. They seem to have been arrested with many others on the same day. The petitioners say that Lee must have been killed by other whites, but that we leave on one side, as what we have to deal with is not the petitioners' innocence or guilt, but solely the question whether their constitutional rights have been preserved. They say that their meeting was to employ counsel for protection against extortions practiced upon them by the landowners, and that the landowners tried to prevent their effort; but that again we pass by as not directly bearing upon the trial. It should be mentioned, however, that O. S. Bratton, a son of the counsel who is said to have been contemplated, and who took part in the argument here, arriving for consultation on October 1, is said to have barely escaped being mobbed; that he was arrested and confined during the month on a charge of murder, and on October 31 was indicted for barratry, but, later in the day, was told that he would be discharged, but that he must leave secretly by a closed automobile to take the train at West Helena, four miles away, to avoid being mobbed. It is alleged that the judge of the court in which the petitioners were tried facilitated the departure and went with Bratton to see him safely off.

A Committee of Seven was appointed by the Governor in regard to what the Committee called the "insurrection" in the county. The newspapers daily published inflammatory articles. On the 7th a statement by one of the committee was made public, to the effect that the present trouble was "a deliberately planned insurrection of the negroes against the whites, directed by an organization known as the 'Progressive Farmers' and 'Household Union of

America' established for the purpose of banding Negroes together for the killing of white people." According to the statement the organization was started by a swindler, to get money from the banks.

Shortly after the arrest of the petitioners a mob marched to the jail for the purpose of lynching them, but were prevented by the presence of United States troops and the promise of some of the Committee of Seven and other leading officials that, if the mob would refrain, as the petition puts it, they would execute those found guilty in the form of law. The committee's own statement was that the reason that the people refrained from mob violence was "that this committee gave our citizens their solemn promise that the law would be carried out." According to affidavits of two white men and the colored witnesses on whose testimony the petitioners were convicted, produced by the petitioners since the last decision of the supreme court hereafter mentioned, the committee made good their promise by calling colored witnesses and having them whipped and tortured until they would say what was wanted, among them being the two relied on to prove the petitioners' guilt. However this may be, a grand jury of white men was organized on October 27, with one of the Committee of Seven, and, it is alleged, with many of a posse organized to fight the blacks, upon it, and, on the morning of the 29th, the indictment was returned. On November 3 the petitioners were brought into court, informed that a certain lawyer was appointed their counsel, and were placed on trial before a white jury, — blacks being systematically excluded from both grand and petit juries. The court and neighborhood were thronged with an adverse crowd that threatened the most dangerous consequences to anyone interfering with the desired result. The counsel did not venture to demand delay or a change of venue, to challenge a juryman, or to ask for separate trials. He had had no preliminary consultation with the accused, called no witnesses for the defense, although they could have been produced, and did not put the defendants on the stand. The trial lasted about three quarters of an hour, and in less than five minutes the jury brought in a verdict of guilty of murder in the first degree. According to the allegations and affidavits there never was a chance for the petitioners to be acquitted; no juryman could have voted for an acquittal and continued to live in Phillips county, and if any prisoner, by any chance, had been acquitted by a jury, he could not have escaped the mob.

STATE POWER AND FREE TRADE IN IDEAS 351

The averments as to the prejudice by which the trial was environed have some corroboration in appeals to the governor, about a year later, earnestly urging him not to interfere with the execution of the petitioners. One came from five members of the Committee of Seven, and stated, in addition to what has been quoted heretofore, that "all our citizens are of the opinion that the law should take its course." Another from a part of the American Legion, protests against a contemplated commutation of the sentence of four of the petitioners, and repeats that a "solemn promise was given by the leading citizens of the community that if the guilty parties were not lynched, and let the law take its course, that justice would be done and the majesty of the law upheld." A meeting of the Helena Rotary Club, attended by members representing, as it said, seventy-five of the leading industrial and commercial enterprises of Helena, passed a resolution approving and supporting the action of the American Legion post. The Lions Club of Helena, at a meeting attended by members said to represent sixty of the leading industrial and commercial enterprises of the city, passed a resolution to the same effect. In May of the same year, a trial of six other negroes was coming on, and it was represented to the governor by the white citizens and officials of Phillips county, that, in all probability, those negroes would be lynched. It is alleged that, in order to appease the mob spirit, and, in a measure, secure the safety of the six, the Governor fixed the date for the execution of the petitioners at June 10, 1921, but that the execution was stayed by proceedings in court, — we presume, the proceedings before the chancellor, to which we shall advert.

In *Frank* v. *Mangum*, 237 U. S. 309, 335, it was recognized, of course, that if in fact a trial is dominated by a mob, so that there is an actual interference with the course of justice, there is a departure from due process of law; and that "if the state, supplying no corrective process, carries into execution a judgment of death or imprisonment based upon a verdict thus produced by mob domination, the state deprives the accused of his life or liberty without due process of law." We presume, in accordance with that case, that the corrective process supplied by the state may be so adequate that interference by *habeas corpus* ought not to be allowed. It certainly is true that mere mistakes of law in the course of a trial are not to be corrected in that way. But if the case is that the whole proceeding is a mask, — that counsel, jury, and judge were swept to the fatal end by an irresistible wave of public passion, and that the state courts failed to correct the wrong, neither perfection in the machinery for correction nor the possibility that the trial court and counsel saw no other way of avoiding an immediate outbreak of the mob can prevent this court from securing to the petitioners their constitutional rights.

In this case a motion for a new trial on the ground alleged in this petition was overruled, and, upon exceptions and appeal to the Supreme Court the judgment was affirmed. The supreme court said that the complaint of discrimination against petitioners by the exclusion of colored men from the jury came too late, and, by way of answer to the objection that no fair trial could be had in the circumstances, stated that it could not say "that this must necessarily have been the case"; that eminent counsel was appointed to defend the petitioners, that the trial was had according to law, the jury correctly charged, and the testimony legally sufficient. On June 8, 1921, two days before the date fixed for their execution, a petition for *habeas corpus* was presented to the chancellor, and he issued the writ and an injunction against the execution of the petitioners; but the supreme court of the state held that the chancellor had no jurisdiction under the State law, whatever might be the law of the United States. The present petition, perhaps, was suggested by the language of the court: "What the result would be of an application to a Federal Court we need not inquire." It was presented to the district court on September 21. We shall not say more concerning the corrective process afforded to the petitioners than that it does not seem to us sufficient to allow a judge of the United States to escape the duty of examining the facts for himself, when, if true, as alleged, they make the trial absolutely void. We have confined the statement to facts admitted by the demurrer. We will not say that they cannot be met, but it appears to us unavoidable that the district judge should find whether the facts alleged are true, and whether they can be explained so far as to leave the state proceedings undisturbed.

Order reversed. The case to stand for hearing before the District Court.

MALT WHISKY AND THE EXTERNAL STANDARD

Peck v. Tribune Co.
214 U. S. 185 (1909)

>   This case presents another continuity with Holmes's past as a judge on the Massachusetts Court. He had there written a dissent in Hanson v. Globe Company,[1] and now a similar approach to the problem of libel was adopted by the Supreme Court. In both cases he used the external standard to determine liability for a tort. The present case is an important one in libel law. In libel suits two issues are generally raised: the reference to the plaintiff and the defamatory nature of the publication. To the first Holmes answers that the plaintiff was referred to through the publication of her picture, even though the intent may have been to publish someone else's picture, since, in Lord Mansfield's words, a man "publishes at his peril." To the second question he answers by a sort of moral functionalism that the test of whether it is defamatory is not whether it would be held so by a majority, but whether "a considerable and respectable class in the community" might so regard it. In this case to be associated with the drinking of malt whisky might in certain circles prove harmful.
>   Here, as elsewhere, there is a hardness and lack of sentimentality in Holmes's thinking about the law that links him with the great common law judges. If one pushes this hardness back, and asks the cui bono, the answer seems to be that there is a social value to be conserved — the protection from invasion of the privacy of the individual personality. Thus, although not a case in constitutional law, this becomes at least a marginal civil liberties case, and Holmes manages to link Lord Mansfield with John Stuart Mill.

Holmes, J., for the Court:
  This is an action on the case for a libel. The libel alleged is found in an advertisement printed in the defendant's newspaper

[1] See p. 96.

The Chicago Sunday Tribune, and so far as is material is as follows: "Nurse and Patients Praise Duffy's — Mrs. A. Schuman, One of Chicago's Most Capable and Experienced Nurses, Pays an Eloquent Tribute to the Great Invigorating Life-Giving and Curative Properties of Duffy's Pure Malt Whiskey. . . ." Then followed a portrait of the plaintiff, with the words "Mrs. A. Schuman" under it. Then, in quotation marks, "After years of constant use of your Pure Malt Whiskey, both by myself and as given to patients in my capacity as nurse, I have no hesitation in recommending it as the very best tonic and stimulant for all weak and run-down conditions," &c., &c., with the words "Mrs. A. Schuman, 1576 Mozart St., Chicago, Ill.," at the end, not in quotation marks, but conveying the notion of a signature, or at least that the words were hers. The declaration alleged that the plaintiff was not Mrs. Schuman, was not a nurse, and was a total abstainer from whiskey and all spirituous liquors. There was also a count for publishing the plaintiff's likeness without leave. The defendant pleaded not guilty. At the trial, subject to exceptions, the judge excluded the plaintiff's testimony in support of her allegations just stated, and directed a verdict for the defendant. His action was sustained by the Circuit Court of Appeals. . . .

Of course the insertion of the plaintiff's picture in the place and with the concomitants that we have described imported that she was the nurse and made the statements set forth, as rightly was decided in *Wandt* v. *Hearst's Chicago American,* 129 Wisconsin, 419, 421. *Morrison* v. *Smith,* 177 N. Y. 366. Therefore the publication was of and concerning the plaintiff, notwithstanding the presence of another fact, the name of the real signer of the certificate, if that was Mrs. Schuman, that was inconsistent, when all the facts were known, with the plaintiff's having signed or adopted it. Many might recognize the plaintiff's face without knowing her name, and those who did know it might be led to infer that she had sanctioned the publication under an alias. There was some suggestion that the defendant published the portrait by mistake, and without knowledge that it was the plaintiff's portrait or was not what it purported to be. But the fact, if it was one, was no excuse. If the publication was libellous the defendant took the risk. As was said of such matters by Lord Mansfield, "Whenever a man publishes, he publishes at his peril." *The King* v. *Woodfall,* Lofft, 776, 781. See further *Hearne* v. *Stowell,* 12 A. & E. 719, 726; *Shep-*

STATE POWER AND FREE TRADE IN IDEAS

heard v. *Whitaker,* L. R. 10 C. P. 502; *Clark* v. *North American Co.,* 203 Pa. St. 346, 351, 352. The reason is plain. A libel is harmful on its face. If a man sees fit to publish manifestly hurtful statements concerning an individual, without other justification than exists for an advertisement or a piece of news, the usual principles of tort will make him liable, if the statements are false or are true only of some one else. See *Morasse* v. *Brochu,* 151 Massachusetts, 567, 575.

The question, then, is whether the publication was a libel. It was held by the Circuit Court of Appeals not to be, or at most to entitle the plaintiff only to nominal damages, no special damage being alleged. It was pointed out that there was no general consensus of opinion that to drink whiskey is wrong or that to be a nurse is discreditable. It might have been added that very possibly giving a certificate and the use of one's portrait in aid of an advertisement would be regarded with irony, or a stronger feeling, only by a few. But it appears to us that such inquiries are beside the point. It may be that the action for libel is of little use, but while it is maintained it should be governed by the general principles of tort. If the advertisement obviously would hurt the plaintiff in the estimation of an important and respectable part of the community, liability is not a question of a majority vote.

We know of no decision in which this matter is discussed upon principle. But obviously an unprivileged falsehood need not entail universal hatred to constitute a cause of action. No falsehood is thought about or even known by all the world. No conduct is hated by all. That it will be known by a large number and will lead an appreciable fraction of that number to regard the plaintiff with contempt is enough to do her practical harm. Thus if a doctor were represented as advertising, the fact that it would affect his standing with others of his profession might make the representation actionable, although advertising is not reputed dishonest and even seems to be regarded by many with pride. See *Martin* v. *The Picayune,* 115 Louisiana, 979. It seems to us impossible to say that the obvious tendency of what is imputed to the plaintiff by this advertisement is not seriously to hurt her standing with a considerable and respectable class in the community. Therefore it was the plaintiff's right to prove her case and go to the jury, and the defendant would have got all that it could ask if it had been permitted to persuade them, if it could, to take a contrary view. . . .

It is unnecessary to consider the question whether the publication of the plaintiff's likeness was a tort *per se*. It is enough for the present case that the law should at least be prompt to recognize the injuries that may arise from an unauthorized use in connection with other facts, even if more subtlety is needed to state the wrong than is needed here. In this instance we feel no doubt.

Judgment reversed.

"THREE GENERATIONS OF IMBECILES"

Buck v. Bell
274 U. S. 200 (1927)

Justice Holmes has several times, notably by Justice Clarke in United Zinc and Chemical Co. v. Britt,[1] *been accused of taking a "Draconian" view of the law. And it is true that for all his humanism, he despised the sentimental outlook. There was a strain of social Darwinism in his thought. "Every society," he often wrote, "rests on the death of men." It is not surprising therefore that in the present case he should uphold a 1924 Virginia statute permitting sterilization of inmates in institutions for the feeble-minded. Over against the invasion of individual liberty he set the decisive social value of preventing the deterioration of the race. Carrie Buck was the daughter of a feeble-minded mother and had a feeble-minded child. "Three generations of imbeciles," he wrote, "are enough." He spoke for an almost unanimous Court, Justice Butler dissenting without opinion.*

Holmes, J., for the Court:

This is a writ of error to review a judgment of the supreme court of appeals of the state of Virginia, affirming a judgment of the circuit court of Amherst county, by which the defendant in error, the superintendent of the State Colony for Epileptics and Feeble Minded, was ordered to perform the operation of salpingectomy upon Carrie Buck, the plaintiff in error, for the purpose of making her sterile. 143 Va. 310. The case comes here upon the contention that the statute authorizing the judgment is void under the Fourteenth Amendment as denying to the plaintiff

---

[1] 258 U. S. 268 (1922); see above, p. 201.

STATE POWER AND FREE TRADE IN IDEAS 357

in error due process of law and the equal protection of the laws.

Carrie Buck is a feeble-minded white woman who was committed to the State Colony above mentioned in due form. She is the daughter of a feeble-minded mother in the same institution, and the mother of an illegitimate feeble-minded child. She was eighteen years old at the time of the trial of her case in the circuit court, in the latter part of 1924. An Act of Virginia, approved March 20, 1924, recites that the health of the patient and the welfare of society may be promoted in certain cases by the sterilization of mental defectives, under careful safeguard, &c.; that the sterilization may be effected in males by vasectomy and in females by salpingectomy, without serious pain or substantial danger to life; that the Commonwealth is supporting in various institutions many defective persons who if now discharged would become a menace but if incapable of procreating might be discharged with safety and become self-supporting with benefit to themselves and to society; and that experience has shown that heredity plays an important part in the transmission of insanity, imbecility, &c. The statute then enacts that whenever the superintendent of certain institutions including the above named State Colony shall be of opinion that it is for the best interests of the patients and of society that the inmate under his care should be sexually sterilized, he may have the operation performed upon any patient afflicted with hereditary forms of insanity, imbecility, &c., on complying with the very careful provisions by which the act protects the patients from possible abuse.

The superintendent first presents a petition to the special board of directors of his hospital or colony, stating the facts and the grounds for his opinion, verified by affidavit. Notice of the petition and of the time and place of the hearing in the institution is to be served upon the inmate, and also upon his guardian, and if there is no guardian the superintendent is to apply to the circuit court of the county to appoint one. If the inmate is a minor notice also is to be given to his parents if any with a copy of the petition. The board is to see to it that the inmate may attend the hearings if desired by him or his guardian. The evidence is all to be reduced to writing, and after the board has made its order for or against the operation, the superintendent, or the inmate, or his guardian, may appeal to the circuit court of the county. The circuit court may consider the record of the board and the evidence before it and such other admissible evidence as may be offered, and may affirm, revise, or reverse the order of the board and enter such order as it deems just. Finally any party may apply to the supreme court of appeals, which, if it grants the appeal, is to hear the case upon the record of the trial in the Circuit Court and may enter such order as it thinks the Circuit Court should have entered. There can be no doubt that so far as procedure is concerned the rights of the patient are most carefully considered, and as every step in this case was taken in scrupulous compliance with the statute and after months of observation, there is no doubt that in that respect the plaintiff in error has had due process of law.

The attack is not upon the procedure but upon the substantive law. It seems to be contended that in no circumstances could such an order be justified. It certainly is contended that the order cannot be justified upon the existing grounds. The judgment finds the facts that have been recited and that Carrie Buck "is the probable potential parent of socially inadequate offspring, likewise afflicted, that she may be sexually sterilized without detriment to her general health and that her welfare and that of society will be promoted by her sterilization," and thereupon makes the order. In view of the general declarations of the legislature and the specific findings of the court obviously we cannot say as matter of law that the grounds do not exist, and if they exist they justify the result. We have seen more than once that the public welfare may call upon the best citizens for their lives. It would be strange if it could not call upon those who already sap the strength of the state for these lesser sacrifices, often not felt to be such by those concerned, in order to prevent our being swamped with incompetence. It is better for all the world, if instead of waiting to execute degenerate offspring for crime, or to let them starve for their imbecility, society can prevent those who are manifestly unfit from continuing their kind. The principle that sustains compulsory vaccination is broad enough to cover cutting the Fallopian tubes. *Jacobson* v. *Massachusetts,* 197 U. S. 11. Three generations of imbeciles are enough.

But, it is said, however it might be if this reasoning were applied generally, it fails when it is confined to the small number who are in the institutions named and is not applied to the multitudes outside. It is the usual last resort of constitutional arguments to point out shortcomings of this sort. But the answer is that the law does all that is needed when it does all that it can, indicates a policy, applies to all within the lines, and seeks to bring within the lines all similarly situated so far and so fast as its means allow. Of course so far as the operations enable those who otherwise must be kept confined to be returned to the world, and thus open the asylum to others, the equality aimed at will be more nearly reached.

Judgment affirmed.

THE "DIRTY BUSINESS" OF WIRE TAPPING

Olmstead v. U. S.
277 U. S. 438, 469 (1928)

Threads running back to the "searches and seizures" of colonial times, the social history of Prohibition, and forward to whatever future a political police may have in America, converge in this case. Olmstead was a far from savory character — head of a bootlegging and rum-running combine with headquarters in Seattle, which was operated on a big-business scale, with an annual profit of over two million dollars. For months the wires of this ring were tapped by federal Prohibition officers, who accumulated almost eight hundred pages of conversation proving the violation of Prohibition laws. The problem before the Court was whether this wire tapping was constitutional, Olmstead claiming that it violated the guarantee against searches and seizures in the Fourth Amendment and against self-incrimination in the Fifth. The Supreme Court upheld the federal Government, in a five-to-four decision. Chief Justice Taft, again — as in the Myers *case (see p. 285) — viewing the problem with the conditionings of an administrator, held that wire tapping could not be classified as a "search and seizure." There was no entry into home or office: only the act of listening. Congress could, if it wished, protect the secrecy of telephone messages by direct legislation, but where it had not chosen to do so the Court could not act in its place by extending the language of the Fourth Amendment to guarantee telephone privacy.*

Justices Holmes, Brandeis, and Butler each wrote dissenting opinions, while Justice Stone joined with Holmes and Bran-

deis, and with Butler partially. Each of the dissents was characteristic of its writer. Justice Brandeis took a dynamic view of the history of the Fourth and Fifth Amendments. At the time they were adopted the methods of preserving privacy and of interfering with it were relatively simple. But with the march of technology, "subtler and more far-reaching means of invading privacy have become available to the Government." And looking ahead he sees that in the future more "advances in the psychic and related sciences may bring means of exploring unexpressed beliefs, thoughts and emotions." Against this process of extension the Constitution must offer an adequate safeguard for privacy. Justice Butler held that, by the very nature of telephones, wire tapping "literally constituted a search for evidence."

Holmes in his dissent brushed aside the constitutional question as less important than the problem of competing "objects of desire" — to catch criminals and to keep the integrity of the government. Wire tapping he saw as a "dirty business" — particularly since it was a crime by the Washington state law. "We have to choose, and for my part I think it a less evil that some criminals should escape than that the government should play an ignoble part." Further light is shed on his opinion by a letter to Pollock: —

The C. J. who wrote the prevailing opinion, perhaps as a rhetorical device to obscure the difficulty, perhaps merely because he did not note the difference, which perhaps I should have emphasized more, spoke of the objection to the evidence as based on its being obtained by "unethical" means (horrid phrase), although he adds & by a misdemeanor under the laws of Washington. I said that the State of Washington had made it a crime and that the Government could not put itself in the position of offering to pay for a crime in order to get evidence of another crime. Brandeis wrote much more elaborately, but I didn't agree with all that he said. I should not have printed what I wrote, however, if he had not asked me to.[1]

The Olmstead decision was not, however, the last word. Several attempts were made to get Congress to prohibit wire

[1] H–P, II:222 (June 20, 1928).

tapping by federal officials, but without success. In Nardone v. U. S., *302 U. S. 379 (1937)*, however, a clause in the *1934 Federal Communications Act* was interpreted to mean that intercepted interstate telephone conversations were not admissible in evidence, and this was further re-enforced by Justice Frankfurter in the second case of Nardone v. U. S., *308 U. S. 338 (1939)*.[2]

In 1941 a bill was introduced into the House by Representative Hobbs of Alabama providing that when the Attorney General had reason to suspect espionage, sabotage, kidnapping, or extortion, he might authorize wire tapping by Department of Justice officials. Holmes's opinion in the Olmstead case was an important factor in the debate. The opponents of the bill used Holmes's phrase "a dirty business" to such good effect that Mr. Hobbs felt it necessary to make a speech in which he interpreted the Holmes position to say that the "dirty business" was not wire tapping in itself, but wire tapping in the face of a state law against it; and he quoted from the letter to Pollock. But however right he may have been (and it is not too clear what Holmes meant as between these two versions) it was hard to fight the phrase. The bill was defeated by the close vote of 146–154.

Thus the Holmes opinion proved decisive both in the later Court decisions and in the Congressional debate.

Holmes, J., dissenting:

My Brother Brandeis has given this case so exhaustive an examination that I desire to add but a few words. While I do not deny it, I am not prepared to say that the penumbra of the Fourth and Fifth Amendments covers the defendant, although I fully agree that courts are apt to err by sticking too closely to the words of a law where those words import a policy that goes beyond them. *Goch v. Oregon Short Line R. R. Co.*, 258 U. S. 22, 24. But I think, as Mr. Justice Brandeis says, that apart from the Constitution the government ought not to use evidence obtained, and only obtain-

---

[2] But in *Goldstein* v. *U. S.* (decided April 27, 1942) the Court held, in a five-to-three opinion by Justice Roberts, that even when the government had used wire tapping to build a criminal case, one who was not a party to the intercepted messages could not invoke the Federal Communications Act against the government's use of wire tapping. Justice Murphy wrote a dissent, in which Chief Justice Stone and Justice Frankfurter joined.

able, by a criminal act. There is no body of precedents by which we are bound, and which confines us to logical deduction from established rules. Therefore, we must consider the two objects of desire both of which we cannot have and make up our minds which to choose. It is desirable that criminals should be detected, and to that end that all available evidence should be used. It also is desirable that the government should not itself foster and pay for other crimes, when they are the means by which the evidence is to be obtained. If it pays its officers for having got evidence by crime I do not see why it may not as well pay them for getting it in the same way, and I can attach no importance to protestations of disapproval if it knowingly accepts and pays and announces that in future it will pay for the fruits. We have to choose, and for my part I think it a less evil that some criminals should escape than that the government should play an ignoble part.

For those who agree with me, no distinction can be taken between the government as prosecutor and the government as judge. If the existing code does not permit district attorneys to have a hand in such dirty business, it does not permit the judge to allow such iniquities to succeed. See *Silverthorne Lumber Co.* v. *United States*, 251 U. S. 385. And if all that I have said so far be accepted, it makes no difference that in this case wire tapping is made a crime by the law of the state, not by the law of the United States. It is true that a state cannot make rules of evidence for courts of the United States, but the state has authority over the conduct in question, and I hardly think that the United States would appear to greater advantage when paying for an odious crime against state law than when inciting to the disregard of its own. I am aware of the often repeated statement that in a criminal proceeding the court will not take notice of the manner in which papers offered in evidence have been obtained. But that somewhat rudimentary mode of disposing of the question has been overthrown by *Weeks* v. *United States*, 232 U. S. 383 and the cases that have followed it. I have said that we are free to choose between two principles of policy. But if we are to confine ourselves to precedent and logic the reason for excluding evidence obtained by violating the Constitution seems to me logically to lead to excluding evidence obtained by a crime of the officers of the law.

PART III

The Savor of Life

1. Men and Ideas
2. Letters
3. Last Words

The Savor of Life

Carlyle, in his Heroes and Hero Worship, *quotes a remark about Robert Burns to the effect that "his poetry was not any particular faculty; but the general result of a naturally vigorous original mind expressing itself in that way."* [1] *The same might be said of Holmes as a judge. Even in his opinions he displayed the many-sidedness of a naturally vigorous original mind. He was over sixty when he came to the Supreme Court, and as he grew older he turned increasingly to a wide swathe of reading and reflection. This might have led to the philosophic forays of a William James or the shelf of critical essays of a Paul Elmer More. With Holmes it did not, perhaps because he disliked diffusion of energy, perhaps because he felt it more important to get the full and complex savor of life as an amateur than to fail as a multiple professional. As a result he focused his energy upon his judicial work, allowing what could not be contained within those channels to overflow into essays or speeches, and particularly into his letters.*

Holmes did no organized writing after The Common Law. *He was at his best as an occasional writer, in his letters, speeches, introductions, and memorials. In fact, there has perhaps been no better occasional writer in the American language. He had grace of phrasing, and with it a deliberateness that enabled him to take expressions worn thin by currency and give them a freshness of meaning and a new stamp of authority. He had the daring to break into the kind of poetry that one finds at the end of his Marshall speech,*[2] *or even more in the last two paragraphs of his speech on "Law and the Court."* [3] *But the daring was linked with a delicate restraint which led him almost always to skirt the margin of the unutterable and to treat weighty things with lightness and indirection. And in these occasional statements, as in his letters, he did not have to make intellectual ends meet with the finality demanded in a more organized work. He could resort to paradox and whimsy, to satire and exaggeration: and while they brought out new values they tended also*

---

[1] *Heroes and Hero Worship,* Temple Classics edition (1900), 232.
[2] See p. 388.
[3] See p. 391.

to blur the edges of what was left unassimilated. In these forms he could be expansive, indulging his bent.

As one reads him, one cannot help feeling that Holmes was a man who knew how to enjoy himself. Despite disquieting glimpses into the depths of the human fate ("We are all," he once wrote, "near despair"), there was in him a deep core of serenity that enabled him without envy to taste the best of what had been said and written, and without self-consciousness to strike a note of authority.

1. Men and Ideas

"We are very quiet there," Holmes remarked about the Supreme Court in one of his best speeches,[1] "but it is the quiet of a storm centre." Holmes was speaking of the criticisms that were being directed against the Court at the time. But it is equally true that, serene as Holmes's life seemed, he lived at the center of lashing intellectual storms. The essays and speeches in this section are part of Holmes's response to these storms. They include his more important later nonjudicial writings, except for his letters and his few valedictory words which are gathered together in the remaining sections of this book.

In form, these pieces are diverse — several speeches, some prefaces, an essay in a memorial volume, and the remainder law review articles. Nevertheless, there is a unity in them. Their theme is the relation of law to the complex forces of society, and the relation of men to the known and unknowable forces of the cosmos. They were the mature reflections of a judge on men and ideas, and an attempt to translate his own experience in both law and life into some general propositions. Holmes was getting a growing audience for these views as well as for his judicial opinions. So much so that during the last quarter-century of his life he emerged as easily the most important legal philosopher of America.

Rarely has so vast an influence been built upon so slight a body of legal writing. Perhaps because of the very slenderness of the text and the gnomic quality of its utterances, each commentator has seen in Holmes something different, and generally something to suit his own preconceptions. To one, Holmes has been a pragmatic philosopher, to another a rationalist, to a third a legal statesman, to still another a knightlike figure smashing intellectual windmills. The traditionalists have been unwilling to fight him openly, for there was a deep strain of traditionalism in him. Yet it is interesting to note that modern writers on the law are his most fervent champions. Jerome Frank, for example, in his Law and the Modern Mind

---

[1] See "Law and the Court," p. 387.

(*1930*), sees Holmes as illusionless, one who limits himself to the logic of probabilities and is contemptuous of certainty, an unsparing thinker who approaches law from the angle of what the bad man can get away with, a "completely adult jurist" — in short, a legal Realist. In fact, those who have attacked every school of law and even the law itself have either exempted Holmes or sought to enroll him on their side.[2] That these strains of legal realism exist in Holmes may go without challenge. But that they are not balanced by strains of traditionalism rather than change, of belief rather than skepticism, it would take a bold man to say.

In his early essay on "The Path of the Law" (*1897*) Holmes had taken as a vantage ground the viewpoint of the "bad man" who "has as much reason as a good one for wishing to avoid an encounter with the public force," and who wants "to know what the Massachusetts or English courts are likely to do in fact." (See above, pp. 73–75.) From this vantage ground Holmes defined the law as "the prophecies of what the courts will do in fact, and nothing more pretentious." On this suggestion, dropped almost casually in *1897*, was built the school of American legal "realism" which is our characteristic contribution to legal thought. Holmes's friend, John Chipman Gray (whom Holmes discusses below), took up the suggestion in *1909*, in his Nature and Sources of the Law. Gray blundered a bit by speaking of law as the "rules *laid down by the courts*," rather than "what the courts *will do* in fact." He blundered in shifting the discussion from behavior to doctrine, but the later members of the realistic school have returned to Holmes's view.

The conflict between the realists and the "natural law" theorists, who argue for an ethical basis of law, has influenced some of the recent evaluations of Holmes's work. Thus Lon L. Fuller, in his able lectures, The Law in Quest of Itself (*1940*), guesses that the reason why Holmes left so little influence upon private, as contrasted with public, law was the strain of legal "positivism" in him which drove him to effect an unreal separation between law and morality. I agree that Holmes's influence on private law was relatively slight, without agreeing with Fuller's statement of the cause. I also agree with Fuller that much of the attractiveness of the positivist, or hard-boiled, conception of law for us may be traced to the glamour and sense of philosophic breadth with which Holmes

[2] See F. Rodell's *Woe Unto You, Lawyers* (1939), and my comment on it in *Ideas for the Ice Age* (1941) 321–328.

invested this view. But it would be attributing too much to Holmes to see his influence as the decisive one. The fact is that Holmes's "bad man" standard, his rejection of natural law, and his definition of law as what the courts will in fact do, were all congenial to the mood and quality of a pragmatic America in whose practical business life the realm of fact had elbowed out the norms of morality. Holmes was, in that sense, part of a great tide. And his triumph in American jurisprudence was thus linked with the same social forces that brought the triumph of William James and John Dewey in American philosophy and education.

In making up this section I have drawn principally upon Holmes's writings after he came to the United States Supreme Court. I have, however, carried over from the earlier period two selections, on Montesquieu and John Marshall, simply because both in scope and mood they go more conveniently with the later writings. With them I have included a somewhat insubstantial yet graceful memorial essay on John Chipman Gray. These three men were diverse. One was a man of the world who was also an intellectual; the second was a man of action who found himself by circumstance in a place where he had great shaping influence on what later men did and thought; the third was a scholar who was also a man of affairs. They differed in their sensitivities, their coarseness or fineness of grain, their preoccupations. Yet their diversity shows Holmes's range of sympathy, and his capacity to get inside of a person. Holmes was able to write on all of them because each of them represented a facet of his own personality.

The essay on Montesquieu, for all its fluid quality and its insight, is without political depth. Holmes seems more interested in Montesquieu the littérateur *and the man of the world than in Montesquieu the thinker, more interested in his love affairs and his* Persian Letters *than in the* Spirit of the Laws. *On Montesquieu as thinker Holmes speaks principally of his sense of the relativism of laws and institutions. To Holmes's comment that Montesquieu's remarks on the balance of powers in England were from the start fictional, Pollock wrote him a dissenting letter. Holmes replied, "You discourse with a learning that I do not attempt to emulate as to Montesquieu and the balance of political powers. The little I ever knew is, I am afraid, pretty well forgotten. So I accept your remarks in respectful silence."* [3] *The likelihood is that the political elements in Montes-*

---

[3] H–P, II:267 (June 9, 1930).

quieu's thinking — he was a traditionalist with a strong sense of the complexity of society [4] — parallel similar elements in Holmes's thought. For that reason Holmes felt that there was not much in Montesquieu that seems fresh today. His essay would grace a new edition of Montesquieu for the lay reader; but it does not add much to scholarship nor does it flow from a great knowledge of the intellectual history of eighteenth-century Europe.

On Marshall, Holmes is magnificent. This is one of the rare instances of a memorial speech which approaches its subject with detachment and judgment. Holmes denies any originality to Marshall and shows that his greatness consists in his being part of the campaign of history. But having placed him in this perspective he gives him his proper meed of greatness in shaping history. Holmes was mightily pleased when the Harvard Law School hung his full-length portrait opposite that of John Marshall.[5] This is the speech, incidentally, which almost cost Holmes his Supreme Court appointment: when President Theodore Roosevelt read it he expressed some doubts as to whether a man who had reservations about Marshall's greatness would fit into the Court.[6] In this speech, as in the essay on Montesquieu, there is a lightness of language and a fluidity of manner along with a justness of observation that recalls Sainte-Beuve. But there is also, particularly at the end, a very non-Gallic intensity of feeling.

I have placed after this trilogy of comments on men another of comments on ideas. "Law and the Court," "Ideals and Doubts," and "Natural Law" are Holmes's best writing on legal philosophy, and on them his reputation as a legal philosopher, as distinguished from a judge, rests. The first is a speech delivered at a Harvard Law School banquet, the other two are law review articles. All three differ from the bulk of his law review writings, which tended to be on such technical subjects as equity, agency, and liability. To this trilogy I have added the essay on "Law and Social Reform," less well known, but as acid and quotable as the other three and in essentially the same strain.

The speech on "Law and the Court" is Holmes's most sharply

[4] See the striking summary of Montesquieu's thought by P. R. Rohden, *Encyclopedia of Social Sciences*, Vol. 10, pp. 637–639.
[5] H–P, II:253 (Sept. 27, 1929).
[6] *Letters of Theodore Roosevelt and Henry Cabot Lodge* (1925), Vol. I, pp. 517–519. For a discussion of this episode, see my introduction to this book "Holmes: a Personal History."

defined and most militantly phrased legal utterance outside of his opinions. Holmes takes as his starting point the attacks which were being leveled on the Court at that time (it was 1913, under Wilson's "New Freedom" and after the Theodore Roosevelt campaign for judicial reform). From that he seeks to give a long-range view of the factors affecting the Court's power and position. He hits at both the economic interpretation of the Court's function ("I admit it makes my heart ache") [7] *and, on the other hand, "the vague terror" that the advance of socialism strikes into the hearts of conservatives. The speech is an injunction to both sides to "think things instead of words." It is an injunction also to the "naïf simple-minded men" who are judges to "transcend their convictions," to get an "education in the obvious," and to understand that the fate of the United States does not depend on the fate of judicial review. What it adds up to is a plea for evolutionary progress in the law. Put thus it sounds trite, yet Holmes's genius lay in taking so middle-of-the-road a position and freshening it, as an animal might lick its formless cub into shape, by his vitality and his ardor.*

"Ideals and Doubts" and "Natural Law" were written out of an impulsive reaction against some Continental writers who made law out to be too rational, idealistic, and absolute for Holmes to stomach. In each case, Holmes says he wrote the article "currente calamo, in a kind of rage of writing one day." [8] *The essays have a quality of passion and even indignation. In them, as in the speech on "Law and the Court," Holmes is essentially the conservative. He attacks the legal rationalism and conceptualism which tend to cement the* status quo, *but even more he attacks the same ideas when they seek to reshape the legal and social order by sheer intellectuality. He hits both at the idea of the future as already inevitably shaped, and also at the idea that men can shape their law at will. He hits at the theme of law as absolute and at the idea that certainty is obtainable and expressible in law. And he suggests as the best sort of relativism a notion that progress is obtainable*

---

[7] Holmes does not mention in this speech Charles Beard's *Economic Interpretation of the Constitution*, but it is clear from his correspondence with Pollock (H-P, I:237, July 12, 1916) that when he came to read Beard three years later he thought very badly of his book. In 1913 Beard was being fiercely discussed, as also was Gustavus Myers' *History of the Supreme Court*. I have discussed elsewhere at some length the intellectual temper of this period: see my *Ideas Are Weapons* (1939), pp. 152-169, 430-436.

[8] H-P I:271 (Oct. 31, 1918).

if only you know what you want, estimate the specific means for achieving it, calculate the price you will have to pay as well as the benefits you will receive. But although his general position in these essays is that of one who has been through the wars of ideas and is ready to thrust his rapier through the sawdust warriors of both camps, Holmes's most explicit attention is given to what he considers the naïvetés of the reformers. This is especially clear in the essay to which I have given the heading "Law and Social Reform."

Pollock did not like Holmes's essay on "Natural Law." "If you mean to imply that no one can accept natural law . . . without maintaining it as a body of rules known to be absolutely true, I do not agree. . . . If you deny that any principles of conduct at all are common to and admitted by all men who try to behave reasonably — well, I don't see how you can have any ethics or any ethical background for law." [9] To which Holmes replied, "I didn't expect you to agree with me altogether. As to Ethics I have called them a body of imperfect social generalizations expressed in terms of emotion. Of course I agree that there is such a body on which to a certain extent civilized men would agree — but how much less than would have been taken for granted fifty years ago, witness the Bolsheviki." [10]

Note that Holmes here suggests a relativism of attitude, but both in his letters and in his essay on "Natural Law" it is a relativism that does not exclude the need for deep convictions as to values. "Deep-seated preferences," he wrote in a characteristic vein, "cannot be argued about. . . . and therefore, when differences are sufficiently far-reaching, we try to kill the other man rather than let him have his way. But that is perfectly consistent with admitting that, so far as appears, his grounds are just as good as ours." [11] And to those who would sum Holmes up as a skeptic one may point out, at the end of "Natural Law," Holmes's almost mystical belief "that the universe has in it more than we understand, that the private soldiers have not been told the plan of campaign, or even that there is one. . . . It is enough for us that the universe has produced us and has within it, as less than it, all that we believe and love."

The essay on "Natural Law" is thus as good a summary of Holmes's maturer views on the nature of law as one can find in his

[9] H–P I:274–275 (Dec. 20, 1918).
[10] H–P II:3 (Jan. 24, 1919).
[11] See below, p. 396.

writings. "A right," he says in a famous phrase, "*is only the hypostasis of a prophecy — the imagination of a substance supporting the fact that the public force will be brought to bear upon those who do things said to contravene it.*" And then he adds that this does not exclude "*the fighting will of the subject to maintain*" the rights: "*A dog will fight for his bone.*" [12] *We have here the behavioristic definition of law, squeezing it dry of all morality and sentiment; and we have also the attempt to bring in the element of faith and energy as a natural part of the human mind. I tend to agree with Fuller and some others that Holmes did not adequately bridge the gaps between the two worlds. There was in him a deep conflict between skepticism and belief, between mind and faith, between a recognition that men act in terms of a cold calculation of interests, and a recognition also that they are moved by symbols which, if you squeeze the life and energy out of them, become merely tinsel and rag. He tried to construct a legal theory, as he tried to construct a philosophy of life for himself, which would allow him to take account of both strains. He was not wholly successful logically in the attempt, but he made a going concern out of it. And because he did he leaves with us the sense of a full-statured person far more than do those who sought to trim their energies to the narrow confines of one or the other partial view.*

MONTESQUIEU [1]

"There is no new thing under the sun." It is the judgment of a man of the world, and from his point of view it is true enough. The things which he sees in one country he sees in another, and he is slightly bored from the beginning. But the judgment is quite untrue from the point of view of science or philosophy. From the time of Pericles to now, during the whole period that counts in the intellectual history of the race, the science or philosophy of one century has been different from that of the one before, and in some sense further along. By a corollary easy to work out, we have the paradox that the books which are always modern, the thoughts which are as stinging to-day as they were in their cool youth, are the books and thoughts of the men of the world. Ecclesiastes, Horace, and Rochefoucauld give us as much pleasure as they gave

[12] See below, p. 397.
[1] Introduction to a reprint of the *Esprit des Lois*. (1900.)

to Hebrew or Roman or the subject of Louis XIV. In this sense it is the second rate that lasts. But the greatest works of intellect soon lose all but their historic significance. The science of one generation is refuted or outgeneralized by the science of the next; the philosophy of one century is taken up or transcended by the philosophy of a later one; and so Plato, St. Augustine, and Descartes, and we almost may say Kant and Hegel, are not much more read than Hippocrates or Cuvier or Bichat.

Montesquieu was a man of science and at the same time a man of the world. As a man of science he wrote an epoch-making book. And just because and in so far as his book was a work of science and epoch-making, it is as dead as the classics. The later investigations which it did so much to start have taken up what was true in it and have refuted what needed refutation, and without the need of controversy they have killed many pale shoots of fancy and insufficient knowledge simply by letting in light and air. For a beginner to read Montesquieu with the expectation that there he is to find his understanding of the laws of social being, would be as ingenuous as to read Plato at eighteen expecting to find in him the answers to the riddles of life when they begin to perplex and sadden the mind of youth. He would learn a good deal more from Lecky. Montesquieu is buried under his own triumphs, to use his own words with a different application.

But Montesquieu also was a man of the world and a man of *esprit*. That wit which deals with the daily aspect of life and offers trenchant solutions in two or three lines is a dangerous gift. It hardly is compatible with great art, and Flaubert is not without reason when he rails at it in his letters. It is no less dangerous to great thinking, to that profound and sustained insight which distrusts the dilemma as an instrument of logic, and discerns that a thing may be neither A nor not A, but the perpendicular, or, more plainly, that the truth may escape from the limitations of a given plane of thought to a higher one. Montesquieu said that Voltaire had too much *esprit* to understand him. Nevertheless, Montesquieu had enough of it to have sustained the *Saturday Review* when Maine and Fitzjames Stephen or Venables were its contributors, and as a man of wit he still is fresh and pleasant reading. When one runs through the *Lettres Persanes* one feels as he does after reading Swift's *Polite Conversation,* struck with a wondering shame at the number of things he has been capable of feeling pleased with himself for saying, when they had been noted as familiar two hundred years before. He is in the realm of the ever old which also is the ever new, those middle axioms of experience which have been made from the beginning of society, but which give each generation a fresh pleasure as they are realized again in actual life. There is a good deal more than this, because Montesquieu was a good deal more than a man of the world, but there is this also in which we escape from the preliminary dulness of things really great.

We find the same thing in the *Esprit des Lois,* and one might read that work happily enough simply as literature. One may read it also as a first step in studies intended to be carried further and into later days. But to read it as it should be read, to appreciate the great and many-sided genius of the author and his place in the canonical succession of the high priests of thought, one must come back to it in the fulness of knowledge and the ripeness of age. To read the great works of the past with intelligent appreciation, is one of the last achievements of a studious life. But I will postpone what more I have to say of this book until we come to it in following the course of the author's career.

Charles de Secondat, Baron de la Brède, was born at the Château de la Brède, near Bordeaux, on January 18, 1689. His family had gained distinction both by the sword and in the law. His father was a magistrate, and intended that he should be one. His mother was pious, and no doubt hoped that he might be like her. Neither wish was entirely fulfilled.

At the moment of his birth a beggar presented himself at the château, and was retained that he might be god-father to the young noble, and so remind him all his life that the poor were his brothers. He was nursed by peasants, and he kept through life a touch of Gascon speech, and, the Frenchmen say, something of the Gascon in his style. His early education was by churchmen, but at twenty he showed the tendency of his mind by composing an essay to prove that the pagan did not deserve to be eternally damned. The essay has not been preserved, but perhaps an echo of his reflections is to be found in the thirty-fifth of the *Lettres Persanes,* in which Usbek, who, not without dispute, has been taken for the author, asks the "sublime dervish" Gemchid whether he thinks that the Christians are to be damned forever for not having embraced the true religion of which they never have heard.

He studied law. "When I left college," he said, "they put law books into my hands. I tried to find their inner meaning" (*J'en cherchais l'esprit*). The *Esprit des Lois* was the outcome, but not the immediate outcome, of his studies. The immediate result was that, at twenty-five, on February 24, 1714, he was admitted to the Parlement de Bordeaux as *conseiller*. On July 13, 1716, he succeeded to the office (*président à mortier*) and fortune of an uncle, on condition of assuming the name of Montesquieu. Meantime he had married, and he had a son this same year, and later two daughters. As a magistrate he seems to have been not without weight. In 1722 he was intrusted with the shaping of a remonstrance to the king against a tax on wines, which for the time was successful. As a husband he was not wanting in decorum. But neither magistracy nor marriage seems to have filled his life.

He made a reasonable amount of love in his day, I infer not wholly before 1715. Whether or not he would have said that the society of women makes us "subtle and insincere," he did say that it spoils our morals and forms our taste. I suspect also that it added a poignancy to his phrase when he came to write, as it certainly gave him a freedom and alertness of interest in dealing with matters of sex. He took his passions easily. As soon as he ceased to believe that a woman loved him, he broke with her at once, he says, and elsewhere he tells us in more general terms that he never had a sorrow which an hour's reading would not dispel. At times his detachment seems to have been too visible, as one lady reproached him with writing his book in society. Perhaps it was timidity, which he says was a plague of his life. So much for his relations, domestic and otherwise, with women. As to the magistracy, he resigned his place in 1726. He found procedure hard to master, and it disgusted him to see men upon whose talents he justly looked down excelling in a matter that was too much for him.

About the same time that he succeeded his uncle he joined a society in Bordeaux, in which for a while he devoted himself to science. He made some experiments, wrote some scientific memoirs, planned a physical history of the earth, and sent out circulars of inquiry in 1719, but happily it all came to nothing, and this failure, combined with the shortness of his outward and the reach of his inward sight, helped to fix his attention upon his kind. He had the "disease of book-making," and as early as 1721 he published his *Lettres Persanes*. The putting of the criticism of his own times into the mouth of an intelligent foreigner, and all the Oriental coloring, seem a trifle faded nowadays. But these are merely the frame or excuse for a series of essays — somewhat like those in the nearly contemporary *Spectator* — on social subjects and subjects of social interest, running all the way from God to the Fashions.

In almost every letter there are things which have been quoted so often that one is afraid to repeat them. In one he makes a few reflections upon suicide that are hard to answer, and which had a practical aim, in view of the monstrous condition of the law. In another he is equally outspoken with regard to divorce, and says, not without some truth, that wishing to tighten the knot the law has untied it, and instead of uniting hearts, as it proposed, has separated them forever. Before Adam Smith he remarks the activity of dissenting sects, and he points out with unorthodox candor their service in reforming the abuses of the established faith.

In the person of Usbek he says: "Everything interests me, everything excites my wonder. I am like a child whose immature organs are keenly struck by the most insignificant objects." Montesquieu proves it in these letters. Alongside of such grave discussions as the foregoing he has portraits, or rather types, that still live. The *parvenu* tax farmer, the father confessor, the old soldier who can not hope for preferment "because we" (very sensibly) "believe that a man who has not the qualities of a general at thirty never will have them," the *homme à bonnes fortunes* who has hair, little wit, and so much impertinence, the poet (Montesquieu despised the poets, at least those whom he saw) — the poet, with grimaces and language different from the others, who would stand a beating better than the least criticism, the grand seigneur who personates himself. "He took a pinch of snuff so haughtily, he wiped his nose so pitilessly, he spit with so much phlegm, he fondled his dogs in a way so insulting to men, that I could not weary of wondering." The *décisionnaire:* "In a quarter of an hour he decided three questions of morals, four problems of history, and five points of physics. . . . They dropped the sciences and talked of the news of the day. . . . I thought that I would catch him, and spoke of Persia. But I hardly had said four words when he contradicted me twice. . . . Ah! *bon Dieu!* said I to myself, what sort of man is this? Soon he will know the streets of Ispahan better than I."

The letter on fashion ought to be quoted entire. When he says in the next one that what is foreign always seems ridiculous to the

French, of course he is only noticing an instance of the universal law, but he makes us remember that Little Pedlington is everywhere, and that this day there is no more marked Little Pedlingtonian than the Parisian boulevardier man of letters. It is true that Montesquieu limits his remarks to trifles. They readily will admit that other people are wiser, he says, if you grant them that they are better dressed. His talk about the Spaniards is equally good. The Spaniards whom they do not burn, he says, seem so attached to the Inquisition that it would be ill-natured to deprive them of it. But at the end he gives them their revenge. He imagines a Spaniard in Paris and makes him say that they have a house there in which they shut up a few madmen in order to persuade the world that the rest are not mad. After things of this sort, two pages further on we read that the most perfect government is that which attains its ends with the least cost, so that the one which leads men in the way most according to their inclination is best. What have two hundred years added? What proximate test of excellence can be found except correspondence to the actual equilibrium of force in the community — that is, conformity to the wishes of the dominant power? Of course, such conformity may lead to destruction, and it is desirable that the dominant power should be wise. But wise or not, the proximate test of a good government is that the dominant power has its way.

There are considerations upon colonies, upon population, upon monarchy, a striking prophecy that the Protestant countries will grow richer and more powerful and the Catholic countries weaker. There is, in short, a scattering criticism of pretty nearly everything in the social order, of a sceptically radical kind, but always moderate and rational, with hints and germs of his future work, interspersed with many little sayings not too bright or good for human nature's daily food, and with some which are famous, such as, "It sometimes is necessary to change certain laws, but the case is rare, and when it occurs one should touch them only with a trembling hand"; or, "Nature always acts slowly and, so to speak, sparingly; her operations are never violent." This last is said by Sorel to be the whole philosophy of the *Esprit des Lois,* and suggests a more extensive philosophy still, which no doubt was more or less in the air, which found expression a little later in Linnaeus's *Natura non facit saltus,* and which nowadays in its more developed form we call evolution.

The *Lettres Persanes* came out anonymously, ostensibly from Amsterdam, when Montesquieu was little more than thirty, and ran through four editions in the first year. The name of the author became known to everybody. He went to Paris, and there frequented the society of men and women whose names to us of this country and time are but foam from the sea of oblivion, but who were the best of their day. There, to please the ladies, or a lady, he wrote in 1725 the *Temple de Gnide* and *Cephise et l'Amour,* which need not delay us. He says that only well-curled and well-powdered heads will understand them. At the beginning of 1728 he was elected to the Academy, which he, like other Frenchmen, had made sport of but desired to enter. He had been elected before, but had been refused by the king. This time he had better luck. Voltaire and D'Alembert tell a tale of how it was managed. Entrance to the Academy is apt to be an occasion for the display of malice on the one side or the other; the address of welcome twitted him with having no recognized works to justify the election, under the form of a compliment on the certainty that the public would give him the credit of clever anonymous ones. For this or other reasons he did not go much to the Academy, and he soon set out upon a tour of Europe. He went to Vienna, and there met the Prince Eugene. He applied for a post as a diplomat, and again, luckily for the world, he failed. He visited Hungary, then Venice, where he met the famous John Law and became a friend of Lord Chesterfield; then Switzerland and Holland by way of the Rhine. From Holland he went with Lord Chesterfield to England, where he remained for nearly two years, returning in August, 1731, to La Brède, his family, and his writing.

In 1734 he published his *Considérations sur les causes de la grandeur des Romains et de leur décadence.* He was drawing nearer to his great work; from sporadic *aperçus* he was turning to systematic exposition. It often is said, and with a good deal of truth, that men reach their highest mark between thirty and forty. Perhaps the statement seems more significant than it really is, because men generally have settled down to their permanent occupation by thirty, and in the course of the next ten years are likely to have found such leading and dominant conceptions as they are going to find; the rest of life is working out details. Montesquieu and Kant either are exceptions to the rule or illustrate the qualification just suggested. In their earlier life as you look back at it you see the *Critique* and the *Esprit des Lois* coming, but the fruit did not ripen fully until they were in the neighborhood of sixty. In 1734 Montesquieu was already forty-five.

Roman history has been rewritten since his day by Niebuhr and his successors. But Montesquieu gives us the key to his mode of thought and to all fruitful thought upon historic subjects when he says that "there are general causes, moral or physical, at work in every monarchy, which elevate and maintain it or work its downfall; all accidents are the result of causes; and if the chance of a battle — that is, a special cause — has ruined a state, there was a general cause at work which made that state ready to perish by a single battle. In a word, the main current carries with it all the special accidents."

Montesquieu the ladies' man, Montesquieu the student of science, Montesquieu the lover of travel both real and fictitious, Montesquieu the learned in the classics and admirer of that conventional antiquity that passed so long for the real thing in France — all these Montesquieus unite in the *Esprit des Lois,* as is pointed out most happily by Faguet, whose many-sided and delicate appreciation of the author I read just as I was writing this sentence. The book, he says, is called *Esprit des Lois;* it should have been called simply *Montesquieu.* Perhaps the fact is due in part to the subject's not having become a specialty. In the same way Adam Smith's *Wealth of Nations* has many interesting and penetrating remarks that, alas! hardly would be allowed in a modern political economy, even if the writer had the wit to make them. At all events, after his Roman history, the rest of Montesquieu's life may be summed up as the production of this volume. In the preface he calls it the labor of twenty years. It appeared in 1748. When it was done his hair had whitened over the last books, and his eyes had grown dim. "It seems to me," he said, "that the light left to me is but the dawn of the day on which my eyes shall close forever." He published a defence of the work in 1750, attended to the sale of wine from his vineyards, noticed with pleasure that the sale seemed to have been increased in England by the publication of his book, and died in Paris on February 10, 1755, watched, if not like Arthur by weeping queens, at least by the Duchess d'Aiguillon and a houseful of loving and admiring friends. According to Maupertius, he was well proportioned, careless in dress, modest in demeanor, candid in speech, simple in his mode of life, and welcomed in society with universal joy. The medallion gives him a distinguished face.

It would be out of place to offer an analysis of a book which is before the reader, and it would take a larger book to contain all the thoughts which it suggests. The chapters on the feudal law are so far separable from the rest that it had been thought a mistake of Montesquieu to add them. The modern student naturally would turn to Roth or whatever still later man may displace Roth. With regard to the main body of the work, one might say that it expressed a theory of the continuity of the phenomenal universe at a time when, through no fault of the author, its facts were largely miraculous. He was not able to see history as an evolution, he looked at all events as if they were contemporaneous. Montesquieu's Rome was the Rome of fable uncritically accepted. His anthropology was anecdotic. His notion of a democracy suggests a Latin town meeting rather than the later developments in the United States and France. He made the world realize the influence of the climate and physical environment — which in our day furnished the already forgotten Buckle a suggestive chapter — but had not the data to be more than a precursor.

His England — the England of the threefold division of power into legislative, executive and judicial — was a fiction invented by him, a fiction which misled Blackstone and Delolme. Hear Bagehot in his work upon the subject: "The efficient secret of the English Constitution may be described as the close union, the nearly complete fusion of the executive and legislative powers." And again: "The American Constitution was made upon a most careful argument, and most of that argument assumes the king to be the administrator of the English Constitution, and an unhereditary substitute for him — viz., a president — to be peremptorily necessary. Living across the Atlantic, and misled by accepted doctrines, the acute framers of the Federal Constitution, even after the keenest attention, did not perceive the Prime Minister to be the principal executive of the British Constitution, and the sovereign a cog in the mechanism."

It is worth remarking that, notwithstanding his deep sense of the inevitableness of the workings of the world, Montesquieu had a possibly exaggerated belief in the power of legislation, and an equally strong conviction of the reality of abstract justice. But it is vain to attempt to criticize the book in detail. Indeed, it is more important to understand its relation to what had been done before than to criticise. There is not space even to point out how many seeds it sowed. Montesquieu is a precursor, to repeat the word, in so many ways. He was a precursor of political economy. He was the precursor of Beccaria in the criminal law. He was the precursor of Burke when Burke seems a hundred years ahead of his time. The Frenchmen tell us that he was the precursor of Rousseau. He was an authority for the writers of *The Federalist*. He influenced, and to a great extent started scientific theory in its study of societies, and he hardly less influenced practice in legislation, from Russia to the United States. His book had a dazzling success at the moment, and since then probably has done as much to remodel the world as any product of the eighteenth century, which burned so many forests and sowed so many fields.

And this was the work of a lonely scholar sitting in a library. Like Descartes or Kant, he commanded the future from his study more than Napoleon from his throne. At the same time he affects no august sovereignty, but even gives us one or two discreet personal touches full of a sort of pathetic charm — the "*Italiam! Italiam!*" when the long day's work was done and the author saw his goal before darkness closed upon him; the suppressed invocation at the beginning of Book XX; the proud epigraph, "*Prolem sine matre creatam*"; and above all the preface, that immortal cheer to other lonely spirits. It is the great sigh of a great man when he has done a great thing. The last words of that are the words with which this introduction should end. "If this work meets with success, I shall owe it largely to the majesty of my subject. However, I do not think that I have been wholly wanting in genius. When I have seen what so many great men in France, England, and Germany have written before me, I have been lost in admiration, but I have not lost my courage. 'And I too am a painter,' I have said with Correggio."

JOHN MARSHALL [1]

As we walk down Court Street in the midst of a jostling crowd, intent like us upon to-day and its affairs, our eyes are like to fall

[1] In answer to a motion that the Court adjourn, on February 4, 1901, the one hundredth anniversary of the day on which Marshall took his seat as Chief Justice. From *Speeches* (1913) 87–91.

upon the small, dark building that stands at the head of State Street, and, like an ominous reef, divides the stream of business in its course to the gray cliffs that tower beyond. And, whoever we may be, we may chance to pause and forget our hurry for a moment, as we remember that the first waves that foretold the coming storm of the Revolution broke around that reef. But, if we are lawyers, our memories and our reverence grow more profound. In the Old State House, we remember, James Otis argued the case of the writs of assistance, and in that argument laid one of the foundations for American constitutional law. Just as that little building is not diminished, but rather is enhanced and glorified, by the vast structures which somehow it turns into a background, so the beginnings of our national life, whether in battle or in law, lose none of their greatness by contrast with all the mighty things of later date, beside which, by every law of number and measure, they ought to seem so small. To us who took part in the Civil War, the greatest battle of the Revolution seems little more than a reconnoissance in force, and Lexington and Concord were mere skirmishes that would not find mention in the newspapers. Yet veterans who have known battle on a modern scale, are not less aware of the spiritual significance of those little fights, I venture to say, than the enlightened children of commerce who tell us that soon war is to be no more.

If I were to think of John Marshall simply by number and measure in the abstract, I might hesitate in my superlatives, just as I should hesitate over the battle of the Brandywine if I thought of it apart from its place in the line of historic cause. But such thinking is empty in the same proportion that it is abstract. It is most idle to take a man apart from the circumstances which, in fact, were his. To be sure, it is easier in fancy to separate a person from his riches than from his character. But it is just as futile. Remove a square inch of mucous membrane, and the tenor will sing no more. Remove a little cube from the brain, and the orator will be speechless; or another, and the brave, generous and profound spirit becomes a timid and querulous trifler. A great man represents a great ganglion in the nerves of society, or, to vary the figure, a strategic point in the campaign of history, and part of his greatness consists in his being *there*. I no more can separate John Marshall from the fortunate circumstance that the appointment of Chief Justice fell to John Adams, instead of to Jefferson a month later, and so gave it to a Federalist and loose constructionist to start the working of the Constitution, than I can separate the black line through which he sent his electric fire at Fort Wagner from Colonel Shaw. When we celebrate Marshall we celebrate at the same time and indivisibly the inevitable fact that the oneness of the nation and the supremacy of the national Constitution were declared to govern the dealings of man with man by the judgments and decrees of the most august of courts.

I do not mean, of course, that personal estimates are useless or teach us nothing. No doubt to-day there will be heard from able and competent persons such estimates of Marshall. But I will not trench upon their field of work. It would be out of place when I am called on only to express the answer to a motion addressed to the court and when many of those who are here are to listen this afternoon to the accomplished teacher who has had every occasion to make a personal study of the judge, and again this evening to a gentleman who shares by birth the traditions of the man. My own impressions are only those that I have gathered in the common course of legal education and practice. In them I am conscious, perhaps, of some little revolt from our purely local or national estimates, and of a wish to see things and people judged by more cosmopolitan standards. A man is bound to be parochial in his practice — to give his life, and if necessary his death, for the place where he has his roots. But his thinking should be cosmopolitan and detached. He should be able to criticise what he reveres and loves.

The Federalist, when I read it many years ago, seemed to me a truly original and wonderful production for the time. I do not trust even that judgment unrevised when I remember that *The Federalist* and its authors struck a distinguished English friend of mine as finite; and I should feel a greater doubt whether, after Hamilton and the Constitution itself, Marshall's work proved more than a strong intellect, a good style, personal ascendancy in his court, courage, justice and the convictions of his party. My keenest interest is excited, not by what are called great questions and great cases, but by little decisions which the common run of selectors would pass by because they did not deal with the Constitution or a telephone company, yet which have in them the germ of some wider theory, and therefore of some profound interstitial change in the very tissue of the law. The men whom I should be tempted to commemorate would be the originators of transforming thought. They often are half obscure, because what the world pays for is judgment, not the original mind.

But what I have said does not mean that I shall join in this celebration or in granting the motion before the court in any half-hearted way. Not only do I recur to what I said in the beginning, and remembering that you cannot separate a man from his place, remember also that there fell to Marshall perhaps the greatest place that ever was filled by a judge; but when I consider his might, his justice, and his wisdom, I do fully believe that if American law were to be represented by a single figure, sceptic and worshipper alike would agree without dispute that the figure could be one alone, and that one, John Marshall.

A few words more and I have done. We live by symbols, and what shall be symbolized by any image of the sight depends upon the mind of him who sees it. The setting aside of this day in honor of a great judge may stand to a Virginian for the glory of his glorious State; to a patriot for the fact that time has been on Marshall's side, and that the theory for which Hamilton argued, and he decided, and Webster spoke, and Grant fought, and Lincoln died, is now our corner-stone. To the more abstract but farther-reaching contemplation of the lawyer, it stands for the rise of a new body of jurisprudence, by which guiding principles are raised above the reach of statute and State, and judges are entrusted with a solemn and hitherto unheard-of authority and duty. To one who lives in what may seem to him a solitude of thought, this day — as it marks the triumph of a man whom some Presidents of his time bade carry out his judgments as he could — this day marks the fact that all thought is social, is on its way to action; that, to borrow the expression of a French writer, every idea tends to become first a catechism and then a code; and that according to its worth his unhelped meditation may one day mount a throne, and without armies, or even with them, may shoot across the world the electric despotism of an unresisted power. It is all a symbol, if you like, but so is the flag. The flag is but a bit of bunting to one who insists on prose. Yet, thanks to Marshall and to the men of his generation — and for this above all we celebrate him and them — its red is our lifeblood, its stars our world, its blue our heaven. It owns our land. At will it throws away our lives.

The motion of the bar is granted, and the court will now adjourn.

JOHN CHIPMAN GRAY [1]

The affectionate intimacy of a lifetime may not be the best preparation for an attempt to characterize a friend whom one has known and loved so long. His qualities come to be felt too instinctively for articulate enumeration just as one ceases to be conscious of the judgments that govern one's walk in the streets. But with so marked a personality as that of John Gray, there were features that no one could forget.

He came of a family in which scholarship was in the blood; and I think that perhaps the first thought that would occur to me would be that he was a scholar born. He was a scholar of a type that is growing rare. For his knowledge, his immense reading, his memory were not confined to the actualities of the day. Alongside of mathematics, and the latest German works on jurisprudence, alongside of his mastery of the law, equally profound and available for teaching in the Law School and advising upon great affairs, he not only kept up the study of Greek and Roman classics, but he was familiar with a thousand bypaths among books. I think he could have given a clear account of the Bangorian controversy, the very name of which has been forgotten by most of us, and he could have recited upon all manner of curious memoirs or upon pretty much any theme that falls within the domain of literature, properly so-called. He loved books, and his beautiful collection ranged from the Theodosian code to curious eighteenth-century tracts.

He brought this scholarship to bear unobtrusively but powerfully when he came to write. His treatise on *Perpetuities* is a quiet masterpiece that stands on an equal footing with the most famous works of the great English writers upon property law. His last little book is worthy of the German professors who might seem to have made that theme their private domain. But unlike much German work, instead of pedantry, it is written with the light touch and humor of a man of the world. For his knowledge not only was converted into the organic tissue of wisdom, but flowered with the quiet humor that sometimes emerged in his writing and that gave habitual delightfulness to his talk.

He was a very wise man. So wise that those who met him in affairs perhaps would say that wisdom was the first thing to be

---

[1] From *John Chipman Gray* (Boston, 1917), a memorial volume.

mentioned with his name. He was able as no one else has been to unite practice in Boston, in which he was consulted and relied upon in matters of the largest import, with teaching at the Law School, where his subjects required study of subjects that seemed most remote from every day; and both with equal success.

In this connection, it is worth recalling that when he was in the army he was the first officer to meet Sherman at Savannah after the march to the sea, and that he is referred to in Sherman's report of his operations as "a very intelligent officer whose name I have forgotten," a striking tribute to one who barely had reached manhood from the great commander at the crowning moment of his success.

Such capacity as Gray's for voluminous occupation is apt to go with a loose fibre, or, one might say, a somewhat coarse grain, but Gray was delicate, accurate, and fine grained. Like all his race, he was keenly observing without showing it, seeming to see from the sides of his eyes like a woman. Any one of his remarkable qualities and capacities remained isolated or futile, but they all united to give character to the stream of his thought. It will be seen that I am trying to describe a master, one who fairly may be called a master, who was listened to with equal respect by clients, by courts, and by all students of the law, and at the same time an extraordinary and delightful man, whose conversation gave equal pleasure to specialists and men of the world. When I add to this that he was a most faithful and affectionate friend, I have said enough perhaps to show, I will not say what a loss is his death, for he had lived as long as a man can hope to live, but what a gain, not only to us who loved him, but to the world, was his life, a life rich in fruits and ending surrounded by honor and by love.

LAW AND THE COURT [1]

MR. CHAIRMAN AND GENTLEMEN: —

Vanity is the most philosophical of those feelings that we are taught to despise. For vanity recognizes that if a man is in a minority of one we lock him up, and therefore longs for an as-

[1] Speech at a dinner of the Harvard Law School Association of New York, February 15, 1913. This was reprinted as Senate Doc. 1106, 62nd Congress, 3rd session.

surance from others that one's work has not been in vain. If a man's ambition is the thirst for a power that comes not from office but from within, he never can be sure that any happiness is not a fool's paradise — he never can be sure that he sits on that other bench reserved for the masters of those who know. Then too, at least until one draws near to seventy, one is less likely to hear the trumpets than the rolling fire of the front. I have passed that age, but I still am on the firing line, and it is only in rare moments like this that there comes a pause and for half an hour one feels a trembling hope. They are the rewards of a lifetime's work.

But let me turn to more palpable realities — to that other visible Court to which for ten now accomplished years it has been my opportunity to belong. We are very quiet there, but it is the quiet of a storm centre, as we all know. Science has taught the world scepticism and has made it legitimate to put everything to the test of proof. Many beautiful and noble reverences are impaired, but in these days no one can complain if any institution, system, or belief is called on to justify its continuance in life. Of course we are not excepted and have not escaped. Doubts are expressed that go to our very being. Not only are we told that when Marshall pronounced an Act of Congress unconstitutional he usurped a power that the Constitution did not give, but we are told that we are the representatives of a class — a tool of the money power. I get letters, not always anonymous, intimating that we are corrupt. Well, gentlemen, I admit that it makes my heart ache. It is very painful, when one spends all the energies of one's soul in trying to do good work, with no thought but that of solving a problem according to the rules by which one is bound, to know that many see sinister motives and would be glad of evidence that one was consciously bad. But we must take such things philosophically and try to see what we can learn from hatred and distrust and whether behind them there may not be some germ of inarticulate truth.

The attacks upon the Court are merely an expression of the unrest that seems to wonder vaguely whether law and order pay. When the ignorant are taught to doubt they do not know what they safely may believe. And it seems to me that at this time we need education in the obvious more than investigation of the obscure. I do not see so much immediate use in committees on the high cost of living and inquiries how far it is due to the increased production of gold, how far to the narrowing of cattle ranges and the growth of population, how far to the bugaboo, as I do in bringing home to people a few social and economic truths. Most men think dramatically, not quantitatively, a fact that the rich would be wise to remember more than they do. We are apt to contrast the palace with the hovel, the dinner at Sherry's with the working man's pail, and never ask how much or realize how little is withdrawn to make the prizes of success (subordinate prizes — since the only prize much cared for by the powerful is power. The prize of the general is not a bigger tent, but command). We are apt to think of ownership as a terminus, not as a gateway, and not to realize that except for the tax levied for personal consumption large ownership means investment, and investment means the direction of labor towards the production of the greatest returns — returns that so far as they are great show by that very fact that they are consumed by the many, not alone by the few. If I may ride a hobby for an instant, I should say we need to think things instead of words — to drop ownership, money, etc., and to think of the stream of products; of wheat and cloth and railway travel. When we do, it is obvious that the many consume them; that they now as truly have substantially all there is, as if the title were in the United States; that the great body of property is socially administered now, and that the function of private ownership is to divine in advance the equilibrium of social desires — which socialism equally would have to divine, but which, under the illusion of self-seeking, is more poignantly and shrewdly foreseen.

I should like to see it brought home to the public that the question of fair prices is due to the fact that none of us can have as much as we want of all the things we want; that as less will be produced than the public wants, the question is how much of each product it will have and how much go without; that thus the final competition is between the objects of desire, and therefore between the producers of those objects; that when we oppose labor and capital, labor means the group that is selling its product and capital all the other groups that are buying it. The hated capitalist is simply the mediator, the prophet, the adjuster according to his divination of the future desire. If you could get that believed, the body of the people would have no doubt as to the worth of law.

That is my outside thought on the present discontents. As to the truth embodied in them, in part it cannot be helped. It cannot be helped, it is as it should be, that the law is behind the times. I told a labor leader once that what they asked was favor, and if a decision was against them they called it wicked. The same might be said of their opponents. It means that the law is growing. As law embodies beliefs that have triumphed in the battle of ideas and then have translated themselves into action, while there still is doubt, while opposite convictions still keep a battle front against each other, the time for law has not come; the notion destined to prevail is not yet entitled to the field. It is a misfortune if a judge reads his conscious or unconscious sympathy with one side or the other prematurely into the law, and forgets that what seem to him to be first principles are believed by half his fellow men to be wrong. I think that we have suffered from this misfortune, in State courts at least, and that this is another and very important truth to be extracted from the popular discontent. When twenty years ago a vague terror went over the earth and the word socialism began to be heard, I thought and still think that fear was translated into doctrines that had no proper place in the Constitution or the common law. Judges are apt to be naïf, simple-minded men, and they need something of Mephistopheles. We too need education in the obvious—to learn to transcend our own convictions and to leave room for much that we hold dear to be done away with short of revolution by the orderly change of law.

I have no belief in panaceas and almost none in sudden ruin. I believe with Montesquieu that if the chance of a battle—I may add, the passage of a law—has ruined a state, there was a general cause at work that made the state ready to perish by a single battle or a law. Hence I am not much interested one way or the other in the nostrums now so strenuously urged. I do not think the United States would come to an end if we lost our power to declare an Act of Congress void. I do think the Union would be imperiled if we could not make that declaration as to the laws of the several States. For one in my place sees how often a local policy prevails with those who are not trained to national views and how often action is taken that embodies what the Commerce Clause was meant to end. But I am not aware that there is any serious desire to limit the Court's power in this regard. For most of the things that properly can be called evils in the present state of the law I think the main remedy, as for the evils of public opinion, is for us to grow more civilized.

If I am right it will be a slow business for our people to reach rational views, assuming that we are allowed to work peaceably to that end. But as I grow older I grow calm. If I feel what are perhaps an old man's apprehensions, that competition from new races will cut deeper than working men's disputes and will test whether we can hang together and can fight; if I fear that we are running through the world's resources at a pace that we cannot keep; I do not lose my hopes. I do not pin my dreams for the future to my country or even to my race. I think it probable that civilization somehow will last as long as I care to look ahead — perhaps with smaller numbers, but perhaps also bred to greatness and splendor by science. I think it not improbable that man, like the grub that prepares a chamber for the winged thing it never has seen but is to be — that man may have cosmic destinies that he does not understand. And so beyond the vision of battling races and an impoverished earth I catch a dreaming glimpse of peace.

The other day my dream was pictured to my mind. It was evening. I was walking homeward on Pennsylvania Avenue near the Treasury, and as I looked beyond Sherman's Statue to the west the sky was aflame with scarlet and crimson from the setting sun. But, like the note of downfall in Wagner's opera, below the sky line there came from little globes the pallid discord of the electric lights. And I thought to myself the Götterdämmerung will end, and from those globes clustered like evil eggs will come the new masters of the sky. It is like the time in which we live. But then I remembered the faith that I partly have expressed, faith in a universe not measured by our fears, a universe that has thought and more than thought inside of it, and as I gazed, after the sunset and above the electric lights there shone the stars.

IDEALS AND DOUBTS [1]

For the last thirty years we have been preoccupied with the embryology of legal ideas; and explanations, which, when I was in college, meant a reference to final causes, later came to mean tracing origin and growth. But fashion is as potent in the intellectual world as elsewhere, and there are signs of an inevitable reaction. The reaction, if there is one, seems to me an advance, for it is toward the ultimate question of worth. That is the text of an ex-

[1] *Illinois Law Review,* Vol. X (1915).

cellent article, "History versus Value," by Morris R. Cohen in the *Journal of Philosophy, Psychology and Scientific Methods,* and although perhaps rather in the form of conservation than of advance, of Del Vecchio's *Formal Bases of Law* in the Modern Legal Philosophical Series. To show that it has my sympathy I may refer to the *Law Quarterly Review.*[2] But perhaps it will not be out of place to express the caution with which I am compelled to approach any general recension from which the young hope so much.

The first inquiry is for the criterion. If I may do Del Vecchio the wrong of summing up in a sentence or two what from a hasty reading I gather to be his mode of reaching one, it is that of a Neo-Kantian idealist. Experience takes place and is organized in consciousness, by its machinery and according to its laws, such as the category of cause and effect. Therefore consciousness constructs the universe and as the fundamental fact is entitled to fundamental reverence. From this it is easy to proceed to the Kantian injunction to regard every human being as an end in himself and not as a means.

I confess that I rebel at once. If we want conscripts, we march them up to the front with bayonets in their rear to die for a cause in which perhaps they do not believe. The enemy we treat not even as a means but as an obstacle to be abolished, if so it may be. I feel no pangs of conscience over either step, and naturally am slow to accept a theory that seems to be contradicted by practices that I approve. In fact, it seems to me that the idealists give away their case when they write books. For it shows that they have done the great act of faith and decided that they are not God. If the world were my dream, I should be God in the only universe I know. But although I cannot prove that I am awake, I believe that my neighbors exist in the same sense that I do, and if I admit that, it is easy to admit also that I am in the universe, not it in me.

When I say that a thing is true, I mean that I cannot help believing it. I am stating an experience as to which there is no choice. But as there are many things that I cannot help doing that the universe can, I do not venture to assume that my inabilities in the way of thought are inabilities of the universe. I therefore define the truth as the system of my limitations, and leave absolute truth for those who are better equipped. With absolute truth I leave absolute ideals of conduct equally on one side.

[2] 25 *Law Quarterly Review,* 412, 414, October, 1909.

But although one believes in what commonly, with some equivocation, is called necessity; that phenomena always are found to stand in quantitatively fixed relations to earlier phenomena; it does not follow that without such absolute ideals we have nothing to do but to sit still and let time run over us. As I wrote many years ago, the mode in which the inevitable comes to pass is through effort. Consciously or unconsciously we all strive to make the kind of a world that we like. And although with Spinoza we may regard criticism of the past as futile, there is every reason for doing all that we can to make a future such as we desire.

There is every reason also for trying to make our desires intelligent. The trouble is that our ideals for the most part are inarticulate, and that even if we have made them definite we have very little experimental knowledge of the way to bring them about. The social reformers of today seem to me so far to forget that we no more can get something for nothing by legislation than we can by mechanics as to be satisfied if the bill to be paid for their improvements is not presented in a lump sum. Interstitial detriments that may far outweigh the benefit promised are not bothered about. Probably I am too skeptical as to our ability to do more than shift disagreeable burdens from the shoulders of the stronger to those of the weaker. But I hold to a few articles of a creed that I do not expect to see popular in my day. I believe that the wholesale social regeneration which so many now seem to expect, if it can be helped by conscious, coördinated human effort, cannot be affected appreciably by tinkering with the institution of property, but only by taking in hand life and trying to build a race. That would be my starting point for an ideal for the law. The notion that with socialized property we should have women free and a piano for everybody seems to me an empty humbug.

To get a little nearer to the practical, our current ethics and our current satisfaction with conventional legal rules, it seems to me, can be purged to a certain extent without reference to what our final ideal may be. To rest upon a formula is a slumber that, prolonged, means death. Our system of morality is a body of imperfect social generalizations expressed in terms of emotion. To get at its truth, it is useful to omit the emotion and ask ourselves what those generalizations are and how far they are confirmed by fact accurately ascertained. So in regard to the formulas of the law, I have found it very instructive to consider what may be the postulates implied. They are generically two: that such and such a condition or result is desirable and that such and such means are appropriate to bring it about. In all debatable matters there are conflicting desires to be accomplished by inconsistent means, and the further question arises, which is entitled to prevail in the specific case? Upon such issues logic does not carry us far, and the practical solution sometimes may assume a somewhat cynical shape. But I have found it a help to clear thinking to try to get behind my conventional assumptions as a judge whose first business is to see that the game is played according to the rules whether I like them or not. To have doubted one's own first principles is the mark of a civilized man. To know what you want and why you think that such a measure will help it is the first but by no means the last step towards intelligent legal reform. The other and more difficult one is to realize what you must give up to get it, and to consider whether you are ready to pay the price.

It is fashionable nowadays to emphasize the criterion of social welfare as against the individualistic eighteenth century bills of rights. I may venture to refer to a book of mine published thirty-four years ago to show that it is no novelty.[3] The trouble with some of those who hold to that modest platitude is that they are apt to take the general premise as a sufficient justification for specific measures. One may accept the premise in good faith and yet disbelieve all the popular conceptions of socialism, or even doubt whether there is a panacea in giving women votes. Personally I like to know what the bill is going to be before I order a luxury. But it is a pleasure to see more faith and enthusiasm in the young men; and I thought that one of them made a good answer to some of my skeptical talk when he said, "You would base legislation upon regrets rather than upon hopes."

NATURAL LAW[1]

It is not enough for the knight of romance that you agree that his lady is a very nice girl — if you do not admit that she is the best that God ever made or will make, you must fight. There is in

[3] *The Common Law*, pp. 43, 44, 48.
[1] First published in 32 HLR (1918) 40. Suggested by reading François Geny, *Science et Technique en Droit Positif Privé*, Paris, 1915.

all men a demand for the superlative, so much so that the poor devil who has no other way of reaching it attains it by getting drunk. It seems to me that this demand is at the bottom of the philosopher's effort to prove that truth is absolute and of the jurist's search for criteria of universal validity which he collects under the head of natural law.

I used to say, when I was young, that truth was the majority vote of that nation that could lick all others. Certainly we may expect that the received opinion about the present war will depend a good deal upon which side wins (I hope with all my soul it will be mine), and I think that the statement was correct in so far as it implied that our test of truth is a reference to either a present or an imagined future majority in favor of our view. If, as I have suggested elsewhere, the truth may be defined as the system of my (intellectual) limitations,[2] what gives it objectivity is the fact that I find my fellow man to a greater or less extent (never wholly) subject to the same *Can't Helps*. If I think that I am sitting at a table I find that the other persons present agree with me; so if I say that the sum of the angles of a triangle is equal to two right angles. If I am in a minority of one they send for a doctor or lock me up; and I am so far able to transcend the to me convincing testimony of my senses or my reason as to recognize that if I am alone probably something is wrong with my works.

Certitude is not the test of certainty. We have been cock-sure of many things that were not so. If I may quote myself again, property, friendship, and truth have a common root in time. One can not be wrenched from the rocky crevices into which one has grown for many years without feeling that one is attacked in one's life. What we most love and revere generally is determined by early associations. I love granite rocks and barberry bushes, no doubt because with them were my earliest joys that reach back through the past eternity of my life. But while one's experience thus makes certain preferences dogmatic for oneself, recognition of how they came to be so leaves one able to see that others, poor souls, may be equally dogmatic about something else. And this again means scepticism. Not that one's belief or love does not remain. Not that we would not fight and die for it if important — we all, whether we know it or not, are fighting to make the kind of a world that we should

[2] See "Ideals and Doubts," p. 391.

like — but that we have learned to recognize that others will fight and die to make a different world, with equal sincerity or belief. Deep-seated preferences can not be argued about — you can not argue a man into liking a glass of beer — and therefore, when differences are sufficiently far reaching, we try to kill the other man rather than let him have his way. But that is perfectly consistent with admitting that, so far as appears, his grounds are just as good as ours.

The jurists who believe in natural law seem to me to be in that naïve state of mind that accepts what has been familiar and accepted by them and their neighbors as something that must be accepted by all men everywhere. No doubt it is true that, so far as we can see ahead, some arrangements and the rudiments of familiar institutions seem to be necessary elements in any society that may spring from our own and that would seem to us to be civilized — some form of permanent association between the sexes — some residue of property individually owned — some mode of binding oneself to specified future conduct — at the bottom of all, some protection for the person. But without speculating whether a group is imaginable in which all but the last of these might disappear and the last be subject to qualifications that most of us would abhor, the question remains as to the *Ought* of natural law.

It is true that beliefs and wishes have a transcendental basis in the sense that their foundation is arbitrary. You can not help entertaining and feeling them, and there is an end of it. As an arbitrary fact people wish to live, and we say with various degrees of certainty that they can do so only on certain conditions. To do it they must eat and drink. That necessity is absolute. It is a necessity of less degree but practically general that they should live in society. If they live in society, so far as we can see, there are further conditions. Reason working on experience does tell us, no doubt, that if our wish to live continues, we can do it only on those terms. But that seems to me the whole of the matter. I see no *a priori* duty to live with others and in that way, but simply a statement of what I must do if I wish to remain alive. If I do live with others they tell me that I must do and abstain from doing various things or they will put the screws on to me. I believe that they will, and being of the same mind as to their conduct I not only accept the rules but come in time to accept them with sympathy and emotional affirmation and begin to talk about duties and rights. But for legal purposes a right is only the hypostasis of a prophecy — the imagination of a substance supporting the fact that the public force will be brought to bear upon those who do things said to contravene it — just as we talk of the force of gravitation accounting for the conduct of bodies in space. One phrase adds no more than the other to what we know without it. No doubt behind these legal rights is the fighting will of the subject to maintain them, and the spread of his emotions to the general rules by which they are maintained; but that does not seem to me the same thing as the supposed *a priori* discernment of a duty or the assertion of a pre-existing right. A dog will fight for his bone.

The most fundamental of the supposed pre-existing rights — the right to life — is sacrificed without a scruple not only in war, but whenever the interest of society, that is, of the predominant power in the community, is thought to demand it. Whether that interest is the interest of mankind in the long run no one can tell, and as, in any event, to those who do not think with Kant and Hegel it is only an interest, the sanctity disappears. I remember a very tenderhearted judge being of opinion that closing a hatch to stop a fire and the destruction of a cargo was justified even if it was known that doing so would stifle a man below. It is idle to illustrate further, because to those who agree with me I am uttering commonplaces and to those who disagree I am ignoring the necessary foundations of thought. The *a priori* men generally call the dissentients superficial. But I do agree with them in believing that one's attitude on these matters is closely connected with one's general attitude toward the universe. Proximately, as has been suggested, it is determined largely by early associations and temperament, coupled with the desire to have an absolute guide. Men to a great extent believe what they want to — although I see in that no basis for a philosophy that tells us what we should want to want.

Now when we come to our attitude toward the universe I do not see any rational ground for demanding the superlative — for being dissatisfied unless we are assured that our truth is cosmic truth, if there is such a thing — that the ultimates of a little creature on this little earth are the last word of the unimaginable whole. If a man sees no reason for believing that significance, consciousness and ideals are more than marks of the finite, that does not justify what has been familiar in French sceptics; getting upon a pedestal and professing to look with haughty scorn upon a world in ruins. The real conclusion is that the part can not swallow the whole — that our categories are not, or may not be, adequate to formulate what we cannot know. If we believe that we come out of the universe, not it out of us, we must admit that we do not know what we are talking about when we speak of brute matter. We do know that a certain complex of energies can wag its tail and another can make syllogisms. These are among the powers of the unknown, and if, as may be, it has still greater powers that we cannot understand, as Fabre in his studies of instinct would have us believe, studies that gave Bergson one of the strongest strands for his philosophy and enable Maeterlinck to make us fancy for a moment that we heard a clang from behind phenomena — if this be true, why should we not be content? Why should we employ the energy that is furnished to us by the cosmos to defy it and shake our fist at the sky? It seems to me silly.

That the universe has in it more than we understand, that the private soldiers have not been told the plan of campaign, or even that there is one, rather than some vaster unthinkable to which every predicate is an impertinence, has no bearing upon our conduct. We still shall fight — all of us because we want to live, some, at least, because we want to realize our spontaneity and prove our powers, for the joy of it, and we may leave to the unknown the supposed final valuation of that which in any event has value to us. It is enough for us that the universe has produced us and has within it, as less than it, all that we believe and love. If we think of our existence not as that of a little god outside, but as that of a ganglion within, we have the infinite behind us. It gives us our only but our adequate significance. A grain of sand has the same, but what competent person supposes that he understands a grain of sand? That is as much beyond our grasp as man. If our imagination is strong enough to accept the vision of ourselves as parts inseverable from the rest, and to extend our final interest beyond the boundary of our skins, it justifies the sacrifice even of our lives for ends outside of ourselves. The motive, to be sure, is the common wants and ideals that we find in man. Philosophy does not furnish motives, but it shows men that they are not fools for doing what they already want to do. It opens to the forlorn hopes on which we throw ourselves away, the vista of the farthest stretch of human thought, the chords of a harmony that breathes from the unknown.

LAW AND SOCIAL REFORM [1]

Law is a plant that lives long before it throws out bulbs. It is rooted for millenniums before it gathers the food and develops the nucleus for a new life that inquires into the reason for its being and for the directions and character of its growth. A book in which the leading institutions of the law are discussed in this way and defended or condemned by representatives of different sides hardly would have been possible until within the last hundred, perhaps the last fifty, years. But within that time it has become popular to believe that society advantageously may take its destiny into its own hands — may give a conscious direction to much that heretofore has rested on the assumption that the familiar is the best, or that has been left to the mechanically determined outcome of the co-operation and clash of private effort. We have seen even attempts to create a new and universal language. A first step toward such social control is to take an account of stock and to set a valuation upon what we have. To make a code that should do more than embody the unreasoned habits of the community it would be desirable in the beginning to determine our ideal — the remote but dominant end that we aim to reach — and then to consider whether one measure rather than another would help us toward it. I confess that I do not think that as yet we are very well prepared for wholesale reconstruction. But even if it never led to reconstruction it would gratify the noble instinct of scientific curiosity to understand why we maintain what now is.

Since the time when I was in college embryology has taken the place of explanation, and even in the law a good deal of attention has been given to inquiring through what stages the law has come to its present form and content. But as law is human and can be altered the present inquiry is more important than any investigation of the past. We want reasons more than life history. At times the reader may feel disappointment — he may feel that, as in some fruits, there is a large constituent of water. But that is partly due to the fact that any idea that has been in the world for twenty years and has not perished has become a platitude although it was a

[1] First published as an Introduction to *The Rational Basis of Legal Institutions* (1923), Vol. XI, Modern Legal Philosophy Series.

revelation twenty years ago. One might also venture on the paradox that by the time that a proposition becomes generally articulate it ceases to be true — because things change about as fast as they are realized.

The present time is experimenting in negations — an amusing sport if it is remembered that while it takes but a few minutes to cut down a tree it takes a century for a tree to grow. Perhaps, however, more is to be apprehended from ungrounded hopes than from criticisms without a fulcrum. A very common mode of argument, made popular by the abolitionists, is to prophesy a change as bound to come and then to discount this promise for the future and to treat it as cash — as a present fact and a premise for further conclusions. Those who reason thus are more common and, I suspect, more dangerous than people who speak of the injustice of men being born with unequal faculties — criticising the order of the universe as if they were little gods outside it. The logic of the latter would seem to require that the cosmos should reduce itself to a single set of waves of equal length. We do not bother ourselves very much about them. But the optimists who are ready to make fundamental changes upon prophecies of the millennium to ensue may do real harm. When I am told that under this or that regime selfishness would disappear, I cannot but reflect that my neighbor is better nourished by eating his own dinner than by my eating it for him, and I recall the tale of the men of Gotham who got hopelessly tangled up in their public meeting until a philosopher came by and said: Every man pull out his own legs. For the most part men believe what they want to. Humbugs through whose vitals Malthus ran a rapier a hundred years ago are alive and kicking to-day. But reason means truth and those who are not governed by it take the chances that some day the sunken fact will rip the bottom out of their boat.

The subjects dealt with in this book are so interesting that it is hard to refrain from expressing one's own views upon some of them at least. But in one place or another I have said what I think about the foundations, and I will go no farther than to repeat that most even of the enlightened reformers that I hear or read seem to me not to have considered with accuracy the means at our disposal and to become rhetorical just where I want figures. The notion that we can secure an economic paradise by changes in property alone seems to me twaddle. I can understand better legislation that aims rather to improve the quality than to increase the quantity of the population. I can understand saying, whatever the cost, so far as may be, we will keep certain strains out of our blood. If before the English factory acts the race was running down physically I can understand taking the economic risk of passing those acts — although they had to be paid for, and I do not doubt that in some way or other England was the worse for them, however favorable the balance of the account. I can understand a man's saying in any case, I want this or that and I am willing to pay the price, if he realizes what the price is. What I most fear is saying the same thing when those who say it do not know and have made no serious effort to find out what it will cost, as I think we in this country are rather inclined to do.

The passion for equality is now in fashion, and Mr. Lester Ward has told us of the value of discontent. Without considering how far motives commonly classed as ignoble have covered themselves with a high sounding name, or how far discontent means inadequacy of temperament or will, the first step toward improvement is to look the facts in the face. To help us to do so is, I take it, the object of the book.

OPINIONS AND CHAMPAGNES[1]

For obvious reasons I should not care to speak upon your subject except as from time to time I have to.

I see no impropriety, however, in suggesting the isolated reflection that with effervescing opinions, as with the not yet forgotten champagnes, the quickest way to let them get flat is to let them get exposed to the air.

A PREFACE[2]

This collection has been made by the kindness of a friend, Mr. Harold J. Laski, and I owe him thanks for gathering these little fragments of my fleece that I have left upon the hedges of life. They are printed as they appeared and I have been unable to do more than run my eye over them, but I am glad to see them put

[1] Letter to the Harvard Liberal Club, Jan. 1920.
[2] To the *Collected Legal Papers* (1920).

together in a book, as they offer some views of law and life that I have not expressed elsewhere so fully. . . .

A later generation has carried on the work that I began nearly half a century ago, and it is a great pleasure to an old warrior who cannot expect to bear arms much longer, that the brilliant young soldiers still give him a place in their councils of war.

2. Letters

Holmes made of his letters a minor art. He was not a voluminous and certainly not an indiscriminate letter writer. But there were five or six friends with whom he maintained a steady exchange over the years. Three of these bodies of correspondence have been published — a few letters to William James, a considerable number to John C. H. Wu, and the massive exchange with Sir Frederick Pollock. Of those that remain to be published the exchange with Harold J. Laski promises to be the most substantial and exciting. The two men had enough in common to move in the same intellectual universe, and enough divergences to strike fire when they clashed.

The letters to William James were first published by Ralph Barton Perry in an article, "The Common Enemy," in the Atlantic Monthly, *and later in his book* The Thought and Character of William James *(2 vols., Little, Brown and Company, 1935). Holmes and James knew each other when the former was a student at the Harvard Law School and the latter was pursuing his medical studies in and out of Cambridge. For about five years they were the closest of friends. In a letter from Berlin written in 1868 in reply to the first letter from Holmes printed below, James gives a glimpse of how deeply moved he was by his friendship. To lay "the ghosts of the past," he had decided to write "a few lines to one of the most obtrusive ghosts of all — namely the tall and lank one of Charles Street. Good golly! how I would prefer to have about twenty-four hours' talk with you up in that whitely lit-up room — without the sun rising or the firmament revolving so as to put the gas out, without sleep, food, clothing or shelter except your whiskey bottle, of which, or the like of which, I have not partaken since I have been in these longitudes! I should like to have you opposite me in any mood, whether the facetiously excursive, the metaphysically discursive, the personally confidential, or the jadedly cursive and argumentative." (Perry, op. cit., I: 507–508.)*

But the friendship cooled, partly (as James himself thought) because of Holmes's increasing preoccupation with the study of law. There can be no question that Holmes was studying terribly hard during his years at the Law School; and the same applied during his early years on the American Law Review, when he was preparing his edition of Kent's Commentaries.[1] In writing to another friend in 1868 James lamented the increasing distance between him and Holmes due to the fact that each was concentrating on a different life work. "The mystery of the Total is a rather empty platform to be the only one to meet a man on." (Perry, op. cit., I: 290.)

Yet one may guess that the reasons for the estrangement were deeper. In a letter in 1869, to his brother Henry, William James lamented "the cold-blooded conscious egotism and conceit of people," and then went on to say that "all the noble qualities of Wendell Holmes, for instance, are poisoned by them." In 1876, after his third visit with the Holmeses at Mattapoisett, James wrote that Holmes was "a powerful battery, formed like a planing machine to gouge a deep self-beneficial groove through life." (Perry, op. cit. I: 371.) The fact was that the two men differed deeply not only in their philosophical outlooks but even more in their essential natures. Holmes was confident, self-contained, determined on the deflation of emotion and sentiment; James was nervous, too eager, excessively introspective, and tending always to over-explain himself. A long-sustained friendship needs minds more congenial. Professor Perry says rightly that "James and Holmes had been drawn together chiefly through their common negations and defiances." Early in their friendship Holmes had struck off the phrase "the common enemy" as a somewhat mystical embodiment of the forces each of them was fighting, and the eagerness with which James took the phrase up showed how avid he was to find a basis for their friendship. But as they grew older James's need for greater affirmations was not satisfied by Holmes. When the latter, then Chief Justice of the Supreme Judicial Court of Massachusetts, made his speech before the Boston Bar Association in 1900,[2] and ended "life is an end in itself, and the only question as to whether it is worth

[1] A letter in 1873 from the James family to Henry James, William's brother, recites the following: "Wendell Holmes dined with us a few days ago. His whole life, soul and body, is utterly absorbed in his *last* work upon his Kent. He carries about his manuscript in his green bag and never loses sight of it for a moment. He started to go to Will's room to wash his hands, but came back for his bag, and when we went to dinner, Will said, 'Don't you want to take your bag with you?' He said, 'Yes, I always do so at home.' His pallid face, and this fearful grip upon his work makes him a melancholy sight." (Perry, *op. cit.* I: 519.)

[2] See above, p. 40.

living is whether you have enough of it," James was irritated. *"I must say,"* he wrote in a letter to a friend, *"I'm disappointed in O. W. H. for being unable to make any other than that one set speech which comes out on every occasion. It's all right for once, in the exuberance of youth, to celebrate mere vital excitement,* la joie de vivre, *as a protest against humdrum solemnity. But to make it systematic, and oppose it, as an ideal and a duty, to the ordinarily recognized duties, is to pervert it altogether. . . . Mere excitement is an immature ideal, unworthy of the Supreme Court's official endorsement."* (Perry, op. cit. II: *251*).

That Holmes felt a reciprocal annoyance with James's writings is even more evident in his chance remarks about James in the letters to Pollock than it is in the formal responses printed below on the occasions when James sent Holmes his books. Holmes had great respect for James's "Irish" charm and temperament and for his literary insights, but thought he was weak as a logician and abstract philosopher. He suspected that his philosophy was a wishful construction and "that the aim and end of the whole business is religious." [3]

The letters to Wu are good Holmes quality. They were built upon what was almost wholly a letter-friendship, which was touching without being deep. Wu was a young Chinese student who brought to his correspondence with the legal great in America and England an elaborate Chinese courtliness of style and a Chinese reverence for learning and intellectual distinction.[4] He seems to have sent Holmes an article of his on Chinese law. He was twenty-two; Holmes was eighty. Holmes answered gracefully but in a noncommittal fashion. Gradually his interest was stirred, and the letters ripened into a steady exchange of correspondence over thirteen years, including a period when Wu was in China as professor and judge and a period when he came to Cambridge on a fellowship. In all Holmes sent him some seventy letters, and it is a striking fact, as

---

[3] On William James's death in 1910, Holmes wrote to Pollock: "Wm. James's death cuts a root for me that went far into the past, but of late, indeed for many years, we had seen little of each other and had little communication except as he occasionally sent me a book. Distance, other circumstances and latterly my little sympathy with his demi spiritualism and pragmatism, were sufficient cause. His reason made him sceptical and his wishes led him to turn down the lights so as to give miracle a chance." (H–P I:167, Sept. 1, 1910.)

[4] The rest of this paragraph and the next are largely taken from my essay, "The Scar Holmes Leaves," in my *Ideas Are Weapons* (1939), pp. 58–63.

Wu puts it, that "whenever there was a lapse in our correspondence, I invariably was the culprit." [5] One suspects that Holmes, never impervious to attention, was touched by the eager admiration of the young Chinese and by his utterance of things which the New England restraint of Holmes had generally kept him shy of. And since Holmes had no children of his own, these letters express the rather moving paternal strain in him.

They are the letters of an old New England aristocrat, laden with years and honors, to a young student of law and philosophy. But they are also the letters of a gallant and graceful old man, expecting to die any year, but taking the time to dip into his rich experience and nourish a hungry youth. We see a general in the campaign of life painstakingly teaching a soldier the rules of warfare. We see a man who has found success and a deep core of peace within himself gently nurturing the troubled spirit of a young man just starting out in life. We see a teacher writing to a student with infinite frankness and infinite tact. And if at times a hint of the stuffiness of a Polonius creeps into the older man's letters, the amazing thing is that there is only a hint of it and that it occurs so rarely.

Holmes's letters to Wu were first published in the Chinese Ti'en Hsia Monthly in 1935. Several excerpts from them appeared in the Saturday Evening Post after Holmes's death, and the body of them was later republished in Harry C. Shriver's edition of Holmes's Book Notices and Uncollected Letters and Papers (1936). I have chosen what seem to me the letters of more enduring importance, and in several instances have omitted introductory and closing paragraphs as being of only transient interest.

The story of the letters to Sir Frederick Pollock is of a very different sort. The recent publication of these letters [6] has been perhaps the most important single scholarly event in the study of Holmes's thought and personality. I wish for that reason that it had been possible to include more of these letters in the present volume. But I must thank the publishers and editor of the letters for their kindness in permitting me the ten I have chosen, and refer the more avid reader to the volumes themselves.

A lifelong sustained correspondence, like a lifelong unbroken friendship or happy marriage, requires explaining: all the cards are

[5] John C. H. Wu, *The Art of Law and Other Essays* (Shanghai, 1936), 176.
[6] *Holmes–Pollock Letters*, edited by Mark DeWolfe Howe. Two vols., Harvard University Press, 1941.

normally stacked against it.[7] *In the case of Justice Holmes and Sir Frederick Pollock the explanation lies in temperaments congenial without being too similar, interests similar without getting in each other's way — and distance. The two men came from two national cultures that rose from the same sources and flowed by different routes into the same sea. They first met in England in 1874 when Pollock was not quite thirty and Holmes thirty-three, both already certain of their professional interest in life but with all the possibilities of their world stretching before them. During the close to sixty years of life that remained to them they met again scarcely half a dozen times, on those rare occasions when one or the other crossed the Atlantic to deliver a course of lectures or receive some honor. And yet this frail foundation of intimacy was to support one of the notable structures of correspondence in the language.*

It is notable for reasons very different from those which make Flaubert's correspondence notable, or Poe's, or D. H. Lawrence's. There are few flashes of revelation, and at no time does either man let down his guard. The letters are highly literary, casual but with a finished casualness. The fire that burns in them is a gentle literary fire. They have superbly the qualities of one class of letters which are in their essence simply good conversation, carried on under the difficult conditions of distance and delay but for that very reason even better suited to their purpose. For their purpose is that of a set of diary entries and critical notebooks meant for the eye of another who is near enough for informality but not so near as to evade the unremitting diligence of one's internal censor. The result is that there are many delightful letters but none that are searing, many that are quotable but few that are unforgettable, many for the chronicler of the mind but few for the biographer of the heart. The themes of the letters are what one might expect from the preoccupations of two men who are lawyers, scholars, men-of-letters. Their mood is the mood of two gentlemen who feel so secure about their status that they can afford to be gay and irreverent and to gibe at the sanctities of their gentlemanly universe. They talk freely about shop, especially in the earlier and more earnest letters, but decreasingly as they grow older. And shop for them is an absorption not with the practice of the law but with law as history and law as civilization. Their sense of community in the legal field is great.

[7] In what follows I have borrowed liberally from my review of the *Holmes–Pollock Letters* in the *Harvard Law Review* for April, 1942.

Both of them have essentially operational and non-absolutist conceptions of law, and common-sense definitions of scientific method in law. But what links them even more is a common devotion to "Our Lady, the Common Law," a common conviction of great work still to be done in legal thinking, a common feeling for craftsmanship, a common delight in the learning and observations that illumine the dark spaces in men's behavior. For this illumination they ransacked their reading and experience, exchanging views on English and American law, on Frankish and Salic, on Hindu and Filipino. The two of them formed in themselves an entire Institute of Comparative Law.

But each of them was a great legal scholar because he was so much more than a legal scholar. And after the first half-volume, most of the talk is of books and reading, of people and politics, of amenities and philosophy in life. It would be strange if two men so close together in their legal views were very far apart in their social and political thinking. And they were not. Holmes was an economic conservative, although the unthinking at times thought of him as a dangerous radical. Pollock was a Tory. The difference between the two men in this respect lay not so much in the specific gravity of their views as in the way they carried it. But the gulf of quality between two men that made one, however interesting and rich a personality, merely a very good second-rater and the other a first-rater, shows up best neither in their law nor in their politics, but in the whole range of taste, imagination, and value that makes the imprint of a personality. Holmes can fashion a phrase that leaves a scar on us because the idea and the experience behind the phrase have been whittled over years to a fatal sharpness. Pollock overwhelms us, as he overwhelmed Holmes, by his precise command of facts, the sweep of his learning, his sheer virtuosity in a dozen fields. But for all this, we do not feel when he has passed us that we have been brushed by greatness.

The volumes of Holmes–Pollock letters will be most a treasure-trove to those who are interested in criticism. And by criticism I mean not only evaluations in literature but in the whole sweep of intellectual history, and not only of books and ideas but of men as well. "The literature of the past is a bore," writes Holmes, breaking a lance in the centuries-old Battle of the Books. Nevertheless, along with his usual literary diet of lightweight French novels and his (I fear) too conscious enjoyment of Nize Baby and Gentlemen

Prefer Blondes, *he turned increasingly to the classics as he grew older. The fact is not that Holmes was a modernist in the Battle of the Books but that he insisted that each book, old or recent, prove its worth for him rather than for someone else. The result is a set of independent judgments of men and ideas that must rank high in the history of criticism.*

The differences in style and mood between the three sets of Holmes letters from which selections are here reprinted are striking. The early letters to James are adolescent, more delightfully so when they are rhapsodizing about spring weather without and within the heart of a young man than when they are mired in heavy philosophizing; the later letters are slightly on the formal side. The letters to Wu tend to be homilies, and their charm is part of the rambling discursiveness of an older man talking to a younger. The letters to Pollock are less self-conscious and easier flowing. They are less likely than the Wu letters to repeat what Holmes has written and said before. They are gayer, fuller of whim and paradox. They go along, impelled, seemingly, by little logic save that of free association, much as his father's talk flowed along in the volumes of the Autocrat, the Professor and the Poet holding forth at the Breakfast Table. Perhaps for that reason they express, better than anything else Holmes wrote, the pattern of a mind and a life.[8]

TO WILLIAM JAMES

Boston, Dec. 15, 1867

DEAR BILL, —

I shall begin with no apologies for my delay in writing except to tell you that since seeing you I have written three long letters to you at different intervals on *vis viva,* each of which I was compelled to destroy because on reflection it appeared either unsound or incomplete. But I was talking yesterday with Fanny Dixwell and she told me to fire away anyhow — that she thought it would please you to hear from me even with *vis viva.* So here goes. Writing is so unnatural to me that I have never before dared to try it to you unless in connection with a subject. Ah! dear Bill, do me justice. My

---

[8] In the case of the letters to James and Pollock, I must thank the respective editors from whose volumes I have taken the selections — Professors Ralph Barton Perry and Mark DeWolfe Howe — for the use of their clarifying footnotes.

expressions of esteem are not hollow nor hyperbolical — nor put in to cover my neglect. In spite of my many friends I am almost alone in my thoughts and inner feelings. And whether I ever see you much or not, I think I can never fail to derive a secret comfort and companionship from the thought of you. I believe I shall always respect and love you whether we see much or little of each other. . . .

For two or three months I debauched o' nights in philosophy. But now it is law — law — law. My *magnum opus* was reading the *Critique of Pure Reason* and Schulze's *éclaircissement* — which on the whole, though an excellent abridgment, doesn't much by way of *éclaircissements*. . . . Assumed that logic exhaustively classifies judgments according to their possible forms, it [Kant's *Critique*] has then implicitly classified concepts in like manner. But all experience to be thought must be thought through concepts. The forms of concepts, then, are inherent in all organized experience as an *a priori* element. Hence it is explained *inter alia* why, given phenomenon A, we say it must have had a cause in an antecedent phenomenon. The phenomenon only became thinkable through that form and others. You see how ingenious and audacious was his attempt — yet its fallacy seems obvious when the reasoning by which it was arrived at is grasped.

Thus, the logical categories have reference only to the form in which judgments are expressed. The conceptions of substance, causal relation, etc., belong to the content and are not given in the form. Thus, take the hypothetical judgment, "If A then B." This form is not coterminous with the causal judgment, as Thomson [1] (reasoning *alio intuitu*) points out; e.g., "if this be poetry, poetry is worthless," is as much hypothetical in form as "if the moon attracts in same line as the sun the tides are at their highest." Thomson says the only case of causal relation is when the four terms are all different: "if A is B then C is D." But whether even this last is always so may be doubted — e.g., "if I am right then tomorrow will be warm." Again, he and Mansel have both shown — I should think successfully, but I am no logician — that all of these can be reduced to categorical judgments. And then what becomes of a theory based on their fundamental distinctions? But the other objection is, I think, insuperable — that if the concept cause and effect be only a form of thought corresponding to the hypothetical judgment, that

---

[1] Sir William Thomson. The book is presumably his *Treatise on Natural Philosophy*, I, 1867.

judgment ought never to express any but causal relations. . . . It's puerile stuff enough, I admit, to waste energy on. But it seems necessary to read a good deal of useless stuff, in order to know that it is so and not to depend only on surmise. At present, I say it's nothing but law; though, by the by, I am reading Tyndall's book on *Heat* — what a yellow-whiskered, healthy, florid-complected, pleasant English book it is, to be sure. Aren't the foreigners simpler than we? See what one of the great lights of English law says in the preface to a book I'm reading (he is speaking of Savigny): "I have used great exertions, but without effect, to make myself sufficiently master of the German language to read this work in the original." If a man here had three cents' worth of secondhand knowledge would he confess that he didn't know anything under the sun? Talking of Britons, there have been a lot here of late — one, a Mr. Henry Cowper — brother of the present Earl C., made a decided impression on me. He had the cosmos at heart, it seemed to me, and we hammered at it late into the night several times. . . .

Oh! Bill, my beloved, how have I yearned after thee all this long time. How I have admired those brave, generous and magnanimous traits of which I will not shame thee by speaking. I am the better that I have seen thee and known thee, — let that suffice. Since I wrote the last word I have been to see your father. By a rather remarkable coincidence, your last letter referred to Kant and to Schulze's book. It is rather strange, isn't it? It is now evening and the whole day has been yours with the exceptions noted and meals. I expect Gray directly. May this get to you in time to wish you a Happy New Year. By Heaven I do, — *vis viva* must wait. There are stickers I can't answer. But I rather think you found difficulty — at least I did — in the insufficiency of facts. As one is shaping his views he wants to say, Is this experiment so or so? I got more out of Cooke[2] on terms by way of translating mathematics into English than anyone else. But I found my first explanations in great measure *chimæra bombinans in vacuo* when I went into the matter a second time in order to write you. As it is I just see that force isn't destroyed, without having mastered the formulae. What a passion your father has in writing and talking his religion! Almost he persuadeth me to be a Swedenborgian, but I can't go it so far — will see whether

---

[2] Josiah Parsons Cooke, whose books on physics and chemistry were current at this time.

the other scheme busts up first, I think. Good-bye, dear Bill — don't forget me quite.

Affectionately yours,
O. W. HOLMES

Boston, April 19, 1868

DEAR BILL, —

The icy teeth have melted out of the air and winter has snapped at us for the last time. Now are the waters beneath my window of a deeper and more significant blue than heretofore. Now do the fields burn with green fire — the evanescent hint of I know not what hidden longing of the earth. Now all the bushes burgeon with wooly buds and the elm trees have put on bridal veils of hazy brown. Now to the chorus of the frogs answers the chorus of the birds in antiphony of morning and evening. Now couples, walking round Boston Common Sundays after sunset, draw near to each other in the dark spaces between the gas lights and think themselves unseen. Now are the roads around Cambridge filled with collegians with new hats and sticks and shining schoolboy faces. Now the young man seeks the maiden nothing loath to be pursued. Spring is here, Bill, and I turn to thee, — not with more affection than during the long grind of the winter, but desiring if it may be to say a word to thee once more.

Since I wrote in December I have worked at nothing but the law. Philosophy has hibernated in torpid slumber, and I have laid "sluttishly soaking and gurgling in the devil's pickle," as Carlyle says. It has been necessary, — if a man chooses a profession he cannot forever content himself in picking out the plums with fastidious dilettantism and give the rest of the loaf to the poor, but must eat his way manfully through crust and crumb — soft, unpleasant, inner parts which, within one, swell, causing discomfort in the bowels. Such has been my cowardice that I have been almost glad that you weren't here, lest you should be disgusted to find me inaccessible to ideas and impressions of more spiritual significance but alien to my studies. Think not, however, that I distrust the long enduring of your patience. I know that you would be the last of all to turn away from one in whom you discerned the possibility of friendship because his vigils were at a different shrine, knowing it was the same Divinity he worshipped. And the winter has been a success, I think, both for the simple discipline of the work and because I now go on with an ever increasing conviction that law as well as any other series of facts in this world may be approached in the interests of science and may be studied, yes and practised, with the preservation of one's ideals. I should even say that they grew robust under the regimen, — more than that I do not ask. To finish the search of mankind, to discover the *ne plus ultra* which is the demand of ingenuous youth, one finds is not allotted to an individual. To reconcile oneself to life — to dimly apprehend that this dream disturbing the sleep of the cosm is not the result of a dyspepsy, but is well — to suspect some of the divine harmonies, though you cannot note them like a score of music — these things, methinks, furnish vanishing points which give a kind of perspective to the chaos of events. Perhaps I am fortunate in what I have often made a reproach to myself.

Harry never lets up on his high aims, — somehow it connects itself with the absence of humor in him which himself avows. I *do*. There are not infrequent times when a bottle of wine, a good dinner, a girl of some trivial sort can fill the hour for me. So for longer spaces, work, — of which only at the beginning and the end do I perceive the philosophic *nexus,* and while performing forget the Great Task Master's Eye. This makes life easier though perhaps it does not deserve approval.

Let me give another example of "if A is B, then C is D" (in my last letter) which does not denote a causal connection — the one I gave was open to objection as standing on peculiar grounds. Take all judgments of universal or assumed universal concomitants: "If the barometer falls suddenly, there will be a gale"; "If the sun shines in Boston, the stars are out in China." In these, etc., there is no causal connection between protasis and apodosis, although *by going outside of the judgment* to an induction we may say with more or less confidence that where two facts are always found together, if one is not the cause of the other then they are both (probably) referable to a common cause. . . . Is it not clear that . . . the relation of the *if* and the *then* to a common cause is not in any way given in the form of the judgment, and that said *if* and *then* don't stand to each other in the relation of cause and effect? . . .

Dear old Bill, I haven't said anything about your illness to you — there is nothing, perhaps, which particularly belongs to me to say. But for God's sake don't lose that courage with which you have faced "the common enemy" (as you well have it). Would that I could give back the spirits which you have given to me so often. At all events doubt not of my love.

Let me not be sad,—at least for this letter. There is a new fire in the earth and sky. I, who through the long winter have felt the wrinkles deepening in my face and a stoop settling in my back— I, who have said to myself that my life henceforth must and should be given only to severe thought, and have said to youth, "*procul esto*,"—I feel the mighty quickening of the spring.

The larches have sprouted.

I saw a butterfly today just loosed from the bondage of winter, and a bee toiling in sticky buds half opened.

O! passionate breezes! O! rejoicing hills! How swells the soft full chorus—for this earth which slept has awakened, and the air is tremulous with multiplied joyous sound.

Sing, sparrow—kissing with thy feet the topmost tassels of the pines.

Cease not thy too much sound, O! robin. Squirrels grind thy scissors in the woods. Creak, blackbirds. Croak, frogs. Caw, high-flying crows, who have seen the breaking of the ice in northern rivers and the seaward moving booms.

A keen, slender, stridulous vibration—almost too fine for the hearing, weaving in and out, and in the pauses of the music dividing the silence like a knife—pierces my heart with an ecstasy I cannot utter. Ah! what is it? Did I ever hear it? Is it a voice within answering to the others, but different from them—and like a singing flame not ceasing with that which made it vocal?

Dear Bill, to whom should I vent this madness but to you? Goodbye. You know my sentiments—I will not repeat them. Affectionately yours,

O. W. HOLMES

Apr. 25. It is snowing again. S' help me.

Boston, May 24, 1896

DEAR WILLIAM,—

Thank you very much for the little book which I have read with much pleasure. With its general aim or end I sympathize deeply —I mean the justification of the idealizing impulse; in detail, I somewhat diverge. I think the demands made of the universe are too nearly the Christian demands without the scheme of salvation. I long ago made up my mind that all that one needed was a belief in the significance of the universe. And more lately it has come to seem to me that even that might be ambiguous. For all I know "significance" is an expression of finiteness and incompleteness, and the total, if there is one, is too great a swell to condescend to have a meaning. The basis of my content is precisely the denial of the possibility of that attitude of rejection and scorn for which you quote Carlyle and the *City of Dreadful Night*. Of course a man may say, "I hate it," as a mere fact of temperament, and may talk big against God while the lightning is quiet. But what warrant a sceptic can have for assuming that he is a god outside the show, with a ποῦ στῶ for criticizing it, I don't understand. This you will recognize as my ever recurring view ever since we have known each other. I won't write a lecture, but just hint my reserves and repeat my thanks. Affectionately yours,

O. W. HOLMES

Washington, March 24, 1907

DEAR BILL, —

I have read your two pieces about pragmatism [1] (pedantic name) and am curious to hear the rest. Meantime I will fire off a reflection or two. For a good many years I have had a formula for truth which seems humbler than those you give . . . but I don't know whether it is pragmatic or not. I have been in the habit of saying that all I mean by truth is what I can't help thinking. The assumption of the validity of the thinking process seems to mean no more than that: I am up against it — I have gone as far as I can go — just as when I like a glass of beer. But I have learned to surmise that my *can't helps* are not necessarily cosmic can't helps — that the universe may not be subject to my limitations; and philosophy generally seems to me to sin through arrogance. It is like the old knight-errants who proposed to knock your head off if you didn't admit that their girl was not only a nice girl but the most beautiful and best of all possible girls. I can't help preferring champagne to ditch water, — I doubt if the universe does.

But a reference to the universe seems to let in the Absolute that

---

[1] "Pragmatism's Conception of Truth," *Jour. of Philos.*, IV (1907); and "A Defense of Pragmatism," *Pop. Sci. Mo.*, LXX (1907).

in form I was expelling. To that I answer that I admit it to be but a guess. I think the despised *ding an sich* is all right. It stands on faith or a bet. The great act of faith is when a man decides that he is not God. But when I admit that you are not my dream, I seem to myself to have admitted the universe and the *ding an sich*, — unpredictable and only guessed at, as somewhat out of which I come rather than coming out of me. But if I did come out of it, or rather, if I am in it, I see no wonder why I can't swallow it. If it fixed my bounds, as it gives me my powers, I have nothing to say about its possibilities or characteristics except that it is a kind of thing (using this phraseology sceptically and under protest) that has me in its belly and so is bigger than I. It seems to me that the only promising activity is to make *my* universe coherent and livable, not to babble about *the* universe. Truth then, as one, I agree with you, is only an ideal — an assumption that if everyone was as educated and clever as I he would feel the same compulsions that I do. To a limited extent only do men feel so in fact, so that in fact there are as many truths as there are men. But if we all agreed, we should only have formulated our limitations. . . . I think the attempt to make these limitations compulsory on anything outside our dream — to demand significance, etc., of *the* universe — absurd. I simply say it contains them, and bow my head. To defy it would be equally absurd, as it would furnish me the energy with which to shake my fist. Most of us retain enough of the theological attitude to think that we are little gods. It is the regular position of sceptical French heroes, — like the scientific man in Maeterlinck's "Bees."

I have written more of a letter than I have time to write, but I add that I don't think fundamental doubt at all inconsistent with practical idealizing. As long as man's food produces extra energy he will have to let it off, i.e., to act. To act affirms, for the moment at least, the worth of an end; idealizing seems to be simply the generalized and permanent affirmation of the worth of ends. One may make that affirmation for purposes of conduct, and leave to the universe the care of deciding how much it cares about them. Again I bow my head and try to fulfil what seems to me my manifest destiny. . . . As to pain, suicide, etc., I think you make too much row about them, and have had thoughts on the need of a society for the promotion of hard-heartedness. It is as absurd for me to be spearing my old commonplaces at you as it would be for an outsider to instruct me in the theory of legal responsibility, but you see, *mon vieux,* although it is years since we have had any real talk together, I am rather obstinate in my adherence to ancient sympathies and enjoy letting out a little slack to you.

I think your "Defense of Pragmatism" an admirable piece of writing. Also it commands my full sympathy so far as I see. Its classification reminded me (in the freedom merely) of Patten's *Development of English Thought* — a most amusing and suggestive book — one of those that like your piece makes me say, "Give me the literature of the last twenty-five years and you may destroy the rest" (when I want to horrify the cultured). In general nowadays I would rather read sociology than philosophy; though I was interested by Santayana's four volumes, spite of their slight tendency to improvise; and though I devoted a certain time, the summer before last, to enough study of Hegel's *Logic* to enable me for the moment to say specifically what I thought the fallacies, and then dismissed it from my mind. Adieu. Yours ever,

O. W. HOLMES

P. S. I have just read your other paper,[2] also good. Your general line of thought has been used by protectionists — that protection unlocks energies and gets more out of men.

Washington, April 1, 1907

DEAR BILL, —

Thanks for the additional article[3] which I have read. We start from surprisingly similar premises, and our conclusions fit as opposites sometimes do. Your world is convex and mine is concave, but I don't see but you come out on the arbitrary as I do. That is, unless your *better for us* means what feels better, you still are defining truth by truth, which is like seeking the limit of space in terms of space. Starting with a feeling, and starting with a can't help, seem to me a good deal alike except in their implications. I am reminded by some things you say of an observation of mine to which I attach some value in the legal aspect. I say that truth, friendship, and the statute of limitations have a common root in time. The true explanation of title by prescription seems to me to be that man, like a tree in the cleft of a rock, gradually shapes his roots to

[2] "The Energies of Men," *Philos. Rev.,* XVI (1907).
[3] Second installment of "A Defense of Pragmatism," *Popular Sci. Mo.,* LXX (1907).

his surroundings, and when the roots have grown to a certain size, can't be displaced without cutting at his life. The law used to look with disfavor on the statute of limitations, but I have been in the habit of saying it is one of the most sacred and indubitable principles that we have; which used to lead my predecessor Field to say that Holmes didn't value any title that was not based on fraud or force. Yours ever,

O. W. HOLMES

TO JOHN C. H. WU

December 12, 1921

MY DEAR MR. WU,

Your very kind letter which comes this morning deserves an immediate answer, and luckily I have no case to write this week and am able to send one. By a coincidence, the moment I came upstairs to my library I had been talking about war with a guest who served in France. I am afraid that my talk was a little more sceptical than you would approve, perhaps because I am old and have seen many wars. It is shortly this. We all try to make the kind of a world that we should like. What we like lies too deep for argument and can be changed only gradually, often through the experience of many generations. If the different desires of different peoples come in conflict in a region that each wishes to occupy (especially if it is a physical region) and each wishes it strongly enough, what is there to do except to remove the other if you can? I hate to discourage the belief of a young man in reason. I believe in it with all my heart, but I think that its control over the actions of men when it comes against what they want is not very great. A century ago Malthus ran his sword through fallacies that one would have thought must die then and there, but men didn't like to believe him, and the humbugs that he killed are as alive as ever today. I will not go on with a subject which is rather a sad one.

I am glad that you have the opportunity to study in Paris. I am not well informed as to present conditions, but just before the late war, or a little earlier, the French seemed to me to be turning out masterpieces. Such were to my mind, Girard's *Manuel de droit romain*, and Giraud's *Histoire du droit français*. On your subject I am not well informed, but if the atmosphere is like that indicated by books such as I have mentioned, the world has nothing better. I mention only two books, but I might mention others that made a similar impression. I suppose Paul Viollet must be dead before this. Indeed, I talk like an old fogey who has not kept up with the movement of the world. *Que voulez-vous?* A man must accept limits, at least after eighty. He must accept Hegel's notion that one becomes a person only by determination, that is, by accepting limits. To be *this* is to be *not that*.

I have written to the Harvard Law Review to send you a copy of the number you asked for, if one is to be had. I am afraid that I cannot venture into the realm of self-criticism to which you invite me, but I may say that I think that what you say about Platonian and Aristotelian is pretty keen. The two little pieces, "Ideals and Doubts" and "Natural Law," indicate some of my starting points. I write amid many distractions and will not attempt to say more now, although I should like to. With every good wish to you, I am,

Sincerely yours,
O. W. HOLMES

April 1, 1923

MY DEAR MR. WU,

Your letter came just after I had written to the *Mich. Law Review* enclosing stamps for a copy of the number with your article. I have a glimpse of it elsewhere and was much pleased, but I have not received it yet. I will not undertake to discuss your German article for several reasons. I do not read the language very easily. I shall have to begin too far away, and I am absorbed in my work, so that I cannot do you justice with the time and strength at my command. You speak of going deeply into the philosophy of Hegel. Hegel impresses me as other Germans have done, as having had real and profound insights which remain and as having thought it necessary to make a system which I think as dead as other systems generally are in a hundred years. The summer before last (last summer I spent in the hospital) I reread the translation of his logic. When I first read it the only proposition that remained to me was that he could not persuade me that a syllogism could wag its tail. In other words his attempted transition from logic to life I think a humbug — subject to the judgment of those who know more about him than I do. So of his philosophy of law — *aperçus* that are flashes of lightning — a system for which I care nothing. That I summed up by saying that he could not persuade me that his King of Prussia was God. But after you have steeped yourself in him, I fear that you will think that I have been flippant and superficial. I love the enthusiasms that you feel — including that for me. It will grow less I fear as you grow older, but I trust that enough will remain to be a pleasant memory to you, when I am no longer above ground. I passed 82 since I last wrote to you. I have very little time to read, but the other day I read with pleasure the 4th volume of Salomon Reinach's *Cultes, Mythes, et Réligions,* that came out years ago but that I got only lately. I should think that he believed in Frazer's *Golden Bough* rather more than I should, but he is delightful, whether discussing some forgotten belief or God, or becoming polemic on the Inquisition and Catholicism. His free thinking makes his discourse more amazing and perhaps more picturesque. But you are too much occupied with philosophy to bother about him, I hope not too much to take pleasure in art. I have a hobby for etchings and engravings, especially old ones that I indulge (a very little). I have just bought one of Albert Dürer's copper engravings (I have a lot of his woodcuts that I bought during our Civil War), also a modern English etching that I like. But this is in the breathing space of an adjournment of the Court. The adjournment does not leave me idle, as I shall send to the printer tomorrow a dissent from the prevailing judgment in a case that interests me a good deal. So now adieu for the present. With every good wish for your successful study.

Sincerely yours,
O. W. HOLMES

May 14, 1923

MY DEAR MR. WU,

When you come to see me at Beverly Farms in the summer, we will, perhaps, try to twist the tail of the cosmos.

You make me chuckle when you say that you are no longer young, that you have turned 24. A man is or may be young to after 60, and not old before 80. But since last summer, although I feel much the same eagerness as ever, I have taken a step possibly I may get back again, but I doubt. I walk slowly and use an elevator to get to my library. When two years ago, except when I remembered that on general principles I ought not to, I went upstairs two steps at a time and at a run. However, it is true that in one sense a man is no longer young at 24. He has reached an age when his opinions are entitled to respect, when in a general way he is anybody's equal, when at least no one is entitled to bully him. If we meet, perhaps you will bully me, for I venture to have reserves, considerable reserves, on the Kantian philosophy, but I am no longer fresh in his terminology. Probably you will find as I do, that ideas are not difficult, that the trouble is in the words in which they are expressed. Every group, and even almost every individual when he has acquired a definite mode of thought, gets a more or less special terminology which it takes time for an outsider to live into. Having to listen to arguments, now about railroad business, now about a patent, now about an admiralty case, now about mining law and so on, a thousand times I have thought that I was hopelessly stupid and as many have found that when I got hold of the language there was no such thing as a difficult case. There are plenty of cases about which one doubts, and may doubt forever, as the premises for reasoning are not exact, but all the cases when you have walled up and seized the lion's skin come uncovered and show the old donkey of a question of law, like all the rest. . . .

Sincerely yours,
O. W. HOLMES

June 16, 1923

MY DEAR MR. WU,

. . . I am sorry at your disappointment about the Carnegie Fellowship, but it may turn out a blessing. The test of an ideal or rather of an idealist, is the power to hold to it and get one's inward inspiration from it under difficulties. When one is comfortable and well off, it is easy to talk high talk. I remember just before the battle of Antietam thinking and perhaps saying to a brother officer that it would be easy after a comfortable breakfast to come down the steps of one's house pulling on one's gloves and smoking a cigar to get on to a horse and charge a battery up Beacon Street, while the ladies wave handkerchiefs from a balcony. But the reality was to pass a night on the ground in the rain with your bowels out of order and then after no particular breakfast to wade a stream and attack the enemy. That is life. I hope that your interest in philosophy (and philosophy wisely understood is the greatest interest there is) will not lead you too far from the concrete. My notion of the philosophic movement is simply to see the universal in the particular, which perhaps is a commonplace, but is the best of commonplaces if you realize that *every* particular is as good as any other to illustrate it, subject only to the qualification, that some can see it in one, some in another matter more readily, according to their faculties. The artist sees the line of growth in a tree, the business man an opportunity in a muddle, the lawyer a principle in a lot of dramatic detail. Great as is my respect for Stammler I am a little afraid that he may tend to keep you too remote from daily facts. I noticed that he criticized my remark about experience and logic, I think I appreciate logic — see e.g. my *Collected Legal Papers* if you have time, p. 180, in *The Path of the Law,* but I am afraid that I should differ fundamentally as to the absolute value of his forms — but that goes back to fundamentals which it would take too long to write about. I don't believe or know anything about absolute truth. I hinted at my generalities in "Ideals and Doubts" and "Natural Law" in the same book. I noticed once that you treated it as a joke when I asked how you knew that you weren't dreaming me. I am quite serious, and as I have put it in an article referred to above, we begin with an act of faith, with deciding that we are not God, for if we were dreaming the universe we should be God so far as we knew. You never can prove that you are awake. By an act of faith I assume that you exist in the same sense that I do and by the same act assume that I am in the universe and not it in me. I regard myself as a cosmic ganglion — a part of an unimaginable and don't venture to assume that my *can't helps* which I call reason and truth are cosmic *can't helps*. I know nothing about it, but I am being led too far. I can only send you my good wishes and still hope that I may have a glimpse of you this summer.

Sincerely yours,
O. W. HOLMES

February 5, 1924

DEAR MR. WU,

Your letter finds me feeling a little feeble this morning and so I shall not write at length, glad as I am to hear from you. I hope you will not yield to the Bacon–Shakespeare mystics. It seems to me that Brandes was quite right when he pronounced the notion the product of American Demi-culture. I never have given the matter any great study but I have heard enthusiasts talk. It is one of many matters on which one must be governed by prejudices — preliminary judgments based on a knowledge admitted not to be exhaustive but on which at the peril of one's soul one has to act as life is short. If we have eternity I suppose it might be our duty to have an articulate answer to every imbecility that can be found from the words in the dictionary. Very likely I told you of William James once asking me why I did not join the society for psychical research. I replied why don't you study Mahometan religion. Millions of men think you will be damned if you don't join it, yet you don't bother. The answer is the same. We have to divine which is likely to be the highroad and which a *cul de sac*. We may be wrong but we have to take the risks. I put Bacon–Shakespeare and spiritualism into the same bag. I interrupted this letter to write as you desired to James Brown Scott. I don't know him well but was glad to write as it seems cruel that Stammler should be so poor.

I hope you won't forget my recommendation of Tocqueville's *Ancien Régime*. I think it was not to you but to Laski that I wrote *apropos* of the book that the men who teach us to disbelieve general propositions are only less valuable than those who encourage us to make them. It is merely as an illustration of the danger of obvious truths in politics that I recommend it. If I felt a little more comfortable (only a belly-ache) I should be perusing literature. I have won adorable leisure. I have read a little French and might conceivably reread *Faust* but I doubt if I shall.

Ever sincerely yours,
O. W. HOLMES

April 10, 1924

MY DEAR MR. WU,

. . . You interest me greatly by what you say about China and your plans. I am not likely to live to see how you work them out, but my hopes and prophecies go with you. Probably the direction of your efforts will be modified by your experience at home, but part of life is to feel a direction for effort before it is definitely and articulately known and to persevere with faith. That at least was my case. If I were dying my last words would be: Have faith and pursue the unknown end. I hope to see you before you go back but it seems a close fit, as we don't adjourn till June 9, and I suppose that we shall go to Boston two or three days later.

During the adjournment I had a little dash into the classics — a few hours turning over the pages of Seneca, finding one or two fine things, but rather long-winded moralizing. Some of Plutarch's Essays in the translation; a play of Plautus, rudimentary humors like the circus; and then two books of Tacitus's History, which I never had read. There is a man who could write. You care nothing for the events but he tells them so that you are absorbed — as the world knows, a master of pungent brevity. Then I wound up with Santayana's *Scepticism and Animal Faith*. I should think that our starting points are the same or very similar. But he pours out such a volume of charming but not too lucid words that the theme is almost lost in the variations and arabesques. It is agreeable literature but doesn't seem to me a book that will last. He has too an air of ironic superiority that seems to come from his having been a Catholic, and some categories of thought that seem to echo the same fact. I don't suppose that he can be recognized by the Church as a member, but he seems to keep the scheme for aesthetic delectation and to pity the Philistines who don't. But I get this from my general impressions from other books more than from this.

Now I am a law machine, and even the little time that I have taken for this is stolen from duty as I ought to be examining a case. When this sitting is over on May 5 I expect more leisure, I can't yet tell how much. Meantime, I send you my affectionate good wishes.

Sincerely yours,
O. W. HOLMES

January 27, 1925

MY DEAR WU,

It was a great pleasure and relief to get your letter. You had been silent so long that I had begun to fear that you were suffering from the troubles in China. I am so ignorant about them that I know not how far or to what way things affect you. The request for a cable and the mention of you gave me a chance to poke a message at you in the hope of evoking a return shot. I am much interested and a little surprised at the subjects of your teaching. I don't doubt you do more than half in setting your class on fire. When you do that you do the best and the rarest thing that a teacher can do. I used to say that Emerson's great gift was that of imparting a ferment. Of course teaching is a great way to learn.

As you say, there is no short cut to scholarship, nor is there to anything else in the way of achievement. I wish that I might know more of your circumstances if discretion does not require you to be silent. Your "this miserable world" makes me anxious. I imagine that you are at the time of life when the staying power of your enthusiasm will be most tried. For me at least there came moments when faith wavered. But there is the great lesson and the great triumph if you keep the fire burning until, by and by, out of the mass of sordid details there comes some result, be it some new generalization or be it a transcending spiritual repose. I am working away as usual. While we are sitting, each week is like the last. The assignment of a case or cases to be written comes after our conference on Saturday and then there is an intellectual spasm until I get opinions printed and distributed, usually by Tuesday or Wednesday mornings and then a lapse into relative repose, although there is always something to be done. I may send you one or two of the latest just as samples. I have no time to read seriously except in the adjournment when I profit by having written my cases as they come along. For the next leisure I have bought a book by F. H. Bradley — *Essays on Truth and Reality* — as some people think he is the first English philosopher since Hume. I always have shied away from him doubting if he would say much to me, and I still doubt, but after talking with my friend Cohen I concluded I ought not to die without knowing something of him. In the summer and after I made a few excursions into literature and philosophy, including laboring with a dictionary through the first volume of a stimulating humbug of a book, *Der Untergang Des Abendlandes*. At least I thought it need not be taken too seriously. And with reasonable profit I read two volumes published by the *Encyclopedia Britannica*, "These Eventful Years," giving a pretty good account of the War from all sides — the economic question, the new nation, and even something as to the science, art and literature of the country. I took it as a compensation for my failure to read the newspapers and felt as if I had done something to catch up.

I must stop, because as usual there are other things I must attend to, but I repeat that I was delighted to hear from you and send you all good wishes.

Ever sincerely yours,
O. W. HOLMES

March 26, 1925

MY DEAR WU,

As I have said I haven't been good for much beyond my duties in the last fortnight, my duties and the dentist. So I have read nothing but a few French plays. A week ago I took a flying look at Ovid whom I never have read and who I think can wait. Age increases my conviction that one cannot afford to give much time to the classics. Some time, yes. But one needs to enlarge and enrich one's view of life and the universe. The ideas of the classics, so far as living, are our commonplaces. It is the modern books that give us the latest and the most profound conceptions. It seems to me rather a lazy makeshift to mumble over the familiar. I was saying this to a lady the other day and she said where do you get such a scheme of life as in the New Testament? I replied that I didn't believe the economic opinion there intimated and that to love my neighbor as myself did not seem to me the true or at least the necessary foundation for a noble life, that I thought the true view was that of my imaginary society of the jobbists, who were free to be egotists or altruists on the usual Saturday half holiday provided they were neither while on their job. Their job is their contribution to the general welfare and when a man is on that, he will do it better the less he thinks either of himself or of his neighbors, and the more he puts all his energy into the problem he has to solve. I have said this a thousand times before and I ought to apologise for repeating it, but it comes home to me afresh from time to time. It is what I think best men believe although they often suppose that they believe something else that they hear on Sundays. I wish I loved my fellow men more than I do, but to love one's neighbor as oneself, taken literally, would mean to realize all his impulses as one's own, which no one can, and which I humbly think would not be desirable if one could. Do not imagine from what I said above that I am not well now. I am, though languid, through the season and perhaps also from age. When I have a case to write I am all there, but when it is over I incline to lie down and often to sleep. I hope to see another birthday on the Bench, but I am a little slack about improving my mind in the interests of work. I send you all possible good wishes, and hope and expect that you will get satisfaction out of life, in spite of your speaking of it as if it were a miserable business. One sometimes feels so, but we know nothing of its ultimate significance, if the cosmos knows the significance. If it doesn't, it is because it is bigger than that. For it has significance in its belly.

Ever sincerely yours,
O. W. HOLMES

May 30, 1925

MY DEAR WU,

Ever since your letter came a few days ago, it has been a weight on my mind that I should disappoint you. Your exalted feeling for me adds to my anxiety. If I had stopped work, perhaps I should not feel so, but as I am still in harness I feel an added apprehension that the future may change your opinion of the past. However it is foolish to write this last as long as one is in the battle and must take the chances, and thus far all has gone well.

We have been very busy and I have read little. The Chief sent me the other day a rather charming book by Morgan about John Morley, with a portrait in the front that reminded me of Newman by a look of holiness. But perhaps that very thing indicated what I have felt in reading Morley in former years, that he missed the fierce electric high light. He is very civilized and rational, and for all his being an agnostic he lives in the atmosphere of those who believed more than he did. But I used to think that in his world Harriet Martineau was the Virgin and John Stuart Mill the prophet. It is so long however since I read any book of Morley's that perhaps I should change my judgment now. Nothing else except an excellent little study of the history of trade-marks, and a few of Pliny's Letters, always good reading. He quotes a friend of his: It is better to be idle than to do nothing — *otiosum,* I suppose more accurately to enjoy leisure, but I like the paradoxical form.

With very good wishes, I am always
Sincerely yours,
O. W. HOLMES

Beverly Farms, Massachusetts
July 21, 1925

DEAR WU,

. . . Since the latter part of June I have been at my regular summer abode with my work done and seemingly at leisure, but leisure always is busy even though I get considerable time to motor about on this beautiful and interesting Capetown and intervals of slumber. A letter of Laski's led me to take up Sainte-Beuve's *Port Royal* — 5 stout volumes — and it filled my spare time until lately. I don't like Ste.-Beuve and apart from Pascal and some pages given to Racine and Moliere, the book deals with the actors in an almost forgotten theological controversy, about which I care nothing, and but for Laski's wise discourse I should feel as if I rather had wasted my time. I had a brief counter-irritant in a book called *Post Mortem* by a doctor which opened a promising view by suggesting medical explanations of the conduct of some famous characters. He thinks Henry VIII had the pox and that Joan of Arc is more or less accounted for by suppressed *menses*. Per contra, he thinks Napoleon was *not* epileptic. A good deal of the short volume I didn't care for. Now I am on a stout octavo of Laski's writing — A Political Grammar — just received and just begun. I fear that I shall not agree with it as much as friendship would make me wish to. I hardly think of man as so sacred an object as Laski seems to think him. I believe that Malthus was right in his fundamental notion, and that is as far as we have got or are likely to get in my day. Every society is founded on the death of men. In one way or another some are always and inevitably pushed down the dead line. I think it a manifest humbug to suppose that even relative universal bliss is to be reached by tinkering with property or changing forms of government so long as every social improvement is expended in increased and unchecked propagation. I shall think socialism begins to be entitled to serious treatment when and not before it takes life in hand and prevents the continuance of the unfit. In answering you, above, I neglect to say that I think you are right in devoting yourself to what you call cultural achievement. A new and valid idea is worth more than a regiment and fewer men can furnish the former than can command the latter. Also I have on hand typewritten chapters of the *Life of Lincoln* on which my neighbor ex-Senator Beveridge is at work. After that I hope for some literature and real leisure. I go back to Washington at the end of September and expect to be much refreshed, though I left in better condition than some of the others. I am relieved to infer that you are able to keep on notwithstanding the disturbances of which I hear only an echo.

Affectionately yours,
O. W. HOLMES

Beverly Farms, Massachusetts
September 6, 1925

DEAR WU,

... The papers now speak of me as the Venerable Justice, and when I pass 85 next March, if I do, as seems likely, I suppose I should be called a very old man. My reason tells me not to expect much now, although my feelings still have some of the illusions of youth.

... I have been reading old books this summer with an exception for my friend Laski, *A Grammar of Politics* — I don't agree with its premises or conclusions, and only partially with its aspirations; but he writes for England about which I cannot speak. Just now I am finishing the *Odyssey*. I read it rather slowly even with a translation alongside. It has suggested some reflections to me — too long to put on paper — but I have been surprised to find that it gave me very considerable pleasure. My excursions into the past are interrupted occasionally by my neighbor Ex-Senator Beveridge with some chapters of a life of Lincoln that he is writing. If he has patience to finish it, I think it will be *the* Life — and show the rise of a great figure out of the primitive ooze. Also for two hours I drive and motor about this beautiful and interesting region, which I am sorry that you did not see. One may gaze over lonely cliffs upon the seas or pass along smooth boulevards by crowded beaches, or skirt windswept downs and fine inland farms, or evoke the past by visiting houses built two centuries and a half ago. That is not long for China but it is long enough for romance. I say that all society is founded on the death of men. Certainly the romance of the past is. So much so that the memorial tablets of a great war have the effect of two centuries added. I could run on for a good while, but I must stop. I send you my affectionate best wishes and am,

Sincerely yours,
O. W. HOLMES

May 5, 1926

MY DEAR WU,

... As to Taylor's note 126, *Faust* Part II, of course you refer to Goethe's suggestion concerning our permanent existence and W. von Humboldt *ad idem*. I hesitate a little to speak freely because of my impression as to your beliefs or hopes, but I will say a few words. I think men even now, and probably more in Goethe's day, retain the theological attitude with regard to themselves even when they have given it up for the cosmos. That is, they think of themselves as little gods over against the universe, whether there is a big one or not. I see no warrant for it. I believe that we are in the universe, not it in us, that we are part of an unimaginable, which I will call a whole, in order to name it, that our personality is a cosmic ganglion, that just as when certain rays meet and cross there is a white light at the meeting point, but the rays go on after the meeting as they did before, so, when certain other streams of energy cross, the meeting point can frame a syllogism or wag its tail. I never forget that the cosmos has the power to produce consciousness, intelligence, ideals, out of a like course of its energy, but I see no reason to assume that these ultimates for me are cosmic ultimates. I frame no predicates about the cosmos. I suspect that all my ultimates have the mark of the finite upon them, but as they are the best I know I give them practical respect, love, etc., but inwardly doubt whether they have any importance except for us and as something that with or without reasons the universe has produced and therefore for the moment has sanctioned. We must be serious in order to get work done, but when the usual Saturday half holiday comes I see no reason why we should not smile at the trick by which nature keeps us at our job. It makes me enormously happy when I am encouraged to believe that I have done something of what I should have liked to do, but in the subterranean misgivings I think, I believe that I think sincerely, that it does not matter much. This is private talk, not to be quoted to others, for one is shy and sensitive as to one's inner convictions, except in those queer moments when one tells the world as poets and philosophers do. I am writing under difficulties for want of time, and because the great English Strike fills me with sadness and apprehension. I am wondering if my friends there will suffer and whether that noble people is facing ruin. This, like our other ups and downs is but for a little while in world history, but the moment has its right to sorrow, however much one may look beyond. I hope I shall live to see you here or in the country. It gives me joy to have your affection and to anticipate fine things for you.

Ever sincerely yours,
O. W. HOLMES

Beverly Farms, Massachusetts
August 26, 1926

MY DEAR WU,

Your letter comes none too early. For with my ignorance of conditions in China I had begun to feel anxious. It is most consoling to hear that everything is going well with you, and it touches and delights me that your affection has not grown dim with time and absence. I come at once to your essay. But I begin with a preliminary. Since I last wrote, I think, I have read Stammler's book. I don't want to run the risk of repeating what I may have said before and therefore will only say a word. I did not find it instructive. I liked your appendix better than anything else in it. The body of the book seems to me to elaborate the obvious in scholastic language or maintain propositions that I don't believe. And I can't help feeling that the German method of over-systematizing has too much influence on you. To name the most august, Kant's and Hegel's systems seem to me to have gone into the waste-paper basket. They each had profound *aperçus* here and there, and these were their real contributions, and the world would have been less bothered and bored if they had stopped with them. You may remember Schopenhauer's remark that of Kant's categories cause and effect was genuine and the rest was blind windows put in for architectural effect. How I hate to say anything discouraging to you, but I do not perceive in what you have written anything likely to influence profoundly, as you expect, the development of legal science. Perhaps your phrase legal *science* indicates the beginning of our divergence. Formerly at least you were inclined with your German teacher to believe in *a priori* ultimates. I don't, except in the limited sense of human *can't helps* in the way of thinking, which may or may not have cosmic validity. I don't believe that it is an absolute principle or even a human ultimate that man always is an end in himself — that his dignity must be respected, etc. We march up a conscript with bayonets behind to die for a cause he doesn't believe in. And I feel no scruples about it. Our morality seems to me only a check on the ultimate domination of force, just as our politeness is a check on the impulse of every pig to put his feet in the trough. When the Germans in the late war disregarded what we called the rules of the game, I don't see there was anything to be said except: we don't like it and shall kill you if we can. So when it comes to the development of a *corpus juris* the ultimate question is what do the dominant forces of the community want and do they want it hard enough to disregard whatever inhibitions may stand in the way. If a given community has a definite ideal, for instance, to regulate itself so as to produce a certain type of man, other communities would have a different one — and that community might change in a hundred years. But suppose the ideal accepted, there would be infinite differences of opinion as to the way in which it was to be achieved, and the law of a given moment would represent only the dominant will of the moment, subject to change on experiment or for deeper reasons. But I am beginning too far back. You assume a body of law in force and start to formulate the principles of juristic development. I should think the only principles worth talking about were the existing notions of public policy. How those notions have changed and still change I don't need to illustrate to you. I can't say that I find much illumination in the thought that analogy and hypothesis are used for justification in the law and for explanation in physical science. Supposing it is true it does not seem to me to tell much, and personally I should not speak of justification which presupposes an absolute criterion, whereas I should think that the only problem was: does this decision represent what the lawmaking power must be taken to want. Taking it this way, you may say, your distinctions still are valid. I am willing to assume it but I do not see that they reveal anything helpful or new. It seems to me to be superfluous systematizing and hashing. That decisions follow earlier decisions that are not identical on the ground that the policy implied covers the present case is well known. The process is understood and I don't see what is gained by a new ticket upon them. That the consequences are to be weighed is equally familiar. I always should be sorry if I could not get any reason more definite than in consonance with our sense of justice, but whether it was that or some more definite policy (*i.e.* lawmaker's desire) to be derived from statutes or earlier cases, the consideration of consequences is a most familiar basis of argument. I think the word juralogical is bad — it unites a Latin (*Jus*) with a Greek (*logos*) root. I should rather think, if used, it should be jurilogical, and I hardly see the need of it. I omit some remarks on the notes that occurred to me — they show your learning. I shall send the paper to Pound for his judgment, for it very well may be that he will see more than I do in the work. I repeat that I hate to write discouragingly, but you ask me to give you a serious opinion and *ich kann nicht anders.* If the essay had not taken all the discourse I should talk about Höffding's *History of Modern Philosophy* which I have been reading with pleasure and add a few words as to why I think what he and his like call the "problem of evil" a humbug and putting the problem in the wrong place.

I shall ask Pound to write either to you or to me after reading your essay, and I shall be very glad if I see you again, but we both must remember that I am eighty-five.

Ever sincerely yours,
O. W. HOLMES

January 27, 1927

MY DEAR WU,

Your letter gives me the happiness that you anticipated in telling me that you have been appointed Judge of so important a Court. To have everything exactly as I could have wished I should like you to have had a little experience in practice, but you will get hold of the actualities, and that is what I want to see happen to you. I would much rather see you deciding cases and realizing how the law takes hold of people in life than continuing to speculate before you have taken in a lot more raw material. You write as if you might be Mr. Emerson in Concord and refer in no way to disturbed conditions in your country. It may be philosophical abstraction. It may be that they do not affect you. The echoes that I hear make me a little uneasy on your account, but I hope that there is no real ground for apprehension. I am as ignorant as a child about it.

At your suggestion I read Dewey's *Experience and Nature.* I began it sceptically in spite of what you said, but I agreed with you. I was very much impressed by it, although it seemed to me as badly written as possible. I could not have given an account of any page or chapter and yet he seemed to me to have more of our cosmos in his head than I ever had found in a book before. I think I may read it over again in the effort to render my knowledge articulate. You seem to me right in calling it a great book. I haven't much else to report in the way of reading. Professor Redlich dined here the other night — a very agreeable and interesting man — and told me to read Gilbert Murray's volume of Essays — called *Tradition and Progress* — which I have done with pleasure. He has taken the time to live into the classics and his reverence and enthusiasm are contagious. If I have the time I am expecting, I shall read a play of Euripides and a little Ovid. I suspect somehow a want of the hard steel underneath in Gilbert Murray but he thinks and perceives and takes life in a lofty way, and writes I might almost say charmingly. In the main I have been listening to arguments and turning out decisions — one or two involving interesting points of theory — the average having no more than the interest that every decision has, but that is considerable to the one who writes them.

How should I address you on a letter? The Hon'ble or Prof. I shall stick to the latter until you tell me that you are established. In between 6 and 7 weeks, if I count right, I shall be 86. I remember my father, when he was younger than I am (indeed he did not live to quite my present age), saying "the time will come when you will hold me up to the light and see the light through me (that is from the thinness of age) but I shall not know it." I feel something of that self-distrust of age, but not enough to discourage me from keeping on. I once thought, perhaps you remember, that you would have got over your present feeling for me before this. I am proud that you have not and am confident now that however you may change in the future you will remember your old friend in a way that would not give him pain if he knew it. It proves your constancy more than my merit but it is very encouraging and touching.

Affectionately yours,
O. W. HOLMES

Beverly Farms, Massachusetts
June 21, 1928

MY DEAR WU,

... As you see, the term has finished and I am in the country with relative leisure. It has been a very busy eight months, hardly a half hour when I didn't feel that there was something waiting to be done. I have written more dissents than I liked to this term, but they are dissents from decisions that I regretted and as to which I felt deeply. I am reading a very interesting book — Parrington's *Main Currents of American Thought* which I find full of instruction as to the intellectual history of the country from the very beginning, but displeasing to me from a sort of dogmatic implication of the obvious connection of views that I don't share. He seemingly has followed the suggestion of Beard that really the adoption of the Constitution was due to the moneyed interests and I don't readily give up the belief that Washington and the rest had for their dominant motive a patriotic desire to see a powerful nation take the place of squabbling states. If the change helped their investments, I should suppose that it was because they invested in the belief that what they thought best would come to pass, not that they talked patriotism because they had invested. Also, if there is a form of speech for which I have less sympathy than another it is talk about "exploitation," as a hostile characterization of modern commercial life, and an implication that dominant brains are to blame. I think it is drivelling cant and I have a standing war with my dear friend Laski, as to his passion for Equality, with which I have no sympathy at all. Yet in my youth I was an abolitionist and shuddered at a Negro Minstrel Show, as belittling a suffering race and I am glad I was and did. Well, my dear boy, I could ramble on if you were here, but this is enough for writing, especially as there are those who say that my Ms. is [not] good to read. I tell my brethren when they complain that they ought to go to a night school. Awaiting for the news.

Ever sincerely yours,
O. W. HOLMES

Beverly Farms, Massachusetts
July 1, 1929

MY DEAR WU,

A good letter from you comes today and I like your talk in it, except that I am more than surprised at what you say about Ehrlich although your criticisms may be just. I thought one book of his about the best of modern books on legal subjects. I am tickled by the "healthy sense of justice" business. I have said to my brethren many times that I hate justice, which means that I know if a man begins to talk about that, for one reason or another he is shirking thinking in legal terms.

Cardozo I am sure that I should really love if I knew him better. I not only owe to him some praise that I regard as one of the chief rewards of my life, but have noticed such a sensitive delicacy in him that I should tremble lest I should prove unworthy of his regard. All who know him seem to give him a superlative place. I have seen him but once, and then his face greatly impressed me. I believe he is a great and beautiful spirit. These things still interest me, but I regard myself substantially as finished. You may have heard before this of the death of my wife, which not only takes away a half of my life but gives me notice. She was of the same age as I and at 88 the end is due. I may work on for a year or two, but I cannot hope to add much to what I have done. I am too sceptical to think that it matters much, but too conscious of the mystery of the universe to say that it or anything else does not. I bow my head, I think serenely, and say as I told some one the other day, O Cosmos — Now lettest thou thy ganglion dissolve in peace.

I hope that I shall live to see you here.

Yours always,
O. W. HOLMES

March 14, 1932

MY DEAR WU,

Thank you for your letter. I have been wondering about you and whether things were going well. I can't give you an adequate answer because writing has become difficult to me. I have no other reason than 91 years. Perhaps you know that shortly before my last birthday I resigned my seat on the Bench. I am well but don't want to do any work at present. My secretary reads to me some philosophy and economics but more modern stories. With a daily drive and long hours in bed, calls made upon me and some necessary letters, I find my hands full. Frankfurter was quoted the other day for a suggestion that I might write a book about the law. I can think of a first sentence, but after that I should like to study and I doubt if I shall study any more. At all events I mean to take life easy for a time.

Since I began this I have had a call from Cardozo. I think you would love him as I do and have from the first moment I saw him — a beautiful spirit.

Affectionately yours,
O. W. HOLMES

Thanks also for the article which seems to me good.

TO LADY POLLOCK

Beverly Farms, *August 12, 1895*

DEAR LADY POLLOCK:
While I was taking my lesson some friends of mine walked by and with them a girl with a roving eye who seemed to take more notice than the usual tame bird. So the next day, to wit, after beginning this letter, I strolled up to my friend's house and soon was at it hammer and tongs with m'mselle. Of course she had been brought up in London, though of an American mother. You may say what you like about American women — and I won't be unpatriotic — but English women are brought up, it seems to me, to realize that it is an object to be charming, that man is a dangerous animal — or ought to be — and that a sexless *bonhomie* is not the ideal relation. I always say you can get your tragedy of any desired length in England, from thirty seconds to a lifetime. I had one adorable one of twenty-nine minutes by the watch. At the end of that time I started for my train. Woman I'd had a glimpse of in London — walk. She sat on a style, I below her, gazing into her eyes — then, "remember this lane," "while memory holds its seat, etc." "Adieu." And I still do and ever shall remember her, and I rather think she does me a little bit. What imbecilities for an old fellow to be talking. But if one knows his place and makes way for younger men when he isn't sure, it is better perhaps not quite to abandon interest in the sports of life. . . .

Your affectionate friend,
O. W. HOLMES

TO SIR FREDERICK POLLOCK

Boston, *Feb. (September?) 23, 1902*

DEAR FRED:
I am just back from this week's circuit and must vent a line of unreasoning — rage I was going to say — dissatisfaction is nearer. There have been stacks of notices of me all over the country and the immense majority of them seem to me hopelessly devoid of personal discrimination or courage. They are so favorable that they make my nomination a popular success but they have the flabbiness

of American ignorance. I had to get appreciation for my book in England before they dared say anything here except in one or two quarters. There were one or two notable exceptions. And now as to my judicial career they don't know much more than that I took the labor side in *Vegelahn v. Guntner* and as that frightened some money interests, and such interests count for a good deal as soon as one gets out of the cloister, it is easy to suggest that the Judge has partial views, is brilliant but not very sound, has talent but is not great, etc., etc. It makes one sick when he has broken his heart in trying to make every word living and real to see a lot of duffers, generally I think not even lawyers, talking with the sanctity of print in a way that at once discloses to the knowing eye that literally they don't know anything about it.

Believe me I am not exaggerating.

The legal periodicals are generally in vacation. I hope some one of them may have an intelligent word, but you can understand how at a moment of ostensible triumph I have been for the most part in a desert — when I hoped to see that they understood what I meant, enough not to bully me with Shaw, Marshall and the rest. If I haven't done my share in the way of putting in new and remodeling old thought for the last 20 years then I delude myself. Occasionally some one has a glimpse — but in the main damn the lot of them. This is a confidential ebullition of spleen to an intimate which will do me good. I ought to be doing other things but first stopped for a moment to unpack my heart.

Yours,
O. W. H.

Washington, *May 25, 1906*

Dear Pollock:

... I have finished my (presumably) last case and am free to answer at once. Brooks Adams sent me the book you mention and Bigelow also wrote to me about it.[1] I acknowledged it at once with necessary excuses but read it later and felt the same embarrassment that you do. Bigelow is a good and most creditable creature,

---

[1] In Holmes's Journal for 1906 appears, "*Centralization and the Law* [1906] (Melville M. Bigelow, Brooks Adams *et al.*)." A brief account of Adams' early association with Holmes and Bigelow may be found in Adams' "Melville M. Bigelow," 1 *Boston University Law Rev.* 168 (1921).

but you must have noticed before now that he never hits the first rate and that at times he assumes an air of significance hardly warranted by the facts. I couldn't see that he had anything important to say. Brooks Adams I still find it hard to formulate with confidence of justice. I have known him from boyhood. I have found him more suggestive than almost anyone, generally with propositions which I don't believe, and yet I still don't quite know what to say or think. He will hand you out a statement with an august air, and you can't tell whether it is the result of ten years' study or a fellow told it to him just before he met you — or for the matter of that whether you didn't tell it to him yourself within half an hour. Whatever matter he is interested in, generally a question of property, a brief history of the world winds up with his solution. I imagine that dissatisfaction with the treatment of Spokane, where he had land, has stirred him up on the rate bill, and you hear the echo of his grievances in his first chapter.[2] This of course can't be said. I thought his customary picture of a class gradually rising through self protection to knocking the one previously dominant in the head was amusing and not without stimulating power. On the other hand I think his talk about the world being slaves to the man who commands the necessaries of life, rot. If Jim Hill (the great railroad man) does not follow the economically necessary course he comes to grief. I remember what a very able man who made a fortune on the Stock Exchange once said to me. "They talk about our leading the procession — we only *follow it ahead* like little boys. If we turn down a side street it doesn't." Under modern conditions the crowd presents the inevitable to itself as the fiat of some great man, and hates him, but it is very silly. Brooks at present is in a great stir and thinks a world crisis is at hand, for us among others, and that our Court may have a last word as to who shall be master in the great battle between the many and the few. I think this notion is exaggerated and half cracked. But I don't read the papers or otherwise feel the pulse of the machine. I merely speculate. My hobby is to consider the stream of products, to omit all talk about ownership and just to consider who eats the wheat, wears the clothes, uses the railroads and lives in the houses. I think the crowd now has substantially all there is, that the luxuries of the few are

[2] The first of the two lectures by Adams was entitled "Nature of Law: Methods and Aim of Legal Education."

a drop in the bucket, and that unless you make war on moderate comfort there is no general economic question. I agree however that there are great wastes in competition, due to advertisement, superfluous reduplication of establishments, etc. But those are the very things the trusts get rid of. But I am wandering far afield. I think I should damn with faint praise — recognizing the streak of suggestiveness in B. A. and the unpretentious virtues of Harriman (who is original in his book on Contract) and Haines.[3] I still have not read your notes to Maine because since they have arrived I have been constantly loaded with work. I have read a part with the expected pleasure and profit, and ever recurring wonder at your accomplishments. . . . We adjourn next Monday. Dinner to Brown,[4] who retires, on the 31st & then freedom and Beverly Farms as soon as we like — one of the first days in June. . . . It has been a satisfactory year, although I have had comparatively few cases that had a very general interest. There is always the fun of untying a knot and trying to do it in good compact form. By the by — I ought to tell you that in *Commonwealth* v. *Pierce*,[5] cited on p. 432 of *Torts*, 7th Ed., I struck out "personal equation or" to please some one or more of my brethren, before the case went into the reports,[6] although it was printed with the words in some of the periodicals, I think *Amer. Law Register,* e.g. I got them in however in *The Germanic,* 196 U. S. 589, 596.[7] One of time's revenges. . . .

Yours ever,
O. W. HOLMES

---

[3] Edward A. Harriman's lecture was entitled "Law as an Applied Science"; the paper by H. S. Haines, "An Object-Lesson in Extension: Rate Making," was the final lecture in the volume.

[4] Henry Billings Brown.

[5] 138 Mass. 165, 176 (1884).

[6] At the page to which Holmes refers, Pollock had quoted from Holmes's opinion in *Commonwealth* v. *Pierce:* "If a man's conduct is such as would be reckless in a man of ordinary prudence, it is reckless in him. Unless he can bring himself within some broadly defined exception to general rules, the law deliberately leaves his *personal equation or* idiosyncrasies out of account, and peremptorily assumes that he has as much capacity to judge and foresee consequences as a man of ordinary prudence would have in the same situation." (Italics added.)

[7] In discussing negligence in *The Germanic,* Holmes, for the Court, said, "The standard of conduct, whether left to the jury or laid down by the court, is an external standard, and takes no account of the personal equation of the man concerned."

Washington, *February 26, 1911*

DEAR POLLOCK:

Leonhard sent me his essay.[1] He translated my book into German but found trouble in getting a publisher. I believe he has lectured on it. But I have not done more than glance at his discourse as I don't read German as easily as you do. I wrote to you apropos of your contribution. The few odd minutes I have had to spare I have given to Plato, recurring to his *Symposium* after fifty years; with a translation alongside I find the Greek easy. My successive reflections have been these: How natural they talk. But it is the "first intention" common to the classics. They have not a looking glass at each end of their room, and their simplicity is the bark of a dog, not the simplicity of art. But they seem to say things that no human being really would say and think. But that criticism shows how small a part of the field of human possibilities any one man realizes. On the other hand, platitudes. But is not this simply an illustration of the flatness of an original work when it has wrought its effects and been followed by centuries — millennia — of development, so that we take for granted what it took a man of genius to say? More specifically, just as Christianity is taken to have brought a new note of love into the world, was not Plato the first to make articulate the high idealizing that we recognize as the best thing in man? No doubt the divine gossip — Aristophanes hindered from discoursing by the hiccups — and Alcibiades more or less drunk describing Socrates — have done much toward floating the dialogue down to us, but is there not a more portentous significance in it, of the kind I mention? I am not quite sure. When I have finished it I may reach conviction.

If I didn't believe that socialism rested on dramatic contrasts and not on a serious consideration of what changes it could be expected to make in the nature or distribution of the stream of products, I should listen to it with more respect. But the argument never gets much farther than look at the big house and the little one. It never becomes quantitative, asking how much does the tax levied by the rich for the pleasures of the few amount to. Also

---

[1] Presumably, Rudolf Leonhard, "*Ein Amerikanisches Urteil über die Deutsche Besitzlehre*," in *Festschrift Otto Gierke* (1911), p. 19. The essay was concerned with Holmes's discussion of possession in his *Common Law*. Pollock apparently had mentioned that essay and other matters in a letter which is missing.

it never proposes to begin by taking life in hand, which seems to me the only possible starting point for an attempt at social renovation. κ. τ. ν. . . . .

Yours ever,
O. W. H.

I shall be 70 March 8! but I probably have said it more than once as it impresses one.

Washington, April 5, 1919

DEAR POLLOCK:

. . . I am glad that the hitches in Jack's coming over are coming to an end. You know that I have sympathized with you both, but I didn't dare to write while you were in doubt. I am beginning to get stupid letters of protest against a decision that Debs, a noted agitator, was rightly convicted of obstructing the recruiting service so far as the law was concerned. I wondered that the Government should press the case to a hearing before us, as the inevitable result was that fools, knaves, and ignorant persons were bound to say he was convicted because he was a dangerous agitator and that obstructing the draft was a pretence. How it was with the Jury of course I don't know, but of course the talk is silly as to us. There was a lot of jaw about free speech, which I dealt with somewhat summarily in an earlier case — *Schenck* v. *U. S.* . . . also *Frohwerk* v. *U. S.* . . . As it happens I should go farther probably than the majority in favor of it, and I daresay it was partly on that account that the C. J. assigned the case to me.

Your mention of Boethius made me want to get it but our book sellers in this one horse place no longer keep the Loeb series. I believe I have mentioned before what a shame I think it that such a good plan should be so spoiled by not giving critically accurate translations. As to Harlan's qualified concurrence in *Kawananakoa* v. *Polyblank,* that sage, although a man of real power, did not shine either in analysis or generalization and I never troubled myself much when he shied. I used to say that he had a powerful vise the jaws of which couldn't be got nearer than two inches to each other.

For the moment my work is done and I hope for a little leisure during the next week. I propose to devote it first to Laski's new book *Authority in the Modern State,* which he dedicates to me and Frankfurter. Do you know anything about him in Oxford? People in Boston [1] seem to have got the idea that he is a dangerous man (they used to think me one). I don't know whether because he is inspired by Figgis [2] more or less in his discourse on sovereignty or because (as I am told) his wife has written some come-out or subversive articles — I know not what. I have had the greatest pleasure in his conversation as he is a portent of knowledge though still very young. There is also a prejudice against Frankfurter; I think partly because he (as well as Laski) is a Jew. I believe him to have been very valuable as a stimulus in the Law School,[3] but Boston is nothing if not critical. It never occurs to me until after the event that a man I like is a Jew, nor do I care, when I realize it. If I had to choose I think I would rather see power in the hands of the Jews than in the Catholics', — not that I wish to be run by either. I have let the League go its way without much study. I have my hands full and am too old and too busy to take a part, and futile worry is waste.

I got a rattling good French book on Rembrandt's etchings the other day — *Coppier,* the author.[4] Just now I am looking a gift horse in the mouth and trying to ascertain whether an Ostade is first, second, or third state: also I read with great interest Rhodes's *History of the Civil War* — a real work of art I think — although I hate to read about those times and read this only because his sister sent it to me. My love to Lady Pollock.

Yours ever,
O. W. H.

Washington, *May 26, 1919*

MY DEAR F. P.:

What an aggravising (a good child's word) cuss you are! To give me your admirable aphorisms and leave me — me who have so little time here to read anything but records — to guess what

---

[1] Laski was a lecturer and instructor in History at Harvard University, 1916–1920.

[2] Rev. John Neville Figgis (1866–1919). Figgis, a distinguished churchman and political philosopher, was largely concerned with the conflicts between church and state, and was insistent upon the value and significance of the independence of church from state.

[3] Felix Frankfurter had been appointed Professor of Law at the Harvard Law School in 1914.

[4] André Charles Coppier, *Les Eaux-Fortes Authentiques de Rembrandt* (1917).

inspired them. I haven't the slightest idea. I *have* just read Marvin, *The Century of Hope,* an interesting conspectus of the modern period inspired by a rather deeper belief in the spiritual significance of man than I am able to entertain and a consequently greater faith in the upward and onward destiny of the race. But the note of hope is the best for achievement and so the book seemed to me worth writing and reading. Laski suggested it to me and then sent to me Graham Wallas's *Life of Francis Place* which I have begun. Until I read the first mentioned volume I am afraid I never heard of Place. . . . To recur to your aphorisms and to avoid a possible misinterpretation of my criticism of Marvin: I fully agree to the *nulla in Deo Vanitas* — in the sense of the little article that I sent to you some time ago.[1] I only don't believe, i.e. have no affirmative belief, that man was necessary to God in order to find out that he existed (if the cosmos wears a beard, as to which I have no opinion). It seems to me probable that the only cosmic significance of man is that he is part of the cosmos, but that seems to me enough.

Brandeis the other day drove a harpoon into my midriff with reference to my summer occupations. He said you talk about improving your mind, you only exercise it on the subjects with which you are familiar. Why don't you try something new, study some domain of fact. Take up the textile industries in Massachusetts and after reading the reports sufficiently you can go to Lawrence and get a human notion of how it really is. I hate facts. I always say the chief end of man is to form general propositions — adding that no general proposition is worth a damn. Of course a general proposition is simply a string for the facts and I have little doubt that it would be good for my immortal soul to plunge into them, good also for the performance of my duties, but I shrink from the bore — or rather I hate to give up the chance to read this and that, that a gentleman should have read before he dies. I don't remember that I ever read Machiavelli's *Prince* — and I think of the Day of Judgment. There are a good many worse ignorances than that, that ought to be closed up. I don't know how it will come out. The spring here is enchanting. Since the last sentence I have been over in Georgetown with my wife and had a glimpse of the park — noble oaks — the air full of the smell of box and roses and

---

[1] Presumably his "Natural Law," 32 *Harv. L. Rev.* 40 (1918); *CLP* 310. (Included above, p. 394.)

what Bob Barlow[2] once called the yelling of birds. Really if a glance at the *New Republic* had not thrown the customary gloom over life it would seem fair once more. With which I close my potato-trap — for speech — to open it again to take in luncheon. . . . My work is done for the moment and there can't be much more of any sort before vacation.

Yours ever,
O. W. HOLMES

Washington, *February 9, 1921*

DEAR F. P.:

A good letter from you, just after reading *Theodore Roosevelt & His Time,* a class of work that I eschew. Of course I pretty well made up my package about him a good while ago, and I don't think I was too much disturbed by what you admit to and what was formulated by a Senator in his day, thus: "What the boys like about Roosevelt is that he doesn't care a damn for the law." It broke up our incipient friendship, however, as he looked on my dissent to the *Northern Securities* case as a political departure (or, I suspect, more truly, couldn't forgive anyone who stood in his way). We talked freely later but it never was the same after that, and if he had not been restrained by his friends, I am told that he would have made a fool of himself and would have excluded me from the White House — and as in his case about the law, so in mine about that, I never cared a damn whether I went there or not. He was very likeable, a big figure, a rather ordinary intellect, with extraordinary gifts, a shrewd and I think pretty unscrupulous politician. He played all his cards — if not more. R. i. p.

Hohfeld was as you surmise an ingenious gent, taking, as I judge from flying glimpses, pretty good and keen distinctions of the kind that are more needed by a lower grade of lawyer than they are by you and me. I think all those systematic schematisms rather bores; and now Kocourek in the *Illinois Law Rev.* and elsewhere adds epicycles — and I regard him civilly but as I have written don't care much for the whole machinery. I even doubt the profit of the terminology of rights (the hypostasis of a prophecy); as Hohfeld used to crack me up naturally I thought well of him, but his industry was not of a kind that I should give much time to. I took another flying glimpse at your man Vinogradoff's new

[2] Robert Shaw Barlow, Boston lawyer and personal friend of Holmes.

book.[1] It gave me the impression of the Chinaman who ran three miles to jump over a hill — but I just looked, yawned and passed on.

Well, my Frederick, shortly after you receive this I shall have turned the eighty corner. I was so much pleased with a notice by Cohen of my book in the *New Republic*[2] that I thought I might do up the past into a package — have it insured by Cohen as valuable and pass the residue of my life in such amusement as I could find. But the moment you turn a corner you see another straight stretch ahead and there comes some further challenge to your ambition — were it only that, that I probably have mentioned to you from my youth, of being carried in a civic procession as a survivor! My love to Lady Pollock.

Yours ever,
O. W. HOLMES

I take *Punch*.

Washington, April 2, 1926

MY DEAR POLLOCK:

It is a month from the date of your last letter and must be two or three weeks since I sent a bulletin.

I was overwhelmed with letters, telegrams, and papers on and after my birthday, and they with my work drove me to the limit of my powers. I was surprised and no little pleased at some of the articles. But that is over now and for the rest of this and next week I am as near the feeling of leisure as I am likely to get. I need it and mean to be as idle as I can. The only book I read, at odd minutes, is Horace Walpole's Correspondence — just the thing for such moments. He once in a while is surprisingly ahead of his beef-eating contemporaries, and his style is so pleasant that one can read on indefinitely without fatigue. For all round, I think you might put him at the head of English letter writers, of course Charles Lamb is more pungent and has more genius, and very possibly Byron whom I don't remember so well, but take the world he tells you about and the way he tells it, I think one could read him longer with undiminished pleasure. But, oh, my dear Pollock, I began talking about leisure and since I began this letter

[1] *Outlines of Historical Jurisprudence* (Vol. 1, 1920).
[2] Holmes's *Collected Legal Papers* was reviewed by Morris R. Cohen in 25 *New Republic* 294 (Feb. 2, 1921).

three opinions have come in that I must read carefully, and a man has called to jaw with me about writing something to be engrossed on parchment and put under a corner stone! (a decent chap though) and one of my brethren is coming later, and I have a polite letter from Belgium with a signature that I can't read but concerning which I must consult the Belgian Embassy. I may say with Betsy Prig — leisure, I don't believe there's no sich a person. Even when I am ready to be idle I say to myself what duty am I neglecting? I turn to your last letter. I think I met your brother in former days but I knew only his name. You speak for the need of a certain modicum of intelligence for justice. It seems to me that the whole scheme of salvation depends on having a required modicum of intelligence. People are born fools and damned for not being wiser. I often say over to myself the verse "O God, be merciful to me a fool," the fallacy of which to my mind (you won't agree with me) is in the "me," that it looks on man as a little God over against the universe, instead of as a cosmic ganglion, a momentary intersection of what humanly speaking we call streams of energy, such as gives white light at one point and the power of making syllogisms at another, but always an inseverable part of the unimaginable, in which we live and move and have our being, no more needing its mercy than my little toe needs mine. It would be well if the intelligent classes could forget the word sin and think less of being good. We learn how to behave as lawyers, soldiers, merchants, or what not by being them. Life, not the parson, teaches conduct. But I seem to be drooling moralities and will shut up and go up to the Belgian Embassy as I said. My love to Lady Pollock.

Yours ever,
O. W. H.

Beverly Farms, June 20, 1928

MY DEAR YOUNG FREDERICK:

It is good to see your handwriting again and to welcome you back from your youthful larks — my time for them has gone by. The fatigue of Washington to Boston and Boston to Washington is enough for me, and I walk very little. I am interested by what you tell of Charybdis and the truant Scylla. I dissented in the case of tapping telephone wires. The C. J. who wrote the prevailing opinion, perhaps as a rhetorical device to obscure the difficulty, perhaps merely because he did not note the difference, which perhaps I should have emphasized more, spoke of the objection to the evidence as based on its being obtained by "unethical" means (horrid phrase), although he adds & by a misdemeanor under the laws of Washington.[1] I said that the State of Washington had made it a crime and that the Government could not put itself in the position of offering to pay for a crime in order to get evidence of another crime. Brandeis wrote much more elaborately, but I didn't agree with all that he said.[2] I should not have printed what I wrote, however, if he had not asked me to. I am reading an able book: Parrington, *Main Currents in American Thought*, which gives a very interesting picture, or rather analysis, of the elements at work from the beginning. But I shall not easily believe the thesis running through it and started by earlier works of Beard (*An Economic Interpretation of the Constitution*, etc.) to the effect that the Constitution primarily represents the triumph of the money power over democratic agrarianism & individualism. Beard I thought years ago when I read him went into rather ignoble though most painstaking investigation of the investments of the leaders, with an innuendo even if disclaimed. I shall believe until compelled to think otherwise that they wanted to make a nation and invested (bet) on the belief that they would make one, not that they wanted a powerful government because they had invested. Belittling arguments always have a force of their own, but you and I believe that high-mindedness is not impossible to man. The result is that I am not taking unmixed pleasure in one of the ablest and most instructive books that I have read for a long time. I have brought with me Bertrand Russell's *Philosophy*, but that must wait till I have finished Parrington's second volume. I have let in a little sweetness and light by reading *en passant, But Gentlemen Marry Brunettes*, a sequel to *Gentlemen Prefer Blondes*, with which perhaps you improved your mind. But sexual talk or innuendo is displeasing from a woman, I

---

[1] *Olmstead* v. *U. S.*, 277 U. S., p. 466. (See above, p. 359.)

[2] In his dissenting opinion Justice Brandeis stated that the tapping of telephone wires and the use of evidence so obtained violated the constitutional provisions against unreasonable searches and seizures (4th Amendment), and against compelling a person in a criminal case to become a witness against himself (5th Amendment). Holmes in his dissent said: "While I do not deny it, I am not prepared to say that the penumbra of the 4th and 5th amendments covers the defendant, although I fully agree that Courts are apt to err by sticking too closely to the words of a law where those words import a policy that goes beyond them."

think. Perhaps because we know, though the older literary tradition is the other way, that they take less interest in the business than we do. We have been here a week and a half and are settling into our routine, the main event a motor drive of two hours, which is about my limit. (I interrupted myself here to write to the Clerk to send you the opinion and dissents in the above mentioned case if he still has copies.) Please give my love to Lady Pollock. I rarely see anyone but am happy in solitude. Most of the places here now to me are sockets from which the occupants that I knew have been extracted by the final dentist.

Yours ever,
O. W. H.

. . . The Prayer Book is a mystery that I do not touch.

Washington, April 21, 1932

MY DEAR POLLOCK:

Probably you will have returned from your I hope successful trip to and on the Mediterranean. I envy you, but I am being happily idle and persuading myself that 91 has outlived duty. I can imagine a book on the law, getting rid of all talk of duties and rights — beginning with the definition of law in the lawyer's sense as a statement of the circumstances in which the public force will be brought to bear upon a man through the Courts, and expounding rights as the hypostasis of a prophecy — in short, systematizing some of my old chestnuts. But I don't mean to do it or to bother about anything. We are reading Spengler, *The Decline of the West,* a learned, original book, written with incredible German arrogance, and not in all believed by me, but wonderfully suggestive — an odious animal who must be read. A lot of other stuff is being waded through and I am lightly skipping through the little book on Marcel Proust.[1] The cherry trees around the Potomac basin have been as beautiful as ever but probably are near their end. My love to Lady Pollock.

Yours ever,
O. W. H.

[1] Leon Pierre-Quint, *Marcel Proust* (1925, translated 1927).

3. Last Words

Holmes was graceful and epigrammatic to the end. On his resignation from the Court, his more than ninety years did not prevent him, in his letters to his colleagues who had sat with him and the members of the Bar who had argued cases before him, from turning a phrase and placing a punchline as effectively as ever. Some months before he resigned he agreed to take part in a celebration of his ninetieth birthday and spoke from his home over the radio. "To live is to function," he said. ". . . 'Death plucks my ears and says, Live — I am coming.'" I have thought it best for these words to close this volume. It is worth noting that in his three last utterances the figures Holmes uses for life are the sun's course, a Japanese picture, the arrow in the chase, the horse race, fire. "We live by symbols," Holmes once said, and the symbols he used were not without meaning. The race, the chase, the sun, the flame, the picture that does not end with the margin — these come closer than any words of our own could to delineating Holmes from the inside of his mind and faith.

"GOLD TO THE SUNSET"

Supreme Court of United States [1]
Washington, D. C.
January 12, 1932

MY DEAR BRETHREN: —

You must let me call you so once more. Your more than kind, your generous, letter touches me to the bottom of my heart. The long and intimate association with men who so command my respect and admiration could not but fix my affection as well. For such little time as may be left for me I shall treasure it as adding gold to the sunset.

Affectionately yours,
OLIVER WENDELL HOLMES

[1] In response to a letter from his Supreme Court colleagues on his resignation.

THE ARROW IN FLAMES

Washington, D. C.
February 29, 1932

GENTLEMEN OF THE FEDERAL BAR ASSOCIATION: —

Your kind invitation for March 8 has been answered, I believe, in due form. But I cannot say Farewell to life and you in formal words. Life seems to me like a Japanese picture which our imagination does not allow to end with the margin. We aim at the infinite and when our arrow falls to earth it is in flames.

At times the ambitious ends of life have made it seem to me lonely, but it has not been. You have given me the companionship of dear friends who have helped to keep alive the fire in my heart. If I could think that I had sent a spark to those who come after I should be ready to say Goodbye.

O. W. HOLMES

"DEATH PLUCKS MY EARS"[1]

In this symposium my part is only to sit in silence. To express one's feelings as the end draws near is too intimate a task.

But I may mention one thought that comes to me as a listener-in. The riders in a race do not stop short when they reach the goal. There is a little finishing canter before coming to a standstill. There is time to hear the kind voice of friends and to say to one's self: "The work is done."

But just as one says that, the answer comes: "The race is over, but the work never is done while the power to work remains."

The canter that brings you to a standstill need not be only coming to rest. It cannot be while you still live. For to live is to function. That is all there is in living.

And so I end with a line from a Latin poet who uttered the message more than fifteen hundred years ago:

"Death plucks my ears and says, Live — I am coming."

[1] March, 1931: A radio talk on the occasion of a national celebration of his ninetieth birthday.

Holmes Revisited: An Afterword Essay

1

An author is lucky to have the chance to revisit as early a book as this one, and to get his licks in once again. I gathered these utterances of Justice Holmes and wrote prefaces for them half a lifetime ago when I was instructing the young at Williams College in constitutional history. At forty, in 1943, I was already a veteran of the passions and actions of the New Deal constitutional wars. Whatever impulse incited me to these labors, I recall the excitement that sustained me in grappling with the character and thinking of so enigmatic a figure.

The original version of one's work—if it amounts to anything—is always a hard act to follow. As I reread the book the thing of wonder to me is my youthful brashness in daring to plan a venture a third of whose pages comprised my comments on the two-thirds that were Holmes's. Given his magisterial brevity, my prefaces to his opinions were often longer than what they prefaced. It was, I fear, a case of the context swallowing the text. What saw me through it was the effort to present a total rather than a specialized view of Holmes—to integrate the personal journey with the professional and intellectual, the mind and character with the style, the strengths and vulnerabilities of a thinker with his impact on history.

Happily the book had a sturdy life over the years, enduring the constitutional tumults that tested its viability. The occasion for republishing it is also an occasion for reviewing the scholarship of the intervening years, taking the measure of Holmes again, charting afresh the stages of his constitutional journey and the trajectory of his reputation, rethinking his relevance for an America almost a half-century after his death.

In the case of a federal judge his constitutional journey[1] starts well before his actual decisions, with the early history and the turning points in the ideas that bear directly on them. Slow step-by-step growth may be part of the story, but also the creative leaps—mutations, as it were—which are at times all but inexplicable.

The seminal period for Holmes was the triad of the Civil War, the law school student years, and the long days and nights spent writing his formative essays for the *American Law Review*. They were the source from which the river of legal history began its strong flow for him. Holmes was twenty-one when he was first wounded at Ball's Bluff. He was in his late thirties when he began to write *The Common Law*—unillusioned, sceptical, stoic, yet with a deep fire of insight and purpose.

During his years of intense study he shaped the leading ideas he put together in the *Common Law* lectures—the anthropology, history, economics, psychology, the deep experiential and pragmatic thrust, the epigrammatic style, the shying away from certitudes and absolutes, the legal philosophy that he saw (in Voltaire's phrase) as "history teaching by example."[2]

We have the sense in reading his letters to Pollock and Laski that Holmes did everything with an easy grace. Yet his years of early labor suggest that it was a hard-won grace. He spoke later of the "icy night" that enveloped him in the harsh law school years, which must have seemed a continuance of the Civil War traumas, on other battlefields, with other enemies. Holmes had in those years something like Yeats's knotty "fascination with what's difficult." He later gave the impression of a conjurer's capacity to untie the knots, presto, or to cut through them with a swift decisiveness. But he had prepared the ground in his years of ordeal. Compared with the disciplined mastery he had to achieve early, everything after that was made to seem easy.

The Common Law, which he completed at age forty, was thus the deftly prepared turning point that made everyone take him seriously as a comer. It forked off into two roads that were swiftly opened to him—as legal scholar and professor and as State Supreme Court judge. Like Robert Frost, another Yankee of ribbed words, Holmes could not take both. He chose the second, I suspect, because it enabled him "to think for action upon which great interests depend." It is tantalizing to speculate about where the road not taken might have led.

Holmes never wrote another book. Yet in his two Court tenures, of twenty and thirty years, he wrote a sheaf of opinions that led to his becoming in time a kind of judicial Philosopher-King, somewhat disdainful of the crown he wore with an amused tilt—but he nonetheless wore it.

2

In my commentary on the State Court opinions I drew a distinction between the Holmes of private and of public law. I might have made it sharper. His public law opinions formed a transition to his Supreme Court views, especially in his deference as a judge to majoritarian decisions of legislative bodies. But the reputation he achieved on both courts thrust his earlier importance for private law into the shadow. We all worked and wrote in that shadow.

What we missed was the shift in Holmes's private law thinking under the nitty-gritty testing of his State Court duties. As a scholar he had been an intellectual radical, like his friends in the "Metaphysical Club," and was influenced by the positivist science of the time. It added a strong conceptual strain to his pragmatic inclinations. It didn't negate his recoil from formalism and from the heavy constrictions of philosophical idealism. But it made him willing to apply standards and strike principled approximations to resolve the hardest problems of legal thinking.

If the conceptual Holmes survived the State Court experience it was in a considerably altered state. He still aimed at clear principles and an "external standard," whether in torts, contracts, or property law. But the dividing line between the clashing sets of social desires was more blurred in action than it had been in the scholarly cloister. He couldn't fall back on the "not unreasonable" legislative bodies, as he did in public law. Nor was he willing to rely on the judgment of juries beyond their findings of fact. He saw no certainties in the competing social interests that clustered around every case. He saw instead a shadowy continuum that led to something like an "uncertainty" principle. He had to draw a line somewhere, however, make a choice between "irreconcilable desires"— and thereby play something of an activist role in "making law."

It must have been a chastening experience for him, but also a growth experience. It was in these years that he moved decisively from the law as a set of rules linked with "rights" or "duties" or moral imperatives to the law as a prediction of what the courts will operatively do. This led him inevitably into the depths where certainties as well as logics dissolved and where at times arbitrary choices had to be made. A half-century later (as G. Edward White notes) the efforts to dig into Holmes's importance as a private law thinker led to "a larger rediscovery of the history of private law."

Meanwhile Holmes led a relaxed life, took vacations in Europe, read French novels, corresponded widely—and waited for the Godot of the coveted prize. We tend to see a kind of inevitability in his progression to the summit. Yet it was a near thing, hanging on the hairbreadth of Henry Cabot Lodge's reassuring response to Theodore Roosevelt's anxiety. Holmes had become Chief Justice of the Massachusetts Court by the 1900 term and was attracting national attention. But he was already sixty-one when the choice was made, and he wouldn't have been *papabile* much longer. A lot of history would have come out differently if T.R. had insisted on a "safer" man.[3]

3

This emphasis on law as what the courts will actually do led ineluctably to a focus on the judge himself and the workings of his mind—articulate or not, conscious or unconscious. There are hints of this in his State Court opinions—this journey into the interior of a judge's mind—but the flowering came soon after he reached the Supreme Court.

It is clearest in his *Lochner v. N.Y.* dissent (1905), which created a new jurisprudence—one of self-awareness of a judge's unstated philosophical premises and his social priorities. It led to the recognition of the need to come to terms with this underlying set of personal premises, at the peril of "playing God" with judicial lawmaking.[4]

It was a turning point in Holmes's intellectual journey but also in that of successive generations of students. I read the dissent as a graduate student in the mid-1920s, as did my generation. It created a school of "legal realism" in the law school culture later in the 1930s. Yet little note has been taken of its strategic aspect from 1905 to the New Deal attacks on the Court in the mid-1930s.

Holmes was on polite terms with his Court brethren, but their succession of rigid decisions furnished the laboratory in which he developed his strategy for meeting and overcoming them. He was a solitary fighter, and had no one to talk with until Brandeis came to the Court in 1917. Brandeis brought a sociological jurisprudence with him from his Populist progressive years, and he documented the new "felt necessities" of the time. But Holmes dug deeper, into the hidden logic of the "unarticulated major premise" that underlay the conservative lawmaking, and also into the fears and commitments that shaped the priorities of judges like the formidable Justice Peckham who wrote the Court opinion in *Lochner*.

This led Holmes to his doctrine of "judicial deference." The important fact about it was that it brought all of Holmes's insights together and served as a strategic weapon in the doctrinal wars for generations. I don't say it was all calculated. I do say that without Holmes's shrewd conceptualizing capacity it would not have happened that way or that soon.

In his address on John Marshall, with its guarded praise, Holmes asserted that his influence lay in being *there* at a strategic point in the campaign of history.[5] We can turn his remark about and see that it was true of Holmes as well. He was *there*, exactly when a Court of resourceful conservatives was creating a set of doctrines—notably "liberty of contract" and "due process of law"—to protect an archaic property system against its challengers.

We all declaimed and wrung our hands over these indignities. Yet it devolved on Holmes to bear the burden of contriving an equally resourceful doctrinal strategy to counter them. He achieved it with the concept of judicial deference to reasonable legislative majorities. By the mid-1930s and their constitutional battles we were calling it "judicial restraint" and using it against the "judicial supremacy" of the conservative Court majority.

In Holmes's relations with the liberal law school professors the ardor was all on their side, and it increased with his decisions and dissents on free trade in ideas. He saw these opinions of his as meditations on how to reconcile the clashing imperatives of speech—of a nation seeking to guard its very existence and of the same nation striving to retain its soul by refusing to quench the fires of competing ideas.

Holmes was not one of the "First Amendment voluptuaries" (as Alexander Bickel has dubbed them), drunk with an absolutism that sees only one of the imperatives. Holmes saw both and picked his way warily between them. To have moved in a brief period from the majority "clear and present danger" test of *Schenck v. U.S.*, to the majority opinion upholding the *Debs v. U.S.* conviction, to the ringing *Abrams v. U.S.* dissent was in itself a daring and scrupulous journey. Holmes performed his conceptual differentiations between them with a scalpel-like precision and couched them in quicksilver phrases that still dance and live in the memory of every constitutional scholar. The final product was his own, yet this was one phase of his journey where a notable dialogue took place, involving exchanges with (among others) Brandeis, Laski, and especially Learned Hand.[6]

4

Much has been written on the "apotheosis" of Holmes by the "legal realists" of the 1930s and more generally by the New Deal liberals. As an unchartered member of both groups I can bear witness that the charge of our "hero worship" and "mythmaking" is overdone. I had few illusions, either in the book or the *Nation* and Law Review articles that preceded it, about Holmes as a liberal. We knew that he was an economic, social, and neo-Darwinian conservative and that his judicial doctrine—however powerful a strategic weapon it proved—was based on an intellectual austerity that few of us as combatants in the liberal wars could muster. Holmes never walked on water for us. There was no liberal canonizing of him as there was of Brandeis and supremely of Franklin Roosevelt.

Of the principal "Realists," Karl Llewellyn was poetic about Holmes because that was his style, but he was also sophisticated in his insights; Walton Hamilton saw his importance, but he was astringent about "dating Holmes"; and Thurmond Arnold was caustic about everyone, not excluding Holmes. Only Jerome Frank was a bit excessive in his often quoted final chapter (in *Law and the Modern Mind*) about Holmes as a paradigm of a "mature man."

For a time the Realists were fascinated by Holmes. They needed him more than he needed them. He was the symbol that gave cohesion to them as a "school." It was a passing phase. They have regrouped since, found other symbols, rallied behind more exotic causes, under other banners.[7] Even when they marched to the same drum, neither Holmes nor they allowed themselves to be diverted from their own campaign of history.

Holmes left the Supreme Court just as the New Deal entered history. They barely bowed to each other in passing, although the White House and many of the new agencies were staffed by Holmesians. It was well that Holmes was no longer on the Court during FDR's attacks on the "Nine Old Men": had he stayed he would have been the oldest—and the wisest. The Court-packing plan would doubtless have been anathema to him, as it was to Brandeis and Hughes. Yet Holmes's opinions not only laid a base for attacking judicial supremacy; they also furnished a rationale for accepting legislative social experiments like the New Deal and validating an executive power adequate to the nation's survival.

Holmes could not have known—nor could I—that the Roosevelt constitutional revolution of the 1930s would first enshrine and then undermine his reputation. The trajectory of the rise and fall—and rise again—of the Holmes heritage is a richly theatrical chapter in the history of ideas. It has had echoes in the legal scholarship and is worth tracing for its ironies and paradoxes.

Broadly put, the Holmes legacy flourished in the 1930s, tottered in the 1940s and 1950s, collapsed in the 1960s and early 1970s, and revived in the later 1970s and 1980s. These vagaries of his reputation, curiously, had less to do with his constitutional doctrines than with his larger philosophy and indeed with the perceptions of his character. Most of all they were governed by what was happening in the law school culture as it watched the Roosevelt Court and its successors and responded to the pressures of the larger political culture. Holmes became part of history, and the story of his reputation is a story of the ways in which a dominant legal elite deploys the uses of history.

5

In retrospect the most radical thing about my book was its title and therefore its central theme—that Holmes possessed not only a striking mind but a unique faith. This was heresy at the time and became even greater heresy during the decades when he was under attack. Is it possible (his critics asked) that this agnostic, sceptic, Darwinian had a faith? Yet the faith informs his thinking, which cannot be studied without it.

We must not forget that his core experience was the near encounters with death in the Civil War when brother fought and killed brother, each convinced of the rightness of his cause—a conviction that Holmes came to call a "fighting faith." He knew that time withers every faith but also knew that we need it as a symbolic mode of giving meaning to life in an uncaring universe. His "can't helps" represented a way of coming to terms with the urgency of ultimate and absolute truths. It was as far as he was willing to go toward universal as well as unique patterns, and he made them personal, not general.

The liberals came to see Holmes as a disembodied mind, lacking compassion for the welfare of his fellows, unwilling to use his judicial gifts to elevate their condition. Yet to see him thus is to miss the point of the Holmes enigma. Compassion was not one of his prime values, but neither was force—certainly not the force of the state. Competition and struggle were the essence of life, death was its sanction, and faith transcended both.

Hence the "dark" quality that many have seen in Holmes. The attack was only in part on doctrinal grounds. It was largely characterological. Paradoxically it united the liberal Left, which dominated the legal culture, with the catholic and traditionalist Right, which had its own agenda of opposition to Holmes—the doctrine of "natural rights." For a time both Left and Right found common ground in seeing Holmes as a strange creature—the Left depicting his as a cold, uncaring spectator, the Right as a savage pre-Hitler totalitarian.

There is little question that there was in fact a side of Holmes that was extraordinarily detached from the everyday pressures and urgencies of life. Only a warrior who had been through the battles and had experienced death as closely as Holmes could be so consistently "above the battle." There was an archetypal Jungian "shadow" in Holmes that not only furnished his dark side, but also gave him his rocklike strength of character and his steadiness of vision.

True, his death experiences also left a scar on his life perception, making him less open to humanist thinking, so that he made short shrift of any liberalisms other than free trade in ideas, and wrote too much off as "uplift." Edmund Wilson, writing in the early 1960s, spoke of "the carapace of impregnable indifference to current pressures and public opinion" that marked Holmes. G. Edward White, in 1971, wrote of his "articulated refusal to take pride in being human," which made him "the least heroic of America's heroes."[8]

Had Holmes lived longer, all this would have throughly disqualified him from membership in the Warren Court. It kept Holmes from being proudly and generously accepted, even during the recent decades of his "revival." But to ask for a Holmes with these added "enlightened" and "progressive" qualities would miss the point of the total Holmes and how his critical life experiences had made him what he was. They account for the flaws in his thinking but account also in part for the strength both of his mind and faith.

One gets in Holmes the sense of life and death entangled with each other in an *agon* without end. He didn't use Eros and Thanatos as his symbols for it, unlike Freud, who wrote after another war as he came to recognize the role of death. Both men, strikingly, went through a similar experience of starting with a positivist belief in the science of their day, getting fascinated by the hidden agenda of the mind, and moving ever closer to the dark imperatives of the instinctual drives expressed in life and death.

6

If Holmes fell from grace as an idol of the liberal Left, he was anything but a darling of the conservative, traditionalist, and moralist Right. How could they not oppose him? His positivism and realism enabled him to define law operatively without recourse to the dimension of "ought" that conservative as well as liberal moralists have found indispensable. In bringing the "bad man" into his theory of law Holmes used the adjective almost wryly to mean, matter-of-factly, whatever got him entangled with the law's sanctions. As a young editor he read all the Continental theorists of "natural law" and "natural rights," including the windy ones—and rejected them. Natural law was too static and absolute for an evolutionary thinker who knew how the conception of "nature" had changed over the ages. The breezy authority with which Holmes dismissed a whole phalanx of weighty scholars made him all the more exasperating.

I had to confess myself somewhat troubled, in my original prefaces, by the gap I found in Holmes's thinking: "Holmes did not adequately bridge the gap between [his] two worlds. There was in him a deep conflict between scepticism and belief, between mind and faith, between a recognition that men act in terms of a cold calculation of interests, and a recognition also that they are moved by symbols . . ." I added that his effort "to take account of both strains . . . was not wholly successful," but that it stretched him into becoming "a full-statured person," more than he would have been if he had restricted his energies "to the narrow confines of one or the other partial view."[9]

I still hold this a viable view, although I shall add some further reflections below on the "natural rights" (rather than "natural law") philosophy of both Left and Right.[10]

When Holmes left the bench, in 1932, it was not yet clear how any coalition war effort against Hitler might fare. There had been premonitory scholarly articles, from 1941 to 1943, mostly by Jesuit legal thinkers, on Holmes as forerunner of the ideas of Hitler, Göring, Goebbels, and Himmler, but it was left to Ben Palmer, in the year the war ended (1945), to put the same thesis in a popularized form, yielding to the alliterative seduction of his title, "Hobbes, Holmes and Hitler." Admitting that Holmes "did not go around like a storm trooper, knocking people down," he nevertheless saw Holmes as a source of "totalitarian" philosophy.

The controversy raged through the rest of the 1940s and the 1950s, engaging more time and verbiage than it deserved. It also evoked some necessary reassessments of Holmes's evolutionary approach to legal philosophy, which he had always put more nakedly—almost perversely—than he had to. What happened to Holmes's legacy, starting a decade after his death, came with a fantastic irrelevance out of the full revelation of the Holocaust, which would have been as alien to him as he to it.

We see the roots of Nazism more clearly now. They had nothing to do with the Hobbesian doctrine of sovereignty nor with Holmes's legal pragmatism. They shed a cruel light on the German intellectual tradition of a Europe in which Nazism emerged and flourished. One has to ask what good the centuries of French Enlightenment and German "natural law" thinking did when it came to confront the radical evil of Hitler. Holmes never had a love affair with either of them. Nor has

Hannah Arendt's foray into the Enlightenment thinkers, on the intellectual origins of totalitarianism, tempered the continuing criticism of Holmes. The critics have not taken adequate account of the role of "social engineering" strategies and fantasies, both Right and Left, in the genocides of Hitler and Stalin.

There is a key passage in Holmes in which he concludes that he is "in the universe," not the universe in him—that he is therefore not God in it and disdains to "play God" in shaping the destinies of others in the same universe. In a deep sense, his working theory of judging was grounded on this metaphysic.

The liberals who found Holmes and his gnomic language so engaging in the 1920s and 1930s did so not because they liked all his judicial outcomes and his philosophy, and certainly not because of his metaphysic. They were willing to overlook his departures from their liberal ideal in his *Schenck* and *Debs* opinions because they fixed on *Abrams*, *Gitlow*, and *Schwimmer*. They too lived by symbols, and Holmes was for them a symbol of resistance to the reactionary Court majority, a symbol also of enlightenment on the Bill of Rights, and—in the case of the Realists—a symbol of a down-to-earth willingness to reckon with the here and now that they equated with a kind of liberal modernism. As with love and marriage, their disillusionment with him came out of their initial illusions. When they looked closer and found that this wasn't the love object that had once enchanted them, they recoiled more strongly.

As it happened, their recoil (like that of the "natural law" conservatives) came at the war's end, in the mid-1940s. It lasted for some thirty years, mounting during the Warren 1960s. The dynamics of the recoil are not analyzed clearly in the accounts of it in the legal literature. In the 1940s and after, a series of generations came into the law schools sharply different from the constitutional generation I knew in the 1920s and 1930s. The true key to their change was the succession of activist Supreme Courts, starting with a Court appointed almost entirely by Franklin Roosevelt. Behind this in turn is the story of the political cultures that we call the New Deal, the Fair Deal, the New Frontier, and the Great Society, and their impact at once on the Supreme Court members and on the law school culture that served as their support system.

Despite Holmes's half-century of judging, including thirty years on the Supreme Court, his impact on constitutional law proved narrower than seemed likely in the early 1940s. The *Holmesian moment*—if we may call it that—was his burst of creative fire between *Lochner* in 1905 and the free-speech cases in the early 1920s. The fact that many of his great opinions in this period were dissents is witness to Holmes's fate in having to spend his best years on a Court whose majority saw him as marginal to the judicial culture of the time. In fact, this brief spell saw the mature harvest of the great sowings in his hungry young years and the years of manhood on the State Court.

Aside from the force of his basic decisional philosophy, Holmes's doctrinal resourcefulness in sheer constitutional terms was not great. On that score it didn't match Justice Hugo Black's on the Roosevelt Court or the doctrinal fertility of the later Warren group. The reason is clear enough. The burden of Holmesian thinking was to define the judicial power narrowly and set limits to it. The burden of the later activist thinking of the Roosevelt and Warren Courts was to expand the judicial power, and to that end a doctrinal fertility was an imperative.

After Holmes's retirement in 1932 the Holmesian moment continued its brief triumph, in "a little finishing canter before coming to a standstill"—the horserace metaphor he used in his ninetieth birthday.[11] It lasted as long as his strategic legacy was useful in helping to fight the anti-New Deal decisions and later to validate the New Deal legislation. But with the first Roosevelt appointments to the Supreme Court in the closing 1930s the new masters of the Court no longer needed the Holmesian doctrine. After that it stayed alive until the Warren Court, but only as an element of contention in the great feud between two Court factions. The impetus of the new *Zeitgeist* succeeded in ending the Holmesian moment.

7

The nature of this *Zeitgeist* is worth some probing for the light it sheds on what happened to the Holmes legacy and why. The episode of Holmes's meeting with Franklin Roosevelt has a symbolic importance. Flanked by FDR's intimate, Felix Frankfurter, and Holmes's former law clerk, Tom Corcoran, the President-elect visited the ancient Justice. Asked later what he thought of his visitor, Holmes replied, "A first-rate temperament, a second-rate mind." Whether Holmes was right or not, the episode was premonitory of the collision between the Holmes legacy and the New Deal. Holmes was wide of the mark in one respect. This "second-rate mind" was resourceful enough to use Holmes's judicial strategy, and then became impatient of it and exploded in the militancy of the "Court-packing"[12] plan. Roosevelt ended by appointing a Supreme Court that fused the expanded executive power with a new liberal judicial activism.

There were powerful minds and personalities on the Roosevelt Court, clearly the ablest in American Constitutional history. No one's *epigoni*, they were masterful men in their own right. The most talented of them came out of the assertive New Deal political culture. They were *novi homines*, a new, aggressive breed of political men: an Alabama redneck from Clay County who became a brilliant lawyer and Senate militant; a Jewish immigrant from Austria who worked with FDR in World War I and whose law students planned and staffed half the New Deal administrative agencies; a farm boy from Yakima, Washington, who became a law professor and ran the Security Exchange Commission; a Buffalo lawyer who skipped law school and became FDR's creative Attorney-General.

These four men, forming as vivid a core for a Court as any we have seen, became involved in a doctrinal feud that continued into the Warren Court. Hugo L. Black and William O. Douglas found the Holmes legacy both irrelevant and obstructive to their aims, while Felix Frankfurter and Robert H. Jackson used it still as a strong, shaping, decisional force.[13]

They all strove to be resourceful tacticians in their doctrinal maneuvers. Of the first pair, Douglas had the less original mind, distracted by sprawling interests that went beyond law to a liberated philosophy of life, both private and public. He tended to follow Black's doctrinal leads, combining them with an adherence to Brandeisian concepts, including notably the "right of privacy," which was to prove expansive in later Courts.

Next to Holmes, Hugo Black may prove to be the strongest, most original judicial mind since Holmes. His aim was to translate the New Deal revolution into constitutional law, and he succeeded. Largely an autodidact, he used historical excursions (not always accurate) to discover the original intent of the Fourteenth Amendment in order to enlarge its impact. He built a bridge between a literalist absolutism on civil liberties and an expansionism of social protections, using historicism, the "incorporation" doctrine, "equal protection," and the Establishment clause. His writing had a crude power in place of style but he was a constitutional warrior in the Roosevelt, Vinson, and Warren Courts, with an unmatched doctrinal creativeness.

Felix Frankfurter had a richer, more intricate, more complex mind than Black or any Justice since, and his style reflected it. His problem was that he was overprepared for his Court role. He had lived too many lives when Roosevelt named him to the Court—as reformer and professor at Cambridge, as Brandeis's alter ego, as Holmes's most fervent adherent, as FDR's close friend and adviser on every issue of state. He was Faustian, reaching out to all his competing hungers, while Holmes was Lucretian, with a long view of how the evolutionary gods play with human destinies.

In terms of internal mental struggle Frankfurter was the central dramatic figure of the Court's history—a neo-Holmesian at heart, striving to reconcile the Holmes legacy of a constrained judicial doctrine with his commitment to a strange mixture of Brandeisian and New Deal social progressivism. It made for great intellectual theater and resulted in some remarkable (if unpopular) opinions in which he balanced the conflicting pulls on a perilous edge of decision. Yet it couldn't overcome the thrust of social forces that sustained Black's views. In the end, in his historic meeting of minds with Chief Justice Warren in *Brown* (1952), Frankfurter achieved his ultimate ideal of judicial statesmanship, moving beyond the Holmes doctrine in a time and area so fraught with the clear and present danger of ethnic divisiveness that Holmes might well have reached the same result. For Holmes didn't like a vacuum of action and *Brown* filled a great one.

Robert H. Jackson went along with Frankfurter and Warren on *Brown*, although more reluctantly than any of the others. He had an asperity of thought and word that made him the best stylist of the group. He wrote eloquently against judicial supremacy in any form and was quick to note the twistings and turnings of his liberal brethren in trying to avoid the charge. But he too suffered, as Frankfurter did, from the constraints of a decisional method that left most of the juicy doctrinal inventiveness to the opposing camp.

From FDR's appointments through Truman's and Eisenhower's the constitutional wars raged, with varying results. But the long trend line of the political and legal cultures was liberal-activist, and the Holmes heritage seemed distasteful, even repugnant, to generations of the young. The impact of this era on his reputation can scarcely have come as much of a surprise. The dominant liberal group didn't like either the austerities of Holmes or his doctrine of judicial deference. Quite naturally they honed in on their own philosophy of judicial activism, social engineering, and doctrinal inventiveness—all of which had been alien to Holmes. The Eisenhower appointees, Warren and Brennan (paradoxically liberals), fed the fires of the Court generation that went by Warren's name, while the Johnson appointees renewed and sustained them. It was the apogee of constitutional activism, which makes some sense of the fact that the Holmes legacy reached its nadir during the Warren 1960s.

The perceptions of Holmes by the Law School culture were too narrow. While Holmes was the source and father of judicial deference, it was only one of the principles he judged by. Since he was wary of "general propositions" and shied from making an absolute of any, he made no absolute of this doctrine either. It was a star to steer by, but no chart for rough waters. He saw it as useful for a time in keeping the reactionary activism of his brothers from seizing a new America that was coming to birth and holding it unconstitutional. He also saw his deference doctrine as a way of keeping the contending powers of a democracy in balance, giving leeway to the majoritarian principle in legislative bodies—except when the threatened rights were basic to the competition of ideas and of values systems that underlies all social change.

Yet Holmes never turned his doctrine rigid, never carried it into historical excursions in search of "original intent," never read the Constitution with a literalism that would leach out its meaning, any more than he read it with an expansionism that would bloat it beyond coherence. He recognized that the Constitution is a changing organism, as the nation is. Yet he also saw that both Constitution and nation need power to make them effective.

He refused to turn any of the three powers—executive, legislative, judicial—into an eidolon. Each had its functions. But when confronted by an aggressive expansion from any of the others, the deepest power of the judiciary was to establish a principle and draw a line of separation. "A line there must be" was Holmes's constant imperative, from the time of his early State Court decisions to his great national organismic ones on the executive and taxing powers.[14]

8

Two current schools of constitutional thought present the strongest challenge to the Holmes legacy. One from the Left, the other from the Right, both strike at the vulnerable point the Holmes legacy presents in terms of finding firm criteria for confronting a constantly transforming world with a document two centuries old. Law is not like literature, art, and philosophy, which can be distanced from the daily immediacies. It is caught in their whorl. When the immediacies change, in the form of instant media, "Artificial Intelligence," global money markets, missile systems in space, biotechnics, born-again faiths, drug addictions, terrorisms, and AIDS, we spot the archaisms in the document and demand new judgments and constitutional relationships that will meet the current discontents.

The Holmes answer was that there is a plenitude of power in the total constitutional system, and the Courts must draw a line between its claimants, but not to the enhancement of the judicial power when others have acted or can act. This didn't satisfy the challengers from the Left, from Black and Douglas through Warren, Fortas, and Brennan.

If I call them the "Warrenites" for convenience, I refer to the Warren Court as symbol. I mean also to include their philosophical support system in the universities and law schools, those who feel that too many "rights," of individuals and groups, will slip through the crevices of the Holmesian doctrine, leaving them unprotected unless the Courts act to do the protecting—whence the need for their activism. Ronald Dworkin found a phrase, "taking rights seriously," that summed up their concern.

The Holmes legacy was vulnerable to this concern. It failed to meet the fear that in the absence of judicial action—given prejudiced, fearful, or apathetic legislatures and executives—the cases of voting reapportionment, desegregated schools, the right to counsel, the *Miranda* warnings, affirmative action, the access to abortions, and the protections against sexual harassment would all have failed to be taken seriously enough to fill the social void or meet the social injustice. More than anything it was this fear and the failure to meet it that turned the courts and law school culture away from Holmes for so long. His "felt necessities" applied to the shaping of the common law, but failed to still the clamant social urgencies that besieged constitutional law.

The trouble was of course that the expanding universe of liberal activism had no moral philosophy of its own to set limits to its rising entitlements and the interest-group incitements they provoked. The embrace of an unlimited rights dynamic within such a society heightens the centrifugal forces in it, diminishes the centripetal ones, and makes it all but impossible to govern from a center that will hold. It was the growing awareness of this, since the early 1970s, that reached the electorates and courts, undercut the liberal legal culture, and sent Holmes's reputation into an upward arc.

While the liberal aversion to Holmes came from his deflating of all utopianisms, the conservative attack focuses on his pragmatism and his values relativism. Unlike the liberals who read selective "rights" into the Constitution through the "penumbra" around them, the traditionalists make the stronger case against Holmes from their "natural right" base, with a firm belief that the essential nature of man can be used to ground a good society and keep it from the ravages both of a grandiose activism and a laissez-faire particularism.

It is an insight that has given the Straussians (if I may use them as a counter to the Warrenites) a considerable entrance into constitutional history and law.[15] If they have a strong case to make against Holmes it is not because they are right about their version of "natural right" and Holmes wrong in his scepticism of all such philosophies. It is rather because the fault line between his pragmatism and his evolutionism kept him from offering a principle of cohesion to keep a postmodern society from disintegrating under its centrifugal pressures.

The problem of the Warrenites was their failure to set limits. The problem of the Straussians is that their flight from relativism and their quest of the single "truth" expose them to the enticement of absolute thinking. No movement of thought has yet succeeded in finding the common ground of truths and values in the history of human experience on which an absolute "natural right" can be based. Yet the anthropological approach, which the young Holmes used in his researches on *the Common Law,* might still yield a cluster of intersecting values that would be useful for constitutional thinkers as well. This might give judges a direction for meeting the strong social urgencies of the time, and for adding a measure of statesmanship to the Holmes legacy of judicial deference.

9

A word about the Holmes style. Almost every attack on him pays tribute to it, but only as a kind of adornment, even an excrescence, which obscures the "savagery" or "bleakness" of his doctrine. It makes no sense, however, to garland Holmes for being an artificer of beautiful passages while dismissing him for being wrong-headed. There are in fact some flowery passages in Holmes, especially in his perorations, and over the years he repeated favorite expressions in his speeches and correspondence. Yet in the judicial opinions themselves there is hardly ever a surplus word, a self-indulgent adjective, an unnecessary phrase. It is style that cuts to the marrow of the issue at hand.

"A word is the skin of a thought," he wrote. It is more than an epigram; it is a thought that sheds light on his style. Holmes became a jurist but never ceased to be what he had all along dreamt of being, long before his law school years—a philosophical writer. There is no separation in him between style and substance; they are one. The word encloses and illumines the thought, which gives content and meaning to the word. Both his word and thought have the same crispness, economy, cutting edge, the same sparkling sense of playfulness, the same perversity in the face of fashions, the same unerring aim at the jugular—the same essence and permanence.

I add a personal note about my own perception of Holmes. Several years before the book's publication, Walton Hamilton, then at Yale Law School, wrote an influential *Law Review* article, "On Dating Mr. Justice Holmes." It said in effect that Holmes had come to seem both timeless and dateless, yet he was in fact a creature of his time and needed to be dated. As it happens, Hamilton was my teacher at the Robert Brookings Graduate School, where I learned some constitutional law in 1925 and first encountered the great Holmes decisions. One thing Hamilton taught us was to "place" a thinker in time and in social and personal circumstance. I sought to do it in this book, especially in the introductory essay on Holmes's "personal history."

Where the critics of Holmes (including Hamilton) had it wrong was in believing that the act of placing a thinker or artist in time strips him of what timelessness he has achieved. This has not proved true of Emerson, Whitman, O'Neill, and Faulkner, or of either William or Henry James who were of Holmes's generation and social circle. Like them all Holmes was a creature of his time and circumstance, but—also like them—he reached beyond it to universals. In his case the universals involved the process of judging, including the complex and intrusive role of the judge himself.

Because judicial review is the greatest American achievement in the arts of the polity, we have needed thinkers with insights that start with particulars and reach to the universal. It cannot be said of Holmes that he was free of the judgment of successive generations. Yet, however savaged, he has survived and somehow prevailed. Of all the American judges in time and circumstance there is a quality of *gravitas* in Holmes that gives him a measure of this timelessness.

There have been a number of attempts to write Holmes's life, but all have been partial or truncated. He is a hard subject to seize. Grant Gilmore, the custodian of the Holmes papers after the death of his biographer, Mark DeWolfe Howe, saw more "darkness" in Holmes than he could handle and gave up. Yet he stated: "To the extent that I can follow the dark outlines of his thought Holmes was both a greater man and a more profound thinker than the mythical Holmes ever was."

I never took either of the Holmes myths as final—the mythologizing of the 1920s and 1930s or the counter-mythologizing of the mid-1940s to the mid-1970s. Holmes is indeed a mythic figure, but in a different sense from myth seen as unreality. He has become mythic in the sense that his constitutional journey has become part of the journey taken in each generation—including the journey of those who resisted and attacked him.

Nor do I take the Holmes "revival" of the past decade as decisive or final. His critics made law school reputations by him, only to be dismayed by the refusal of his reputation to lie down and die. The faithful on the Burger and Rehnquist Courts in the 1980s picked only a single strand of Holmes for their fealty—judicial restraint—but they turned it into a historicism of "original intent" that attenuated what he meant and missed the richness of his range.

There will be other dips and rises in his reputation. A figure like Holmes becomes a way of looking into the mirror of ourselves and our time. He will rise and fall with the "felt necessities" of time and selfhood, with attitudes toward civilizational change and continuity, with perceptions of the life and death principles, and with the imperatives of the most difficult of all arts of governing—the art of adjudication.

This is especially true in an America that has suffered convulsive changes since Holmes's death, becoming not only a nation of competing pluralisms but a kingpin of the Western imperium, in a world of terrorism but also of an emerging community of law. Holmes couldn't have foreseen it, yet it is wholly compatible with his long perspectives. In such an America of changes and chances there is—more than anything else— a need for cohesion through permanences. I say "permanences," not "absolutes." "Continuity with the past," Holmes noted, "is not a duty. It is only a necessity."

Holmes didn't think much of engineered changes in which politically minded judges decide what is good for others. He did very much believe in broad evolutionary change and wanted judges to be part of it and to help set its channels and limits. With such a philosophy he defined the judicial tasks of his own age—and of ours—more trenchantly than any of his assailers or followers. This is his relevance for today and tomorrow.

Notes

1. I discuss this concept in my forthcoming *The Constitutional Journey: Selected Essays on Ideas and Power in Supreme Court History (1931-1988)*, which deals with Holmes along with other constitutional "greats."
2. I tried to express this in my commentary on the first two sections of Holmes's writings: it has been enriched and fortified by the research and scholarship since I wrote—notably the first two volumes of Mark DeWolfe Howe's great unfinished biography, *Justice Oliver Wendell Holmes: The Shaping Years* (1957) and *The Proving Years* (1963), Edmund Wilson's shrewd and quirky essay in *Patriotic Gore* (1962), and the two volumes of Holmes-Laski correspondence (1953).
3. For a discussion of the Roosevelt-Lodge correspondence see infra, p. 454 (Notes on the Holmes Literature).
4. See "Herbert Spencer in N.Y. Bakeries," my preface to the *Lochner* dissent, pp. 143-148 infra.
5. See infra, p. 382.
6. Hand held out for a more absolute First Amendment standard of "direct incitement" before state intervention would be warranted. The Brandeis test was whether there is still time for "education." On the *Abrams* case see my comment, infra p. 304; also see Richard Polenberg, *Fighting Faiths* (1987). For the Hand incident see Frederic R. Kellogg, "Learned Hand and the Great Train Ride," *American Scholar* (1987), pp. 471-486, drawing on letters in a forthcoming biography of Hand by Gerald Gunther.
7. Their more extreme descendants, now known as the Critical Legal School ("Crits"), have merged some extensions of "Realist" thinking with residues of the "Critical" Frankfurt School, along with Deconstructionism. It is a far cry from Holmes, yet it suggests how he anticipated a century ago much that is now seen as radical and strangely new.
8. White wrote later and more equable reassessments in 1982 and 1986 (see citations in bibliography).
9. See my preface to "Men and Ideas," Part III, Sec. 1 infra 367, especially p. 373. Note also Holmes's almost "mystical belief" that "the universe has in it more than we understand, that the private soldiers have not been told of the

plan of campaign, or even that there is one ... It is enough for us that the universe has produced us and has within it, as less than it, all that we believe and love" (Essay on "Natural Law," id., p. 398).
10. Infra, p. 394.
11. See infra, "'Death Plucks My Ears,'" p. 451.
12. I can bear witness to the way the angry young New Deal militants felt, since I backed the Court plan as an expression of a daring executive supremacy to counter the judicial. See my *It Is Later Than You Think* (1938), in a forthcoming new edition with a new afterword essay (Transaction Publishers).
13. For some writings of mine on all four see my forthcoming *The Constitutional Journey*.
14. See my prefaces to *Missouri v. Holland* (infra. pp. 273-275 "They Created a Nation, Not a Document") and to *Schlesinger v. Wisconsin* (infra, pp. 257-258, "Tax Law and the Penumbra").
15. For a discussion of the impact of Leo Strauss and the "Chicago School" upon American constitutional history and law see Gordon Wood, "The Fundamentalists and the Constitution," 35 *New York Review of Books*, 33ff (2/18/88).

Selected Additional Literature on Holmes (Since the First edition)

Aleinikoff, T. Alexander, "Constitutional Law in the Age of Balancing," 96 YALE L. JRL. 943 (1987)

Atiyal, Patrick S., "The Legacy of Holmes Through English Eyes," 63 B.U.L. REV. 341 (1983)

Barnett, Vincent M., "Mr. Justice Murphy, Civil Liberties and the Holmes Tradition . . .," 32 CORNELL L. REV. 177–221 (Nov. 1946)

Belz, Herman, "The Realist Critique of the Constitution in the Era of Reform," 15 AMER. J. OF LEGAL HISTORY 288

Berger, Raoul, *Government by Judiciary: The Transformation of the 14th Amendment* (1977)

Bernstein, Irving, "The Conservative Mr. Justice Holmes," 23 NEW ENG. QUART. 435–452 (Dec. 1950)

Bickel, Alexander M., "Portrait of Justice Holmes," NEW REPUBLIC (11/6/61) p. 19

―――, *The Supreme Court and the Idea of Progress* (1970)

―――, *The Morality of Consent* (1975)

Bickel, Alexander M., *The Judiciary and Responsible Government 1910-21*, with Benno C. Schmidt, Jr., Vol. 9 in the Holmes Devise *History of the Supreme Court of the United States*

Bogen, David S., "The Free Speech Metamorphosis of Mr. Justice Holmes," 11 HOFSTRA L. REV. 97 (1982)

Boudin, Louis B., *Government by Judiciary* (1932)

―――, "Justice Holmes and His World," 3 LAW. GUILD REV. 24–41 (July/Aug. 1943)

Brody, Burton F., "The Pragmatic Naturalism of Mr. Justice Holmes," 46 CHI. L. REV. 9 (1969)

Burton, David H., *Oliver Wendell Holmes, Jr.: What Manner of Liberal?* (1979)

―――, "Justice Holmes and the Jesuits," 27 AM. J. JURIS. 32 (1982)

Burton, David H., ed., *Progressive Masks: Letters of Oliver Wendell Holmes, Jr., and Franklin Ford* (1982)

Collins, Ronald K. L. & Skover, David M., "The Future of Liberal Legal Scholarship: A Commentary," 87 MICH. L. REV. (Oct. 1988)

Cover, Robert M., *Justice Accused* (1975)

Cox, Archibald, *The Court and the Constitution* (1987)

Currie, David P., "The Constitution in the Supreme Court: 1910–1921," DUKE L. JRL. 1111 (1985)

―――, "The Constitution in the Supreme Court: Full Faith and the Bill of Rights, 1889–1910," 52 U. CHI. L. REV. 867 (1985)

Curtis, Charles T., Jr., *Lions Under the Throne* (1947)

Darasz, Kathy A., "A Review of the Personal Correspondence of Justice Oliver Wendell Holmes, Jr.," 15 RUTGERS L. JRL. 114 (1984)

Davis, Horace B., "The End of Holmes' Tradition," 19 U. KAN. CITY L. REV. 53-65 (Dec. 1950 & Feb. 1951)

Domnarski, William, "Style and Justice Holmes," 60 CONN. B.J. 251 (1986)

Dudziak, Mary L., "Oliver Wendell Holmes as a Eugenic Reformer: Rhetoric in the Writing of Constitutional Law," 71 IOWA L. REV. 833 (1986)

Dworkin, Ronald, *Taking Rights Seriously* (1977)

———, *Law's Empire* (1986)

Eldridge, F. Howard, "Justice Holmes: Another Aspect of His Life," 10 U. CHI. L. REV. 417-436 (July 1943)

Elliott, E. Donald, "Holmes and Evolution: Legal Process as Artificial Intelligence," 13 J. LEGAL STUD. 113 (1984)

Ely, John H., *Democracy and Distrust: A Theory of Judicial Review* (1981)

Fallon, Perlie P., "The Judicial World of Mr. Justice Holmes," 14 NOTRE DAME L. REV. 52-102, 163-208 (Nov. & Jan. 1937-1938)

———, "Some Influences of Justice Holmes' Thought on Current Law . . .," 29 MINN. L. REV. 318-338 (April 1945)

Ferguson, Robert A., "Holmes and the Judicial Figure," 55 U. CHI. L. REV. 506 (1988)

Fisch, Max H., "Justice Holmes, the Predictive Theory of Law, and Pragmatism," 39 J. PHILO. 85-97 (Feb. 1962)

Ford, John C., "The Fundamentals of Holmes' Juristic Philosophy," 11 FORDHAM L. REV. (1942)

———, "Totalitarian Justice Holmes," 159 CATHOLIC WORLD 114-122 (May 1944)

Frank, Jerome, *If Men Were Angels: Some Aspects of Government in a Democracy* (1942)

Frankfurter, Felix, "Mr. Justice Holmes," *Dictionary of American Biography*, Supplement One (Vol. 21, p. 417), (1944), reprinted in Felix Frankfurter, *Of Law and Men* (1956)

———, *Felix Frankfurter Reminiscenses*, edited by Harlan B. Phillips (1960)

———, *From the Diaries of Felix Frankfurter*, edited by Joseph P. Lash (1975)

Fredrickson, George M., *The Inner Civil War* (1965)

Freund, Paul A., *On Understanding the Supreme Court* (1949)

———,"Holmes and Brandeis in Retrospect," 28 BOSTON BAR J. 7 (Sept./Oct. 1984)

Garraty, John A., "Holmes' Appointment to the U.S. Supreme Court (1902)," 22 NEW ENG. QUART. 291-303 (Sept. 1949)

Gilmore, Grant, *The Ages of American Law* (1977)

Gordon, Robert V., "Holmes' *Common Law* as Legal and Social Science," 10 HOFSTRA L. REV. 719 (1982)

Gregg, Paul L., "Pragmatism of Mr. Justice Holmes," 31 GEORGETOWN L. JRL. 262–295 (March 1943)

Gunther, Gerald, "Learned Hand and the Origins of Modern First Amendment Doctrine: Some Fragments of History," STAN. L. REV. 27 (1975) 719–773.

Handler, Milton & Ruby, Michael, "Justice Holmes and the Year Books," 59 N.Y.ST. B.J. 58 (July 1987)

Hart, H.L.A., "Positivism and the Separation of Law and Morals," 71 HARV. L. REV. 593–629 (Feb. 1958)

Hart, Henry, "Holmes' Positivism—an Addendum," 64 HARV. L. REV. 924–937 (April 1951)

Hickman, Martin, "Mr. Justice Holmes: A Reappraisal," 5 WESTERN POLITICAL QUARTERLY 66 (1952)

Hofstadter, Richard, *Age of Reform* (1955)

Holmes, Oliver Wendell Jr., *The Common Law*, edited with Introduction and Glossary by Mark DeWolfe Howe (1963)

Howe, Mark DeWolfe, "The Letters of Henry James to Mr. Justice Holmes," 38 YALE L. REV. 410–433 (March 1949, #3)

———, "The Positivism of Mr. Justice Holmes," 64 HARV. L. REV. 529 (1951)

———, *Justice Oliver Wendell Holmes: The Shaping Years*, Vol. 1 (1957), *The Proving Years*, Vol. 2 (1963)

Howe, Mark DeWolfe, ed., *Touched with Fire: Civil War Letters and Diary of Oliver Wendell Holmes, Jr.* (1947)

———, *Holmes-Laski Letters*, 2 vols. (1953)

———, *Holmes-Pollock Letters*, 2nd ed. (1961)

———, *The Occasional Speeches of Justice Oliver Wendell Holmes* (1962)

Kairys, David, *The Politics of Law* (1982)

Kalman, Laura, *Legal Realism at Yale, 1927–1960* (1986)

Kaplan, Benjamin, "Encounters with O. W. Holmes, Jr.," 96 HARV. L. REV. 1828 (1988)

Kelley, Patrick J., "A Critical Analysis of Holmes' Theory of Torts," 61 WASH. U.L.Q. 681 (1983)

Kellogg, Frederic R., *The Formative Essays of Justice Holmes* (1984)

———, "Laws, Morals and Justice Holmes," 69 JUDICATURE 214 (1985)

———, "Learned Hand and the Great Train Ride," AMER. SCHOLAR 471–489 (Autumn 1987)

Komisar, Yale, "Taking Institutions Seriously," 51 U. CHI. L. REV. 316 (1984)

Konefsky, Samuel J., *The Legacy of Holmes and Brandeis* (1956)
Krislov, Samuel, "Oliver Wendell Holmes: The Ebb and Flow of Judicial Legendry," 52 NW. U. L. REV. 514–525 (Sept./Oct. 1957)
Kurland, Phillip, "Portrait of the Jurist as a Young Mind," 25 U. CHI. L. REV. 206 (1957)
Lash, Joseph P., ed., *From the Diaries of Felix Frankfurter* (1975)
Laski, Harold J., "Ever Sincerely Yours, O. W. Holmes," NEW YORK TIMES MAGAZINE (2/15/48) p. 11 et. seq.
———, *Holmes-Laski Letters*, 2 vols., Mark DeWolfe Howe, ed. (1953)
Lerner, Max, "Bork's Progress," THE NEW REPUBLIC (9114,21/87)
———, "Courting Rituals," THE NEW REPUBLIC (2/1/88)
———, "A Judge Touched with Fire," CONNOISSEUR (Oct. 1988), forthcoming
———, *The Constitutional Journey: Selected Essays on Ideas and Power in Supreme Court History (1931–1988)*, forthcoming
Lippmann, Walter, "Mr. Justice Holmes," *Public Persons*, Gilbert A. Harrison, ed. (1976)
Little, Eleanor N., "Early Reading of Justice Oliver Wendell Holmes," HARVARD LIBRARY BULLETIN VIII, Spring 1954, 163–203
Llewellyn, Karl N., *Jurisprudence: Realism in Theory and Practice* (1962)
Lucey, Francis, "Jurisprudence and the Future Social Order," 16 SOCIAL SCIENCES (1941)
———, "Natural Law and American Legal Realism," 30 GEORGETOWN L. JRL. (1942)
Mason, Alpheus W., *The Supreme Court from Taft to Warren* (1958)
McCloskey, Robert G., *The American Supreme Court* (1960)
McKinnon, Harold R., "The Secret of Mr. Justice Holmes," in David H. Burton, ed. *Oliver Wendell Holmes Jr.: What Manner of Liberal?*
Mellen, Francis J., Jr., "Ralph Waldo Emerson, Mr. Justice Holmes and the Idea of Organic Form in American Law," 14 NEW ENG. L. REV. 147 (1978)
Michelman, Frank I., "Forward: Traces of Self-Government," 100 HARV. L. REV. 4 (1986)
Millar, James D., "Holmes, Peirce and Legal Pragmatism," 84 YALE L. REV. 1123–1140 (April 1975)
Monagon, John S., "Holmes' Common Law: An Originating Venture," 67 A.B.A.J. 312 (1981)
Murphy, Paul L., *The Constitution in Crisis Times: 1918–1969* (1972)
O'Connell, Jeffrey & O'Connell, Thomas E., "Mencken and Holmes," 2 CONST. COMMENTARY 277 (1985)
———, "From Doctor Johnson to Justice Holmes to Professor Laski," 46 MD. L. REV. 320 (1987)

SELECTED ADDITIONAL LITERATURE 477

Oppenheim, Leonard, "The Civil Liberties Doctrine of Mr. Justice Holmes and Mr. Justice Cardozo," 20 TUL. L. REV. 177–219 (Dec. 1945)
Palmer, Ben, "Hobbes, Holmes and Hitler," 31 A.B.A. JRL. 569 (Nov. 1945)
Paper, Lewis J., *Brandeis* (1983)
Patterson, C. Perry, "Jurisprudence of Oliver Wendell Holmes," 31 MINN. L. REV. 355–370 (March 1947)
Peabody, J., ed., *The Holmes-Einstein Letters* (1964)
Pohlman, Harold L., *Holmes' Legal Philosophy and Utilitarian Jurisprudence* (1985)
Posner, Richard, "The Meaning of Judicial Self-Restraint," 59 IND. L. J. 1 (1983)
____, *Law and Literature: A Misunderstood Relation*, Ch. 7, forthcoming.
Rehnquist, William H., *The Supreme Court: The Way It Was—The Way It Is* (1987)
Reiblich, Kenneth, "The Conflict of Laws Philosophy of Mr. Justice Holmes," 28 GEORGETOWN L. JRL. 1 (1939)
Reid, John P., "Experience or Reason: The Tort Theories of Holmes and Doe," 18 VAND. L. REV. 405–436 (1965)
Rodell, Fred, "Justice Holmes and His Hecklers," 60 YALE L. JRL. 620–624 (April 1951)
____, *Nine Men: A Political History of the Supreme Court*, 1790 (1955)
Rogat, Yosel, "Mr. Justice Holmes: A Dissenting Opinion," (Pts. 1 & 2) 15 STAN. L. REV. 3, 254 (Dec. 1962–March 1963)
____, "Mr. Justice Holmes: Some Modern Views . . .," 31 U. CHI. L. REV. 213 (1964)
____, "The Judge as Spectator," 31 U. CHI. L. REV. 213 (1964)
Rogat, Yosel & O'Fallon, James M., "Mr. Justice Holmes: A Dissenting Opinion—The Speech Cases," 36 STAN. L. REV. 1349 (1984)
Schmidt, Benno C., Jr., *The Judiciary and Responsible Government 1910–21*, with Alexander M. Bicket, Vol. 9 in the Holmes Devise *History of the Supreme Court of the United States*
Shriver, Harry C., *What Justice Holmes Wrote and What Has Been Written About Him, A Bibliography, 1866–1976* (1978)
Speziale, Marcia Jean, "Oliver Wendell Holmes, Jr., William James, Theodore Roosevelt, and the Strenuous Life," 13 CONN. L. REV. 663 (1981)
Strauss, Leo, *Liberalism: Ancient and Modern* (1968)
Sunstein, Cass, "Constitutionalism After the New Deal," 101 HARV. L. REV. 421 (1987)
____, "The Legacy of Lochner," 87 COL. L. REV. (1987)

Symposium, "Mr. Justice Holmes: The Man and His Legacy, 28 U. FLA. L. REV. 365 (1976), including articles by Larry Martin Roth, Julius J. Marks and a number of Holmes' law clerks.

Touster, Saul, "Holmes: The Years of the Common Law," 64 COLUM. L. REV. 230–247 (Feb. 1964)

———, "In Search of Holmes from Within," 18 VAND. L. REV. 437 (1965)

———, "Holmes a Hundred Years Ago: The Common Law and Legal Theory," 10 HOFSTRA L. REV. 673 (1982)

Tushnet, Mark, "The Logic of Experience: Oliver Wendell Holmes on the Supreme Judicial Court," 63 VA. L. REV. 975 (1977)

Vetter, Jan., "The Evolution of Holmes, Holmes and Evolution," 72 CALIF. L. REV. 343 (1984)

Wechsler, Herbert, "Toward Neutral Principles of Constitutional Law," 73 HARV. L. REV. 1 (1959)

White, G. Edward, "The Rise and Fall of Justice Holmes," 39 U. CHI. L. REV. 51–77 (1971–1972)

———, American Judicial Tradition (1976)

———, "The Integrity of Holmes' Jurisprudence," 10 HOFSTRA L. REV. 633 (1982)

———, "Looking at Holmes in the Mirror," 4 LAW & HIST. REV. 439 (1986)

White, Morton G., "Revolt Against Formalism in American Social Thought of the Twentieth Century," 8 JRL. HIST. IDEAS 131–152 (April 1947)

Wilson, Edmund, *Patriotic Gore* (1962), "Holmes, the Last Roman"

Wolgast, Elizabeth, *The Grammar of Justice* (1987)

Wood, Gordon, "The Fundamentalists and the Constitution," 35 NY REVIEW OF BOOKS 33ff (2/18/88)

Wyzanski, Charles E., Jr., "The Democracy of Justice Oliver Wendell Holmes," 7 VAND. L. REV. 311–324 (April 1954)

Note on the Holmes Literature

I. *Collections of Holmes's Writings*
Shriver, Harry C. (Ed.), *The Judicial Opinions of Oliver Wendell Holmes* (1940) (State court opinions)
Lief, Alfred (Ed.), *Representative Opinions of Mr. Justice Holmes* (1931)
Lief, Alfred (Ed.), *Dissenting Opinions of Mr. Justice Holmes* (1929)
Shriver, Harry C. (Ed.), *Justice Oliver Wendell Holmes: His Book Notices and Uncollected Letters and Papers* (1936)
Howe, Mark DeWolfe (Ed.), *Holmes–Pollock Letters* (1941)

II. *Bibliographical Sources*
There is as yet no reliable biography of Holmes. Silas Bent's volume is discussed below. As this goes to press a brief life by Catherine Drinker Bowen is promised for early publication. Just as I had finished reading the proofs of the present book, Attorney General Francis Biddle's *Mr. Justice Holmes* (1942) came to hand, but too late for me to make use of it. The lay reader will find it colorful and evocative, much of it written in Holmes's own words. A definitive full-length biography is in preparation by Professor Mark DeWolfe Howe of the University of Buffalo Law School, to whom Holmes's executor has entrusted the Holmes papers. Lacking these papers the road of a biographical essay is dusty, uncertain, and beset with thorns. Holmes's life was in its outlines one of the most exciting, as his personality was one of the richest, in American history. Yet the details that would give substance to these outlines are thus far lacking. I have in my biographical essay not sought to go beyond the needs of a brief sketch as an introduction of Holmes to the lay reader, and have used only the available published material.

The richest published material on Holmes's life and work will be found in the *Holmes–Pollock Letters*, edited by Mark DeWolfe Howe. I have borrowed freely from these letters not only for facts about his life but also for light on his opinions. Without them it would have been impossible to edit this book or to write the prefatory notes. Next to the

Letters the most convenient general biographical material is in Silas Bent's rambling, occasionally incorrect, frequently padded, and yet shrewd and suggestive biography, *Justice Oliver Wendell Holmes* (1932), and in the memorial volume of tributes to Holmes on his ninetieth birthday, *Mr. Justice Holmes* (1931), edited by Professor (now Justice) Felix Frankfurter, particularly the delightful essay by Elizabeth Shepley Sergeant, "Justice Touched with Fire," which is also reprinted in her *Fire Under the Andes* (1927). The most authoritative is the biographical material included in John Gorham Palfrey's introduction to the *Holmes–Pollock Letters,* cited above.

For the various phases of Holmes's life the following have been useful: On the elder Holmes there is a discursive two-volume *Life and Letters,* by John T. Morse, Jr. (1886) which is worth paging through and which contains some homely family material on the son. The best discussion of Dr. Holmes that I have found is the extended introduction by S. I. Hayakawa and Howard Mumford Jones in their book of Representative Selections from his writings in the "American Writers' Series" (1939). There are some readable and evocative chapters on him (chs. 18 and 26) in Van Wyck Brooks, *The Flowering of New England* (1936) and (ch. 1), *New England: Indian Summer* (1940). The section on Dr. Holmes in Vernon L. Parrington, *Main Currents in American Thought,* vol. 2 (1927), 451–459, is a harsh estimate of him, but well worth study for the social milieu in which Holmes grew up. The climate and mood of this milieu are more sympathetically presented in the volumes by Brooks cited above. The Boston of the 1840's is also well described in Henry Steele Commager's *Theodore Parker* (1936), ch. 6, "The Hub of the Universe." F. O. Matthiessen, *American Renaissance* (1941), without any direct bearing on Holmes, is a brilliant introduction to the literary history of New England during his boyhood.

Holmes's *Lehrejahre* have been excellently treated in F. C. Fiechter, Jr., "The Preparation of an American Aristocrat," *New England Quarterly,* vol. 6 (1933), 3–28. There is no history of Harvard which covers this period, S. E. Morison having begun the construction of his monumental history Union-Pacific fashion, working from both ends toward the middle, and the golden spike not yet having been driven. For Holmes's Civil War experiences see Bent, op. cit., Colonel George A. Bruce, *The Twentieth Regiment of Massachu-*

NOTE ON THE HOLMES LITERATURE 481

setts Volunteer Infantry (1906), and Dr. Holmes's "My Hunt After the Captain," to be found in his *Collected Works*, vol. 8 (1892), 16–77. On this episode see also 33 *Maryland Historical Magazine* (1938), 109–126. Alexander Woollcott has done some historical sleuthing on a Civil War episode when Holmes is supposed to have met President Lincoln: see his article, "Get Down, You Fool," 161 *Atlantic Monthly* (1938), 169–173. There is no good account of the Harvard Law School during the period when Holmes studied there. Ralph Barton Perry's *Thought and Character of William James* (2 vols., 1935) contains not only the exchange of letters between Holmes and James, but lights up also what young people thought about and talked about in the Harvard and Boston of the sixties and seventies. On the trips to England see Palfrey, op. cit. Harold J. Laski, in an article on "Henry Adams: an Unpublished Letter," in 151 *Nation* (1940), 94–95, suggests the possibility that Holmes may have met Pollock on his trip to England in the 1860's rather than in the 1870's, but Palfrey (op. cit., p. xv) is inclined to doubt it. For the years of Holmes's editorship of the *American Law Review*, Professor Felix Frankfurter blazed the trail by his study of "The Early Writings of O. W. Holmes, Jr.," 44 HLR (1931), 717–724. Harry C. Shriver has since collected a number of Holmes's book reviews and articles in the *American Law Review*, in *Justice Oliver Wendell Holmes: His Book Notices and Uncollected Letters and Papers* (1936).

A study of Holmes as a judge of the Supreme Judicial Court of Massachusetts still remains to be written, and would be extremely rewarding. Silas Bent devotes to the period three chapters of his biography, op. cit., with copious quotations from cases, and Shriver, in his *Judicial Opinions of Oliver Wendell Holmes* (1940), has brought together the more important opinions bearing on Constitutional issues. But the best material as yet available on the twenty years that Holmes spent on the Court, as also on his speeches and reading during the period, is in the letters to Pollock. For Holmes's friendship with Brooks Adams, see the latter's article on his relations with Holmes and Bigelow in 1 *Boston University Law Review* (1921), 168. For Theodore Roosevelt's letters to Lodge regarding the Holmes appointment to the United States Supreme Court, see *The Letters of Theodore Roosevelt and Henry Cabot Lodge* (1925), vol. 1, 517–519.

Owen Wister has left an interesting description of the "Roosevelt Familiars" in *Roosevelt: The Story of a Friendship* (1933); it must, however, be read carefully because of its savage unfairness to Justice Brandeis and its strange mouthings about Brandeis as an "Oriental" mind. Henry F. Pringle's *Theodore Roosevelt, a Biography* (1931) and Matthew Josephson's *The President Makers* (1940), 142–143, have also been helpful for an insight into Roosevelt's relation to his circle. The Court at the time Holmes came to it and in later years is discussed in Charles Warren, *The Supreme Court in United States History* (1922), vol. 2. No good biographies are available as yet of Holmes's colleagues with the exception of Henry F. Pringle's *Life and Times of William Howard Taft*, 2 vols. (1939), from which I have drawn for Taft's opinions of Holmes. Alfred Lief's *Brandeis: The Personal History of an American Ideal* (1936) is also valuable for the friendship between Holmes and Brandeis; and the forthcoming definitive biography of Brandeis by Alpheus T. Mason should shed more light.

Of Holmes in his later years on the Court we have had very few reliable glimpses. This gap could be repaired; since Holmes's legal secretaries, one of whom came to him each year from the Harvard Law School, were also his almost constant companions, a book made up of their recollections and whatever records they may have kept would be of great value. Meanwhile the following may be consulted: an interview with Holmes in 1925 by Walter Tittle in 110 *Century* (1925), 181–186; F. Frankfurter, "October Days," 3 *Today* (1935), 5; Richard W. Hale, *Some Table Talk of Mr. Justice Holmes and "the Mrs."* (1935); Derby, "Recollections of Mr. Justice Holmes," 12 *New York University Law Quarterly Review* (1935), 345–353.

III. *Commentary on Holmes*

1. Collection of articles:

    Harvard Law Review, vol. 29 (April 1916), 565–704; a symposium in honor of Holmes, dedicated to him on his seventy-fifth birthday; articles by Sir Frederick Pollock, John H. Wigmore, Morris R. Cohen, Felix Frankfurter, Eugene Ehrlich, Learned Hand, and Roscoe Pound, either on Holmes or inspired by him
    Illinois Law Review, vol. 10 (1916), 617; dedicated to Holmes on his seventy-fifth birthday

Harvard Law Review, vol. 34 (March 1921), 449–532; dedicated to Holmes on his eightieth birthday; only the article by Roscoe Pound, however, is on Holmes

Columbia Law Review, vol. 31 (March 1931), 349–532; dedicated to Holmes on his ninetieth birthday; articles by Frederick Pollock and Morris R. Cohen on Holmes

Harvard Law Review, vol. 44 (March 1931), 677–828; dedicated to Holmes on his ninetieth birthday; articles by Charles Evans Hughes, Lord Sankey, W. A. Jowitt, Benjamin N. Cardozo, Sir Frederick Pollock, Roscoe Pound, Theodore Plucknett, Felix Frankfurter — all directly on Holmes

Yale Law Journal, vol. 40 (March 1931), 683–842; dedicated to Holmes on his ninetieth birthday; articles by Harold J. Laski and Hessel E. Yntema on Holmes, and an article by Karl Llewellyn inspired by Holmes

Mr. Justice Holmes, a symposium volume, ed. by Felix Frankfurter (1931). Contains articles by Charles Evans Hughes, Benjamin N. Cardozo, John Dewey, Felix Frankfurter, Learned Hand, Harold J. Laski, Walter Lippmann, Philip Littell, Josef Redlich, Elizabeth Shepley Sergeant, John H. Wigmore

2. Other Commentary

The list below is an imperfect selection, in which space has compelled me to omit much that is of value. It will, however, give some indication of the richness of the body of Holmes scholarship and commentary. For more exhaustive bibliographies, see Harry C. Shriver, *Justice Oliver Wendell Holmes: His Book Notices and Uncollected Letters and Papers* (1936), 247–276; Karl Llewellyn, "Holmes," 35 CLR (1935), 490–492; and John C. Ford, S.J., "The Fundamentals of Holmes's Juristic Philosophy," *Proceedings of the Jesuit Philosophical Association* (1941), 77–81

Aitchison, Clyde B., "Justice Holmes and the Development of Administrative Law," 1 *George Washington Law Review* (1933), 165–171

Beard, Charles A., "Justice Oliver Wendell Holmes," 33 *Current History* (1931), 801–806

Bent, Silas, *Justice Oliver Wendell Holmes, a Biography* (1932)

Boorstin, Daniel, "The Elusiveness of Mr. Justice

Holmes" 14 *New England Quarterly* (1941), 478–487

Cardozo, Benjamin N., "Mr. Justice Holmes," 44 HLR (March 1931), 682–692; reprinted in Frankfurter, ed., *Mr. Justice Holmes* (1931)

Chafee, Zechariah, Jr., *Freedom of Speech* (1920); rev. ed. *Free Speech in the United States* (1941)

Clark, Charles E., "Case Study of a Liberal," 6 *Saturday Review of Literature* (December 21, 1929), 581–582

Cohen, Morris R., "Justice Holmes," 25 *New Republic* (1921), 294–296, a review of *Collected Legal Papers*: reprinted in Frankfurter, ed., *Mr. Justice Holmes* (1931)

"Justice Holmes and the Nature of the Law," 31 CLR (March 1931), 352–367; reprinted in Cohen, *Law and the Social Order* (1933), 198–218

"Justice Holmes," 82 *New Republic* (1935), 206–209

"A Critical Sketch of Legal Philosophy in America," *Law — A Century of Progress,* vol. 2 (1937), 266–302

Cook, Walter W., "Oliver Wendell Holmes, Scientist," 21 *Am. Bar Assn. J.* (April 1935), 211–213

Dewey, John, "Justice Holmes and the Liberal Mind," 53 *New Republic* (January 11, 1938), 210–212; reprinted in Dewey, *Characters and Events,* ed. Joseph Ratner (1929), vol. 1, 100–106; also in Frankfurter, ed., *Mr. Justice Holmes* (1931)

Fisch, M. H., "Mr. Justice Holmes, the prediction theory of law, and pragmatism," *Journal of Philosophy* (1942), 85–97

Frank, Jerome, *Law and the Modern Mind* (1930)

"Are Judges Human?," 80 *University of Pennsylvania Law Review* (November 1931), 17

"Mr. Justice Holmes and Non-Euclidian Legal Thinking," 17 *Cornell Law Quarterly Review* (June 1932), 568–603

Frankfurter, Felix, "The Constitutional Opinions of Justice Holmes," 29 HLR (April 1916), 683–699

"Twenty Years of Mr. Justice Holmes' Constitutional Opinions," 36 HLR (June 1923), 909–939

"Mr. Justice Holmes and the Constitution: A Review of His Twenty-Five Years on the Supreme Court," 41 HLR (December 1927), 121–173; reprinted in Frankfurter, ed., *Mr. Justice Holmes* (1931)

"The Early Writings of O. W. Holmes, Jr.," 44 HLR (March 1931), 717–724

Bibliography of Holmes's writings and decisions, 44 HLR (March 1931), 797

Mr. Justice Holmes and the Supreme Court (1938)

Fuller, Lon L., *The Law in Quest of Itself* (1940)

Grinnell, Charles E., Review of *The Common Law*, 2 *American Law Review* (May 1881), 331–338

Hamilton, Walton H., Review of Lief's *Dissenting Opinions of Mr. Justice Holmes*, 19 *Yale Review* (1930), 611–614

"Legal Philosophy of Justices Holmes and Brandeis," 33 *Current History* (February 1931), 654–660

"On Dating Mr. Justice Holmes," 9 *University of Chicago Law Review* (December 1941), 1–27

Hand, Learned, Review of *Collected Legal Papers*, 36 *Political Science Quarterly* (September 1921), 528–530

"Mr. Justice Holmes," 43 HLR (April 1930), 857–862; reprinted in *Mr. Justice Holmes*, ed., Felix Frankfurter (1931)

Holdsworth, W. S., *The Historians of Anglo-American Law* (1928)

"In Memoriam," 51 *Law Quarterly Review* (April 1935), 264–265

Hough, Charles M., Review of *Collected Legal Papers*, 21 CLR (March 1921), 296–298

Hughes, Charles Evans, "Mr. Justice Holmes," 44 HLR (March 1931), 677–679; reprinted in Frankfurter, ed., *Mr. Justice Holmes* (1931)

"Justice Holmes at Ninety," 83 *Review of Reviews* (April 1931), 69–70; 17 *Am. Bar Assn. J.* (April 1931), 251–253. Radio address in honor of Justice Holmes's ninetieth birthday

Kagan, Louis R., "Justice Holmes and His Contribution to the Sherman Anti-Trust Law," 39 *Commercial Law Journal* (April 1934), 207–208

Kirchwey, George W., Foreword to Lief's *Dissenting Opinions of Mr. Justice Holmes* (1929)

Kocourek, Albert, Review of *Collected Legal Papers*, 16 *Illinois Law Review* (June 1921), 156–161

Laski, Harold J., "Mr. Justice Holmes: for his Eighty-ninth Birthday," 160 *Harper's* (March 1930), 415–423; reprinted in Frankfurter, ed., *Mr. Justice*

Holmes (1931); also in Laski, *The Danger of Being a Gentleman* (1939)

"Political Philosophy of Mr. Justice Holmes," 40 YLJ (March 1931), 683–695

Foreword to Lief's *Representative Opinions of Mr. Justice Holmes* (1931)

"Mr. Justice Holmes," 6 *Political Quarterly* (1935), 351–354

Lerner, Max, "Justice Holmes: Flowering and Defeat," 142 *Nation* (June 10, 1936), 746–747; reprinted in Lerner, *Ideas Are Weapons* (1939)

"The Scar Holmes Leaves," 46 YLJ (March 1937), 904–908; reprinted in Lerner, *Ideas Are Weapons* (1939)

"Holmes, Frankfurter, and the Austerity Theory," 147 *Nation* (Nov. 19, 1938), 537–539; reprinted in Lerner, *Ideas Are Weapons* (1939)

"The Mind and Faith of Justice Holmes," *Ideas for the Ice Age* (1941), 100–115

Review of the *Holmes–Pollock Letters,* 42 HLR (April 1942), 1069–1073

Levy, Beryl H., *Our Constitution: Tool or Testament?* (1941)

Llewellyn, Karl, Review of *Mr. Justice Holmes* (ed., Felix Frankfurter), 31 CLR (May 1931), 902–905

"What Price Contract? An Essay in Perspective," 40 YLJ (March 1931), 704–751

"On Philosophy in Our Law," 82 *University of Pennsylvania Review* (January 1934), 210–212

"Holmes," 35 CLR (April 1935), 485–492

Fragments in Tribute, a booklet, includes portions of the above articles

Mencken, H. L., "The Great Holmes Mystery," review of Bent's *Justice Oliver Wendell Holmes, a Biography* and *Mr. Justice Holmes,* ed., Felix Frankfurter, 26 *American Mercury* (1932), 123–126

Nelles, Walter and Mermin, Samuel, "Holmes and Labor Law," 13 *New York University Law Quarterly Review* (May 1936), 517–555

Otto, Max, "On truth, majority vote, free will and necessity," 38 *Journal of Philosophy* (1941), 389–392

Plucknett, Theodore, "Holmes: The Historian," 44 HLR (March 1931), 712–716

Pollard, Joseph P., "Justice Holmes Dissents," 85 *Scribner's* (January 1929), 22–29
Pollock, Sir Frederick, "Abrams v. United States," 250 U.S. 616. 36 *Law Quarterly Review* (October 1920), 334–338
"Mr. Justice Holmes," 44 HLR (March 1931), 693–696
"Ad Multos Annos," 31 CLR (March 1931), 349–351
"Mr. Justice Holmes," 48 HLR (June 1935), 1277–1278
Pound, Roscoe, "Liberty of Contract," 18 YLJ (1909), 454–487
"Judge Holmes' Contributions to the Science of Law," 34 HLR (March 1921), 449–453
Powell, Thomas Reed, "Holmes and Pollock," a review of the *Holmes–Pollock Letters*, 152 *Nation* (1941), 589–590
Richardson, Dorsey, *Constitutional Doctrines of Justice Oliver Wendell Holmes* (1924)
Smith, T. V., *Creative Skeptics* (1934), ch. 6; revised in *The Democratic Tradition in America* (1941), ch. 4
Tully, Nettleton, "The Philosophy of Mr. Justice Holmes on Freedom of Speech," 3 *Southwestern Social Science Quarterly* (March 1923), 287–305
Wigmore, John H., "Justice Holmes and the Law of Torts," 29 HLR (April 1916), 601–616; reprinted in Frankfurter, ed., *Mr. Justice Holmes*
Wu, John C. H., "The Juristic Philosophy of Justice Holmes," 21 *Michigan Law Review* (March 1923), 523–541; reprinted in Wu's *The Art of Law* (1936)
"The Mind of Mr. Justice Holmes," 8 *China Law Review* (August 1935), 77–108; reprinted in Wu's *The Art of Law* (1936)
Yntema, Hessel E., "Mr. Justice Holmes' View of Legal Science," 40 YLJ (March 1931), 696–703

Note on Acknowledgments

To John Gorham Palfrey, executor of Justice Holmes, for his generosity with respect to reprinting permissions

To Dumas Malone and the Harvard University Press, publishers of the *Holmes–Pollock Letters,* and to Mark DeWolfe Howe, their editor, for the letters from Holmes to Pollock and Lady Pollock

To Dean J. M. Landis and Acting Dean E. M. Morgan of the Harvard Law School, and to the editors of the *Harvard Law Review,* for the following: "The Path of the Law," 10 HLR (1897), 457–478; "Law and the Court"; "Natural Law," 32 HLR (1918), 40

To John C. H. Wu and the *T'ien Hsia Monthly* for the letters of Holmes to Wu

To Henry James, Ralph Barton Perry, Little, Brown and Company, and the *Atlantic Monthly* for the letters from Holmes to William James

To Little, Brown and Company for selections from Holmes's *Speeches* (1913) and from *The Common Law* (1881)

To Harcourt, Brace and Co. and to Harold J. Laski for selections from Holmes's *Collected Legal Papers* (1920)

To the Macmillan Co., for "Law and Social Reform," from *The Rational Basis of Social Institutions,* ed. J. H. Wigmore and A. Kocourek

To the editors of the *Illinois Law Review,* for "Ideals and Doubts"

To the *Christian Science Monitor* and the *New Republic* for "Opinions and Champagnes"

To the editors of the *American Law Review* for "Masters and Men," originally published as "The Gas-Stokers' Strike," 7 *American Law Review* (1873), 582

NOTE ON ACKNOWLEDGMENTS

To F. C. Fiechter, Jr., and the *New England Quarterly* for Holmes's "Autobiographical Sketch," from "The Preparation of an American Aristocrat," 6 (1933), 3–28

To Alfred Lief and H. C. Shriver for their valuable spadework and for the help given by their editorial notes

Note on Abbreviations

ALR — *American Law Review*
CLP — Holmes's *Collected Legal Papers* (1920)
CLR — *Columbia Law Review*
HLR — *Harvard Law Review*
H–P — *Holmes–Pollock Letters* (1941), ed. Mark DeWolfe Howe
Selected Essays — *Selected Essays on Constitutional Law* (1938), ed. Douglas Maggs (5 vols.)
Speeches — Holmes's *Speeches* (1913)
YLJ — *Yale Law Journal*

Table of Cases

Abrams v. *U.S.*, xlv, 129, 299, 304–313
Adair v. *U.S.*, 150–152, 153, 154
Addyston Pipe and Steel Co., 232
Adkins v. *Children's Hospital*, 135, 145, 148, 172–179, 192
Allen v. *Flood*, 111, 120
Allgeyer v. *Louisiana*, 145
American Column and Lumber Co. v. U.S., 246–249
Arizona Employers' Liability Cases, 135, 160–165

Bailey v. *Alabama*, 336–341
Bailey v. *Drexel Furniture Co.*, 167, 173
Bakeshop Case. See *Lochner* v. *New York*
Baldwin v. *Missouri*, 261–264
Baltimore and Ohio R.R. Co. v. Goodman, 45, 205–208
Bartels v. *Iowa*, 317–321
Bauer and Cie v. O'Donnell, 240
Berry v. *Donovan*, 120
Black and White Taxicab Co. v. Brown and Yellow Taxicab Co., 135, 193–201
Blackstone v. *Miller*, 261, 262
Bleistein v. Donaldson Lithographing Company, 208–213
Block v. *Hirsh*, xliii, 129, 136, 278–285
Board of Trade of the City of Chicago v. Olsen, 233
Bridges v. *California*, 333
Brown v. *Mississippi*, 348
Buchanan v. *Warley*, 347
Buck v. *Bell*, 356–359
Budd v. *New York*, 144
Bunting v. *Oregon*, 148, 172, 178

Cement Manufacturers' Protective Assoc. v. U.S., 248
Chambers v. *Florida*, 348
Champion v. *Ames*, 169, 171
Chastleman Corp. v. *Sinclair*, 280
Commonwealth v. *Davis*, xliv, 106–108
Commonwealth v. *Hunt*, 111
Commonwealth v. *Perry*, 92–95
Commonwealth v. *Pierce*, 162
Coppage v. *Kansas*, 135, 152–156

Davis v. *Mass.*, 107
Debs v. *U.S.*, xliv, xlv, 106, 290, 291, 297–304

De Jonge v. *Oregon*, 323
Diamond Glue Co. v. U.S. Glue Co., 137
Dr. Miles Medical Co. v. Park and Sons Co., 135, 239–246

Emergency Rent Case, xliii, 129, 136, 278–285. See *Block* v. *Hirsh*
Erie R.R. Co. v. Tompkins, 198
Evans v. *Gore*, 264–268, 333

Farmers Loan and Trust Co. v. Minnesota, 262
First Child Labor Case. See *Hammer* v. *Dagenhart*
First National Bank of Boston v. Maine, 262
Fiske v. *Kansas*, 323
Flag Salute Case, 320. See also *Minersville School District* v. *Gobitis*
Frank v. *Mangum*, 338, 342–347, 348
Frick v. *Pennsylvania*, 262
Frohwerk v. *U.S.*, 292, 298
Frost v. *California*, 252–254
F.T.C. v. Beech-Nut Packing Co., 240

Gas-Stokers' Case, 44, 110
German Alliance Insurance Co. v. Lewis, 177
Gilbert v. *Minnesota*, 322
Gitlow v. *New York*, xliv, xlv, 290, 291, 321–325
Grover v. *Townsend*, 330
Guinn v. *U.S.*, 347

Hague v. *CIO*, 106
Hammer v. *Dagenhart*, 129, 165–171, 173
Hancock v. *Yaden*, 95
Hanley v. *Kansas City R.R. Co.*, 137
Hanson v. *Globe Newspaper Company*, 96–102, 353
Hardwood Case. See *American Column and Lumber Co.* v. *U.S.*
Herbert v. *Shanley Co.*, 135, 216–217
Herndon v. *Lowry*, 323
Hitchman Coal and Coke Co. v. Mitchell, 155
Humphrey's Executor v. U.S., 287, 288

Income Tax Cases, 147

Jackman v. *Rosenbaum Co.*, 197
Jones v. *City of Opelika*, 107

TABLE OF CASES

Kuhn v. Fairmont Coal Co., 194, 201

Linseed Oil Case, 248
Lochner v. New York, xxxviii, xxxix, 44, 143–150, 154, 178
Louis K. Liggett Co. v. Baldridge, 254–257
Louisville Gas Co. v. Coleman, 259–261

McCray v. U.S., 169
Maple Flooring Manufacturers' Assoc. v. U.S., 248
Marcus Brown Co. v. Feldman, 278, 279
Masses Publishing Co. v. Patten, 293
May v. Wood, 120
Meyer v. Nebraska, 290, 291, 317–321, 359
Miles v. Graham, 265
Milwaukee Social Democratic Publishing Co. v. Burleson, 313–317
Minersville School District v. Gobitis, 107, 319, 320
Missouri v. Holland, xliii, 273–278
Missouri, Kansas, and Tennessee Railroad v. May, 141–143
Moore v. Dempsey, 338, 343, 347–352
Morehead v. Tipaldo, 175
Moyer v. Peabody, xliii, 136, 268–273
Muller v. Oregon, 148, 172, 174, 177, 178
Munn v. Illinois, 144, 191, 192
Myers v. U.S., 285–288

Nardone v. U.S., 361
Near v. Minnesota, 314, 322
Nixon v. Herndon, 328–332
Noble State Bank v. Haskell, 135, 136, 179–185, 280
Norris v. Alabama, 348
Northern Securities Company v. U.S., xxxiii–xxxvi, xxxviii, 110–111, 143, 217–231, 232, 445
Nye v. U.S., 333

Oleomargarine Case. See McCray v. U.S.
Olmstead v. U.S., 359–362, 447–448
O'Malley v. Woodrough, 265
Opinion of the Justices (Municipal Ownership), 95–96
Opinion of the Justices (Woman Suffrage), 103–105
Otis v. Parker, xxxviii, 136–141

Palko v. Connecticut, 323
Peck v. Tribune Co., 353–356
Pennsylvania Coal Co. v. Mahon, 185–190
Pierce v. Society of Sisters, 319

Pierce v. U.S., 292
Plant v. Woods, xxx, 117–122, 219, 241
Poisoned Pool Case. See United Zinc and Chemical Co. v. Britt
Powell v. Alabama, 348
Powell v. Pennsylvania, 250
Prudential Insurance Co. v. Cheek, 322

Railroad Crossing Case, 45, 205–208. See also Baltimore and Ohio R.R. Co. v. Goodman
Rice v. Albee, 120

Sacco-Vanzetti Case, xliv
Schaefer v. U.S., 292
Schenck v. U.S., xlv, 106, 280, 292–297, 298
Schlesinger v. Wisconsin, 250, 257–259
Schneider v. New Jersey, 107
Scottsboro Cases, 348
Second Child Labor Case. See Bailey v. Drexel Furniture Co.
Sioux City and Pacific Ry. Co. v. Stout, 202, 203, 204
Slaughter House Cases, 95, 145
Southern Pacific Co. v. Jensen, 195
Stafford v. Wallace, 233
Standard Oil Case, 247
Sterling v. Constantin, 269
Stettler v. O'Hara, 172
Storti v. Commonwealth, 122–123
Stromberg v. California, 323
Sugar Trust Case. See U.S. v. E. C. Knight Co.
Swift v. Tyson, 155, 193–201, 207
Swift and Co. v. U.S., 231–239

Toledo Newspaper Co. v. U.S., 165, 332–336
Towne v. Eisner, 257
Truax v. Corrigan, 156–160, 173
Turntable Cases, 202–205
Tyson Brothers v. Banton, 135, 190–193, 280

Union Pacific Ry. Co. v. McDonald, 202–205
Union Refrigerator Transit Co. v. Kentucky, 262
U.S. v. American Linseed Oil Co., 248
U.S. v. American Tobacco Co., 247
U.S. v. Classic, 330
U.S. v. Colgate and Co., 240
U.S. v. Darby, 168, 176
U.S. v. E. C. Knight Co., 232–233
U.S. v. General Electric, 240
U.S. v. Macintosh, 326

TABLE OF CASES

U.S. v. *Schwimmer,* 325–328
United Zinc and Chemical Co. v. *Britt,* 45, 201–205, 205–208, 356

Vegelahn v. *Guntner,* xxx, xxxvii, 109–116, 117, 119, 120, 154, 219, 438

Walker v. Cronin, 120
Weaver v. *Palmer Bros. Co.,* 249–251
West Coast Hotel Co. *v.* Parrish, 176
White-Smith Music Co. v. *Apollo,* 213–215
Whitney *v.* California, 323

Index

Abbott, Edith, 168
Abbott, Grace, 166
absentee ownership, 255
accident insurance, 160–165
Adams, Brooks, 109, 129, 438, 439, 440, 454
Adams, Henry, xix
Adams, John Quincy, 280
Aitchison, Clyde B., 456
Allen, Justice William, 109
American Civil Liberties Union, 322
American Law Journal, xxvi
American Law Review, 44, 90
Ames, James B., xxv, 85
anti-Semitism, 342
anti-trust, 134–136, 217–239, 246–249. See also Sherman Act
army, 19
Arnold, Thurman, 111
art, 208–213
"attractive nuisance" doctrine, 201–205
Austin, John, 79

Bagehot, Walter, xlv, 44, 289
bank deposits, 179–185
Barker, Justice, 102
Beard, Charles A., xxxiv, xxxviii, 371, 435, 448
Bent, Silas, 8, 452, 453, 454, 456
Bentham, Jeremy, 57, 79, 140
Beowulf, 21
Berger, Victor, xlv, 313
Beveridge, Albert J., xxxiii, 166, 429
Biddle, Francis, 315, 452
Bigelow, Melville M., 85, 109, 120, 438, 454
Black, Forrest R., 298
Black, Justice Hugo L., 333
Böhm-Bawerk, Eugene von, 241
Bonaparte, Napoleon, *see* Napoleon
Boorstin, Daniel, 456
Boston, xx
Boudin, Louis B., 144, 145, 192
Bowen, Catherine D., 452
boycott, 109–116, 117–122
Bradley, F. H., 129, 425
Bradley, Justice Joseph P., 145, 196
Brandeis, Justice Louis D., xxxvii, xxxviii, xl, xli, xliv, 28–29, 132, 133, 148, 157, 158, 161, 166, 167, 172, 173, 175, 186, 191, 196, 247, 248, 250, 252, 255, 256, 260, 262, 264, 286, 288, 291, 298, 299, 304, 313, 314, 316, 318, 322, 325, 326, 333, 359–360, 444, 448, 455
Brewer, Justice David J., 131, 137, 218
Brooks, Van Wyck, xxii, 453
Brown, Justice Henry, xxxvii, 440
Brown, Ray A., 181
Brown, Robert C., 262
Bruce, George A., 453
Burke, Edmund, 36
Burleson, Albert S., 313
Burns, James M., ix
Burns, Robert, 365
business, 18
Butler, Bishop Joseph, 57
Butler, Justice Pierce, 106, 175, 196, 249, 250, 265, 325, 359–360

Cannon, James P., 324
Cardozo, Justice Benjamin N., 90, 323, 330, 435, 436, 456, 457
Carlyle, 365
Carnegie, Andrew, xxxiv
Chafee, Zechariah, xlvi, 106, 292, 298, 299, 304, 305, 322, 457
chain stores, 254–257
Chicago *Tribune*, xlv, 315
child labor, 165–171
children, 203
Children's Bureau, 166
circus, 212
citizenship, 325–328. See also diversity of citizenship
civil liberties, xxxviii, xliii–xlvi, 106–108, 289–362, (England) 307
Civil War, xxiii–xxv, xxxix, 3–27, 443
Clark, Judge Charles E., 457
Clarke, Grenville, 106
Clarke, Justice John H., 157, 161, 166, 196, 202, 203, 247, 304, 305, 313, 332, 356
classics, xlix
Clayton Act, 158–159
clear and present danger, xlv, 289–317
Cleveland, Grover, 150
closed shop, 117–122
coal industry, 185–190
Cohen, Morris R., 392, 425, 446, 455, 456, 457
collective bargaining, 117–122, 150–156
combinations, industrial, 115–116, 217–231, 246–249
commerce power, 220, 221, 231–239

496　INDEX

Commager, Henry S., 453
common law, 135–136, 195, 196, 197, 199, 219–220, 239. *See also* federal common law
competition, 217–231, 239–246
conservatism, xlvii
contempt of court, 332–336
contract, 76, 77, 93. *See also* freedom of contract
contributory negligence, 206
Cook, Walter W., 457
Cooke, Josiah P., 411
Coppier, 443
copyright, 134–136, 208–217
Corwin, Edward S., 166, 175, 233, 287, 305
Coughlin, Charles, xlv, 315
crime, 51–64
criminal syndicalism, xlv, 321–325
Cushman, Robert E., 150

Darwin, Charles, xxii, 44, (Darwinism) xxxv, 219, 306, 356
Day, Justice William Rufus, 146, 153, 155, 166, 202, 203, 214, 332, 337
Debs, Eugene V., xlv, 106, 297–304, 442. *See also* Table of Cases, *Debs v. U.S.*
Degas, 212
Del Vecchio, Giorgio, 392
deposit insurance. *See* bank deposits
DeRautz, Marguerite, x
Dewey, John, 129, 369, 433, 456, 457
diversity of citizenship, 193–201
Dixwell, Fanny. *See* Holmes, Mrs. Fanny Dixwell
Douglas, Justice William O., 333
Dowell, Eldridge F., 322
draft obstruction, 292–304
due process of law, xxxvii, 127, 134–136, 136–141, 156–160, 249, 255
dueling, 23
Dunne, Finley P., xxxiii
Dürer, Albrecht, 209, 420

Eastman, Max, 298
Ebb, Lawrence F., ix
economic theory, xxx, 119–122, 135, 146, 148, 217–231, 239–243, 389–391
Edgerton, Judge Henry W., 265
education, 317–321
Ehrlich, Eugene, 455
Eighteenth Amendment. *See* prohibition
electrocution, 122–123
Ely, Richard T., 243
Emerson, Ralph W., xx, xxxix, 197, 424
eminent domain, 185–190, 282–283
England, xxvi, xxix, xlii, xliv

Erdman Act, 150
evidence, 359
executive power, 134–136, 268–288
external standard, 45, 56–64, 97, 146, 353

Fair Labor Standards Act, 168, 176
fair trial, 342–352
Fairman, Charles, 93, 269
federal common law, 134–136, 193–201, 203, 205–207. *See also* common law
Federal Trade Commission Act, 242
federalism, 197
Federalist, The, 384
Feld-Crawford Act, 242
fictions, legal, 190–193
Fiechter, F. C., Jr., 6, 453
Field, Justice Stephen J., xxxvii, 93, 109
Field, Chief Justice Walbridge, 418
Fifth Amendment, 150–152
Fisch, M. H., 457
food and drug control, 170
Ford, Henry, 325
Ford, John C., 456
Foster, William Z., 324
Fourteenth Amendment, 137, 143–152, 156–160, 172–179, 185–190
Frank, Jerome, 367, 457
Frank, Leo, 342–347
Frankfurter, Justice Felix, ix, xlix, 107, 120, 130, 157, 159, 167, 172, 174, 192, 194, 265, 285, 319, 320, 361, 436, 443, 453, 454, 455, 456, 457, 458
freedom of the press, xlv, 313–317, 332–336. *See also* civil liberties
freedom of speech, xliv, 293, 297–313, 321–328. *See also* civil liberties
Freund, Ernst, 298, 299, 326
Friedrich, Anton A., 279
Fuller, Lon L., 368, 373, 458
Fuller, Chief Justice Melville, xxxvi, xxxvii, 218, 231
Fuller, Raymond G., 167

Girard, Paul F., 418
Giraud, Jean B., 418
Glass-Steagall Banking Act, 181
Godkin, E. L., xxx
Goethe, J. W., 430
Gordon, T. M., 166
Goya, Lucientes de, 209, 212
Gray, Justice Horace J., xxxi, xxxii, 218
Gray, John C., 368, 369, 386–387
Greene, Nathan, 120
Grinnell, Charles E., 458

INDEX

HAINES, CHARLES G., 175
Haines, H. S., 440
Hale, Sir Matthew, 144, 192
Hale, Richard W., 455
Hamilton, Walton H., xlvi, 130, 144, 145, 191, 232, 242, 458
Hammond, Justice, 117
Hand, Justice Learned, 293, 455, 456, 458
Harding, Warren G., 300
Harlan, Justice John M., xxxvii, 131, 146, 147, 150, 195, 209, 218, 250, 337, 442
Harriman, Edward A., 440
Hart, Henry, 285
Harvard College, xxi–xxii, 7, 17, 25
Harvard Law Review, 90, 95, 110, 118, 148
Harvard Law School, xxv, xxvii, xl, xlii
Hawthorne, Nathaniel, xix, xx
Hay, John, xxxiii
Hayakawa, S. I., 453
Hays, Will H., 314
Haywood, William, 269
Hegel, G. W. F., 58, 88, 419, 431
Hill, James G., xxxiv, 218, 221, 439
Hobbes, Thomas, 79, 104, 105
Holdsworth, W. S., 458
Holmes, Dr. Oliver Wendell, xix, xx, xxi, xxiv, xxviii, xlviii, 6, 453, 454
Holmes, Oliver Wendell, Jr., Life, *passim;* Writings (items in italics are the titles of books): Autobiographical Sketch, 6–8; Civil War Speeches, 9–27; *Collected Legal Papers,* 401–402; *Common Law,* xxvii, xli, 44–47, 51–71; Gas-Stokers' Strike, 44–45, 48–51, 110; George Otis Shattuck, 37–40; Ideals and Doubts, 371, 391–394; John Chipman Gray, 386–387; John Marshall, 382–386; Kent's *Commentaries,* xxvi, 44, 197; Last Words, 450–452; Law and the Court, 387–391; Law and Social Reform, 399–401; Legal profession speeches, 29–43; Letters, 403–449; Montesquieu, 373–382; Natural Law, 371, 372–373, 394–399; Path of the Law, 47, 71–89, 368; Privilege, Malice, Intent, 45; *Speeches* (1913), 9, 17, 29, 37, 40, 382; State Court opinions, 90–123; Supreme Court opinions, 134–362
Holmes, Mrs. Fanny Dixwell, xxvi, xli, 409, 436
Holmes–Pollock Letters, xxxvi (H), xlix (H), 95 (H), 103 (H), 111 (P), 118 (H), 129, 130 (H), 131 (H), 132 (H), 133 (H), 136 (H), 154 (H), 161 (P,H), 162 (P,H), 165 (H), 167 (H), 173 (P), 185 (H), 186 (H), 196 (H), 203 (H), 207 (P), 213 (H), 222 (P,H), 233 (H), 243 (H), 246 (H), 251 (H), 261 (H), 299 (H), 300 (H), 306 (P), 307 (H), 326 (H), 333 (H), 347 (H), 360 (H), 369 (H), 372 (P,H), 405 (H), 406–409, 452, 453, 454, 437–449
honor, 33–34
Hoover, Herbert, 287
Hough, Charles M., 458
hours of labor, 143–150, 165–171, 172
Howe, Mark DeWolfe, ix, xlvi, 347, 409, 452
Hudson, Manley O., 202
Hughes, Chief Justice Charles E., xl, xlii, 130, 131, 153, 155, 157, 175, 176, 240, 242, 269, 314, 323, 326, 337, 338, 342, 456, 458
Hughes, Thomas, xxvi
humanitarianism, 19, 203

INJUNCTION. See labor injunction
interstate commerce, 165–171, 217–239

JACKSON, ANDREW, xxxvii, 286
Jackson, Charles, xxviii
Jackson, Justice Robert H., 193, 287
James, William, 129, 369, 403, 404, 405, 409–418, 423, 454
Jehovah's Witnesses, 107, 320
Jevons, Stanley, 144
Johnson, Andrew, 286
Jones, Howard M., 453
Josephson, Matthew, 455
Jowitt, W. A., 456
judges, (salaries) 264–268, (appointment) xxxii–xxxiv, xxxvii, 437, (outlook) 387–391, (power) 190–201, 261, (on Supreme Court) 127–136, (judicial review) xxxvii–xxxix, 41, 90, 127–133, 137, 148, 197, 371, 387–391
Jusserand, Jules, xxxiii

KAGAN, LOUIS R., 458
Kant, Immanuel, 58, 410, 421, 431
Keating-Owen Act, 166
Keats, John, xlviii
Kelley, Florence, 166
Kent, James, xxvi, 44, 197
Kirchwey, George W., 458
Knowlton, Justice (Mass.), 93
Knox, Philander C., 218
Kocourek, Albert, 445, 458

LABOR, xxxix, 48–51, 93–94, 103, 109–116, 117–122, 143–150, 151–152, 152–156, 156–160, 160–165, 171–179
labor contract, 172–179

498 INDEX

labor injunction, 109–116, 117–122, 156–160
laissez faire, 163, 167, 172
Lamb, Charles, 446
Landis, Judge K. M., 313
Langdell, C. C., xxv, 34
Laski, Harold J., 180, 401, 423, 428, 429, 442–443, 444, 454, 456, 458, 459
Lathrop, Julia, 166
law, (legal theory) 28–92, 71–87, 127–133, 148, 367–370, 387–401; (legal profession) viii, xxvii, xxxix, 3, 28, 29–31, 36–37, 71–87, 386–387
Leonhard, Rudolf, 441
Lerner, Edna, 313
Lerner, Max, 128, 313, 368, 371, 459
Levy, Beryl H., 459
Lewinson, Paul, 328, 329
Lewis, W. D., 118
liability, 51–56, 90, 160–165, 201–208
libel, 96–102, 353–356
liberty of contract, 127, 136–141, 144, 145, 150–152, 152–156, 173, 190, 318
Lief, Alfred, 452, 455
Lippmann, Walter, 456
lithographs, 208–213
Littell, Philip, 456
Llewellyn, Karl, xix, 456, 459
Lodge, Henry Cabot, xxxii, xxxiii, xxxiv, 166, 218, 454
lotteries, 191, 193
Lowell, Charles Russell, 17
Lowndes, Charles L. B., 262
Lurton, Justice Horace H., xxxiv, 240, 337
Lusk Committee, 322
lynching, 343

McAllister, Breck P., 96
McKenna, Justice Joseph, xxxvii, 151, 162, 166, 195, 196, 209, 247, 279, 322
McReynolds, Justice James C., 162, 175, 195, 252, 261, 262, 279, 286, 318, 319, 322, 330, 348
McWilliams, Carey, 165

Machiavelli, N., 444
Maine, Henry S., 44
Maitland, Frederick W., 85
Malthus, Thomas R., xxii, 400, 418
Manet, Edouard, 212
Mansfield, Lord, 96, 353
Maritime law, 195
Marshall, Alfred, 243
Marshall, Chief Justice John, xxxi, xxxii, xxxiv, xlix, 130, 274, 342, 369, 370
martial law, 269

Marvin, F. W., 444
Marx, Karl, 173
Mason, Alpheus T., 455
Matthiessen, F. O., 453
Melville, Herman, xx
Mencken, H. L., 459
Mermin, Samuel, 459
migratory birds, 273–278
militarism, 5–6
Mill, John Stuart, xxvi, xlv, 289, 290, 353
Miller, Justice, xxxvii, 93, 130
Milton, John, xlv, 289, 290, 306
Milwaukee Leader, xlv, 313–317
minimum wage, 172–179
minorities, cultural, 317–321
monopoly, 217–231, 231–239, 246–249
Montesquieu, xlix, 369
morals, 172–179
Morgan, J. P., xxxiv, 218, 229
Morgan, J. H., 427
Morison, S. E., 453
Morse, John T., Jr., 453
Morse, Robert, 40
Morton, Justice, 102
Muckrakers, 144, 166, 232
Muller, 211
municipal ownership, xxx, 95–96
Murray, Gilbert, 433–434
music, 213–215

Nansen, F., 36
Napier, Sir William, 19
Napoleon, 41
Nation, xxx
N.A.A.C.P., 347
National Consumers' League, 166, 175
National Labor Relations Act, 120, 155
national power, 150–152, 165–179, 217–239, 273–288
natural law, 369, 370, 371, 372, 373, 394–399
natural rights, 163
naturalization, *see* citizenship
Negroes, 328–332, 347–352
Nelles, Walter, 459
New England, xx, xxi, 12
New Republic, 299, 300, 445
Nineteenth Amendment, 174
Norris-La Guardia Anti-Injunction Act, 159

O'Hare, Kate Richards, 301
Olney, Richard, 150
Otto, Max, 290, 459

Pacifism, xlii, 6
Palfrey, John G., 453, 454
Parker, Theodore, xx
Parkinson, Thomas I., 175

INDEX 499

Parrington, Vernon L., 434, 448, 453
patriotism, xlii
Pearson, Karl, 147
Peckham, Justice Rufus W., xxxiv, xxxvi, xxxix, 137, 144–148, 218, 231
Pelley, William D., xlv, 315
penumbra theory, 250, 257–258
peonage, 336–341
Pepper, Senator G. W., 286
Perry, Ralph B., 403, 404, 405, 409, 454
Phillips, Wendell, xx
philosophy, 129
picketing, 156–160
Pitney, Justice Mahlon, 153, 157, 161, 196, 275, 278, 342
Plato, 289, 318, 441
Plautus, 424
Plucknett, Theodore F., 455, 459
poetry, xlviii
police power, 90, 134–136, 137, 141, 153, 172, 179–190
Pollard, Joseph P., 460
Pollock, Sir Frederick, xxvi, xli, xlii, 85, 87, 111, 129, 145, 161, 162, 173, 202, 222, 343, 369, 372, 403, 406, 407, 408, 440, 454, 455, 456, 460
Pollock, Lady, 437
populism, xxix, 128
Pound, Judge Cuthbert, 206
Pound, Roscoe, 148, 175, 455, 456, 460
Powell, Thomas R., ix, 156, 172, 175, 186, 198, 460
pragmatism, 148, 415
presidential power, 270, 285–288
price fixing, 190–193, 239–246, 246–249
price regulation, 190–193
Pringle, Henry F., 132, 167, 455
prohibition, 170, 191, 193
propaganda, 314–316, 321–328
property, 158, 185–190, 203, 279
Proust, Marcel, viii, 449
public interest, 134–136, 179–185, 190–193, 280
punishment, 56–64
Puritanism, 12, 13

RACE, xliii, 23, 391
race discrimination, *see* Negroes
Radin, Max, 326
Railway Labor Board, 150
Rankin, Robert S., 270
Redlich, Josef, 433, 456
Reed, Justice Stanley F., 107
referendum, 103–105
Reinach, S., 420
Rembrandt, 209, 211
removal power, 285, 286
resale price maintenance, 239–246

restraint of trade, 220, 231–239, 239–246
revenge, 51–56
Rhodes, James F., 443
Richardson, Dorsey, 460
Riesman, David, 291, 330
Roberts, Justice Owen J., 330
Robins, Raymond, 305
Rodell, Fred, 368
Rohden, Richard, 370
Roosevelt, Franklin D., xxxv, xlix, 261, 287
Roosevelt, Theodore, xxxi–xxxvi, xxxviii, 110, 132, 217–222, 370, 371, 445, 454
Ruskin, John, 209

SAINTE-BEUVE, C. A., 428
Saint-Gaudens, A., xxxiii
Sanford, Justice Edward T., 191, 260, 322, 325
Sankey, Lord, 456
Santayana, George, 129, 147, 417, 424
Sayre, F. B., 175
Schaub, E. L., 279
sedition, 289–317
Seligman, E. R. A., 242
Seneca, 424
Sergeant, Elizabeth S., xxiii, 453, 456
Shakespeare, William, 41
Shattuck, George O., xxviii, 37–40
Shaw, Chief Justice Lemuel, 111
Shaw, Colonel Robert G., 17
Sherman Anti-trust Act, xxxv, 217–231, 231–239, 239–246, 247
Shriver, Harry C., 343, 406, 452, 454, 456
Sinclair, Upton, 232
Smith, Alfred E., 324
Smith, Jeremiah, 202
Smith, T. V., 6, 460
social legislation, 45, 134–136, 143–150, 160–165, 249–251
Socialism, xxix, 297–304, 389–391, 394
social reform, 399–401
Spencer, Herbert, 44, 80, 144, 147, 149
Spengler, Oswald, 425, 449
Stammler, R., 422, 431
state power, 143–150, 152–165, 179–201, 249–264, 268–273, 317–325, 328–332, 336–342, 356–359
states-rights, 166, 254–257, 274
Steffens, Lincoln, xxxiii
Stephen, Sir James, 57, 87
Stephen, Leslie, xxvi, 88
sterilization, 356
Stetson, Francis L., 218
Steunenberg, Governor, 269
Stokes, Rose Pastor, 301

Stone, Chief Justice Harlan F., xlix, 168, 175, 191, 196, 250, 260, 262, 264, 319, 326, 359
Storey, Moorfield, 347
Story, Justice Joseph, 201
strike, 117–122, 156–160
Sutherland, Justice George, xxiv, 173, 174, 175, 191, 252, 255, 256, 259, 287, 318, 326, 348

TACITUS, 424
Taft, Chief Justice William H., xl, 132, 133, 156, 157, 158, 167, 174, 202, 203, 233, 286–288, 359
Taney, Chief Justice Roger B., xxxii, xxxvii, 130, 146
Taussig, F. W., 120
taxation, 134, 257–268
Tennyson, Alfred, 22
Tenth Amendment, 166
Thackeray, W. M., 36
Thayer, James B., 85
theater, 191, 193, (tickets) 190–193
Thomson, Sir William, 410
Thoreau, Henry D., xx
Till, Irene, 232
Tittle, Walter, 455
torts, 64–71, 134–136
trade associations, 246–249
trade unions, 93–94, 109–122, 150–152, 152–156, 156–160
treaty-making power, 273–278
Tully, Nettleton, 460

UNITED STATES SUPREME COURT, xxxii, xxxvii, 134–362

VAN DEVANTER, JUSTICE WILLIS, 162, 175, 264, 275, 278, 279
Veblen, Thorstein, xxi, xxxviii–xxxix, 255

Velasquez, 210
Volgmuth, Doris, x

WAGE FUND THEORY, 117–122
wage regulation, 92–95, 117–122, 172–179
Waite, Chief Justice Morrison R., 192
Walker, Frank C., 315
Walpole, Horace, 446
war, xlii–xliii, 5–6, 9–16, 10, 17–18, 18–25, 20, 21, 23, 24, 392
war powers, xliii, 134–136
Ward, Lester, 401
Warren, Charles, 323, 455
Watkins, Edgar, 181
Wechsler, Herbert, xlv
Whistler, James, 210
White, Justice Edward D., xxxvi, xxxvii, 106, 131, 146, 162, 195, 196, 218, 220, 231, 262, 279, 332
Wickersham, George W., 180
Wigmore, John H., 297, 306–307, 455, 456, 460, 461
Wilson, Woodrow, xlii, 28, 300, 371
wire tapping, 359–362, 447–448
Wister, Owen, xxix, xxxiii, 455
Witte, Edwin, 111
woman suffrage, 103–105
women, social position, 172–179
Woollcott, Alexander, 454
workmen's compensation laws, 160–165, 181, 195
World War I, xli–xlii, xliii
World War II, ix
Wormser, I. M., 175
Wu, John C., 343, 403, 405, 406, 409, 418–436, 460

"YELLOW DOG" CONTRACT, 150–152, 152–156
Yntema, Hessel E., 456, 460